W9-CSC-559

Contemporary
Curriculum
Discourses

Studies in the
Postmodern Theory of Education

Joe L. Kincheloe and Shirley R. Steinberg
General Editors

Vol. 70

PETER LANG
New York • Washington, D.C./Baltimore • Boston
Bern • Frankfurt am Main • Berlin • Vienna • Paris

Contemporary Curriculum Discourses

Twenty Years of JCT

EDITED BY

William F. Pinar

PETER LANG
New York • Washington, D.C./Baltimore • Boston
Bern • Frankfurt am Main • Berlin • Vienna • Paris

Library of Congress Cataloging-in-Publication Data

Contemporary curriculum discourses: twenty years of JCT /
[edited by] William F. Pinar.
p. cm. — (Counterpoints; vol. 70)
Includes bibliographical references and index.
1. Curriculum planning—United States—Philosophy. 2. Curriculum
change—United States—Philosophy. I. Pinar, William. II. JCT.
III. Series: Counterpoints (New York, N.Y.); vol. 70.
LB2806.15.C6753   375'.001'0973—dc21   99-21198
ISBN 0-8204-3882-0
ISSN 1058-1634

Die Deutsche Bibliothek-CIP-Einheitsaufnahme

Contemporary curriculum discourses: twenty years of
JCT / ed. by William F. Pinar. –New York; Washington, D.C./Baltimore;
Boston; Bern; Frankfurt am Main; Berlin; Vienna; Paris: Lang.
(Counterpoints; Vol. 70)
ISBN 0-8204-3882-0

All royalties go to *JCT*
Cover design by Nona Reuter

The paper in this book meets the guidelines for permanence and durability
of the Committee on Production Guidelines for Book Longevity
of the Council of Library Resources.

© 1999 Peter Lang Publishing, Inc., New York

All rights reserved.
Reprint or reproduction, even partially, in all forms such as microfilm, xerography,
microfiche, microcard, and offset strictly prohibited.

Printed in the United States of America.

For all those who worked on the journal
and the conference over the years, especially for
Janet L. Miller

TABLE OF CONTENTS

INTRODUCTION

A Farewell and a Celebration

William F. Pinar
1998

This is a celebration and a farewell. Twenty years have passed since *JCT* and its conference appeared on the scene: twenty years of innovative and provocative articles, essays, several book-length pieces, and many remarkable conference presentations. I have used the term "reconceptualization" to describe what occurred in the field during the 1970s, but the term is not dramatic enough to express the role that *JCT* and the Bergamo Conference have played. Perhaps "intellectual breakthrough" is more descriptive. You will, I think, agree with my choice of phrases once you've moved through this remarkable collection. Of course, the book excludes as much as it includes. I have had to pass over—for reasons of space—many exciting and important pieces. But I believe that the ones I have chosen aptly celebrate *JCT*'s position as *the* avant-garde journal, not only in North American curriculum studies, but perhaps in all of education. Let us celebrate what is truly a collective achievement.

This book represents as well my farewell to the journal and the conference. My departure has already occurred; this volume allows me to formalize it, to make it public. While I passed on the active editorship of *JCT* to Bill Reynolds in 1986 (then to Jo Anne Pagano in 1989 and to Dennis Sumara and Brent Davis in 1994), I did remain in a kind of "overseeing" relationship to the journal and conference I had started in 1978. I attended my last conference in 1995, detached myself from both it and the journal the year following, determined they would survive on their own without me.

While I started both *JCT* and the conference, I have hardly worked alone. Janet Miller was my partner from the beginning. Long phone calls to Janet in Columbus (studying for her Ph.D. with Paul Klohr at Ohio State) from

California (where I had gone in winter 1979 to spend the semester with my son who was living in Berkeley) helped to shape and sustain the project in its early and fragile phases. Later that year Janet and I met the buses that transported conference registrants from National Airport (Washington, D.C.) to the Airlie conference site (near Warrenton, Virginia). Janet has remained very much engaged, serving often as director of the conference and always as managing editor of the journal. I am more grateful than I can say for your friendship, Janet, your colleagueship, your commitment, and your strength, both psychological and intellectual. I said something (clumsily) to this effect at the 1994 meeting in Banff, but I want to repeat it here, in print. What JCT and the conference have amounted to over these past twenty years has to do in no minor way with your labor and leadership. This book is dedicated to everyone who has worked on the journal and the conference, and, most particularly, to you.

As hard as you have worked, Janet, you would be the first to acknowledge the labor of others. Paul Klohr has been there all along, from the beginning, encouraging me to take it on, advising me on issues large and small. For instance, it was Paul who traveled with me to Dayton and helped me settle on the Bergamo conference site after we decided we could not return to Airlie House in Virginia. My colleague and friend Bill Doll has also been a longtime supporter of the journal and the conference. It was Bill who made the trip with me to Monteagle, Tennessee, and while he opposed the site (he turned out to be right…the majority did not find the place to their liking), he kindly deferred to my enthusiasm. Bill has generously contributed his own funds to the journal from time to time, as well as organizing the Saturday seminars he held with others for several years. Others have helped as well, including several institutions that provided financial support from time to time. My thanks to the University of Dayton (Ellis Joseph and Joe Watras were key); the University of Rochester (Jim Doi was dean and supported both the University of Rochester conference in 1973 and JCT); LSU; Simon Fraser University; York University; as well as the universities of Lethbridge and Alberta.

And then there is Margaret Zaccone. Margaret has been there almost from the beginning. What would I have done without you, Margaret? Margaret and Dorothy Horton are known to all conference registrants; they have worked long and hard on what amounts to a volunteer basis. I want to thank you, Margaret, especially, for your commitment, labor, and loyalty. You have been a remarkable friend, to me, to JCT, and to the conference.

There are others who are almost as familiar as Margaret and Dorothy—well, almost. You Bergamo regulars know who you are. Seeing you each year at the meeting was for me like coming home for the holidays. You are too numerous to name individually, but many of you have published in the pages of JCT at one point or another; if you did, your name will appear alphabetically in the appendix. Look there too for Craig's Kridel's commentary on the conference.

Also there can be found the names of the editors whom I have mentioned already: William Reynolds, Jo Anne Pagano, and, since 1994, Brent Davis and Dennis Sumara. I want to express my thanks especially to Dennis and Brent, for their intelligence, creativity, and energy brought new life to the project, new life that also allowed me to feel finally that I could leave.

I have departed for several reasons; two are pertinent here. I am leaving because my own work has drawn me elsewhere. One must, of course, follow one's heart, one's intellectual heart, wherever it leads, and loyalty to one's intellectual journey has typified, I think, all of us associated with the journal and the conference. Of course, JCT and Bergamo would have accommodated my new direction; for my own psychological reasons I felt the work must take me elsewhere. Secondly, I left because I decided (after thinking about it for several years) that for the project to be true to its origin—that is, the support of new work, to allow the next wave to break—it needed to sweep away the father. It would have done so in time; the process was well underway, or so it felt. What finally became clear to me was that it was past time to step aside and allow the younger ones to do whatever it is they deem appropriate without looking over their shoulder at me. True, Bill or Jo Anne didn't then and Dennis and Brent don't now look back at me very much, nor can I imagine any of you accusing me of constraining you in any way. But it is also true that I have been there, that you have consulted me about the big issues, that it has been assumed—out of deference perhaps for the one who started it, if nothing else—that I *should* be consulted. Now I am no longer there to be consulted. Things will proceed without me, but if I am surprised and they do not, I will feel no regret. The point has never been about building monuments or traditions, it has been about tearing them down, allowing new ideas to emerge and take hold. The point has been to nurture work that AERA or ASCD or PES or even AESA would not. The point has been to support the experimental point of view.

In doing so there has been what I call in *Understanding Curriculum* some degree of "speculative excess," but that is the price to be paid. When respectability and caution rule the day, intellectual experimentalism is the casualty. In this I believe we have succeeded, some critics would say to a fault. As you will read here (perhaps for the second time, if you have been a subscriber to JCT) and as you have heard at the conferences, there have been remarkable performances of intellectual creativity, originality, and erudition. I know I have learned much from what I have read in JCT and what I have seen at the Bergamo meetings over the past twenty years. Those who have written for the journal and who have spoken at the conferences deserve much praise. In no incidental way this book is for you, to help you remember and appreciate what has been achieved. But the book is intended also to encourage beginning students to remake a field that—in our time—we helped to refashion. Whatever royalties this book generates go to *JCT*, to support what might become future "intellectual breakthroughs."

The reconceptualization of American curriculum studies has been described in detail in *Understanding Curriculum*; there is no point in repeating the history here. My anecdotal version is reprinted in the appendix; it introduced the 1988 collection that anticipated the map of the field I used in *Understanding Curriculum*. Janet Miller's autobiographical remembrance of *JCT*'s role in the reconceptualization is also reprinted in the appendix. Suffice to say here, for those readers for whom this is all new, that my generation rejected the position that history and tradition had fashioned for us. The curriculum—especially the secondary school curriculum—had been settled, more or less, in its official senses; it would be directed toward, and articulated with, postsecondary destinations, key among them the university and the workplace. What remained of the progressive dream—education for democratization, which meant schooling for psychological and social as well as intellectual development—was over, as Bill Pilder (Pinar et al. pp. 1995, 222-223) said at the first conference in Rochester. We found ourselves—in the aftermath of the 1960s national curriculum reform movement—invited to be, in a word, bureaucrats, to assist curriculum to be the means to those ends specified by politicians and corporatists and our well-meaning if narrowly and vocationally focused arts and sciences colleagues in the university. We were to help teachers forget their historical calling to practice academic freedom, to be authentic individuals, not automata. We were to help them become skillful implementers of others' objectives, something like an academic version of the postal service, delivering other people's mail. We were not to author what we delivered to the children, nor were we permitted to modify it (except for the sake of its more efficient transmission); our job was to see that the mail—the curriculum—was delivered, opened, read, then learned. "Accountability" was—remains—the watchword of the day.

We rejected that occupational description and sought from the outset to understand, not just implement or evaluate, the curriculum. The project of understanding—which we always took to be a form of *praxis*—took us various places: history, politics, race, gender, phenomenology, postmodernism, autobiography, aesthetics, theology, the institution of schooling, the world. These are chapter headings of *Understanding Curriculum*, and with the notable exception of the explosive growth of cultural studies since the early 1990s (by which time *Understanding Curriculum* had been completed), they remain today the major domains of scholarship in the field. [And in these pages—taken from the pages of *JCT*—you will read provocative examples of this hybrid, interdisciplinary area (for a brief description and history of cultural studies, see Edgerton 1996, p. 18 ff).] So, in a phrase, we traded the safety of bureaucracy for the excitement of intellectual exploration, hoping all along that we could influence our colleagues and friends in the schools to do the same. We remain, despite the odds, determined (see Thomas & Schubert, 1997, p. 280 ff., for one illustration of this determination).

THE ESSAYS

How to organize this book was not obvious to me. At first I thought I would expand the schema I had used in the 1988 *Contemporary Curriculum Discourses* collection, that is, the basic format of *Understanding Curriculum*. For the book to be helpful to the journal it must be taught, and that hope would be more likely realized if the book could be easily used as a reader alongside the textbook. But as I worked on the project I changed my mind. I think chronology rather than thematics makes the more powerful and revealing organizer. By serializing the essays according to the year of their publication (and within any given year alphabetically by the author's name), readers can quickly see who was thinking what and when. When one realizes, for instance, that Florence Krall was thinking about ecology fifteen years before it became a major preoccupation in the field—one thinks of Chet Bowers's (1995) provocative work as well as Noel Gough's (1994, 1996, 1997)—one appreciates just how "cutting edge" Flo was. And she spoke in such a disarmingly powerful autobiographical voice! Flo Krall was unafraid, direct, and wise; those of us who witnessed her conference presentations will not forget the spell she cast. Her essay opens the collection. Henry Giroux was an assistant professor at Boston University when he wrote "Dialectics and the Development of Curriculum Theory" (chapter 2). Soon after, he edited with Tony Penna and me—using the tripartite map of the field then in place (traditionalists, conceptual-empiricists, reconceptualists)— *Curriculum and Instruction: Alternatives in Education*. Soon after that Henry left curriculum for "critical pedagogy," and a decade later he would move again, this time to cultural studies. He has been a pioneer for a long time. Speaking of pioneers, Madeleine Grumet first connected "Conception, Contradiction and Curriculum" in 1979, nearly a decade before brilliantly elaborating on the three in *Bitter Milk*. Given how important and widely read that book is, I have chosen not to reproduce "Conception, Contradiction and Curriculum" but two other pieces, one that succinctly captures her early thinking on autobiography (chapter 3) and a second that is post-*Bitter Milk* (chapter 15). Next is Janet Miller's early (1982) and beautiful meditation on women and education, in which we hear clearly her lyrical and courageous voice speak the "sound of silence breaking." Following Janet's essay are three pieces from the 1980 John Dewey Society meeting (organized by Bill Doll), which *JCT* then printed. At that Dallas

meeting Nel Noddings tried out her idea of "caring"—Mary Anne Raywid and I
tried to be helpful (chapter 5). Herb Kliebard's intriguing piece on Dewey's early
history—his flirtation with the Herbartians—is next (chapter 6), followed by Jo
Anne Pagano's very helpful historical study (chapter 7), an important
contribution she made several years before formulating her provocative feminist
theory of teaching and curriculum, published as *Exiles and Communities* (1988).

Chapter 8 is Mary Aswell Doll's insightful "Beyond the Window." Here my
friend explores, from a Jungian perspective, themes and concepts she expresses
even more fully in *Beckett and Myth* (1988) and in her thoughtful and moving *To
the Lighthouse and Back* (1995). Michael Littleford is one of the most overlooked
and brilliant theorists of her generation; I am pleased to reproduce one of the
several pieces she did for *JCT* (chapter 9). Her knowledge of Vico and Blake, her
sensitive reading of the present historical moment, and her commitment to
democracy and education are evident in this example of her superb scholarship.
"Brilliant" is an adjective one must associate with Philip Wexler too, whose
provocative elaboration of "body and soul" is chapter 10. Shigeru Asanuma's
intriguing description of autobiographical method is next (chapter 11), followed
by the legendary Ted Aoki in a powerfully phenomenological meditation on
computers (chapter 12). Ted moved off phenomenology proper toward
poststructuralism and deconstruction, modes of analysis and critique evident in
Alan Block's sophisticated and literary explication of the school as text (chapter
13). Kathleen Casey has made two significant contributions: first is her
autobiographical studies of teachers, and second is her rethinking of the role of
religion in education (chapter 14). Next is Madeleine Grumet's clarifying
reflection on curriculum criticism (chapter 15) mentioned earlier. Patti Lather
has become a key figure in the 1990s; her *Getting Smart* was a major and early
statement of postmodernism in the field. She has become even more well known
for her perceptive analyses and theorizations of issues in research methodology.
In chapter 16 we can see why. David Jardine's "A Bell Ringing in the Empty
Sky" (chapter 17) is next. Jardine is one of the most gifted individuals in the
field; his brilliance is quite evident here, as he contemplates the legacy of the
West not only for the field, but for his son as well. Like Kathleen Casey, Patrick
Slattery (chapter 18) has transgressed religious borders in his scholarship; here I
reproduce his exciting elaboration of the eschatological in curriculum theory.
"Of Seagulls and Glass Roses" is next (chapter 19), Dennis Sumara's stunning
elaboration of curriculum as reading, relationality, and transformation. Dennis's
essay is followed by Michael W. Apple's memorable autobiographical appeal for
class analysis (chapter 20). In chapter 21 Brent Davis quietly reconceptualizes
mathematics education. Next is that Renaissance man named Joe Kincheloe; in
this occasion my friend reintegrates academic and vocational education (chapter
22). Cameron McCarthy gives us a strong example of postcolonial cultural
studies in his commentary on Wilson Harris (chapter 23). Once again Cameron

is out in front of an important discursive development in the field. Deborah Britzman, whose sophisticated psychoanalytic and queer theorizing promise to move her center stage, comments on "a polymorphously perverse curriculum" in chapter 24. The brilliant Suzanne de Castell's rumination on "literacy as a technology of self-formation" comes next (chapter 25), followed by Marla Morris's provocative analysis of parody and drag as instances of "ludic pedagogy" (chapter 26). Petra Munro's very smart "Resisting 'Resistance': Stories Women Teachers Tell" is chapter 27, followed by David Geoffrey Smith's insightful "Identity, Self, and Other in the Conduct of Pedagogical Action: An East/West Inquiry" (chapter 28). Concluding the collection is the remarkable Shirley Steinberg, here rethinking "Early Education as a Gendered Construction."

Even this very cursory review of these contents suggests something about the nature of the "intellectual breakthrough" in which JCT participated. In a word, the field shifted from a preoccupation with the narrow proceduralism associated with the Tyler Rationale to theoretical understanding broadly conceived. Even while political conditions eroded our capacity to influence schools in any jurisdictional sense, our effort to understand curriculum—not just implement or evaluate it—hardly means we have given up our hopes for the school or our sense of pedagogical and political solidarity with teachers, especially those who find their way into our university classrooms. Those who read *Understanding Curriculum* as somehow a "retreat from practice" are not reading very carefully. When I concluded that curriculum had become a highly symbolic concept over the course of the last twenty years, that hardly meant it was no longer an institutional one. By virtue of understanding curriculum as what the older generation chooses to tell the younger generation, one is inevitably engaged in everyday life, caught up as that is in the practical and the political. But what we now understand is that deciding how to proceed in our everyday engagement with students and ideas is not a self-evident matter; it cannot be reduced to protocol or social engineering.

The thoughtful practice of everyday educational life requires us to understand practice theoretically. So understood, curriculum becomes intensely historical, political, racial, gendered, phenomenological, postmodern, autobiographical, aesthetic, theological, and international. When we say that curriculum is a site on which the generations struggle to define themselves and the world, we are engaged in a theoretically enriched practice. When we say that curriculum is an extraordinarily complicated conversation, we are underscoring human agency and the volitional character of human action. When curriculum specialists understood their work only in institutional terms, they had in fact retreated from politically engaged and phenomenologically lived senses of practice. When curriculum was understood only institutionally, the classroom became a mausoleum, not a civic forum. We rejected a bureaucratization of the everyday, what was in fact pseudopractice. We embraced *praxis*. Over the past twenty years the American "curriculum" field has attempted "to take back" curriculum from the bureaucrats, to make the curriculum field itself a conversation, and in so doing, revitalize practice theoretically. That qualifies as an intellectual breakthrough in my book, and that is what is evident in these pages, pages taken from the pages of JCT.

It is winter 1998 as I write this; let us now return to a winter twenty years ago. In that first issue of JCT, I express—with Janet—our aspirations (not all of which were to be realized) and ask for a collective engagement in the reconceptualization of American curriculum studies ("Editorial Statement," 1979). Thinking about the relation of JCT to the field it wanted to serve engaged me the year after. "Notes on the Relationship Between a Field and its Journals" is the second part of the introduction to this collection. Kuhn's work on the concept of "paradigm shift" was still relatively fresh at the time; it seemed to describe well enough what was underway in American curriculum studies. I close that brief piece with a description of the kinds of work we hoped to publish in JCT and an announcement regarding the first conference, to be held at the Airlie House, near Warrenton, Virginia. There is mention of a foundation: ah, how our aspirations exceeded our fate. So it goes. Fate was kind enough, perhaps. Welcome to twenty years of JCT.

A C K N O W L E D G M E N T S

Many thanks to Dennis Sumara and Brent Davis for preparing sections four, five, six, and seven of the appendix. Thanks as well to Toby Daspit (general assistance), Craig Kridel (appendix and cover concept), Anne Pautz (cover photographs), and Janet Miller (appendix). Thanks as well to Shirley R. Steinberg and Joe L. Kincheloe for taking an interest in the project.

R E F E R E N C E S

Bowers, C. A. (1995). *Educating for an ecologically sustainable culture.* Albany: State University of New York Press.

Doll, M. A. (1988). *Becket and myth.* Syracuse, NY: Syracuse University Press.

Doll, M. A. (1995). *To the lighthouse and back.* New York: Peter Lang.

Edgerton, S. H. (1996). *Translating the curriculum.* New York: Routledge.

Giroux, H., Penna, A., & Pinar, W. F. (Eds.). (1981). *Curriculum and Instruction: Alternatives in education.* Berkeley, CA: McCutchan.

Gough, N. (1994). Playing at catastrophe: Ecopolitical education after the post-structuralism. *Educational Theory*, 44 (2), 189-210.

Gough, N. (1996). Virtual geography, video art and the global environment: Postmodernist possibilities for environmental education research. *Environmental Education Research*, 2 (3); 379-389.

Gough, Noel (1997). Weather* Incorporated: Environmental education, postmodern identities, and technocultural constructions of nature. *Canadian Journal of Environmental Education*, 2; 145-162.

Grumet, M. R. (1979). Conception, contradiction and curriculum. Paper presented to the Airlie Conference, Virginia. [Also, JCT, 1981, 3 (1), 287-298.]

Grumet, M. R. (1988). *Bitter milk.* Amherst, MA: University of Massachusetts Press.

Lather, P. (1991). *Getting smart: Feminist research and pedagogy with/in the postmodern.* London; Routledge.

Miller, J. L. (1982). The sound of silence breaking: Feminist pedagogy and curriculum theory. JCT, 4 (1), 5-11.

Pagano, J. A. (1990). *Exiles and communities: Teaching in the patriarchal wilderness.* Albany, NY: State University of New York Press.

Pinar, W. F. (Ed.). (1988). *Contemporary curriculum discourses.* Scottsdale, AZ: GSP.

Pinar, W. F., Reynolds, W. M., Slattery, P., & Taubman, P. M. (1995). *Understanding curriculum.* New York: Peter Lang.

Thomas, T. P. & Schubert, W. H. (1997, Spring). Recent curriculum theory. *Educational Theory, 47* (2), 261-285.

EDITORIAL STATEMENT

William F. Pinar
1979

Herbert Kliebard has written: "The task of the next fifty years in the curriculum field is one of developing alternatives to the mode of thinking that has so clearly dominated our first fifty years."[1] *The Journal Of Curriculum Theorizing* is interested in providing a medium through which this task can be achieved.

This work has commenced already. The University of Rochester conference in 1973, and the yearly conferences, which have ensued[2] represent evidence of what we have termed—not without controversy—the "reconceptualization." The phenomenon is, in one essential sense, this work of developing alternatives. It is more ambitious however; we aspire to fundamental reconceiving of current ideas of curriculum.

There are other signs that this work is underway: the publication *Of Heightened Consciousness, Cultural Revolution, and Curriculum Theory* (1974), *Curriculum Theorizing: The Reconceptualists* (1975), *Schools In Search Of Meaning* (1975), *Toward A Poor Curriculum* (1976), and *Ideology And Curriculum* (1979).[3] *The Journal Of Curriculum Theorizing* intends to encourage this work, and in several ways.

The journal plans to sponsor, as its financial condition permits, a series of activities, activities we hope will stimulate scholarly activity in a field some have characterized as "moribund." One major activity will be conferences, annually if circumstances and need suggest them. A second will be smaller occasional meetings, at which six to ten participants can focus on one or two papers. Third, the journal intends to publish a small book series—perhaps three titles a year—

in curriculum theory, history, and criticism. These will be important to the field, but of insufficient market potential to interest commercial publishers. The ambition in each of these projects is to increase the frequency and intensity of dialogue in the field.

The journal will not be afraid to publish writers who are not well known, including work by graduate students. We are especially interested in work that is intellectually experimental. We are willing to take risks, publishing material more conservative journals would reject. Some of these articles will be controversial—at least we hope so. We reject the notion that only polished, finished scholarly products are worthy of publication. After all, our interest is education, including the process of formulating views, the process of articulating experience. Thus, some of the pieces will be rough and clearly unfinished, primarily calls for further work. We hardly eschew refinement, but we will not sacrifice our commitment to the experimental attitude—experiment extended to the forms of scholarship and theory themselves—for the sake of quick and wide acceptance.

We intend to print pieces, which speak to school teachers and administrators, to interested laymen, as well as to our colleagues in colleges and universities. It follows we will print material written in varying degrees of abstraction, what some will see—with raised eyebrows—as varying degrees of theoretical sophistication. We will not be unduly concerned with such judgments. On occasion, we will print articles written with the often powerful simplicity of the autobiographical voice.

At the same time we remain conscious that the journal is responsible to the field as it is presently constituted. Our primary commitment is to assisting the field to take its "next step", but we recognize that such a step can only finally be taken by us all, by traditionalists and conceptual-empiricists, as well as by reconceptualists. We want to minimize the rigidifying effect ("here I stand, there you stand") such categories often have. We want exchange, including criticism. Thus we will occasionally print traditional and conceptual-empirical work when it addresses issues of mutual interest. George Posner's "Curriculum Research" in the first issue is an example.

The journal has received its financial start from royalties from the sale of *Curriculum Theorizing: The Reconceptualists*. It receives modest but important support from the Graduate School of Education and Human Development of the University of Rochester. In order to survive, however, it must receive subscriptions. And if it is to offer leadership to the field, through its program of activities, it must receive contributions above the basic fee.

These are hard times. Many are out of work, and this is especially so in the curriculum field. We do not ask such people to contribute more than the basic fee. But many of us continue to hold well-paying positions. We do ask that those of us in this category recognize the importance of the journal, and send according to our means.

We look forward with you to an important contribution to the intellectual life of the curriculum field.

N O T E S

1. Kliebard, H., (1975). Persistent Curriculum Issues in Historical Perspective, in W. F. Pinar (ed.), *Curriculum Theorizing: The reconceptualists*. Berkeley: McCutchan.

2. University of Rochester, (1973), chaired by Pinar; Xaiver University, Cincinnati (1974), chaired by Timonthy Riordan; University of Virginia (1975), chaired by Charles W. Beegle; University of Wisconsin, Milwaukee (1976), chaired by Alex Molnar and John Zahorik; Kent State University (1977), chaired by Richard Hawthorne; Rochester Institute of Technology (1978), chaired by Ronald E. Padgham; and Georgia State University (1978), chaired by Dorothy Huenecke.

3. Pinar, W. F. (ed.). (1974). *Heightened consciousness, cultural revolution, and curriculum theory*. Berkeley: McCutchan.   Pinar, W. F. (ed.). (1975). *Curriculum theorizing: The reconceptualists*. Berkeley: McCutchan. Macdonald, J. B. & Esther Zaret. (eds.). (1975). *Schools In Search Of Meaning*. Washington, D.C.: Association for Supervision and Curriculum Development. Pinar, W. F. & Grumet, M. R. *Toward a poor curriculum*. (1976). Dubuque, IO: Kendall/Hunt. Apple, M. W. (1979). *Ideology And Curriculum*. London: Routledge and Kegan Paul.

Notes on the Relationship
Between a Field and Its Journals

William F. Pinar
1980

As I begin to discuss *The Journal Of Curriculum Theorizing* and its relationship to the field, I realize that I speak in a different voice than when I discuss autobiography as a mode of curriculum research or when I describe and propose the reconceptualization of curriculum studies. When engaged in these latter activities, I am partisan to some extent. That is, I feel a loyalty to the point of view that I am proposing. My stance tends to be argumentative. However, the present assignment elicits another voice. The loyalty here is to the field itself, regardless what theoretic and methodoligic direction it may take. As is clear, I have opinions regarding that direction, but these are suspended for this occasion. Today I speak in the "base-line" way, in which we are allies, not only colleagues. We can agree here; we are speaking of our commitment to the field in which we were trained, in which we work, and the future of which is inextricably linked to our individual futures. We share this investment and commitment to the curriculum field, although we may not share ways of expressing that investment and commitment. Partly this is because our field is in what Kuhn terms crisis; partly it is the healthy and perennial condition of dissension.

I acknowledge that the Kuhn material has been misused and overused. Part of the lasting criticism of it has been the facility with which opposing points of view have appropriated the concept of "paradigm shift" to support contrasting positions. And there is the considerable controversy regarding Kuhn's vague and shifting use of the concept "paradigm." This important criticism acknowledged, there are aspects of the Kuhnian view of the history of science—and by extension the history of any field—that are not only true, but useful in discussing the relationship of a journal to its field.

One invaluable insight is the political character of field formation and disintegration. The conventional and usually publicly expressed view tends to be that a field proceeds rationally, according to the logical power of certain arguments. The image is of relatively emotionless, high-minded men [only a few women allowed] deliberating over various ideas, their own self-interests absent, deciding logically which ideas warrant further study and which do not. Kuhn, as well as our experience, tells us otherwise. Yet acknowledgement that scientists and academicians generally are not especially selfless, and in fact employ a variety of nonrational strategies to advance ideas they prefer [usually advancing their careers also], has caused very heated controversy. Many are shocked and angered that someone, namely Kuhn, could suggest such a thing. This response strikes me as odd, given that even superficial participation in a field discloses the profoundly political character of its movement.

Recognizing this political character is not equivalent to endorsing it. In my view it is regrettable. To the extent we allow our differences to be settled nonrationally, through political maneuvering, is the extent to which we diminish not only our field but our individual intellectual energy as well. It is facile and inescapably anti-intellectual, for instance, to ignore a new thinker, simply refuse to respond, and by so ignoring her, attempt to dispel her. One safeguards the status quo and conserves one's energy by refusing to engage with another. It is entropy. Such reliance upon political means—she is not invited to speak at conferences for instance—ensures intellectual parochialism, guarantees a static field. It is understandable that the "old boys" wish to protect their position, and explains why paradigms *shift* rather than *melt* gradually into each other, why a field goes into crisis when a dominant paradigm loses majority support rather than gracefully proceeds to new paradigms. The old boys hold on to their field as long as it is politically possible, and many would rather see the field die than give it over to the next generation. Thus, when the *ancien regime* does fall, it falls hard, and possibly the field does die in the ensuing power struggle. Awareness of the complex psycho-political dynamics of a field's internal process is important, not in order to legitimate these dynamics, but to assist us in becoming more rational in our participation in the development of our field.

It is obvious that the curriculum field is now, and has been for maybe 20 years [though this number is arguable], in a period of breakdown, or in Kuhn's term, "crisis." In fact, it has been near death for at least ten years as two prominent theoreticians have noted—Schwab in 1970 and Heubner six years later. Every field, Kuhn tells us, goes through such periods in its history. A dominant paradigm—a shared sense of what our work is and how we are to conduct it—is missing, and without a conceptual center several inchoate points of view vie for center stage. If a field passes through this period successfully, it will settle on some small number of these for a time. At the least it will agree which points of view are major, which are minor, and which are not to be considered further.

In the curriculum field's current crisis period, a majority of scholars and theorists cannot so agree. A majority cannot even agree upon a characterization of the crisis; witness the controversy surrounding my writing on the notion of reconceptualization. Whether the curriculum field will resolve its present crisis is, in my mind, an open question. It may not, and may simply pass from the scene altogether. There is some evidence to support this, and several prestigious schools of education are deleting the designation from the appropriate departments. Many curriculum faculty at less prestigious schools tend to ignore, astonishingly enough, the debate; i.e., the contemporary discussion of the crisis, and they retain curriculum ideas, such as the Tyler rationale, which are embarrassingly dated.

These questions—will the field survive, and if so in what form—are finally not merely interesting questions for me. I am invested in the field's survival, and I will experience relief and pleasure at the resolution of the present crisis, even if that resolution does not include in it continuing and serious investigation of autobiography as method and theme. This realization returns me to the initial reflection that this topic elicited, namely that one only feels a loyalty to one's field that is more basic than one's thematic and methodologic loyalties within that field.

What is the relationship of a journal to its field? In times of consensus or normal science, as Kuhn calls them, it seems it is primarily a servant. Its function is to print the best work available, and the determination of "best" is not problematic, as the majority of researchers share the same vision of their work and its advancement. In a time of crisis, the relationship is somewhat more complicated. True enough, a journal must remain faithful to the field and its point of view, for if it strays too far from mainstream perspectives, or even from the tradition that is in decline, it will not have a readership. Yet, because the tradition no longer controls the field, because it is clear that one of the now-nascent points of view will someday become the new tradition, constitute the paradigm (that is if resolution occurs at all), the journal can choose to ally itself with one or more of the nascent and competing points of view. Thus it will print, and this is true for *The Journal Of Curriculum Theorizing*, work according to two or more sets of criteria of quality. Of course, should these ideas of quality fade from the scene so will the journal, unless it shifts emphases accordingly. This fact underscores my view that, even in times of considerable fluidity, a journal remains, if it is to survive, a servant of the field. Perhaps I can portray this relationship more completely if I briefly discuss what I see as the position of the journal editor.

This position is a dual one; it contains elements of servant and leader. He is servant to the field insofar as he must publish, to some extent, the mainstream dialogue of the field. Obviously, he has some freedom to choose what he prints, and possibly it seems to those of us who have had manuscripts rejected, he has considerable and arbitrary freedom. Yet, further reflection reveals that he must remain intellectually loyal to a significant number of colleagues by printing work they agree is important, else he loses the journal's readership. For this reason I see the basic relationship between a journal and its field, between the journal editor and his field, as primarily servant to master. In times of "normal science" or consensus, this relationship is more stable than in periods of crisis, but the relationship fundamentally is unchanged.

In a time of crisis the editor can choose to ally himself and the journal with one or more points of view. One factor in the resolution of the crisis and the predominance of one perspective over another is the power of publication. The power to publish is part of the power to define the dialogue of a field because as what is printed becomes historical record in libraries, to be studied by graduate students, i.e., prospective disciplinary participants. Again, this power to publish is sharply circumscribed according to the interests of journal subscribers. A field cannot be hijacked by extremists who print in their journal only their own point of view. Such partisans, who demonstrate by their exclusivity their self-interest and unwillingness to converse with their colleagues, may survive over a period of time, but the lack of a broad constituency will eventually ensure they are not included in what we may call—tongue in cheek—the new coalition government. Those who constitute the mainstream, even if that mainstream is not conceptually coherent, maintain a kind of veto over their field's direction, simply by political strength of numbers. Thus, in a period of crisis, a journal and its editor may exercise some leadership; however, this leadership is carefully circumscribed by the intellectual limits and political power of his mainstream colleagues.

I want to stress that I do not view the process of change (and more specifically the crisis resolution) as exclusively political. It is logical. As well, it is psychological and economic, but even the briefest consideration of these aspects is beyond the scope of this obviously limited exposition. These matters could well be the subject of several studies, studies that would not only provide helpful information to us in attempting to navigate our way through the present crisis, but as well would contribute to our knowledge of how fields—nonscientific fields that to my knowledge are virtually unexplored from a Kuhnian perspective— resolve crises and go through change generally. The role of the journal in this complex process is a modest and primarily passive one.

▼▼▼

In the remainder of this article I would like to shift my comments considerably, from the more generalized focus of the preceding to a more concrete focus on *The Journal Of Curriculum Theorizing* itself. We are interested in three orders of work: theory, history, and criticism. While distinguishable, these categories overlap.

We see historical work as important for the commonsensical reason that it makes more discernible the origins of the present situation. As well, the history of the field is interesting in its own right, regardless of its use in understanding the present. I see criticism broadly as assessment of both historical and contemporary trends in curriculum theory and practice. As the historical, the critical voice is primarily a scholarly one. That is, it carefully portrays others' work, and through argumentation, appraises that work. The third order of work, the theoretical, is by its nature less scholarly. Its emphasis is the construction of new points of view, not "new" in the sense of being unconnected with past and present perspectives, but new insofar as it aspires to extend these views. You note that I am not employing theory in any scientific sense. A scientific sense of theory is, of course, warranted in the field, but it is of little interest to me. I am interested in theoretical work that is intellectually experimental and that is born in study characteristic of the humanities and the arts. Because our field has not been a scholarly field, many of us are presently preoccupied, and rightly, with standards of careful scholarship. Such persons I see as working in the historical and critical modes of research. However, there need to be, if our field is to advance, those of us who abandon such caution, refuse to be intellectually conservative. We must, if our field is not always to lag 10 to 20 years behind avant garde work in the other disciplines, be willing to intellectually experiment and create points of view for which there are no exact precedents. Only by such risk can we hope to offer important leadership to our colleagues in the university and in the schools. I have been deliberately vague about the meaning of the theoretical, partly due to considerations of time, and in order not to stipulate in advance what form this work will take.

To honor these interests *The Journal Of Curriculum Theorizing* will publish all three orders of work. We will do so in essay and book form. The books we intend to publish will be of high scholarly and theoretical quality, but given their subject matter are of insufficient financial promise to interest commercial publishers, or of too limited focus to interest university presses. The first book appeared in the issue that preceded this one. It is John Schwartz's comprehensive study of objectivity and the work of Harold Rugg. As you know, Rugg is just now beginning to receive the serious attention his importance to the field merits. The Schwartz study is particularly timely as it examines a question—objectivity—which is of at least peripheral concern to most of us. Further, Schwartz connects Rugg's work and the methodologic issues that preoccupied him as a curriculum writer and theorist, to the contemporary scene. Further publications include Leonard Berk's interesting study of biography as a mode of curriculum research; the proceedings of the 1974 Xavier, the 1975 Virginia, and the 1978 Georgia State conferences; and my own recently completed study of life history and educational experience. We anticipate publishing approximately two books a year in this Rochester Series in Curriculum Theory, History, and Criticism.

One difficulty I see in the field at present is the lack of occasion for scholars and theorists to address each other. It is something of the nature of curriculum and of other education subfields for university faculty to address their work to schoolpeople. Texts tend to be written for those who will enroll in curriculum courses. This is necessary, but it does tend to restrict dialogue among university researchers. It tends to keep the work more introductory, as one is forever introducing the few principles and concepts that have accumulated over the years to a new audience each term. Often, the university scholar speaks in a popular, journalistic mode to present preoccupations of school personnel and ignores his own theoretical interests. The result is the "trendy" quality to much curriculum writing. Not until university curriculum faculty are willing to work with themselves as well as with school personnel will any curriculum knowledge and methods of lasting value be formulated, To further this development, the journal will sponsor a series of conferences, possibly yearly, expressly to offer university faculty the occasion to speak explicitly to each other, to consider the question of the field, and its advancement. The first meeting will be held this fall in north central Virginia, at the Airlie House. The opening address will be given by Professor Theodore Brown of the University of Rochester's Department of History. Brown took his Ph.D. with Kuhn at Princeton, and he will offer us a generalized model of how fields—such as curriculum—pass through crisis and change. Other speakers will be selected from those proposing papers.

Depending upon financial success, we are interested in establishing *The Journal Of Curriculum Theorizing* Foundation, a not-for-profit organization dedicated to the advancement of curriculum studies. In addition to publication of the journal and sponsoring conferences, the foundation would offer faculty study grants and graduate student fellowships for advanced study of curriculum. Finally, the foundation would consider, as its financial condition permits, hiring a lobbying unit to argue in Washington and elsewhere for the importance of curriculum studies.

The extent to which these proposals are realized depends, as my earlier comments make evident, on the interests of the majority of you.

CHAPTER ONE

Living Metaphors

The Real Curriculum
in Environmental Education

Florence R. Krall
1979

PART I

I am about to backpack into a trailess wilderness. Physically and psychologically tired before beginning, I am filled with ambivalence. The divide at 12,000 feet and the descent into the drainage on the other side are our goal; we have planned long for this journey. But now with the moment at hand I dread the days ahead, the beginning, the climb, the struggle, the unknown. I feel the weight of inertia, the resistance to change, the longing for the status quo. I wonder why I am here doing this.... A feeling, deep down begins to emerge. A quick breath. A rush of excitement bubbles up. "To plunge in; to choose; to disclose; to move: this is the road...." (Greene, 1975). I pick up my pack and head out.

Fallen logs to straddle. Boulders to hop. The tension of the unknown passes as I am absorbed with the task at hand. Distracted, I lose my way. A game trail appears suddenly. I borrow it. It disappears as suddenly and I am confronted once more with finding my own way. The divide becomes secondary as all of my attentions are directed to the present. The here and now becomes my motive.

A flash of color brings my binoculars, hanging readily accessible on my backpack, to my eyes. I bracket a Western Tanager, black, red, white, and yellow on the limb of a spruce. I escape body, place, and time and for a brief moment (or is it an eternity?) I am the bird, free and beautiful.

The quiet, cool forest engulfs me. The musty smell of decomposition, fungi benefiting. Lichen eating at the pink facies of feldspar, crystalline quartz, reducing rock to something life can take hold of. New creations synergizing. Unique meetings. New forms uniting.

The canyon narrows. The stream, till now my companion, forces me against the mountain. I must cross but, first, a rest. My backpack off, eyes close, I lean against a tree. The soothing sound of water cleansing, refreshing, rushes through my mind.

I rouse myself and walk to the stream's edge. Reflections on a quiet pool hide the savage, underwater world with an inverted image of sky and tree. Kneeling, I look deeper and see a hint of the bottom distorted by current and refraction.

I prop myself on two boulders polished by time, lower my face to the water, and drink deeply. Clear, cleansing, common, liquid-ubiquitous, unique. Water.

Two deep breaths. I submerge my face and open my eyes. The reflections, refractions gone, I am a part of the watery world: a caddis fly, crawling in an improvised home of stream debris, spinning a net, an opportunist, snatching whatever comes my way; a black fly larva, barely hanging on, clinging to the rock ledge as the world rushes by; a vicious beetle larva, predatory, attacking; a schizophrenic whirligig living at the interface of two worlds with eyes to see both. Which am I?

I come out of the water, wipe my face with a bandanna. Aerobe that I am, I cannot detach myself from the water world. I stare at a cascade and feel myself slipping over the smooth boulders, falling, splashing down. Trapped in turbulent flow, I stagnate in a back-eddy. Then once more caught in the stream, I flow, at times conforming to my surroundings, at other times, creating my own path. Down, down, to base level, to the open ocean, mingling with the waters of the world, rising in a new vapor.

With aching muscles and relishing the sweetness of fatigue, I pick up my pack. I dream of the top, fantasize the view. Ah! To look as far as eyes can see! To breathe as deeply as lungs can hold!

Flowers along the path beckon to me. Old friends telling their stories. Adapted, they know their place. Beautiful diverse forms with but one common goal: a seed.

> In the forest
>   wind-thrown firs,
>   flat-roofs, on edge,
>   giant webs.
> Below timberline
>   weathered snags
>   fuel of ancient fires,
>   twisted monuments.
> At timberline

crumholtz
flagged and wind-pruned
carrying on.
TREES
reminders of the past
sprouting in ashes
growing tips, heaven-bound.

We camp at timberline. Half-sleeping, I hear picas rummaging around my tent the night through. Early the next morning, climbing west toward the summit, I find ice crystals, strange remnants of the previous day. As I gaze at them, wondering how they came to be, they disappear before my eyes, the tiny basin containing them filling with water, dissolving them away. The rising sun shining on the snow field above answers my question. I marvel at the perfect timing so often bringing answers, so often guiding my footsteps to singular crossings.

The top at last! A moment to rest and enjoy the view, the air. Stretched supine, I see above me a cloud. "But the view," my friends are saying. Racing ahead yet standing still, leading edge dissipating, trailing edge condensing, streams of vapor folding back, transcedent. I came for the view and found THE CLOUD!

"The view!" my impatient students remind me. But wait! At my feet, hidden by the brown, frost-tipped alpine carpet, an arctic gentian. Prone, now, eye to eye, I stare into the delicate, pale-green bell; the salmon anthers, bulging into pollen; the funnel-shaped corolla, flecked. My breath leaves me. How could I have overlooked anything so beautiful? I came for the view and found THE FLOWER.

"The view!" Ah, yes, the view. "I am a transparent eyeball; I am nothing, I see all...the health of the eye seems to demand a horizon. We are never tired so long as we can see far enough" (Emerson, 1927). So I look across the boulder field, down into the deep canyon below. I look back at the hazy mountains in the distance. I look ahead at the trail leading on endlessly. I look. I become: the canyon, the forest, the path winding up, crossing others, fading into the future.

P A R T   I I

I am floating the Colorado River with a group of students, deep in the red womb of Earth Mother. Spence is lying motionless, lost in thought. Leslie flirts with the boatman. Cal reviews his bird list. Lynne reads a novel. Jay declares impatiently that we need a geologist. I sit and brood. Who needs a geologist! It is so clear: each layer upon layer, laid down in succession uniformly, plateau lifted, river entrenched. Protoplasmic intrusion, we, one with the layered rock, the standing walls, the river flowing.

I stare up at the smooth, red-walled alcove, tiger-striped. I am reminded of Dubai's description of sculptors, African, Oriental, Eskimo. Recognizing the structure within their wood, jade, ivory, they then create the external form. The Eskimo carver attempting to release the spirit within the ivory, talks to the fragment, whispering *"Who are You?"* (Dubos, 1972). What lies within these fossil sands? The weathered face of an elder, its spirit, revealed.

The sinking sun tells us it's time to camp, to explore the canyon before nightfall. I hike up the creekbed, the canyon walls at each turn, a mosaic of shadow and light. I peer into an alcove heavy with the musk of woodrat. Above a shelf of petrified excrement, two giant luminous eyes, framed by juniper branches, watch me. Scraps dropped in eating add to the centuries of waste, a monument to plant and woodrat history.

I walk on. A cavity in the side wall, my size, entices me in. Coiled in a fetal position from my shadowy womb/tomb. I look out at the blazing red wall. Walking down the creekbed once more, I look through dark tunnels, carved by water, into the light beyond. The sun at my back, I take a picture of my shadow against a rock backdrop. The box canyon ends at the falls, inky waters gushing from a high crevice outlined in god by the day's last rays. In camp that night, lying in my sleeping bag, I see the crescent moon barely revealing its dark side shining through a skyline notch.

P A R T   I I I

Back in the faculty meeting in Room 121, Milton Bennion Hall, I am trying to convey to my colleagues the essence of my environmental education curriculum. I deny that I am teaching science, geography, philosophy, creative writing, or whatever. No, I do not stress survival, the physical challenge of the human against the elements; nor recreation, for "nature never became a toy to the wise spirit" (Emerson, 1927).

I teach through metaphors. Living, not literary. What are they? Encounters. Encounters with nature, purely sentient and personal in their conception. Vivid, intense, clear, they grow and go on living in my heart and mind, tapes, replayed over and over telling me more and more about my Earth niche. Tools of pedagogy? Perhaps. Sometimes. But shared with students with great care and humility only when a common ground is sensed. Parcels of existential reality they carry a deeper meaning transferable as it is remembered—useful only in pedagogy if "they evince feelings or predispose others [students] to act and feel" (Black, 1962). Where are they found? Wherever. Rainbows, they come as gifts after the rain. Seeking them unintentionally, I discover them in proper time for "The shows of the day...if too eagerly hunted, become shows merely, and mock us with their unreality" (Emerson, 1927).

And what of the curriculum? It is a "poor curriculum stripped of the distractions...of videotape, audiotape, fancy books and buildings, values clarification and individualized instruction. Stripped of all the clothing we drape around us to keep us from seeing" (Pinar, Grumet, 1976). DA practical curriculum uniting scientific and interpretive ways of knowing while freeing the individual (Van Manen, 1976) to "adjust inward and outward senses to each other" (Emerson, 1927). An emancipating curriculum with the elements of praxis, action and reflection, joined (Freire, 1970). A general curriculum, a multidisciplinary way of looking at the world, (Nash, 1976) essential to persons who intend teaching the children of this planet.

My colleagues sit waiting; their eyes impatient, unbelieving. I recall the tension of the unknown; long for the release with reflection, the sense of wisdom and wholeness, the interactive process between the world, students, and myself, bringing attributes of the world, parcels of reality woven into a fabric with brilliant threads throughout; the practical knowledge; the spiritual healing; the destruction of old ways of knowing leading to the creative act, a reconceptualization of what teaching and learning are all about (Pinar, 1975). Why can't I bring these moments into this meeting? I flush with frustration and feeling and mutter: "Perhaps some day soon I'll write a position paper."

6 FLORENCE R. KRALL

E F E R E N C E S

Black, M. (1962). Models and metaphors, studies in language and philosophy. Ithaca, NY: Cornell University Press.

Dubos, R. (1972). *A God within*. New York: Scribner's Sons.

Emerson, R. W. (1927). Nature in *The Works Of Ralph Waldo Emerson*. New York: Walter J. Black.

Freire, P. (1974). *Pedagogy of the oppressed*. New York: Herder and Herder.

Greene, M. Curriculum and Consciousness. In *Curriculum Theorizing, The Reconceptualists*, edited by W. Pinar. Berkeley, CA: McCutchan Publishing.

Nash, R. (1976). *Logs*, Universities, and the Environmental Education Compromise. *Current Issues In Environmental Education, II*, edited by R. Martlett. Columbus, OH: ERIC/SMEAC.

Pinar, W. F. & M. R. Grumet. (1976). *Toward A Poor Curriculum*. Dubuque, IO: Kendall/Hunt Publishing.

van Manen, M. Linking Ways of Knowing with Ways of Being Practical. Mimeographed paper presented at the Milwaukee Curriculum Theory Conference, November, 1976.

CHAPTER TWO

Dialectics and the Development of Curriculum Theory

Henry A. Giroux
1980

One of the major tasks of the curriculum field is to demonstrate in consistent fashion the process of self-criticism and self-renewal. Unfortunately, such a task is more easily stated than accomplished. Yet, while the reasons for the loss of this critical capacity are varied and complex, the underlying source for the atrophy of self-reflection in the curriculum field may be traced to a general failure, particularly among members of the dominant tradition, to understand how the interface of ideology, dominant institutional interests, and curriculum theory contribute to the latter's incomplete development.

Walter Benjamin provided one clue when he wrote, "In every era the attempt must be made to wrest tradition away from a conformist that is about to overpower it."[1] What this implies is that no field of inquiry, including the curriculum field, is immune from the self-complacency that threatens it once the field gains status as an "acceptable" mode of discourse and inquiry. Thus, the institutionalization of the curriculum field points to the need to develop a mode of analysis that educates its members to the language and logic of its own political and ideological center of gravity. What this means is that if the curriculum field is going to resist the conformity that threatens to overtake it, its members will have to reassess its possibilities for critique and growth against the influence and mediations of those dominant institutional forces that often work to limit the curriculum field's power as a mode of critical discourse and inquiry.

The role of curriculum theory as a vehicle of critique and vision has a long and valued tradition. If that tradition is to be maintained, we will have to begin with an acknowledgement of its decline within the last few decades. At the core of this acknowledgement is the notion that such a tradition consistently needs to

replenish itself in the face of changing historical situations and the development
of new social formations. This suggests that we must consider new forms of
discourse and practice in order to maintain the field's critical posture as well as
its ability for self-renewal. This paper represents one step in the process of self-
renewal. It attempts to show the significance of the concept of the dialectic for
curriculum theory and practice. It posits a general framework that points to new
ways to examine the relationships and ensuing questions that result when we use
a different conceptual model to critique the curriculum field. The model used in
this paper is neither altogether new, nor is it intended to be complete. In part, it
modestly demonstrates both the strengths and weaknesses of the dialectic itself:
the dynamic of an unfolding process whose very existence points to an incessant
struggle against a series of conflicts and contradictions that underscore the
curriculum field, the wider society, and the perceptions that shape our
understanding of the world in which we live and work. Moreover, these conflicts
and contradictions are rooted in real life situations, and if they are to be
understood by educators, they will have to be examined at their source, for only
then can they be overcome. The concept of the dialectic helps to shake us from
the boredom and indifference that accompanies the belief that we live in the
best of all worlds. In essence, it speaks to the existence of contradictions that are
a part of every age. Its message is neither a celebration of relativity nor cynicism,
but rather an acknowledgment that the search for the truth must begin by seeing
beyond the false harmony between subject and society. Such "harmony" must be
seen for what it is: a piece of ideology that smoothes over the existence of those
contradictions that call into question the meaning and consequence of our work
as educators and the role that such work has in reproducing the inequities that
mark the larger society.

The meaning of the dialectic has an elusive quality. Variations on its
meaning and application extend from Plato to Hegel to Mao Tse Tung. The
concept has been defined in purely idealist terms by Hegel as well as in vulgar
materialist terms by a score of orthodox Marxists.[2] In its many versions, it has
been used as a rationale to support repressive ideologies and social systems as
well as radical world views and social orders. Given the mixed history of the
concept, it will be a major goal of this essay to delineate what I believe are the
most useful and central categories of the dialectic.

Instead of being viewed as a universal method, characterized by rigid rules
and magical qualities, the concept of the dialectic is defined here as a critical
mode of reasoning and behavior, one that represents both a part as well as a
critique of the conflicts and solutions that define the nature of human existence.
In effect, the real meaning of the concept of the dialectic is rooted in the major
assumptions that give its categories their driving and critical power. Similarly,
the categories themselves both reflect and develop out of those aspects of human
knowledge that reflect and critically penetrate "the process of natural and social
development."[3] But if these categories of the dialectic are to become functional,

the assumptions that reveal both their interests and intent must be clarified. It is to the latter task that I will now turn.

It is my belief that the notion of the dialectic becomes important only with a commitment to the notion of emancipation, one that seeks to liberate human beings in both subjective and objective terms. In other words, a notion of emancipation that penetrates the world of everyday life with critical concepts that link the preconceptual, the ritualized experiences and the routine practices of daily existence with forms of reflection that reveal their objective and social roots. It is in the tension between the recognized oppression that underlies our daily lives and the critical understanding that demands a call to rectify it that the dialectic becomes more than a neutral social science category.[4]

Given this context, it would be inappropriate to reduce the dialectic to a form of epistemology that functions solely as a tool of rational understanding. Nor can the dialectic in this case be viewed simply as a ready made formula or "method" whose laws exist outside of history or human action. Both positions strip the dialectic of its critical force. In the first instance, the dialectic is reduced to mere cognition. Lost there is the concertinas of the dialectic, concertinas rooted in the very basis and origins of being itself.[5] In other words, the dialectic is more than a comprehension of reality, it is the "designation for aspects of being within being itself...human existence in its reality, in its events, within the world as it is conceived and formed."[6] Karol Koki captures this point in his claim that "dialectics does not enter cognition from without as an afterthought...Rather cognition is dialectics itself, in one of its forms."[7] Cognition, in this sense, is not simply contemplation, it is the understanding of reality insofar as humankind shapes it in the process of living it.

On the other hand, it is important to understand that the dialectic is not simply a methodology governed by universal laws. Such a perspective has more to do with "frozen" ideology than a critical concept of the dialectic. Removed from the necessity of constant self-renewal through the process of reflective criticism, this view of the dialectic becomes synonymous with a petrified, omniscient system of universal laws. Not only does methodology stand alone as a measure of truth in such a view, it also denies the notion of human intentionality and the interplay between human consciousness and specific historical circumstances. Such a position has more to do with vulgar forms of positivism than with the dialectic. T.W. Adorno has noted that the latter position can only degenerate into a form of ideological shorthand that extends unqualified support to the status quo. He writes:

> A rigorous dialectical thinker should not in fact speak of method, for the simple reason—which today has almost entirely disappeared from view—that the method should be a function of the object, not the inverse. This notion, which Hegel elaborated very convincingly, is one which has been all too simply repressed by the positivistic spirit, such that the over-valuation of method is truly a symptom of the consciousness of our time. Sociologically speaking, it is

truly closely related to the general tendency to substitute means for ends. In the last instance, this tendency is related to the nature of the commodity: to the fact that everything is seen as functional, as being-for-another and no longer something which exists in itself.[8]

Of course, this is not meant to imply that methodological reflections should be dispensed with. What it does mean is that method should allow educators to get a clear perception of how they should resolve predefined issues; but the ultimate meaning of such issues must be dealt with before methodological considerations can be taken into account. Thus, the dialectic does not begin with a methodology, it begins with the fact of human existence and the contradictions and disjunctions that, in part, shape it and problematize its meaning in the world. This is not meant to suggest that the concept of the dialectic does not have its limitations. In some cases, the dialectic is useful, in others it is not. It is clear that there are microphenomena and projects that under certain conditions yield valuable insights when analyzed according to the rules of formal logic, rules which are distinctly undialectical. For example, there are laws of formal logic such as the law of exclusion, i.e., either A, or non −A, that are more applicable to a specific problem than the concept of the dialectic might be. Yet, while formal logic has a certain valuable specificity and application, in the final analysis it is the dialectic that helps us to understand the limitations of formal logic. To ignore the limitations and strengths of the dialectic is to expand it into its opposite: an empty concept with no boundaries or possibilities for self-reflection and correction. In the final analysis, we can say that the dialectic represents an interpenetration of reasoning and method, an interpenetration that belies both an abstract objectivism and abstract subjectivism. If the driving power of the dialectic is to dissolve into metaphysical smoke, it must be seen as a form of radical critique and action, each of which act on and penetrate the other.

This brings us to another assumption that gives critical power to the concept of the dialectic. Any emancipatory notion of the dialectic has to be grounded in the process of critique and praxis. In general terms this means that the dialectic functions so as to help people analyze the world in which they live, to become aware of the constraints that prevent them from changing that world, and, finally, to help them collectively struggle to transform that world. As a form of critique, the dialectic functions to bring to awareness underlying contradictions that support existing forms of alienation. It is based on the use of a language and discourse that is capable of looking at the world in a different way: that is, from a perspective that transcends the world of "facts" and "natural" laws that serve to smother reality and to flatten contradictions. Although it must be recognized that as a first step toward praxis critique is as difficult as it is necessary. In other words, critique in itself in this country is a difficult task. This is particularly true in the United States since the dominant social science paradigm eschews critical categories of social thought.[9] It comes as no surprise to find that categories like social class, ideology, false consciousness, and class conflict are either missing from the language of mainstream social science or conveniently stripped of any analytical power. Under such circumstances, the relationship between dialectical reasoning and critical thought becomes lost.

In brief, a critical concept of the dialectic moves beyond mainstream social analysis by presenting itself as both the form and experience of critique. As an epistemology it gives power to the concept of negative thinking. Herbert Marcuse illuminates the latter with his claim that "dialectical thought starts with the experience that the world is unfree; that is to say man and nature exist in conditions of alienation, exist as other than they are."[10] Thus, the driving force of negative thinking resides in its ability to penetrate reality and to search and reveal the source and genesis of the contradictions that give it meaning. Put another way, negative thinking is an attack on the pseudoconcrete, i.e., the collection of phenomena that reproduce and support forms of mystification and ideology that conceal the essence of reality. Kosik describes the pseudoconcrete as "the collection of phenomena that crowd the everyday environment and the routine atmosphere of human life, and which penetrate the consciousness of acting individuals with a regularity, immediacy and self-evidence that lend them a semblance of autonomy and naturalness."[11] Clearly, there is no room in this type of analysis for those positivistic assumptions that suggest: (1) that the relationship of theory to practice is primarily technical; (2) that there is only one scientific method, (3) that knowledge is inherently neutral, and (4) that scientific inquiry itself is value free.[12] The importance of critique as a fundamental dimension of the dialectic rests with its ability to peel away the layers of meaning that give shape to our everyday lives; moreover it serves as a guide to action designed to alter those life forces that embody the power of an oppressive reality. As such, the concept of the dialectic used here is closely tied to an acknowledgement of the importance of a critique that embraces critical categories that serve to illuminate the intersection of the social and the personal, history and private experience. This allows us to further extend our definition of "praxis" as a guiding assumption of the dialectic.

Praxis as we use it has a number of important moments, all of which overlap and interpenetrate. Praxis, as one moment, represents the transition from critical thought to reflective intervention in the world. Paulo Freire captures the importance of this general conception of praxis when he writes:

> Men will be truly critical if they live in the plenitude of praxis, that is if their action encompasses a critical reflection which increasingly organizes their thinking and thus leads them to move from a purely naïve knowledge of reality to a higher level, one which enables them to perceive the causes of reality.[13]

But praxis, as another moment, suggests more than a struggle against the forces of oppression; it further suggests a struggle that defines freedom in social and not merely personal terms. Emancipation is linked in this case to groups of people struggling against the social forces that oppress them. It also suggests that the struggle affirms the power of human agents to act in a self-determining fashion out of a context that is as deeply historical as it is critical. Praxis then, as another moment, typifies a conception of freedom that analyzes the content and form of existing struggles within the contest of their historical genesis and development.

Praxis, as a third moment, translates a historical sensibility into a critical sensibility.[14] More specifically, it is argued here that modes of reasoning, interpretation, and inquiry develop a critical capacity to the degree that they pay attention to the flow of history. In the absence of an attentiveness to history, criticism is often muted by the dominant ideology, which often parades under the banner of absolute verities and "natural" laws. This type of "assault" on historical sensibility is no small matter. Marcuse rightfully claims that this represents a form of false consciousness, "the repression of society in the formation of concepts…a confinement of experience, a restriction of meaning."[15] Understandably, a critical notion of the dialectic grounds itself in historical sensibility because not to do so represents an attack on the very process of thinking itself. In more specific terms, the dialectic incorporates a historical sensibility in the interest of liberating human beings not only from those traditions that legitimate oppressive institutional arrangements, but also from their own individual history, i.e., that which society has made of them. This is the critical point that links praxis and historical consciousness. For we must turn to history in order to understand the traditions that have shaped our individual biographies and intersubjective relationships with other human beings. At the core of the dialectic is the notion that underlying the mediations that form the intersubjective space in which we live, work, study, and dream are social relationships, relations between people and not things. All the material things around us, whether they are the buildings we live in or the money that we use to pay our rent, represent the objectification of human labor and social formations operating under specific socio-historical conditions. These are both part of the dialectic and serve as well as an object of study and analysis through one form of the dialectic, i.e., dialectical reasoning.

In short, if the concept of the dialectic is to become useful in the service or radical pedagogy, it will have to be grounded in assumptions that give its central categories an emancipatory purpose. I have specified what these assumptions are by arguing: (1) that the dialectic is a form of praxis that links critical reasoning with a critical intervention in the world; (2) that the dialectic is not guided by absolute laws but is a process of critique and praxis that under different historical circumstances takes different forms; (3) that the dialectic necessitates human agents acting collectively to transform the world in which they live; (4) that the dialectic is grounded in a vision that links historical and critical sensibilities as modes of reasoning that inform and enrich each other; and (5) that the dialectic is not value-free, but rests on interests that oppose oppression in all of its forms.

This section will briefly spell out what the central categories of the dialectic are and attempt at the same time to provide brief examples of how these categories relate to educational theory and practice.

Totality represents one of the central categories of the dialectic. Its meaning is based on the insight that for any fact, issue, or phenomenon to become meaningful it must ultimately be examined within the context of the social totality that gives it meaning. This represents one of the fundamental tenets of the dialectic, one that underscores context in the methodological sense as well as in the sense of grasping the importance of "historical totality." For instance, Herbert Marcuse writes:

> To comprehend an historical object completely in its concrete reality, one has to grasp the totality of events. Such a comprehension is impossible if the historical object is considered rigid and isolated from its historical context, and treated as an identity free of contradictions "throughout time," instead of seeing it as a many-faced coming into being, acting and passing away in time. Not only its positive moments should be brought into view but also its negative moments which equally belong to it—what the historical object has been—and what it is becoming, and what it is not contributes to its reality, since this is what determines it and moves it.[16]

Moreover, the category of totality stresses that the "irreducible unit of reality is the relation and not the thing."[17] Within the context of human history and understanding, socio-political reality is seen as the "unity of production and products, of subject and object, of genesis and structure."[18] Thus, the category of totality speaks to the importance of seeing things relationally in their many sided development; moreover, it points to a world in which things, meanings, and relations are not conceived as objects removed from human history and action, but rather are seen as products of human praxis. Within the notion of totality there is little room for a reified, positivistic vision of the world, one that celebrates a posture that is at once fragmented, isolated, and ahistorical.

In concrete pedagogical terms this means that the role of schools, curriculum development, and pedagogy itself must be examined in a context that reveals their development historically, as well as their relationship to the larger social order. Michael W. Apple has voiced this concern with his claim that:

> education as a field of study does not have a strong tradition of such "situating." In fact, if one were to point to one of the most neglected areas of educational scholarship, it would be just this, the critical study of the relationship between ideologies and educational thought and practice, the study of the range of seemingly commonsense assumptions that would lay bare the political, social, ethical, and economic interests and commitments that are uncritically accepted as "the way life really is" in our day to day life as educators.[19]

As a mode of reasoning, the category of totality in the dialectic allows educators not only to become more critically interpretive, it also suggests new ways of acting in the world. It helps teachers and students alike to link knowledge with specific normative interests, with specific frames of reference. The latter point necessitates one important qualification about the category of totality, and that is, for this category to become viable it must be connected to notions of causality and ideology. The category of totality ceases to be dialectical when it becomes nothing more than a methodology for asserting that everything is connected with everything else. The importance of totality lies in its value in helping us answer fundamental questions about the truth content and nature of reality. [20] It focuses on the ideological and objective structures of society and looks at how they function in their contradictions and correspondence to distort as well as reflect reality. Totality in this sense points to causal relationships as part of an effort to ascertain the truth. This leads us to the next category, the notion of mediation.

Mediation is a core category of the dialectic that enriches and deepens the notion of totality. It does this by dispensing with the trivial notion that reality is merely a reflection of the sum of forces that make up the world in which we live. In essence, mediation rejects simple "reflection" theories by claiming that "all active relations between being and consciousness are inevitably mediated..."[21] This suggests two important points: (1) mediation is a process that embodies the object itself, i.e., those forces that shape our perceptions of the world are not just in our minds, but are a material and constitutive part of our everyday routines and practices; and (2) pure immediacy in its various forms: perception, commonsense, "facts," and sensation is an illusion. Mediation is thus a process, an internalized force, and a critical category. It can be used to reveal how the mechanisms of social and cultural reproduction both determine and legitimate the meaning of various socio-cultural institutional arrangements, modes of knowing, ways of behaving, patterns of interaction, etc. In short, the category of mediation provides the framework for looking at various cultural phenomena in terms of their essences and not in terms of their "legitimated" commonsense meanings. Thus, mediation indicates a search for the essence of a phenomenon, a peeling away of its different layers of meaning until one finds the combination of objective and subjective forces that made it what it is and, therefore, constitute its true nature. Mediation is both a process and a statement against the notion that phenomena reveal themselves immediately. It posits the need for human beings to look for the structure of meaning beyond the distorting fabricated "reality" of ideology. It points to another level of reality, one that suggests not distortion but reality in its unmasked form.[22]

The value that the category of mediation has for educators is noteworthy. It calls into question the static and petrified commonsense assumptions that underlie much of our thinking about curriculum and classroom pedagogy. It forces us to think relationally about the nature of knowledge, classroom social relationships, and values. Similarly, it points to ever-widening levels of mediation and correspondence between schools and the larger society. Not only does it continually prod us to make problematic the selection, organization, and distribution of meanings and values that structure classroom learning, it also serves to open to examination the very belief and values that guide actions in and out of the classroom.

In brief, the category of mediation is crucial to the dialectic because it lifts our commonsense perceptions and experiences to new levels of understanding, complexity, and concreteness. In doing so, it serves to illuminate the way in which specific social and political forces mediate between ourselves and the larger society. As a critical category, it replaces the myth of the autonomous individual with the problem of what one has to do to struggle to become a self-determining social agent acting on, rather than responding to, the world in which we live.

The next category of the dialectic I have labeled is the category of appropriation. Unlike the Hegelian version of the dialectic, the unfolding process at work in history, in my view, is not abstractly spiritual, it involves a subject. This means that at the heart of the dialectic is a human agent who is never merely a passive being removed from the historical arena, but instead is an acting subject, who with qualitatively different levels of reasoning and action, appropriates and penetrates the reality in which he or she lives. Appropriation, as it is used here refers to human beings who in varying degrees both reproduce and act upon the socio-cultural matrix in which they find themselves.[23] The driving force of appropriation is the recognition of the value of consciousness and action in the service of praxis. Appropriation rejects the overly determined and passive view of man that is inherent in various forms of behaviorism and vulgar Marxism. But appropriation represents more than a celebration of subjectivity, it further represents a rejection of all world views and social formations that support an objectified, and oversocialized model of human behavior. In other words, it both rejects and struggles against forms of objectivism that deny human consciousness, subjectivity, and action.[24]

Within the context of schooling, the category of appropriation posits reflective thought and action as a central concern of both teachers and students. This points to forms of classroom interaction that promote critical dialogue and communicative patterns stripped of unnecessary institutional control. In addition, it helps us to focus on the way in which various aspects of the schooling process reproduce in both material and ideological terms the mechanizations of social conformity and control. Thus, it helps us to focus more critically on questions concerning the nature of the hidden curriculum, the patterns of social control that underlie student-teacher relationships, and the forms of ideology embedded in the use of specific types of knowledge and modes of classroom evaluation.[25] But if appropriation is to move beyond a hermeneutic function, it will have to be linked to a notion of transcendence, and this leads us to the final category of the dialectic.

As the final category of the dialectic, transcendence (*Aufhebung*) subsumes a number of other characteristics that are often associated with the dialectic, i.e., the driving force of contradictions, the unity of opposites, and the negation of the negation.

The essence of the category of transcendence lies in its refusal to accept the world as it is. Its posture is based on the political and moral imperative that things must change. Inherent in its aforementioned nature is a commitment to a world view that calls for the "emancipation" of sensibility, imagination, and reason in all spheres of subjectivity and objectivity."[26]

Transcendence distinguishes itself by its acknowledgement that the contradictory forces that steer, shape, and characterize specific historical moments and social formations must be measured against their emancipatory and repressive possibilities. They must be seized by human beings acting as subjects in the intervention and shaping of history and dealt with as part of a "struggle for their liberation."[27]

On one level, transcendence represents what Agnes Heller has called:

> the simple consciousness of alienation, the recognition that the social relations are alienated: from this there follows [or this constitutes the base for] the need to overcome alienation, to overturn the alienated social and productive relations in a revolutionary way, and to create general social and productive relations which are not alienated.[28]

Thus, transcendence as a category of the dialectic is a call to action informed by an emancipatory vision. It is a call to develop an awareness of our own historically conditioned self-formative processes as well as an awareness of those socially unnecessary modes of domination that shape the larger society. In different terms it is a call to reveal how the antagonistic character of social reality manifests itself in both personal and social terms and how both of these realms affect, change, and reproduce each other.

Put another way, transcendence is more than an explanatory concept, it is a categorical demonstration of the negation of the negation. That is, it traces the contradictions that characterize existing society to their fractured source and tries to overcome them.[29] As the negation of the negation, transcendence is at first a form of refusal and secondly an act of reconstruction. Resistance gives way to the search for qualitatively better modes of existence. The medium of transcendence is informed consciousness and reflexive action, and its goal is a society free of alienating and oppressive social institutions and life forms.

While it is impossible to detail here how this overarching category of the dialectic might specifically shape the process of schooling, one aspect of its pedagogical application can be clarified. The category of transcendence forcefully supports an educational philosophy based on the assumption that the purpose of education should be to educate youth not for the present "but for a better future condition of the human race, that is for the idea of humanity."[30] Transcendence posits the need for all educational workers to examine their most fundamental assumptions about pedagogy next to a clearly delineated set of emancipatory intentions. In this case, commitment is substituted for objectivism, and a critical and visionary posture toward the world is substituted for a "professional" noncommittal manner. Thus, what all of this means is that we need a critical pedagogy that links pedagogical processes to radical modes of reasoning, both of which support each other and act as a catalyst for students and teachers to fight against those ideological and material forces that prevent such a synthesis from manifesting itself, whether it is inside or outside the school. A number of radical educators have already begun to lay the foundations for such a pedagogy.[31]

The concept of the dialectic as presented in this essay is both a conceptual tool as well as a mode of experience that is useful in developing pedagogical theory and practice. Its basic categories are not universals, but social processes steeped in specific assumptions about schools, society, human nature, and freedom. Moreover, these categories provide a powerful analytical scheme for analyzing, modifying, and changing the complex mediations that influence the many levels of human consciousness and action, both in schools and the wider society. The dialectic points not only to the contradictions of schooling, but also to the need for tracing and resolving those contradictions in the larger society. I will now finish up this essay by suggesting a few specific ways in which the concept of the dialectic can be applied to classroom pedagogy.

P A R T   I I I

If the concept of the dialectic is to become relevant for classroom pedagogy, teachers can begin by using its central categories to examine the curriculum as a selection from the larger culture. By doing so, they can begin to look at their own educational philosophy within a particular social, cultural, and historical context. The notion of schooling as a cultural phenomenon not only calls into question the basic assumptions that structure one's view of classroom pedagogy, it also forces teachers to examine the role schools play as agents of social and cultural reproduction. The dialectic, in this case, illuminates for teachers the way in which the dominant beliefs and values in the wider society and their own world views interpenetrate. Schooling, in this case, is stripped of its innocence. The foundation for a progressive form of classroom pedagogy can be now developed since schooling can be understood as a study in ideology and values. Questions concerning totality, mediation, and appropriation now become essential in developing a form of pedagogy in which teachers carefully examine how the structural and ideological determinants of the dominant society affect the behavior, attitudes, and speech of all those involved in the classroom encounter.

The concept of the dialectic is particularly useful in making teachers attentive to the specific ways in which cultural forms in the classroom reproduce, redefine, and affect the selection of meanings and social relationships that receive institutional support. One major task of classroom teachers will be to help students understand the social and economic meanings that stand behind various forms of classroom knowledge and pedagogical encounters. This means that we have to make clear to students, depending upon the levels we are working with, the valuative underpinnings and limitations of different forms of knowledge. Just as teachers must come to recognize the theoretical assumptions that underlie their own pedagogical concepts and practices, students must also learn to recognize the meaning for frame of reference, and how the latter concept is instrumental in deciding, selecting, and organizing the "facts" that go into everything from their social studies texts to their health textbook.[32] The foundation for such an approach can begin by developing classroom pedagogy around social processes and conceptual models that raise and demonstrate questions such as: (1) What counts as knowledge? (2) How is what counts as knowledge organized and produced? (3) How is such knowledge transmitted? (4) Who has access to such knowledge? (5) Whose interests does such knowledge serve?

If organized around the above questions, classroom pedagogy of this sort would have to develop a view of students that recognizes them as appropriators or self-conscious agents in the classroom encounter. This means teachers would have to take seriously those cultural experiences and meanings that students bring to the day-to-day process of schooling itself. Problematizing knowledge becomes meaningful only if students are allowed to explore such knowledge within their own modes of knowing and understanding. The important notion of schooling as a selection from the wider culture becomes meaningful when teachers begin by acknowledging not only the source and meaning of their own cultural capital, but also the importance and meaningfulness of the cultural capital that characterizes their students. If we take the experiences of our students as a starting point for dialogue and analysis, we give them the opportunity to validate themselves, to use their own voices. Once students become aware of the dignity of their own histories and perceptions, they can then make a leap to the theoretical and begin to examine critically the truth value of their meanings and perceptions, particularly as they relate to the dominant culture.[33]

William Pinar has written of the need for students to be able to formulate questions that will help them to capitalize on, use, and learn within their own experiences.[34] This is an important point. Teaching students to step outside the somewhat reified world of schooling represents more than supplying them with critical modes of reasoning. Critical reasoning becomes an empty exercise if students don't learn how to both reflect on as well as transform the nature and meaning of their own lived-worlds. In other words, students must be given the opportunity to learn how to use and interpret their own experiences in a manner that reveals how the latter have been shaped and influenced by the dominant culture. Subjective awareness becomes the first step in transforming those experiences.

One important step in helping teachers develop a pedagogy that will assist students to move beyond the taken-for-grantedness that shapes part of their view of the world lies in providing them with a new language and conceptual scheme through which they can view the world more critically. It goes without saying that dialogue and supportive interaction represent crucial media in the development of a dialectical pedagogy, but they become meaningful only if students have a language that allows them to move toward a critical stance, "a way of looking at the world which can serve as the foundation of subsequent analysis and criticism."[35] In concrete terms this means that students must learn a language that is both hermeneutic and emancipatory. Such a language would help both teachers and students to become more interpretive, but it would also reveal the structures and limitations present in different modes of language. For instance, a distinction should be made between a dialectical and nondialectical approach to language. The latter can be designated as a language that is confined to the boundaries of a given subject, confined to the operations, principles, and inner space of a given topic. This is the "inside" language of technocratic rationality, i.e., the language of means, techniques, etc. We often hear it among lawyers, music theorists, mathematicians. And so on. A more dialectical language is characterized by the way it draws from a variety of subjects to examine any given topic. It draws upon the "languages" of psychoanalysis, sociology, history, psychology, and a wide variety of other subjects in order to examine a specific problem or issue. It is the language of connections and mediations. It refuses to support a mode of reasoning that reinforces the artificial constructs between the various disciplines and subjects.

The use of a dialectical language will make it easier for teachers to enable students to understand the meaning of frame of reference. By looking at issues from a variety of perspectives, students can learn something about the interpretive screens that people use in constituting and creating reality. The latter is of profound insight and has enormous political significance. When applied to the content and process of classroom pedagogy, it "tells us that our most basic thought-processes and our very image of reality are neither neutral, inevitable, or fixed but merely the product of the particular society in which we live."[36] The link between human knowledge, values, and the nature of truth becomes an operational pedagogical principle within this approach. One qualification must be made here. Teaching students critical conceptual categories that help them to confront their own unexamined and implicit views of the world should not be reduced to a mere celebration of subjectivity, i.e., "you have your views and I have mine." The latter is a form of "bad subjectivity" and can be avoided by teaching students to challenge and test the relationship between what they know and reality as it objectively exists. The world does not necessarily correspond to the way people view it. Not to understand this is to ignore the importance and meaning of false consciousness and to end up supporting a mystifying form of cultural relativism. Students must be taught to look beyond the immediate, they must learn how to test the truth claims inherent in any interpretation, including their own.

Hopefully, this paper has demonstrated successfully the need for curriculum theorists and other educators to reexamine the most basic assumptions and values that guide their work. It has provided a rationale and some suggestions for using the concept of the dialectic as a step toward the process of renewal and self-criticism in our field. If the spirit of critique and social commitment is to be kept alive in the curriculum field, we are going to have to work hard to sustain such a tradition. This suggests not just developing new conceptual models through which to view our work, more importantly it means committing ourselves to a notion of truth and justice that makes our view of what we do and who we are meaningful. It is the consequence of what we do that makes the concerns of this paper imperative. The rest is up to us.

N O T E S

1. Walter Benjamin, "Theses on the Philosophy of History," in *Illuminations* (New York: Schocken, 1969), 255.

2. Maurice Cornforth, Historical Materialism (New York: International Publishers, 1962). The classic example is Joseph Stalin, "Dialectical and Historical Materialism," in *History Of The Communist Party Of The Soviet Union* (New York: International Publishers, 1939). For an insightful analysis of Stalin's purging of the dialectic, see Herbert Marcuse, *Soviet Marxism* (New York: Vintage Books, 1961). Two interesting general critiques of the orthodox Marxist position can be found in Michael Albert and Robin Hahnel, *Unorthodox Marxism* (Boston: South End Press, 1978); James Miller, *History And Human Existence: From Marx To Merleau-Ponty* (Berkeley: University of California Press, 1979).

3. Howard Sherman, "Dialectics as Method," *The Insurgent Sociologist 3* (Summer, 1976): 62.

4. T.W. Freiberg, "Critical Social Theory in the American Conjuncture," in *Critical Sociology* (New York: Halsted Press, 1979), 1-21.

5. Herbert Marcuse, "On the Problem of the Dialectic," *Telos 27* (Spring, 1976), 12-39. M. Merleau-Ponty, *On The Adventures Of The Dialectic*, trans. By Joseph Bien (Evanston: Northwestern University Press, 1973). T.W. Adorno, *Negative Dialectics* (New York: Seabury Press, 1973).

6. Marcuse, IBIC., 22.

7. Karol Kosik, *Dialectics Of The Concrete* (Boston and Dardrecht-Holland: D. Reidel Publishing Company, 1976).

8. T.W. Adorno, "Goldman and Adorno: To Describe, Understand and Explain," in Lucien Goldman, *Cultural Creation In Modern Society*, trans. Bart Grahl. (St. Louis: Telos Press, 1977), 130-31.

9. Freiberg, op. cit., pp. 7-8. Also see Richard Bernstein, *The Reconstruction Of Social And Political Theory* (Philadelphia: University of Pennsylvania Press, 1976), Xi-54.

10. Herbert Marcuse, *Reason And Revolution* (Boston: Beacon Press, 1970), eighth printing, p. 1x.

11. Kosik, op. cit., p. 2.

12. Fred R. Dallmary and Thomas A. McCarthy, "Introduction: The positivist Reception," in *Understanding And Social Inquiry*, eds. Fred R. Dallmary and

Thomas A. McCarthy (Notre Dame: University of Notre Dame Press, 1977), 77-78. Also see Theodore W. Adorno, Hans Albert, Ralf Dahrendorf, Jurgen Habermas, Harold Pilot, and Karl R. Popper, *The Positivist Dispute In German Sociology* (London: Heinemann Educational Books, Ltd., 1976).

13. Paulo Freire, *Pedagogy Of The Oppressed* (New York: Seabury Press, 1970), 125.

14. Henry A. Giroux, "Schooling and the Culture of Positivism: Notes on the Death of History," *Educational Theory* (in press).

15. Herbert Marcuse, *One Dimensional Man* (Boston: Beacon Press, 1964), 204.

16. Marcuse, "On the Problem of the Dialectic," 20-21.

17. Bertell Ollmann, "On Teaching Marxism," *The Insurgent Sociologist* (Summer, 1976), 42.

18. Kosik, op. cit., p. 7.

19. Michael W. Apple, *Ideology And Curriculum* (Boston and London: Routledge and Kegan Paul, 1979), 17-18

20. Kosik, op. cit., p. 19.

21. Raymond Williams, *Marxism And Literature* (London: Oxford University Press, 1977), 98.

22. George Lukacs, *History And Class Consciousness* (Cambridge: MIT Press, 1968).

23. Paul Willis, *Learning To Labour; How Working Class Kids Get Working Class Jobs* (Lexington, Mass.: Lexington Books, 1977).

24. Henry A. Giroux, "Paulo Freire's Approach to Radical Educational Reform," *Curriculum Inquiry* 9 (3), (Fall, 1979): 257-72.

25. Jean Anyon, "United States History Textbooks and Ideology: A Study of Curriculum Content and Social Interest," *Harvard Educational Review*, in press. Jean Anyon, "Education, Social 'Structure' and the Power of Individuals," *Theory And Research In Social Education*, 7(1), 49-59. Henry A. Giroux and Anthony N. Penna, "Social Education in the Classroom: The Dynamics of the Hidden Curriculum," *Theory And Research In Social Education* 7(1), (Spring, 1979): 21-42

26. Herbert Marcuse, *The Aesthetic Dimension* (Boston: Beacon Press, 1978), 9.

27. Freire, op. cit., p. 33.

28. Agnes Heller, *The Theory Of Need In Marx* (London: Allison and Busby, 1976), 95.

29. Russell Jacoby, *Social Amnesia* (Boston: Beacon Press, 1975), p. 61.

30. Herbert Marcuse, *Counterrevolution And Revolt* (Boston: Beacon Press, 1972), 27-28.

31. This list is far from inclusive: See the collection of writings in William F. Pinar, ed., *Curriculum Theorizing* (Berkeley: McCutchan Publishing, 1975); William F. Pinar and Madeline R. Grumet, *Toward A Poor Curriculum* (Dubuque: Kendall/Hunt Publishing Company, 1976); Maxine Greene, *Landscapes Of Learning* (New York: Teachers College Press, 1978); Jerome Karabel and A.H. Halsey, eds., *Power And Ideology In Education* (New York: Oxford University Press, 1977); Apple, op. cit.,; Willis, op. cit.; Henry A. Giroux, *Ideology, Culture And The Process Of Schooling* (in press).

32. Henry A. Giroux, "Writing and Critical Thinking in the Social Studies," *Curriculum Inquiry* 8(4), 291-310.

33. Maxine Greene, "Curriculum and Consciousness," in *Curriculum Theorizing*, op. cit., p. 304.

34. William F. Pinar, "Currere: Toward Reconceptualization," in *Curriculum Theorizing*, op. cit., pp. 396-414.

35. Jean Tethke Elshtain, "The Social Relations of the Classroom: A Moral and Political Perspective," TELOS 27 (Spring, 1976), p. 108.

36. Kenneth Dolbeare, "Alternatives to the New Fascism," *The Massachusetts Review* 17(1), Spring, 1976, 77.

CHAPTER THREE

Autobiography
and Reconceptualization

Madeleine R. Grumet
1980

Literally, reconceptualization means to conceive again, to turn back the conceptual structures that support our actions in order to reveal the rich and abundant experience they conceal. To some, this reflexive scrutiny may suggest a relentless descent into abstraction and introspection, and there are probably moments we can all recall when reflection drew us down and into eddies of confusion and anxiety.

The reconceptualization of curriculum is spared this paralyzing doubt that accompanies an infinite regression of questions because it is firmly anchored in the world. The concrete event that is experienced by a particular person is its mooring. Curriculum is the child of culture, and the relation is as complex and reciprocal as are any that bonds the generations. Curriculum transmits culture, as it is formed by it. Curriculum modifies culture even as it transmits it. Similarly, as with culture, we live curriculum before we describe it. The event and the thought about the event are never simultaneous, never identical. We live curriculum as we drive to work, take a quick stop in the faculty washroom before class, make our way past students stuffing bulky coats into narrow lockers, past tiled walls and display cases, into the room where the curriculum we describe is or is not experienced. Curriculum as lived and curriculum as described amble along, their paths sometimes parallel, often not, occasionally in moments of insight intersecting. So it is possible that experience and description diverge now and then and that paeans of praise to participative democracy are sung in autocratic classrooms, individualization degenerates into depersonalized programming, and inquiry method requires that I search for answers to someone else's questions.

Reconceptualization of curriculum requires a more than reflexive somersault that scoops up our old, flat ideas and turns them over. It is a reflexive project that attempts to reclaim curriculum as we have lived it and to test our conceptual schemes and descriptions of it against the evidence of our experience. Tonight I may find that evidence in the image of my father bending over my textbooks at the dining room table, covering them with deep red, durable paper, rolled up and carried home from work on the subway just for that purpose. The evidence surprises me, presenting itself abruptly, like the ticket stubs from *South Pacific* wedged into the pocket of an old purse. Or it may be the memory of the young man with the curly hair and angular face who came to teach us junior high social studies and called us "people." "People did you finish the assignment" and "I want to ask you people some questions." Or it may be the day he asked us to grade ourselves for the term and Bobby Aaronson became a hero because he gave himself an F, explaining that he knew he had not done his best. It's Miss Leahy telling a thirsty third grade classmate to bite his tongue and drink the blood, and it's the penny that glowed in the puddle on Broadway and 118th Street as I walked out into the twilight after hearing Stravinsky's *Symphony Of Psalms* played in class.

My students tell their own stories, of speaking Spanish in a kindergarten where everyone speaks English, of talking to a kid from the "slow" class one day in the girl's bathroom, of understanding the discipline of natural science while rehearsing an ensemble scene from *Richard III*.

THE METHOD EXPLAINED

The method is autobiography. Curriculum reclaimed in this manner is, of course, inevitably reconceptualized, even in the most meticulous and ingenuous retelling. The selection of some events and the exclusion of others, the repudiation of some feelings and the acknowledgement of others, remind us that these accounts never can exactly coincide with our experience. The event-in-itself defies re-presentation, slipping away from our grasp like the landscape outside the window of a railway car. Nevertheless, the abstractions of primary experience presented in these autobiographical reflections are vulnerable to critical scrutiny. The writer can turn back upon her own texts and see there her own processes and biases of selection at work. It is here that curriculum as thought is revealed as the screen through which we pass curriculum as lived. Miss Leahy did make that sadistic comment. The student teacher (was he appended to Miss Leahy?) did call us "people," and my father did cradle his paper for my books under his arm and bring it home, battling the rush hour crowds and his own fatigue to cover my books. Those things did happen then but why do I tell them rather than other tales? What principle of selection excludes the story about Mrs. Dobkin who called my mother to urge her to consult another pediatrician when I had been out of school for two or three weeks with a mysterious ailment? Why is Leahy's sadism a more successful candidate for recycling than Dobkin's solicitous concern? Perhaps one question may illuminate another. Why "people?" The designation flattered us, suggesting that we were all peers, even though we knew that the status the student teacher extended to us so generously was tentative because he survived from day to day only by Leahy's (yes, it was Leahy) leave. And even Bobby Aaronson's martyrdom was staged. We weren't real people and Bobby Aaronson wasn't a real martyr. We played at human dignity and our gestures confirmed our impotence and degradation. And finally, that's why Dobkin is in the piece, not because she cared enough to call but because she assumed that my parents needed her advice, that her pediatrician would be better than the one they had chosen, and because they resented her patronizing intrusion even as they appreciated her concern. Tales of power, its use and abuse.

The gaps in the tale are brimming with information for the reader who is the writer of such an autobiography. And that information is not about what it was to be seven, nor is it about Leahy and Dobkin. It is information that pulls the past into the present, drawing it together to confirm what I anticipate will be my next move. Today, as I teach students who would be teachers and encourage them to be agents of their own visions and commitments, am I also posturing with my "people" while Leahy smirks?

H O W   T H E   M E T H O D   R E C O N C E P T U A L I Z E S   C U R R I C U L U M

Through this critical reflection upon educational experience, curriculum is reconceptualized in two ways. The first phase of this reflexive research is free-associative. The content that will be specified by that word, curriculum, is reclaimed by a reflective process that allows the mind to wander but notes the path and all its markers. In this essay Leahy, Dobkin, "people" are the souvenirs of that side trip. When the method has been extended by any students, they have been asked to write an essay that provides at least three narratives of events in their lives that they would call educational experience. The stories need not concern schooling, but they may. The persuasion of autobiography resembles that of fiction. Detail is required to demonstrate lawful possession of the tale. It is detail that reveals that my father brought the bookcovers back from the "place," the term we used to refer to the loft across the river that housed my father's manufacturing company. It is the shelter and authority of "the place," with its slamming presses, and piles of cardboard from floor to ceiling that my father applies to the fragile binding of my social studies text. Anything brought home from the place contained a potency absent in items purchased at Woolworth's or at the corner candy store. These imports, the five hundred rubber bands, the packing tape, paper clips, the red paper, were passports back to the world across the river, to the loading dock, to the union, to the machines, to the business, the commerce, the power of "the place."

The reconceived curriculum is the curriculum reclaimed by what Merleau-Ponty calls the body-subject. It is the relation of the knower to the known (and to the unknown) that is manifested in the concrete images of lived worlds. It is the body-subject who ran her fingers over the sharp folds and card corners of that bookcover, heard the music, felt the rain, and imagined the salty taste of my own blood. It is the curriculum of bitten nails that were noted on the report card, of crayola cranberry vines decorating each page of the report on New England, of singing *The Battle Hymn Of The Republic* on the high school steps after chorus rehearsal on the night Julius and Ethel Rosenberg were executed. This concrete reclamation reconceptualizes the curriculum, for it literally reconceives it by gathering it from the specific associations that represent our experience of it. The themes repeat themselves. The bitten nails, the energy turned back upon myself, expressiveness shunted into decorative margins. And those early stirrings of political awareness, of identification and protest, sentimentalized and nationalized and moved out of the building, after hours, on to the steps.

As we analyze the narrative we reveal interests and biases we rarely see because they are threaded through the thick fabric of our daily lives. This is the second phase of reconceptualizing that illuminates the ways we organize and interpret our experience by framing those choices in an aesthetic object, the autobiography. Within those pages those choices, which, when embedded in the activity of our daily lives seem obligatory and unavoidable, stand as expressions of our freedom. I organize my story as I organize my world, and it is my story of the past that can tell me where I am and where I am going.

Because I question the reality of my own power, the brave but ultimately hollow gestures return to remind me that oppression is most insidious when the oppressed are placated with the false but flattering slogans and poses that disguise their experience. The possibility that schools may become places where students understand their own powers is never realized through rhetoric but through the choices and actions that fill the minutes we spend together.

The faculty bathroom is clean and has a door. I enjoy its privacy. The student's bathrooms have no outer doors, and when I visit them, demonstrating my egalitarianism, all conversation stops, cigarettes are quickly flushed, and I destroy whatever privacy that peer solidarity and separate facilities have provided.

In schools, the exercise of power is institutionalized and disclaimed. Reclaiming it requires attention to the initiatives we take and the responses we make.

If "people" and "the place" have washed up on the shore to remind me of the power the child didn't own, power the student merely imitated or borrowed, they also remind me of the power I now claim as teacher and as parent. And if when I push it and prod it like a jellyfish, it turns out to have a real string, what use shall I make of it?

THE METHOD USED

I have used this method of reflexive analysis with students in teacher education courses (Pinar, Grumet, 1976), in theatre courses (Grumet, 1978), and in in-service work (Grumet, 1978a). (The theatre students organized their reflective writing around the concept, theatrical experience in one case and around play, in another.) While there is initial anxiety, for students have little practice in finding and telling their own stories, there is usually a rush of fluency once the choices are made. It is rare that these pieces are burdened with poor writing. People usually make sense when they know what they are talking about.

I attempt to reply to the pieces in ways that will extend both the concrete and abstract sources of information that the autobiographical exercise can offer. I footnote my comments that I append on a separate sheet; my questions sometimes request information, drawing out the particular details that are not yet visible but may hold, I suspect, the clue as to why the story is important. I may help the writer to ascertain what is missing in the text as well as to recognize patterns and themes that often surface in each of the apparently disparate narratives. The writer of the piece maintains possession and authority over his own prose. He need not respond to any questions that call him into territory he'd rather not tread. It is his recognition and acknowledgement that establishes the authority of any of the interpretations I may offer. The essays initiate reflexive writing in other forms. Journals may be kept. Additional essays may follow.

This work is pursued in the aspiration that it will enable the student to become the active interpreter of his past, as well as to heighten his capacity to be the active agent of his own interests in a present that he shares with his community. As curriculum is reconceptualized through the selection and criticism that reorders educational experience into a usable past, it may also be transformed into a usable present by students who see themselves as responsible for the shape and texture of their own experience.

A N D S O

Which brings me to the penny in the puddle. I can still see it glimmer, clean rain water on pebbly cement, its copper purity adding a pecuniary fallacy to the natural one that accompanied Stravinsky. Although it is not without some guilt that I dishonor this cherished moment with condescending labels culled from lit. crit., I cannot make use of this memory as an image of my current concerns. That evening provided the organic continuity that pepper attributes to aesthetic experience, the music, the City, the rain, the penny all arranged around me, fused and glowing. But now I am the arranger and look to aesthetics not to create perfect wholes but to reveal those cracks in the smooth surface of our conceptual world that may suggest new interpretations of human experience.

R E F E R E N C E S

Pinar, W. & Grumet, M. (1976). *Toward a poor curriculum*. Dubuque:
Kendall/Hunt, 274–315.

Grumet, M. (1978). Songs and situations. In *Qualitative Evaluation*, edited by
george Willis. Berkeley: McCutchan Publishing Corp.

Grumet, M. (1979). Supervision and Situations. In *The Journal Of Curriculum
Theorizing, 191–257.*

A C K N O W L E D G M E N T S

I appreciate Joan Didion's essay *On Keeping A Notebook* (New York: Dell.
1961) for providing a form that contains both autobiography and its theory.

CHAPTER FOUR

Women

The Evolving Educational Consciousness

Janet L. Miller
1980

Everyone repeatedly has to break through to a new vision if she/he is to keep living.[1]

That women function within the realm of education, both as students and as educators, does not appear, at first glance, to be a unique or particularly volatile statement. Since the inception of formalized education in the United States, women have found a welcome refuge within the teaching profession, in recent years, educational opportunities for women have become more plentiful, and, in certain cases, more lucrative. However, I am concerned with the "educational consciousness" of women; that is, to what extent and in what manner do the layers of society, was well as personal expectations, shape women's perceptions of themselves and their potential to be educated as well as to educate? These issues and questions arise initially from situations within my own biographic experience, and it is within this personal context that I must begin my explorations of heretofore unexamined aspects of the nature of my educational experience. Only after attending to the complexities that have shaped my own present educational consciousness might I then move to examine the larger generalities of the underlying political, economic, racial, and sexual situations that surely have influenced the educational consciousness of women collectively.

In attempting to find grounding for educational consciousness in my personal history, I initiate a critical step in connecting to the commonalities that link us all. I attach primary significance to the fact that each of us achieved contact with the world from a particular vantage point, in terms of a particular biography. All of this underlies our present perspectives and affects the way we look at things and talk about things and structure our realities. To be in touch with our landscapes is to be conscious of our evolving experiences, to be aware of the ways in which we encounter our world.[2]

Only recently have I become aware of the dichotomy within myself in terms of my work; only recently have I even questioned the tensions and confusions that I feel about my professional self, my personal self, and the seeming lack of cohesion between the two. In finally acknowledging the fragmentation that I have been experiencing in various forms for several months, I feel release in confronting the separation. Now, as I explore the underlying expectations that color my tensions, I become curious—this tension, this fragmentation, on surface inspection appears to be the result of pressures that characterize the lives of all who perform the daily tasks and routines that specific positions dictate. And so to work in one sense means to function within the restrictions of time, relationships, and responsibilities. The initial appraisal, then, of my specific situation would indicate that I am able to manage well the effects of these confines. I have taught school for ten years, and I now do work in curriculum for a private research institute; these facts alone would attest, some would say, to a certain perseverance, a dedication, a freely chosen professional course.

I must delve more deeply, then, into the grayer recesses of my discomfort. I must trace the evolvement of my uneasiness in an attempt to understand its sudden surfacing, for, indeed, in terms of my professional life, the intensity of my feelings of a dichotomous self are somehow frightening in their immediacy. Could I have been unaware of such a fissure within myself for such a long time? Perhaps, but what appears more likely is that my changing perspectives about myself as a professional educator as well as a woman have allowed the slow unfolding of many of my own expectations for myself in my professional as well as my private world. As these layers of expectations—my own for myself as well as my perceptions of others' for me—are exposed, I perceive the bared root of the dichotomy; I am a professional educator and I am a woman. Historically, within the confines of society's roles and expectations, the relationship is neither consonant nor life-giving.

The protestations bubble to the surface; women always have found a place in education. Teaching has been an acceptable and desirable position for women. Today, however, I question the sources of such assessments. In tracing the evolution of women in education, one notes that those men who first administered the schools pointed to the necessity of imposing the qualities of dutifulness, respect for righteousness, and obedience to existing social authorities upon the lives of children. In attempting to socialize large numbers of children into a life increasingly dominated by industry, and later, technology, American educators throughout the nineteenth and into the twentieth century have internationalized the notion of subordination as a primary framework for behavior within the classroom.

> Whether the dominating concern was to create a literate and disciplined working class, to impose a middle-class and Protestant ethos, or to erect barriers against corruption and disorder, the expressed commitment was to "social control"...Anti-social energies and appetites were to be tamped down; "impetuosity" was to be subordinated to "voluntary compliance." The entire effort and the prevailing atmosphere were thought of as redemptive, humane, and benign.[3]

And who better than women to project such ideals? Certainly, women could provide the gentility and docility needed to maintain such an atmosphere, for, in the 1830s, with the rise of the common schools and the efforts to establish an effective public school system, women were in no position, economically or socially, to question their roles as dutiful and dependent subordinates.

In examining the role of women in education, I, of course, acknowledge that the situation has changed, in some aspects, from the subordinate roles that women played, not only in education, but also in their daily lives. Women today are gaining positions of leadership in educational administrations and organizations. However, these facts do not eradicate the dichotomy that I deeply feel. Somehow, even in the light of a professional career, of a position in which I may explore a variety of educational possibilities, I still am responding to a deeply internalized conception of myself as I "should be" within the world. It is not sufficient to merely acknowledge the historical antecedents of my perceptions of the roles that women play. I must go further to unravel the entangled layers of my expectations of myself as woman and to perhaps then understand why those personal expectations clash with those of my professional self.

As I remember and review my entry into the professional teaching world, I am aware that I came to teaching, like many others, I suspect, for a variety of reasons. As a newly married young woman, teaching seemed to offer reliability, security, and a chance to work with students—certainly, to me, an exciting and rewarding prospect. Now, as I engage in the retrospective process, I further explore the basis for my conception of teaching as a rewarding endeavor. What was I seeking for myself and what did I hope to give to others? Although not conscious of this concept at the time, I realize now that an important vision of myself rests upon my ability to give to others, to do something, in some way, to help, to enrich, to embellish others' lives. I could accomplish this in my relationships with my students. Through the giving of myself in the teaching process, through the sharing of the literature to which I so deeply responded, I could feel as though I were contributing and as though my work, and thus my life, were meaningful. Only now, in retrospect, am I able to expose the deeper concept around which such actions in my life are based: women's lives, in many ways, are organized around the principle of serving others.

> women have been led to feel that they can integrate and use all their attributes if they use them for others, but not for themselves. They have developed the sense that their lives should be guided by the constant need to attune themselves to the wishes, desires, and needs of others. The others are the important ones and the guides to action.[4]

This is not to say that dedicating oneself in the service of others is a negative action, per se; it is to say that, specifically for a woman, such action is colored by internalizations of her role as nurturer and server of others' needs. The act of giving is negatively internalized when women "are forced to serve others' needs or when they are expected to do so because it is the 'only thing women are good for.'"[5]

In my biographical situation, teaching provided me with a supposedly positive outlet for such internalized expectations. I was able to fulfill my desire to serve others and, at the same time, was able to enlarge upon my perception of myself as a productive and worthwhile person.

The danger with such a perception of myself was that I had developed no personal, individual, unique way of perceiving and confronting my relationships to the world. I had, without thinking and without questioning, transferred an expectation of myself as woman, which largely was a societal creation, to my professional role. Although appearing to be my conscious and free choice, the profession of teaching became a vehicle for positing many of my internalized, but unexamined, expectations for myself.

Thus, the dichotomy I feel even now, after working within a professional mode for twelve years, is partly the result of my inability to articulate those expectations for myself that I truly feel are appropriate for me. I struggle to identify the constructed realities of others that I falsely have identified as my own. As I attempt to extricate the vision of myself as I thought others might have defined me, and struggle, in its place, to construct a conception of myself that is grounded in my own wishes and goals, I must reconceive the very ways in which I approach myself and my world.

> Freedom is the power of vision and the power to choose. It involves the capacity to assess situations in such a way that lacks can be defined, openings identified, and possibilities revealed. It is realized only when action is taken to repair the lacks, to move through the openings, to try to pursue real possibilities.[6]

I merely have begun, then, to become aware of the countless ways in which I have internalized conflicting views of my professional and my private self. The dichotomy I express has much to do with my perceptions of myself as woman and as educator. I acknowledge that my work signifies one important way of taking action upon the world: "Our attitudes toward work become the touchstone of what we do, since it is by means of work that freedom comes into being in individual lives."[7] I respond to the reality in which I may share my work with others. At the same time, I recognize that constant attention must be paid to the sources of my motivations. I have become conscious of the pervasive internalization of the conception of woman as helper, nurturer, subordinate "other."[8] I must now attempt to incorporate a new vision of myself, choosing freely among those characteristics that I feel will enhance my strength as an individual. As I work to bring the dichotomous self into a whole, I need not reject those characteristics or goals that may be regarded by some as feminine or as masculine. The task is one of redefinition within an awakened consciousness. I cannot turn back; I cannot settle for less that constant attention to the awakening of a self-definition than "might transform both men's and women's common world."[9]

In offering a vignette of some of the conflicts that characterize my experiences as a woman educator, I in no way attempt to transfer particular biographical observations to the collective experiences of women. Rather, by revealing a portion of my personal situation, I wish to emphasize the extent to which the unexamined consciousness may conform to forms and modes of action that are shaped by external factors and the extent to which unthinking compliance with prescribed images may lead to a dissonance that promises only further fragmentation and distance from oneself. Thus, the biographic vignette becomes a conceptual tool with which to examine underlying assumptions and expectations that guide the person who chooses to work as an educator; specifically, it allows the framing of a focus upon the processes by which women are educated and upon the manifestations of those educational processes within women who are educators. I maintain that the educational processes differ for women and men, and, further, that the effects of those differing processes, if unexamined, may have debilitating consequences for all.

Thus, this work is an initial inquiry into the multifaceted nature of women's educational consciousness. As part of a larger work in progress, then, I wish to concentrate now upon implications of such work for teacher educators.

In earlier work,[10] I have envisioned a teacher preparation program that provides opportunities for future teachers to examine and define the context of their objective and subjective relationships and connections to their specific subject-matter disciplines, as well as to their perceptions and projections of themselves in the role of teacher. The intent in my desire to reconceive the nature of a preparation program for teachers reflects my concerns with schooling, and specifically, with curriculum that involves students as well as teachers in the process of living. A thematic strand throughout the conceptual design, evolving in part from the critical thinking and philosophical tenets of Maxine Greene's work, is the creation of curriculum that is intricately bound together with the individual's search for meaning. The curricular design itself provides the contexts of a setting, a community, in which future teachers may explore the private, political, historical, and social aspects of teaching. Thus, by confronting one's assimilations of the role of teacher, and by becoming aware of the subjective and, at times, unconscious connections one creates between public role and personal expression, future teachers may conceive of their function within education in the broadest sense, "as it refers to the multiple modes of becoming, of confronting life situations, of engaging with others, of reflecting, forming, choosing, struggling to be."[11] This quest for a preparation program that attends to both the subjective and objective realms of inquiry and of being is predicated upon the belief that before teachers can present vehicles and create atmospheres in which their students may explore and develop their connections to the active world, teachers first must have opportunities to perform their own explorations and create their own authentic ways of uncovering, reflecting, and acting upon the potentialities within their lives.

Obviously, such a curricular design for future teachers challenges complacent acceptance of existing norms in a time, especially when attempts to further awareness of self are constantly juxtaposed against the demands of an advanced technological society. The incorporation of personal awareness into the dialogical relationships in which individuals engage becomes a difficult contemporary project, given the inundation of the back-to-basics proposals, with their accompanying competency requirements, minimum performance levels, and basic skills assessments. Thus, to encourage future teachers to delve into philosophical, psychological, and sociological considerations that underlie the myriad ways in which they may perceive themselves and their relationships with students and peers becomes a project to which many educators would assign lowest priority. It is exactly at this time, I would maintain, that we need programs that allow time for future teachers to experience those very processes, interactions, and materials that they, in turn, will expect and wish their students to experience. At no other time in the history of American education has the future teacher been crushed with such a plethora of external restraints, measurements, and expectations. At no other time have teachers so needed the time and context in which to align their private selves into authentic relationships with their public selves and with others.

> If the teacher agrees to submerge himself into the system, if he consents to being defined by others' views of what he is supposed to be, he gives up his freedom "to see, to understand, and to signify" for himself. If he is immersed and impermeable, he can hardly stir others to define themselves as individuals. If, on the other hand, he is willing to take the view of the homecomer and create a new perspective on what he has habitually considered real, his teaching may become the project of a person virtually open to his students and the world…. He will be continuously engaged in interpreting a reality forever new; he will feel more alive than he ever has before.[12]

Part III

The task of "interpreting a reality forever new" becomes a particularly poignant one for the woman who hopes to teach others. She must try to demystify the myriad issues that characterize the state of the field in education; she must become aware of the historical forms and underlying assumptions that pervade her view of the roles and functions of teachers, students, and schooling institutions. However, before she is able to move into an analysis of these complex situations that influence her actions as teacher, she first must examine the tenets of her perceived reality and the extent to which these tenets have been constructed from the overriding patriarchal nature of the generally accepted social reality. Thus, to "create a new perspective" becomes a two-fold endeavor for the woman educator. She first must attempt to uncover the layers of the hypothetical self to reach her own essence; only then is she free to begin explorations of the relationships of the private self and the public, professional self.

In truth, then, the woman is, as ever, one step behind her male counterpart. The man who wishes to prepare for a teaching career is able to examine role expectations and functions that have been created by a predominantly male vision; thus, as a man prepares for his career in education, he is less likely to perceive a dichotomy within his self image and his career image. He is moving into a realm that has been shaped by men, and which, to a large extent, continues to serve a function that is dictated by the controlling forces of society. Thus, as schooling continues to serve, in part, the assigning of individuals to their respective places within society, so men will continue to find positions of dominance within such a structure. Of course, a hopeful evolvement here is that men who are encouraged to go through the self-reflective processes in a teacher preparation program may well reject the manifestations within themselves of a schooling system that maintains the dominant/subordinate framework.

However, in confronting the *status quo*, I hold that, as teacher preparation programs generally now are structured, a woman, if she is to become cognizant of her educational consciousness and its varied manifestations, must uniquely investigate her motivations, expectations, and conceptions for herself as teacher. A man may, and should, perform the same reflective processes; the difference for man and woman is that the underlying structures for conceptions of self and of self as educator evolve from separate sources.

The source for much of women's concept of self is the state of existing in oppression. Obviously the literature that focuses upon the nature and the roots of women's oppression is vast, and the varied theories are complex. However, as Gayle Rubin notes, the issue is not a trivial one,

> since the answers given it determine our visions of the future, and our
> evaluation of whether or not it is realistic to hope for a sexually egalitarian

society;...the analysis of the causes of women's oppression forms the basis for any assessment of just what would have to be changed in order to achieve a society without gender hierarchy.[13]

The causes of women's oppression are complex and call for extensive study and analysis beyond the scope of this particular paper. I do wish, however, to point to the place of such analyses within the context of programs for future teachers. Woman no longer can assume the comfortable confines of a teaching career without challenging the very sources from which her perceived role derives. To do so at this juncture is to insure the continuation of the "part of social life which is the locus of the oppression of women, of sexual minorities, and of certain aspects of human personality within individuals."[14] This part of social life, as defined by Rubin, is a "sex/gender system," which is the "set of arrangements by which a society transforms biological sexuality into products of human activity, and in which these transformed sexual needs are satisfied."[15]

Within the context of the conception of the prevailing "sex/gender system," then, I have been able to begin to scrutinize my need to nurture others, for example, in light of a prevailing sexually defined notion that derives not from my own self initially, but rather from a function culturally determined and obtained. I may choose to accept such a characteristic within myself as a positive strength; however, I may now do so in terms of my conscious choice, not in terms of my perceptions of what others expect of me. As I briefly have revealed biographical manifestations of socially organized values and role definitions, I wish to emphasize the nature of such self-reflective processes, the importance of such work to those working in education, and the scope of such an undertaking.

I find it necessary, in calling for an integration of analyses of the roles of teacher in terms of sex/gender as well as social, economic, and political systems, to heed the note of caution that Rubin applies to such analyses. In her attempt to construct a "theory of women" oppression by borrowing concepts from anthropology and psychoanalysis, Rubin notes that the major theorists within these disciplines write from within an intellectual tradition produced by a culture in which women are oppressed. Thus, she recognizes the danger in her enterprise "is that the sexism in the tradition of which they are a part tends to be dragged in with each borrowing."[16]

So too must we acknowledge dangers inherent within analyses of the educational consciousness of men and women. As we work to discover the context and possibilities of our lived worlds, we constantly must attend to the structures that have shaped the very processes and methodologies that we utilize in the search. Particularly women, as they seek to define themselves and their roles as educators, must monitor the foundations upon which their present conceptions rest.

> The organization of sex and gender once had functions other than itself –
> it organized society. Now, it only organizes and reproduces itself. The kinds of

relationships of sexuality established in the dim human past still dominate our sexual lives, our ideas about men and women, and the ways we raise our children. But they lack the functional load they once carried. One of the most conspicuous features of kinship is that it has been systematically stripped of its functions—political, economic, educational, and organizational. It has been reduced to its barest bones—sex and gender.[17]

The task is immense; the work must be extensive. We must expose the bases of the predicaments of women, as Maxine Greene so eloquently reminds us.[18] We must work to eradicate the feeling, as described by Simone de Beauvoir, in the closing lines of *Force Of Curcumstance*, of being gypped as a woman: in looking back toward the young girl she had been, she measures her "adult astonishment in remembering her illusions when she was sixteen."[19] We must attend to the implications of what some see as the dominant force of patriarchal consciousness and resulting human action—the image and worship of death in its most violent forms.[20] We must perceive the meanings of the internalization of the concept that "it is not in giving life but in risking life that man is raised above the animal; that is why superiority has been accorded in humanity not to the sex that brings forth but to that which kills."[21]

Such profound and dramatic perceptions of life and of our attempts to move beyond the implications of imposed prescription upon our lives may serve as impetus for us all to examine the dichotomies within ourselves. We share the juxtapositioning of youth and maturity, the subjective and objective selves, personal and political identities. As educators, our responsibilities extend beyond ourselves to the lives of those who will internalize and extend the foundational perceptions that we as teachers have helped to shape. The particular nature of women in their roles as educators poses problems that are complex in their origins and in their manifestations. However, as women begin to define their educational consciousness as part of the conscious search for some kind of coherence, some kind of sense, they cannot help but suggest to others something of what it signifies to pursue or to understand.[22] Such work promises to liberate women, but, more importantly, to liberate the human personalities of us all.

N O T E S

1. Jean Baker Miller, *Toward A New Psychology Of Women* (Boston: Beacon Press, 1976), 44.

2. Maxine Greene, *Landscapes Of Learning* (New York: Teachers College Press, 1978), 2.

3. Ibid., 227

4. Miller, 60-61

5. Ibid., 61.

6. Greene, 223.

7. Ibid., 252.

8. Simone de Beauvoir, *The Second Sex*, trans. and ed. H.M. Parshley (New York: Vintage Books, 1974). The reader is referred to this classic analysis of woman as "Other,…the incidental, the inessential as opposed to the essential."

9. Greene, 241.

10. Janet L. Miller, *Curriculum Theory Of Maxine Greene: A Reconceptualization Of Foundations In English Education* (Rochester, NY: The Press of *The Journal Of Curriculum Theorizing*, forthcoming).

11. Maxine Greene, ed., *Existential Encounters For Teachers* (New York: Random House, 1967), 4,

12. Maxine Greene, *Teacher As Stranger* (Belmont, CA: Wadsworth Publishing Company, Inc., 1973), 270.

13. Gayle Rugin, "The Traffic in Women: Notes on the 'Political Economy' of Sex," in *Toward An Anthropology Of Women*, ed. Rayna Reiter (New York: Monthly Review Press, 1975): 157.

14. Ibid., 159.

15. Ibid.

16. Ibid., 200.

17. Ibid., 199.

18. Greene, *Landscapes Of Learning*.

19. Axel Madsen, *Hearts And Minds: The Common Journey To Simone De Beauvoir And Jean-Paul Sartre* (New York: William Morrow and Company, Inc., 1977), 251.

20. Phyllis Chesler, *About Men* (New York: Simon and Schuster, 1978), xx.

21. De Beauvoir, 72

22. Greene, *Landscapes Of Learning*, 3.

CHAPTER FIVE

Caring

Nel Noddings
1981

What does it mean to care? Our dictionaries tell us that "care" is a state of mental suffering or of engrossment; to care is to be in a burdened mental state, one of anxiety, fear, or solicitude about something or someone. Alternatively, one cares for something or someone if one has a regard for or inclination toward that something or someone. If I have an inclination toward mathematics, I may willingly spend some time with it, and if I have regard for you, what you think, feel, and desire will matter to me. And, again, to care may mean to be charged with the protection, welfare, or maintenance of something or someone.

These definitions represent uses of "care" but, in the deepest human sense, we shall see that elements of each of them are involved in caring. In one sense, I may equate "cares" with "burdens"; I have cares in certain matters (professional, personal, or public) if I have burdens and worries, if I fret over current and projected states of affairs. In another sense, I care for someone if I feel a stir of desire or inclination toward him. In a related sense, I care for someone if I have regard for his views and interests. In the third sense, I have the care of an elderly relative if I am charged with the responsibility for his physical welfare. But, clearly in the deep human sense that will occupy us, I cannot claim to care for my relative if my caretaking is perfunctory or grudging. In this paper, I shall for the most part restrict discussion to caring for human beings.

I shall claim that there are three aspects of caring relationships. The first two contain elements that are necessary, that is, constitutive of caring; the last reveals elements that are characteristic. There is engrossment, a first-person condition in which the consciousness of the person who is caring is focused on the cared-for. This engrossment induces a displacement of motivational focus from the one-caring to the cared-for. There is an attitude of the one-caring that is received by and reflected in the cared-for (a second-person aspect). This attitude conveys the regard for the one-caring to the cared-for; its reception in the cared-for completes the caring. We shall see that one may properly claim to care for another if the first-person conditions are met, but that the relation itself cannot be called "caring" unless the caring is completed in the cared-for. Finally, there is usually some observable action (a third-person aspect) in behalf of the cared-for. It will be clear, however, that an action criterion cannot be used as an infallible external test for caring; that is, we cannot say with certainty that X cares for Y on the basis of characteristic acts that we, as outsiders to the (X,Y) relation, may observe.

T H E   O N E - C A R I N G

In the ordinary course of events, we expect some action from one who claims to care, but action is not all we expect. How are we to determine whether Mr. Smith cares for his elderly mother who is confined to a nursing home? It is not enough, surely, that Mr. Smith should say, "I care." (But the possibility of his saying this will lead us onto another path of analysis shortly. We shall have to examine caring from the inside.) We, as observers, must look for some action, some manifestation in Smith's behavior that will allow us to agree that he cares. To care, we feel, requires some action in behalf of the cared-for. Thus, if Smith never visits his mother, nor writes to her, nor telephones her, we would be likely to say that, although he is charged formally with her care—he pays for her confinement—he does not really care. We point out that he seems to be lacking in regard, that he is not troubled enough to see for himself how his mother fares. These is no desire for her company, no inclination toward her. But notice that a criterion of action would not be easy to formulate from this case. Smith, after all, does perform some action in behalf of his mother; he pays for her physical maintenance. But we are looking for a qualitatively different sort of action.

Is direct, externally observable action necessary for caring? Can caring be present in the absence of action in behalf of the cared-for? Consider the problem of lovers who cannot marry because they are already committed to satisfactory and honorable marriages. The lover learns that his beloved is ill. All his instincts cry out for his presence at her bedside. Yet, if he fears for the trouble he may bring her, for the recriminations that may spring from his appearance, he may stay away from her. Surely, we would not say in such a case that the lover does not care. He is in a mental state of engrossment, even suffering; he feels the deepest regard; and, charged by his love with the duty to protect, he denies his own need in order to spare her one form of pain. Thus, in caring, he chooses not to act directly and tenderly in response to the beloved's immediate physical pain. We see, then, that there is an act of commitment on the part of the one-caring, but there need not be an action observable in the external world.

Engrossment is the fundamental aspect of caring from the inside. When I look at and think about how I am when I care, I realize that there is invariably this displacement of interest from my own reality to the reality of the other. Kierkegaard has said that we apprehend another's reality as possibility.[1] To touch me, to arouse in me something that will disturb my own ethical reality, I must see the other's reality as a possibility for my own. This is not to say that I cannot try to see the other's reality differently. Indeed, I can. I can look at it objectively by collecting factual data; I can look at it historically. If it is heroic, I can come to admire it. But this sort of looking does not touch my own ethical reality; it may even distract me from it. As Kierkegaard put it:

> Ethically speaking there is nothing so conducive to sound sleep as admiration of another's ethical reality. And again ethically speaking, if there is anything that can stir and rouse a man, it is a possibility ideally requiring itself of a human being.[2]

But I am suggesting that it is not only the logical possibilities for becoming better than we are that we see when we struggle toward the reality of the other. We also have aroused in us the immediate feeling, "I must do something." When we see the other's reality as a possibility for us, we must act to eliminate the intolerable, to reduce the pain, to fill the need, to actualize the dream. When I am in this sort of relationship with another, that the other's reality becomes a real possibility for me, I care. Whether the caring is sustained, whether it lasts long enough to be conveyed to the other, whether it becomes visible in the world, depends upon my sustaining the relationship or, at least, acting out of concern for my own ethicality as though it were sustained.

In this latter case, one in which something has slipped away from me or eluded me from the start (in a particular case) but in which I strive to regain or to attain it, I experience a genuine caring for self. This caring for self, for the ethical self, can only emerge from a caring for others. Now, of course, a sense of my physical self, a knowledge of what gives me pain and pleasure, precedes my caring for others. Otherwise their realities as possibilities for my own reality would mean nothing to me. But this sense is anticipatory to caring; it is not caring itself. When we say of someone, "He cares only for himself," we mean that, in our deepest sense, he does not care at all. He has only a sense of that physical self—of what gives him pain or pleasure. Whatever he sees in others is preselected in relation to his own needs and desires. He does not see the reality of the other as a possibility for himself but only as an instance of what he has already determined as self or not-self. Thus, he is ethically both zero and finished. His only "becoming" is a physical becoming.

Now I need not be a person who cares only for myself in order to behave occasionally as though I care only for myself. Sometimes I behave this way because I have not thought through things carefully enough and because the mode of times pushes the thoughtless in its own direction. Suppose that I am a teacher who loves mathematics. I encounter a student who is doing poorly, and I decide to talk with him. He tells me that he hates mathematics. Aha, I think, here is the problem. I must help this poor boy to love mathematics and then he will do better at it. What am I doing when I proceed this way? I am not trying to grasp the reality of the other as a possibility for myself. I have not even asked: "How would it feel to hate mathematics?" Instead, I project my own reality onto my student and say, "You will be just fine if you only learn to love mathematics." And I have "data" to support me. There is evidence that intrinsic motivation is associated with higher achievement (Did anyone ever doubt this?), so my student becomes an object of study and manipulation for me.

But if I care, I do not make the cared-for into an object of study; at least, I do not allow this change to become permanent. The "feeling with" of caring precedes rational determination of what might be done in behalf of the cared-for, and I must continually turn back to this feeling, to the receptive mode that allows me to apprehend the other. As I convert what I have received from the other into a problem, something to be solved, I move away from the other. I clean up his reality, strip it of complex and bothersome qualities, in order to think it. The other's reality becomes data, stuff to be analyzed, studied, interpreted. All this is to be expected and is entirely appropriate provided that I see the essential turning points and move back to the concrete, the personal, and the receptive. If I care, I must consider the cared-for's nature, his way of life, needs, and desires. I enter into a relation with him and tie my objective thinking to a relational stake that stands at the heart of caring. By this tie, I allow myself to be continually pulled back into direct communication . If I fail to do this, I may climb into clouds of abstraction, moving rapidly away from the cared-for into a domain of objective and impersonal problems upon which I impose whatever structure satisfies it. If I do not turn away from my abstractions, I lose the cared-for. Indeed, I lose myself as one-caring, for I now care about a problem instead of a person.

Caring involves, for the one-caring, a "feeling with" the other. This "feeling with" is not synonymous with "empathy" as it is usually defined. It does not involve projection into the other, nor does it imply a full understanding of the other. Rather it involves receiving the other. When I care, I receive this variable and never fully understand other into myself. I become a duality.

Suppose, for example, that I am having lunch with a random group of colleagues. Among them is one for whom I have never had much regard and for whom I have little professional respect. I do not care for him. Somewhere in the light banter of lunch talk, he begins to talk about an experience in the war-time navy and the feelings he had under a particular treatment. He talks about how these feelings impelled him to become a teacher. His expressions are unusually lucid, defenseless. I am touched—not by sentiment—but by something else. It is as though his eyes and mine have combined to look at the scene he describes. I know that I would have behaved differently in the situation, but this knowledge is in itself a matter of indifference. I feel what he says he felt. I have been invaded by this other. Quite simply, I shall never again be completely without regard for him. My professional opinion has not changed, but I now care.

Apprehending the other's reality, feeling what he feels as nearly as possible, is the essential part of caring from the view of the one-caring. For if I take on the other's reality as possibility and begin to feel its reality, I feel also that I must act accordingly; that is, I am impelled to act as though in my own behalf, but in reality on behalf of the other. But, of course, this feeling that I must act may or may not be sustained. I must make a commitment to act or to refrain from acting. The commitment to act in behalf of the cared-for, the continued interest in his reality, and a continual renewal of commitment are the essential elements of caring from the view of the one-caring. The renewal of commitment spans the temporal space of caring. It may endure for a brief interval as I aid a stranger in minor distress, or it may endure for a lifetime with family and friends. So long as it endures, I care.

T H E   C A R E D - F O R

Caring is, at the outset, a relation between the one-caring and an apprehended reality that represents the cared-for. But to be completed in the world it depends upon the receptivity of the cared-for. You may care for me, for example, without my knowing it; further, I may not believe that you care for me simply because you say that you do. Assuming that I am unresisting and even receptive, what will convince me? Generally, I look more for an attitude than a specific kind of action. I look for something that tells me that you have regard for me, that you are not behaving perfunctorily or merely out of obligation.

Gabriel Marcel characterizes this attitude in terms of "disposability (disponabilite), the readiness to bestow and spend oneself and make oneself available, and its contrary, indisposability."[3] One who is disposable recognizes that she has a self to invest, to give. She does not identify herself with her objects and possessions. She is present to the cared-for. One who is indisposable, however, comes across even to one physically present as absent, as elsewhere. Marcel says:

> When I am with someone who is indisposable, I am conscious of being with someone for whom I do not exist; I am thrown back on myself.[4]

The one-caring, in caring, is present in her acts of caring. Even in physical absence, acts at a distance bear the signs of presence: engrossment in the other—regard—desire for the other's well-being. Caring is largely reactive and responsive. Perhaps it is even better characterized as receptive. The one-caring is sufficiently engrossed in the other to listen to him and take pleasure or pain in what he recounts. Whatever she does for the cared-for is embedded in a relationship that reveals itself as engrossment of the one-caring and in an attitude that warms and comforts the cared-for.

The caring attitude, this quality of disposability, pervades the situational time-space. So far as it is in my control, if we are conversing and if I care, I remain present to you throughout the conversation. Of course, if I care and you do not, then I may put my presence at a distance, thus freeing you to embrace the absence you have chosen. This is the way of dignity in such situations. To be treated as though one does not exist is a threatening experience, and one has to gather up one's self, one's presence, and place it in a safer, more welcome environment. And, of course, it is the way of generosity.

The one cared-for sees the concern, delight, or interest in the eyes of the one-caring and feels her warmth in both verbal and body language. To the cared-for no act in his behalf is quite as important or influential as the attitude of the one-caring; an act done grudgingly may be accepted graciously on the surface but resented deeply inwardly, whereas small act performed generously may be accepted nonchalantly but appreciated inwardly. When the attitude of the one-caring bespeaks caring, the cared-for glows, grows stronger, and feels not so much that he has been given something as that something has been added to him. And this "something" may be hard to specify. Indeed, for the one-caring and the cared-for in a relationship of genuine caring, there is no felt need on either part to specify what sort of transformation has taken place.

The intangible something that is added to the cared-for (and often, simultaneously, to the one-caring) will be an important consideration for us when we discuss caring in social institutions and, especially, in schools. It may be that much of what is most valuable in the teaching-learning relationship cannot be specified and certainly not prespecified. The attitude characteristic of caring comes through in acquaintance. When the student associates with the teacher, feeling free to initiate conversation and to suggest areas of interest, he or she is better able to detect the characteristic attitude even in formal, goal-oriented situations such as lectures. Then a brief contact of eyes may say, "I am still the one interested in you. All of this is of variable importance and significance, but you still matter more." It is no use saying that the teacher who "really cares" wants her students to learn the basic skills that are necessary to a comfortable life; I am not denying that, but the notion is impoverished on both ends. On the one extreme, it is not enough to want one's students to master basic skills. I would not want to choose, but if I had to choose whether my child would be a reader or a loving human being, I would choose the latter with alacrity.

On the other extreme, it is by itself too much, for it suggests that I as a caring teacher should be willing to do almost anything to bring my students to mastery of the basic skills. And I am not. Among the intangibles that I would have my students carry away is the feeling that the subject we have struggled with is both fascinating and boring, significant and silly, fraught with meaning and nonsense, challenging and tedious, and that whatever attitude we take toward it, it will not diminish our regard for each other. The student is infinitely more important than the subject.

The cared-for responds to the presence of the one-caring. He feels the difference between being received and being held off or ignored. Whatever the one-caring actually does is enhanced or diminished, made meaningful or meaningless, in the attitude conveyed to the cared-for. This attitude is not something thought by either the one-caring or the cared-for although, of course, either one may think about it. It is a total conveyance of self to other, a continual transformation of individual to duality to new individual to new duality. Neither the engrossment of the one-caring nor the attitude perceived by the cared-for is rational; that is, neither is reasoned. While much of what goes on in caring is rational and carefully thought out, the basic relationship is not, and neither is the awareness of relatedness. The essentially nonrational nature of caring is recognized by, for example, Urie Bronfenbrenner when he claims: "In order to develop child needs the enduring, irrational involvement of one or more adults in care and joint activity with the child."[5]

In answer to what he means by "irrational," he explains: "Somebody has got to be crazy about that kid!"[6]

Now, of course, philosophers are certain to point out that being "crazy" about a child is not necessarily "irrational." There is equivocation here. But Bronfenbrenner's way of talking nonetheless underscores the essential point I have been trying to make. The caring relationship is, at bottom, nonrational. However rational the decision making processes that enter it, however rational the investigation of means-ends relationships, the commitment that elicits the rational activity precedes it and gives it personal meaning. The one-caring stands ready to engage in play, to embrace, to take wild and desperate chances in behalf of the cared-for. All this the cared-for sees and, in the absence of pathology, he grows and glows with it.

So far, I have proceeded phenomenologically. I have been exploring situations that all of us are familiar with, and I have subjected these situations to analysis. But it is important to realize that there are both logical and empirical factors that contribute to the analysis. In the logical domain, I have claimed that reception by the cared-for of an attitude of caring on the part of the one-caring is partially constitutive of caring. This attitude and its reception are not just characteristic of caring. Does this mean that I cannot be said to care for X if X does not recognize my caring? In the fullest sense, in evaluating the relation, I think we have to accept this result. Caring involves, essentially, two parties: the one-caring and the cared-for. It is complete when it is fulfilled in both. We are tempted to say that the caring attitude is characteristic of caring, that when one cares, she characteristically exhibits an attitude. But, then, it could be missed by the cared-for. If I meet the first-person requirements of caring for X, I am tempted to insist that I do care—that there is something wrong with X that he does not appreciate my caring. We want to allow my claim without committing ourselves to call the relation caring. For consider: If X is looking at this relationship, X would have to report, however reluctantly, that something is missing. X does not feel that I care. Therefore, sadly, I must admit that, while I care, X does not perceive that I do and, hence, the relationship cannot be characterized as one of caring. This result does not necessarily signify negligence on my part. There are limits in caring. X may be paranoid or otherwise pathological. There may be no way for my caring to reach him. But, the caring has been only partially actualized.

Logically, we have the following: "(W,X) is a caring relationship if and only if W cares for X (as described in the one-caring), and X recognizes that W cares for X."

When we say "X recognizes that W cares for X," we mean that X receives the caring honestly. He receives it; he does not hide from it or deny it. Hence, its reception becomes part of what the one-caring feels when he receives the cared-for. We do not need to add a third condition and a fourth, as in, "W is aware that X recognizes," "X is aware that W is aware that..." and so on. Caring requires the typical engrossment and motivational displacement in W and, also, the recognition of caring by X.

Now, of course, the relationship can be mutually (or doubly) caring if we can interchange W and X and retain true expressions. This seems the correct logical analysis of caring, and, of course, it has the merit that it accounts for the ambivalence that may arise in such a situation. By that, I mean it allows me to say, "I care for X," even if I must admit that (I, W) is not a fully caring relationship.

There is, also, empirical confirmation of much that we have explored phenomenologically. Space prevents extended discussion, but we may note that the empirical literature contains many references to the effects of attitude (both positive and negative) on the one-to-be-cared-for. Sanger,[7] Montague,[8] and Wengraf,[9] for example, present evidence that even a fetus is affected by the feelings of acceptance or rejection in its mother. Speaking of maternal hostility, Zilboorg says that it

> has its rather mysterious ways of conveying itself to the child and of provoking a considerable number of undesirable and at times directly pathological reations.[10]

Further, studies have shown that significant differences in child personality and behavior cannot always be traced to specific differences in child-rearing practices but are often correlated with parental attitudes toward their children.[11]

Hence, a claim that attitude is crucial to an analysis of caring, that feeling is somehow conveyed faithfully and directly, is supported both logically and empirically.

CARING ACTS

We have seen that externally observable action is not necessary to caring, but we can agree readily that it is characteristic of caring. Our motivation, in caring, is directed toward the welfare, protection, and enhancement of the cared-for. When we care, we should, ideally, be able to present reasons for our action/inaction, which would persuade a reasonable, dis-interested observer that we have acted in behalf of the cared-for. This does not mean that all such observers have to agree that they would have behaved exactly as we did in the caring situation. They may, indeed, see preferred alternatives. They may experience the very conflicts that caused us anxiety and, as a result, suggest a different course of action. But our reasons should be so well connected to the objective elements of the problem that our course of action clearly stands a chance of succeeding in behalf of the cared-for.

The problems a third-person (observer) has in judging a chain of action for caring seem somehow extraneous or unimportant to the actual caring. There are, after all, two persons in a unique position to judge: the one-caring and the cared-for. Over time, the cared-for should recognize and acknowledge the caring; from the start, the one-caring should be aware of a displacement in attention from the self to the cared-for. But the problems of the observer become important when we consider how care may be entrusted. When we consider the possibility of institutional or societal caring, these problems become critical.

Clearly, the motive of one claiming to care may properly yield either partial support for a claim to care, or it may reveal a desire merely to be thought of as caring. But motives are not always revealed. There is, also, an attitude characteristic of caring; the one-caring is engrossed in the other, not in herself. There is a move away from egoism. But how is this revealed in action?

It seems likely that the actions of one-caring will be varied rather than rule-bound. Variation is to be expected if the one claiming to care really cares, for her engrossment is in the variable and never fully understood other, on the particular individual in a particular set of circumstances. Rule-bound responses in the name of caring lead us to suspect that the claimant wants to be credited with caring. A person who "cares" for animals and whisks every stray promptly to the county shelter may be suspect. To care, after all, is to have an inclination toward, to protect. Most animals, once at the county shelter, suffer death. Does one who cares choose swift and merciful death for the object of her care over precarious and perhaps painful life? Well, we might say, it depends. If we live in a quiet area, relatively free of traffic, we might feed strays for a while, watching for signs of illness and inquiring in various ways after the owners. We might adopt some of them. If, however, we live on a street where traffic presents a continual threat to life and if we cannot ourselves provide shelter, we might properly turn often to the institutional shelter. But, by and large, we do not say with any conviction that a person cares if that person acts routinely according to a fixed rule.

Caring involves stepping out of one's own personal frame of reference into the other's. When we care, we consider the other's point of view, his objective needs, and what he expects of us. Our attention, our mental engrossment, is on the cared-for, not on ourselves. Our reasons for acting, then, have to do both with the other's wants and desires and with the objective elements of his problematic situation. If the stray cat is healthy and relatively safe, we provide food, water, and encouraging affection. Why condemn it to death when it might enjoy a vagabond freedom? If our minds are on ourselves, however, our reasons for acting point back at us and not outward to the cared-for. When we want to be thought of as caring, we act routinely in a way that may easily secure that credit for us.

A teacher describes a series of incidents that occurred in a team teaching situation. The students had entered into contracts for the grades they would like to receive in mathematics. One bright boy achieved his "B" relatively early in the marking period and decided to use the rest of his time on nonmathematical studies. The teacher telling the story accepted his decision, but the other teachers on the team did not. They felt that they could not properly allow a student to "waste" his obvious talent and that they were obligated to insist that he strive for the "A," of which he was clearly capable. They insisted that they cared and that they were helping the student. The teacher who accepted the boy's decision was not so sure. Were they helping or hindering?[12] For this teacher, the boy's motives and attitude toward mathematics and other studies were respectable possibilities. She "felt with" him and respected his decision. This is not to say that she refrained from trying to influence him, but she did refrain from attempting to control him "for his own sake."

This is, I think, an important point about caring in the teaching relationship. When we care, we are touched by the other and expect to touch him. We enter into a relation with the student, but that relation need not be one of interference and control. Martin Buber describes it as a master-apprentice relation:

> the master remains the model for the teacher. For if the educator of our day has to act consciously he must nevertheless do it "as though he did not." That raising of the finger, that questioning glance, are his genuine doing. Through him the selection of the effective world reaches the pupil. He fails the recipient when he presents this selection to him with a gesture of interference.... Interference divides the soul in his care into an obedient part and a rebellious

part. But a hidden influence proceeding from his integrity has an integrating force.13

To care, then, is not to act by rule but by affection and regard. We act not to achieve for ourselves a commendation but to protect and enhance the welfare of the cared-for. Because we are inclined toward the cared-for, we want to act in a way that will please him. But we wish to please him for his sake and not for ours. Even this reason—to act so that the happiness and pleasure of the cared-for will be enhanced—may not be a sure sign of caring. We are sometimes thrown into conflict over what the cared-for wants and what we think would be best for him. As caring parents, for example, we cannot always act in ways that bring immediate reactions of pleasure from our children. But our decisions are accompanied by conversation that is open to influence.

The one-caring desires the well-being of the cared-for and acts to promote that well-being. She is inclined toward the other. An observer, however, cannot "see" the crucial motive and may misread the attitudinal signs. The observer, then, must judge caring, in part, by the following: first, the action under consideration either brings about a favorable outcome for the cared-for or seems reasonably likely to have done so; second, the one-caring displays a characteristic variation in her actions—she acts in non rule-bound fashion in behalf of the cared-for; third, decisions are often made through deliberation with the cared-for and through mutual influence rather than interference.

CAN INSTITUTIONS CARE?

We want to ask, how, whether a society or large community can care. In light of our analysis, the initial response to this question must be "no." A society cannot be "present" to the cared–for; only an individual can be disposable in this important sense. Strictly speaking, only an individual has a motive. But in a modified sense, it would seem that a society can care. It can allocate funds to enhance the well-being of groups to be cared for; it can structure its laws and institutions in ways that make it clear that, at least, the existence of the group to be cared for is recognized. It can provide systematically for caretaking.

The motive for caring arises in individuals. As groups of individuals discuss the perceived needs of another individual or group, the imperative changes from, "I must do something!" to "Something must be done." This change is accompanied by a shift from the nonrational to the rational. What should be done? How shall it be done? Who should do it? Why should the persons named do it? The danger, as we have already seen, is that caring which is essentially a nonrational response to the needs and wants of the cared-for is transformed into an analytically prescribed system of caretaking. The result is a pervasive complaint against our caretaking institutions and agencies: "Nobody cares!"

Is there an alternative to this rational transformation of caring? I would like to suggest that institutions, agencies, and large groups should not undertake what is clearly impossible for them to accomplish; that is, they should not try through any sort of rational transformation to care directly. Rather, the individuals planning for these large groups should consider how they might best provide supportive environments for caring. This means that planners will have to ask how they can provide opportunities for those entrusted with caretaking to care. The engrossment constitutive of caring and its reception in the cared-for require that relations be developed. Persons in a caring relationship need time to talk to each other, to share, to influence each other. Space prevents the extended discussion that must eventually be engaged on this, but some recommendations compatible with our analysis can be made.

Provisions for extended interactions must be made. Working groups might be kept small. Their association over time might be extended. In schools, for example, "schools within schools" or some such device might be tried. Advisors might stay with students, by mutual consent, for the students' entire school attendance. Similarly, teachers might stay with their classes for two or three years instead of the traditional one year. Several desirable outcomes might emerge from such arrangements. First, and most important, caring has a better chance of developing in longer, closer relationships. Second, teachers might predictably develop a greater sense of responsibility for the growth of students with whom they will have extended contact. Third, teachers might gain greater proficiency in the subjects they teach by following the subjects longitudinally instead of teaching the same thing year after year. It is sometimes protested, in reaction to this recommendation, that there are teachers we would not wish to entrust our children to for such extended periods. This is a poor argument. We should not entrust our children to such persons for one year or even for part of a year. A fourth, final, advantage to this arrangement, then, is that we might finally—and quite naturally—begin to force out of the profession those who are least caring and least competent.

Next, rules must be converted, wherever possible, to principles and guidelines. Those entrusted with caretaking must also be entrusted with making judgments. Variability in treatments must be expected and encouraged with appropriate justification. Caring reduces the necessity for justice. Where we can, we respond to the felt needs and longings of the cared-for. We establish expectations, and our regard makes it likely that the expectations will be met. But decisions are not necessarily easily made in caring relationships; they are not made by formula. When we care, we personally are addressed, and we must respond. We can turn to others for help, but we cannot turn to others, or to "society," to relieve us of responsibility. Always we turn away from rules and abstractions to the real, concrete, present cared-for, and organizations that entrust us with caretaking must encourage us to do this.

As Bronfenbrenner suggests, organizations might themselves be rewarded for encouraging caring in their personnel. Organizations might, then, make it acceptable for parents to stay home with sick children; to make and receive phone calls from family members; to bring infants to work under suitable conditions (a baby is no more a distraction in an office than in a kitchen); to participate in community activities requiring one-to-one interactions.

The intrinsic rewards of caring must also be acknowledged, and persons must be freed of the constraints that now prevent their harvesting of these rewards. In schools, this means a shift away from rule-bound accountability, and from product-oriented evaluation, away from insistence on uniform competencies. It means a move toward personal responsibility, toward helping rather than rating, toward increased opportunities for dialogue, toward long-term and, perhaps, joy filled personal relationships.

CLOSING COMMENTS

Caring is a large, complex topic. In this paper, I have outlined an analysis of personal caring and caring relationships, and I have tried to suggest some ways in which large organizations might foster caring among their personnel. Many intriguing aspects of caring remain to be explored: how caring develops in the young, the ontological status of caring, how caring for nonhuman living things contributes to the quality of human life, what it means to care for things, ideas, and principles, and what "caring schools" might look like. Then, too, I have not discussed in detail the conflicts of caring, the role of contiguity in caring, or the formal and informal chains that bind us lightly in a state of preparation to care."

There is work enough, I suspect, to occupy many of us for some time to come.

N O T E S

1. Soren Kierkegaard, *Concluding Unscientific Postscript*, trans. by David F. Swenson and Walter Lowrie (Princeton University Press, 1941).

2. Ibid., 322.

3. See H. J. Blackman, *Six Existentialist Thinkers* (New York: Harper & Row Publishers), 66-85.

4. Ibid., 80x

5. Urie Bronfenbrenner, "Who Needs Parent Education?" *Teachers College Record* (May 1978): 773-74.

6. Ibid., 774.

7. Margaret Sanger (Ed.), *The Sixth International Neo-Malthusian And Birth Control Conference*, Vol. 4: *Religious And Ethical Aspects Of Birth Control* (New York: American Birth Control League, 1926).

8. M. Γ. Λ. Montagu, *Prenatal Influences* (Springfield, Ill.: Thomas, 1962).

9. F. Wengraf, *Psychosomatic Approach To Gynecology And Obstetrics* (Springfield, Ill.: Thomas, 1953).

10. G. Zilboorg, "The Clinical Issues of Postpartum Psychopathological Reactions," *American Journal Of Obstetrics And Gynecology* 73, 308.

11. See, for example, R. R. Sears, et al, *Patterns Of Child Rearing* (Evanston, Ill.: Row, Peterson, 1957) and E.S. Schaefer and R.O. Bell, "Patterns of Attitudes Toward Child Rearing and the Family," *Journal Of Abnormal Social Psychology* 54, (1957): 391-95.

12. For a discussion of "hindering" in the helping professions, see David Brandon, *Zen In The Art Of Helping* (New York: Dell Publishing Co., Inc. 1978), ch. 3.

13. Martin Buber, "Education," in *Between Man And Man* (New York: The Macmillan Company, 1968), 90.

Caring:
Gender Considerations

William F. Pinar
1981

A   R E S P O N S E   T O
N E L   N O D D I N G S '   " C A R I N G "

I find this paper interesting, thematically and methodologically. "Caring" is not a
a common theme of scholarly papers, certainly not in curriculum studies,
probably not in philosophy of education. Because as Noddings suggests, caring is
"nonrational,"[1] I think it tends not to readily lend itself to an analysis of its
properties. Because it is an attitude (disposability is the inelegant translation of
Marcel's word) and not a specifiable set of behaviors, it does not readily lend
itself to empirical research, as conducted by mainstream social scientists. Even
so, Noddings manages to mend this incongruence of method and theme. How
she manages this mend, and why the study of caring is methodologically
complicated, can be partially explained by situating these issues in a body of
work just now entering curriculum discourse: gender analysis. In a word, gender
analysis refers to the reconstruction of the process of gender formation, and can
be regarded as loosely allied with psychoanalytic strands of feminist thought. It
almost goes without saying that I have time to sketch this connection only
lightly. Doing so might, however, bring into sharper relief the phenomenon of
caring, and Noddings' deft analysis of it. To begin, let us return to her paper.

Early on we learn that "we shall have to examine caring from the inside."[2]
This she achieves, and without abandoning linguistic analysis, without resorting
to autobiography or poetry, two more likely methods of portraying "the inside."
Her depiction of lovers, for instance, who care for one another while remaining
married to others,[3] does not slow the progression of her argument. But it does
contextualize that argument in emotion and experience, sacrificing neither the
experience to the argument, nor the argument to the experience. This
methodological success is evident again in her portrait of "objectification."
Describing the mathematics teachers and the poor student, Noddings notes the
delusion of the former who thinks they "must help this poor boy to love
mathematics, and then he will do better at it."[4] She observes:

What am I doing when I proceed this way? I am not trying to grasp the reality of the other as a possibility for myself. I have not even asked: How would it feel to hate mathematics? Instead, I have projected my own reality onto my student and say, You will be just fine if you only learn to love mathematics. So my student becomes an object of study and manipulation for me.5

She returns us to the world of everyday experience. It penetrates her prose, not permitting the reader to escape into a discrete world of ideas, the interrelationships of which become the consuming interest. Instead, it is my life, and the lives of others I am pointed to. In a quiet, disarmingly simple way she clarifies the psychologically complex and perennial confusion of need and caring. "[Caring] does not involve projection into the other, nor does it imply full understanding of the other. Rather it involves receiving the other."6 This last idea is central to her conception. "Caring is largely reactive and responsive. Perhaps it is even better characterized as receptive."7

"Receiving the other" is, classically and specifically heterosexually, the woman's posture. It suggests a certain passivity, a certain openness to the Other. Classically and specifically heterosexually, the male is the asserting, even aggressive one. Gender analysts argue that these classical and to an extent stereotypic, postures are not anatomical givens. Rather, they are the psychosexual consequences of contemporary childrearing practices in advanced industrial societies. That is another story, too long and too complex for present purposes. For present purposes I want to suggest that "caring" is classically a woman's preoccupation, especially when it is described as receptivity. (That is why it is rare in the literature. There are few women among us.) Further, I want to speculate that linguistic analysis may have its psychogenesis in the classic male resolution of the oedipal crisis. That Noddings has made use of the latter to clarify the former is a methodological achievement, although perhaps not a feminist one. Finally, it is necessary to suggest that in the effort to establish institutional support for caring (as Noddings calls for),8 gender considerations are probably crucial. It may be, as some feminists have concluded, that man—by virtue of his gender formation—has "stunted relational potential,"9 to use Nancy Chodorow's phrase. In a word, we men may have reduced capacities to care. With that unpleasant thought, let us back up a bit, sketch this problematic process of gender formation, and link it to the idea of subjectivity and objectivity. For this we turn to Madeleine R. Grumet who, in her seminal essay "Contradiction, Conception, and Curriculum"10 argues that the capacity to experience, understand, and articulate subjectivity tends to remain intact in the woman, while becoming repressed in the man. Grumet relies on Chodorow's reconstruction of the oedpial crisis for her argument that men lose this capacity as they lose their pre-oedipal identification with the mother. This identification they must repress in order to construct a male identity, an identification with the father. Thus at its inception the male's identification of himself as a man is characterized by a cognitive construction. He is like his father, the absent one, the one who inhabits a world outside the child's, a world the child can only imagine. He becomes unlike his mother, the present one, from whom he has hitherto been undifferentiated, whose world he shared as she shared his. The complicated result is that the male makes virtue out of necessity: he rationalizes the denial of undifferentiated experience of and with the mother, and he celebrates the conceptualization of himself after an embodied idea, his father. He becomes an object to himself as he is a son to his father. The female child, because she is permitted to remain identified with the mother, adds desire for the father. She remains immersed in the intersubjective and undifferentiated experience of mother and child. The male tends to disparage that which he has lost—subjectivity becomes "soft," too "messy"—and admire what he has gained: the facility to construct and infer, symbolically systematized in science, law, and logic. As an adult he posits cause and ownership of the child that his woman only "carries"; Grumet describes the father's compensation for his abstract and inferred paternity and—more generally—identity. Grumet writes:

> As a parent the father contradicts the inferential and uncertain character of his paternity by transforming the abstraction that has been felt as deficiency into a virtue, into virtue itself. Co-opting the word, and transforming it into the law the fathers dominate communal activity. Typing procreation and kinship to the exchange of capital the fathers master the pernicious alchemy of turning people into gold, substituting the objectification of persons for the abstraction paternity implies and technology and capitalism amplify. The project to be the cause, to see the relation of self and other as concrete is expressed in monologic epistemologies of cause and effect, either/or construction of truth, and of social science that denigrates the ambiguity and dialectical nature of human action to honor the predictability and control of physical and mechanistic phenomena.[11]

It is the objectification of persons that Noddings underscores as not caring.[12] It is the situation of persons in Idea—whether that idea be excellence in mathematics or for capitalists the accumulation of capital—which idolizes the object,[13] and forgets or merely manipulates the Subject. These politico-economic tendencies parallel the epistemological ones in the tendency to objectify and naturalize contingent and variable human experience into invariant laws and objective truth. What sometimes seems like an obsession with logic and language in twentieth-century philosophy (the parallel perhaps of positivism in social science) likewise suggests the virtue of cognitivism, the idolatry of symbol, and the neglect of nonrational experience, which can be linked to the male's repression of his female identity, and with it, the repression of feeling and undifferentiated experience. What is striking about Noddings' paper is that she sacrifices neither feeling nor logic. She returns us to that nameless domain that is primal emotion and conceptually unmediated experience, but we do not lose our analytic mode of conveyance. Consider the following passage in which she subtly describes the experience of the "one cared-for."

> When the attitude of the one-caring bespeaks caring, the cared-for glows, grows stronger, and feels not so much that he has been given something as that something has been added to him. And this "something" may be hard to specify. Indeed, for the one-caring and the cared-for in a relationship of genuine caring, there is no felt need on either part to specify what sort of transformation has taken place.[14]

Noddings observes that the unspecified nature of this "something added" parallels that which cannot be specified, and yet which is central, in a "teaching-learning relationship." We are told that through eye contact the teacher communicates to his student that he cares for him. "I am still the one interested in you. All of this is of variable importance and significance, but you still matter more."[15] Simply and powerfully Noddings notes that "the student is infinitely more important the subject."[16] I submit that this is not the language of the Father, whose final commitments are to achievement and career; it is the language of the Mother, for whom, even in failure, her baby remains her baby, irreducibly important.

That caring is at heart something "added on," something "unspecified," may be—given present childrearing patterns and oedipal resolutions—the woman's experience. It is the daughter who adds on desire and love from her father, although complete in her relationship with her mother. That caring is something unspecified in Noddings' paper may illustrate the woman's comfort with subjective experience. Our (meaning we men) possible discomfort may derive from our particular oedipal experience. It is the male's repression of his subjectivity, the repression of his identification with the mother, which demarcates his estrangement from the primordial, the undifferentiated, the formless, from pure emotion. It is the male who consequently insists upon the specification of experience, the analysis of concepts, the objectifications of persons. His caring often takes mediated form: providing for his family for instance, rather than being lovingly present for and disposable to them.

Noddings' paper is important because it refers to that which is unspecified while not abandoning or repudiating what is. She makes use of her words to recreate and clarify the experience of caring, not to reductionistically call attention only to words themselves. Honoring the experience of her mother with the words of her Father, she unites an androgynous prose which in the present historical moment is usually dissociated. For this I appreciate her, and I look forward to more from her.

NOTES

1. Nel Noddings, "Caring," unpublished manuscript, 14.

2. Noddings, 3.

3. Noddings, 4.

4. Noddings, 7, emphasis removed.

5. Noddings, 7, emphasis in original.

6. Noddings, 8, emphasis in original.

7. Noddings, 11

8. Noddings, 23ff.

9. Nancy Chodorow, *The Reproduction Of Mothering* (Berkeley: University of California Press, 1978.)

10. Madeleine R. Grumet, "Contradiction, Conception and Curriculum," paper presented to *The Journal Of Curriculum Theorizing*, 1979 Conference, Airlie, Virginia.

11. Grumet, 17-18.

12. Noddings, 8.

13. Noddings, 10.

14. Noddings, 12.

15. Noddings, 12.

16. Noddings, 13.

Up from Agapé

Mary Anne Raywid
1981

RESPONSE TO "CARING"
BY NEL NODDINGS

Nel's decision to examine the concept of caring—with its ramifications for schooling and to her institutionalized activities—is much to be applauded. For the lack of caring in these institutions, and the absence of the conditions that would permit and encourage it, are not just accidental. I find that my students, and many of my colleagues, too, tend to contrast the carers with the noncarers as though these were innate and immutable traits, likenable to good and evil, kind and callous. The trouble with this kind of thinking is not only that it is dysfunctional for making things better; it is dysfunctional even for understanding what they are.

I believe that the absence of caring from the current institutional scene is neither individual failure nor casual accident; it is the inevitable consequence, the played out logic, of what we have explicitly sought as the articulating spirit of these institutions. We have systematically substituted the virtues of noncaring relationships for those of caring. Such ideals as justice, equality, impartiality, due process, and decision by law, not individuals, surface first in government. But they have made the long march through our public institutions, coming increasingly to order the activities and priorities of all of them. Nel is right in saying that "Caring reduces the necessity for justice" (p. 147). It introduces an entirely different set of concerns to be heeded, and principles for guiding institutions, and quite different attitudes for relating to one another within them. Coming to understand what caring entails—and how we have quite systematically excluded it from our public interactions—may prove important steps to restoring it within schools—which I deem a much-needed move. Thus, I want to begin by applauding Nel's effort.

Before examining the parts of her concept in detail, it is important to identify her general strategy. Note first that Nel chose to explore caring—in preference, e.g., to loving or esteeming, or cherishing or liking or being fond of. She is interested, I take it, in all of these—in what sustains any positive relationship between two human beings. And she is also interested in what this answer might or should mean for the way we operate institutions, particularly schools. Her search, then, is for a concept with sufficient scope to encompass all human relationships marked by positive affect. Her next move is to extract the essential elements common to all such relationships.

I'm afraid the strategy yields difficulty. The more I pursue the provocative questions her paper raises for me, the more I doubt that there is much that can informatively be said about "caring"—because the concept represents such a high level of generalization or abstraction, so remote from any context. The "caring" of a lover, a parent, a friend, a co-worker, a teacher, a child, and an air traffic controller seem so vastly different in nature, as well as in intensity, that an analysis of what is common to all must encounter considerable risks of error on the one hand, versus vague and inapplicable generality on the other. The most likely way out of such a predicament is to settle on a model or paradigmatic form of caring to deal with, which is what I think Nel has done. But this is a move that must prove reductionist in proportion to the variability of the types or forms of "caring" rolled into the original concept. I think there remains a sizable job to be done in demonstrating that what is true of the "caring" she talks about is, indeed, true of all forms of human caring. Short of such demonstration, her analysis seems repeatedly to take on the flavor of a programmatic definition—by means of which one is admonished that one is not a real carer unless one feels or acts or responds in the ways specified.

What is the particular form of caring that Nel has taken for her model? What she selects as logical requirements and empirical attributes of caring seem to mark her paradigm as being in love—and perhaps only one phase of being in love, at that. Recall that the constitutive elements of caring are "engrossment" and "an attitude...which is received by and reflected in the cared for" (p. 140), who is thus aware of and receptive to be cared for (p. 143). On her part, the career has made, and continually renews, her "commitment to act in behalf of the cared-for" and to maintain a "continued interest in his reality" (p. 141). On the other side of the relationship, the cared-for must feel that the one-caring is continually "present" to him and, in rough translation, "at his disposal" (p. 142). "The cared-for responds to the presence of the one-caring" (p. 143) and "the cared-for glows, grows stronger, and feels not so much that he has been given something as that something has been added to him" (p. 142). "The one cared-for sees the concern, delight, or interest in the eyes of the one-caring and feels her warmth in both verbal and body language" (p. 142). What the one-caring offers is "a total conveyance of self to other, a continual transformation of individual to duality to new individual to new duality" (p. 143).

Now this simply is not logically or empirically descriptive of any caring relationship except the first phase of being in love. Even in such a rare relationship as this one, after the initial phase the figure-ground focus is allowed to shift at least occasionally, so that the beloved is not the only and continuously dominant figure in the consciousness of the one caring. (Otherwise there could be only one caring relationship at a time in our lives, and it would, of course, preclude getting any work done!—two consequences of Nel's account of caring that would have particularly serious ramifications for the teacher.) But notice that when such a figure-ground shift takes place, the one-caring is no longer constantly marked by "engrossment" in the cared-for, and is not "present" nor disposable to him at all times. When working, neither my husband nor I tend to be psychically available to the other in the sense that Nel's logical requisites would seem to require of us. What I would want to insist, of course, is that the caring is nevertheless still there. But if so, then caring is not as Nel has described it, and its constitutive elements are other than those she has identified.

There is a haunting scene from Thornton Wilder's "Our Town"—a play that became a classic largely, I suspect, for its portrayal of caring—which for me offers a powerful counter instance to Nel's account. It is the scene in which Emily returns to earth for the one day she has chosen to re-live, her twelfth birthday—and as her Mother stands at the stove cooking breakfast, Emily-returned, silently cries, "Oh, Mama, just look at me one minute as though you really saw me...[It is] just for a moment now we're all together. Mama, just for a moment we're happy. Let's look at one another." (Act Three, New York: Franklin Watts, 1938, p. 99). I don't think Wilder's point is, as Nel's analysis would have it, that Emily's Mother doesn't care for her: it is that this is simply the nature of people and the stuff of life. At least after adolescence, we can care very much about an individual, yet be occupied with others, or with things or ideas—which would have to disqualify us as caring, according to Nel's requisites.

The reason for some of these apparent difficulties in Nel's account seem clear. She wants to find one form of positive human disposition toward another that can subsume all forms. This necessitates that she choose the most intense mode—a move that subsequently obligates her to perceive all our positive dispositions toward others as approximations of this most intense form, differing from it only as a matter of degree. And this, it seems to me, is simply unfaithful to human experience. The quality of affect marking the initial phase of being in love is probably for most of us quite atypical of the range of caring relationships that involve us most of the time—rather than paradigmatic of these multiple kinds of caring. And treating it as though it is the ideal or model form seems likely to mislead us into all sorts of false expectations about the way we can and should feel about people, that we simply don't. It is at least partly what leads Nel to conclude that "institutions...should not undertake what is clearly impossible for them to accomplish; that is they should not try...to care directly" (p. 146).

Although I found Nel's concept of caring fascinating, I want to call attention to only one additional feature of it, or I'll have no time left to explore its institutional ramifications. Nel is obviously right in suggesting that caring is at root affective and nonrational in nature. But I am bothered, nevertheless, by what seems to be her tendency to split it off so completely from the rational. It seems to me that the attempt to "feel with" and to help the cared-for may frequently call for cognitive activity. Granted, if the caring-one focuses too exclusively on just how to help, at some point she has come to "care about a problem instead of a person" (p. 141). But short of such an obsessional switch, rationality seems to me incumbent on the one-caring, not somehow inimical to or disruptive of the caring. I tend to feel more comfortable about a surgeon I believe cares about or for me as an individual. Similarly a lawyer or a teacher. But in none of these cases would I want to see the carer's rationality circumscribed. There are some things we want and need from others—including teachers—to which rationality and objectivity are essential. The remoteness from others and correcting of my frame of reference may be exactly what I most need from a lawyer or a teacher.

For me, then, there is an obligation to effectiveness in genuine caring. The caring one who rushes to save his beloved from a bee, but knocks her over a cliff in the process, has not exhibited the kind of caring we can admire. If he simply knocks her flat instead, he's just a klutz instead of a tragic figure, but that's no model of caring either. And effective caring, it seems to me, calls for a rationality that Nel's concept seems to minimize at best. I prefer Mayeroff's conception in this regard. He says quite bluntly "To care for someone, I must know many things." (Milton Mayeroff, *On Caring*, New York: Perennial Library, 1971, p. 13).

The importance of the effectiveness requirement becomes even clearer when we begin to explore the possibilities of institutionalized caring. Here, the harm that teachers or social workers or surgeons can do is written so large and bold that effective caring seems as incumbent upon them as mere caring. As Bettelheim has told us, "Love is Not Enough." And as the film "The Prime of Miss Jean Brodie" demonstrated for us, some caring—particularly of the adult for the young—can have tragically destructive effects. (I am thinking of the girl—a favorite of Miss Brodie's—who acted on her mentor's romanticized view of the Spanish Civil War and was killed.)

Nel doesn't make it explicit why, but she feels that teachers should be caring people. She even wants to force noncaring teachers out of the profession (p. 147). Yet in the way she defines caring and caring relationships, she makes it very difficult for teachers to be carers—and, to the extent that they care, she may make it difficult for them to be teachers. How can an individual share the caring relationship Nel has described with an entire class, or even with several members of a class? Nel's caring relationships are highly selective in the first place. We would also have to note that only sometime in adolescence would most youngsters become able to enter into a caring relationship as Nel has described it. Prior to this time, they typically lack the awareness of others, and the logical capacities Nel implicates in the receiving and reflecting of caring. On her idea of caring, then, the teacher's caring must remain "only partially actualized" (p. 143) and incapable of being "completed in the world" (p. 141)— since caring involves two parties and is complete only when fulfilled in both (p. 142).

While this one sidedness seems accurate enough, mightn't it be more helpful to construe the teacher's caring in terms that acknowledge and accept the asymmetry of adult-child relations, instead of casting them as unsatisfactory imitations of adult relations? I have found Buber's discussion of nonmutuality of teacher-student relationships extremely insightful in this regard. He distinguishes the educational relation from the relationship of friends precisely by virtue of its one-sidedness. Furthermore, for Buber, if the educational relation loses one-sidedness it loses its essence (*Between Man And Man*).

But I am bothered even more by the priority Nel assigns "feeling with" in a caring relationship. The one-caring must maintain a focus on sharing the reality of the cared-for and perceiving the world in his terms. I am ambivalent about the wisdom of that for the teacher. For many teachers, it would be a very desirable corrective to try to do so. We seem so often in education to be indifferent to the phenomenology of our students—and when interested at all, it is typically with the way their heads will be at some future time, not now. On the other hand, however, the teacher's "feeling with" the student needs also to be contained, alternated perhaps with another perspective. The teacher's obligation is to mediate between the child's present perceived reality and other realities. She has the task of introducing these new realities—a charge that cannot be fulfilled without stepping outside the child's reality.

In sum, then, I would have to say that the institutional application of Nel's caring concept to schools suggests that it does not respond well to the realities of children and of the teaching task. But I am very much interested in caring teachers, and in trying to frame a conception of caring that could shed light on the elements of teacher caring. How might that be done? I think first that we must begin with another mode of caring altogether—rather than with what appears to be the most intense kind of caring. Two possibilities arise. One is that we look to a kind of "impersonalized" or public sort of caring—the sort epitomized in its most extreme form, perhaps, by the sort of selfless gallantry John Jacob Astor is supposed to have displayed as the Titanic went down. At more mundane levels, this is simply the kind of depersonalized caring exhibited in good manners—the concern that the door you let go of may strike and injure a stranger. I'd love to see this kind of caring restored in the world, but I don't think its chances are very good. It would appear that genuinely impersonal caring is highly improbable, at least under the conditions of mass society and extensive anonymity.

The other possibility is that we attempt somehow to restore a personalized caring within public institutions. I am very much committed to this and have been focusing for the last several years on a form of education specializing in it: alternative schools. The single most prevalent feature of alternative education is its emphasis on interpersonal relationships within the school. Alternatives make loud and specific reply to the question "why should teachers care?" by suggesting that no other kind of institution can be healthy for—or even minimally injurious to—children. Moreover, claim alternative educators, human relationships are themselves among the most educative features of a school. Accordingly, within an alternative school, a fair amount of time is likely to be given to an activity many call "community building." The explicit purpose is to promote a very personal kind of caring among all the members of the group. My observations of alternative schools suggest many succeed at this to a remarkable degree. Note that the caring in such cases is not just teacher to student, but student to student as well. I've come to believe that that is important. Another way of putting it is that the secondary associations we have been content with in other institutions—and have even cultivated in the school—simply will not do there, and must be converted to primary associations.

Acting on such a conviction calls for extensive changes in schools. For openers, you cannot confront a teacher with 150 students each day, divided into groups claiming 45 minute time slots, and say you're serious about caring relationships between that teacher and his or her students. Nor can you haphazardly schedule a student into eight different peer groupings a day—with what could conceivably be a total of 240 different classmates—and say you are serious about developing caring relationships among students.

But the rearrangements this suggests are just the beginning if we want to cultivate caring relationships in the school. And perhaps the first thing we must do is to understand the extent to which secondary associations have come to constitute our taken-for-granted reality with respect to what schooling must be—and understanding that must precede any very promising attempt at change: the school's culture makes secondary associations the norm—and friendships are assumed to be irrelevant at best, and more usually, prospectively disruptive of classroom procedures.

Were we to take seriously the idea that a caring relationship ought to obtain between teacher and student, we would have to allow students and teachers to choose one another—because we know it is as impossible for a teacher to genuinely care for all her students as it is for a student to feel that way about all his teachers. We should probably begin thinking much more seriously about such questions as "What draws one human being to another?" and "What makes us like one and want to keep our distance from another?" We know very little about such matters, but several years ago, David Epperson worked up a fascinating theory in response: he speculated that we are drawn to people who see the world generally, and themselves within it, as we do; and seeing ourselves and the world similarly is very largely a matter of sharing fundamental discontents. Epperson listed eight such pervasive discontents that, he believed, gave rise to eight different sorts of relationships or alliances that bind those who share them to one another (David Epperson, "Assessing Alternative Teaching— Learning Alliances," in *Theories For Learning*, edited by Lindley J. Stiles. New

York: Dodd, Mead (1974, pp.97-117). Perhaps some such theory as this one might figure prominently in our grouping projections for schools. It surely makes as good sense as an organizing principle as some of the others we have tried as the basis for dividing youngsters into groups.

To take caring seriously—as something institutional policy ought to promote instead of discouraging—would also make for considerable change in the institutions with which most of us here are most immediately familiar. As decline has replaced growth in higher education, and as openly adversarial relations have come to mark many of our interactions, the impersonality and detachment of secondary associations have frequently given way to active animus. Collective bargaining has exposed the adversarial character of faculty-administration relationships. But what many of us have failed to acknowledge is that the departmentalized system that brings us into interaction with fellow faculty from other departments only in committees is also an adversarial context, particularly in a contracting (and contractual) universe. Under such circumstances, if we are to make campuses viable places for faculties to live, we will need to think about how to stimulate positive interactions among them in order to let caring develop. Structures offer much more promise for doing so than the occasions we have depended upon (the Christmas party and annual picnic). So we will need to restructure our colleges and universities as well as our schools once we begin to take caring seriously—as something to be encouraged among faculties as well as among students, and between the two.

I think Nel is right in singling out caring for attention. It has been the missing element in many of our attempts to change and improve schools—and ironically so, since I suspect it lies close to the crux of determining what will work there. A number of our best-intentioned plans for bettering education have led instead to what has well been called the "thingification" of human beings. It was hauntingly appropriate that one of the slogans of the student revolution of ten years ago was the notice "I am a human being. Do not bend, fold, spindle, or mutilate." Nel's interest in caring seems centrally concerned with acknowledging and nurturing what is at the heart of that humanness. It thus makes so much better sense to follow her lead than to turn toward such bromides as ombudsmen and student advocates and court decisions to render uncaring institutions minimally viable. Caring, and caring relationships, may be a long way from a sufficient condition for good education. But we need reminding that they are probably a necessary condition. More power to Nel for so suggesting.

CHAPTER SIX

Dewey and the Herbartians: The Genesis of a Theory of Curriculum

Herbert M. Kliebard
1981

When at the age of 20, John Dewey was offered a teaching position in Oil City, Pennsylvania, by his cousin, the principal of the high school, he readily accepted. It is likely, however, that this decision was reflective of a young man uncertain about himself and his future rather than an early manifestation of Dewey's interest in education. During the time that he held the position in Oil City High School, between 1879 and 1881, Dewey taught Latin, science, and algebra. It was in 1881 that Dewey submitted his first article to the *Journal Of Speculative Philosophy*, accompanied by a letter to the editor, William Torrey Harris, America's leading Hegelian, describing himself as "a young man in doubt as to how to employ my reading hours" and asking Harris for advice as to whether his article on metaphysics showed "ability enough of any kind to warrant my putting much of my time on that sort of subject."[1] After he left Oil City, Dewey taught for a time in a village school in Charlotte, Vermont, near his home in Burlington.

Dewey did not mention his early experiences as a schoolteacher in his only published autobiographical account,[2] and it remains a relatively obscure chapter in his life. Although he appears to have been a rather successful high-school teacher, there is still no reason to believe that, at this point in his life, he seriously entertained the idea of devoting a major portion of his career to professional education. Rather, the earliest indications of Dewey's interest in education as a major scholarly pursuit seem to have had their inception in his graduate work in psychology, particularly in his latter years at Johns Hopkins

University, as well as in certain opportunities that were available to him as a faculty member at the University of Michigan.

Dewey began his graduate work at Johns Hopkins in 1881 working under George Sylvester Morris, but when Morris returned to his regular academic post at the University of Michigan in 1883, Dewey concentrated his graduate study in psychology under G. Stanley Hall. Dewey's choice of a Ph.D. dissertation topic, "The Psychology of Kant," a dissertation completed early in 1884, reflected Dewey's growing identification with psychology as a major scholarly focus. Dewey is known, for example, to have delivered a paper entitled, "The New Psychology" to the Metaphysical Club at Johns Hopkins in March of 1884, which was later published in the *Andover Review*.[3] Although this article, unlike Dewey's four earlier philosophical articles, has been appropriately described as "incomprehensible,"[4] it does reflect a high optimism, a euphoria, about the future of psychology.

DEWEY'S APPOINTMENT AT THE UNIVERSITY OF MICHIGAN

There is little doubt that George Sylvester Morris was responsible for Dewey's offer of an appointment as instructor in philosophy and psychology at the University of Michigan when he completed his Ph.D. degree in 1884. Apart from Morris' apparent recognition of Dewey's ability, he was probably concerned about the growing dissatisfaction among the students at Michigan about the preoccupation of the philosophy faculty with German idealism and the neglect of what was regarded as "the whole modern scientific school of philosophy."[5] Although philosophically committed to idealism himself, Dewey also possessed the "scientific" credentials that the students apparently felt were needed, and it was this feature of Dewey's scholarly interests, rather than as a Hegelian, that seems to have been his early professional identification at Michigan. Morris himself taught the course in History of European Philosophy, Ethics, Aesthetics, and Real Logic, while Dewey's teaching responsibilities included Empirical Psychology, Experimental Psychology, Speculative Psychology, and Special Topics in Psychology (Physiological, Comparative, and Morbid).[6] Dewey's work in these courses undoubtedly led to the publication of his first book, *Psychology*, which he began writing within a year of his arrival in Ann Arbor.

Apart from his work in psychology, Dewey participated in at least two other major activities during his tenure at the University of Michigan. His principal extracurricular activity seems to have been in the field of religion. Dewey became a trustee of the Students' Christian Association and involved himself actively in their work.[7] His numerous lectures on religious topics in behalf of the Association led one Ann Arbor newspaper to comment, "no one can afford to miss the privilege of hearing him."[8] One of these lectures, entitled "Christianity and Democracy," drew an audience of about 400.[9] While these activities did not lead to an abiding interest in theological issues, one of Dewey's other university activities, his gradual and tentative involvement in education at the elementary and secondary levels foreshadowed a lifelong commitment to philosophy of education, which reached its peak in the period of the Laboratory School at the University of Chicago between 1896 and 1904.

The University of Michigan, in the late nineteenth century, offered its faculty a rare opportunity to see education beyond the university setting. In 1869-70, the University had undertaken a program of admissions based on the observations and evaluations of its faculty in secondary schools. In essence, this was an attempt to assess the preparation of applicants to the University through direct examination of the secondary schools they attended. The University of Illinois and the University of Wisconsin adopted similar plans, and, by 1895, this approach to college admission culminated in the creation of the North Central Association, a voluntary association of secondary schools and colleges designed to provide "accreditation" for the secondary schools that met their standards. In this respect, its functions were similar to other regional associations such as the Association of Colleges and Preparatory Schools of the Middle States and Maryland and the Preparatory Schools of the Southern States. In 1886, two years after Dewey's arrival at the University of Michigan, the Michigan Plan, as it was then called, evolved into the Schoolmaster's Club, and Dewey was a founding member. At its first meeting, Dewey, still reflecting his fascination with psychology, read a paper entitled "Psychology in High Schools from the Standpoint of the College."[10] (His first article related to education and his only publication of the previous year was a brief commentary on a study conducted by the association of Collegiate Alumnae on the question of the effects of college life on the health of women.)

During the remainder of his tenure at the University of Michigan, Dewey published almost nothing concerned directly with education. Although he is listed as a co-author of Applied Psychology, originally published in 1889, and while it is true that book is sub-titled Principles And Practice Of Education, it is difficult to find in it anything that reflects Dewey's distinctive psychological interpretations or any educational ideas not directly tied to the standard psychology of the period. There is even much that is substantially different from Dewey's position. The book is a typical, even pedestrian, normal-school textbook of the period. It appears to be almost entirely the work of McLellan, a director of normal schools in Ontario, Canada, rather than Dewey. In fact, Dewey was not listed as co-author in the first edition of the book but is thanked for his contribution and cited by McLellan in the preface as someone "whose work on Psychology has been so well received by students of philosophy."[11] It is likely, as Boydston had suggested, that Dewey's name was added as a co-author in later printings in order to take advantage of his then established position in education.[12]

If *Applied Psychology*, a popular textbook, is indeed only nominally attributable to Dewey, then it is difficult to find any concrete basis for the outstanding reputation he was unquestionably building in education. There is some evidence to indicate that Dewey, despite his shy manner, had a powerful effect on people with whom he came into contact, and it may have been through his personal associations with teachers' groups, professional educational associations, and speaking engagements, rather than through his published writings for formal teaching, that Dewey's reputation in the field of education became established in this early period.

One particular event during his tenure at the University of Michigan seems to have had a profound effect on the course of Dewey's evolving theory of education. When the National Education Association met in Saratoga Springs, New York, in 1892, a prominent group of educators, including Charles DeGarmo, Frank and Charles McMurry, Elmer E. Brown, Nicholas Murray Butler, and Joseph Mayer Rice organized the Herbart Club. By becoming a charter member of the group and later involving himself actively in its affairs, Dewey aligned himself with a particularly zealous group of educational reformers who had undertaken to challenge the existing order in American education. Several of the leading Herbartians had studied pedagogy in Germany, particularly at Leipsig and Jena. By 1895, they reorganized into the National Herbart Society for the Scientific Study of Education and, in that same year, they took the occasion of the committee of fifteen's sub-committee report to mount an attack on the dominant figure and conservative spirit in American education, William Torrey Harris, who was the principal author of the report. The atmosphere at that meeting was so charged and the clash of ideologies so strong that 38 years later, DeGarmo, at the age of 85, was moved to write his friend Nicholas Murray Butler, "No scene recurs to me more vividly than on that immortal day in Cleveland, which marked the death of the old order and the birth of the new."[13] In America, the Herbartians were regarded as the major force for progressive educational ideas; and Dewey's association with them set in motion a lifelong commitment to educational reform.

D E W E Y   A N D   T H E   H E R B A R T I A N S

Apart from the sheer zeal they brought to the cause of reforming American education, the Herbartians came equipped with a particular set of concepts and ideas that they used to challenge "the old order." Whether these ideas were faithful to the work of the German philosopher Johann Friedrich Herbart, who died about a half a century before, is open to serious question,[14] but they did present a more or less coherent system of thought with respect to education. At the very least, the Herbartians were successful in introducing a new vocabulary into the educational discourse of the late nineteenth and early twentieth centuries, and Dewey became involved in the controversies surrounding the definition of their key terms and the clarification of the concepts they represented. Dewey, for example, was drawn into the fray over the Herbartian concept of interest. The concept of interest had become a focal point in the clash between Herbartian psychology and the then dominant faculty psychology. Characteristically, Dewey found fault on both sides.[15]

Dewey also became involved in the controversy over the meaning and utility of the central Herbartian concept in curriculum, culture epoch. His attempt to reinterpret the concept of culture epochs provides the best illustration of how his early involvement with the American Herbartians profoundly influenced his thinking in curriculum matters. The first *Yearbook* of the National Herbart Society included a long and presumably definitive article on the subject by C. C. Van Liew, a major American Herbartian theorist. Van Liew reviewed the historical development of the idea that "the individual recapitulates the experience of the 'race'" through the work of such philosophers as Kant, Goethe, and Pestalozzi, with particular attention, however, to the application of the idea to curriculum by Tuiskon Ziller, a leading disciple of Herbart's.[16] The parallelisms that Ziller and others perceived between the historical stages in the development of the human race and the stages of development in the individual human being were seen as applicable to certain major curriculum questions. "This parallelism, applied to curriculum," said Van Liew, "suggests not only a motive for the approach to the study of nature, but also the general character of the material in the various grades"[17] In other works, the Herbartian concept of culture epochs provided not only a justification for teaching certain things at various levels of schooling, but the very materials from which these things would be taught. Thus, "the superstitious fear of the savage race...finds its parallel in the fears of the child in its earliest years" and the products of this epoch in race history provide the materials for the child to study while undergoing that stage in his development. This was generally interpreted to be a "natural" order of studies in which the interest of the child could be evoked. As Van Liew put it, "the principal [sic] of succession in the curriculum must be sought in the humanistic institutional movement in culture; that material which is selected on the principal [sic] of culture epochs will be able to call forth lasting interest in the child."[18]

Dewey took issue with this position on at least two counts. First, Dewey argued that unless the parallel stages were exact (which admittedly it was not), it made a great difference, educationally speaking, if we start with race history and make inferences to child development or vice versa. To Dewey, it was obvious that the sequence of development in the child was the critical factor whether or not a parallel could be found in race history. Dewey put it this way:

> We must, in all cases, discover the epoch of growth independently in the child himself, and by investigation of the child himself. All the racial side can do is to suggest questions. Since this epoch was passed through by the race, it is possible

we shall find its correlate in the child. Let us, then, be on the look-out for it. Do we find it? But the criterion comes back in all cases to the child himself.[19]

Dewey also objected to the inferences the Herbartians were drawing from culture epochs regarding the amount of time devoted to the various stages. Even if we were to accept the idea that there is a stage in individual development that corresponds to the hunting epoch in human history, do we have a right, Dewey asked, to "condemn" children to a whole year of study corresponding to that epoch?

Dewey's second major objection to the culture-epochs curriculum pertained to its assumption that the products of each of the historical stages were the appropriate objects of study for the child undergoing the parallel stage in individual development. Herbartians assumed, in other words, that a child who is experiencing the "agricultural" phase in his development should study the products—particularly the literary products—of the parallel historical epoch. If the theory makes any sense at all, Dewey argued, "the agricultural instinct requires...to be fed in just the same way in the child in which it was fed in the race—by contact with earth and seed and air and sun and all the mighty flux and ebb of life in nature."[20] In this sense, Dewey's objection was not to the general idea of a parallelism between individual development and the historical development of the human race, but to the interpretation of this parallelism as a kind of mystical union between the individual and his ancestors through the works of those ancestors. What was implied by that parallelism according to Dewey was direct participation in the activities that characterized the historical period.

Dewey's criticism of the central Herbartian concept of culture epochs evoked no less than three published replies. Charles McMurry, a leading Herbartian spokesman, was the first to spring into the fray. He conceded one of Dewey's major points—that the child, not the historical epoch, is the proper "center" from which to draw curricular inferences. He denied, however, that present manifestations of a particular epoch are to be preferred over historical ones. "First find out," McMurry argued, "what present society has to offer that the child needs. If the child is the center, the argument against imposing materials on him is just as strong on one side as on the other. Present society, just as past history, has a great many things for which the child has no use at all."[21] McMurry's argument against Dewey's notion of substituting direct experiences for cultural products was a much weaker one. He suggested that since the child comes to school already having experienced much direct activity through his senses, the school should provide the influence from history and literature that the child presumably lacks. Naturally, these "cultural products" should be tested so as to ascertain their relationship to children's interests.

A second response to Dewey's criticism of culture epochs was wholly laudatory. The superintendent of schools of Great Bend, Kansas, wrote the editor to say that the article "by Professor Dewey is worth a whole year's subscription to *The [Public School] Journal.*"[22] He went on to speculate that the "greater part of the culture epoch theory comes from the inner consciousness of the pedagogical philosopher"[23] rather than from the true instincts and interests of the child, a noteworthy insight. Van Liew's own response initially criticized Daum, the school superintendent, for interpreting culture-epochs doctrine in terms merely of the interest that children allegedly show in the products of historical epochs, such as myths or fairy tales. In turning to Dewey's criticism, Van Liew accused Dewey of not actually attacking the theory of culture epochs "rightly understood,"[24] referring rather mysteriously to a letter he received from "Dr. Dewey" in which culture epochs is "viewed in the light of [Dewey's] philosophy." According to Van Liew, Dewey's letter revealed him to be "not an opponent of the doctrine in question."[25]

Van Liew's puzzlement regarding Dewey's position on this key curriculum issue is probably due to an assumption that Dewey's criticism of the master's teaching amounted to a rejection of the concept of culture epochs as the basis of curriculum organization. Dewey's writing on curriculum during the period of his direct association with the Herbartians indicates that while he was obviously critical of certain features of the theory, he accepted the overall framework of recapitulation along with his fellow Herbartians. Acceptance of this basic frame of reference is especially significant since this was the period in Dewey's development when he was beginning to move away from the mere translation of psychological concepts into educational terms and starting to consider the curriculum principles that were later to form the basis of the program of studies at the Laboratory School at the University of Chicago.

D E W E Y ' S   B R I G H A M   Y O U N G   L E C T U R E S

Dewey's early fascination with Herbartian educational theory was also reflected in a little known series of ten lectures that Dewey delivered at Brigham Young Academy in 1901.[26] They were published by the Brigham Young Summer School under the title, *Educational Lectures By Dr. John Dewey.* The lectures reflected not only Dewey's early interest in psychology, and the application of psychology to educational affairs (which was actually the major thrust of the lectures), but also the new directions in which his interaction with Herbartian concepts was leading him.

In line with Dewey's predominantly psychological approach to education during this early period, his summer session lectures were drawn heavily from his maturing psychological theory. In his very first lecture, for example, Dewey announced that his lectures would deal with "psychological topics in their bearing upon education."[27] Indeed, most of the lectures deal with the conventional psychological topics of the day, including "How the Mind Learns,"

"Imagination," and "Habit" Interestingly, Dewey's ideas on these psychological matters did not reflect direct Herbartian influence; for example, in evoking an image of the mind, he specifically rejected the idea that "the mind is like a piece of blank paper, to which it is sometimes compared, nor like a waxed tablet on which the natural world makes impressions."[28] Instead, Dewey invoked a digestive metaphor, declaring the child's "hunger to be an active thing, so active that it causes him to search eagerly for food."[29] In extending the metaphor, Dewey asserted that "The Child supplies the hunger but he does not supply the food."[30] Why, then, Dewey asked, do children so often find their school studies so repulsive? The answer Dewey supplied is that, "The food is not being presented in the shape they recognize as food."[31] Such an active concept of mind is more reflective of Hegel than it is of Herbart.

In two of the lectures, however, (the second and the eighth) Dewey departed from the basic psychological orientation of the course. In these instances, the influence of a Herbartian frame of reference was unmistakable. In his lecture on the "Social Aspects of Education," for example, Dewey dealt with the curriculum question of how the school subjects may be interrelated. In this context, Dewey introduced the Herbartian concept of correlation, first in connection with tying the educational opportunities in the home with those in the school. Pointing out that the school is only one of the educational agencies within a community, Dewey applauded the introduction of cooking, sewing, and household management into the schools curriculum, seeing it as a way of correlating family life with the work of the school.[32] Here, Dewey, characteristically, took a familiar educational concept and twisted it. By correlation, the Herbartians meant, generally, the interrelationship among school subjects. Thus, a single topic could be used to "correlate" the various schools subjects around a central theme; for example, if fish were the theme, a day's activity in geography, arithmetic, science, and literature would all revolve around the topic, thus achieving, presumably, a unifying effect. Dewey conceived of this unity in terms of the child's overall experience rather than in traditional Herbartian terms. Of even greater significance to Dewey was that the connection between home and school afforded an opportunity for the child to understand and experience the social origins of school subjects. People did not invent arithmetic, Dewey pointed out, in an advanced abstract form. Arithmetic, like all school subjects, arose out of practical necessity. As Dewey put it, "we may trace one study after another to a period where it grew originally out of the actual necessities of social life."[33] Ultimately, this epistemological development from basic social activities to abstract subject matter became the core of Dewey's curriculum theory.

As soon as Dewey introduced this principle, he turned to the general notion of recapitulation, which was then already popular as a basis for curriculum—one particularly favored by the Herbartians. Dewey described the position as holding that "just as the race goes step by step from the lower to the higher plane, so the child must go thru similar stages of evolution."[34] Dewey twice described this idea as "absurd" but was careful to qualify this judgment on both occasions by indicating that this opinion was confined to those who took it too literally. Obviously, the young child was not actually a savage, comparable in any literal sense to the "savage" stage in human history. In fact, when Dewey returned to the question of the value of school subjects, he asserted a qualified, but unmistakable, endorsement of the theory. "So far as these branches [of study] are concerned": Dewey said, "we might accept the statement of the race development theory."[35] What Dewey seemed to be reaching for, but which he did not enunciate fully until later in his career, was a refinement and reinterpretation of the recapitulation metaphor as central to his curriculum theory, a metaphor that he recognized was constantly being misinterpreted as a literal statement.

When Dewey turned his attention once more to curriculum issues in his eighth lecture, his staring point was again Herbartian doctrine, this time referring to it explicitly by name. Using the terms "correlation" and "concentration" more or less interchangeably, Dewey objected particularly to the use of literature as the integrating core around which the school subjects should be concentrated. (In later years, Dewey expressed the idea that geography as a study possessed such integrating properties.) Dewey regarded the Herbartian emphasis on literature as leading toward artificiality, pointing out that in German schools, where the race-development theory had both a religious and a secular side, German children, at one state in the curriculum, "get their arithmetic by adding, dividing, multiplying, and subtracting the Twelve Tribes, and by dealing numerically with the various incidents of history, the number of people engaged in battle, the number of miles in Palestine from this point to that and so on."[36] Apart from the sheer artificiality of this organization of the curriculum, Dewey again objected to the attempt merely to correlate subjects with one another. Correlation must be achieved not only among the various school subjects, Dewey insisted, but between the school subjects as a whole and the life experiences of the child.

It is in the context of trying to explicate this idea that Dewey first used the term "occupations," a concept that was crucial in developing the curriculum of the Laboratory School in Chicago. As Dewey introduced the concept there, occupations were to be pursued not for specific didactic purposes, but for their own sake. Children, Dewey said, "cook for the fun of cooking...not for the sake of making a scientific study of the chemistry of foods."[37] Occupations such as cooking, furthermore, not only "follow out the child's own end," but "recapitulate" the social world that surrounds the child. Dewey argued that if such fundamental human activities as woodwork, ironwork, cooking, and weaving "were to be made part of the curriculum they would give the child a chance to reflect from within the school and social interests and activities of the home."[38] As yet, Dewey did not seem to have incorporated the notion of occupations fully into his general recapitulation theory. Against the possible charge that these activities may be too utilitarian, for example, Dewey argued only that much of the activity of mankind is directed toward utilitarian pursuits and that the school may be a good place to "idealize" them. Later, he would have denied that occupations, as part of the curriculum, had any direct utilitarian purpose.

Apparently, however, Dewey did have in mind an overall plan for the curriculum based on three distinct groups of studies that would be arranged more or less sequentially. The first group, "hardly studies in the technical sense," would be those occupations that "the child must shortly follow for a livelihood,"[39] a characterization that Dewey would not have used in more sophisticated versions of his curriculum theory. Even here, however, Dewey argued that the basic occupations "can be made to teach a broader view of the evolution of civilization down the avenues of history."[40] As an example of the first group of studies, Dewey cited the making of clothing from the raw wool of sheep through the various stages required to bring it to a refined and useful state. Accounts of the activities of the Dewey School actually report this as a major activity of the youngest age groups.

The second group of studies would be directed mainly to providing the background for social life and comprised, essentially, history and geography (including nature study). Dewey deplored the emphasis on history on the "military side," arguing that its proper focus should be on "finding out how people lived, and how they came to live as they did—I mean the common people—the difficulties they were laboring under, the struggles they had to make, the victories they won—not the military victories so much as the human victories—the artistic advances, the educational movements, and the moral and religious conquests."[41] History, Dewey said, ought to be "a sort of moral telescope"[42] through which we can gain a perspective on the present. In the same vein, geography should be seen as "a study of the theatre of life," with an emphasis on human value. One of the problems here, according to Dewey, was that the specialist so influences what should be taught in fields like history and geography that technicalities begin to dominate what is taught instead of elements of our common experience. The child, Dewey argued, does not even need to know the particular names of the subjects he is studying. "The very moment you put one of those labels on the study," Dewey said, "you isolate it."[43]

THE HERBARTIAN INFLUENCE ON DEWEY'S CURRICULUM THEORY

Dewey's interaction with the ideas of the American Herbartians had not only earned him a reputation as a promising educational leader and reformer, but provided him with the anvil on which he was to forge his major educational theories. Herbartian concepts such as correlation, concentration, and culture epochs represented ways by which central curriculum issues could be addressed. His early work at the University of Chicago Laboratory School gave him a chance to test these theoretical concepts in an actual school setting. Although Dewey ultimately did not accept the traditional Herbartian interpretations of these concepts, he did accept them as potent ways of considering those issues that almost inevitably arise when one undertakes to construct a curriculum.

Of particular significance was Dewey's acceptance of recapitulation as the central frame of reference for his curriculum theory. Although he rejected any kind of strict or literal notion of race recapitulation in the individual, he seems to have accepted the idea of a temporally ordered curriculum paralleling stages of individual growth. Delivered a year before Dewey's major essay on curriculum, "The Child and the Curriculum," the Brigham Young lectures indicate that Dewey was thinking in terms of individual stages in human development on one hand, and, on the other, the stages by which the human race moved from one state of knowing to a higher one. While Dewey saw no special merit in a curriculum that simply recapitulated the history of the human race, he began to see some promise in the idea that, through the curriculum, children may recapitulate the stages in which the human race acquired knowledge, from the most primitive and direct ways of knowing to the most sophisticated and abstract.

Dewey's reconstruction of the theory of culture epochs began to take shape shortly after his appointment at the University of Chicago. In particular, Dewey took the first tentative steps toward substituting a social and epistemological basis for the historical and literary one that the Herbartians favored. It seems clear that Dewey did not reject the fundamental metaphor by which an individual's growth and development are seen as paralleling a historical dimension of the human experience. It was the particular conception of the historical side of that analogy and not the recapitulation analogy itself that Dewey rejected. In fact, his own theory of curriculum rests on almost the same metaphor. Instead of the naïve conception of discrete stages in human history, which the Herbartians favored, Dewey took as his parallel to individual development, the growth of ever more refined ways of knowing over the course of man's social history.

ACKNOWLEDGMENTS

I am indebted to the John Dewey Foundation of Carbondale, Illinois, and the Research Committee of the Graduate School of the University of Wisconsin for grants that supported research reported here in part.

No copy of Dewey's Ph.D. dissertation is known to exist.

Only Dewey's article in *Educational Review* in 1893, "Teaching Ethics in High School," can be regarded as dealing with precollegiate education. Even that was probably an offshoot of his syllabus for a course in ethics that he published a year later.

REFERENCES

1. John Dewey to W.T. Harris, 17 May 1881, quoted in George Dykhuizen, *The Life And Mind Of John Dewey* (Carbondale: Southern Illinois University Press, 1973), 23.

2. John Dewey, "From Absolutism to Experimentalism," in George P. Adams and William P. Montague, eds., *Contemporary American Philosophy*, 2 vols. (New York: Macmillan, 1930), 2: 13-27.

3. John Dewey, "The New Psychology," *Andover Review*, II (September, 1884), 278-289.

4. Neil Coughlan, *Young John Dewey* (Chicago: University of Chicago Press, 1973), 42.

5. Dykhuizen, *Life And Mind Of John Dewey*, 45.

6. Ibid., 46

7. John A. Axelson, "John Dewey:" *Michigan Educational Journal*, XLIII (May, 1966), 13.

8. Ibid., 14.

9. Ibid.

10. John Dewey, "Psychology in High-Schools from the Standpoint of the College," Michigan Schoolmaster's Club, *Papers* (Lansing, Mich: H.R. Pattengill, 1886).

11. James A. McLellan, *Applied Psychology* (Toronto: Copp, Clark and Company, 1889), vi.

12. Jo Ann Boydston, "A Note on Applied Psychology, " *John Dewey: The Early Works*, 1882-1898 III: 1889-1892 (Carbondale: Southern Illinois University Press, 1969), xiii-xix.

13. Charles DeGarmo to N. M. Butler, 15 December 1933, Butler Papers, Columbia University, quoted in Walter H. Drost, "That Immortal Day in Cleveland—The Report of the Committee of Fifteen," *Educational Theory*, XVII (April, 1967), 178.

14. Harold B. Dunkel, *Herbart And Herbartianism*. (Chicago: University of Chicago Press, 1970).

15. C. C. Van Liew, "Culture Epochs," *First Yearbook Of The National Herbart Society* (Bloomington, Ill.: The Society, 1895), 70-123.

16. Ibid., 97.

17. Ibid., 106.

18. Ibid., 117

19. John Dewey, "Interpretation of the Culture-Epoch Theory," *Public School Journal*, XV (January, 1896), 234.

20. Ibid., 235.

21. C. A. McMurry, "The Culture Epochs," *Public School Journal*, IX (February, 1896), 298.

22. N. F. Dam, "Culture Epoch Theory," *Public School Journal*, XV (May, 1896), 509.

23. Ibid., 509-10.

24. C. C. Van Liew, "Culture Epoch Theory," *Public School Journal*, XV (June, 1896), 546.

25. Ibid.

26. John Dewey, *Educational Lectures* (Provo, Utah: Brigham Young Academy Summer School, n.d.)

27. Ibid., 1.

28. Ibid., 3.

29. Ibid., 4.

30. Ibid., 6.

31. Ibid., 7.

32. Ibid., 38.

33. Ibid., 45.

34. Ibid., 45.

35. Ibid., 46.

36. Ibid., 175.

37. Ibid., 180.

38. Ibid., 181.

39. Ibid.

40. Ibid., 186.

41. Ibid., 188.

42. Ibid., 189.

43. Ibid., 192.

CHAPTER SEVEN

The Curriculum Field

Emergence of a Discipline

Jo Anne Pagano
1981

Future scholars of the curriculum field may come to think of the past 20 years in the field as the era of uncertainty. The period is remarkable for the enormous volume of literature devoted to the task of legitimatizing a claim to disciplinary status of education and its subfield, curriculum. Typically, papers bear titles that are some variant on the questions "Is education a discipline?" and "Is curriculum theory possible?"[1] Also typical of the period was the 1961 symposium held at Johns Hopkins that was addressed solely to the issue of the disciplinary status of education.[2] The prevailing opinion among participants in the debate was that education was not, and logically could not be, a discipline, and that curriculum theory was, in principle, impossible.

Nearly all of the writers concerned followed similar patterns of argument. They first established general criteria for determining disciplinary status. These criteria were drawn from the natural sciences, both at the theoretical and practical levels. After establishing the unique claim of the sciences to the title of "discipline," the presentation usually proceeded to a demonstration of the dissimilarity of education to science. The inevitable conclusion was that since education was not like a natural science, it was not a discipline but something else.[3] That something else varied from writer to writer. More interesting than the particular conclusions reached, however, is the apparent ease and unreflectiveness with which these writers accepted science as the model for all disciplines.

A plausible explanation of the bare fact of the questions being raised at this time makes comprehensible the ready abdication of disciplinary status. We may suppose that events consequent on the Sputnik hysteria provoked an identity crisis in the field commensurate with the collective identity crisis suffered by the country at large. The selection of Jerome Bruner to chair the Woodshole conference, and the subsequent domination by psychologists and scientists on the new national curriculum projects, was doubtless seen as a threat to the integrity of the curriculum field. In this context, the question of disciplinary status can be viewed as an attempt at institutional legitimation beyond anything else. But what could have been the source of legitimation? The self-reflective questioning attendant on this goal was an activity not much engaged in since the consolidation of the field as a university specialty in the 1930s. Therefore, there was no ready foundation on which to build the case for legitimacy. Given the national preoccupation with science, indeed the social and intellectual domination of the scientific rational framework, combined with the loss of institutional power to scientists, it is not surprising that the ideal model of a discipline should have been seen as the scientific.

Had we not been so preoccupied with science at the time, arguments might have taken a different form. It is by no means certain (or even uncontroversial) that a discipline is to be identified in terms of some sort of internal and inexorable logic and subject matter unique to it. (It is by no means uncontroversial that that is an accurate characterization of science.) At the 1961 symposium one dissenting voice was audible among the chorus. James McClellan argued:

> The most visible sense of discipline is the social one. A great many persons in this world are socially identified with one or more recognized branches of study. With the typically American genius for establishing voluntary associations for worthy purposes we have organized learned societies by the score. If we want to see the discipline we attend an annual meeting of the learned society, we read its journals, and we watch the typical patterns of speech and action that distinguish its members from those in other learned societies.[4]

What is suggested here is a need to reconceptualize "discipline" in terms of sociointellectual communities. This means that in order to identify and characterize a disciplinary community, we must attend not only to subject matter, theoretical propositions, and research methodology, we must be equally attentive to social networks and boundaries that are constituted by scholars in the field. Theories and methodologies do not, after all, exist independently of persons elaborating and communicating within them. An investigation of the early days of the curriculum field reveals both the intellectual and sociological components required for a field's qualification as a discipline.

The history of the curriculum field discloses another interesting aspect of the disciplines as well. Not only is knowledge of the sociological features internal to a disciplinary community essential to understanding the community, but such communities are in varying degrees permeable to social and political features of the larger cultural communities within which they are situated.[5]

This permeability to sociopolitical influences is particularly striking when we look at education and its subfields. That there is an ineluctable bond between intellectual development and sociopolitical factors is doubtless as striking as it is in this case because of the social reform roots of American education. This historical circumstance does not require us to conclude along with Peters, however, that education and reform are identical in all respects.[6] A look at the intellectual developments in the 1920s, while revealing the influence of social reform concerns, also demonstrates that in terms of sociointellectual development, education and its subfields are more similar to the sciences than they are to the Salvation Army or the A.A.

In this paper we will look at the development of the curriculum field in terms of social and institutional developments filtered through a growing communications network of theorists and researchers addressing the same issues. We will see how particular social and institutional arrangements (and we will focus on three institutions here) have crystallized in intellectual orientations that persist in the field today.

The sociointellectual traditions that guide work in the curriculum field today can be traced to the efforts of a small group of scholars at three educational institutions established during the first two decades of this century. At this point we should note the intellectual debt that the curriculum field owes to William James and John Dewey, among others whom we will not discuss here, since their work in education represents but one aspect of their work. Our discussion will be limited to those whose sole intellectual commitment was to education.

Early activity that resulted in the development of the curriculum field is exemplified by the work of educators at the University of Chicago, Columbia University Teachers College, and the Ohio State University. The men associated with these institutions and those primarily responsible for the emergence, first of education as a discipline and then of the curriculum field within it, are Charles H. Judd, Franklin Bobbitt, and Ralph Tyler of the University of Chicago; Boyd Bode, Harold Alberty, Burdette Buckingham, and W. W. Charters of the Ohio State University; and James Earl Russell, William F. Russell, Harold O. Rugg, Edward L. Thorndike, William Heard Kilpatrick, Jesse H. Newlon, and George S. Counts of Teachers College. These men and their work can be seen as the intellectual fathers of the major orientations that characterize curriculum study in the 1970s. Recognizing that for the present the distinctions are crude and that there is considerable overlap of categories and scholars assigned to them, we can derive some conceptual utility from characterizing the University of Chicago group as the forefathers of the logico-empirical approach to curriculum study;

the Ohio State faculty as the instigators of the critical conceptual approach; and the Teachers College group as uniquely representative of a social hermeneutical approach.

Since the workers whom we have mentioned have, in some cases, remarkably similar intellectual backgrounds, many having studied with Charles Juddan understanding of their unique and differential contributions to the development of the curriculum field requires an investigation of particular social and institutional mediations. Such an investigation reveals two things: 1) It supports the claim made earlier that curriculum scholars do constitute a disciplinary community in sociointellectual terms, and 2) It provides a framework within which to comprehend and explain the development of different intellectual perspectives.

Looking at the early academic and intellectual histories of James Earl Russell, Boyd Bode, and Charles Judd, one might be tempted to conclude along with the numerous writers who have so concluded that curriculum is not in itself a proper discipline, but is rather an activity involving the practical application of the "real" disciplines. Given their historical status as pioneers, they had to have been trained someplace else. A New Yorker who moves to California does not remain forever a New Yorker.

James Earl Russell was trained as a philosopher at Cornell University. After completing his studies, he worked for a time as a headmaster at a private academy in Ithaca, New York, an experience that gave birth to a personal rebellion against what he judged to be a rigid and outmoded educational system. He was certain that there must be a better way to teach, and so he went to Germany to look for it. Germany during the late nineteenth and early twentieth centuries was considered the mecca of those scholars interested in psychology and pedagogy. In Germany he studied psychology with Wilhelm Wundt and pedagogy with the Herbartian Wilhelm Rein.[7] It was in Germany that he first became aware of the intimate links between schooling and society when he noticed that attitudes and behaviors of students in the schools mirrored the behaviors expected of German citizens. This realization marked the beginning of Russell's lifelong concern for the notion of educating for a democratic society.[8]

It is not surprising that the founders of Columbia Teachers College should have sought as their first dean someone with Russell's vision to give shape to the new professional school. The Teachers College is clearly the child of a collective reformist social conscience, having grown out of the 1881 Kitchen Garden Association, a philanthropic institution whose primary goal was the preparation of working-class children for life in an urban society. In 1884, the Kitchen Garden Association became the Industrial Education association in recognition of the increasing demand for skilled manual laborers in an increasingly industrial society. The demand for more sophisticated training of children if they were to become productive members of the society led ultimately to a demand for more sophisticated training of teachers. The demand for competent teachers resulted finally in a shift from a purely philanthropic perspective to a decidedly professional educational one. By 1897, the College maintained a school for teachers and a model school for children that was to serve as a laboratory for the training of teachers.[9]

The absorption of the College into Columbia University and the concurrent arrival of Russell marked the beginning of the shaping of a discipline. Russell's vision of the educative concept as extending beyond the boundaries of the schools has informed the entire course of development of the field at Teachers College.

The nature and strength of Russell's commitments are clearly seen in the faculty he called to the College. His view of professional education was multidimensional and that view is reflected in the composition of the faculty. John Dewey and Edward L. Thorndike, the men often credited with establishing the framework of twentieth-century educational theory, were brought to Teachers College during Russell's early days. Dewey is responsible, as everyone knows, for "child-centered" or "progressive" education, and Thorndike for the invention of performance scales and the introduction of statistical methods in the study of education. Frank McMurray, an early Herbartian who is known for his application of Thorndike's principles to teaching methods, and William Heard Kilpatrick, a student of Dewey's and a schoolman, also came at this time, as did Paul Monroe, a historian, sociologist, and test expert. The psychologist William C. Bagley and his intellectual and ideological opponent, David Snedden, arrived at Teachers College at about the same time and as a result of their having been recruited by Russell. Snedden was a fervent proponent of tracking and testing, while Bagley argued that good teaching demands a solid background in culture and scholarship. Bagley was also a harsh critic of testing. Teachers College has maintained a conscious policy of hiring and recruitment to retain such diversity.[10]

In its early days, the granting of graduate degrees at Teachers College was under the control of the Department of Philosophy. By 1902 the separation of education from philosophy was complete. At this time the student body was composed primarily of young girls seeking undergraduate preparation for elementary school teaching. In 1907 only 50 graduate degrees were conferred. By the 1920s, largely owing to postwar developments and the increasing momentum of the testing movement, the situation had changed. By the time of Russell's retirement in 1927 the College was primarily a graduate professional school and the student body composition had changed accordingly.[11]

The era of curriculum expansion that characterized Columbia Teachers College after the war was accompanied by increased activity in, and reorganization of, educational research. The Department of Educational

Research, established in 1916, became the Institute of Educational Research in 1921.[12] A case can be made for the claim that it was during the 1920s that education and its subdivisions began to emerge as a legitimate discipline in their own right.

> the demands upon the College for large-scale educational surveys were increasing, and, without solicitation, the sale of Teachers College publications was continually mounting. ...In an interview with the New York TIMES Dean Russell explained that "the need for research in education was a result of the new type of students coming to Teachers College, that it is experienced teachers, administrators, supervisors for whose problems the Institute is set up to investigate and to help.[13]

At about this time Teachers College began populating more colleges and universities than public schools with its graduates.[14] The generation of the 1920s is the first generation of educationists to have been specifically trained in education. They were perhaps the first recipients of a coherent and organized body of knowledge that could be termed the subject of education.

Harold O. Rugg is a good example of this new breed of professional at Teachers College. He took his undergraduate training in civil engineering at Dartmouth College in 1907. This training led him first to a position as a railroad surveyor and then to one as an instructor in civil engineering at the James Milliken University. According to Rugg, the progression from engineering instructor to Ph.D. candidacy in Education and Sociology was a logical one. He received his doctoral degree under the direction of William Bagley in 1915 while Bagley was still at the University of Illinois. There then followed a five-year period during which Rugg was associated with Charles Judd at the University of Chicago. This time was devoted to experimental and statistical studies in the social sciences. In 1918 Rugg worked for a while for the U.S. Army, and at that time he met John Coss of Columbia University. Coss started him thinking about the possibility of integrating the social sciences with the study of contemporary civilization. Because of his connection with Coss, Rugg accepted with alacrity when he was offered a position at Teachers College in 1920. He was appointed associate professor of education at the College and educational psychologist at the experimental Lincoln School. His move to New York resulted in his developing close associations with the intellectual and artistic community of Greenwich Village. These associations were crucial to his later intellectual development, as were his contacts at Teachers College.[15]

The retirement of Dean Russell in 1927 and the subsequent appointment of his son William F. Russell in that same year marked the beginning of more changes at Teachers College. William F. Russell was a true child of Teachers College, having received his early education at Horace Mann Elementary and High Schools and having received his doctorate from Teachers College. The period of the younger Russell's leadership was one of instinct, with self-appraisal and "intellectual soul-searching" for the College faculty. During the first decade of his administration 20 professors retired. While none of these men had been trained in education, the newcomers in the 1920s had been, for the most part, students of the original College faculty. Russell's fear was that the College was beginning to show signs of inbreeding, and he feared that this would have a debilitating effect on the intellectual vitality of the College. To guard against such possible deleterious effects, he instituted a conscious program of recruitment from outside the ranks of Teachers College graduates.[16]

All of Counts' academic training was in education. His doctoral dissertation, completed in 1915 under the direction of Judd, was on work with arithmetic scales in a survey of Cleveland public schools. Cremin tells us that "Counts early abandoned the science of education for a career of social analysis and criticism." A reason for this conversion is never given.[19]

Counts' educational criticism is an early statement of the themes dominating the work of the revisionists in the 1970s. In *The Selective Character Of American Secondary Education* he argued that the organization of the public high school system acted so as to perpetuate pernicious class differences and hence social and political inequalities.[20] He called in this book, and in others, for a transformation of the schools and a concomitant transformation of society along progressive political lines. Counts' fundamental belief in this regard was that it was not only possible for schools to do so, but it was incumbent on them to act as agents for social change.[21]

Jesse Newlon was also a professionally trained educator; however, his early career was practical rather than academic, as had been Count' and Rugg's. Newlon was brought to the attention of the academic education establishment as a consequence of a program of curriculum revision that he had instituted and directed while he was superintendent of schools in Denver. The assumptions underlying the Denver program were 1) that a vital, even a viable school program needs continual revision; 2) that this revision must be doubly grounded, first in the needs and capacities of children, and second in the goals of society for the development of children into productive adults; and 3) those people most competent to decide on curriculum revisions were the ones who had the most contact with the curriculum and with children, i.e., teachers. A curriculum committee under the Denver plan was set up so as to comprise both active classroom teachers and professional educationists from colleges and universities whose function was to be advisory. Teachers were given release time from their teaching duties, and the teachers on the committee were rotated so that all of the school system's teachers were involved in curriculum writing. The intent behind this arrangement was to keep a constant flow of fresh ideas coming to the committee. Word of the success of the program spread rapidly, and nearly as rapidly as it spread similar programs were institution in other communities.[22]

In 1927 Newlon left Denver and went to Teachers College to become director of the Lincoln School. By 1934 he was chairman of the Division of Instruction at the College.[23] Newlon's commitments to the idea of social change and his notion of the intimate connection between schooling and society are apparent but still nascent and largely inchoate in the Denver plan. His work at Teaches College is marked by increasing articulation of these nascent ideas. *Education For Democracy In Our Time*, published in 1939, is the culminating statement of Newlon's intellectual development. By this time he was a critic of scientific method in education, a method which the Denver plan with its emphasis on articulation of measurable objectives at least tacitly embraces.

As the social and economic crisis deepened after the World War, the more thoughtful students of social and educational affairs saw that the most difficult problems simply would not yield to quantitative and statistical methods. Statistical data do not interpret themselves. It cannot be demonstrated by these techniques that controversial social issues should be studied in schools or what issues should be studied or how. It cannot be demonstrated scientifically that the individual should be regarded as the end and not the means of government, that democracy is preferable to fascism. The hope that the problems of education could be solved solely by the application of the scientific method proved to be an illusion. The idea that the worth of a program of education for democracy can be in any sense finally evaluated by any test other than the test of time is also a dangerous illusion. It is also true that science has given us many techniques of conditioning that can be made to serve the ends of a dictatorship as well as those of a democracy.[24]

We may imagine that this statement reflects partly the effects of the years of interaction with scholars like Rugg and Counts and Dewey and the particular situation of Teachers College during the crisis of the Depression years.

In comparison with other colleges and universities, Teachers College was unique with respect to its financial arrangements. It operates almost solely on the tuition charged it students, and so, has never been in a position to compete with other institutions financially. Initially, the Teachers College student population came mostly from the Northeast and primarily from New York. By 1927 only 64% of the student population was represented by this geographic area. Students from other areas of the country were returning to these areas and teaching at teachers' colleges there. There was no longer any need for students to move to New York City to study with faculty comparable to those at Teachers College. Teachers College had in effect supplied its competitors.[25]

There was, during the Depression years, a concerted effort made by the faculty and administration of the College to reorganize the divisions under its jurisdiction. One might argue that the Depression acted as a catalyst but that other factors were equally important in the changes that occurred during the 1930s. Among these factors were the new Dean's concern for "soul-searching," resulting before the Depression in the constitution of numerous committees charged with appraising the College's current offerings. Another important factor was the presence on the faculty of extraordinary men such as those mentioned. Their response to the crisis of the Depression was to outline and design a program that would contribute to building a society capable of avoiding the disintegration that they saw as threatening American society at that time.

In 1929 the College was organized in two main divisions: a faculty of education, which, included foundations, subject matter, and curriculum and methods experts, and a faculty of practical arts, which taught such subjects as health, music, and industrial arts. The function of the practical arts faculty had been primarily to serve the needs of undergraduates preparing for public school teaching careers. The increased emphasis on graduate education that grew during the 1920s obviated the need for such a function. By 1934 the College had been reorganized into five divisions: Foundations, Administration, Guidance, Instruction, and Measurement and Research.[26]

The committee that directed the reorganization was actually in the beginning an informal group meeting bi-monthly over dinner and drinks to discuss the purpose and future of American education. The group consisted of professors who eventually became the Department of Social and Political Foundations of Education, among whom were Rugg, Counts, Kilpatrick, Newlon, and occasionally John Dewey. The problem that they set themselves was to "define a program which would prepare teachers for a socially conscious American school."[27]

A first step toward this end was to recognize that a firm grasp of the foundations of education was necessary for all educationists. The consensus opinion was that foundations could only be mastered by a multidisciplinary approach at the most basic level of study. The theme around which the multidisciplinary foundations course would be organized was school, child, and society relationships.

The formalized committee on reorganization was led first by Kilpatrick, who was replaced by Newlon in 1937. Its first accomplishment was to establish a course taught by seven professors—four from the foundations division and three from other divisions—which "attempted to draw from the various foundational disciplines certain understandings, outlooks and terminologies which would eventually be the common property of the entire education profession."[28] By the time the group held the last of its meetings in 1937 the entire administrative structure of the college had been reorganized, and all divisions were operated on what was characterized as a multilevel, multidisciplinary academic arrangement. The final accomplishment of the committee is noted in Dean Russell's announcement that a separate department of curriculum and teaching would be formed under the Division of Instruction. The department was headed by Hollis Caswell, who was instrumental in forming the first curriculum societies and in publishing the first volumes devoted exclusively to curriculum.[29] Jesse Newlon was at this time transferred to the chairmanship of the foundations department.[30] These moves are doubtless significant for establishing the rootedness of the curriculum perspective at Teachers College in social and philosophical foundations.

It seems safe to say that the emergence of the curriculum field as an isolable subdivision of education depended on the development and growth of a community of scholars and researchers with similar intellectual and social commitments framed in a shared vocabulary; the development of a technology of social science—the tests and statistical tools of Thorndike, the experimental quantifications of Judd and the generalized American faith in the power and obligation of schools in the shaping of society. The threats to the integrity of American society that accompanied the Depression were perhaps more keenly felt by educationists than by any other academic groups because of the shared reformist history of American schools and American society. The making of the curriculum acquired closer conscious identification with the shaping of the American character, and so acquired a new academic importance.

The dominance of the social reconstructionist orientation at Teachers College was clearly a function then of three main factors: 1) the social and intellectual interactions of a disciplinary community, 2) the growth of both theory and technology, and 3) the unique institutional character of Teachers College. We shall see that these same three factors contributed to the differing orientations of the University of Chicago and Ohio State University groups.

The orientation to curriculum study at the University of Chicago was from its inception the exact opposite of that which characterized Teachers College. Where the Teachers College approach to curriculum was child centered, the University of Chicago's was society centered; where Teachers College stressed collective responsibility and the necessity for understanding of social structure and dynamics, the University of Chicago approached education as essentially a matter of individual ability and responsibility. Once again, an investigation of institutional historical and individual biographical factors in social context illuminate this development.

The University of Chicago is unique in many respects. From the time of conception of the idea of the University of Chicago, the founders intended that it should be an intellectually rigorous and socially conscious research and professional institution.[31] What this "intent translated into action" became was a quantitative experimentally based program emphasizing research in the social sciences. Undergraduate programs were often criticized as being haphazard and the suggestion was made more than once that the University should get rid of the undergraduate colleges and restrict its efforts to research and professional work. The rationale for retaining the colleges as stated in his "The Future of the University" speech on February 24, 1923, according to the then President

Burton was that the school of educational research required the colleges "to complete our own educational laboratory."[32]

William Rainey Harper, the first President of the University of Chicago (1891-1906), was a man committed to a conjoint ideal of education and research. Before his acceptance of the position at the new University, he had made an exemplary reputation for himself at Muskingum and at Yale as both a scholar and a pedagogue.[33] His task at Chicago was not only to run the University, but to formulate its programs and commitments as well. He became president while the University was still an idea. The following statement is excerpted from Harper's plan for the organization of the University.

> It is expected by all who are interested that the university idea is to be emphasized. It is proposed to establish, not a college, but a university...A large number of the professors have been selected with the understanding that their work is to be exclusively in the Graduate Schools. The organization, as it has been perfected, would be from the college point of view entirely a mistake. It has been the desire to establish an institution which should not be a rival with the many colleges already in existence, but an institution which should help these colleges...To assist these numerous colleges, to furnish them instructors who shall be able to do work of the highest order; to accomplish this purpose, the main energies of the institution have been directed toward graduate work. ...The chief purpose of graduate work is, not to stock the student's mind with knowledge of what has already been accomplished in a given field, but rather so to train him that he himself may be able to push out along new lines of investigation. Such work is, of course, of the most expensive character. Laboratories and libraries and apparatus must be lavishly provided in order to offer the necessary opportunities. ...Here also is to be found the question of the effort to secure the best available men in the country as the heads and directors of departments. It is only the man who has made investigation who may teach others to investigate. Without this spirit in the instructor and without his example students will never be led to undertake the work. Moreover, if the instructor is loaded down with lectures he will have neither the time nor strength to pursue his investigations. Freedom from care, time for work, and liberty of thought are prime requisites in all such work. An essential element, moreover, is the opportunity of publishing results obtained in investigation. To this end it is provided that in each department there shall be published a journal or a series of separate studies which shall in each department embody the results of the work of the instructors in that department. It is expected that professors and other instructors will, at intervals, be excused entirely for a period from lecture work, in order that they may thus be able to give their entire time to the work of investigation. Promotion of younger men in the departments will depend more largely upon the results of their work as investigators than upon the efficiency of their teaching, although the latter will by no means be overlooked. In other words, it is proposed in this institution to make the work of investigation primary, the work of giving instruction secondary.[34]

All of the departments of the University were in fact organized according to this plan. In contradistinction to other colleges of education developed within university structures, the School of Education at the University of Chicago was from its inception research oriented. The usual pattern was normal school to undergraduate degree granting program to graduate program. The School of Education at Chicago began with the acquisition by the University in 1901 of the Chicago Institute, a normal school, along with elementary schools, a secondary, and a manual training school. Once merged with the University all of these units were treated as laboratories for research.[35]

By 1923 the School of Education has quadrupled in size of enrollments and amount of expenditures.[36] At this time the University's position with regard to the relationship between education and research was firmly entrenched. In a speech entitled "The University as It Should Be in 1940," President Burton said in 1925:

> The third view (of education) is that there is no fixed formula of school organization or teaching that any generation can adopt without reformulation of the practices of an earlier day.... Our school of Education is an embodiment of this third view. While teaching the various subjects of the school curriculum with the cooperation of the other departments of the University and training its students in the Laboratory Schools, it devotes its chief energies to constructive studies looking toward the improvement of methods and the enlargement of the content of teaching and at the same time looking toward more efficient organization of the school systems of the country.[37]

The rest of this passage enumerates the "scientific" accomplishments of Judd and others. A statement prepared for the members of the Chicago Bar in the mid-1920s proudly states:

> A still broader test of scientific accomplishment is that made by James McKeen Cattel, president of the American Association for the Advancement of Science, who has selected the thousand leading "American Men of Science" on the basis of a ballot taken among authorities in twelve branches of science. Of these leading American scientists 113 are identified with the University of Chicago.[38]

The ideal of science in the service of society, as perhaps the exemplary service to society, is one that has persisted at the University of Chicago. The School of Education was always considered part of the social sciences and today continues its existence as a department under the Division of Social Sciences. The hiring policy first articulated by President Harper is doubtless one reason for this continued research emphasis.

The selection of Charles H. Judd as head of the Department of Education in 1909, a position that he held until 1938, represents another instance of the University's unique intellectual commitment. Judd had first distinguished himself in 1907 by translating Wundt" OUTLINE OF PSYCHOLOGY into English. He was at that time directing a psychological laboratory at Yale.[39] Harold Rugg's sketch of Judd's career probably best summarizes his approach to the study of education.

> Judd believed in having a small, highly selected body of students who would work with meticulous care at the laboratory analysis of human behavior. He had returned from Leipzig imbued with two of Wundt's lifelong interests. The first was the exact instrumental analysis of human behavior. This led him to develop the famous psychological laboratory at the School of Education, from which he and his students, from 1910 to 1930, reported a score of objective investigations. Judd, in contradistinction to Thorndike's lifelong measurement of products of education, fixed his study on the processes of education.[40]

He also focused his attention on the social aspects of these processes of education.[41]

During his career, Judd was commissioned to make a number of surveys of public school systems in most of the large cities of the country, including St. Louis, Denver, Grand Rapids, and Cleveland.[42] One can speculate that Judd's rigorous quantitative approach to the surveys not only acted as a model for future survey work, but it may also have been responsible for the increasing popularity of the survey during this time. Professor Judd was also credited with having been instrumental in establishing the junior-senior high school since the model of this system was first instituted in the University laboratory school.[43]

Judd's experimental and measurement work had a tremendous effect on the developing work of his University of Chicago colleague, Franklin Bobbitt. Cremin is correct in attributing to Bobbitt the beginning of awareness of curriculum making as a specialized professional activity, but curriculum as a field of study is still nascent at this point. Bobbitt's contribution was a first attempt to define and systematize the curriculum in terms of analyzing school experiences and activities.

Bobbitt's early work in education was as an administrator setting up a school system in the newly acquired Philippines. He went from this position to Clark University, where, as a graduate student, he was influenced by G. Stanley Hall's research on the stages by which a child repeats the developmental history of its race. This exposure consolidated a line of thought that had occurred to Bobbitt during his period in the Philippines: that there is a relationship between society and the curriculum and a primary purpose of schooling is the proper socialization of children.[44]

In 1909, the same year as Judd's arrival, Bobbitt joined the University of Chicago as an instructor in Educational Administration. His contact with Judd introduced him to the new and exciting world of educational measurement, an introduction that opened the door to his later work.

Another equally important influence was the publication in 1911 of Frederick Winslow Taylor's *The Principles Of Scientific Management*. Bobbitt's administrative background, his allegiance to quantitative research in education, and the ideas that he took from this book resulted in one of the persistent and dominant themes in American education today. The raw material, process, product metaphor was inspired by this combination of factors.[45]

Bobbitt thought that schools would be more efficient, and incidentally, that efficiency was the desideratum, if they were managed and that the tasks of management are the same whether in the context of an industry or in the context of schools. He saw the job of the schools as the production of a high-quality standard product, namely a productive adult citizen. Elaboration of the metaphor involved systematic quantitative analysis of the functions of a productive adult citizen and the discovery of classroom goals and activities that could be guaranteed to produce citizens able to perform such functions.[46] This work was an early formulation of Tyler's later articulation of the curriculum-making process.

The tradition being established at the University of Chicago was fully realized in the work of one of Judd's graduate students, Ralph Tyler. Tyler's dissertation, completed in 1927, was an analysis of statistical applications in curriculum evaluation. The notion of curriculum evaluation was relatively new at this time, and Tyler has often been referred to as the father of curriculum evaluation. It is with the development of systematic evaluation procedures that we have a foundation for a technology and method for the scientific approach to curriculum work.

Tyler's impact on the development of the curriculum field, in terms of numbers of disciples and critics alike, is equaled only by that of John Dewey. The Tyler Rationale is the model for the entire behavioral objectives approach that has dominated public school curriculum making over the last forty years.

The Tyler Rationale dictates an operationalized sequence of linear steps leading from the formulation of goals and specification of outcomes, identification of classroom experiences presumed to yield desired outcomes, and precise articulation of evaluation procedures to measure achievement or nonachievement of specified goals. The specification of goals and experiences is to be derived from careful study of the nature of the "learner," the needs and purposes of the society, and a coherent philosophy of education.

The work that culminated in the precise statement of the rationale is among the most significant studies in the evolution of the curriculum field. The Eight-Year Study, which was directed by Tyler and a group of measurement experts, was commissioned by a committee of the Progressive Education Association, the members of which included Harold Rugg.[48] According to Tyler, the Study was precipitated by a crisis in American secondary education, which was directly related to the Depression.

> By 1930, several features of the typical elementary school in the United States were clearly different from those of 1915. ...The high schools, however, were still very much like those of 1910, particularly in terms of curriculum content

and learning activities. ...with the onset of the Great Depression of 1929, new
demands for change came with such force that they could no longer be denied.
Youth in large numbers, unable to find work, enrolled in high school. Most of
these new students did not plan to go to college, and most of them found little
meaning and interest in their high-school tasks. But still they went to school;
there was no other place for them to go.[49]

In response to this crisis the Progressive Education Association Commission
on the Relation of School and College recommended a pilot program that would
allow 30 schools to develop curricula that would not be dictated by college
entrance requirements and would, therefore, be responsive to the needs of all
high school students. The study ran from 1932-1940 and included the efforts of
Harold Alberty of the Ohio State University in the development of subject
matter and activities that would draw upon current studies of adolescents.[50]

Tyler's evaluation team looked at the effectiveness of the program by
studying college students' performance and achievement in 1,475 matched pairs,
each pair consisting of a graduate of one of the study schools and a graduate of
some other secondary school.[51]

Tyler lists the following significant results of the Eight-Year Study:

1. Widespread acceptance of the idea that schools could develop
   educational programs that would meet the needs of all students.
2. Recognition by colleges that entrance testing was a viable selection
   tool.
3. The development of the in-service workshop in teacher education.
4. The supercession of individual student testing as the assessment tool for
   program success by the concept of educational evaluation.
5. The recognition by educational practitioners of the value of defining
   educational objectives in terms of the behavior patterns students are
   encouraged to acquire.[52]

Two other important results of the study should be noted: 1) the scientific
approach to curriculum became a real alternative, with communicable subject
matter and method; and 2) Ralph Tyler became a highly visible figure in
American education, a factor that led to his being made chairman of the
Department of Education at the University of Chicago on Judd's retirement.[53]

If we now compare the emergence of the curriculum field at Teachers
College with the developments coming from the University of Chicago, we can
see that the development of the field in general grew out of commonalities in the
general American education situation, and that the differences in the approach
to the field are owing largely to differences both in institutional history and
faculty composition and interaction. Most striking among the similarities are the
presence of a growing technology of educational research immediately preceding
the social crisis of the depression as it was perceived by educationists. The social
reconstructionist orientation that emerged at Teachers College can be seen as a

function of the reformist history of the institution, and likewise the emergence of the scientific approach at Chicago must be seen as directly related to the research commitment of the University.

The development of the curriculum field at the College of Education at the Ohio State University was a function of the same sort of constellation of faculty personality, institutional structure, and increasing technological sophistication.

The College of Education at Ohio State was founded neither as a professional school nor as a philanthropic agency. It was intimately connected with the land-grant movement when Ohio State University proper was founded as a mechanical and agricultural college under the Morrill Act of 1862. The purpose of the Morrill Act colleges was "to promote the liberal and practical education of the industrial classes in the several pursuits and professions of life."[54] The main idea was to provide education for all citizens beyond that received in the common school, which children typically completed around the age of fourteen. However, in order to enter the University, pupils were required to pass an entrance examination for preparatory classes. This circumstance demanded training for common school teachers so that that quality of instruction received therein would be adequate to prepare pupils to take and pass these examinations. For a number of reasons, however, economic and political, the college was not founded until 1907. The first faculty consisted of a professor of school administration, a professor of psychology, and a professor of history and philosophy of education.[55]

During the first years of its life the College functioned primarily as a training facility for young girls preparing for careers in public schools. The program was a two-year course of study, admission to which required 90 hours of general college work. The course of study in the College of Education was devoted to sociology, history, and psychology of education, with some study of methods and practice teaching.[56] While this preparation was quite different from normal school training, it was still largely a course of practical preparation.

The college began to develop as an institutional force in 1913 with the appointment of George Arps as chairman of the department. He was trained in philosophy and education at the University of Berlin and had studied experimentalism under Wundt. He began to select colleagues who were trained in current methods and in philosophical and psychological traditions, where as prior to his appointment the faculty had been largely imported from normal and secondary schools. Among Arps' major accomplishments were the hiring of Boyd Bode and Burdette Buckingham in 1921, the organization of the Educational Research Bureau, and the establishment of the Ohio State Educational Conferences.[57]

Buckingham organized the Educational Research Bureau under Arps' supervision and advice. Among the projects carried out by the Bureau during the 1920s were the development of improved scales for the teaching of spelling and arithmetic, an investigation of the holding power of junior high schools, and an investigation into the utility of intelligence tests in classroom tracking. It was under the auspices of the Research Bureau that the Eight-Year Study was begun, and it was this Bureau that was responsible for publication in 1921 of the first journal devoted to research in education. The first issue of the *Educational Research Bulletin* began a series of articles on "Common Sense in the Use of Tests." The particular activities of the Bureau and the general method of problem selection employed by it, namely, letters were sent to school administrators asking for statements of school problems, reflects the College's commitment to research in service to practice. This sort of commitment was necessary to the development of a curriculum field.

In 1928 W. W. Charters was made editor of the *Bulletin* and head of the Bureau.[59] Current literature in the field presents Charters as coauthor of the scientific management movement along with Franklin Bobbitt. Actually, it seems as if the similarities are superficial. It is true that Charters was involved in the same sort of activity analysis as Bobbitt, but the focus and the intention of his analyses were very different. Charters' approach remained always faithful to Dewey's philosophy concerning child interest and child activity. He had, in fact, studied under Dewey while at the University of Chicago.[60] Charters' concern remained always with the structure of knowledge while Bobbitt was concerned to discover the components of adult functioning.

The Ohio State Educational Conferences reflected the same kinds of school concerns as did the Bureau of Educational Research. The conferences were organized around the following aims.

1.   To promote professional interests of teachers and prospective teachers.
2.   To aid in solving educational problems.
3.   To stimulate the public interest in education and to gain the cooperation of the public in its improvement.

The speakers at the first conference in 1921 included W. W. Charters, Charles Judd, and William Bagley.[61] These are all men who would later be identified as the nucleus of the group of curriculum theorists and researchers.

One of the most influential members of the Ohio State faculty during the 1920s expansion was Boyd H. Bode, who was brought to the University in 1921 by Dean Arps. Bode spent the first 20 years of his career as a philosopher and professor of philosophy. His move from philosopher to educationist was an outcome of his conversion from idealism to pragmatism. In this he was influenced by his reading of the work of William James, John Dewey, Josiah Royce and others. Pragmatism, with its function view of knowledge, led naturally to concern for the educational processes.[62]

During his career as an educationist and Chairman of the Department of Principles and Practice, Bode was a frequent and outspoken critic of both the progressive and scientific education movements. Bode during his career was sympathetic to the ideals of the Progressive Movement; the purpose of his criticism, he said, was to save the Progressive Movement from its supporters. He was particularly critical of Kilpatrick's project method of teaching. In *Progressive Education At The Crossroads* Bode chastised the tendency of Progressives to neglect logically organized subject matter in favor of some nebulous romanticized vision of the nature of the child.[63] He maintained always that education has to do with enabling the child to search for meanings within the framework of discipline and subject matter.

In *Modern Educational Theories* Bode was especially critical of what he termed "the method of instrumental or incidental learning," with its spirit of immediate practicality on which Kilpatrick's project method seemed to rely.

> This is no objection to the method, unless we apply it too widely. If we do so, we find that our practicality over-reaches itself. Learning that is too limited to this method is too discontinuous, too random and haphazard, too immediate in its function, unless we supplement it with something else. Perhaps children may learn a great deal about numbers from running a play store or bank, but this alone does not give them insight into the mathematics that they need to have. They may learn a great mass of historical facts from staging a play, but this is not a substitute for a systematic study of history. Learning for immediate purposes, or incidental learning, is too much a hit-and-miss affair — it dips in here and there, but it gives no satisfactory perspective, no firm hold on fundamental principles.[64]

Bode was equally critical of the scientific movement in education on the ground that it neglected the child's own role in the construction of knowledge and on the ground that scientific management could be antithetical to the interests of democracy and the common man.[65]

What is particularly interesting about the development of the Ohio State perspective is that this singular critical conceptual posture evolved despite the broad communications network established through the Conferences and the research interaction channeled through the Bureau. We must wonder about the unique social and institutional features of the Ohio State University that contributed to the development of this critical intellectual temperament. We know that the Eight-Year Study, for example, was executed as part of a cooperative effort among Teachers College, University of Chicago, and Ohio State faculty. We know that the conferences included many of the targets of Bode's criticism. The numerous surveys carried out from the Ohio State base were also often the product of cooperative efforts. Yet rather than developing along one of the two lines mentioned in connection with the University of Chicago and Teachers College, the Ohio State University embodied a perspective quite distinct from either of those.

Once again we must speculate about unique social and institutional arrangements. Unlike Teachers College, the Ohio State University was not situated in a rapidly overcrowding urban area beset with all of the problems attending the influx of immigrants. The student population at Ohio State was relatively homogeneous, drawn primarily from its own geographic area.[66] The ever-present urban poverty that must have influenced the concerns of Teachers College faculty was not so great a problem in this part of the Midwest. Unlike the University of Chicago, Ohio State was not a wealthy, heavily endowed institution created primarily for the purpose of the scientific advancement of human knowledge. Its land-grant roots must have influenced the shaping of its commitment of scholarship always in service to practice. And the commitment to practice as shown by the research programs and the tenor of the conferences may have surfaced in an intellectual attitude that saw itself as maintaining a balance between the perceived excesses of the foremost scholars of the day. Admittedly this conclusion requires a certain amount of fantasizing, but it is a plausible fantasy.

The emerging curriculum field can be seen to have consolidated in the 1930s with the signal event of publication of two journals devoted solely to curricular matters. Prior to this time articles on curriculum were spread haphazardly among general education publications. In 1933 the Teachers College informal group began regular publication of *The Educational Frontier* edited by William Kilpatrick. In 1937 the Society for Curriculum Study was organized and its publication of *The Changing Curriculum* began. There were a number of other collections devoted to curriculum study that also began to appear during the 1930s and regular contributors included all of the men who have been mentioned in this paper.

If we agree to accept the sociointellectual definition of a discipline, any argument that the history outlined above is not a picture of growth and consolidation of an academic discipline in untenable. There are no clear problems belonging to the area of curriculum being raised and attacked by scholars specifically trained to deal with them. The subject matter is clearly defined in the context of school questions (at least in these early days), and there is a record of communication among workers who must be identified as curricularists and not as anything else. Certainly it is the case that the pioneers in the field were immigrants from other disciplines, but it is equally certainly that by the 1930s there was a whole generation of scholars who had been born into the discipline of curriculum.

This sociointellectual approach to the history of the field also suggests a way to make sense of the various orientations to the field currently existing. We can see clearly the role of institutional mediation, compellingly in the case of the University of Chicago and Teachers College. The former can be seen to have given us the hard social science research perspective and the latter the concern for moral action in the social arena, which is a dominant theme in the work of some theorists today. A task for the future is the explication of the present in these terms.

N O T E S

1. R. S. Peters, "Must an Educator Have an Aim?" in R. S. Peters, *Authority, Responsibility And Education* (London: George Allen & Unwin Ltd., 19 83-95; Israel Scheffler, "Is Education a Discipline?" in John Walton and James L. Kuethe (eds.). *The Discipline Of Education* (Madison: University of Wisconsin Press, 1963), 47-60; Dwayne Huebner, "Implications of Psychological Thought for the Curriculum," in Arno Bellack and Herbert Kliebard (eds.) *Curriculum And Evaluation* (Berkeley: McCutchan, 1977) 68-76, first appeared in Gladys Unruh and Robert Leeper (eds.), *Influences In Curriculum Change* (Washington, D.C.: Association for Supervision and Curriculum Development, 1968), 28-37; Joseph J. Schwab, "The Practical: A Language for Curriculum," in Bellack and Kliebard (eds.), first appeared in *School Review* 78 (November 1969), 1-23.

2. Papers collected in John Walton and James L. Kuethe (eds.), *The Discipline Of Education* (Madison: University of Wisconsin Press, 1963).

3. In particular this is the kind of argument used by Scheffler, Schwab, and Peters in the papers cited above.

4. James E. McClellan, Comments on "Is Education a Discipline?" by Israel Scheffler in Walton and Kuethe, 125-38.

5. Theodore M. Brown, "Putting Paradigms into History," photocopy of revised draft, 1979.

6. This is essentially Peters' argument in the paper cited above.

7. Lawrence Cremin, et. al., *A History Of Teachers College, Columbia University* (New York: Joh Wiley and Sons, 1975).

8. Ibid.

9. Ibid.

10. Ibid.

11. Ibid.

12. Ibid.

13. Ibid., 80-81.

14. Ibid.

15. Peter F. Carbone, *The Social And Educational Thought Of Harold Rugg* (Durham: Duke University Press, 1977).

16. Lawrence Cremin, *A History Of Teachers College*.

17. Lawrence Cremin, *The Transformation Of The School* (New York: Vintage Books, 1964).

18. Ibid.

19. Ibid.

20. Ibid.

21. Ibid.

22. Ibid.

23. Cremin, *A History Of Teachers College*.

24. Jesse H. Newlon, *Education For Democracy In Our Time* (New York: McGraw-Hill, 1939), 11-12.

25. Cremin, *A History Of Teachers College*.

26. Ibid.

27. Ibid., 154.

28. Ibid., 151.

29. Mary Louise Seguel, *The Curriculum Field: Its Formative Years* (New York: Teachers College Press, 1966).

30. Cremin, *A History Of Teachers College*.

31. Thomas Wakefield Goodspeed, *The Story Of The University Of Chicago*, 1890-1925 (Chicago: University of Chicago Press, 1925); William Edward Murphy and D. J. R. Bruckner, (eds.), *The Idea Of The University Of Chicago* (Chicago: University of Chicago Press, 1976).

32. Murphy and Bruckner, *The Idea Of The Univesity Of Chicago*, 307.

33. Thomas Wakefield Goodspeed, *The Story Of The University Of Chicago*.

34. Ibid., 60, 61.

35. Ibid.

36. *The University Of Chicago: A Statement Prepared For members Of The Chicago Bar* (Chicago: University of Chicago, n.d.).

37. Murphy and Bruckner, *The Idea Of The University Of Chicago*, 364.

38. A statement prepared for members of the Bar, 10.

39. Seguel, *The Curriculum Field*.

40. Ibid., 72, 72 fn. 16.

41. Ibid.

42. Ibid.

43. A statement prepared for members of the Bar.

44. Seguel, *The Curriculum Field*.

45. Ibid.

46. Cremin, *The Transformation Of The School*.

47. Ralph Tyler, *Basic Principles Of Curriculum And Instruction* (Chicago: University of Chicago Press, 1950).

48. Cremin, *The Transformation Of The School*.

49. Ralph Tyler, "Educational Benchmarks in Retrospect: Educational Change Since 1915," in Tyler, *Perspectives On American Education* (Chicago: Science Research Associates, 1976), 38.

50. H. G. Good, *The Rise Of The College Of Education Of The Ohio State University* (Columbus: Ohio State University Press, 1960).

51. Cremin, *The Transformation Of The School*.

52. Tyler, "Educational Benchmarks in Retrospect," 40, 41.

53. John Goodlad, *Introduction* to Tyler, *Perspectives On American Education*.

54. H. g. Good, *The Rise Of The College Of Eduation Of The Ohio State University*, 4.

55. Ibid.

56. Ibid.

57. Ibid.

58. Ibid.

59. Ibid.

60. Seguel, *The Curriculum Field*.

61. Good, *The Rise Of The College Of Education Of The Ohio State University*.

62. J. J. Chambliss, *Boyd H. Bode's Philosophy Of Education* (Columbus: Ohio State University Press, 1963).

63. Boyd H. Bode, *Progressive Education At The Crossroads* (New York: Newson and Company, 1938).

64. Boyd H. Bode, *Modern Educational Theories* (New York: Mcmillan, 1927), 150-51.

65. Bode, *Modern Educational Theories*, 171-91.

66. Good, *The Rise Of The College Of Education Of The Ohio State University*.

CHAPTER EIGHT

Beyond the Window

Dreams and Learning

Mary Aswell Doll
1982

This semester I devised a course on the child from a Jungian perspective. Our reading centered on Jung's essay "The Psychology of the Child Archetype" and included accounts of a fictional child in myth, fairytale, the bible, and literature. My interest was to place the child inside a symbolic framework, seeing the child as an archetype and culturally rather than empirically and realistically. This was in accord with Jung's distinction between symbol and fact: "The mythological idea of the child is emphatically not a copy of the empirical child, but a symbol clearly recognized as such; it is a wonderchild, a divine child, begotten, born, and brought up in quite extraordinary circumstances, and not—this is the point—a human child."[1]

From the start of this venture in the classroom it occurred to me that seeing the child in an archetypal manner is an act of major educational importance. I was asking the students to make two moves. First, I was asking them to draw connections between modern and ancient writing, back and forth continually, until time became more of an ebb and flow than a line. Second, I was asking the students to tap time's flow within themselves, by attending to their dream images. While the first move is accepted procedure in thematic courses, the second move to inner introspection is definitely nonstandard.

Indeed, Jung's psychology is nonstandard. His is a psychology not of science but of art, not of ego but of archetype. Freud, on the other hand, is standard, with his scientific approach to the psyche. His acceptance by psychology departments and his litanizing by literature departments further attests to the ease with which colleges and universities have adopted mainstream thought.

According to this orthodox view, the unconscious is a thing, capable of manipulation. But Jung's approach is different. Basing his psychology on archetypes, he delves deeper into the unconscious, showing it to be not a thing but a person, and not even one person but many types of persons. One facet of the inner self may be like the Trickster, another like the Great Mother, or the Hero, or the Child: all figures familiar in folk tales and wisdom writings. Jung thus makes an astounding point. The unconscious is a poetic not a scientific reality. It can only be apprehended in an "as-if" manner, through personification and metaphor. So embedded are we in orthodoxy, however, that most of us are ignorant of the poetic nature of inner life—just as we are unaware of the rich deviations of our own culture. The task for the teacher, as for the analyst, is to teach how to read psychic speech, if the individual is to be brought together with the nurturing symbols of culture.

Such a rapprochement views the unconscious as a hidden, creative power that sustains culture and self-hood alike. The alchemists of old understood this concept, calling their project of changing base lead into gold the Great Work. For them, the transmutation of metals was really a poetic analogy for another transformation, far more exciting and dangerous than any tinkering with flasks and fire. Instead of treating matter as a thin, the religious alchemists coexisted with matter in an act of imagining. They wanted to acquire the "gold" of reborn consciousness. Centuries later Jung identified the psychological principle underlying the alchemical experiment. In his most mature writings Jung labeled it the principle of compensation, according to which no thing is merely itself: a solid, literal reality.[2] This notion has tremendous implications for education. To learn to see archetypally is to see the self poetically. This is a Great Work, indeed. It could turn a classroom into an alchemical lab.

Jung's highly heterodox theories may leave us feeling less comfortable than do Freud's. For Jung, man is not master in his own house.[3] The terrible error of empirical science, however, has been the overvaluation of the role of the ego. The ego has one big role to perform: like the hero of myth, he must slay and win. But the house of the self has many rooms and many roles, as anyone with the slightest introspective sense knows. A study of the child archetype is a study of the nonheroic, nonegoistic side of human experience, filled with risk, fear, and failing. Such a study can cause discomfort. But I wonder if the time has not come when the classroom, like orthodoxy itself, should not rattle the bars of creed. Archetypal images have been safely caged for too long.[4] Their livingness, as an other side of the self, must be felt if we are to avoid projecting our furies blindly on to others.

My plan for seeing archetypally was to integrate readings from the folk tradition with jottings in dream diaries. My colleague Bob Sidwell, with whom the course was taught, and I wanted to make conscious the connection between theory and practice, reading and imagining, talking and dreaming. It was our intention to bring together the shadow side of Western culture (fairy tale, myth, wisdom writings) with the shadow side of consciousness (the unconscious). What is common to both is poetic expression. Both have a logos of the psyche. The "psyche logic" of pattern and image formed the core of the course.

It seems appropriate that we met at twilight, from 4:30 until 7:00 at evening. We were between times of day when the students, many of them teachers, felt that the day's work had been done. We were also between meals, when hunger was most keen. Precisely at these between moments does the unconscious function best, Jung claims, for the waking mind then is least focused.[5] Like a thief at the gates, the unconscious slips through the cracks of conscious control. Bob would begin our sessions by narrating from memory a folk tale. The students settled down to listen; some dozed. After storytime, we moved to a consideration of one of the readings. Either Bob or I would lecture briefly on such topics as initiatory structures in myth, the role of the Night Journey, the meaning of archetype, or the two modes of Western thought: rational and nonrational. The remainder of classtime was spent in group work, where the students applied the lecture theme to the reading, discussing among themselves the initiatory pattern in "Snow White," for instance, or the motif of the night journey in "Pinocchio," or Jung's paradox, "smaller than small, bigger than big," as exemplary of the role of the dwarf in fairy tales. One student remarked that she always left our class with a headache. She said she was using a part of her head that had never been used before!

The Great Work of the course, however, was done at night. We asked the students to jot down their dreams into a special dream book, for a period of four weeks. Our hope was that the material of the course, reminiscent of childhood readings, would fertilize their imaginations and connect each dreamer with the symbolical child within. We wanted to give the students the real opportunity to feel again the mysteries of the nonhero, who lives just below the surface in the embers of being.

Our first set of papers was to be the fruit of these night labors. We asked the students to cull through their dream books and select one or two dreams for focus. They were to pay particular attention to specific image patters, in accordance with Jung's advice for dealing with nonrationality. "Give [the emerging content of the unconscious] your special attention," he said, "concentrate on it, and observe its alterations objectively. Spare no effort to devote yourself to this task, follow the subsequent transformations of the spontaneous fantasy attentively and carefully. Above all, don't let anything from outside, that does not belong, get into it."[6] This dictum, based on the writing of an alchemist, allows the dream to speak with its own "psyche logic," complete with absurdities. The dreamer's task is not to figure out the images, but to figure them in: to see, in other words, the figure each image makes. To help the students with the simple art of dream recording, I read from my own dream book. What follows is an excerpt of a dream in which I return to the house I grew up in.

> When I got to the house I was very scared. I don't remember being let in. I just remember being on the second floor, where the owner, a young woman, was showing me around. I wanted to see my old bedroom. When I went into it, it had been changed, made smaller and more crude. It had the feel of a camp, as if people come to it only for short visits. It was clear to me that the house was in very bad shape. I kept thinking of the young woman guide, "She has made a bad bargain." When I looked down, the wainscoting had come loose from the floorboards. There was green ooze at the corners, indicating to me that the place was rotting out.

I wanted to share this dream to illustrate an important Jungian motif; namely, that the archetypal child is both beginning and end.[7] Unlike the empirical child, who outgrows his condition, the archetypal child recurs through time to remind us of our poetic origins. Dreams, for Jung, are our best natural resources, whose treasures need to be carefully mined.

I told the students that the dream had left me uneasy but that I came to see it as a gift. It seemed to be warning me against too much intellectualizing about the house of the self. My ascent, after all, to the second floor of the dream house was without regard or knowledge of any foundations. And it was the foundation of the house that was rotting out, as if to underscore a danger to my selfhood. Perhaps in actuality I was viewing the child from a superior-instructional perspective, instead of the symbolical one Jung spoke of. In not feeling the child as real in a symbolic way I was setting my inner life apart from my intellectual life, viewing the inner space as smaller, cruder and more camp-like. One loses connection with one's total being, however, if the self is split off into camps. Further, my dream self was harboring a secret thought against my dream guide, thinking the guide had "made a bad bargain." There is no way to make deals with the unconscious or to bargain-away psychic facts. Really it was I who was on the losing end. As if to draw my gaze to the source of difficulty, the dream shifted direction to the wainscoting. Down there lay the gift in the moist, green ooze. Its greenness and dampness imply a life-giving factor. In that image the dream was showing me what I understood intellectually but needed to see more archetypally: the way to integrated wholeness is not up, but down, to the littler, smaller things that connect us to ourselves.

Self-knowledge involves seeing more clearly into our unacknowledged prejudices and fears—what Jung calls the shadow. Judith Morris Ayers, writing in the JCT newsletter, says of Jung's shadow theory that it enables teachers to see better their problems in dealing with particular students.[8] I think we can go one step farther and say that dreams enable all of us to confront what shades our perceptions—of ourselves as well as of others. The teacher's role can be expanded to include teaching insight into the hidden archetypes that provide our foundation, both culturally and personally. In such a way the dream becomes part of a vast hermetic subculture, entirely consistent with the images of Western heterodoxy: from the alchemists and folklorists, from the secret book of Revelation and the parables of Jesus, up to and including Jungian archetypal psychology and visionary poetry. If we as humanists are to transmit our culture, let us consider carefully the shadow side of mainstream thought, for therein lies the treasure that is hard to attain: the gold of self-knowledge.

The dream papers the students wrote were to contain two parts; first, a description of a dream or dreams dreamt during the semester; and second, an analysis of image patterns, keeping close to the image. How did dream images bring out the shadow, giving it depth and texture, so that the dreamer could face fears and see lurking problems from another, fictional perspective? One student responded, "I feel these dreams are telling me that I have not yet adjusted to (my mother's) loss sub-consciously. All three of the dreams had me travelling in the dark. I feel that this may be symbolizing a period of liminality." Another wrote, "in the dream I was torn between accepting my uncle's righteous advice or joining with my cousin to satisfy my personal pleasure.... The fish represented a test for me, to choose between pleasing myself or doing what is right." And another student concluded, "In getting to know the child better we can see that most everything the child does has some kind of meaning, even though we may not know exactly what it is. Even in regards to oneself we can conclude that our actions are not stupid or foolish, but real expressions that are being held within all of us, and these expressions are released when we need to escape from the real world for a while."

At the most, acknowledging the child as archetypally alive in ourselves allows us in the West a peculiar luxury. It allows us a path to self individuation not practiced by the East. Jungian archetypal psychology, rooted in Western heterodoxy, is not transcendental. It does not hold that one should go beyond this world to another state where all is bliss, nor does it advocate that one should "let go" of one's negative feelings. One need only read Jung's startling essay, "An Answer to Job," to see the highly paradoxical nature of Jungian thought, which includes the heretical notion that even our godhead is not a total positive, all one in goodness and light.[9] The transcendental Self, in its egolessness, is reductively singular in its search for purity, love, and happiness. According to Yoga practice, through meditation one finds the still center of bliss. As the Swami Muktananda puts it, "Absorbed in the little bliss of sleep, we forget the pains of the waking state."[10] But for us in the west neither forgetfulness nor bliss will lead to selfhood. The violence that surrounds us is of our own making and cannot be ignored. Our soul searching must take us into the heart of darkness. If we fail to read our dream messages we could deny the one motif that undergirds our entire culture, the lesson of the "Happy Fall." The archetypal child is divine not because it is above our suffering but because it shares in the suffering moment. The child is bringer of light to our shadows.

The child functions as a herald of change because it allows us the opportunity in dream to see our own opposite. Sometimes the opposite awakens a deep sense of yearning, showing the psyche's desire to incorporate both poles of the opposition between child and adult. One student dream in particular combined many of the motifs surrounding the child archetype.

> There is this one particular dream I remember: looking out of this window. As I look out this window I see a young girl. She must be a child of ten. She is skating on an ice ring. I remember trying so hard to open the window to get at the child but just couldn't. I realize as the child runs past me, it is I. Looking out of this window, I feel I am trying to reach that person, me, who was on the ice. This window is keeping me from the child me. I think that maybe the window side is the reality of myself, the true me. Beyond the window out on the ice rink is the child part of me I just can not get ahold of. I do remember enjoying ice skating but this child was like a gifted skater. I can't skate at all. I have always wanted as a child to be good skater, but, to save my life, I couldn't. I still can not. When my girl friends went skating I sat and watched.... This time I am watching myself. I can not believe, though that I had this dream at my age.[11]

For most of us, windows are barriers to reflection in the psychological sense. That is, they only allow one to see what is Out there, literally and really.[12] But this dream window enables the dreamer to see a poetic image, another imagined reality of the self. A different kind of seeing is required. As if to dramatize the dream's importance, the metaphor of ice pervades. While the dreamer can't quite get ahold of the gifted child, she is given ample opportunity to view her motions against a frozen backdrop. The dream has caught time's flow but yet is filled with flowing motion: the other person "runs" past and skates "like a gifted skater." The whole thing defies reality, utterly, as the dreamer concludes with her statement of disbelief.

The dream's un-reality is further felt by the discrepancy between the two selves. There is the "true me" on one side of the window—the side that watches and wishes but cannot perform on ice—and the "child me" that does the impossible, gifted act. What the dreamer does not quite recognize is that the "true me" is not just the side that sits in reality, watching and wishing. The "true me" is both sides. Indeed, recognizing that simple truth of conjoined opposites is life-saving. It would save the life of the soul to have the gifted child skater brought into full psychic awareness of the dreamer. The dreamer's sense of frustration and yearning suggests that she is sympathetic to the dream's "psyche logic": which is circular, flowing, and on-going.

My claim in this paper has been that seeing archetypally is educationally significant. A curriculum that uses dream speech provides a new dispensation for learning about the self and culture. A course could be designed from the inside out, turning current curriculum practice around. Teachers skilled in following images could connect students first to their prime dream images and then to cultural expressions of these same prime images. In such a way a student is brought together with those symbolic expressions that have the most deep, personal meaning. Nor should these images be drawn from one period or genre. Once they had been elicited from dreams they could be researched in various fields and media. Students could present their research (a searching—again of what had already been imagined in the dream) in a variety of ways: expositionally, fictionally, artistically, dramatically, or whatever.

Modern Western man has lost his soul. Our poets tell us that we are hollow: "shape without form, shade without colour."[13] But there are ways to fill the hollow within our own cultural dispensation. We can allow the pains of the waking state to take on form and color in our dreams. We can learn to see our shadows. Education should not just lead out; it should lead in. Let us follow the child archetype into fantasy's reality and psyche's logic. These await our insight, just beyond the window.

NOTES

1. C. G. Jung, "The Psychology of the Child Archetype," in Psyche And Symbol, ed. Violet S. de Laslo (Garden City: Doubleday & Co., 1958), 124n.

2. Jung's compensatory principle stands in direct contradiction to the sort of literalism characterized, for instance, by Bishop Butler's statement, "Everything is what it is, and not another thing."

3. Freud's ego psychology, setting ego as master, can be seen by his saying, "The ego...is the libido's original home, and remains to some extent its headquarters." See Sigmund Freud, Civilization And Its Discontents, trans. James Strachey (New York: Norton, 1961), 49.

4. Samuel Beckett's archetypal old man expresses this idea of the caged beast wanting to escape from the bars of rationalism: "While within me the wild beast of earnestness padded up and down, roaring, ravening, rending." See his "Malone Dies," Three Novels By Samuel Beckett, trans. Patrick Bowles (New York: Grove Press, 1965), 194.

5. C. G. Jung, The Symbols Of Transformation, trans. R. F. C. Huss (Princeton: Princeton University Press, 1952), Collected Works 5, 25.

6. C. G. Jung, Mysterium Conjunctionis, CW 14, 526.

7. See C. G. Jung, The Archetypes And The Collective Unconscious, CW 9, 177-79.

8. JCT Newsletter, (May, 1981), 4.

9. C. G. Jung, "Answer to Job," in Psychology And Religion: East And West, CW 11.

10. Mediate (Albany: State University of New York Press, 1980), 16.

11. I am indebted to my student Deirdre Fitzgerald for letting me use her dream.

12. For more on seeing out and seeing in, read James Hillman, Re-Visioning Psychology (New York: Harper & Row, 1975), 140-45.

13. T. S. Eliot, "The Hollow Men," in The Complete Poems And Plays (New York: Harcourt, Brace and Co., 1958), line 11.

Curriculum Theorizing and the Possibilities and Conditions for Social Action Toward Democratic Community and Education

Michael S. Littleford
1982

Last year at the Curriculum Theory Conference I was in the midst of attempting to articulate connections between individual growth and self reflection and sane and effective social action.[1] My interest in these relationships evolved from a realization that has been dawning within me for a long time. This realization has tended to structure my professional interests, including my choice to enter the field of foundations of education and my attraction to much of what is going on in the reconceptualizing of the curriculum field.[2] Specifically the realization is that the "democratic" conception of society that allegedly emerged in Western civilization and came to fruition in the new world is at worst simply a lie and at best a cruel distortion. Many recoil at such a stance, but my position is not without support in the literature.[3] Some few others now or in the past have also asserted that something fundamental is wrong; something that cannot be fixed by legislative tinkering, constitutional amendment, or curriculum reform narrowly conceived.

This is, however, not to deny that there were good intentions and bright hopes to begin with. As one ally, Lewis Mumford, puts it:

> This attempt to make a new beginning rested on the valid perception that at various points something had profoundly gone wrong with man's development.[4]

Unfortunately, however, the attempt to wipe the slate clean and begin all over again took the infantile form of escape from origins and the past rather than genuine confrontation, struggle, and transcendence. There was, in short, a futile attempt to escape history and tradition—the cumulative effects of time—by simply trading these for unoccupied land. Quoting Mumford again:

> Western man explored every wilderness except the dark continent of his own soul.[5]

Failing that, his entry on the American continent brought the same psychology of dominance and fear that had shaped the institutions of the old world. There was no real transformation. No genuine cultural creation occurred. Such "democracy" as existed was the happy and temporary accident of an abundant, rich, and beautiful land.

The land ran out rapidly; and since that time, except for increasing levels of technological cleverness, material prosperity, and military power, nothing much has happened. We fought a bloody internal conflict followed by a period of barbaric industrialization. During this time an economic oligarchy was successfully formed and passively accepted by most people. Next we participated in a world war; then another world war, and the trend continues. Throughout all of this the health and well being of most people has been a very low priority in our "democratic" society. A few specific examples follow.

1. In the early part of the century small children were addicted to opium in various forms while their overworked (and often pregnant) mothers were assured of the harmlessness of those calming (and profitable) teething tonics.[6] (Moreover, a safe and effective contraceptive still does not exist, and the necrophillic "right to lifers" are hard at work trying to make the situation even more difficult).

2. Sane public transportation systems have been continuously undermined and subverted in order to pave the way for all to be thoroughly dependent upon the private automobile. Much more could be said concerning this issue but in the interest of brevity I shall refrain.

3. Our present economic system is based upon a job structure that generally relegates on to a soft and sedentary job or to a harsh and one-sided use of the body. Moreover, the leisure time activities that are most heavily emphasized and serve the most people are sedentary and vicarious. Although there are hopeful signs away from this, it still seems, in general, correct to say that we have fallen too much into sedentary and vicarious life.

Example after example could be given to demonstrate our spiritual, ethical, and aesthetic bankruptcy. The third example is intended to convey that this condition is mirrored among other things by an accompanying physical degeneration: by the conspicuous lack of overall generally good bodily health. In short, our fallen spiritual, ethical, and aesthetic selves have their visible side— our fallen bodies.[8] The situation is grim and needs to be portrayed as such by all levels of curriculum reconceptualizing and educational philosophizing. Our country seems to be in the position of the character in Pink Floyd's "The Wall," who cries in anguish:

> There must be some mistake. I didn't mean to let them take
> away my soul. Am I too old? Is it too late?

The seeming necessity of a genuine confrontation with the past, of understanding origins and development from origins, led me to the notion of "cultural psychoanalysis":[10] a process applicable to cultural forms which parallels and provides a context for individual self reflection. Both processes involve attempts to confront the past, transcend limiting structures of thought, and retrieve that which has been suppressed and denied by these limiting structures.

In last year's paper, toward the end of arguing for the necessity of thorough self reflection as a complement of responsible social action, I used the concept of cultural psychoanalysis to examine the dominant thought trends (world views or symbolic forms) in Western civilization. Among other things, I concluded that since these trends have been dualistic and increasingly mechanical, they have also acted to progressively deny and suppress the poetic, imaginative, and organic nature of ourselves and the qualitative aspects of reality. This is another way of saying they have alienated ourselves from ourselves, from others, and from nature.

My most general conclusion from all of this is that it is "closing time"[11] on Western civilization as we have known it; and that genuine democracy, if it arises at all, will arise out of the ruin, demise, and collapse of the dominant forms of this civilization. The remainder of this paper contains a more specific and concentrated application of cultural psychoanalysis to ourselves, our history, and present society. The aim is to yield and stimulate insights into the conditions and possibilities for social action toward a higher form of democratic community than we have known or than is perceived possible within the dominant modes of the past.

Those involved with the origins and foundations of present day American institutions are examples par excellence of the mechanical, dualistic, and abstract thought patterns of Western man. The bases of our revolution and our constitution are the interlocking trio of Lockean philosophy, Newtonian mechanics, and Deism. This is the case of even the more "radical" figures who were involved with the American situation. For example, in The Age of Reason, Thomas Paine[12] admits of an early interest in, and perhaps talent for, poetry, but says that he deliberately repressed it "as leading too much into the field of imagination."[13] In the same book Paine asserts in a similar vein that a mill is the universe in microcosm and that only in mechanics can God be revealed. Hence, when we confront our past in sufficient depth we find that our much daunted

American Revolution was at core based upon a tired and mechanistic materialism.[14]

The poet William Blake was a contemporary of Paine and an admirer of his honesty as a thinker. He was also initially a warmly sympathetic observer of both the American and the French revolutions. He wrote poems about each of them expressing his high hopes for their eventual positive outcomes. As time passed, however, he became increasingly disillusioned and prophesized with amazing accuracy the dismal consequences of both revolutions.[15]

As suggested, Blake did not deny that authentic revolutionary impulses were present in both instances. The overt intent was to smash the structure of tyranny and create a better world. However, neither the American nor the French revolutionaries had an adequate grasp of what creation implies or a reliable vision of what a better world is. Their lack was spiritual and aesthetic; under such conditions a revolution, even if it smashes a tyrant, will not be successful in the end, i.e., it will not smash the structure of tyranny. Either another personal tyrant will replace the earlier one (as in the French Revolution), or a tyranny of custom will become established so powerful that a personal tyrant will not be necessary (as in the American Revolution).

Blake's visionary prophecies still ring out to us today with surprising relevance. Among others his work can provide inspiration, insight, and tools to confront and transcend our current stalemate. For instance, his assessment of the American Revolution includes the notion that the failure to awaken man's imagination and spirit brings an inadequate and fallen concept of liberty as a leveling out and as granted by external nature. Locke, Paine, et. al., were champions of human rights, but the rights were conceived as "out there," automatically granted by the natural order and passively received by man. Such an inadequate conception of liberty, according to Blake, leads to "a placid ovine herd of self-satisfied mediocrities."[16] It encourages an atmosphere of pervasive dull mindedness in which exist many persons who are not vigilant of the actual quality of life or have any awareness that it depends largely upon them.

In short, the current habits and forms of our society have been derived from a philosophy that posits basic reality as a static and rational form separate from us that we are obliged to accept passively. Such qualified democracy as there is occurs within the preformed reality. Perception, the beginning of knowledge, is a passive affair, which by definition deemphasizes the human powers to form images and to make these images into art forms. Beginning with a subject-object dichotomy, Lockean consciousness posits the object as impressing itself upon the passive senses of a passive subject who then turns completely away from the object to "reflect" upon its abstracted qualities.

Such liberty as exists in this situation exists within a group of uniformly dulled-out perceivers; the modes of thought that bring humans to a passive acceptance of reality also bring a shutdown consciousness. A good citizen is one who puts desire in bondage to reason and shuts down her/his potentially active powers of perception. He or she is one who perceives without effort or struggle and thus adds to the security of common perception. In short, communal perception of reality based upon the least common denominator, blank slates receiving the same abstract messages, become the valued modes. Active, imaginary, visionary perception is feared and, this being the case, the fully present person who refuses to be the blank slate is often resented and hindered.

The resentful responses are not surprising because the passive modes of perception upon which our democracy is based lead only to despair in the end.[17] Through our passive modes we see but a "fallen world," i.e., the so-called physical world as it presents itself to the passive senses is a fallen world to active, imaginary perception. What we call observable reality is not the same to the awakened imagination as it is to subject-object consciousness,[18] the normal consciousness for our present and historical forms of democracy. The "normal" consciousness is a vicious cycle. We derive the idea of necessity from the passivity with which we see things and we tend toward passivity the more necessity seems to reign.[19]

For Blake the central problem for social and political emancipation is the release of the creative imagination—the freeing of ourselves from the fears and restraints that shut down our visionary powers and prevent our full presence in the ongoing struggle to create. Moreover, Blake is by no means alone in his attitude; there are other potential allies in our attempt to reconceive the meaning of democratic community. Contributing to the remainder of this paper is a diverse and motley group: 1)Giambattista Vico, the eighteenth-century Italian philosopher who challenged the assumptions of the mechanistic and materialistic philosophy of the Enlightenment; 2) Walt Whitman, America's poet and seer of democracy and the creative imagination; 3) Harold Rugg, a key founder of the foundations of education field, an important historical influence in curriculum theorizing, and a twentieth century philosopher of the imagination; and 4) Mary Daly as a representative of the current feminist theology movement.

Vico's major work, The New Science of Giambattista Vico, is a book concerning the origins and transformations of the human world—of human institutions and knowledge and various modes of human consciousness. This philosophical and historical work confirms the intuitive notions of visionaries like Blake and Whitman that true origins derive from the creative imagination and are sacred. They are poetic an possess religious inspiration.[20] From the Vichian perspective, we have as yet no true origins. Again, our early leaders lacked the necessary vision. The only thing dulled-out Lockean-Newtonian-Deistic thought could do with religion was to separate it from the state and relegate it officially to the "private world." The "founding fathers" feared the excesses of religious conflict and understandably so, but in vain did they attempt to vanish their presence from public life and discourse.

Overt religious practice was admittedly left a matter of private conscience, yet the "public" god was also there in the form of that passively perceived, objective, material order and its absolute laws. Moreover, the private sphere reinforced this as most theologies, regardless of differences in detail, presented the same external and separate form of god. These gods, although a bit more mysterious and irrational that the god of the Lockean philosophy and Newtonian mechanics, are equally effective in shutting down creativity and inducing passivity. In short, whether we are speaking of a Baptist or a bureaucrat (or the likely combination of the two), the overt private and covert public religions work to exalt routine and passivity, to produce boredom and banality, and above all to confirm an uninspiring conception of moral good as conformity. Once more the outcome is dullmindedness, and what we must never forget—the repressed violence and destructiveness that is its shadow side (Eichmann was, after all, a good bureaucrat).

All of this, according to our own poet-seer, works squarely against the very conception of religion that is necessary for authentic democratic communion. Whitman continually insisted that without a religious foundation our democratic politics and plentiful economy are worthless.[21] He spoke often of the necessity of a completely new sense and appreciation of religion for any democracy of the future. Moreover, the sense of religion he referred to is the same as what Blake referred to as "true" religion, as opposed to religious idolatry or false religions that postulate some kind of unknown and mysterious God outside of man to which man must give unquestioning obedience.[22] The only religion that can provide a foundation for a democratic community is one which, in Whitman's words, is based upon the "divine pride of man in himself."[23]

From this perspective, if we are to move toward a higher form of democracy, we must not continue to cower in the unreal separation of church and state. We must take a stand to proclaim the desirability of heightened religious consciousness implied by the common ground of all major world religions, the poetry of visionaries like Blake and Whitman, the philosophers of the imagination, and the most inclusive aspects of contemporary feminism. That is, we must not be afraid to say in our curriculum theorizing and our educational philosophizing that women and men must stop looking outside of themselves for salvation: that human development will be severely arrested until we move toward full consciousness that what we call god, the divine, dwells in every person; that all humans are capable of the same cosmic consciousness as the Buddha, Jesus Christ, Blake, Whitman.[24]

After asserting the universal and infinite potential, however, we must hasten to add that its development is neither natural nor given. It does not come without ceaseless struggle for the perfection of our being in order to engage in authentic creative work and communication. Moreover, one can only endure the struggle if one has a passionate commitment. This mention of passion brings us to another fatal flaw in our conception of democracy, which was recognized early on by Vico.[25] It rests upon a philosophy that grew out of a fear of passion. Yet only passionate commitment can bring trustworthy allegiance.

In our new religious communities it should be obvious that we are no longer speaking of priests and congregations. Rather we are speaking of communities of artists who identify the divine with the creative imagination and for whom the worship of God is self-development. This is what Whitman points to in his poetry when he writes:

> Each is not for its own sake, I say the whole earth and all
> the stars in the sky are for religions sake.

> I say no man has ever been half devout enough,
> None has ever yet adored or worship'd half enough,
> None has begun to think how divine he himself is, and how
>   certain the future is.

> I say the real and permanent grandeur of these states must
>   be their religion,
> Otherwise there is no real and permanent grandeur;
> (Nor character nor life worthy the name without religion,
> Nor land nor man or woman without religion.)[26]

Whitman also spoke of this near the beginning of "Democratic Vistas" when he writes:

> Our fundamental want today...is of a class...of native authors, literatures, far different, far higher in grade than any yet known...and, as its grandest result, accomplishing (what neither the schools nor the churches and their clergy have hitherto accomplish'd and without which this nation will no more stand, permanently, soundly, than a house will stand without a sub-stratum), a religious and moral character beneath the political and productive and intellectual bases of the States. For know you not, dear, earnest reader, that the people of our land may all read and write, and may all possess the right to vote—and yet the main things be entirely lacking?[27]

This is only one of several places that Whitman emphasizes the same point: that a religious consciousness inspired by creative art and vice versa are the deepest and most important structures of a democracy. He says it again in the "Vistas" when he writes that America demands a "poetry that is bold, modern, and all surrounding" and which "must place in the Van and hold up at all hazards the banner of the divine pride of man in himself" (the radical foundation of the new religion).[28]

Harold Rugg, among a few other Americans,[29] saw the problem several decades later and continued the work of Vico, Blake, and Whitman in a twentieth century context. He also had a vision of communities of artists. This vision included a special and important group of "artist-teachers." Rugg had in mind teachers whose perception is visionary and active. In Rugg's words these teachers have put themselves "in the creative path"[30] and "know the creative act internally, in its own terms, through having experienced it within their own bodies."[31] Rugg later did extensive interdisciplinary research on the creative act, which culminated in his final book published posthumously, Imagination. In this work he speaks of the need of the freedom to create as a second freedom. He elaborates on this notion in several ways, referring to it variously as a state of relaxed concentration, as the freedom to associate freely, as freedom from self censorship, which comes from the internalized conflict of "I" and "They."[32]

The idea of this latter freedom brings us back to undivided consciousness— the cosmic consciousness we mentioned earlier—and for which another name is androgynous. This term implies that a vitally important condition for a higher form of democracy is a feminist revolution in the most inclusive sense of the word. Such inclusiveness is manifested currently by aspects of the feminist theology movement. This movement in its most vital and lively dimensions seems definitely the heir apparent of the visionary artists and philosophers of the creative imagination—Vico, Blake, Whitman, Rugg, and others. In short, the feminist theology movement is perhaps the nearest thing that we have to the beginnings of an appropriate new religion and is certainly one of the most fertile sources for promoting a new religious-aesthetic consciousness. Within this movement God, Be-ing, the creative imagination are one. In the words of Mary Daly, "the form destroying, form creating transforming power which makes all things new."[33] To participate in God, means, among other things, to cease being the projected "Other." More specifically it means to cease nurturing the bureaucrat so that he is forced to face himself in all of his weakness, insecurity, and dependency. With no one to project upon he can perhaps begin to dimly perceive that he is a hideous botch compared to what he could be and probably the more so, the more economic and political power he possesses.

In short, women are speaking of the possibilities and conditions of a higher form of democratic community, and women must speak before the works of Blake et al. can contribute to a workable vision and provide real inspiration for the modern. They are speaking, among other things, of beginning by negating the transcending dulled-out, bureaucratized patriarchal space now. One important concept is boundary living,[34] which implies a mode of being that refuses to drain all of our energies fighting for equal rights in that dull-minded space. Instead the idea is to work now to create a new social reality at the boundaries or just outside established institutions in which there is support for repudiating traditional duties and obligations. Within that space and emanating from it can come an all-out exuberant and creative attack upon dull mindedness and its fascistic shadow. Through wrath, humor, defiance, art, and many other modes, the banal and boring bureaucratic monster can be slain, and the ground that supports him—the false tolerance of the dull that has emerged from Lockean liberalism—can be thoroughly exposed and discredited.

Within the new space also can emerge a celebration of creative existence as well as multiple expressions of the conditions necessary for such existence. For example, through dialogue, poetry, painting, drama, play, and other forms we can live and portray the alternating rhythms of the creative path. First there is the movement from the subject-object awareness of ordinary consciousness to a merging of these into a world of lover and beloved, or in Buber's words, I and Thou. This is the plane of sexual love and wonder. It includes childlike delight in the beautiful and varied forms and processes of the natural world. This moment in the creative process is a relaxed and restful stage in which imaginative receptivity is at its height and in which energy is garnered for later creative effort. The active moment in the creative process brings us beyond the union of lover and beloved to an active struggle to forge a union of creator and creature, of energy and form. Blake called the active, formative moment of the creative process "Eden," or the higher paradise.[35]

To live according to these rhythms rather than in conformity to external cues and stereotypical molds is one important way of developing personal presence or what Daly calls the "Power of Being"[36] and Whitman calls "the main thing."[37] Such development is necessary in order to become an artist-teacher capable of functioning in a community of peers working to turn education toward the fulfillment of democratic communion and creation.

If small visionary communities of artists and other such means seem to be puny measures in light of overkill, overpopulation, and nuclear wastes, we can return to Blake for a dose of qualified optimism. His ideas of the historical process are the opposite of Hegel's and seem to illuminate our present situation much more fruitfully: every advance of truth and freedom (triumph of the creative imagination) forces error and tyranny to consolidate into more obviously erroneous forms. History exhibits a series of crises in which a sudden flash of imaginative vision bursts out, is counteracted by a more ruthless defense of the status quo, and then subsides again. The evolution comes in the fact that the opposition grows sharper each time and will one day present a clear-cut alternative of eternal life or extermination.[38]

NOTES

1. "Self Reflection, Social Action, and Curriculum Theory Part II," forthcoming in *The Journal Of Curriculum Theorizing* (Winter, 1980), 57-70. A paper of the same title designated Part I and written by my close friend and colleague, James Whitt, will also appear in this issue. The two related papers were presented in a general session at the 1979 Airlie meetings.

2. A major theme in the early emergence and later development of the Foundations field is a vital concern with achieving and maintaining democratic community in the context of the modern industrial social order. Dewey, Rugg, Kilpatrick, Counts, Bode, et. al. all shared this concern however different their individual thrusts might have been in terms of how social and personal reconstruction should proceed toward this goal. An examination of any of their works will reveal that they all grappled constantly with this concern in an interdisciplinary context. See, for example, Harold Rugg, *The Teacher Of Teachers* (New York: Harper and Brothers Publishers), 1952; George Counts, *Dare The Schools Build A New Social Order* (with a new preface by Wayne J. Urban) (Carbondale: Southern Illinois University Press), 1978.

In the past few decades the foundations field has become tragically fragmented so that the early and once developing vision seems to have been eclipsed except in isolated instances of individuals and small groups. The early spirit of the foundations field and its concern for human emancipation seems to be more thoroughly expressed by the reconceptualist group in curriculum than anywhere else in the field of education. They are addressing themselves to the same problems with renewed vigor, new ideas, sources, and experiences, and with a more exclusive emphasis. I first became acquainted with the work of this dynamic group through a work edited by Bill Pinar, *Heightened Consciousness, Cultural Revolution And Curriculum Theory*, (Berkeley: McCutchan Publishing Corporation), 1974, and one written by Pinar and Madeleine Grumet, *Toward A Poor Curriculum* (Dubuque, Iowa: Kendall/Hunt Publishing Company), 1976. The discovery of these works of emancipatory intent was to me like a reprieve from wandering in a virtual wasteland with little or no place to relate and little dialogue about my professional interests and creative inspirations. Since that time I have examined the work of many others in the group and have found similar inspiration and common interests. To mention only a few of the works that have inspired me: Florence Krall, "Navaho Tapestry" and "Indwellings: Reconceiving Pan," both forthcoming in *The Journal Of*

Curriculum Theorizing; Jose Rosario, "Harold Rugg on How We Come to Know: A View of his Aesthetics," *The Journal Of Curriculum Theorizing*, Volume Two, Issue Two (Summer, 1980), 269-74; Janet Miller, "Women: The Evolving Consciousness," *The Journal Of Curriculum Theorizing*, Volume Two, Issue One (Winter, 1980), 238-47; Barbara Mitrano, "Feminist Theology and Curriculum Theory," (Unpublished paper), 1978, 33 pages.

3. See, for example, Lewis Mumford, *The Pentagon Of Power: The Myth Of The Machine*, Volume II (New York :Harcourt, Brace and Jovanovich), 1970.

4. Ibid., 14.

5. Ibid.

6. For a fascinating report on this subject see William Daniel Drake, Jr., *The Connoisseur's Handbook of Marijuana* (San Francisco: Straight Arrow Books, 1971), 54-57. Drake lists a number of teething tonics containing various forms of opium (heroin, morphine sulfate, codeine, powdered opium) and has retrieved old ads exhalting the healthiness of these concoctions.

7. For an excellent recent statement of this problem see Deborah Baldwin, "Off the Track: How America Lost a Sane Transportation System," *The Progressive*, Volume 43, No. 7 (May, 1979), 12-17.

8. Walt Whitman suggests this same notion in his poem, "I Sing the Body Electric":

> Have you seen the fool that corrupted his own live
> Body? or the fool that corrupted her own live body?
> For they do not conceal themselves, and cannot
> conceal themselves.

In *Walt Whitman Complete Poetry And Selected Prose*, edited by James E. Miller, Jr., (Boston: Houghton Mifflin Company, 1959), 75. Norman O. Brown also advances the notion that the outward form of the body is a visible manifestation of one's aesthetic and spiritual condition. See Brown's *Life Against Death," The Psychoanalytic Meaning Of History* (Middletown, Conn: Wesleyan University Press, 1959); and his *Love's Body* (New York: Random House), 1966.

9. Pink Floyd, *The Wall*. Recorded by Pink Floyd Music Ltd., lyrics by Roger Waters, 1979.

10. Littleford, *op. cit.*

11. Norman O. Brown, *Closing Time* (New York: Random House), 1973,

12. There has been a tendency to separate figures like Paine from the more "conservative" figures who actually wrote that such an outlook "can have no

permanent revolutionary vigor, for underlying it is the weary materialism which asserts that the deader a thing is the more trustworthy it is; that a rock is solid reality and the vital spirit of a living man is a rarefied and diaphanous ghost." N. Frye, *fearful symmetry. A study of william blake* (Princeton: Princeton University Press, 1947), 66.

13. Thomas Paine, *The Age Of Reason*. (New York: Modern Library, 1946).

14. I am indebted to Northrop Frye for directing my attention to this aspect of Paine's thought. Frye makes the point that such an outlook "can have no permanent revolutionary vigor, for underlying it is the weary materialism that asserts that the deader a thing is the more trustworthy it is; that a rock is solid reality and the vital spirit of a living man is a rarefied and diaphanous ghost." N. Frye, *Fearful Symmetry. A Study Of William Blake* (Princeton: Princeton University Press, 1947), 66.

15. Ibid.

16. Ibid., 67. Such an attitude of dull mindedness leads to a dismally corrupt and decadent society that tends toward mass hysteria and war fever. This is vividly portrayed in the poem, "Jerusalem," in *Blake Complete Writings* edited by Geoffrey Keynes (New York: Oxford University Press, 1969), 620-747.

17. For a succinct application of these Blakean ideas to the problems of contemporary life see: Theodore Rosak, *Where The Wasteland Ends: Politics And Transcendance In Postindustrial Society* (Garden City, N.Y.: Doubleday & Company, Inc., 1973), 277. Blake expresses these ideas, among other places, in "Vala or the Four Zoas," *op. cit.* 263-372.

18. This point is vividly illustrated in Blake's "A Vision of the Last Judgement," op. cit., p. 671, when he writes: " 'What,' it will be question'd, 'when the sun rises, do you not see a round disk of fire somewhat like a Guinea?' O no, no, I see an innumerable company of the heavenly host crying 'Holy, Holy, Holy is the Lord God Almighty.'" I question not my corporal or vegetative eye any more than I would question a window concerning a sight. I look thro' it and not with it.

19. This idea is also dealt with in Blake's "Jerusalem." op. cit.

20. *The New Science Of Giambettesta Vico*, translated from the 3rd edition by Thomas C. Bergin and Max H. Fisch (Ithaca: Cornell University Press), 1970. For Vico the origin of all human knowledge and corresponding cultural institutions is "poetic wisdom." In the new science he suggests a "tree of knowledge" whose trunk is poetic wisdom or the creative and inventive power of the human psyche (p. 72). A modern scholar, Giorgio Tagliacozzo has taken up where Vico left off and actually constructed such a tree which, if adopted as a model for curriculum building, could be used in

such a way as to make the creative imagination central in the process of general education. For more detailed information on the tree, see: 1) Georgio Tagliacozzo, "General Education as Unity of Knowledge: A Theory based on Vichian Principles, " *Social Research* (Winter, 1977), 768-95; and 2) Michael S. Littleford, "Vico and Curriculum Studies," *The Journal Of Curriculum Theorizing* (Summer, 1979), 54-64.

21. Whitman, "Democratic Vistas," op. cit., 460-61.

22. The God of official and orthodox Christianity was to Blake an example par excellence of false religion. Referring to this God he writes: "So you see that God is just such a Tyrant as Augustus Caesar: and is not this Good and Learned and Wise and Classical?... For thine is the kingship, or Allegoric Godship, and the Power, or War, and the Glory, or Law. Ages after Ages in thy descendents; for God is only an Allegory of Kings and nothing else." From "Annotations to Dr. Thorton's 'New Translation of the Lords Prayer," OP. CIT., 786-87.

23. Whitman, op. cit., 491.

24. This concept is developed among other places in two fascinating books. One is a relatively well known nineteenth century work that is still in print: Richard M. Bucke, *Cosmic Consciousness: A Classic Investigation Of The Development Of Man's Mystic Relation To The Infinite* (New York: E.P. Dutton, 1969). Bucke was a close friend of Walt Whitman's and the latter provided inspiration for Bucke's writing project. The other is a relatively recent and unknown book: Preston Harold, *The Shining Stranger: An Unorthodox Interpretation Of Jesus And His Mission* (New York: Dodd, Mead & Company, 1973). Harold, like Bucke, presents Jesus as only one among several of history's great truth bearers; all of these great persons conveyed the same essential message: that the "Kingdom of God" is within each of us and that human development is arrested as long as we look outside of ourselves for a "savior" to solve our problems.

25. Vico's emphasis on man was always as more than sheer rationality or intellect. Fantasy, passion, emotion are given equal importance in all areas of human life. For instance, in his education work, *On The Study Of Methods Of Our Time*, translated by Elio Gianturco (New York: The Bobbs-Merrill Company, Inc., 1965), he asserts strongly that effective education must consider and address itself to human passion and sensuality.

26. Whitman, "Starting From Paulmanok." op. cit., 18,

27. Whitman, "Democratic Vista," op. cit., 457.

28. Ibid., 491. In particular Rugg was inspired by Waldo Frank, Randolph Bourne, and Van Wyck Brooks.

29. Harold Rugg. op. cit., 274.

30. Ibid., 270.

31. Harold Rugg, *Imagination* (New York: Harper and Row Publishers, 1963), 94.

32. Mary Daly, *Beyond God The Father: Toward A Philosophy Of Women's Liberation* (Boston: Beacon Press, 1973), 43.

33. Ibid., 40-42. In addition to Daly, other important figures in the feminist theology movement include 1) Sheila Collins, *A Different Heaven And Earth* (Valley Forge, PA.: Judson Press, 1974); 2) Rosemary Ruether, *New Woman New Earth* (New York: Seabury Press, 1975).

34. Frye, op. cit. 49.

35. Daly, op. cit. 28.

36. Whitman, op. cit., 457.

37. Frye, op. cit., 260.

CHAPTER TEN

Body and Soul

Sources of Social Change
and Strategies of Education*

Philip Wexler
1982

In the past decade, the United States has experienced a deepening economic crisis and a decline in the quality of life (Castells, 1980). The search for security in material reward and in cultural meanings that offer consolation for material deprivation and uncertainty speeds up and appears in a caricatured and bifurcated form. Careerism in work and fundamentalism in belief are the most evident expressions of the frantic fashion in which individuals try to solve dilemmas posed by the current character of social change.

The social theory of education, despite its claim of detachment as science or critique, is an integral part of these social and cultural changes. The liberal or progressive view of faith in education as the basis of social reform developed during an earlier period of social expansion and belief in a democratic culture (Welter, 1962; Wexler, 1976). The current view of education as cultural reproduction began as a critique of the liberal social theory of education. Cultural reproduction theory belongs to a later time, when commitment to a common culture has become less tenable as a result of the salience of social fragmentation and class division. The most insightful intellectuals see prevailing social arrangements and patterns of culture as partial, deceptive, and socially

---

❖ Reprinted with permission from *British Journal of Sociology of Education*, Vol. 2, No. 3, 1981. Presented at the 1980 Airlie House Conference on Curriculum Theory sponsored by JCT.

oppressive. Withdrawal of faith in education is an aspect of this more general removal of commitment from a system of symbolic interpretation that has lost its claim to universality and its capacity to compensate for socioeconomic deprivation with cultural consolation. Cultural meanings, and the institutions through which they are transmitted, are identified with social domination. The intellectual work of this period is the work of the critique of culture as ideology, and the demonstration of ways in which the acceptance of ideology in general, and through schooling in particular, blocks the realization of the interests and needs of deprived, and potentially ascendant, social groups(Young, 1971; Brown, 1973; Bourdieu, 1977; Apple, 1979a). This disenchantment is connected to an affirmation, among intellectuals, of the endogenous cultures of the oppressed as more authentic and socially accurate than the official culture. It is also marked by a withdrawal of faith in cultural institutions that become identified with social class domination, and begins to seek a social basis for the future outside of cultural institutions such as schools (Bowles & Gintis, 1976).

But the cultural reproduction view, though it has provided valuable criticism of education, is as inadequate to the demands of the current crisis as the liberal view that it supplanted. Though cultural reproduction shows how a suppressed class is created through education, it fails to develop an alternative, liberating perspective, an alternative cultural basis for meaning and personal identity (Dreier, 1980). The open mass withdrawal of commitment to the prevailing culture—which takes a variety of uncertain, ineffective, and distorted forms—makes the intellectual pronouncement of cultural reproduction appear redundant and irritating.

Here, I wish to discuss a third possibility—a critical theory of education, which moves the study of education away from cultural reproduction to cultural change. First, I will review the divergent trends of Marxism—Gramsci, Trotsky, and the Frankfurt School—which are the historical forebears of a critical theory of education opposed to the cultural reproduction view. I will then apply these strands of Marxist theory to the current cultural crisis. Finally, I shall attempt to develop a positive alternative for curriculum in the schools—as an aid to the development of social change movements.

There is an element of romanticism in the vision of education that I am about to present. I share with Buber (1963, p. 157) the feeling that:

> The goal is greater than mere liberation. It is a regeneration of the very being; it is an inner renewal, a rescue from physical and spiritual deterioration, the turning from a fragmentary, contradictory existence to a whole and unified way of life; it is a purification and redemption.

But a romantic element is I think a proper part of a theory of education. It is a refusal to continue the bourgeois disjunction of the "freedom of the soul" and "the poverty, martyrdom and bondage of the body" (Marcuse, 1968, p. 109), in favor of an integral vision: body and soul.

F O U N D A T I O N S   O F   A   C R I T I C A L   T H E O R Y   O F   E D U C A T I O N

The dominant theoretical tendency at present in the critical social theory of education has stressed the extent to which education is social structurally determined, the depth of the operation of cultural domination through schooling, and the ways in which the culture and microstructure of the school enables perpetuation of the macrostructural functions of capital accumulation and social legitimation (O'Connor, 1973; Bowles & Gintis, 1976). These initial insights are then modified. The central tenets in the model of a political economy of schooling and of class cultural rule by the transmission of ideology as educational knowledge, are significantly qualified. The concept of the totality is replaced by an awareness of relative institutional autonomy. Structural integration gives way to the description of internal contradictions (Wexler, 1979). Domination is mitigated by study of class conflict and student resistance within the school (Willis, 1977; Apple, 1979b). From this perspective, the sources of social change are found in a historically unfolding set of structural contradictions located primarily in the economy, in the contradictory character of capital, and also in the cultural autonomy and resistance of a working-class culture against a hegemonic middle-class school culture. While the empirical work necessary to develop this paradigm has only just begun, it is already possible to note its neglect of the historical character of capitalist development; an elaboration of the specific ways in which working-class cultures are or can be mobilized into an effective resistance and opposition; and analysis of the macrostructural and historically changing relationship between cultural and economic patterns. On the whole, however, the school remains, in this view, embedded within the larger dynamic of reproduction.

Marxism is a divergent tradition. Here I will summarize the historical predecessors of a critical theory of education. I must emphasize that it is not my intention to counterpose a group of "true" Marxists who provide the foundation of critical theory with a group of false Marxists who provide the foundation of cultural reproduction. Marx himself was sharply sarcastic about the search for forebears (1978, p. 595).

> And just then they seemed engaged in revolutionizing themselves and things, in creating something entirely new, precisely in such epochs of revolutionary crisis they anxiously conjure up the spirits of the past to their service and borrow from them names, battle slogans and costumes in order to present the new scene of world history in this time-honored disguise and this borrowed language.

But he also recognized the positive side of such activities (1978, p. 596):

> The awakening of the dead in those revolutions therefore served the purpose of glorifying the new struggles, not of parodying the old; of magnifying the given tasks in imagination, not of taking flight from their solution in reality; of finding once more the spirit of revolution, not of making its ghost walk again.

In reviewing some of the divergent trends of Marxism, my intentions follow the second quote, not the first. I wish to magnify and sharpen the alternative to a cultural reproduction theory, not refute it by a recourse to "ghosts." Further, the discussion of divergent views in Marxism represents an attempt to develop dialogue, not an effort at refutation: the cultural reproduction view of education, and its alignment with the structuralist tradition that I oppose, have in recent years developed an interest in previously neglected cultural phenomena. And the tradition that I affirm, critical theory, has sometimes considered the possibilities of emancipatory education while ignoring the social basis for cultural awareness and pedagogy, its actual mode of production.

At their extremes, each of these tendencies represents, theoretically, the current popular caricatured separation of work as careerism and values as fundamentalism. Against the automatic laws of motion of capital are placed noble cultural aspirations. Production is raised against belief, necessity against freedom. The relative merits of materiality and spirituality are debated, but now in the language of social science. This theoretical repeat of the split between the language of the body and the language of the soul, between what exists and what is possible, helps block conscious initiation of effective collective action. For such action, while it moves toward the realization of the cultural goals announced by the emancipators, always moves from some concrete place. Social and educational change is, as in Bubba's description of creative education, "bound up with history and tradition."

To go beyond the present situation, we require a dialogue between cultural reproduction theory and critical theory, and a concrete analysis of the possibilities of social change. The seemingly orthodox answer to the question of the cultural basis of social change is that the working class, as the historically ascendant social group, embodies in its own everyday practices the cultural vision for a future society. If this were so, then the task for education would be to foster the articulation of this historically progressive culture, and to prevent its encapsulation within the falsely universalistic culture of the decadent class. The analysis of working-class cultural expression in the school, the identification of the means for its elaboration, and the emphasis on working-class "resistance" within the schools is correct, and should be theoretically and practically cultivated. The tradition that harbors the future is already contained in the superior vision of the most oppressed. Lukacs (1971, p. 21) believed that orthodox Marxism itself is working-class culture." "Historical materialism grows

out of the 'immediate, natural' life principle of the proletariat." While he admits
of some reservation on this point, I think it is fair to argue that in general Lukacs
saw in proletarian life conditions and culture not merely a valorized cultural
formation, but the only one capable of grasping historical social reality—a
culture whose free enactment coincides with the transformation of the entire
social structure.

> Thus the unity of theory and practice is only the reverse side of the social and
> historical position of the proletariat. From its own point of view self-knowledge
> coincides with knowledge of the whole so that the proletariat is at one and the
> same time the subject and object of its own knowledge. (1971, p. 20).

The proletariat is the universal excluded class, and with the realization of its
practical freedom and cultural expression, class itself is abolished and the new
order initiated.

G R A M S C I

It may be disputed whether Marx shared this faith in the unfettered expression
of traditional working-class culture, even as an adequate point of departure in
the making of social change. For, he wrote that it was only in the practical
activity of revolution that this class could throw off "the much of the ages."

Gramsci's position is less doubtful. While working-class culture contains
"good sense," it also includes much ignorance, superstition, and self-destructive
folklore. Formation of organic intellectuals of the working class requires both
practical activity and an education for discipline, literacy, and knowledge of
classical culture as constituents of self-knowledge. While there are recent
disputations about whether Gramsci favored a conservative social organization of
schools (Entwistle, 1979; Giroux, 1980, pp. 307–15), there is no denying his
belief that effective self-formation requires the integrative incorporation of the
"whole cultural past of modern European civilization" (1971, p. 37).

For Gramsci, one resource of social change is the appropriation of a wider
culture, and its embodiment in the self-production of people working to change
their society. Education and instruction, although not necessarily bureaucratic or
authoritarian schooling, includes attachment to a traditional culture as a source
for cultural change. On school learning, Gramsci wrote: "It is necessary to enter
the 'classical,' rational phase, and to find in the ends to be attained the natural
source for developing the appropriate methods and forms" (Gramsci, 1971, p.
24). A traditional culture, "classical culture," is a cultural resource for the
reformulation of working-class good sense. Education in such a culture can
provide both the vision (ends to be attained) and cultural tools for a "new
humanism," and a transformation of everyday life.

The new culture is not, as it is for Lukacs, a reflection of the natural
conditions of working-class life. On the contrary, it requires formation through a

variety of educations. This view is closer to acknowledging the self-damning aspects of the working-class culture of the lads whom Willis (1977) studied than it is to any exaltation of their culture as "resistance." Nor does Gramsci leave much doubt on the importance of the process of appropriating existing cultures to form a new culture (Gramsci, 1971, p. 325).

> Creating a new culture does not only mean one's own individual "original" discoveries. It also, and most particularly, means the **diffusion in critical form of truths already discovered** (emphasis added), their "socialization" as it were, and even making them the basis of vital action, an element of co-ordination and intellectual and moral order. For a mass of people to be led to think coherently and in the same coherent fashion about the real present world, is a "philosophical" event far more important and "original" than the discovery by some philosophical "genius" of a truth which remains the property of small groups of intellectuals.

T R O T S K Y

Trotsky, unlike Gramsci, is little quoted by contemporary critical cultural theorists. Perhaps that is because it is more difficult to ignore how much the dynamic element of Trotsky was, as he writes, centered in politics, "but very much at the expense of technology and culture" (Trotsky, 1975, p. 189). Trotsky, whose work can less easily be historically abstracted, provides an even more forceful instance of the view that the development of a new culture requires the appropriation of existing, bourgeois cultures. The new culture is hardly a simple, natural expression of the culture of the proletariat. First, cultural change requires the mass diffusion of existing culture (Trotsky, 1975, p. 193).

> The main task of the proletarian intelligentsia in the immediate future is not the abstract formation of a new culture regardless of the absence of a **basis for it** (emphasis added), but definite culture-bearing, that is, a systematic, planful and, of course, critical imparting to the backward masses of the essential elements of the culture which already exists.

Secondly, the creation of a new culture includes no simple-minded reflection of bourgeois culture as "hegemonic," nor a negative interpretation of what is fashionably now called cultural reproduction (Trotsky, 1975, p. 191).

> Our epoch is not yet an epoch of new culture, but only the entrance to it. We must, first of all, **take possession, politically, of the most important elements of the old culture** (emphasis added), to such an extent, at least, as to be able to pave the way for a new culture.

Thirdly, historical materialism is not the inevitable expression of the proletariat. On the contrary, this fundamental theoretical cultural tool of major social structural transformation, this cultural material force in history, this world-historic example of the importance of culture in the process of social change, is created in the process of appropriating a traditional, namely, bourgeois, culture (Trotsky, 1975, pp. 196–97):

> Marx and Engels came out of the ranks of the petty bourgeois democracy and, of course, were brought up on its culture and not the culture of the proletariat. If there had been no working-class, with its strikes, struggles, sufferings and revolts, there would, of course, have been no scientific Communism, because there would have been no historical necessity for it. **But its theory was formed entirely on the basis of bourgeois culture both scientific and political, though it declared a fight to the finish upon that culture** (emphasis added). Under the pressure of capitalistic contradictions, the universalizing thought of the bourgeois democracy, of its boldest, most honest, and most far-sighted representatives, rises to the height of a marvelous renunciation, armed with all the critical weapons of bourgeois science. Such is the origin of Marxism.

Fourthly, the current fetishization of working-class culture generally, and in schools, known as "resistance," has its precursors in the claims of the Russian "Proletcult," or proletarian culture movement. But Trotsky, this appeal to authenticity, as a legitimation of the progressive character of working-class culture, unnecessarily restricts the horizons of future cultural development to the low current standard of a class struggling for material survival. Against the ideal of the authenticity and superiority of working-class culture, Trotsky (1975) writes (p. 209):

> "Give us," they say, "something even pock-marked, but our own." This is false and untrue. A pock-marked art is not art and is therefore not necessary to the working masses. Those who believe in a "pock-marked' art are imbued to a considerable extent with contempt for the masses.... This is not Marxism, but reactionary populism.

Fifthly, and most important, the appropriation of existing cultures is necessary to the construction of a future in which proletariat culture does not simply supplant bourgeois culture, but ceases to exist. The aim is not the circulation of classes and their cultures, but the end of all classes. Toward that end, a "cultural apprenticeship" is necessary (Trotsky, 1975, p. 225): "This class (the proletariat) cannot begin the construction of a new culture without absorbing and assimilating the elements of the old cultures."

THE   FRANKFURT   SCHOOL

Neither the critique of cultural knowledge as ideology, nor the idealization of a working-class culture, nor the simple assertion of emancipatory belief, can provide a theory of education for social change. A recognition of the dialectic of culture is required. The third stream of the critical tradition, which insists on maintaining a complex tension between materialist and idealist moments, the Frankfurt School, offers insight into this dialectic.

Bourgeois culture is, according to Marcuse, an affirmative culture. It contributes to social reproduction not simply through its contents. Education is not just an indoctrination in false consciousness as cultural reproduction theory charges. Rather, the repressive aspect of bourgeois culture is its function, which diverts cultural goals from realization in concrete social relations by assigning culture to a transcendent and segregated realm above and beyond everyday life. It encapsulates cultural goals as high culture and permits, in daily life, the uncritical acceptance of the status quo.

When education contributes to social reproduction, then, it is more by the ephemeral place which it assigns to culture than by the simple fact of class-cultural transmission. Cultural education qua "culture," "surrenders," as Marcuse writes, "the earth to bourgeois society and makes its ideas unreal by finding satisfaction in heaven and the soul" (Marcuse, 1968, p. 100). Not the content of bourgeois culture, but its use as sublimation and substitution for embodiment and realization in actual social relations, is the path by which culture prevents change and contributes to social reproduction. The "freedom of the soul" is an excuse for "the poverty, martyrdom, and bondage of the body" (Marcuse, 1968, p. 109. The "idea of love" prevents the overcoming of competitive individualism and isolation by "real solidarity" (Marcuse, 1968, p. 111). Beauty is identified with an abstract, illusory idealized form, rather than concrete enjoyment and sensuous pleasure.

But the dialectic of this sublimated, socially affirmative culture is that by the enthronement of its social failures as consoling ideals, affirmative culture, and art offers a "counter-image" to existing social reality. This counter-image provides the "critical and revolutionary force of the ideal, which in its very unreality keeps alive the best desires of men (women) amidst a bad reality" (Marcuse, 1968, p. 108). It contains, as Marcuse writes, with customary poetic underlining, "not only quiescence about what is, but also remembrance of what could be...it has planted real longing alongside poor consolation and false consecration in the soil of bourgeois life" (Marcuse, 1968, pp. 98-99). This traditional European culture, even during the bourgeois epoch, gives a vision of the possible from which social reality may be critically grasped and surpassed. "The task to be accomplished," Horkeimer & Adorno wrote as late as 1944, "is not the conservation of the past, but the redemption of the hopes of the past" (Horkheimer & Adorno, 1972, p. xv).

The pedagogic question of how such a vision can be communicated in the midst of social relations which continually disconfirm it, and what the social and educational conditions are which turn affirmative culture into a critical force, was resolved for the Frankfurt School by the events of history. With the spread of the commodity-form as the organizing principle of social life, and the development of a one-dimensional institutional structure that flattens social contradictions and absorbs all opposition, the social means for the realization of the ideals of affirmation culture recedes from historical view (Marcuse, 1966). Not only does the social structure prevent realization, but the ideals themselves, the cultural traditions that provide a vision for social change, disappear. The traditional cultural basis for hope, opposition, and change is itself destroyed. There is no traditional culture to progressively appropriate, as Gramsci and Trotsky thought possible earlier in the century. Even further, the very dispositions and capacities that are necessary to appropriate such a clutter, not to speak of realizing it socially, are receding from reach. We enter a period of barbarism, which is expressed in the Soviet empire as totalitarianism, and in the West, in the one-dimensional, commodity society.

It is not simply that truth is no longer an end in itself, or that objective reason, the shaping of social relations according to valued ends, such as justice, is replaced by subjective, instrumental, calculative, and adjustment-oriented reason. Rather, it is that thinking, thought itself, as the conceptual moment of distance from what is, the cognitive means to go beyond the opacity of "fact," to its historical production and future transcendence—this thinking is so much transformed into adjustive, instrumental calculation that there is no time or inclination for distance from the immediate field that is necessary to create concepts (Horkheimer, 1947). Thought that is socially rooted in momentary conforming adaptation can apprehend, classify and calculate. But it loses the capacity for synthetic construction and the imagination of what is not fact. Thinking splits into cliché on the one hand, and an imitation of the machine on the other (Horkheimer, 1947, p. 56; 1972, p. 25).

> Thinking in itself tends to be replaced by stereotypical ideas. Thinking objectifies itself to become an automatic, self-activating process; an impersonation of the machine that it produces itself so that ultimately the machine can replace it.

Thinking is instrumentalized by its absorption into, and mimesis of, the social necessities of commodity production. Critical reflection, contemplation, indeed, even the desire for meaning, which rest on an aspiration for the contextualizing of fact and experience in relation to some totality, are sacrificed. They give way in the force of surplus mastery, the destructive domination of nature, an internalization of corporate efficiency logic as thought, and the use of subjective reason to maximize social "fitting-in." Spontaneity, joy, sensuality, the very instinctual, bodily bases of cultural hopes, our human claim to happiness, and the moving force for social transformation, are destroyed by the rules of abstractness and extrinsicalty, which typify the dominant mode of social relations: "No object has an inherent value; it is valuable only to the extent that it can be exchanged" (Horkheimer & Adorno, 1972, p. 158). Neither culture nor language can provide the tools for transcending a society where the very goal of individuation itself, "has at last been replaced by the effort to imitate" and where "the most mortal of sins is to be an outsider" (Horkheimer & Adorno, 1972, pp. 150, 156).

The dialectic of affirmative culture collapses with the rise of the culture industry. Culture "amalgamates with advertising." Discourse is "sales talk." Words are "trademarks." Language is used not for elaboration, but as an "incantation." The possibility of a thinking, feeling, imagining, creative subject is reduced to "shining white teeth and freedom from body odor and emotions." Culture is brought down to earth as an ancillary of commodity capital. The possibility of final transcendence is transformed into a constant series of cultural initiation rites, by which the individual attests loyalty to the system. In so doing, the self is abolished. Culture is supplanted by the commercial propaganda of advertising. In this view the prevailing cultural dynamic is not class-cultural reproduction, but cultural destruction, and the translation of all the potentially critical elements of traditional cultures—the cultural "means of resistance"—into the affirmative language of the commodity.

The stand to be taken against such a world is no longer the appropriation of a traditional culture and the struggle to enact its hopes as social reality. Instead, individuality can be preserved by negation, by a refusal to participate. The best that can be hoped for culturally is to preserve the counterimage inherited from the past. The effort to develop motivation by which to effect social change as a redemption of cultural promises gives way to a need only to conserve the hopes of high culture against the corrosiveness of mass culture. The role of the intellectual is reduced to archivist, preserving cultural vision as a record for some future time after the contemporary barbarism has passed. The sad irony of the Frankfurt School is that the critical theorists who sought to develop the dialectical, contradictory core of historical-materialism concluded that history has flattened the contradictory dynamic of change. The social analysts who saw beyond the economist tendency of European Marxism to acknowledge the creative role of culture and the psychological bases of social change ended by documenting the incorporation of the psycho-cultural dimension as another moment of domination. "The realm of freedom," Horkheimer (1978, p. 221) concludes, "is the backwoods. Those who remain loyal to theory are a remnant."

CRITICAL THEORY AND THE PRESENT CONJUNCTURE

Despite the brilliant insights of the Frankfurt School, their vision of contemporary society has, fortunately, not come to pass. The contradictory character of social organization has not given way to complete integration and incorporation by a barbaric social order. Cultural meaning is not simply a vehicle of social domination. There are increasing attempts to create new cultural meaning rather than passively absorb the dominant culture. The sources of these attempts, and the possibility for social change, are based in a society that requires contradictory social patterns for its maintenance. The sources of social change are in a social condition which in the asymmetrical and unsynchronized character of this society unintentionally brings forward and activates the human capacity for interpretive, symbolic, cultural activity as a necessity in the production of individual identity and social legitimation. The "need for meaning" is neither the historical constant suggested by Weber (1946, p. 281), nor is it historically extinguished by commodity logic as Horkeimer & Adorno (1972) believed. Rather, such a need changes, historically, according to the inherent contradictions and disjunctions of the social formation. To fulfill the promise of a critical theory, we need an analysis of current social contradictions.

I can, of course, only sketch the nature of current social contradictions in this paper. In critical theory, the fundamental contradictory social tendency is between the social and the private. The conditions of modern production are social and cooperate, yet the appropriation of the result of production remains private. This contradiction, which is daily enacted in the structurally antagonistic relation between labor and capital, is, of course, the most coercively defended and culturally well-obscured social contradiction of capitalism. One path toward its popular acknowledgement and toward an understanding that a social arrangement like this inhibits social progress and deforms individual development, is in first naming less mystified social contradictions. There are some contradictory tendencies that are readily recognized by those who enact them because they are closer to the surfaces of everyday knowledge, commonsense, and conscious interest. Some contradictions are experienced as well as enacted.

These are "psychological problems," and problems which resonate to the dominant ideals of the culture. One can treat these problems—more salient to the individual—first, by communicating the specific connections between personal stress, conflict, ambivalence, and socially patterned contradictions. The ultimate aim of such understanding is to demonstrate that the full realization of culturally patterned, personally held, and viscerally experienced ideals cannot occur without restructuring the patterns of social organization, which produce ideals and desires, and simultaneously frustrate their realization.

Take for example, the ideal of individuality and self-realization. The competitive individualistic grid placed upon the organization of social production, the dominant popular belief in a utilitarian imagery of a market of free individual exchange, and the ideal of self-gratification in the character of the consumer, are all sociocultural patterns that reinforce the ideal of individual self-realization. Despite the enormous cultural effort to avoid under-consumption through the social production of consumers, the "sales effort"

(Baran & Sweezy, 1966, p. 112) of advertising, and also schooling (Larkin, 1979), the social site for primary identity, for individual self-realization, remains work (Moberg, 1980). For the "new working class" this is expressed in the model of the career. But important segments of this new class of professionals, like the older working class, now face an increasingly uncertain market for employment, and a heightened rationalization of work practices. The continuing need for capital accumulation through exploitation, the current "fiscal crisis of the state" (O'Connor, 1973), and the stagflation of the "second slump" (Mandel, 1978), seriously affects this new, professional, relatively unorganized group.

The social service sector, which once provided opportunities for this rising class-segment, is a place where ideals of individual self-realization are especially task relevant and culturally acceptable. Yet, it is precisely in the social service scene where rationalizing, hierarchizing, standardizing, and routinizing practices, along with budget cuts attendant upon the fiscal crisis, are particularly felt (O'Connor, 1973; Castells, 1980, p. 162). Thus the anchoring of a cultural ideal of self-realization in work is contravened by the expression of economic contradictions as imbalances in labor force supply-demand rations (job insecurity) and a more rationalized and constrictive organization of the workplace.

Individual responses to these developments include reevaluating the ideal, and searching for extra-work gratifications, as adaptations to the identity problems generated by a changing and contradictory social organization of work. The magnitude of these problems, and the depth of the psychological malaise that results, leads also to institutionally sponsored efforts to solve them. Such, for example, is now the case with teachers. The National Education Association reports that in 1980, 41% of teachers say that they would not enter their professions again, compared to 19% just four years earlier. The NEA further reports that it has instituted stress workshops for teachers, and that it "can't keep up with the applicant demand" (*The Wall Street Journal*, October 14, 1980; p. 1). The structural blockage to a realization of a cultural ideal is experienced as psychological stress. The institutional response, in this culture, is the therapeutic solution.

But it no longer suffices. Increasingly, employers and the scientific consultants, driven by the goal of increased social productivity for private profit, begin to locate the problem of productivity in individual dissatisfaction with a de-skilling (Braverman, 1974) and alienation in the organization of work (Shepard, 1977). Elements of social restructuring, such as job-enrichment, flex-time, and even some workplace democracy, are now offered as goals to productivity and profit. Indeed, freedom in work does improve individual satisfaction and productivity (Moberg, 1980); Castells (1980, p. 58) describes the contradiction between the social conditions of innovation and the hierarchically social organization of production. He notes (p. 57):

In other words, the process of technological innovation can only be effective under conditions of production that evade capitalist logic.... It implies, primarily, that there must be a great deal of initiative in the process of production, which basically contradicts the model of authority in the organization of a capitalist firm.

The social situation of employees in the social service sector, such as teachers, and the demands of technology, are both relevant to the cultural ideal of self-realization and freedom. The ideals of individualism and the experience of work are familiar. But, the cultural work of developing knowledge that a realization of other ideals may require social restructuring is more difficult.

In the United States, for example, the ideals of community (Slater, 1970) and internationalism are not as deeply internalized as individualism. It is less obvious how the social production of community can be separated from current tendencies toward imperialism and corporatism, with which it is structurally linked—separated, to then be developed as a distinct social alternative. The present national and international industrial agglomeration heightens economic, social, and informational interdependence. It produces the social conditions that might serve as the occasion for awareness of a human community. But, this awareness currently remains partialized and fragmented according to private interest and socially outmoded parochialisms.

The unintended creation of the material basis of an international human community by the economic-military imperialism of the Eastern and Western blocs is paralleled by less global contradictory tendencies that press forward the possibility of community. For example, a major psychological problem is the experience of loneliness and isolation (Lowenthal et al., 1975). At the same time, the social relations of interdependence and cooperation that already exist are structured in a divisive and disconnecting way. The corporate and privatized structuring leaves both the social bases of community and their potential to alleviate the experienced problem of loneliness and isolation undeveloped. Pervasive individualistic ideologies block recognition of the relation between potential social relations that can meet the vaunted need for intimacy and cultural taboos against "collectivism." Such taboos, which are an intentional part of the sales effort, suppress the social restructuring that could realize the possibilities of community already contained within individualizing corporatism.

One further brief example of contained contradictions derives from Marcuse's analysis of the appropriation of Eros through repressive desublimination, its transformation into an attribute of commercial products, and the simultaneous rationalization of play (Goodman, 1979) as "fun" (Henry, 1963) and "leisure" (Aronowitz, 1973). This systematic appropriation suppresses the possibility for the actualization of Eros and play within social relations. The expression of these possibilities is currently increasingly removed from the range of a broad-scale realization in everyday life. This occurs not only by socially patterned compartmentalization and fragmenting surplus specialization, but also by the translation of a cultural ideal into an assimilable, but opposite form. Freedom becomes consumption.

In each of these examples—self-realization, community, and play—mass personal stress occurs because the social arrangements that might alleviate it, and for which a social basis already exists, remain undeveloped in the face of the opposing conventional, dominant, and culturally buttressed, social tendencies. Self-realization is falsely inhibited in the name of efficiency, community in the name of national, corporate, and tribal interest, and play in the name of "leisure-as-consumption."

CULTURAL MOBILIZATION AND EDUCATION

Knowledge of alternative social and cultural possibilities within the present social order is a necessary condition of social change. An additional requisite for effective change is to make the cognitive connections between individual problems, their social sources, and the existence of social resources that can lead to their solution. But social change does not occur merely by articulating contradictory social tendencies, or even by showing that alternatives are possible that can meliorate individually experienced problems. Social change also requires a reorientation of personal commitments, collective changes in ways of being and seeing. I believe that to accomplish this also requires a process of cultural mobilization.

Social formations are reproduced and maintained because people are attached to their routines as elements of their self-constitution and identity. Even in the face of cognitive counterevidence, they continue to try to solve problems in customary ways. Unconscious commitments, as well as rational cognitions, connect the self to the social. Organized, mass, social changes occur when existing social arrangements are experienced as hopelessly unsatisfying and unrewarding to such an extent that people withdraw their emotional, as well as their cognitive, commitments from the social relations in which they ordinarily constitute themselves (Wallace, 1956). Such a change is also painful, because it includes a self-denial, a renunciation of social identity to pursue untried and unfamiliar solutions.

This is not the kind of change usually described as evolutionary, adaptive change, or as the cumulation of small-scale changes, or as imminent societal development (Moore, 1963; Applebaum, 1970). Rather this type of change has more in common with collective action and social movements (Wallace, 1956, 1961; Smelser, 1963).

There are several reasons for using collective behavior as a model to describe change. If we are indeed living in a period of socioeconomic and cultural crisis, then the type of social changes that are likely to occur have more in common with historical crisis behaviors than with ordinary social change processes. More importantly, collective movements are a possible model for a radical pedagogy. Rather than document the kinds of social and cultural reproduction that currently occurs in schooling, or argue, in the tradition of liberal educational faith, that the task of schools is to provide equality of opportunity, I am suggesting that schools can provide a basis for cultural change.

My intention is to ask what education would be like if collective movements for social change, which usually originate and make claims outside of established cultural institutions, were instead to be developed within existing institutions. What would education be like if the dynamics of cultural revitalization movements, which Wallace (1956, p. 25) describes as "deliberate, organized, conscious efforts by members of a society to construct a more satisfying culture," became the model for pedagogic activity? I recognize, of course, the existing structure of interests and controls that makes such a transformation of education quite difficult. But I also recognize the possibility and need to construct at least the preconditions for social change within existing social institutions.

A collective change movement requires, first, a personal experience and a social sharing of dissatisfactions and unmet needs. Our cultural ideal of self-realization, which places a premium on need gratification and eschews suffering as a moral virtue, makes it easy to find such dissatisfaction. Secondly, knowledge of alternatives and belief that these alternatives can be brought into being decreases willingness to accept frustrating conditions as inevitable. The development of an understanding of social contradictions as alternatives is then a resource in the sequence of producing change. Thirdly, there is a long initial period of "cultural distortion" (Wallace, 1956, p. 269). Early attempts to find new solutions are often very limited, regressive or self-destructive. Current patterns of social "deviance" would suggest that we are now in such a period of partial, personal, and regressive solutions to the collective problems posed by the ascendance of the less progressive aspects of contradictory social tendencies. Fourthly, the early false starts toward cultural mobilization are usually followed by some reformulation of existing social resources as a new cultural vision. Traditionally, this vision begins with the religious inspiration of the person who then becomes the leader of a movement. If, however, cultural norms inhibit traditional authoritarian individual leadership, and if social conditions produce a mass of individual selves with open boundaries, then it is possible for new cultural visions to be developed simultaneously as a collective vision (Wexler, 1981a). If the movement succeeds, social relations are indeed reorganized to meet individual needs more effectively and to generate continuing commitment to the new ideals and social arrangements. The success of the movement is followed, according to Weber (1946, p. 245), by institutionalization, and the "routinization of charisma" into either a traditional or rational-legal basis of authority.

The point of this sketch is that the development of change from a base of contradictory social tendencies is not automatic or inevitable. The individual dissatisfaction produced in the current crisis, for example, is only an initial condition for the realization of existing alternative social possibilities.

I am suggesting that social transformation requires a process of cultural mobilization. In this process, cognitive understanding is combined with experienced individual frustration, and an emotional and imaginative commitment to a sociocultural alternative. Cultural revitalization movements, which are ordinarily religious movements led by a single individual, are an example of a process of basic cultural reformulation and the accomplishment of new commitments. These movements provide an ideal-typical model for cultural change. The question is whether they can also serve as a model for education as cultural change.

T O W A R D   A   P E D A G O G Y
O F   M O B I L I Z A T I O N

It seems far-fetched or romantic to suggest that mass collective change movements could indicate an alternative pedagogy. We are accustomed to thinking of public education as socially neutral and social movements as intensely partisan. But, what the ideology-critique of educational assumptions (Curti, 1935; Wexler, 1976) and the cultural reproduction approach to education (Apple, 1979) have accomplished is to make it more difficult to believe that schooling is now, or ever has been, socially disinterested and culturally neutral. The issue is whose cultural vision is being implemented, and whether it is possible to replace an institutionalized dominant vision with an alternative, through an **interinstitutional** process of reorganization.

Unlike the traditional model of individually led change movements described by Weber (1946), Wallace (1961), and Smelser (1963), Buber sees the creation of the cultural change that occurs in education as a collective, cultural act (Buber, 1963, p. 151):

> Neither the will nor the imagination of an individual, even of a genius, produces these patterns. They express the deepest life of an entire epoch, and its character and desires at the same time.

In the description close to the view that education is an aspect of a cultural movement, Buber (1963, p. 154) indicates that the content of education changes with the development of the collective movement.

> National education is true creative education as long as it strives toward a certain ideal pattern of a human being, the pattern of the liberator. But when

liberation has been effected, the ideal pattern fades and national education ceased to be true creative education. So if education wishes to remain faithful to its task, and not decay into nationalistic convention, it must set itself a new and greater purpose. The educators cannot think up this purpose. They can, however, derive it from the super-national norm of their own national movement, **a norm which must now be developed and expressed particularly in education (emphasis added).**

Our contemporary "supra-national norm" can, I think, be found among those elements of traditional and bourgeois cultures that critical theorists aimed to appropriate by and for a rising class, in part, by means of education. The concrete cultural content of this "supra-national norm" is found in the redemptive hopes of bourgeois culture, and in the critical skills necessary for their social realization. The theorists of the Frankfurt School believed that these hopes and cultural skills were being driven from the stage of history by the ascendance of the commodity society. On the contrary, I think that cultural desires and social patterns, like self-realization, community, and play, exist now as the suppressed aspects of contradictory social tendencies. If, in the present historical conjuncture, the possibility of realization is in the appropriative, collective, democratic transformation of existing cultural institutions, **from the center,** then mass education can become creative cultural activity.

For education to function as a medium of cultural mobilization, it would have to include elaboration of cultural goals and provision of skills necessary for their realization. If schools were to become a site of cultural mobilization, then they would include, as the foundation of curriculum, stages of collective cultural movements. The path of education would then be modeled on the path of collective social action.

First, this would mean that a primary pedagogical task is the production of self-awareness (Pinar, 1975). Personal commitment to a social alternative that experienced deprivation makes possible does not become an effective individual motive as long as awareness of deprivation is blocked by repression, ignorance, and sublimated self-expression. The uncovering of socially enforced individual repression by pedagogic intervention is the beginning of a process of need articulation necessary for cultural mobilization. The articulation of individual needs is then redirected, by a cognitive social pedagogy, to collective historical experience and to the relevance of broad-scale social rearrangements.

Development of this social understanding entails a danger of jettisoning the personally concrete for the conceptually abstract (Pinar, 1980). Abstract assertions of critical terminology like class, contradiction, or totality as curriculum concepts do not by themselves produce cultural mobilization directed toward social liberation. Education for social understanding means to develop the use capacity to process information through the filter of these organizing concepts (Wexler, 1981b). The development of critical social concepts and their transformation into aspects of identity and self-constitution requires communication in a language of social explanation. The development of a language of social understanding means more than the construction of a conceptual social grid. It also facilitates the acquisition of empirical, concrete knowledge. Commitment to ideals of self-realization, community, and play, and to the language of social attribution and understanding, which is a means toward their realization, is incompatible with social ignorance. Communication of social understanding also implies a repertoire of emotions. Without empathy, social understanding also implies a repertoire of emotions. Without empathy, social understanding remains formalistic and unattached to the particular life of the other that stands behind a vitalizing general social language. Without hope, the capacity to imagine social alternatives is a head-game, lacking force and true self-engagement.

These aspects of cultural mobilization—experience and articulation of needs, cognitive social understanding, and communication—can be seen as the first part of an agenda for curriculum. The crucial creative stage in cultural mobilization is the production of a new cultural vision. "Mazeway reformulation" (Wallace, 1956) requires a cognitive capacity for conceptual switching or information reframing. Where education is a medium of cultural mobilization, gestalt-learning and conscious contextualizing of discrete information within a totalizing, but differentiated frame, would be practiced. Cultural visions have also to be legitimated and translated into more familiar and engaging terms. The process of legitimating vision implies an education for an awareness of the values of others, not as pure tolerance, or compartmentalized values-clarification, but as an appreciation of social biography. New cultural visions become popularly transformative when they are embodied in instrumentally effective, practicable forms of social organization. Without the learning of social practicality, cultural vision remains aloft in heaven and hidden in private soul, and so functions as a bourgeois affirmative education (Marcuse, 1968).

CONCLUSION

The cultural reproduction view has enabled us to document aspects of cultural domination in education and its place in a broader dynamic of social reproduction. The present social conjuncture highlights the continued existence of social structural contradictions and the incapacity of current arrangements to accomplish a smooth and integrated reproduction of the social formation. These failures have led, in the United States for example, to the rise of fundamentalist social movements—not to cultural reproduction but to cultural revitalization and mobilization. Rather than accept these movements as aberrations, I suggest that they reveal a possible alternative to cultural reproduction, as a practice and as a theory. The movements demonstrate that reproduction is only one type of collective cultural process. To appropriate the historical possibilities that they indicate, collective action can be explored as an alternative to the structuralist view of social dynamics, both generally and as applied to education. Here I have offered only a beginning toward the exploration of that alternative—one in which collective cultural mobilization is moved from the periphery of an exceptional case, to the center, as a model for understanding and affecting processes of social and educational change.

R E F E R E N C E S

Apple, M. W. (1979a). *Ideology and curriculum*. (London: Routledge & Kegan Paul).

Apple, M. W. (1979b). What correspondence theories of the hidden curriculum miss: An essay review of Paul Willis, learning to labor: How working class kids get working class jobs. *Review of Education*, 5, pp. 101-112.

Appelbaum, R. P. (1979). *Theories of social change*. (Chicago: Markham).

Aronowitz, S. (1973). *False promises: The shaping of American working class consciousness*. (New York: McGraw-Hill).

Baron, P., & Sweezy, P. M. (1966). *Monopoly capital : An essay on the American economic and social order*. (New York, Monthly Review).

Bell, D. (1976). *The cultural contradictions of capitalism*. (New York: Basic Books).

Bourdieu, P. (1977). *Reproduction in education, culture and society*. (London and Beverly Hills: Sage).

Bowels, S., & Gintis, H. (1976). *Schooling in capitalist America: Educational reform and the contraditions of economic life*. (New York: Basic Books).

Braverman, H. (1974). *Labor and monopoly capital: The degradation of work in the twentieth century*. (New York: Monthly Review).

Brown, R. (Ed.) (1973). *Knowledge, education and cultural change: Papers in the sociology of education*. (London: Tavistock).

Buber, M. (1963). On national education, in *Israel and The World: Essays In A Time of Crisis*, pp. 149-163. (New York: Schocken Books).

Castells, M. (1980). *The economic crisis and American society*. (Princeton, N.J.: Princeton University Press).

Curti, M. (1935). *The social ideas of American education*. (Totowa, N.J.: Littlefield Adams & Co.).

Dreier, P. (1980). Socialism and cynicism: An essay on politics, scholarship and teaching. *Socialist Review*, 53, pp. 105-131.

Entwistle, H. (1979). *Antonio Gramsci: Conservative schooling for radical politics*. (London: Routledge & Kegan Paul).

Giroux, H. A. (1980). Review of Harold Entwistle's Antonio Gramsci: Conservative schooling for radical politics. *British Journal of Sociology of Education*, 1, pp. 307-315.

Goodman, G. (1979). *Choosing sides: Playground and street life on the lower east side.* (New York: Schocken Books).

Gouldner, A. W. (1979). *The future of intellectuals and the rise of the new class.* (New York: Seabury Press).

Gramsci, A. (1970). *Selections from the prison notebooks.* (New York: International Publishers).

Habermas, J. (1973). *Legitimation Crisis.* (Boston: Beacon Press).

Henry, J. (1963). *Culture against man.* (New York: Vintage Books).

Horkheimer, M. (1947). *Eclipse of Reason.* (New York: Oxford University Press).

Horkheimer, M. (1972). *Critical theory.* (New York: Herder & Herder).

Horkheimer, M. (1978). *Dawn and decline: Notes 1926-1931 and 1950-1969.* (New York: Seabury Press).

Horkheimer, M., & Adorno, T. W. (1972). *Dialectic of enlightenment.* (New York: Herder & Herder).

Kay, E. (1974). Middle Management, in *Work and The Quality of Life: Resource Papers For Work In America*, edited by J. O'Toole, pp. 106-129.

Larkin, R. W. (1979) *Suburban youth in cultural crisis.* (New York: Oxford University Press).

Lowenthal, M. F., Thurber, M., Chiriboga, D. et al. (1975). *Four Stages of Life.* (San Francisco: Jossey-Bass).

Lukacs, G. (1971). *History and class consciousness: Studies in Marxist dialects.* (MIT Press).

Mandel, E. (1978). *The second slump: A Marxist analysis of recession in the seventies.* (London: New Left Books).

Marcuse, H. (1966). *One-dimensional man: Studies in the sociology of advanced industrial society.* (Boston: Beacon Press).

Marx, K. (1978). The Eighteenth Brumaire of Louis Bonaparte, in *The Marx-Engels Reader*, edited by R.C. Tucher, pp. 586-594 (New York: W. W. Norton).

Merton, R. K. (1957). Social Structure and Anomie, in *Social Theory and Social Structure*, pp. 131-160 (Glencoe, IL: Free Press).

Moberg, D. (1980). Work and American culture: The ideal of self-determination and the prospects for socialism. *Socialist Review*, 19, 19-56.

Moore, W. E. (1963). *Social change.* (Englewood Cliffs, N.J.: Prentice-Hall).

O'Connor, J. (1973). *The fiscal crisis of the state.* (New York: St. Martin's Press).

Pinar, W. F. (1975). *Curriculum theorizing: The reconceptualists*. (Berkeley, CA: McCutchan).

Pinar, W. F. (1980). The abstract and the concrete in curriculum theorizing, in *Introduction To Curriculum*. edited by Giroux, H., Penn, A., & Pinar, W. F. (Berkeley, CA: McCutchan).

Plato. (1947). The Republic, in *Greek and Roman Classics In Translation*. edited by Murphy, C. T., Guinagh, K. & Oates, W. J. pp. 467-564.

Shepard, J. M. (1977). Technology, alienation and job satisfaction." *Annual Review of Sociology*, 3, pp. 1-21.

Slater, P. (1970). *Pursuuit of loneliness*. (Boston, MA: Beacon Press).

Smelser, N. J. (1963). *Theory of Collective Behavior*. (New York: Free Press).

Trotsky, L. (1975). *Literature and revolution*. (Ann Arbor, MI: University of Michigan Press).

Wallace, A. F.C. (1956). Acculturation: Revitalization movements. *American Anthropologist*," 58, pp. 269-281.

Wallace, A. F.C. (1961). *Culture and Personality*. (New York: Random House).

Weber, M. (1946). The social psychology of the world religions, in *From Max Weber: Essays In Sociology*, edited by Gerth, H. H. & Mills, C. W. pp. 267-301 (New York: Oxford University Press).

Weber, M. (1963). *The sociology of religion*. (Boston, MA: Beacon Press).

Welter, R. (1962). *Popular education and democratic thought In America*. (New York: Columbia University Press).

Wexler, P. (1976). *The sociology of education: Beyond equality*. (Indianapolis, IN: Bobbs-Merrill).

Wexler, P. (1979). Educational change and social contradiction: An example. *Comparative Education Review*, 23, pp. 240-255.

Wexler, P. (1981a). Commodification, Self and Social Psychology. *Social Text*. (in press).

Wexler, P. (1981b). Structure, text and subject: A critical sociology of school knowledge, in *Cultural and Economic Reproduction In Education*, edited by M.W. Apple. (London: Routledge & Kegan Paul).

Willis, P. (1977). *Learning to labour: How working class kids get working class jobs*. (Westmead: Saxon House).

Young, M. F.D. (Ed.) (1971). *Knowledge and control: New directions for the sociology of education*. (London: Collier Macmillan).

Reprinted with permission from *British Journal of Sociology of Education*, Vol. 2, No. 3, 1981.

CHAPTER ELEVEN

The Autobiographical Method in Japanese Education

The Writing Project and Its Application to Social Studies

Shigeru Asanuma
1986

This paper introduces a writing project that represents a very important historical experience for contemporary educators in Japan. It is called the "*seikatsu tsuzurikata*," which means writing down one's life experiences (abbreviated as "*tsuzurikata*" in this paper), and was born out of political oppression in Japan before World War II. This writing project shares basic components similar to those of the "autobiographical method" that Pinar (1975) first conceived of and applied to educational practices in the United States. The autobiographical method was initially designed to investigate an individual's personal experiences; its implication is to develop teaching practice on the basis of such experiences. What is needed now is an inquiry into the major goals and procedures by which the individual classroom teacher can embody the proposed ideal in the classroom, as there are not yet many reports about the practical application of the autobiographical method.

Grumet's description (1978) of her experience teaching a college course using the autobiographical method is a rare case study of this type of teaching.

> Students were encouraged to write every day, but to hand in only one journal a week, so that they might develop skills of critical reflection without thinking of those skills as limited to their dialogue with me (Grumet, 1978a; 303)

This quotation illustrates the purpose and a concrete procedure for using the autobiographical method in practical teaching. Grumet concludes her case study as follows.

> In my initial meeting with the theory of estrangement, it was traveling under
> another name, "distancing." This concept was associated with the
> phenomenological practices of bracketing the natural attitude, of suspending a
> habitual, common sense interpretation of experience in order to achieve a
> scrutiny of phenomena that would admit information generally excluded by our
> presuppositions. (Ibid., 308)

The "distancing" or "bracketing" of the natural attitude means that the
student will commence his/her reflecting on everyday life activities. The
reflection from a distant perspective is to encourage the student to obtain insight
into the objective state of his/her ego. A mere statement of goals of the
autobiographical teaching method, however, is not enough to convince
educators of its applicability in practice. We need more empirical examples in
order to refine the theoretical scheme of the autobiographical method applicable
to schooling at elementary and secondary school levels.

Introducing the Japanese autobiographical method, which is not well known
in the United States and which is to some degree taken for granted in current
school practice in Japan, is expected to give impetus to the advancement of the
autobiographical method. In this paper, I discuss the possible use and advantages
of the autobiographical method in classroom instruction.

WHAT IS THE *TSUZURIKATA*?[1]

The *tsuzurikata* is a student's essay on his/her everyday life experiences. The
collection of students' essays is circulated among students in the classroom.
Students are encouraged to write freely and frankly about their experiences. It is
a radical movement to reform not only language education but also the social
consciousness of the Japanese. The Confucian ethos has forced the Japanese
masses to read and write in a certain traditional framework rather than to
express their own experiences freely and creatively. The *tsuzurikata* is one of the
possible approaches to "currere," the prescription of which is stated by Grumet as
follows.

> It is the ambition of *currere* to provide students with the tools of critical
> reflection that they will need to transform their situations, whatever they may
> be, to take the objectivity that they are given and to create yet another
> objectivity from it. In the process of *currere, the* situation becomes *my* situation.
> *The* criticism that liberates must be *my* negation that arises out of *my*
> experience. Ultimately, only I am responsible for what I do with what I am
> given. (Ibid., 296)

To write about one's own everyday life experiences is to write "about" one's
self through reflection. Reflecting on and externalizing the self makes the
individual objectify his/her past experiences as "lived experiences." The
individual eventually attains "self-consciousness" through the reflective action.

The *tsuzurikata* provides the student with opportunities to express him/herself to the world. It spurs dialectical interaction among students and teachers. The world is constituted in the process of interaction by each student's unconscious consideration of others within the internal sensual process.

The *tsuzurikata* is used to develop social scientific perspectives by exposing students to social reality, which has not been discovered as a thematic and problematic topic in their lives. The *tsuzurikata* teacher provokes students to "objectively" observe the reality surrounding them in terms of their own senses without any intervention of anyone else's authority. The *tsuzurikata* teacher notifies students that they are themselves the sources of authority in their judgments. Students understand that they are situated in the center of various inquiries and that the world is constituted through assumptions tested by their own natural perception.

The *tsuzurikata* is an interdisciplinary project for approaching the reality of life. It provides a situation in which individual *intentionality* comes out. It deals with a real world beyond the dimension of cognitive knowledge, which is divided into various subjects. An individual's intention constitutes the real world. Instead of analyzing the world in segments of knowledge, students learn to comprehend reality in its totality with love, hatred, anger, and curiosity.

Merely describing the observed objects and experienced events, however, does not necessarily lead to critical thinking about objective reality. The role of critical thinking should not be confined to paperwork but ought to be accompanied with the real action of reflecting upon one's own naïve attitude, since the individual cannot be aware of his/her potential to dehumanize others without detaching him/herself from such an attitude. As Freire (1972) suggests, subjective reality ought to be mediated by objective reality for the dialectical development of critical thinking. The important thing is that each subject be aware of his/her potential to dehumanize others, as the oppressed hold the potential to become oppressors unless they are aware of the objective perspective. The potential to become oppressors is determined not only by the social structure but also by the oppressed's own choice. Both the oppressors and the oppressed tend to be unaware that their actions might actually be involved in the process of dehumanization. Freire argues:

> To present this radical demand for the objective transformation of reality, to combat subjectivist immobility which would divert the recognition of oppression into patient waiting for oppression to disappear by itself, is not to dismiss the role of subjectivity in the struggle to change structures. On the contrary, one cannot conceive of objectivity without subjectivity. Neither can exist without the other, nor can they be dichotomized. The separation of objectivity from subjectivity, the denial of the latter when analyzing reality or acting upon it, is objectivism. On the other hand, the denial of objectivity in analysis or action, resulting in a subjectivism which leads to solipsistic positions, denies action itself by denying objective reality. Neither objectivism nor

subjectivism, nor yet psychologism is propounded here, but rather subjectivity
and objectivity in constant dialectical relationship (Freire, 1972: 27)

The hidden structure of force, whereby the oppressors as well as the
oppressed dehumanize others, has to be uncovered and shown to the oppressed
as well as the oppressors.

How can we establish an "authentic praxis," as Freire suggested, for
liberation from the individual potential to be an oppressor? Freire (1970)
addressed the concept of "codification" that "mediates between the concrete and
theoretical contexts of reality" (p. 214), or that "transforms what was a way of
life in the real context into 'objectum' in the theoretical context" (p. 215). The
tsuzurikata is one authentic method to accomplish this goal of codification.

WHY IS IT NEEDED?

What social and historical context predisposed the Japanese to create the
tsuzurikata? There were two major reasons for its demand and development
before the war.

First of all, the development of urbanization expanded the demand for an
aesthetically refined educational culture that contradicted the authoritarian
strict teaching. The rigidly formalized teaching method, which was based on the
odd combination of the Confucian traction and the Herbartian method, forced
students to acquire basic skills, knowledge, and habits. The middle class in
urban areas gradually recognized the unsatisfactory circumstances of schooling
for the development of humanistic values. The middle class, which had more
access to higher education, felt the need for more aesthetically refined culture
because their desire was not fulfilled by the technical knowledge that was
routinely transmitted in school. They were driven to seek sophisticated modern
culture. The original form of the *tsuzurikata* was born to satisfy this cultural
need, which grew mainly in urban areas. This type of *tsuzurikata* emerged as one
of the manners of restoring artistic expression.

The need of the middle class for cultural refinement was criticized by the
Marxist intelligentsia as a "bourgeois" disposition because the desire of the urban
middle class did not originate form the needs of life. On the contrary, proletarian
literature at that time was regarded as *avant-garde*. Its assumption was that the
realism that inspires profound human nature springs from the overwhelming life
situation of laborers rather than from fictions such as romantic love, which tend
to be attached to the interests of the middle class. Therefore, in this argument,
only working class people and the intelligentsia who were aware of the social
conflict within the social structure were supposed by the Marxists to be eligible
to create a new culture based on human needs and interests that were not
mediated by the existing distorted communication. The liberation of an
alienated modern person was to be attained only by initiating a cultural

revolution related to his/her physical conditions. Marxist realism in Japanese literature affected the teachers, and they initiated their voluntary educational movements by modifying the previous educational projects such as the *tsuzurikata*.

The *tsuzurikata* method was developed in rural areas in a different style for other reasons. More than one half of the population in Japan lived in rural areas before the war and most of them suffered by being exploited by the land owners in the tenant farm system. The *tsuzurikata* teacher aimed at awakening social consciousness among students by having them write essays reflecting on their social situation. The prevalence of the *tsuzurikata* in the rural areas over industrial areas exemplifies the special characteristics of Japanese capitalism, which had not developed its industrial capital as much as the advanced European countries. The rural areas, especially the northern part of the Japanese main island, maintained the cultural heritage that had stubbornly remained from the feudal age. The goal of the *tsuzurikata* was to expose rural students to social scientific concepts that challenged the feudalistic customs.

The Great Depression produced political instability both in the cities and in the countryside. In addition, the bad crop of rice at that time damaged the family life of farmers, e.g., they sometimes sold their daughters to light industries as manual laborers. The masses demanded social reform to escape from such despair. However, there was no consensus of values among the people. Ultra-nationalists, socialists, and communists clashed under the domination of a nationalistic ethos. One of the prominent endeavors of social reform was to colonize Manchuria; this desire to expand the nation's land motivated the masses to look outside of the nation rather than to pay attention to the internal problems of the society. On the other hand, Marxist and socialist groups struggled to bring about critical consciousness concerning the traditional and capitalistic society. This reform movement gave the *tsuzurikata* teachers a political orientation in their teaching practice. The *tsuzurikata* was a product of this radical movement.

CHARACTERISTICS OF THE *TSUZURIKATA*

It is difficult to define the *tsuzurikata* in terms of a single concept because of its diversity in actual practice. The following characterization is an attempt to develop an interpretation based on the original assertions of *tsuzurikata* educators.[1]

The first characteristic of the *tsuzurikata* is its emphasis on the naïve observation and description of events and things "as they are." The *tsuzurikata* is based simply upon the perceptions of the senses and personal experiences in everyday life. Eyes are the most important apparatus for an unbiased description of objects and events. Students are advised to observe the live world simply, using their own words, and to include essential elements of their life in the community.

The *tsuzurikata* deeply affects students' social attitudes when school teachers are conscious of the importance of their roles as intelligentsia in the community. The following story is a part of an essay written by Koichi, an eighth grade student in Mr. Muchaku's classroom. Koichi's father died when he was an infant and his mother also had recently died. This essay was named the best student essay by the *tsuzurikata* circle of Japan in 1951.

> My home is poor. I guess the poorest in the village of Yamamoto. As tomorrow is the day of the thirty fifth (a special day for a family that had lost someone in the Buddhist custom), I am reminded of my mother and my miserable family. Tomorrow is also a farewell day to Futao who is the youngest child in my home. Although he is still only in the third grade and such a small boy, he has helped me to do our chores such as carrying wood on his back, without any complaints. He will continue to work even after he is adopted by my uncle.
>
> Tsuneko, my sister, will also be adopted by my uncle's family in Yamagata according to the decision of my relatives. But since she has been suffering from whooping cough, she will be taken there after her recovery.
>
> After she goes, my grandmother and I will remain in my home.

M Y   M O T H E R ' S   D E A T H

> My brother and sister have to live away from me because of my mother's death and the poverty of my home. We have only a house and two terraces on our farm.
>
> My mother was anxious to raise us to be good persons in such an economic condition. Since my mother was not so strong, she had to take care of her own health and also she worried about our situation after her death. However, she might have worked too hard because she felt embarrassed by bothering others, by borrowing money and receiving small aids from the village office. I had been absent from school after getting a permit from Mr. Muchaku to do manual labor. I was not overloaded because I was not a head of the family. My mother might have been beaten by the mental stress of worrying about problems such as "how to make a living," "how to pay taxes," and "how to get rationed rice."
>
> Even when she was almost dying in bed in the clinic, she asked deliriously, "Did you wash the cabbage (to make a kind of pickles)?" among other questions. I did not have any words to comfort her in response to her questions and she reminded me only of my house-keeping duties, even in such a critical condition.
>
> The relatives got together around her bed in the clinic after they were informed of her critical condition. I talked about my experiences of the day before, when the villagers helped me collect brushwood, so she smiled without saying anything. I will never forget her last smile at the moment....
>
> I remember my mother had never smiled from deep within her heart in her whole life. She seldom showed her smile, and even if she smiled, she seemed to

smile in order to hide her sorrow. However, the smile at that moment was different and sticks in my mind. I think that she had never known how to smile deep from her heart....

After my mother was hospitalized, suddenly I became busier. Until my mother was hospitalized, I felt at ease because she was in my home. Although I did not feel confidence in my sister's nursing of my mother, I had to keep working without having a chance to see her....

At last my mother died on November 13th. The funeral was held on the 15th. Mr. Muchaku, Ueno, and Tetsuo, representatives of the village of Sakai, also came to the funeral. The people in the village of Sakai were also there. Denjiro brought a condolence gift. I could not say anything. All that I could do was to bow toward all the people there...My classmates also offered condolence to me. I really thanked my classmates. (Muchaki, 1969: 18-24)

This portion of the student's essay indicates a candid observation of his real life. Self-criticism and empathy toward others are dynamically organized in this frank statement. This essay provokes the reader's sympathy with his sorrowful situation.

The *tsuzurikata* was not originally designed to have students obtain preorganized scientific knowledge but to attain social consciousness of their community life. In contradiction to this original stance of the *tsuzurikata*, Kokubu (1955) contended that by describing their lives, students, like the students of Muchaku's classroom, begin a conceptualization for structurally organized social scientific knowledge. Thus the second characteristic of the *tsuzurikata* is its pursuit of the goals of cognitive development in social sciences. The following excerpt from Koichi's essay could be considered as an illustration of conceptualization of his life.

W H A T   I   A M   T H I N K I N G   N O W

I wrote to Mr. Muchaku this noon as follows:

1. As I will be a ninth grade student next year, I will try to keep studying at school in order to gain the ability to make my living after finishing school it is essential for me to work as a day laborer.
2. After finishing school next year, I would like to repay the debt by getting a job with a regular income.
3. I would like to buy a farm even if I need to borrow money after I finish returning the debt. The farm will enable me to make my living.
4. I would like to save money and make an affluent life for my family
5. In order to do so, I have to be smart enough to live in this society.
6. Anyhow, I would like to be a person like others who can make a living without any aid from others.

> After I wrote to him, I reflected on my proposals stated above. First, I
> doubt I can save money. Second, if I buy another's farm, the other person will
> lose the farm and will be poor like me....
> ...I cannot make a living for my family by myself.
> ...Therefore, it was wrong to say that I can have an affluent life. Our family has
> been poor not because my mother has not worked hard enough but because of
> my dream. I wonder if I can really get out of such a miserable life. (Muchaku,
> 1969: 15-29)

Although his conceptualization is not sufficiently scientific in the ordinary
sense of the word, the *tsuzurikata* teacher assumes that science is always rooted
in practical life. Hence, Kokubu believed that the *tsuzurikata* would not
contradict the assumption of a discipline-centered curriculum, which is
constructed according to predetermined conceptual frameworks. He identified
intuitive observation in everyday life with the intuitive process in scientific
discovery.

Third, the *tsuzurikata* is a means by which the individual can engage in
creative work whenever he/she wants. The physical conditions of a classroom
that usually included more than forty students hindered individualization in
classroom teaching in Japan. However, the *tsuzurikata* has provided a means of
individualization in the conventional classroom environment. Free writing
enables the teacher to individualize his/her instruction but still teach all the
students together. Everybody in the classroom is supposed to pursue individual
goals. This method of individualized teaching has developed in a unique way,
though the course of study in general is so rigid that it has contributed to
standardization and bureaucratization in the Japanese educational system.
Individualization had to be practiced within such a rigid administrative
framework in order to create fruitful meanings for the individual's school life.

Individualization is made possible by the diagnostic use of the *tsuzurikata*. In
other words, the *tsuzurikata* is used for evaluating and clarifying students'
understanding of scientific knowledge as well as for developing critical and
rational thinking. Only a story that is built on the stream of subjective
experience can illuminate the state of the individual consciousness. Parts and
moments in the individual's experience cannot be separated from each other
within the world of subjective consciousness. However, the naïvely perceived
world comes to be detached from the self in the individual mind when the
individual reflects on his/her own consciousness.

The *tsuzurikata* offers students chances for their reflective action. The
tsuzurikata is a mirror through which students exchange their internal processes
(which are written in explicit forms) and participate in the group dynamics. Each
student is aware that the implication of his/her statements in the classroom
journal constitutes his/her own social being. Each one's projected language
circumscribes his/her existence in the world because it encourages reflection on

the self, which has been projected in the form of the social context, including other beings.

The ability to reflect, which is an important educational goal of the *tsuzurikata*, is developed by deeply understanding the objective reality on which the subjective reality is founded. The development of the ability to understand another's subjective reality starts with the understanding of the function of the ego that each holds inside. It is possible to identify the development of the reflective ability in the following excerpt from Koichi's essay.

> Tomorrow is the thirty-fifth day after my mother's death. I will tell that to my mother in the grave. I will examine why we have to suffer from poverty and why we cannot save money even though we work so hard. If I buy someone else's farm, however, I might make the other suffer from a miserable state like my mother. Toshio, a classmate of mine, is even more unlucky than me. We can work together. (Ibid., 32)

Fourth, the *tsuzurikata* has a political orientation. The militaristic and oppressive atmosphere before the war hampered the development of the individual self-consciousness based on the individual "ego-identity." The individual has to return to him/herself before others determine what he/she will be. One of the advantages of Marxism is its humanist point of view that the individual obtains the freedom of spirit as a human being by reconstructing a social structure. The political oppression of Japanese peasants was explicitly related to the basic economic structure in rural areas before the war. It is typically illustrated in General MacArthur's order to liberate peasants from the tenant farm system because of the potential for the communist movement to be rooted in a social class struggle on the basis of the ownership of land. The *tsuzurikata* teacher assumed that the *tsuzurikata* could have a political impact on the naïve mentality of students in rural areas because thinking about reality through reflective activity would lead the individual to speculate about a political ideology that was obstructive to self-consciousness. Students were urged to develop critical thinking by discovering the dominance of political ideology in the natural state of their everyday life experience. The *tsuzurikata* teacher claimed that the subjective reality the individual experiences is a foundation for developing a political assumption. Although students cannot logically reason about their own convictions, they can identify their miserable life situations with political issues. The *tsuzurikata* has the advantage of bringing students' attention to social reality in the community and convincing them that the social reality they experience should be a source of the truthfulness of the world. Thus, the political orientation of the *tsuzurikata* differs from the "currere," which tends to be more psychoanalytically focused than politically focused.

Kokubu classified students' political orientations in their *tsuzurikata* in terms of valued categories, as follows:

1. Facts indicating the new consciousness:
   - I want the United States Army to return home since I heard about the U.S. Army camp in Japan.
   - Koichi said, "We should listen to the talks of Soviet Union and China," and others said "Yes. Yes."
   - My father and mother stopped saying "Go away" any more when the people of the Communist party came to my elder brother.
2. Facts indicating the internal conflict and unstable state:
   - Kenichi said, "It does not matter whether we follow Russia or America if only our life becomes better," and others said, "It might be correct."
   - I cannot object to the rearmament of Japan because someone says, "Japan will be at risk if we do not have a military."
3. Facts indicating the external conflict and unstable state:
   - Whenever my father drinks, he says to my elder brother and to me, "Do not become just a red (Communist)."
   - Uncle Kyuichi said in the barbershop, "Japan exists only because of the existence of an emperor. The people of labor unions will starve because they forget that."
4. Facts indicating unfavorable consciousness recently appearing:
   - Uncle Goro said, "We had better belong to the United States rather than the communist party taking over Japan.
   - Toshie said, "I wish I could have been born in the United States." (Kokubu, 1955: 104-105)

INTERNAL AND EXTERNAL CONTRADICTIONS OF THE *TSUZURIKATA*

The *tsuzurikata* was a distinctive project of Japanese education before the war. Its practice is not comprehended in terms of a single Western notion such as Marxism, realism in literature, or personal development through expressive activity. It is important to note that substantial practice preceded the conceptual formation of the *tsuzurikata*, and the *tsuzurikata* teacher has empirically developed the method of autobiography in the classroom situation. Kokubu's later characterization of the *tsuzurikata* stressed its social scientific orientation, which had not been previously formalized.

It is necessary for the further development of the *tsuzurikata* to clarify the internal contradictions within the project itself. The first problem of the *tsuzurikata* is the difficulty in specifying the particular factor that makes the *tsuzurikata* a successful teaching practice. One could easily stress the technical aspect such as its style or its system. On the other hand, one could point out an intangible aspect of the *tsuzurikata* such as the teacher's spiritual or ethical orientation. The *tsuzurikata* empirically shows that the teacher's ability to educate and humanize the student is not measured only in terms of technical skills and methods. The following part of Koichi's essay illustrates the role played by his classroom teacher.

When Mr. Muchaku and the school principal visited my house, I was going to ask questions of Mr. Muchaku, but instead he asked me many questions all at once that I did not have chance to do so.

Machuka: Do you work carrying leaves of tobacco? How many days do you work? After that what will you do?

Koichi:...Spread leaves.

Muchaku: How many days will you take to finish it?

Koichi: I do not know.

Muchaku: Then show me your diary of last year.

Koichi: I did not record it.

Muchaku: Oh, no. Do record the beginning date and days spent for finishing the work in order to plan for next year's project. Do it from today. What will you do after carrying tobacco?

Koichi: Make a snow fence.

Muchaku: What will you do after that?

Koichi: I may be able to go to school after that.

Muchaku: So you will hardly be able to come to school at all, will you? Tomorrow, you are coming to school to pick up the rationed rice, aren't you? So you should come in the morning. You have not come to school for about one and a half months. Please show up and say thanks to your classmates because they cared about you when your mother died. In addition, make your work schedule....

...Next day, I brought the work schedule to Mr. Muchaku and after he thought about it for a while, he suggested that three other classmates and I go to the nightwatchman's room. He handed the work schedule to Tozaburo, one of the classmates, there and asked him to look at it.

After Tozaburo had contemplated it for some time and raised his head, Mr. Muchaku asked whether they could do anything about my problem. After a short time of silence, Tozaburo began to speak to the other classmates, "Yes, our classroom can handle Koichi's problem and help him so that he can come to school. The others agreed with his proposal. Tears almost came to my eyes. Then he added, "Please do not make it a mess by rushing. We need to carefully plan to assign the number of people for the work." I could not stop the tears from flowing.

Eventually, classmates came not only from my own village but also from other villages to help me and we finished all of the long term work by December 3rd.

...I thanked my nice classmates and the teacher for their kindness in helping me to go to school. I could complete the school assignment of social studies titled "Our school." (Muchaku, 1969: 29-32)

As this essay suggests, the teacher's competence in education cannot be replaced by prescribed instructional systems but has its own value in the process of developing human relationships; the meanings and quality of human experiences are created in such interaction as humanistic dialogue, and the whole existence of the student is cared for by the teacher. Therefore, it is difficult to categorize and specify the abilities needed in the interactive process of teaching and guiding the student in everyday life. One of the important areas to be explored in teaching involves a *charismatic* element, which has been rationally explained neither in terms of behavioral objective approaches nor Marxist aesthetic theory based on materialistic realism. It is an important aspect of the common practice of the Japanese teacher. The aspect of counseling in the *tsuzurikata* has been emphasized, rather than the aspect of its writing, since the end of the war. The teacher's concern for the life beyond the mere writing program is a central reason why the emphasis of the *tsuzurikata* has shifted from a simple writing project to social activities involving the student's life out of school.

The external contradiction of the *tsuzurikata*, on the other hand, is related to the fundamental change in the social reality surrounding the school in Japan. The circumstances in which Koichi lived in his school years show a typical life in a poor area. However, the wave of industrialization and commercialization has now struck rural areas, accompanied by mass media culture. The absolute poverty of the proletariat is no longer defined in terms of a minimum level for survival but in terms of the relative degree of the poverty. The people's drive for possessions is stimulated only by knowledge of others' possessions. The alienation of modern human beings is no more generated from the interest in physical conditions, in the industrialized affluent society. As economically deprived proletariats disappear, practical interest in political slogans has also lost its ground. As the real sense of need has been diluted and distorted through the mass media, the *tsuzurikata* has gradually lost its ability to challenge distorted cultural constructs, such as fad comics for children.

There are, however, two possible alternatives to the traditional *tsuzurikata*, which emphasize the conditions of physical reality. One is to approach the development of social scientific orientation through the practice of writing essays. Kokubu attempted to rationalize the *tsuzurikata* as a starting point for scientific inquiry: writing one's own autobiography is assumed to be a means of developing social scientific concepts and critical thinking among students. In this attempt, the process of developing social scientific concepts is organized in advance, and the role of writing is confined to a very small part of creative activity. However, the gap between the theoretical structure of general sciences and the emphasis on materialistic conditions in the *tsuzurikata* is so wide that the *tsuzurikata* teacher cannot actually reconcile these positions in his/her practice. It is necessary to inquire further, to learn how to remove the discrepancy between these positions.

As has been described, Marxist realism directly points to the physical conditions of life and has been dominant in the traditional *tsuzurikata*. However, it should now be asked whether our experiences are occupied exclusively with materialistic problems. Instead, cultural events and human relations constitute the central interest in our consciousness. "Things" have no value in themselves but can be valued only in the process of the interaction among people. For instance, a gem cannot be valuable unless more than one human expresses an interest in it. The assumptive development of values in the exchange of goods among people determines the value and concept of a thing. This creation of surplus and imagined value is the beginning of alienation from intrinsic values as well as the creation of contrived values in life. Thus, the value of life is constituted on a fictitious foundation. Therefore, as long as traditional Marxists adhere to an absolute scale of economic poverty, they fail to recognize the problem of relative cultural poverty that is related to the inequality of the distribution of educational opportunity. The people's starvation and dehumanization are produced and perpetuated mostly through the media, which determine the relations and modes of interaction among the people.

Another alternative to the traditional *tsuzurikata* is the development of aesthetic elements in writing. The controversy between Marxist realism and bourgeois aesthetics has to be dealt with in terms of the contemporary "post-industrial" society. The main problem of Marxist realism is its reduction of the senses to physical and materialistic needs by ignoring complicated constructs such as intellectual curiosity and aesthetics. The realism that emphasizes serious life problems encourages the student to delineate the overwhelming problems of real life, as in the following example:

M Y   H O M E

My family is worrying about the shortage of rice. Although my father ground rice at home yesterday, he complained that it was at most half of last year's yield. "I am shocked. If this rice is taken as land taxes this year, we will be short of rice for a year," he said. My father and mother said, "We cannot do anything about it," and gazed at the sack of rice with deep disappointment. When I saw them and the poor rice crop, I was almost on the verge of crying because I had asked them to buy rain boots for me. I almost burst into tears, seeing the rice in the storage. (7th grade student, 1931; Kaneko in Obara, 1970: 463-464)

This example demonstrates the critical problem of Marxist realism. It represses the positive emotional aspect of the individual's potential for the emancipation of ego identity, rather than encouraging it. The frank disclosure of the cruel life leads not to the expansion of imagination but rather to its hindrance. Cognitive symbols serve only as guidelines of thought, but the full individual potential is actually developed by aesthetic activities. The potential developed in an aesthetic way can be a solid foundation for creating critical thinking toward the individual's future.

Prior to the *tsuzurikata* of Marxist realism, various efforts had been made to create artistic works in essays, poems, fine arts, and music, within an education movement that occurred during the flourishing cultural reformation of the early 1900s. The ultimate goal of those artistic pursuits is emancipation from an individual's strained reality through imaginative ability. There are, for example, humor and light rhythm in the free style of this example.

> My mother came to the meeting with the teacher today. I felt shy about my friends seeing my mother. I hid her. I was too shy to look at my mother's face, but I do not know why, because I do not feel that way at home. (6th grade student, 1924; Kaneko in Obara, 1970: 462)

This student lightly, innocently, and frankly expressed internal feelings and conflicts in poetic style.

The student does not comprehend reality in terms of physical reality, itself, but merely sees and feels reality in an aesthetic process that is innately developed. If cultural constructs in process are built on limited human senses, the student sees reality in terms of his/her poor apparatus, without recognizing the distortion of reality and the crucial elements needed for creation. It should be noted that the crucial elements of creation do not belong to things, themselves, but spring from the interactive process between the environment and the living human senses that we innately possess and use. Dewey pointed out that the meanings of the world are generated from the context, i.e., "Meaning does not belong to the world and signboard of its own intrinsic right" (1958, p. 83). Meaning is created out of the knowledge of past experiences and one's interaction with others. Artistic expression offers important opportunities for the positive development of imagination. When the *tsuzurikata* is used for sharpening the aesthetic senses, it will contribute to the development of positive creative ability. This heritage of the creative *tsuzurikata* is still partially alive in the writing project in Japanese education, demonstrated as follows.

H U R R Y

> You know, teacher (students get the teacher's attention this way in Japan). Yumi's ears are flushing and her face is hot. Hurry, teacher. (1st grade student; Kurusu, 1966: 11)

K E I K O

"Who is sticking his elbow off the desk?" The teacher's voice was suddenly heard. I was scared and pulled in my arms. "Keiko, you are slouching." Keiko's face turned red. I thought she would cry but she laughed, covering her mouth with her hand. The teacher also smiled. I felt good. (2nd grade student; Kurusu, 1966: 140)

Although these essays do not describe the materialistic state surrounding the students, we can identify sentiment and excitement in their minds that cannot be made explicit by someone else. The dynamics in the mind are the movements in the stream of consciousness. The stream of consciousness is occupied not with routine images but with dialectical dynamics of various factors, especially meanings that are created in the relationship with others.

AFTERMATH OF THE *TSUZURIKATA*

Adults who previously had had no opportunity to write about themselves were stimulated by the *tsuzurikata* to organize themselves into writing circles. Many unknown working class men and women started writing their autobiographies in these circles. It was a purely spontaneous mass movement. They reflected on their lives in their communities and working places.

As has been stated, the meaning of their lives was not given in terms of cognitive social scientific frameworks but created through individual imagination based on their natural perceptions in community life. The *tsuzurikata* developed its own cultural tradition, accommodating needs of provincialism and excluding commercial elements in the urban culture, though elaborate aesthetic elements are often generated from the urban culture. The refinement of the aesthetic sense becomes more important than before because the aesthetic sense is expected to be a sound foundation that resists the anonymously imposed mass media culture of the postindustrial society. The laboring class people could develop critical consciousness because they could find the problem in their communication system according to their natural desire for emancipation. Their critical consciousness should be supported by their aesthetic foundation in the prereflective dimension. The people's desire for regaining the lost "home" might also be reified through distorted communication. The tendency to indiscriminately exclude urban culture as decadent commercialism has dimmed the ability of the masses to appreciate sensually important aesthetic values beyond their physically limited conditions. It is necessary to develop keen sensitivity through aesthetic activities, including all kinds of possibilities so as to discern the intrinsic essences in life from more whimsical elements.

The image of ideal life can also be the construct of our imagination, which tends to be provided in the anonymously constructed cultural circumstances of postindustrial society. However, the refinement of natural senses of children can be practiced in the "micro-cosmos" of the school, rather than exposing them to the uncovered reality of the world that is contaminated with various kinds of infusion. As Dewey suggested, experiences cannot be separated from environmental conditions. The arrangement of environmental conditions in aesthetic forms ought to be a primary concern in creating children's experiences for their future life. However, there still remains a central controversy concerning the source of creativity: Is it psychological or environmental? Thus the exploration of an aesthetic dimension is still a crucial and intangible frontier in education.

N O T E S

1. The characterization of the *tsuzurikata* is based on the following materials.

Kaneko, Magoichi. "Shinko kyoiku to seikatsu tsuzurikata undo" (The development of new education and the spelling life), in Obara, K. (Ed.), *Nihon Shin Kyoiku Hyakunenshi*, vol. 1. Tokyo::Tamagawa Kaigaku Shuppan, 1970

Kokubu, Ichitaro. *Seikatsu Tsuzurikata Noto*, vol. 1. Tokyo: Tamagawa Daigaku Shuppan, 1970

Kkuno, Osamu; Tsurumi, Sunsuke; and Fujita, Shozo. *Seng Nihon No Shiso*. Tokyo: Kodansha, 1976.

Umene, Satoru; Ebihara, Haruyoshi; and Nakano, Akira. *Shiryo Nihon Kyoiku Jissenshi*, vol. 2. Tokyo: Sanseido, 1979.

R E F E R E N C E S

Dewey, J. (1958). *Art as experience*. New York: Capricorn Books.

Freire, P. (1970). The adult literacy process as cultural action for freedom. *Harvard Educational Review*, 40:2: 205-255.

Freire, P. (1972). *Pedagogy of the oppressed*. Penguin Books.

Grumet, M. Songs and situations, in *Qualitative Evaluation*, edited by G. Willis. Berkeley: McCutchan.

Kaneko, M. (1970). "Shinko kyoiku to seikatsu tsuzurikata undo," in *Nihon Shin Kyoiku Hyakunenshi* , edited by K. Obara. vol. 1. Tokyo:Tamagawa Daigaku Shuppankai.

Kokubu, I. (1970). *Seikatsu Tsuzurikata Noto*, I. Tokyo: Tamagawa Daigaku Shuppankai.

Kurusu, Y. (1966). (ed.), *Okasan Anone*, i. Tokyo: Taihei Shuppan.

Muchaku, S. (1969). (ed.), *Yamabiko Gakko*. Tokyo: Kadokawa.

Pinar, W. F. (1975). Currere: Toward reconceptualizataion," in *Curriculum theorizing: The reconceptualists*, edited by W. F. Pinar. Berkeley: McCutchan.

CHAPTER TWELVE

Toward Understanding "Computer Application"

Ted T. Aoki
1987

INTRODUCTION

I have labeled my paper, "Toward Understanding 'Computer Application'." The title appears simple, perhaps, even simple-minded. Ten years ago, even five years ago, I would not have thought such a title worthy of a talk, for then, I would have assumed that everyone understands what computer application is. Today, I am provoked to ask the question "How shall we understand 'computer application'?" I am provoked by what I see as partial blindness of high fashion in the world of curriculum wherein I see bandied about with almost popular abandon expressions linked to the computer without a deep understanding of what they are saying.

Within the faculty of education wherein I dwell, I have experienced in the last quarter century three waves of technological thrusts. We first witnessed the grand entrance of educational media instruments such as the overhead projector, the film projector, the slide projector, and the listening labs. The hold of this instrumental interest led to the hiring of Education Media professors and to the creation of media resource centers, which now exist as mausoleums of curriculum packages and instructional hardware. The most atrocious instrumentalization of a school program within my knowledge during this wave was the "Voix et Image" French as a second language program (the slide tape program) my children underwent in junior high school. The second wave within our faculty was the television thrust. Educational television was looked upon to deliver the message. Today, we see, in our faculty classrooms, platforms mounted in corners, empty holding places for television monitors that no longer sit there, monitors that for some reason could not replace professors. They stand as museum pieces in the wake of unfulfilled hopes of dispensing education via television. Today, the third wave is insistently upon us. The times are such that *Time* Magazine is led to announce without qualm the computer as the man of the year. In our own faculty of education, a computer needs committee proposes the creation of a teaching department in computer education. The Provincial Minister of Education doles out millions of dollars as matching grants to schools buying Apples, Commodores, IBMs, and the like. In schools "computer literacy" curricula have the teachers in a semipanic. And, in the United States, the Commission on Educational Excellence announces "computer science" as a component of the new basics.

Reflecting this ferment the curriculum world picks up on in-language of alphabets—CL (computer literacy), CAI (computer assisted instruction), CE (computer education), FUC (friendly use of computers)—all implying application in schools of the *micro-computer*. Computer application is the focal curriculum third-wave activity.

In all this frenzy, the term "computer application" is assumed to be readily understood and stands naively unproblematic. I choose to question.

But what am I questioning when I ask what computer application essentially is? I wish to press for an understanding by entertaining two questions:

1. How shall I understand computer technology?
2. How shall I understand application?

Hopefully, these questionings will lead me to a deeper understanding of what we mean when we speak of computer application.

UNDERSTANDING THE COMPUTER AS TECHNOLOGY

Acknowledging the microcomputer as a high-tech product, I pose the question: "How shall we understand computer technology?" In dealing with the question, I lean heavily on Heidegger's well-known essay, "The Question Concerning Technology" (Heidegger, 1977).

We are aware of the commonplace answers to the question. The first says that the microcomputer is a high-tech tool. As a tool, it extends man's capabilities in rule-governed behavior. It is a sophisticated manmade means of empowering man to achieve specified ends. Hence, as Heidegger would say, this means-ends embedded interpretation is an instrumental definition of computer technology.

That computer technology is a human activity is another commonplace interpretation, one that is related to the foregoing instrumentalist definition. According to Heidegger:

> To posit ends and procure and utilize the means to them is a human activity. The manufacture and utilization of equipment, tools and machines, the manufactured and used things themselves, and the needs and ends that they serve, all belong to what technology is. (Heidegger, 1977, pp. 4–5)

Computer technology as human activity is what Heidegger refers to as an "anthropological" definition of technology.

Today, so pervasive are the instrumental and anthropological understandings, according to which computer technology is both a means and a human activity, that they can be referred to as the current conception of computer technology. This conception, rooted in man's interest in means, reflects his will to master, to control, and to manipulate.

Pointedly, Heidegger says that this current conception is uncannily correct but not yet true. What does Heidegger mean by this? According to him:

> the correct fixes upon something pertinent in whatever is under consideration. However...this fixing by no means needs to uncover the thing in question in its essence. Only at the point where such an uncovering happens does the true come to pass. For that reason the merely correct is not yet the true. (Heidegger, 1977, p. 6)

Accordingly, the instrumental or anthropological conception of computer technology fails to disclose its essence, although the way to the true is by way of the correct. And since the essence of computer technology is not computer technology as means, we must seek the true by understanding computer technology not merely as means but also as a way of revealing. As a mode of revealing, computer technology will come to presence where revealing and unconcealment can happen, i.e., where truth can happen. If, as Heidegger suggests, the essence of computer technology is not computer technology, we must let go of the seductive hold of the whatness of "computer technology" when we are inclined to ask, "What is computer technology?"

How, then, is this essence revealed? It is revealed as an enframing, the ordering of both man and nature that aims at mastery. This enframing reduces man and beings to a sort of "standing reserve," a stock pile of resources to be at hand and on call for utilitarian ends. Thus, the essence of computer technology reveals the real as "standing reserve," and man, in the midst of it, becomes nothing but the orderer of this "standing reserve." But by so becoming, man tends to be forgetful of his own essence, no longer able to encounter himself authentically. Hence, what endangers man, where revealing as ordering holds sway, is his inability to present other possibilities of revealing. In this, it is not computer technology that is dangerous; it is the essence of computer technology that is dangerous.

Hopefully, our exploration, albeit brief, allows us some sense of what it means to understand the computer as technology in its correctness and in its essence. We turn, now, to explore what computer application essentially means.

U N D E R S T A N D I N G
C O M P U T E R   A P P L I C A T I O N

UNDERSTANDING COMPUTER APPLICATION
AS A TECHNICAL REPRODUCTION

In the prevailing way of thought in Western culture, the very idea of making "application" problematic befuddles many. They ask, is not application simply application? What is there really to query about except how well application is accomplished?

Those who see application as nonproblematic are apt to be caught up within a theory/practice nexus wherein *practice* is thought to be *applied* theory, a secondary notion deriving its meaning from the primacy of *theory*. Within this scheme of things, the term application is seen as a linear activity, joining the primary with the secondary. Within this framework, computer application in a mathematics curriculum, for example, is understood as a linear and technical act of joining the computer with the mathematics education curriculum. Applying is to bring into the fold (*plicare*) or crucible of a concrete situation.

But when a phenomenon like computer technology is enfolded in a situation like a mathematics education curriculum, how should we understand application? The traditional view has been that we understand application as the problem of applying computer technology to a particular situation. Application here means adapting the generalized meaning of computer technology to the concrete situation to which it is speaking. Hence, applying is reproducing something general in a concrete situation. This reproductive view of application embraces the view that application is separated from understanding, and, in fact, follows it. It is an instrumental view.

UNDERSTANDING COMPUTER APPLICATION
AS A HERMENEUTIC PROBLEM

For another view of application, I wish to turn to the work of Hans-Georg Gadamer, who in *Truth and Method* explored the hermeneutic problem of application. In it he recollects the early tradition of hermeneutics which, according to him, "the historical self-consciousness of…the scientific method completely forgot" (Gadamer, 1975, p. 274). Gadamer confronts squarely the hermeneutic problem of application in the context of understanding, interpretation, and application, which, to him, are all moments of the hermeneutic act.

He states that "understanding always involves something like the application of the text to be understood to the present situation of the interpreter" (Gadamer, 1975, p. 274) and that application is an "integral or part of the hermeneutical act as are understanding and interpretation" (Gadamer, 1975, p. 275).

Within this view the task of application in our context is not so much to reproduce computer technology, but to express what is said in a way that considers the situation of the dialogue between the language of computer technology and the language of the mathematics education situation. Application thus is an integral part of understanding, arising from the tension between the language of computer technology on the one hand and the language of the situation on the other. Computer technology is not there to be understood historically, but to be made concretely valid through being interpreted. What is being said here is that computer technology, to be understood properly, must be understood at every moment, in every particular situation in a new and different way. Understood in this way, understanding is always application, and the meaning of computer technology and its application in a concrete curriculum situation are not two separate actions, but one process, one phenomenon, a fusion of horizons.

The question concerning application raises the hermeneutic problem of the relationship between the general and the particular. At the heart of this problem is the notion that the general must be understood in a different way in each new situation. Understanding is, then, a particular case of the application of something general to a particular situation.

We can now see that a serious shortcoming of application as reproduction is the way in which the engagement in reproductive activities can obscure the demands to understanding that the situation itself makes. What the situation demands must not be ignored, for the general risks meaninglessness by remaining detached from the situation.

Ignoring the situational prevents the person in the situation from recognizing that application as technical reproduction is forgetful of the being in the situation. Mindfulness of the situation allows the person in the situation to recognize that application is a hermeneutic act, remembering that being in the situation is a human being in his becoming. This mindfulness allows the listening to what it is that a situation is asking. In a human situation, which is often a situation of action, it asks of us to see what is right. But in order to be able to see what is right in a situation, one must have his own rightness, that is, he must have a right orientation within himself. Not to be able to see what is right is not error or deception; it is blindness.

Within this view, application is neither a subsequent nor a merely occasional part of understanding but codetermines it as a whole from the beginning. Here, application is not the mere relating of some pregiven generalized notion of the particular situation. In our case, then, to understand computer technology, one must not seek to disregard himself and his particular hermeneutic situation. He must relate computer technology to this situation if he wants to understand it at all. And if, as it has been earlier given, that the general must always be understood in a different way, understanding computer technology will necessarily have to be restated in each new subject area situation.

Interpretation is necessary where the meaning of "computer technology" in a situation cannot be immediately understood. It is necessary wherever one is not prepared to trust what a phenomenon immediately presents to us. Thus, there is a tension between the appearance that presents immediately to us and that which needs to be revealed in the situation.

Hopefully, the meaning of application is clearer. It is not the applying to a concrete situation of a given general that we first understand by itself, but it is the actual understanding of the general itself that a given situation constitutes for us. In this sense, understanding shows itself as a kind of an effect and knows itself as such (Gadamer, 1960, p. 305).

For those of us confronted with the application of computer technology in curricular situations as the task at hand, understanding of application as a technical reproduction problem shows itself as instrumentally reductive, and inadequate. Understanding of application as a hermeneutic problem seems to overcome the shortcomings of the technical by vivifying the relationship between computer technology and the pedagogical situation.

CONCLUSION

UNDERSTANDING "UNDERSTANDING" AS ESSENTIAL
TO UNDERSTANDING COMPUTER APPLICATION

As I begin to talk about concluding, I need to point to my neglect in my addressing, thus far, a key term in the title I have chosen for this paper. I have mentioned so far the "computer" and "application." I now feel inclined to say a word about "understanding," the third term of the title, for one of my agendas leading to the coming into being of this paper, such as it is, was to flirt with the question, "What does it mean to understand both epistemologically and ontologically?"

Within the frame of this questioning, I have been guided by a minding of how a coming to appearance of any phenomenon is also a concealing, of how in the very appearing of the phenomenon is concealed the essence of what is, and of how a way to understanding the essence of "what is" without violating the appearance of the phenomenon or the phenomenon itself is to allow the essence to reveal itself in the lived situation.

I feel that as a novice I have begun to come to understand that in my question "What is it?", to be caught in the "it" (i.e., being caught by the question "What is *it?*") is to surrender to the "it." But, I am beginning to understand, too, that only an authentic surrender to "it" frees me from my own caughtness, allowing me to see before me even for a moment the "isness" of the it (i.e., being caught by a different question of "What *is* it?" is to dwell in an epistemological world; to be caught in the question "What *is* it?" is to dwell in an ontological world of the "is" and "not yet." This appearance beckons me to move beyond mere flirtation.

My exploration of computer technology and application was situated to some extent in the question concerning understanding. I feel that my reaching for a fuller understanding of computer technology and application was simultaneously a reaching for a fuller understanding of understanding. In this reach for an understanding, it is well formed to remember Gadamer who, quoting Heidegger, said:

> We live in an era, according to Heidegger, when science expands into a total of technocracy and thus brings on the cosmic night of the forgetfulness of being. (Gadamer, 1982, xvi)

A   L E S S O N   L E A R N E D
F R O M   C A R O L   O L S O N

To be allowed to sense concretely what computer technology essentially is, I wish to turn to Carol Olson, a doctoral student in our department, to reveal what she has taught me.

Carol has been for 12 years a child of haemo-dialysis technology. She and her three siblings have been sustained by a dialysis machine at the University of Alberta Hospital, a teaching-reseach medical institute.

She recently wrote of her experiences with technology:

> We acknowledge our indebtedness to technology; we refuse to be enslaved by technology.

Deep understanding seems to come to those who come to know and feel the limits of one's horizon, for it is at the point of limit that a phenomenon reveals itself through the dialectic of the being that is and the being yet to be.

I somehow feel that the children of technology, like Carol, are the first to see beyond technology, for they know technology with their lifeblood. It is people like Carol who are able to say authentically, "We acknowledge our indebtedness to technology."

So she understands deeply, with her lifeblood she understands that most people understand technology as "applied science," i.e., as "means to ends," strictly an instrumental interpretation. She acknowledges that this interpretation is correct, but not yet true. These understandings she has for she understands that the truth of technology is in the essence of technology, as Heidegger insisted, in the revealing of things and people as only resources, as standing-reserves that can be objectified, manipulated, and exploited. Demanding this of subjectivity, man within the world of technology becomes being-as-thing, no longer human.

So through her own experiences in the teaching-research ward of the hospital, Carol knows, for she writes: "Within technology, we become 'standing-reserve'—units of labor" (as in concentration camps); "teaching material and interesting care" (as in the teaching-research hospital).

Carol struggles against such narrow determination of life. She knows the strong presence of the overwhelming power of consensus among medical and the presencing of the machine itself. To become *empty* in such a situation is, according to her, to block our spiritual pain. One who is spiritually empty knows only physical pain, that pain which leads one to ask, "More Demerol, please."

R E F E R E N C E S

Aoki, T. Beyond the technological lifestyle: Re-shaping lived experiences in schools. An invited paper at *Futurescan '83 Conference*, Saskatoon, Sasketchewan, June 8, 1983. (Sponsored by The Government of Saskatchewan, The University of Saskatchewan and the Saskatoon School Board).

Gadamer, H. G. (1982). *Truth and Method*. (New York: Seabury Press).

Gadamer, H. G. (1982). *Reason in the Age of Science*. (Cambridge, MA: MIT Press).

Heidegger, M. (1977). The Question Concerning Technology, in *The Question Concerning Technology and Other Essays*. (New York: Harper Textbooks): 3-35 (English translation).

CHAPTER THIRTEEN

The Answer is Blowin' in the Wind

A Deconstructive Reading of the School Text

Alan A. Block
1988

To live is to read texts, but to be alive is to write them. Reading is the process by which a reality is consumed; writing is the very production of that reality. Henry David Thoreau knew this when he said that, "Every man is tasked to make his life, even in its details worthy of the contemplation of his most elevated and critical hour...it is far more glorious to carve and paint the very atmosphere and medium through which we look?[1] This activity of carving and painting is the process of writing a text, and though Thoreau and Derrida and Barthes and Lacan may employ a different vocabulary, though not so different as I first imagined, it is textuality about which they all speak. To learn to read is to learn to interpret another's text; but to learn to write is to produce one's own. New a text may be defined as a fabric composed by the weaving of either available and/or original codes. Penelope is the eponymous writer,[2] weaving her fabric daily and taking it apart at night to begin anew the following day. To write a text is to weave a conception of the world and depends on your ability to recognize, manipulate, and create codes, and to produce from them a fabric that answers to our situation at the moment. It is what Henry David Thoreau learned during his life at Walden Pond. He says that "I...had woven a kind of basket of a delicate texture, but I had not made it worth any one's while to buy them. Yet not the less, in my case, did I think it worth my while to weave them, and instead of studying how to make it worth men's while to buy my baskets, I studied how to avoid the necessity of selling them" (18). In that production he may sound Walden Pond to find its bottom, and considers that "I am thankful that this pond was made deep and pure for a symbol. While men believe in the infinite some ponds will be thought to be bottomless" (19). How truly empty that pond is, and yet how actively Thoreau creates meaning in it, though the meaning is really not there. The pond is a code in Thoreau's text, threads of his woven baskets, and as has been often shown, not at all a fixed code, but an open and dynamic one, and entry into it can be made in many places, and hence, may become part of a new code and may be written into another's text, as it has been in mine. *Walden* is a writerly text, and I have learned to write with it—and from it!

I would like to suggest a not so radical idea—that everything comes to us as text, as a fabric woven of codes, even as Thoreau's *Walden* comes to me. But few are the texts that offer the opportunities for writing, and fewer the texts that teach writing. A text that may not be written is composed of codes that preclude the ability to write with them. Such a text may only be read, and may certainly not teach writing. Not to teach writing is to deny the opportunity for the production of worlds, to deny the opportunity to produce knowledge, to deny the experience of pleasure. Writing is, to write with Thoreau's formulation, waking "to an answered question, to Nature, and daylight," and is an activity that results in the construction of reality. Reading, on the other hand, is the activity of observing someone else's reality, and results too often in boredom, frustration, and alienation. Only if we view the world as text that we must write, and, therefore, the product of textuality, is there the opportunity for liberatory activity, for meaningful lives, and for freedom.

I would like to suggest here that the school text is a readerly text. Its codes are irreversible and offer limited and solitary moments of access. The codes may be negotiated in a single direction only, and there is little opportunity for the weaving of new codes within it, or from it. The readerly school text offers only two alternatives to its population: either to accept or reject the text. Yet writing is an activity of freedom, and to teach writing is to teach of the possibility and the availability of choices, to offer freedom and its pleasures. The school text, as a readerly text, may teach only the opposite: enslavement, passivity, lethargy, and subservience to the authority of the signified. That signified, or as Barthes refers to it, as the "Law of the Signified," demands closure and glorifies the centralization of meaning, functioning "to arrange all the meaning of a text in a circle around the hearth of denotation" (the hearth: center, guardian, refuge, light of truth).[3] Reading is governed by the signified, and not only demands, but also defines conformity. From reading, we may learn only what others tells us and our horizons only painted canvases and in-close. Possibility may exist only in writing: the way to hump a cow, e e cummings tells us, is "to multiply because and why/Dividing thens by nows/and adding and (i understand)"[4] There is plenitude in plurality. And so it is ironic that the hue and cry of the educators demands concentration in the teaching of writing; as it is now so constituted, and as it is so planned in the future, reading is all that is possible in the school, and all that may even happen, given the structure of the school text. And it is in this contradiction between what the school proclaims as its purpose and what it actually effects, that it denies whatever meaning it might have produced, and destroys whatever education it might ever have inspired. Indeed, for now and in the future, the teaching of writing is inimicable to the school text; even as its structures may be only read, so may it teach only reading.

Bear with me for a brief time while I establish a vocabulary that we must use to understand what is meant by "writing a text." The terms may be familiar, but I want to place them in a different context.

We must first acknowledge that the world, or all that we have available to produce the text of it, begins as signifiers. We may describe these signifiers as "traces of perception."[5] These original signifiers, which constitute for Saussure the basis of language, and for Lacan constitute the unconscious, which is structured like a language, can only be known, as Saussure, Derrida, Freud and Lacan have noted, by an absence, a gap, by a discontinuity.[6] As Lacan notes, "Discontinuity...is the essential form in which the unconscious first appears to us as a phenomenon-discontinuity, in which something is manifested as a vacillation."[7] This vacillation places "existence" or meaning, not at an identifiable site, but outside of that site. The site itself is known only by the movement of the constellation of presences that notes the absence. As traces of perception these signifiers, then, can be defined not by presence, but rather, as absence. A signifier has meaning only as it is not another signifier, and only as it defers its own use as a signifier in another way. This is as equally true for the letter "t" as for the production of the tongue that has come to be called a Freudian slip. Hence, a signifier can only exist as a trace for it is always "not there," and forever "not that." The defining of any certainty is, of course, not possible here, and Derrida puts knowing under erasure: it, the signifier knowing, is marked by the sign but is not held within it, the sign being the mediating concept between the signifier and the signified.[8] The beginning of all meaning lies in these "traces of perception," in signifiers; rather, the beginning of all meaning lies in the acknowledgement of the structure of the signifier. For the signifier is the absence that allows the denial of centrality and the fullness of space. As Barthes says of Tokyo, "the center itself is no longer anything but a frivolous idea, subsisting there not in order to broadcast power, but to give to...(its)...urban movement the support for its empty central, obliging the traffic in a perpetual departure from the normal path." So with the signifier: in its decenteredness, it insists on diversions from the path.

Signifiers are the natural resource of the text; our signifiers come from nature. To produce text is to respect the integrity of the signifier. The plurality of meaning is an obvious result, for if the signifier is merely an absence, then it can only be defined by its difference from all that marks the space. This process by which the nature of the signifier is acknowledged is the work of textuality, of writing a text. For the writerly text is the field of the signifier. Terry Eagleton explains that for some Kabbalists, the scroll of the Torah used in synagogues, without vowels or punctuation, is an allusion to the original Torah as it existed in the sight of God before the creation—no more than a heap of unorganized letters.[9] God had no need of text: God is the Signifier, or as Lacan says, "the true formula for atheism is God is unconscious" (Lacan, 59). When the Messiah comes, it is told, God will annul the existing Torah and compose its letters into other words: God will teach us to read it in accordance with another scriptive arrangement. In some sense, that is, the words on the page are only a temporary figuration based on a present understanding. The letters can be interminably refigured. The integrity of the signifier is here preserved, for its presence is acknowledged as absence. What seems significant here is the idea that the words, the actual signs, are actually allusions to something else: that their meaning exists not within, but without. What we perceive may have form, be a sign, but its meaning is not contained within that sign. Now what is made of the words at any one time is dependent upon the ideological positions of the interpreters who must first recognize text, which is to say, must produce a fabric from codes, and must then set about signifying that text from the particular weave of those codes. This process is writing, and it produces text that may be seen as "material ceremonies, scriptive fields of force to be negotiated, dense dispositions of signs less to be 'read' than meditatively engaged, incanted, and ritually remade" (Eagleton, 117). Interpretation has no place in the text, for as Nietzsche has told us, all interpreting is the "will to power" and, therefore, is always held within the particular consciousness of the ruling hegemony that determines the controlling center. The law of the signifier is the basis of text, and it is from that basis which must begin the understanding of writing and the production of text. Hence, we must teach the idea of text, that it might be recognized, and the means of writing it so that text is produced.

This begins only by the recognition and understanding of codes. For texts are written from the weaving of codes, and the nature of the codes will determine the nature of the text. Codes are systems of connotation, which connotations serve to provide to decentered signifiers. Barthes defines connotation as a "determination, a relation, an anaphora, a feature which has the power to relate itself to anterior, ulterior, or exterior mentions to other sites of the text (or of another text)" (S/Z, 8). These systems of connotation are based on the law of the signified, and act to control meaning by turning signifiers into signifieds. Codes are produced by the tentative fixing of the signifier. Open codes respect the play of the signifier, putting it under erasure, and therefore indicating that it is inhabited by another signifier which is not there. Thus, open codes may provide access to themselves at many entry points and are reversible. They are non-hierarchical: "this speech, at once very cultural and very savage, [is] above all lexical, sporadic; it set(s) up in me, through its apparent flow, a definitive discontinuity: this non-sentence [is] in no way something that could not have acceded to the sentence, that might have been before the sentence; it (is) what is eternally, splendidly, outside the sentence:" (Barthes, Pleasure, 49). Closed codes are based on hierarchical order. All codes, open or closed, are necessary to facilitate communication: they classify and clarify and delimit signifiers, and provide common grounds upon which to begin communication. The formation of civilization requires that this unrestrained play of signifiers be restricted.

The symbolic process after Lacan, and the Oedipal drama, after Freud, are two descriptions of the means by which humans create and enter into the social structure. For in these processes the unrestrained play that is the very nature of the signifier is restricted, and the indeterminable signifier is transformed into a signified. A free play of signifiers existing in total promiscuity, so to speak, denies individuality and identity, but to produce civilization, that identity is essential: "in total promiscuity (total polysemy) no one could in fact be called father, son, or sister and no one would be able to situate himself or recognize others by the particular place they occupied."[10] Social existence requires the fixing of the signifier. That fixing creates the sign, which may be nothing other than a signifier, hence, Derrida's formulation that writing is at least signifier of a signifier. In Derrida's formulation, "The written signifier is always technical and representative. It has no constitutive meaning."[11]

Now, in constructing civilization, it has been deemed necessary to deny the nature of the signifier, which rests in difference, and enter the realm of the symbolic, in which meaning is more or less determined and denied plurality. "An intermediary is necessary between man and the world, between man and man, between self and manifestation of self. The intermediary is the necessary and sufficient condition once men which to come to an agreement with one another on general principles and wish to exchange something in common" (Lemaire, 61). Hence is created the signified, whose signification is determined by the symbolic process. To create that signified one denies the nature of the signifier by fixing meaning in a "symbol." For Lacan, the symbol is "either a signifier whose nature is different from that of the signified, although their characteristics do show some factual similarity, as in the case of metaphors" (Lemaire, 48). It is in the symbolic order that civilization is made possible for it is there that codes may be formed and specificity is decreed. This development, however, necessitates alienation, for as it creates identity, it denies polysemy. To create the symbol, of/for the signified, one must split the psyche and lose an immediate relation of the self to the self, which only exists in the imaginary. The imaginary is the place of the signifier, and is "everything in the human mind and its reflexive life which is in a state of flux before the fixation is effected by the symbol, a fixation which, at the very least, tempers the incessant sliding of the mutations of being and of desire:" (Lemaire, 61). But in the symbolic, play is diminished as definite links are determined between signifier and signified, circumscribing a text and writer in separate fields, disallowing polysemy. The process of symbolization "implies from the start imperfection, reduction, arbitrariness, submission to external constraints and a partial failure to recognize its own mechanisms" (Lemaire, 58). The use of the signified at one time in a specific way denies its existence in difference and determines meaning. But at the same time, this process denies meaning, as it denies the trace that defines the structure of the signifier. By the process of signification, of meaning-making, a signifier becomes a signified, and some of its original de-centeredness is lost. This process results in codes. But the restriction of infinite play, of polysemy, the closing of codes, is only possible according to some power of authority, of law. As Derrida will state, authority condemns writing.

Authority denies writing, for its anarchic reality threatens power. Writing does away with the father, we are told, for only in speech is the father necessary to speak for the son, logos, and to answer for him. So it is the father who would assign value to writing, define it, and who would wish, as necessary, to control it by designating its social functions. As Theuth answers its inventor, writing will not give wisdom to its student: "the pupils will have the reputation for it without proper instruction, and in consequence be thought very knowledgeable when they are for the most part quite ignorant."[12] What Theuth objects to about writing is its autonomy of the father. Without him, writing is empty notation: someone, the father, must supply the signifieds in order that information may be transferred and wisdom gained. The equation between information and wisdom is striking: and the authority of the father in this system is ensured. Socrates adds to this formulation of the myth: "The same holds true of written words; you might suppose that they understand what they are saying, but if you ask them what they mean by anything they simply return the same answer over and over again...it always needs its parent to come to its rescue; it is quite incapable of defending or helping itself" (97). Of course, what Theuth and Socrates object to in writing is its self-sufficiency, and the resultant denial of the father. "From the position of the holder of the scepter, the desire of writing is indicted, designated, and denounced as a desire for orphanhood and patricidal subversion."[13] So it is that in his condemnation of writing, authority maintains control over the symbolic process in the service of order and meaning. The system of codes within a society, which are developed as a result of the symbolic process, and which are the substance out of which texts are woven, is then determined by the authority whose first wish is to deny writing, which process would immediately undermine that authority. And as texts are produced by the weaving of codes, the nature of those codes will determine the type of text that is produced, and will determine the processes that those texts may teach. Now, a society both inherits and creates codes, but the power of the authority legitimizes some and delegitimizes others, makes some codes available, and makes others forbidden, gives credence to some and places others under suspicion. With that power, society controls the production of texts. Writing, the production of texts, is condemned, as are the open codes that make it possible, and reading remains as the sole option of the institution, which is comprised of, and legitimates only, closed codes.

Codes are the substance of the textual fabric, and there is no limit to the numbers and types of codes that may be theoretically available. But I will suggest that codes may be classified generally into either open or closed varieties. I would like to suggest that a closed code is one that is built upon hierarchical structures, and that an open code is one not so constructed. By hierarchical I do not confine meaning to constructions determined by increasing (or decreasing) levels of importance or degrees of power, though these are types of hierarchies. Rather, by hierarchy I mean here a construction in which the spatio-temporal structure is such that entry into it at any but the prescribed sites, and movement along it in any but the prescribed direction, may be undertaken only at great personal risk or at jeopardy to the existence of the entire code. A closed code, based on such a hierarchy, may not exist in fragments: it would cease to exist. The closed code, then, may not respect the structure of the signifier, and must then deny the nature of polysemous meaning that is represented by the signifier. A fabric composed of closed codes is a readerly text that can be available only to consumption; its codes admit no entry, no displacement, and no option for free movement. Barthes says that "the readerly text is a *tonal* text (for which habit creates a reading process just as conditioned as our hearing: one might say there is a *reading eye* as there is a tonal ear, so that to unlearn the readerly would be the same as to unlearn the tonal)" (Barthes, S/Z, 30). And though tone might be complex, its movement is determined, for tonal unity is dependent on the sequential structuring of codes that must be permutable, irreversible, and constrained by time. This *is* the school. A writerly text, on the other hand, is one woven by open codes, and is, thus, available to be written: its codes respect the structure of the signifier, they are permutable, reversible, and unconstrained by time. This should be the school if it is to teach writing.

Derrida says that the term "writing" is used "to designate not only the physical gestures of literal pictographic or ideographic inscription but also the totality of what makes it possible; and also, beyond the signifying face, the signified fact itself.... We say 'writing' for all that gives rise to an inscription in general, whether it is literal or not and even if what it distributes in space is alien to the order of the voice: cinematography, choreography, of course, but also pictorial, musical, sculptural 'writing'" (Derrida, *Grammatology*, 9). Writing, then, is all that is inhabited by the trace, by the signifier. Writing acknowledges the "not there" and the "not that." It is the production of the world, as the imaginary order is given substance in the symbolic one, and exists in a process of engagement with the signifier, which process can only be defined as flux, and, therefore, based on discontinuity. Barthes tells us that "the reader [writer] of the text may be compared to someone at a loose end [someone slackened off from any imaginary;...on the side of a valley, a *oued* flowing down below] (*oued* is there to bear witness to a certain feeling of unfamiliarity); what he perceives is multiple, irreducible, coming a disconnected, heterogeneous variety of substances and perspectives; lights, colors, vegetation, heat, air, slender explosion of noises, scant cries of birds, children," voices from over on the other side, passages, gestures, clothes of inhabitants near or far away. All these incidents are half-identifiable: they come from codes that are known but their combination is unique, founds the stroll in a difference repeatable only as difference."[14] This experience of writing depends on an openness to freedom, and is only available from a text whose codes are so open that the text is already writerly. It is from such an engagement that writing may be taught: the text as both the model and the source of writing. Barthes' description is of a writerly text and it is such a text that might be the school.

A writerly text is "ourselves writing, before the infinite play of the world (the world as function) is traversed, intersected, stopped, elasticized by some singular system which reduced the plurality of entrances, the opening of networks, the infinity of languages" (Barthes, S/Z, 5). A writerly text mobilizes codes that extend as far as the eye can reach, and are indeterminable; a writerly text is impervious to the authority of any system of meaning. Writerly texts "encourage the critic to carve them up, to transpose them into difference discourses, produce his/her semi-arbitrary play of meaning athwart the work itself."[15] The writerly text has no determined meaning, no settled signifier, but is plural and diffuse, an inexhaustible woven fabric comprised of a galaxy of signifiers, a seamless weave of codes and fragments of codes, through which the writer may cut his own path. The writerly text must be first a "non-sentence," must exist before the "sentence," must exist outside of the "sentence," and though it must always be delivered into the sentence, the sentence need not always be finished. To produce a writerly text, one must first be taught to write (and we must bear in mind at all times Derrida's formulation: writing is all that gives rise to the inscription itself, and is not confined to scriptive systems). A readerly text may not ever teach writing, for to do so would be to advocate the abandonment or rules and laws that define the readerly text's authority—and hence, its existence. "The [writerly] text is [should be] that uninhibited person who shows his behind to the *Political Father*" (Barthes, *Text*, 53). It is the nature of text to deny authority, and yet, it is the authority who wished to condemn writing ",,as a desire for orphanhood and patricidal subversion" (Derrida, *Disseminations*, 77). The school is such an authority, established as a readerly text, and therefore incapable of teaching writing, but rather, determined to teach reading.

I have said that the school text is a readerly one, that it is produced from codes that are closed and that offer severely limited and restricted access to the text which may not then be either written or used to teach writing. The school text denies the nature of the signifier, worships at the altar of the signified, and condemns writing by defining it as the pushing of nouns against verbs. I would like to look at the school text itself, and expose the nature of the codes from which the fabric is woven. I do not mean to offer here a description of how the school text came to be produced; this work is being done by such people as Michael Apple, Henry Giroux, and others. Rather, what I would like to observe is the very structure of the text, and show how the school text is made so readerly from the closed nature of its codes. I intend to speak of five codes: they are not necessarily inclusive, nor are they mutually exclusive, but they are whole and complete in themselves. These five codes are in large part responsible for the fabric of the school text, and determine its readerly quality. Finally, these codes are not how I read/write the school, but rather, how the school itself has been written from the codes. I refer to these codes as the hermeneutic code, whose terms treat of enigmas, articulate ways these enigmas are presented, and structures the means of formulating or delaying an answer to those enigmas; the narrative code, by which effects may be predicted from causes and by which behavioral norms are established; the linear code, whose terms organize the conception of time; the semic code, whose terms include the school vocabulary and which is concerned with the connotations of the signifier; and the physical code, whose terms determine the physical shapes and limits of the school text.

First and foremost, the school text is a site, an idea of a location. The physical code of a school establishes and articulates this environment. The school text is, with rare exception, a social place to which one goes; that is to say, the school text exists as a definable, physical site that will serve in no other text except that of the school. This physical site also defines the limits of the text's boundaries and confines. This physical code articulates a site that is separate and apart from other sites, and hence, ensures the validity of the authority of its activities. "Going to school;" is the first independent foray away from the home. The terms of the physical code articulate it as a special location apart from the home or from business: indeed, whatever the activity of the school might be, and to the child the school's activity is often a mystery—an intentionally kept secret—it must be seen to be exclusively the province of this site which is called 'the school,' which is not home and is not the world, the latter being what one is delivered into after attendance at 'school.' Indeed, the physical code of the school acts to isolate the text from both the home and the non-school environment, allocating certain privileges to each, but protecting their separate domains. The physical code of the school articulates the nature of events and activities: there are those which occur at school or those which take place outside of school. Here the physical code determines appropriate and inappropriate actions to the school text. The school site, then, is, in a sense, designated by its physical code as a way station between the home and that world for which preparation is required, but which is definitely not the school. As George Caldwell, a teacher at Olinger High School in John Updike's *The Centaur* says, society has created "jails called schools, equipped with tortures called education. School is where you go between when your parents can't take you and industry can't take you. I am a paid keeper of Society's unusables—the lame, the halt, the insane, and the ignorant."[16] The physical code restricts the school to the idea of a location, and determines either one of two responses: to accept or reject the text, attendance, or nonattendance.

The physical code of a school also involved the shapes and forms that comprise the environment. This code sets the tone and limits of space. The geometrical shape of the classroom determines not only what a person can do, but to a large extent, determines what he can think. In "The Form of Cities," Le Corbusier says that "Man walks straight because he has a goal; he knows where he is going. He has decided to go somewhere and he walks there directly."[17] This belief in angularity, in straight lines, in the vertical and the horizontal, seems to articulate the terms of the physical code, and results from a world view epitomized in Le Corbusier's words: the forms of nature are chaotic, and to ensure his security, the human creates "a zone of protection which is in accord with what he is and with what he thinks…. Free, man tends toward pure geometry. He makes what is called order." The vertical and the horizontal also determine the eye's direction, the extents of the mind's wanderings, and the limits of the body's perambulations. Straight lines deny meanderings. As Thoreau tells us, "roads are made for horses and men of business. I do not travel them much, comparatively, because I am not in a hurry to get to any tavern or grocery or livery-stable or depot to which they lead."[18] These physical forms of the school text determine the play of the inhabitants who reside within, and their ability to play with the signifiers which might be arrayed around them. The horizontal and verticals with their clear and defined angles, permit sorely limited possibility for choices of directions, and end always in clearness, in finality. There is certainty in a straight line, and order in its forms. The school physical code seems posited on Le Corbusier's assertion that "man, functionally, practices order, that his acts and his thoughts are governed by the upright and the right angle; that to him the upright is an instinctive way and that it is, to his way of thinking, a lofty goal" (135). There is very little in a school that is not governed by geometrical forms. Within the cosmetically designed exterior are an array of boxes, in which are primarily rectangular desks arranged either in rows or large squares. In the occasional circular arrangements, there is a clear inside and outside. On each desk is a square notebook or paper or book, and the lines inscribed on them are for guiding scriptive activities. Through the walls one looks through square windows, or at square pictures placed orderly around the room—or at a rectangular bulletin board. Rectangular file cabinets sit on floors which are tiled with square tiles, or more, in square tiles in rectangular patterns.

Even in those classrooms with added furniture, perhaps a couch or an arm chair, these pieces are usually placed against the wall, leaving the middle free—and square. In such rooms movement is limited, the eye is determined to move along certain directions and to proceed, as Le Corbusier stated, from angle to angle, from start to finish, from entrance to exit. The mind has little choice but to acknowledge the strength and dominance of straight lines and eight angles. And the student's movement and access to movement is determined by the limited geometry of the room. The array of signifiers is sorely restricted, as is the possibility of play with them. Reading is possible in such an environment, the following of lines, but never writing. The physical code of the school determines the environment wherein the activity of the school might happen; and becomes reified into a symbol not only for the place for education, but for whatever education might be. This code is, hence, irreversible, and offers the possibility of entrance at no place other than the rectangular door. The physical code of a school offers a limited play of signifiers with which to work and produces a sameness and boredom from its rigidity.

The geometry of the physical code is mirrored in the structuring of time within the school text. Indeed, the text is severely determined by its linearly coded time, by which is meant the articulation of time in an inexorably forward motion and the acceptance of this flow as natural and inevitable. It is obvious, given this construct, how the linear code can admit of only one entrance and insist on only one continuous direction: linear time is conceived as an objective phenomenon, moving, like the tides, forward. (One is reminded here of the aphorism, "Time and tide for no man waits.") There are beginnings and endings, and both can be exactly defined. Between the beginning and the end there is a relatively straight path, which is the mirror image of the articulation of the physical code of the text. All actions are continually and inevitably enacted under the Damoclean sword—the clock—and it is that perceived belief in the movement of that clock from which the code is constructed.

It would seem superfluous to note how the linear code, a dominant weave in the school text, functions to produce a readerly text in which only reading can be learned, but it might be worthwhile to note in passing just a few instances of its signifieds. The length of the day spent at school is externally defined and determined; whatever the school's activities, they are confined to these regularly kept hours. So too are the years allotted to attendance at the school, at which time education is declared concluded, or higher education must begin. Until the age of sixteen, every person is required to attend school, but at sixteen one may leave voluntarily. The activity is defined by the quantity of years spent in school, and not by the quality of those years. Bells separate scheduled periods, which divide the day into inexorably timed segments. Lessons are organized around single periods of regular and predictable length, all governed by the clock and not by the material; an absence represents time lost, opportunity missed, and is considered as a serious interruption in continued and a continuous movement. Textbooks are read from beginning to end, in sequentially numbered chapters which, in history texts at least, are almost always structured on linearly ordered time lines. Life happens, it must be read, sequentially. One progresses through school from grade 1 and leaves after having completed grades 2 through 12, in that order. Tests must be made up within a certain period of time. Period 2 follows period 1 as regularly as Math II follows Math I. In such a manner only, may education be gained. The closed nature of this code is obvious.

And yet linearity is only a function of efficiency, which is a human device for ordering experience. Linearity is simply a system of classification. And as Stephen Jay Gould notes, "classifications both reflect and direct our thinking. The way we order represents the way we think."[19] This linear code, which prioritizes exact dependence upon regularity, and the definition of movement based upon forward directions is inimical to the writerly text. The linear code is designed to limit access and prevent play, to control movement: to practice and to teach reading. For in our internalization of these structures we determine our systems of thought and prevent our ability to play with the limitless signifiers that are arrayed before us. The linear code maintains us in a track and a direction, and permits no carving or weaving with that code. The only possibilities open in this code are to be left back, to repeat a year, or to extend enrollment beyond the accepted and expected four year stay. Each of these options carries with it society's condemnation. And yet, without that play, we may not learn to write or write our text.

The linear code also denies the possibilities of the writing of text by restricting access to the process by which writing might take place. The research would show that "writing" happens not in linear fashion, but in endless patterns of recursive actions.[20] The linear code, in programming students along a preestablished direction governed by a determined time sequence within ordered time frames, denies the possibility of recursive action, and must deny the writing of the text by a student.

The school text is tightly woven by the linear code: the hermeneutic code, by which enigmas are revealed and their solutions posed, exacerbates the weave of the text. For it is certain that the school text is produced by the setting out of enigmas, and by the controlled and various means of formulating answers or holding those answers in suspension. The concept of prerequisites articulates the hermeneutic code and establishes hierarchies and categories which are, at best, unreachable and isolating; but whose promise for engaging in these practices is redemptive. At the end, solutions are promised, and questions are to be resolved. Hence, this code organizes the availability of experience, and it is by this code that the school text begins to establish a theme. As it suggests enigmas, and as it articulates various ways to the question, to the responses, and to the variety of chance events that can either formulate a question or delay its answer, the school text establishes an irreversible and impenetrable path. That there is an enigma produces the hierarchy; that the enigma has a solution is shown from the hierarchy. There is no escape from the system, and the text that is woven brooks no play, no carving up, no restructuring. The paths are determined, even as are the ends. For as the enigma is already answered in the deep structure of the text, so must the paths to that answer be, as a result, determined. Even as it advertises learning, the hermeneutic code inhibits it by dictating the conditions of it and defining its end.

The establishment of prerequisites is an exclusionary device that prevents the development of natural curiosities and interests even as it tantalizes the learner with golden apples that are made to recede even as they are grasped at by eager minds. Each numbered course, each prerequisite, each division into classes—even buildings—are elements in the hermeneutic code which pose the enigma, and delay its answering. These classifications suggest a final answer. Classify learning into time sequences, and establish clear directions of the process of educational development regardless of the true state of the individual learner. Prerequisites deny the development of planning and individual development, discouraging challenge and risk-taking. Prerequisites protect the system even as they reproduce it, and ensure its continuance by determining what may be learned, by whom, and when.

And prerequisites are only one order of our reliance on the hermeneutic code. When one period follows another, we acknowledge that learning happens in discrete time blocks, Math following English, Social Studies succeeding Math. And that tomorrow's Math lesson will, in all probability, be a continuation of today's. Each block represents a piece to a puzzle, the final picture of which is promised, though rarely offered. Each block, too, as in the daytime soap operas to which students are so attached, offers enlightenment tomorrow. Indeed, the very phrase, higher education, suggests that the answer is continually deferrable, and made available only afterward to those who are chosen to continue. To those who stop along the way remains the perennial disappointment of having stopped going to school, and having ceased their education, and of having failed to acquire the answer. The hermeneutic code in not only establishing the enigma, but in articulating the ways of offering questions and of formulating and delaying answers to it, must deny the signifier in which meaning is infinite. It is from the signifier that writing must stem: writing is the signifier of the signifier.

The hermeneutic code provides, we might say, the tonal nature of the text. It organizes the harmonic patterns which are articulated by the semic code, which is responsible for the connotations of the vocabulary by which the school talks about itself. As determined symbols, this vocabulary represents the reification of meaning, epitomizes the law of the signified, and hence, determines the readerliness of the code which produces the textual fabric. The vocabulary is one which the school has devised in order to write itself, and which it chooses to use when it is engaged in discourse with those within or without the site, and which it advertises as the vocabulary that one must employ when discussing the text which has come to be called "the school." There are terms that are especially particular to the vocabulary code of the school text; it is these to which we must look to evaluate the openness of this particular code. This is not intended as a complete listing, but meant, rather, to indicate drift. Among other terms that are part of this vocabulary code are "curriculum," "student," "teacher," and "administrator." What I would note is how these words are both mutually exclusive, and yet paradoxically, mutually interdependent, producing a hierarchy that is intractable and impermeable. Without students, teachers are irrelevant, and because the school's activity must be organized, ensuring the proper placement and future movement of each member along the directed route, an administrative staff is necessary to oversee that construction. The vocabulary code of the school can only produce a text that is readerly, the code of the school can only produce a text which is readerly, the code itself depending on hierarchical structures. The total effect is a text which provides no flexibility, and no entry save at prescribed places. For no matter how the words are defined—even in the most liberal manner—they are mutually distinct categories, and movement between them is, if not prohibited, then severely restricted.

The hermeneutic code determines the connotations of the word "student" in the school text, for the articulation of enigmas is made expressly to them, and the variety of events that are organized to lead to an answer or to postpone an answer is meant to engage that specific body called students. And though they are to arrive, finally, at an end, that end has been already articulated and defined. Hence, a student's place in the hierarchy is determined. They are, interestingly enough, the lowest rung of the hierarchical order of the school text, and it is they whose movement is most restricted within the vocabulary code. Incapacity of movement prevents writing, and encourages reading, as it denies the structure of the signifier and determines signifieds. It is also significant that by this hierarchical structure, the textuality of the students themselves must be denied, for to admit that "the 'I' which approaches a text is already a plurality of other texts, of codes which are infinite, or more precisely, lost (whose origin is lost)" (Barthes, S/Z, 10), would call into question not only the three codes discussed above, but the nature of the entire school text itself as it is constituted in the society.

The curriculum is the written and designed articulation of the hermeneutic code; curriculum is the name given to the sequential hierarchy of materials to be presented within the time and physical constraints of the school text as it exists in its entirety. Curriculum may also be the subject matter to be presented; but though it may change in detail, it is constrained within the text to serve the same function: as result of the text's rigidity. For whatever the subject matter, it must articulate the enigmas and the way to their solutions or artificial deferrals. And these must be clearly set out, or disorder will result from the varying locations of students in a single room along the hermeneutic code. This disorder is inimitable to the text, and threatens to dismantle it. Hence, there is a language arts curriculum, articulated for grades kindergarten through grade 12, as well as English curriculum for Grade 12. Finally, it must be the result of curriculum to lead students to the answer; hence, the deep structure of curriculum is a world view. By this, the end of curriculum must be interpretation and not construction. Rather, the end of curriculum is the discovery of an interpretation. Writing is the production of text: "whether this text be Proust or the daily newspaper or the television screen: the book creates meaning, the meaning creates life" (Barthes, *Pleasure*, 36). The readerly school text denies this opportunity, and denies then, the opportunity for pleasure.

Teachers, then, is the name given to the order of those whose responsibility it is to deliver the materials ordained by the curriculum. Their role, too, is determined by their place in the hierarchy, these hierarchies the result of the codes. Teachers must be those who may present the curriculum, and in the organization, lead students to a determined answer. Hence, it is posited that teachers within the school text are outside the activity which they initiate, are at best catalysts who should remain unchanged by the situation. What a teacher may actually do is determined not by himself, but by an adherence to the codes by which the school text is written and of which she is both a "part" and "apart."

Now a writerly text calls all language into question, for its field is the signifier; if all language is called into question then all language is demanded and there can be no hierarchy, and there can be no judge, arbiter, confessor master analyst or decoder of the text, for no language system could be sufficient. Yet the school text is founded on layers of hierarchies, shown here in its vocabulary, each one defining by its existence the limits of the writing which is possible. These hierarchies, which exist everywhere within the text, actually deny the writerly quality of the school text even as they prohibit the writing of text. For these hierarchies settle meaning, determine signifieds, and close off and deny access to the signifiers which are the raw materials of writing text. The vocabulary code establishes a hierarchy which announces meaning; determines access to materials for writing even as it condemns that writing.

The school is, finally, woven from the narrative code, which I will define here as that code that allows one to predict effects from causes. The narrative code establishes behavioral norms that are absolutely derived from the above articulated codes. It should be clear now that restricted behavior may be given the natures of the linear, hermeneutic, physical, and semic codes. This narrative code seems the most constrained, and any attempt at play only serves to test the limits of the confinements that each person occupies. Causes and effects are determined from the beginning, and behaviors are organized to direct and to facilitate movement through the text. This is the process of reading, for it demands the consumption of product. This readerly text, which must be consumed, does not offer the opportunity to produce the text, to open it out, to "set it going." This text may never be written, for it offers no opportunity or materials with which to write.

This textual fabric known as "the school" is written by the weave of codes. These codes produce a text which is a social site, and which is classified by the society in which it finds itself by the function that is assigned to it: to engage in education. But the text itself determines very clearly what that means, and this readerly text can only define education as a process and a result of reading. Writing must be inimicable to this text, for writing would deny its very structure and place its existence in jeopardy. And this readerly text teaches reading.

For by the weave of these codes, education may only be the orderly process of following designated paths under the guidance of those who know not only the paths but their ends as well, and arrive finally at an image of the reality which must be either accepted...or rejected. These are the only two options in this construct. Knowledge may not be here, then, production? It can not be a process of transformation in which through human labor, materials of the sensate world – signifiers—are turned into problems, more signifiers. This would be writing, as we have earlier defined it. The activity of the school may not be a process by which these solutions to the first problems, to which we may attach the name, signifieds, become signifiers in the next and continuing transformation; this would be writing, and we recall here Derrida's statement that writing is the signifier of the signifier. Rather, knowledge can only be here an end, a body of information that is not a production, but a reproduction, or worse, simply a matter of transport. This delivery is reading, a process of consumption.

And yet, it is only to see knowledge as production, as writing, that can produce the writerly, and how writing may be learned. The knowledge premised by the school, however, offers no promise for change—the essence of work—and cannot offer the possibility for changing the human's relationships to everything about her, resulting in a change in the quality of life. Without change, without production, there is no writing and no writerly text. For change is intrinsic to the nature of the writerly text as the limitless play of signifiers are transformed into signifieds that are then again transformed into signifiers. Writing is all that inhabits the trace: there can be no trace in a defined and definable goal.

The activity of the readerly school text then, may only practice a sifting through, or engaging in, successive approximations of reality to discover or reveal a preexisting reality.[21] It is to read *Hamlet* and discover its meaning. Those approximations must come from outside, and thus places knowledge not within the student, but without him. In this readerly text, knowledge is not a matter of utilizing aspects of preexisting orders in order to allow one to create one's own reality, one's own text. Rather, knowledge is a location to which one arrives later. And our own present locus is always an inferior version of what will happen later.

But writing does posit knowledge as the power of transformation: the ability to employ the things of this world to transform theoretical raw materials into problems that must be solved. These two rocks, which look so dissimilar, have been found in the same back yard? Why? What could that mean? Or, what interested Shakespeare about Hamlet? What interest me about Hamlet that I would read the play through? And now, having done so, who is Hamlet, and who am I now? Knowledge is a process, is the writing of text; neither activity is an end. Knowledge, textual writing, is the basis of education.

As the school text is so woven now, knowledge is a body of received facts: someone else's signifieds. A large quantity of literature exists, exposing this concept of knowledge: revealing it, rather, to be a socially determined, hegemonic construct that denies the possibility of liberatory activity. The school's role in this construct is central. It would seem that this construct represents that aspect of the lacanian process of symbolization wherein the characteristics and nature of the signified are different from that of the signifier, producing a situation where the relationship between the two is fixed and can only be learned. That learning denies the play of the signifier, creates codes that are inflexible, determines meaning, and prohibits entry into, and hence, writing of, the text. A site that advocates this system must be seen as a readerly text, for it denies the very nature of writing, which is based on the free play of signifiers. It denies the solving of problems as well; for a meaning already determined defines the paths to it, the nature and substance of those limited number of paths. Had there been signs at the crossroads in the yellow wood, the poet's choice would have had to have been arrived at differently, and not by writing, but by reading. It is reading, the reading of signs and not the making of them, which is thus taught in school: reading which is a consumption, and not writing, which is a production. Of consumption two responses only are viable: to consume or not to consume.

Knowledge in the readerly text is merely the exposition of a given text, and the objective delineations of specific disciplines: these the preestablished woven patterns which comprise the readerly text, and which serve only to inhibit entry into the school text and preclude writing. These disciplines determine signifiers into signifieds; this reading practice is not the teaching of writing, and it cannot be education.

Yet, writing is the substance of education. One does not necessarily have a *knowledge* of chemistry at the completion of a course by that name, nor can one claim *to know* Shakespeare after having successfully survived a seminar in the major plays. Rather, one can only claim to have acquired materials from which problems can be devised. One should always speak only of a new array of signifiers. Now, the nature of the signifiers is infinite, as are the problems that can be devised from them. Of course, the presented materials determine the nature of the questions that may be posed; they are, in effect, the answered question seen through a particular window upon awakening. But these materials which are really signifiers are to be played with, torn apart, and reconstituted. Only in this way is writing taught. An in the teaching of writing is taught the plethora of meaning; that is the real purpose of education. For to know that meaning is infinite is to know as well that it may be always produced. That production can only occur in the process of writing: all that inhabits the trace. All else must be reading: to read these signifiers as signifieds suggests that they can be explained, explicated, but never taken apart. These materials must be left whole, they are whole codes themselves and not signifiers that may be employed in the creation of text-in writing. Such materials may be read, may be consumed, are icons to be venerated: their value is what can be gotten from them, what one can do with them, but not what can be done to them. From such materials the observer stands apart, remains outside. Freedom, which is created in the act of writing, however, exists not in contemplation, but in action. To teach reading is to teach subjugation: As Gully Jimson, the irrepressible artist in Joyce Cary's *The Horse's Mouth*, says, "Contemplation, in fact, is *On The Outside*. It's not on the spot.... And the truth is that Spinoza was always on the outside. He didn't understand freedom, and so he didn't understand anything.... Freedom, to be plain is nothing but *The Inside of the Outside*...what you get on the inside...is the works—it's *Something That Goes on Going On*."[22] Writing is an activity of freedom, and to teach writing is to teach freedom: the closed code of activity with which is woven the school text teaches the opposite: teaches enslavement, teaches passivity, lethargy, and subservience to the written word. To teach writing is to have no method, but to allow methods.

Education is the name of the complex system whose primary purpose is to facilitate the production of knowledge. It is the locus where the student might realize his own purposes, and give substance to the work of his imagination. It is where the writerly text teaches writing. It is by the educative process that students are encouraged to incorporate into their repertoire means by which they might produce knowledge. Students, and we are all always students, must be taught to write! Education should provide the stimulus for encouraging the \students' development of original means of production. Only the constraints of ideology determine the limits of these techniques, and the acknowledgement of this limitation is the beginning of its dismantlement. One who is involved in education is engaged in the processes of knowledge production. But, knowledge is the text that one writes, and not the materials on which one works. Education should result in the construction of determined structures, signifieds, whose forms are yet undetermined, are, in fact originally signifiers, and which may become so once again. *Hamlet* is different materials than *Macbeth*, and this difference must figure dominantly in the particular formulation which will arise. But the exact nature of the formulations can never be known until they are produced, nor need they be made permanent. The possibilities are infinite: the text is characterized by plurality. When you ask the citizens of Thekla, in Calvino's *Invisible Cities*, where is the blueprint for their edifices, they are too busy constructing to answer until night has fallen. And when "darkness falls over the building site.... The sky is filled with stars. Pointing upwards, the citizens say 'There is the blueprint.'" The expansive universe is the only model and the sole limitation of their imaginations. Building is what they do, and not what they get. The world is a plural text from which plural texts must be written.

As the slave, Jim, sits captive in a shack at the Phelps' farm, Tom Sawyer and Huckleberry Finn plot to free him. Tom orders Huck to "borrow" a shirt from Aunt Sally.

> "What do we want of a shirt, Tom?"
> "Want it for Jim to keep a journal on."
> "Journal your granny—Jim can't write."
> "S'pse he can't write—he can make marks on the shirt can't he, if we make him
> a pen out of an old pewter spoon or a piece of an old iron-barrelhoop."[23]

Of course, for Tom it is of little consequence that Jim can't write: Tom's text has little to do with the captive slave. Indeed, it is inimical to Tom's text that Jim be able to write: were he so able he would not be liable to such manipulation. As Huck acknowledges, "Jim he couldn't see no sense in the most of it, but he allowed we was white folks and knowed better than him; so he was satisfied, and said he would do it all just as Tom said" (Twain, 239). Nor is Tom's text very plural: the codes it mobilizes have limited access, and determine the method of reading, fixing signifieds and denying signifiers: there is a way to read this text, and Tom knows the way. Responding to Huck's complaint about the foolishness in using case knives to dig Jim out of the shack when picks and shovels would do, Tom responds: "It don't make no difference how foolish it is, it's the *right* way—and it's the regular way. And there ain't no *other*way, that ever *I* heard of, and I've read all the books that gives any information about these things" (Twain, 234). Having learned all by reading, Tom can only produce a readerly text. Chastising Huck, who only knows how to write, for his wanting simply to free Jim in the most efficient and safest manner possible, Tom complains, "You *can* get up the infant-schooliest ways of going at a thing. Why, hain't you ever read any books at all" (231)? Tom's text is a readerly one: it makes of people objects, demands passivity and intransitiviness, insists on seriousness, and its codes limit access to the text. As a readerly text, it denies the nature of the signifiers and exalts the signified. It denies the idea of play and offers only two alternatives to the reader: to accept or reject the text. He admonishes Huck, and denies him freedom, and accuses him of "always a-wandering off on a side issue. Why can't you stick to the main point?" (Twain, 235). And if Huck wants to free Jim, and if Jim desires his freedom, than it is absolutely necessary that they accept Tom's text. The signifiers are determined as signifieds, the symbols have only to be learned. Tom's allowance that Jim can't write doesn't in the least affect Tom's pleasure: but the adherence to the code seriously restricts the acceptance of difference and the plethora of meanings available. And it does produce confusion and boredom in the other participants.

Such is the case with the school text. It is a readerly text. And it cannot produce knowledge. We must recall that all of Tom's reading couldn't free Jim, but Jim's writing saved Tom's life.

E N D N O T E S

1. Henry David Thoreau, *Walden* (New York: New American Library, 1960), p. 65.

2. The adjective is Barthes'. He refers to Penelope as the "eponymous speaker." I believe his intent is akin to my own.

3. Roland Barthes, S/Z, trans. Richard Miller (New York: Hill & Wang, 1986), p. 7.

4. e e cummings, *50 Poems* (New York: Grosset and Dunlap, 1940), p. 14.

5. This definition is equally true for Derrida as for Lacan.

6. Freud says that "The system revealed by the sign that the single acts forming parts of it are unconscious we designate by the name "The Unconscious," for want of a better and less ambiguous term" Sigmund Freud, *A General Selection From The Works Of Sigmund Freud*, edit. John Rickman (New York: Doubleday Anchor Books, 1957), p. 53.

7. Jacques Lacan, *The Four Fundamental Concepts Of Pshcyo-Analysis*, trans. Jacques-Alain Miller (New York: W.W. Norton & Co., 1981), p. 25.

8. Many of these ideas are derived from Jacques Derrida's *Of Grammatology*, trans. Gayatri Chakravorty Spivak (Baltimore: Johns Hopkins University Press, 1976).

9. Terry Eagleton, *Walter Benjamin, or Towards a Revolutionary Criticism* (London: Verso Books, 1985), p. 116.

10. Anika Lemaire, *Jacques Lacan*, trans. Charles Denart (London: Routledge & Kegan Paul Lts., 1977), p. 62.

11. Jacques Derrida, *Of Grammatology*, trans. Gayatri Chakravorty Spivak (Baltimore: John Hopkins University Press, 1976), p. 11.

12. Plato, *Phaedrus And Letters VII And VIII, Trans*, Walter Hamilton (New York: Viking Penguin Books, 1986), p. 96.

13. Jacques Derrida, *Dimmeminations*, trans. Barbara Johnson (Chicago: University of Chicago Press, 1981), p. 77

14. Roland Barthes, *Image, Music, Text*, trans. Stephen Heath (New York: Hill and Wang, 1977), p. 159.

15. Terry Eagleton, *Literary Theory*, (Minneapolis: University of Minnesota Press, 1983), p. 137.

16. John Updike, *The Centaur* (New York: Fawcett World Library, 1963), p. 80.

17. Le Corbusier, *Urbanisme* (Paris: Editions G. Cres, 1972) in *Reading Expository French*, ed. Roy Jay Nelson (New York: Harper & Row, 1965), p. 133.

18. Henry David Thoreau, *The Natural History Essays*, ed. Peregrine Smith, (Salt Lake City: Peregrine Smith, Inc., 1980), pp. 101-102.

19. Stephen Jay Gould, *Hen's Teeth and Horse's Toes* (New York: W.W. Norton & Company, 1984), p. 72.

20. See, for example, Sondra Perl, "The Composing Processes of Unskilled College Writers," *Tresearch in the Teaching of English*, Dec. 1979, Vol. 13, p. 317-326.

21. See Kevin Harris, *Education And Knowledge* (London: Routledge & Kegan Paul, Ltd., 1979).

22. Joyce Cary, *The Horse's Mouth* (New York: Harper & Row, 1965), p. 113.

23. Mark Twain, *The Adventures of Huckleberry Finn* (New York: Bantam Books, 1966) p. 238.

CHAPTER FOURTEEN

Teachers and Values

The Progressive Use
of Religion in Education

Kathleen Casey
1989

It has always been difficult to introduce serious discussion of religious issues into public debates on education in this country. While the constitutional separation of church and state is often evoked to justify this exclusion, such an argument does more to obscure than to clarify the problem. The ethical, moral, or religious (in the broadest sense)[1] dimension of education has never been, and indeed cannot be, excluded from our schools Yet, rather than acknowledge the sharply conflicting interpretations of morality which characterize our heterogeneous society, much of American educational theory, policy, and practice is silent on the subject.

The virtual vacuum in this area of public discourse is one reason why the New Right has been able to represent itself as the only moral voice in education. This bid for a monopoly on morality has not gone unchallenged. But, reactions against this shallow program have made the justification of any ethical language in education all the more awkward to sustain. Rather than abandoning the project, however, I would propose a search for alternative versions of a religious vision in education.

A number of curriculum theorists have produced valuable essays on this topic over the years. Huebner, for example, has consistently argued for the importance of an ethical language for valuing the curriculum. For Huebner, religious values are "the essence of education" (1984, p. 112), theological thought, "one of the most exciting and vital language communities" (1975a, p. 257) today. Huebner's contributions to this subject will be noted below.

The main focus of this article, however, will be on life history narratives of a group of anonymous women teachers. Although moral discourse may be absent from the public debate, many teachers, especially those working in parochial schools, organize their whole lives around religious values. The narratives of progressive Catholic nuns that will be presented below demonstrate the power of such a perspective in practice, and show that recent conservative uses of religious language are not the only forms that such concerns can take.

T H E   T H E O R E T I C A L   C O N T E X T

In the late 1960s and early 1970s, the demarcation of competing conceptual frameworks ("paradigms," "discourses," or "languages") and the disclosure of their underlying assumptions became a central project for theorists in a number of academic fields. In curriculum theory, Huebner (1966) delineated a set of "languages for valuing curriculum." An avowed intention of this many-sided model was escape from the confines of the existing one-dimensional way of talking about curriculum; a major effect was the de-centering of the dominant tradition, and the affirmation of alternative perspectives.

Certain fundamental insights of Huebner's (1966) essay stand unchanged. In the contemporary United States, *technical* demands for efficiency, standardization, and rationalization continue to crowd out *political* concerns about the exercise of power and control in education; *scientific* interests in the production of new knowledge; *esthetic* needs for beauty, harmony, and balance in educational activity; and *ethical* responsibilities in the encounter between two human beings, which is "the essence" of life. But, 20 intervening years have seen increasingly complex explorations of the construction of human meaning in language systems, and Huebner's formulations have also changed.

As Huebner's writings have developed, his emphasis has shifted from a stress on the persistence of language and the passivity of its speakers (see 1966, p. 218, 221) to a recognition of the incomplete and unfinished nature of language, and of the "individual men" (*sic*) who "are the source of its vitality and its growth" (1975a, p. 257). The most conspicuous break with his earlier formulations appears in Huebner's (1984) essay entitled "The search for religious metaphors in the language of education." Using the plural pronoun "we," and situating himself with a Christian community, Huebner now supposes that "knowledge, as social meaning, is always constructed with other. Knowledge is a social construction, not an individual construction" (1984, p. 121). Not only has Huebner's concept of the origins of language changed; his understanding of the relationship among languages is clearly different. What this recent work suggests is that Huebner no longer desires a curriculum which is a combination of equal parts of several perspectives, but one which is organized around a religious core.

T H E   S O C I A L   C O N T E X T

There are remarkable similarities between Huebner's writings and the life history narratives of the Catholic nuns[2], which will be presented below. Both sets of texts employ a vocabulary of receptivity, grace, and prayer; explore metaphors of the stranger, the supper, the dance, and the home; pose existential questions; and offer religious answers. All the authors seem to be participating in the same thriving, albeit marginalized, Christian language community.

But, the distinctiveness of these women's narratives is significant. When women organize their life stories, as they have organized their lives, around religion, they use language in special ways. And, because the women in this study are also progressive political activists, they use a particular "dialect" of religious language. Furthermore, in combination with the aforementioned, they talk about themselves as teachers in a specific way.

As nuns, these women are representatives of a significant group of teachers whose contributions to education have been regularly taken-for-granted, ignored, or riduculed[3], even within church circles. A particular kind of feminist analysis of this experience pervades the life histories. Political theorizing is a salient characteristic of the narratives of these activists, for whom ethics are not abstract principles, but a set of actual deeds, within a concrete network of human relationships. Faced with experiences of nothingness and encounters with death[4], these women reestablish meaning and identity in conjunction with others, within a context of community.

DEFINING THE SELF: THE NUN

In the narratives of Catholic nuns, answers to the existential question "Who am I?" flow from a religious matrix. One woman mentions several times that she was born in a house at the apex of a triangle with the parish convent and rectory. Another woman's life story starts with the sentence, "I was professed in 1964"; the beginning of her life as a nun is, from her perspective, the beginning of her life.

Not every nun's narrative explains her decision to become a nun; but two that did describe their apparently inexplicable choice in clearly existential terms. Both recount difficulties in schools taught by nuns, remember generally disliking the nuns they know, and describe themselves as "not the type" to join the convent. So, having lived as nuns themselves for more than 20 and 25 years respectively, they feel a need to explain this puzzle in their stories. One woman tells of an existential crisis and a religious conversation.

> I think what happened was the year before that I was going though a kind of life crisis…something about the meaning of my life. I suppose that this was probably an identity crisis. It seems like all my life I had had Catholic doctrine and stuff shoved into me and I can remember hating the stuff that I did in high school and when they talked about grace I always thought it was boring. I was more interested in sex.

> I guess what happened was I really went through some kind of conversion. Things that I had formerly just laughed at or just had really never thought about except on a superficial level I started to take seriously. I think I really wanted to know what the meaning of life was, and what the meaning was for me, really, I guess. I decided, at that time, and I can remember deciding it so I

know it was important to me...I decided that...if I had something to do with my life, something important...the thing I most wanted to do was to give it to God, and I think I thought that by going into the convent I could find God.

The search for meaning was not settled for all times by this decision; she continues to ask herself this question. Even last year, she recounts:

I remember kneeling at mass in the morning and suddenly I had this very clear gut feeling that what I had done with my life was really good and important and that I still wanted to do it. So however muddled my reasons were then, I guess they still have a quality, have a clarity about them still and now I just think what I did was the right thing.

Being a nun is, furthermore, no guarantee of meaning, according to this narrative; although she herself finds authenticity in her construction of that role, this woman speaks critically of the possibility of becoming what she calls "canned nun."

For the other woman who unpredictably entered the convent, the title "nun" is, in Carol Christ's (1980) vocabulary, a "false naming," because it is used by those who seek to curtail her ministry to gay and lesbian Catholics. She sees the hurling of the epithet "traitor" at a public meeting, together with the affixing of the label, "class clown," in her childhood days, as attacks on her authentic self. Although her original decision to join the convent "all of sudden...just seemed like the right thing," and living in her community still does, she is no longer comfortable with the name "Sister," because of the expectations some people attach to it.

So I more and more don't want this *Sister* thing...to be anything special or different or...I get angry when people say "Oh, but you're a nun!" Right. "Well, you don't dress like a nun." Well that doesn't make any sense, because I am, and...this is how I dress.

Subjected since childhood to experiences of nothingness in the form of destructive devaluations of her self, this woman was nevertheless able to maintain and nurture her authenticity. While her narrative recounts her positive experiences in teaching, contact with nature, friendship with "those who had no other friends," and small group community living, she does not attribute her sense of freedom to any particular source.

So people call me names, so what? I don't really know how I got freed from that. Really, I don't. But I am, and it's a wonderful feeling. When people actually said, "This is the class clown." or "She's a troublemaker," I felt like...that was then who I was. You know, I don't like that, because I'm more than that. I'm bigger than that.

D E F I N I N G   T H E   S E L F :
T H E   T E A C H E R

The passage in which this woman describes entering the convent, to the surprise of "everyone," even to some extent herself, tells how her religious superiors had their doubts, "and *yet*, they didn't tell me to leave." *Without a pause*, the next sentence continues, intensely, "I, all my life wanted to be a teacher. *All my life.*" Elsewhere she reiterates: "I'm a teacher at heart; I will always be a teacher." In her narrative, entering the convent is inextricably associated with becoming a teacher, and teaching takes on an existential quality in this connection, and in the way she links it to nature.

Echoing Christ's (1980) analysis of nature as a place where women can make contact with the meaning and power withheld from them in society, the girl who was always in trouble in school found "the earth" to be one of "the most influential people," and "significant teachers" of her childhood.

> I very much was raised, I believe, by the earth. I was very attentive to myself, as I was growing, and as I say, I learned a lot from the earth. I probably learned more from the earth than I did from any teacher in school.

And , indeed, although she described her own teaching philosophy and methods in thoughtful detail, she was unable to locate their source in any part of her teacher education or any "school of thought."

According to Christ (1980), women are particularly vulnerable to the experience of nothingness because of their powerlessness in society, but this makes them better able to identify with other victims, and to become involved in their struggles. The main reason this woman became a teacher, for example, was because of her recognition of the powerlessness of "little people." She wanted to create something that she herself had never experienced in school: a space in which children's authenticity could flourish.

> I wanted to make education alive for kids. I wanted it to be real. I didn't want them to feel like they were apart from the institution, or that they were separate from it. That somehow there was meaning there for them, that they *could* make a *difference*. I never felt I could make a difference, because I was always in trouble.

While she was a teacher, one of the children in her class confided in her his fears of being homosexual, and a fellow teacher who was a very close friend disclosed that he was gay. She began to realize the oppression of gay and lesbian people and, as she "was always for the underdog," she went to work for their cause.

D E F I N I N G   T H E   S E L F :
T H E   A C T I V I S T

This woman is a very reluctant activist. She does not like the word "political"; she is "intimidated" by government. She describes herself as a shy person who began her ministry as "a simple presence," and was forced to speak out because of the positions taken by local government and the church. Her public debut as a spokesperson was at a city council meeting in support of gay organizations; the right to hold meetings in the Chamber of Commerce building, an action which she recounts in existential terms: "All kinds of people were there. And I said very loudly, and bravely, 'Sister (her own name), members of the Sisters of (name of her religious order) of (name of city).'"

Another version of the formulation, "I/we are, therefore I/we speak, therefore I/we are" appears in relation to her giving of homilies at the blessing of commitment of two gay people; "I am saying I recognize this relationship," and "I am saying very loudly, yes, it does exist, and I affirm it."

The "new naming" by which the gay and lesbian Catholics tell "who they are," and "what is really going on in their lives," has fortified this woman's sense of who she is. The associations to which gay and lesbian Catholics belong are called "Dignity" and "Integrity"; and this woman feels "compelled" to be their chaplain, because she needs "to live authentically," " to find integrity" in herself. She has always spoken out against injustices, but now she is one voice within a newly defined community of voices. Membership in the new community shows her the falseness of the old institution. She has become deaf to what the church hierarchy is saying; it no longer "makes sense: to her. I don't see the Pope as um…the Catholic church. The church is *these* people I am ministering to, yeah, they are the church, and they are saying, from their life experiences who they are."

Yet, the strength that she derives from her work with gay and lesbian Catholics goes beyond "group solidarity." The "prevailing problematic" of gay and lesbian rights has been, in the words of Cornel West (1982), "existentially appropriated." Her quest is rooted in the powers of being. Within the religious discourse of Prophetic Christianity, the final recourse for "the negation of what is" and "the transformation of prevailing realities" is the transcendent God (West, 1982).

Well, maybe I am a traitor to the Pope, and what he says, but I'm definitely not a traitor to the word of God. The reason I'm here, is because it is very clearly what I hear in the scriptures.

Two nuns make a point of distinguishing between political action taken for religious motivations and that which is not. Speaking of the volunteers who work with her in a program for women in prison, one woman emphasizes:

Many of them don't come from a religious *motivation*. And I do, I do, because Jesus said "I've come to announce freedom to captives." And I know that they have been...treated as less than equal in their education, housing, home...job preparation, employment, they've been treated as inferiors. I *know* that. And I feel that each of us have [sic] a responsibility to do what he/she can...to balance the scales of justice.

The other woman, who now works with street people, makes a functional point about her perspective:

And, for me, I see a real difference when, my motive...and my expression of who I am and what I'm about...comes from a belief in the gospel, rather than out of anger. What happens in my experience is that when people act out of anger they burn out quickly. But when people act out of gospel values...there's a better chance that they're also going to be in touch with.... When I came to an interview here, I was told..."If you see yourself as the one who has to do everything, you won't last. If you see yourself as part of the ministry of God's work, you will last. And you'll be one instrument that God can use to work."

This is expressive not only of a distinctive understanding of the process of political practice, but also of the role of the individual, of the nature of the goals, and of the location of ultimate power.

West (1982, p. 96) echoes and expands upon these women's formulations in one of his summaries and defenses of the discourse of Prophetic Christianity.

The Christian project...is impotent in the sense that within the historical process, ultimate triumph eludes it and imperfect products plague it. Yet, more important, there are varying degrees of imperfection and much historical space for human betterment. For Christians, the dimension of impotency of all historical projects is not an excuse which justifies the status quo, but rather a check on Utopian aspirations which debilitate and demoralize those persons involved in negating and transforming the status quo. Ultimate triumph indeed depends on the almighty power of a transcendent God who proleptically acts in history but who also withholds the final, promised negation and transformation of history until an unknown future.

Of course, not every version of the Christian project is progressive, as West (1982) illustrates in his political typology of the varieties of religious discourse. Distinctions need to be made not just between Christian and non-Christian positions, but also within Christian discourse itself. In fact, the definition of what it means to be a Christian is a subject of ideological struggle.

IDEOLOGICAL STRUGGLE OVER "NAMING

The process of self-naming always takes place within the social context, which is also a site of ideological struggle. The "new naming" of themselves by gay and lesbian Catholics has not been left unchallenged. The "false naming" of the gay rights activist by an opponent was an assault in an ideological battle, as was the attempted "un-naming" with which another activist was threatened.

This personally and politically assertive woman was not interested in the anonymity of the research project because, she told me, she would rather have her causes publicized through the use of her name. Throughout her narratives she explicitly announces her identities ("I've been a nun for forty-five years; I have been a teacher more or less in some way or another for forty years; I am Jewish-Christian relations, and women"), and emphasizes their religious foundations ("So I feel that I do...that which is God's will"). Probably for this very reason, her "naming" was being seriously threatened by the church hierarchy at the time of our meeting.

For a number of years she had been one of the leaders of several groups within the Catholic church who challenged the teachings of the hierarchy, particularly on subjects related to women in the church. Then, with a number of other clergy, she became part of a public call for "dialogue" on the subject of abortion, during a national political campaign in which some Catholic bishops were making it a partisan issue.

The way in which this woman structures her narrative of these events is more important than the content that she communicates. Accounts of the episode can be found elsewhere, as it was, and still is, being widely covered by the media. But in this account we can see several sets of assumptions that gave shape to the actions and understandings of the participants themselves.

G R O U P S   I N   I D E O L O G I C A L   S T R U G G L E

Throughout the passage dealing with this issue, this woman speaks in the first person plural ("we signed it"); this was an action taken as a group. In emphasizing the importance of "sticking together," she is critical of the men who were originally part of the group, and who later "conformed." As men, she notes, they have the prospect of gender-exclusive promotion; as men, they do not have the experience of gender oppression, and of solidarity with "women who are in a hard corner." Thus, her definition of the group is, in the last analysis, as women within the church struggling against the male hierarchy.

Gender is a primary issue in this woman's narrative. "My own cause is women," she reiterates throughout her story, and in one strikingly existential definition of her activism, she declares, "I am women." While she extends the circumference of her concern to include women throughout the world, specifically mentioning her own trips to India, Lebanon, and Latin America, it is clearly women living in poverty for whom she works. And within this group, she has now focused on women in prison. At the same time she has been shifting her energies to the specific cause of poor women, she has also been a primary organizer of her own cohort of women coworkers. She was a founder of a cross-congregational association of Catholic women religious, protesting their position in the church; she established the organization of interdenominational church women who work with women in prison; she has connections with the National Organization for Women. The public petition on abortion came out of a preexisting network of a particular group of Catholic women religious and their associates.

The process of "un-naming" was, it appears, to be conducted by remote control. Neither the individuals involved, nor their assembly as a group, were ever directly addressed by the church hierarchy. Instead the process of censure was initiated through the separate religious orders to which the members of the group belonged. But here also, it seems, the solidarity of the institutional group (of women) won out against a hierarchically imposed authority (of men). While this woman recounts other examples of individual members of her religious congregation criticizing her work, in this instance she emphasizes the fact that her religious superiors "stood by us, you know. And in effect, they said 'We can find no cause to dismiss so and so.'"

As the word "dialogue" suggests, this woman, together with her co-signers, took for granted the existence of distinct groups within the Catholic church. The call for "dialogue" also proposes interaction between groups of equal status. Any claim of the church hierarchy to exclusive or higher authority is dismissed ("They are always quoting themselves and each other...to find authority. Find a better authority than that"). Like the nun who was an advocate for gay and lesbian Catholics, this woman finds authority for her actions through the immanent voices of her constituency, women living in poverty, and, ultimately, in the transcendent power of God. The power of the hierarchy is radically undercut when they are not seen as intermediaries to the greater power. Not only does this woman declare: "I don't take vows to the Pope. My vows were made to God"; she has also joined a "non-canonical" community, so she will "always be a nun," even if the makers of the laws say she is not. The approval from the hierarchy, which was previously understood as legitimating religious organizations, is simply by-passed, and groups name themselves as communities dedicated to religious ends.

This woman does not rest her case only on the language of religious belief; she also speaks the language of social scientific analysis. That some of the hierarchy saw the letter as a confrontation with a small group of "minions," rather than a conversation within the whole church, she proposes, is an indication of their lack of understanding of contemporary realities. Research by the National Opinion Research Center, she notes, "showed that only eleven percent of adult Catholic couples, only eleven percent, follow the church's teaching on the use of contraceptives." In a Gallup poll taken in July 1984, she also observes, "of adult Catholics called, 77% believed that abortion was permissible in some instances." For a particular group within the clergy to assert authoritarian power under these circumstances is, in her estimate, an inept miscalculation.

> When we signed it, we didn't think it was gonna be radical. Some man, some man in the church, some bishops we think, here in this country, did not realize what it was gonna do. Unleashed all that energy. We were grateful. Cause it gave us an instrument to tell people how we thought. But he had no idea. He thought we'd just sink in, you know, conform. Well, the men did, be we didn't. And we don't intend to.

Thus, the ideological position articulated by those who signed the newspaper advertisement is grounded not only in the strong network of the signers themselves but also in the (unorganized) majority of the total organization.

I D E N T I T I E S   A N D   I N S T I T U T I O N S

So far we have seen examples in which the individual's identity is created by, and creates, a group identity. But these groups do not correspond to the institutions within which the women live their lives. Working on their political projects, their networks include alliances across religious congregations, and denominations, in coalition with "lay–", and "non–" Catholics, in solidarity with other occupations, and even with their "clients." Even while these women remain members of a particular institution, they are breaching its boundaries by virtue of their wider networks.

But the women's perception of their relationship to the institution of the church is very different from their understanding of their relationship to their own congregations as institutions. The world "institution" is, in fact, always used in a derogatory sense to describe bureaucratic and legalistic trends in church organization. In the early part of this century, one woman complains, bishops were only interested in building institutions. Hence, they "kept pressuring sisters for hospitals and schools," without "thinking in terms of the broader society and each one having an individual gift to do something. They were thinking in terms of big chunks of labor."

The contemporary institutional church is seen as a regressive organization dominated by a privileged male hierarchy who exacerbate tensions by exerting authoritarian control. Nuns are relegated to the powerless periphery. They feel alienated from the institution, and see it as an impediment to their authentic identities. In the words of one woman, "You have to keep an aesthetic distance; otherwise it's cruel on your psyche." Another reiterates: "I don't wana say I didn't *respect* the institution, but...I tried to keep it in perspective, you know, and I always felt...separate from it. And yet a part of it but separate."

At the same time, the women's own religious congregations are becoming less "institutionalized." Their legalistic phase is seen as an aberration, caused in part, according to one woman's interpretation of her order's history, by "the war;" "we were cut off from our origins across the ocean. We had continued to observe every single thing the way it was before, and they had evolved."

Since the Vatican II reforms, communities are creating, and being created by, more democratic participation. "It seems as though the rule is now something that we make through our experience," one woman states; another observes:

> I can't do the institutional kind of living any more. I will never be able to again. This is ordinary living. I'm an ordinary person. I'm very person-oriented. And, I can't deal well with…big institutions.

The women's perceptions of their leaders are not antagonistic, even though there are several ironic comments on inappropriate assignments "they" made in the past. Yet, descriptions of disagreement generally stress processes of consultation, negotiation, flexibility, tolerance, and the contemporary development of "co-responsibility." Other sisters are assumed to be in good faith. There is a strong underlying sense of a common project, of an authentic striving for the common good.

When tension between an individual and the religious congregation do appear, they are often concerned with the individual's work identity. The one woman who left the convent gave as one of her major reasons her discomfiture with the subject and level (college political science) which she had been assigned to teach. Another woman's work history fluctuated between nursing (which was her own interest) and teaching English, depending on the vacancies which the order needed to fill.

Work loads and preservice training are also mentioned as areas that were particularly problematic in the past. While several nuns in this study were selected for further education before they began to teach, one woman's experience is more typical of the common practice thirty years ago.

> I was educated in eight different colleges before I got my degree. At the end of my freshman year it became apparent that there were not enough teachers to fill this grade school that we had. And I was told that I was going to take one set of summer courses and go and teach. And so I said Ok. I was *scared*. I was so scared. I worked *really* hard, and I worried a lot about those kids, because I really loved them. But I, there was a lot I didn't know when I started teaching. On the other hand, what we *did* have was a fine sense of solidarity. So it wasn't like I was entirely on my own. And then I went to school in summer. For fourteen years. It took me fourteen years to get my degree.

I S O L A T E D   I N D I V I D U A L
E N C O U N T E R S   W I T H   D E A T H

In spite of these tensions, the lives of women religious are so tightly interwoven with their communities that changes in identity and/or context are potentially very traumatic.[5] Two women recreate experiences of existential isolation in their narratives by associating the process of change with an encounter with death.

One woman who reluctantly accepted her "re-naming" to a position of leadership in her religious community connects that transition to her escape from a fatal car accident. Her first official act as coordinator was to organize funerals for two friends with whom she would have been traveling had she not taken up her new job one week before. The association of these two experiences in her narrative suggests that she was mourning the loss of her earlier identity, at the same time as she was feeling lonely and isolated by her new managerial role. It must have seemed as though her life was saved so that she could make her special contribution to the community. After she had organized the structural transition that the congregation had mandated for itself, (a whole scale transformation of group relationships and individual identities), she left the (now obsolete) position of coordinator to return to her former occupation and ordinary membership in the community.

Another woman's re-naming originated in her search for more meaningful work, and only indirectly in connection with her congregation. She had chosen her life's work when she joined a religious order dedicated to teaching and had received professional training and certification in that area. But, after teaching for 20 years, and becoming a highly skillful practitioner, she began to feel "hollow"; she had lost her sense of purpose. Around this time, she relates, one of her colleagues was killed in a car crash. It was not only the death of a fellow teacher that shocked her; it was the interpretation of that loss by the school administration[6] that impinged on her own fragile identity.

> I remember when this Brother who was a very nice man died and the principal stood up and said, "Well, we had a problem. I was away in Europe this summer and when I got back I found out that he had died. Brother died, and we didn't have anybody to take his place, but fortunately, we were able to fill the gap." I was just appalled, you know. Like I finally said…that's all the administration want, you know, someone to fill the hole.

Her own doubts about the meaning of her occupation made her susceptible to others' devaluation of it. Her work "wasn't really valued"; she was "just another cog in the wheel" in the eyes of six different principals, who "never knew what had come before and cared less." When she was transferred after 17 years teaching in the same school, she "left without even a plastic plaque with my name on it," symbolic, in her eyes, of the nonbeing accorded to her person. She subsequently laid her teacher identity to rest, and, with the support of another artist, she began to redefine herself as a painter. At the time of our meeting, she was still working out the integration of her new role within her community; this included the major practical project of finding employment, as there was no suitable position within the schools her congregation operates.

Like the accidental deaths with which they are associated, identity changes appear in these two stories as ruptures, which cause disorientation, isolation, and (at least temporarily) destruction, and against which meaning must be recreated. Two of the narratives that include encounters with death present deliberately chosen constructions of identity and meaning through group action. Disjunctures are immediately transformed by the religious and political projects within which whose contexts they appear.

IDEOLOGICAL VICTORY OVER DEATH

The deaths that appear in the narrative of a woman who works with the homeless are neither natural nor accidental; they have social causes. Deaths from exposure of the homeless can be traced to real estate profiteering, and to the allocation of government resources for military purposes. Nuclear research, the building of battleships, and funding of insurgencies, each remove money from social services, and each is in itself a cause of death. "I choose life," this woman declares, in a deliberate reconstruction of the right-wing "pro-life" phrase.

> Trying to help people choose life. Politically that's where I am. Now, it's difficult because I'm not...I cannot classify myself in the group of people who call themselves pro-life. Ok? I'm not in that group, because their idea of pro-life to me is very limited. You know, "Capital punishment is fine," things like that. And, for me, when I choose life, I choose life for all people in all dimensions. And it doesn't matter who the person is or where they live.

One of this woman's religious/political projects is the prevention of socially caused deaths through public manifestations of their existence. Participating in a "lie-in" at a nuclear research facility, a "die-in" on a battleship, and a "sit-in" on the Nicaraguan-Honduran border, this woman has progressed from naming the destructive function of an ordinarily invisible facility, to acting the part of an already deceased victim, to placing herself in danger of death. In each case, she was personally and publicly constructing a religious and political discourse in concert with the groups of which she was a member. Theory and practice, ideology and action, were united in her "experience of putting my body where I believed." Death was defined, and conquered, in a particular formulation; and leadership, defined as the collective taking of public initiative out of personal conviction, was accepted as an identity.

The moment of ideological victory over death is vividly described in this woman's account of her encounter with death on the Nicaraguan border. Ordinary fears are transcended as ideology-put-into-practice becomes an empowering force, and the isolated individual is bonded with the group, and with the transcendent God.

> And I remember saying to someone that, I studied a lot about grace, but being at the border when the soldiers lifted their rifles, it was a real powerful experience of grace. Because there was no other way!
>
> Before I went to Nicaragua, like just a few days before, they had the helicopter incidents and everything, and I was saying, "Oh my God," I said, "I'm carrying a little American flag, and if we have problems, I'm gonna raise it and say 'I'm on your side!' " Everything I believe in goes down the drain when it comes to that. And I, I told people "Now, if someone...tells me to raise my hands and they're gonna shoot me, I'll break every record in the race," I said, "I'll run so fast."
>
> And I remember thinking that when I was at the border, I started to laugh to myself thinking, "God, all the things I said before I came here." And it was like, I just wanted to say, "Shoot me if you want. But you're not going to destroy what we believe in, the power of Christ, is so much stronger than those bullets and everything else." And it, I thought I can't believe I'm really thinking this.
>
> And we shared as a group afterwards, and everybody agreed. Everyone was really afraid. But that fear...was overcome with courage and it was an experience of what we read in...you know, Paul, when he says about the power of the risen Christ is in you. It was a real, I mean, a power that was within, that gave me strength to stand there, that's the resurrection power. And it was, so it was an experience of so much I've studied. Being there.

The idea of "dying for what I really believe in" is now associated in this woman's mind with a feeling of "peace within me." In another woman's narrative, expulsion from religious life is symbolically equated with death and, even while she was making organization maneuvers to prevent this existential unnaming, she willingly accepted the possibility of "dying" for what she believes.

> My dossier is on their top desk in Rome. And I'm sure they want my head, but they won't dare. I don't think they'll dare. If they do, I'll go. I've been a nun for forty-five years. I've been a faithful nun. But, ok, I'll go. It's a good cause to die for. *To stand with women.*

T H E   C O N S T R U C T I O N
O F   T H E   C O N S I S T E N T   S E L F

It was the public manifestation of a particular religious and political stand in a full page national newspaper advertisement signed by this woman and her cohorts that put her in jeopardy of her identity as a nun, threatening her existence within the church. But it is the continuous composition and publication of her ideas (in "over two hundred articles and several books") which contributes to her identity as an activist, giving her other grounds to say "I am."

While I was recording her narrative, she would pause from time to time to find me reprints from national magazines of other interviews she had given, and to show me relevant quotations. I later heard other members of her cohort use the same or similar phrases in their own media presentations about the newspaper advertisement, attesting to the way in which her statements grow out of her political connections, and more often take the form of "we are" than of "I am."

Her publications are contributions to the discourse of the networks to which she is attached; but, her writings have also helped her explain her own life to herself. Faced with existential dread after the death of her parents, she was able to assuage her grief of interpreting the meaning of their lives in terms of their influence on her. Many of her acquaintances say they do not know the source of their activism, she observes; she traces her own back to her parents.

> I have been reflecting deeply about my childhood. And after my parents died, I couldn't talk about it. I was in such grief. We all were. But, I wrote a chapter for a book, and that was a kind of release for me. And after that I could think more about my parents. "Cause I, I was so in grief over their loss. It was natural, I mean it, it was a natural death at a natural time, but it was…and after that then I began thinking. I wrote three chapters for different books on that subject. And, I think it's my parents. I definitely think so.
> Well, my father and mother were very loving and caring. They were the town physician and the nurse. And the two of them took car of migrants, and they took care of everybody, of course, but they were very solicitous. Always. Yes, I think I got it from them. As I look back now, I think I can see the roots there in my parents. For example, I'm sure there was no Jew in our town. And yet my father, who was a very humble, simple, marvelous man, I can remember him saying, "as we treat the Jews, so God will treat us." And I didn't think much about it. But as I look back I think that made a *deep* impression on me, and I think it's true.

Political sociology has investigated the relationship between childhood experiences and political socialization; and it has analyzed the influence of parents on their children's political formation. What is important about this passage is that the speaker, a former political science professor, makes such a connection in her own life. She is asking an existential question: "What was the meaning of my parents' lives?" and, she has constructed a religious/political/sociological answer: "They made me an activist."

In another section of her narrative this woman rejects the suggestion that she was ever not an activist, declaring: "I am consistent; I am very consistent." In the passage above she constructs a narrative consistency that stretches over time, interpreting the past (her childhood) in relationship to the present (her parents' death), and ranges across spheres, bonding together personal, work and political relations (the intergenerational reproduction of professional care for needy clients). Political action is explained in an ethical vocabulary of love, care, and solicitude, for, always at the center of this consistency, organizing all its dimensions, is religion.

T H E   S Y M B O L I C   M A T R I X

A particular normative vocabulary is threaded through all the narratives in this group, and binds together the personal, work, and political relations of all its speakers. Moral imperatives are explicitly evoked throughout the narratives, and they are interwoven with a system of metaphoric representations of what ought to be.

One woman's explanation of the consistency and complexity of her moral identity makes use of several different kinds of metaphors. Calling herself an "existential phenomenologist," she uses vocabulary from her academic studies in that area: "My identity as a Sister of—is the primary focus of my identity, you know. Within that identity, I play lots of roles. But, that's...in the existential jargon, that's my primary 'project'." But she also chooses to explain herself through such symbolic forms as a triangle, a circle, an infinity sign, and a lazy-susan.

The triangle and the circle are configurations of the religious context within which this woman sees her self-formation. The house in which she was born becomes an analog for herself as she describes its position in relationship to the Catholic parish buildings.

> What I learned as a child, growing up in my house, was reinforced in the church and its position in our lives... and while I joke about living in that triangle between the convent and the rectory, I also know that we grew up knowing priests and sisters as people.

When she tells of an early teaching assignment in that parish and a later return to live in the same neighborhood, she describes the feeling of "coming full circle." Using yet another geometric symbol of integration, and moving her and to draw a figure eight as she speaks, she reiterates her interpretation of the process by which she has come to be.

> And my own experience just reinforces that, so that I feel kind of like that infinity sign, that the church has reinforced my identity as a person and my person has been reinforced by the values and the symbols and the rituals and the culture of the church.

"Body language" also reinforces this woman's explication of her identity when, expanding the symbolic mode, she holds up one hand, and points to her palm with a finger of the other hand, saying, "There is this identity. And there is this lazy-susan on which the roles are." Then pointing to each finger she lists such roles as working and praying, emphasizing the way in which they are "infused," so that, for example, "my work is my identity. I am my work."

While some of this woman's metaphors are her idiomatic constructions, she shares others with the larger group, specifically those of family and home. At first glance, there seems to be an irony to discovering these stereotypical female images in the discourse of progressive political activists, who, additionally, have lived their adult lives in the antithesis of a "house-wife" role. Further examination, however, will show a particularly interesting reconstruction of the symbolism of these images.

References to families recur throughout these narratives. Sometimes the focus is on families of biological origin[7], but even that conventionally defined grouping is presented as a social unity that reproduces a particular moral discourse. Family appears in the narrative context together with childhood, religious community, school, church, and state; its meaning is elaborated and developed in relationship to them, finally emerging as the embodiment of what ought to be, as a model for the transformation of those social relations that do not correspond to the speakers' moral discourse.

THE CHILDHOOD FAMILY

With the family, as with other topics, the internal organization of a life history does not often follow a neat, sequential chronology, but places emphasis according to the significations of the speaker. One woman's narrative omits the period of her childhood, and hence, the role her family of origin played in those years; two other women mention these aspects of their lives only briefly. While some narratives describe the families of their childhood in glowing terms, not all the women see their original families as matching their ideas.

One woman describes a childhood experience of existential meaninglessness caused by her mother's schizophrenia.

> It really caused havoc in our family. And, since I was the youngest, and the one at home...I was the only one still in grade school...I got a lot of the...bewilderment. And I was just becoming...I was passing from sixth grade into seventh when the worst happened. The worst being that she decided that the communists were after us and that was why her marriage was...unhappy, and why my father drank...Which was all crazy, and we had one of the large radio consoles with the luminous dial, and she thought the announcers could see into our home. And that they were manipulating her, and so on....
>
> The first year...it was really miserable...my whole seventh grade. She was very unpredictable. I took piano lessons and she was the one who had started me, and she would come and slap my hands at the piano and tell me not to play that...*wicked* music. And I was playing *Brahms*, you know! I'd cry, and I'd say "I

have to learn this! My teacher gave me this to learn." Once I remember she hit
me over the back with a butcher knife, and...some things like that happened
that were really kind of bizarre. And made it very scary.

When her mother was committed to a mental institution, she was sent to a
Catholic girls' boarding school. She never returned home; she joined the
convent directly out of high school.

Denied access to meaning in her fragmented family, she was able to escape
her mother's idiosyncratic discourse in a community of understanding "sisters."
As she was still a child, and, in her own phrase, "just becoming," her identity was
created within this surrogate family.

> When...I entered, I pretty well told my family...I didn't need them any
> more. I had learned to love and respect the people I had gone to school with,
> and I really did love the sisters. I had some real young, good, intelligent
> teachers. Who are still my best friends. They're like five years older than I am.
> And...I really admired what they taught me, and...I was altruistic. I wanted to
> do something for somebody else, but I really needed a family. So I got them
> both!

From this woman's perspective, the religious community is characterized by an
inclusivity that surpasses that of the family of biological origin. She notes, for
example, that counted among the sisters in her congregation

> Is a woman whom we raised from age three, who was left as a child with the
> sisters in our order by her father who didn't want her. Cause she was too sick.
> And we raised her, and she grew up, she worked in the kitchen...She visited
> her father very often. She's now seventy-five, and lives in—, with us still. Her
> parents have been dead a long time. And she was as much a member of our
> order except that she was not mentally real capable.

The religious community, not the family of biological origin, was the
childhood family for these two women, providing them with moral and material
support in their formative years.

R E L I G I O U S   C O M M U N I T Y
A S   F A M I L Y

The number of times the name "sister" is used in these narratives would be
striking to an uninitiated reader. Of course, historically, the Catholic church has
used the language of kinship to describe relationships among its members, and so
such terms are part of the taken-for-granted vocabulary of the narrators. In fact,
the use of the preface "Sister" has somewhat declined among Catholic women
religious in recent years, perhaps to evade the aspects of "false naming" with
which it had become associated, and to signify less formal and more personal
relationships.

However they maybe phrased, constituent familial relationships remain a central focus of the narratives. Whereas "sisterhood" is not the newly constructed, self-conscious naming of the contemporary womens movement, it consistently appears as a consciously valued and deliberately reproduced relationship. So, for example, one woman tells how she came to appreciate her relationships with friends in the convent; when one of them was posted elsewhere, and later left the order, "I went through a terrible kind of loss. It was as though I had lost a member of my family."

Sharing is presented as the essence of sisterhood, and its moments of personal delight: "I mean, just sitting down and sharing a cup of coffee with your sister, I mean, that is a unique gift," and in its ordering of group relations.

> And, if there's anything religious women have really experienced, it's community. How *all kinds* of us from all different attitudes and walks come together, and we made a home for each other. We have some sisters in our order, I thought, "How the hell did they ever get here!" I mean *come on*! But they were part of us. And we included them.

This sharing is not based on such standards of merit as intelligence. An assumption of human equality makes this family compassionate; they learn to "feel *with*" others, rather than to pity from a superior position.

> We have one little sister who was...under four feet. Who was, when you heard her speak, it was really sad. The rest of her family was real intelligent, she was...somewhat retarded. She spoke...She would say something three or four times, and usually in the same, exact same sentences...She was a *good*hearted little person. Worked real hard, did what she was told, cried a lot...but, she wasn't of...an intellectual caliber that she could ever feel like she belonged. Except that's what she did. She did belong, because she contributed to the work. It was good for the rest of us, because we learned.
>
> We learned compassion. We learned, compassion is not pity. Compassion is solidarity with people. Based on the fact that we're both people. Without any other conditions. It's standing with people in their suffering or in whatever, you know. And that's good. You have to learn that. It took me a long time before I had any compassion for that person, cause she was such an annoying person. She'd come and talk to you and say things over, three and four times. When you were trying to get something done, she would come and talk to you. But little—was an asset to our community. When she died, we felt bad.

SCHOOL COMMUNITY AS FAMILY

In these narratives, the norms associated with the religious congregation as family are extended into other spheres of social relations; these women have the same moral expectations in the work arena as they do for their personal relationships. The emblematic tale of the retarded child taken in by the religious congregation is echoed in this same narrator's story of her handicapped student.

And one of the things I always try to do, to bring that back to teaching, is look out for the ones that were on the frazzled edge of it. My first year teaching, I had—. I don't know where— is now, and I hope you don't print his name. — had a clubfoot. He was a third grader who was maybe two inches taller than anybody else in the grade, because he had failed once. He was a little tow-head with a crew cut, with a little toothy grin, skinny little kid, and always went as fast as he could on his little clubfoot.

I remember the highlight of my first awful year as a teacher was that – turned to me and said, "You're the best teacher I ever had!: In all of his three years of school, four years of school, in third grade! Eh! I was so pleased. But I think that kind of kid always attracted me because…I knew what it was like.

Having known the existential nothingness of being on "the frazzled edge" of her fragmented family of origin, this woman feels at one with other lost children, and is moved to connect them, as she herself was drawn in, to a new family. And, in the reciprocal arrangement of her narrative, the givers of the gift of inclusion are themselves rewarded by acceptance, reinforcing her theme that "there's a reason everybody is included."

Coming from the same root as *compassion*, the word *community* is also used in these narratives, and family is frequently presented as its embodiment. Both in its taken-for-granted conventional usage (as in reference to the "religious community"), and in its more deliberately defined examples, this characterization of family accentuates the congruence of the members of the group. Using such a pattern of association, another woman contrasts two different schools in which she taught. In the one that matched her expectations,

> I remember we worked really hard on establishing faith community in the school, and a lot of discussion, and when I was leaving there, people told me that the administrative team really did model to the school what faith community was about.

She chose to leave the other school because she thought it destroyed the equality and authenticity that she considered qualities of a family environment; in its embodiment of violent hierarchical authority (which, we must note, is a competing definition of family), it seemed to her more like a prison.

> And the reason I left that, the school in—was that I didn't agree with a lot of the philosophy in the school. I really believe that a school is a place where people come together, and form some kind of a community, and it's a prison, and if it's likened to anything it's likened to a family rather than a prison. And, my experience in that school was that it was *much* closer to a prison. And I was not into prison ministry at the time!
>
> So I decided, I will get out of here. And I didn't, I just didn't like the way the young men and women were being treated. I didn't think it was practicing what I believe in. I believe in authority, but I believe in nonviolent authority.

And there's such a thing that we each have our own authorship, and we speak out of that.

And I think teenagers in high school, have authority that's rightfully given to them by God, and teachers need to listen to them. And in that school, it was...*we are the faculty*. I mean, one day it was actually announced over the PA, "You will smile at your teachers." I mean, it was *really*...that was the day I said I need to get out of here. And there were just too many games being played.

The school community which is a family is characterized by relationships of love among its members. In one narrative, this love is defined in terms of enthusiasm, close personal ties, and positive encouragement.

Well, when I taught the first twenty years I loved the people I taught. I found great...enthusiasm in myself and in them. I could name any student I ever had, both boys and girls, and I could...For each one I think I could name the five virtues that are outstanding in that person. And I think that's the essence of true teaching. To get to love your students, and then to use their virtues in order to bring them forward. Um, pointing out their virtues only, their faults only through their virtues. The goal is to have the child feel at home. And love school, and run to school.

Another woman creates a narrative parallel between her feelings toward members of her religious congregation and her relationship with her students. In an almost identical construction to one quoted above, she explains her decision to join the convent in terms of love:

And I got very close to the sisters there. Was very close to the sisters of—. Anyway, because they were...the nuns who taught in the schools. And I loved them dearly, although I didn't like some of them personally, I loved them as a whole. I loved the sisters of --. I loved their spirit.

And, she uses the same vocabulary to describe her affinity for the adults and children with whom she worked in schools.

We worked with marvelous people. People whom I still correspond with today and, I love dearly. I had a junior homeroom, and I *loved* juniors. Mm, so much more than any other group in high school. Juniors are really *neat* kids.

CHURCH AS FAMILY

The love described in connection with the religious congregation and the school community is neither that of spouses nor of parents and children, two possible familial versions of that emotion. Rather, it comes closest to love among siblings, so often called "brotherly" (*sic*) love, and historically known in Christian symbolism as "agape." The alternative set of church symbols in which the loving parent exercises benevolent power over the children is explicitly rejected as an acceptable relationship for the religious congregation, for the school, and for the church itself.

Criticisms of the "Holy Father" occur frequently through the narratives. One woman calls him a "macho monster." But the rejection of the male parent's role in the family, which is the church, goes deeper than problems with a specific person. Words etymologically derived from the paternal metaphor are used only in the derogatory versions of their definition. The pontiff and his associates "pontificate," using their position of leadership in a pompous and dogmatic manner. The protective and supportive meanings of "patronage" are lost, for its condescending aspects are more evident.

> And see I don't, I, I think I don't, I don't wanna destroy the whole system. You know, and I don't wanna say, it's no good. But I want to say, we're missing something. You know, we could be so much better…if we listen to people. If we really welcomed people, not patronized people, but I would like to see us be able to, us, the Catholic church, strip the layers away, so that you're not afraid. I feel like we're very afraid…to invite all kinds of people, into our embrace.

In these narratives, the true embrace, a gesture of love, is impossible for the male clergy, "who set themselves up and apart."

T H E   F A M I L Y   E X P A N D E D

Across the narratives, the family of biological origins, the religious community, the school, and the church are each in turn evaluated according to the criterion of inclusion. In certain narratives, the state, and the political, social, and economic relations of the society at large are also judged according to the same demand.

The moral imperative "to invite all kinds of people" is repeated in several similar formulations in these narratives, e.g., "everyone's included at the banquet," "there is a reason why everyone is included," and, in an explicitly familial vocabulary,

> And, I choose life…for all people in all dimensions. And it doesn't matter, who the person is or where they live. You know, there were no boundaries in my idea of…The world is my sister and my brother. Doesn't matter if you live in a certain street, or in a certain country. And, when I think of politics I guess, my stand is, whatever is for life.

The "human family" is the frame of reference for another woman, whose commitment to the Jewish people is based on the "great gift" to that family: keeping "alive the idea of one God on this planet."

Particularly important manifestations of the ideals of inclusivity and reciprocity are the several passages that stress the cross-class basis for the moral/political project. Incorporating the previous mentioned motifs of family, love, and support, one woman asserts a theory of class incorporation, even while noting its impediments.

> My sisters are married and they're all middle class and they love and support me and I love them. And I'm not throwing out the middle class. I'm not being foolish. Because I know that it's from the middle class that I came…and I know that we must move the middle class…in such a way that they will incorporate the poor. See, the middle-middle, the upper-lower, if only the middle class could absorb the upper-lower, and maybe even the middle-lower…. What's happening now is that, the lower-middle class is now becoming the upper-lower. That's a problem. And of course the yuppies have nothing in sight but, they wanna become lower-upper.

This analysis is echoed by another woman who constructs a parallel between the history of her religious congregation and contemporary politics. The person who founded the order

> was outspoken. He was kind, but he was outspoken and he believed in standing up for social change that was needed. And, people who had money, it was their job to make the town work. I was so excited the other day I saw, in the paper that the Democratic party is beginning to speak again about the common good. *Hooray*, for the Democratic Party!
> And that was very much the philosophy under which—operated. That the common good depended upon…those who had the money, and could create the conditions for it. We all were responsible for the common good in some way. Nobody was off the hook. None of this, "I've got money and I can go do what I wanna do." But…they didn't have huge cities. It was so easy to tell what a person was doing with his time and money. And, so easy to be…pulled back…in.

Again, certain impediments are acknowledged, but community, cooperation, and the common good are set forth as ideal.

Service was the keynote of the catholic school program in which one woman approvingly participated; the project was organized to produce (and reproduce) a cross-class and interracial perspective among the participating students.

> It was the coming together of all different schools, within the religion program. And we had fifteen students from each school, and they would be matched, an inner city school with a suburban, very wealthy school. Like we were matched with—Country Day School. Their tuition's like…Then it was $3,200….
> But our kids and their kids would be in groups, doing some kind of service. They might go to a nursing home, a day care center, a hospital. They'd do it as a group. They would be going in the same places….
> But what would happen is, one day a month, they would go together, and one day a month there would be a reflection afternoon. Talking about their experiences. What would, what would happen in that is the kids would learn

about each other, and talk about who *they* were. And, kids from—would hear some of the problems that kids from—had. And what happened was, that they realized that, they came from different backgrounds but they were all kids and they all had different kinds of problems.

And they started looking at each other as people, rather than groups or classes of people. And that was, part of the purpose was that people could work together and...they're still doing that...And, that was a way of trying to get all different cultures together. And that worked really well.

F A M I L Y   T I E S

Of course, these women are particularly connected to specific members of this vast human family, but they explain these attachments in terms of inclusion, rather than exclusion. One woman, for example, was accused of neglecting her "own people" while attending to the needs of others, but, she did not accept the racial and religious boundaries that had been drawn by her critic.

> Huh! You know that during the sixties my work for interracial justice was considered *very* controversial. Well, it was terrible, one of the nuns said to me, "Well, are blacks Catholic?" And I said, "Only two percent," She said, "Well, then when you gonna work for us?" I mean, eh!

The breadth of her definition of a "people" was further demonstrated when, in the course of our conversation, the bombing of the MOVE headquarters in Philadelphia the previous week was discussed, and she remonstrated: "But you don't drop a *bomb* on one of your...I mean, we're dropping bombs on *our own people.*"

V O C A T I O N

Several women use a metaphor of oral/auditory communication to describe their state of receptivity to the needs of particular groups. The "vocation," "the call to service," is of course a long-standing Christian symbol, especially with reference to joining a religious community. Using and transforming this religious notion, one woman explains her "choice" of political projects in terms of her "listening heart."

> So basically I see *all* of those issues as life issues. And I see them all as um...very pertinent to my whole life style, because I've professed obedience. And to me obedience is a listening heart. If I'm going to be faithful to my vow of obedience, it doesn't just mean in my community. It means that I'm going to be faithful to listening to what God is saying, in the realities of life. And then I have no choice...to be out there, you know, protesting the embargo. It's not a choice. I've made the choice...to be faithful to the gospel, and...as a religious I took a vow of obedience. And whether I was a religious or not, to me, it's faithful to

my baptismal promises. But, as a religious I said *publicly* I will profess these. Well then I need to do it publicly. And I need to...whatever's *public* at that moment.

Another woman echoes the idea that one has only to listen to the contemporary debates to know what God is saying: "The motto of our founder was 'The will of the times is the need of God.'"

INTERPELLATION [8]

One woman describes the beginning of her connection to a particular group as a literal "call to service"; she was "hailed" and "petitioned" by the inmates in a prison which she was visiting.

> Well, what happened is that I gave a talk in—, and one of the women there was one of the chaplains, and she said "Would you like to see— prison?" I said indeed I would, because—is a famous prison. *Infamous prison.*
>
> So I went out there and, when I went through the women's division, the women came out of their cells, and they said, "Now, can you read this and what do you think?" And it would be a brief. That they had written. And I said, "Well, I'm not a lawyer, but I do have friends who are lawyers." And then somebody else would bring you something. "Well, now, look, do you see my art?" And, "Would you look at it?" I'd say, "Well, I'm not an artist, but I have some friends who are artists," you know, and so...that's how we began having weekends down in—.

Yet, there must be a correspondence between the "listening heart" and the "interpolating voice" in order for the message to be heard. This is not always clearly spelled out in the narratives. When there seems to be a perfect "fit" between ideology and practice, the appropriateness of one's actions is taken-for-granted.

> To me it's just well this, this is life, this is everyday, so why is it radical? In fact, the first time I was arrested for civil disobedience, I didn't call up the provincial council to tell them. And I remember saying to someone, I remember saying, "well, why, why should I call them? Isn't that a part of who I am? Isn't that a part of life?" And someone said to me, "Yeah, but it's not a part of everybody else's life!" And I understand their reason and I've called ever since.

Most often, there is no visible external source of interpolation; one is called by a voice within one's self. Sometimes this voice is explained as the voice of God; sometimes women just speak in terms of "doing what had to be done," of decisions which "just seem to be the right thing." One woman explicitly rejects voices of external persuasion in connection with religious vocations.

> The other part-time job that I've had was in vocational, you know, congregation, so I was like an army recruiter. And that just wasn't my thing...'cause I just...*believe* that if, if people have a vocation for a religious life,

we don't have to go looking for them. They will come. They will want to be part of us. Um, and I will support, you know, women who come and who *want* to, you know…and encourage…but…it just didn't fit me.

The feeling of "fit" between ideology and practice is also expressed in terms of celebratory moments and rituals. One woman's master of fine arts project was a set of photographs that celebrated the life of her religious community. She describes the emblematic significance of one of these pictures:

> The photos are all of our sisters. Some of them are up close, some of them, I have a great one that I used for the flyer for the show. And…there are three people in the room. One is a woman whom we raised from age three…And she was as much a member of our order except that she was not mentally real capable….
>
> So one was a picture of her with this friend of mine, and an older sister, and they were, they were kind of dancing, in the room. Just the three of them. It's a wonderful picture. I've got this sister with a hat on, with her arms out like this, and a big smile, looking right at the camera with an apron on. And I remember my photography teacher saying, "*These pictures! You never see pictures like this of nuns!*" And I said, "Yeah, yeah, I know you don't." "*You aren't there when they happen.*"

The moment of dancing is spontaneous rejoicing; other celebrations are planned rituals. In the shelter for homeless women, the weekly sharing of a family meal embodies and celebrates the values of community.

> Well, Wednesday night is our community night. We have liturgy, and the women come to liturgy, liturgy twice a week. The women come. And Wednesday night we have supper up here, it's the only night we eat together as a community. But it's almost like a sacred night. No one plans anything on a Wednesday night. And we really choose to be with one another and share a lot of values and, just…I'd say prayer life in this house really does support the ministry.

H A B I T U S [9]

Another way in which these women express their ideological predispositions is through metaphorical descriptions of the terrain upon which they see themselves situated. Physical features only appear on the ideological map when the habituée perceives a particular set of social relationships in that space. On a basic level, nuns are more likely to describe a local area as a "parish" than as a "neighborhood," or a "ward." In the more elaborate pattern of association in these narratives, the symbolism of the human-built landscape is consistently used to embody issues associated with change and problems connected with structure.

THE   COMMUNITY   AS   A   BUILDING

In the architectural metaphors used throughout these narratives, the habitus is not a permanent structure, but an ongoing construction process. Religious communities are criticized because, during their static phases, their structures operated as constraints and restrictions, like frames or boxes. One woman explains:

> See when we were in the, the first twenty years, we were kind locked into a frame. I think I was one of the first in our whole community. But I did it simply because I went to an education department, and it was a national Catholic, but it wasn't run by the church. It wasn't official church organization. But I think maybe my leadership did think so. I don't know. I myself hadn't even thought of it at the time.

Another echoes:

> I couldn't stand it! They were so straight-laced. And the expectations were, the three I was living with, there was one who was just a honey, the other two were like...and I could not stand it! Here I am an artist, you know, and into...alternative life-style stuff, and...it's probably why I joined the convent to begin with, being alternative to what I had. Trying to always find something better, and they were so straight-laced and boxed in, and I just couldn't stand it.

The communities continue to stand, but they have been subjected to drastic renovations due to dramatic changes in the perspectives of the inhabitants.

As the clothing previously worn by nuns was known as a habit, discussion of its meaning is pertinent to an understanding of habitus. In its day, the habit was not necessarily an encumbrance, according to one woman who recalls: "I marched in Selma in full habit. The James Meredith march through Mississippi in full habit." Yet, over time, according to other narratives, it lost its meaning, and became a "habit" in its negative sense, i.e., "a tendency to act in a particular way, acquired by frequent repetition of the same act until it becomes almost or quite involuntary" (O.E.D.).

> Oh heavens. Being a sister...has to do with your attitude. It has nothing to do with, what street you live on and what clothes you wear. It doesn't. It has nothing to do with that. It makes me angry when people say about the habit, you know. It has nothing to do with it! If you can't tell that I am a sister by my commitment or my attitude, then forget it.

W O M E N   A S   B U I L D E R S
A N D   D E M O L I T I O N   W O R K E R S

These women are not content to live out-moded habits, nor in a structure that someone else built. Sometimes they portray themselves as builders. In her discussion of the issues involved in a reproductive freedom campaign, one nun describes both the potential of the women with whom she works, and the need for change in the church, in architectural terms.

> A woman had to be...the architect of her own body. She had to make her decisions. And then she would be willing to *live* by her decisions, if she could make 'em.
> The hardest thing was abortion, and the right of a woman to make her own decision, just because I knew it was a threshold in the church, beyond which...but you see it already *is* a consensus.

Sometimes these women envision themselves as part of a demolition crew. Prisons are presented in these narratives as the epitome of repressive structures, and one woman recalls a moment of religious liberation within such a context using architectural terms.

> The last time we were there, I went to a *huge* gym, and that was gonna be the worship for the men. And...this woman, a Presbyterian minister, the woman was leading them, in prayer, in song, and they practically took the roof off that gym singing the sacred hymns. And I thought, that's wonderful. Yes, it is. In a woman.

T H E   B U I L D I N G   A S   T H E   H O M E

The positive aspects of structure, the healthy components of the habitus, are portrayed in terms of the home. When the social landscape is viewed through the lens of moral expectations, not every collection of people living together is a family, and not every common dwelling place, is a home. Childhood dwellings are not necessarily homes; neither are convents.

Several women make distinctions among the different convents in which they have lived. Comparing two of her early positions, one woman sees the emotional atmosphere of each community embodied in its physical arrangements. In the first situation, "the place was really bare...just a bed and a chest of drawers"; then she was sent to a convent where she "was allowed to pick out (her) own bedroom and...the room was nice and there were so many things about it that (she) really liked." In the first instance, the buildings and the community itself were large, established structures; the second convent and its connected school was brand-new, "and it was as though we were making *our* dent on it, our impression, and it was an easy way to start (teaching) in high school too because there weren't any traditions." So, as she was young and energetic herself, she was glad to move from the first situation to the new convent and school.

> By the time I went on to—, I was just really glad to go. I shook the dust of—off my feet and moved. Jeez, there were just so many things I hated about that that I left behind me. Awful. Anyway. I got to—. And I felt like I had come home.

Beside having a correspondence between her own and the community values, and an appropriate embodiment of those values, this woman needed to be an active maker of the structures within which she lived in order to feel "at home."

T H E   F E M A L E   D O M A I N

In stereotypical representations of women's virtues enacted in a women's domain, the home is seen as the site for care, solicitude, and love. In these narratives that connection holds true; however, the terrain of family relations, like the family itself, is expanded far beyond any narrow, privatized borders. In an emblematic description of her childhood home, one woman remembers that house as a site for the construction of meaning in the middle of a world literally at war. But, in her telling, the house is the very opposite of an involuted, claustrophobic female retreat. It is the male parent who remains inside in this story. And, like the music her father plays, the meaning generated by the world-within flows into the world-without, breaching the boundaries constructed by the state.

> Probably the most influential thing I would guess in my life, in those days, when I was a kid growing up, was that both my parents were musicians. My mother was a professional singer, and my father was her accompanist, and that just meant that music was going to be an important part of my life. For me as well as for others. So, that's been a kind of thread right straight through.
>   You know, I was reflecting the other day with a friend that, in our house where we grew up, on—Street, the one with this great front porch, and during...the...Second World War when there would be air raid drills, we used to sit on the front porch, which was very illegal, "cause you're supposed to be in the basement...And, he would sit inside and play the piano. All during this time. And so it was like, we had the best of both worlds really. Sneaking around on the porch, watching all these air raid wardens in their white hats and...he was playing the piano.

Even when the home has been established as the domain of women, this site need not necessarily stand on the margins of the social world. It can even be the nexus of the social activities for the larger religious community, as Elisabeth Schussler Fiorenza (1985) suggests in her "feminist theological reconstruction of Christian origins." In an analysis that shows a high degree of correspondence with the discourse being discussed here, Fiorenze (pp. 286-288) examines the historical conditions under which the early church shifted its organizational center from the "house church," characterized by communal authority and a central role for women, to the "household of god," with authority vested in the patriarchially defined office of bishops, and women's leadership relegated to marginal positions. In the early church, as in present times, the feminist religious discourse suggests, the church is faced with two competing models of family and home, and the more powerful patriarchal structure wins.

The irony of church organization is that the marginality of Catholic women religious has also given them a great degree of autonomy. It can be argued that, in spite of an overarching patriarchal structure, Catholic women religious have continued to maintain the alternative model of family and home within their gender-segregated space. This model underlies the narrative accounts of recent structural changes in the nuns' immediate surroundings. While still maintaining an environment in which women and women's values are at the center, they have broken their cloistered isolation from the larger society by moving into "ordinary houses" in local neighborhoods; and by living in community with their "clients," in shelters for the homeless and in therapeutic communities. One definition of the home is as a hub of ideologically compatible activity.

THE PROGRESSIVE USE OF RELIGION IN EDUCATION

In a recent study of American values, Bellah et al. (1986, p. 219) observed that "although we seldom asked specially about religion, time and again in our conversations, religion emerged as important to the people we were interviewing." Neither the endurance, nor the expansion, of religious sentiments should not continue to surprise us, given the abundance of empirically observable examples, not only in this country, but throughout the contemporary world. The question no longer seems to be whether or not religion will continue to exist, but, rather, what new forms it will take.

Because language is always incomplete and unfinished, because it is socially constructed, the cultural and political forms that religion takes will depend upon those who participate in various religious language communities. The New Right does not have a monopoly on religious language. In the voices of these progressive nuns, we hear a particular dialect of Christianity, one which cries out with moral indignation over social injustice, one which calls for emancipatory education and social reconstruction. For, to use Huebner's words, this is the story of "a few people, sharing something in common, breaking bread and drinking wine, and then changing the shape of the public world" (1975b, p. 280).

When Huebner speaks of educational practice as human event, he explains that

> the curricularist is also a human being with a biography in conflict and harmony
> with other emerging biographies being played out in historically evolving
> institutions. A concern for the history of practice as human event calls
> attention to the biographical structure of people involved in educational
> environments. The life history of the individuals involved in educative
> situations becomes a potential focal point of the concern and suggests the need
> for conceptual systems that articulate the phenomenon of human events
> (1975a, p. 266).

What these biographies call to our attention is the fact that ordinary
teachers have long understood, and acted upon, ethically important issues in
education. One cannot read the powerful and dramatic discourse constructed by
this community without realizing that these teachers are also curriculum
theorists and their narratives are texts to teach us new lessons about the
relationship of religion, education, and progressive politics.

N O T E S

1. Even though I realize that these words are not always interchangeable, in this article I will not differentiate between "morality" and "ethics," or "ethics" and "religion," and so forth. Here I am more concerned with overlaps of meaning than with distinctions.

2. Tape-recorded narratives of 33 women were collected in five American cities in 1984-1985. All of the women are, or were at some time in their lives, employed as teachers in elementary and/or high schools; all were described by themselves and/or others as working for progressive social change. Transcripts were organized and analyzed according to distinctive social groups. This article is an in-depth analysis of the narratives of one of these cohorts: Catholic women religious who have taught in parochial schools and been politically involved in "social justice ministry." For further details, see my Ph.D. dissertation (1988), Teacher as Author: Life History Narratives of Contemporary Women Teachers Working for Social Change.

   Three of the women quoted in this article belonged to the same congregation but were living in three different cities at the time of the study. One of these women introduced two friends, living in the same city as she, but belonging to two other congregations. One woman who was contacted independently, in yet another city, proved during her narrative to be a former member of one of the orders to which I already had connections. Her narrative, as well as that of another nun, from a fourth congregation, also solicited independently, significantly echoed the life stories that I had heard from those women more directly connected to each other.

3. There is not only a general public disregard of the history of religious women's work; this is also a neglected area of academic research. Sr. Elizabeth Kolmer (1980) observes: "Although Catholic sisters have been active on the American scene since the eighteenth century, the story of their life and work remains largely untold. Significant opportunities exist for serious researchers in this untouched area of social history."

4. In the sections of "defining the self," I am indebted to Christ's (1980) discussion of women's religious experience for the general movement of my argument, as well as for those particular phrases that will be noted.

5. The departure of large numbers of women from religious congregations in the past 20 years can be partially explained by the radical changes in these institutions during those years. It appears that identities and contexts fell out of synchronization for these women. I will not attempt to discuss this

trend here, nor to establish any general relationship between changes in institutions and changes in individual identities. The one woman in this study who had left the convent gave as one of her reasons the fact that she was ahead of her time and wished to do things which her order was not ready to allow. But another woman who is still a nun did not wait for her order to change; she instigated innovations. For many women, personal and institutional change seem to have occurred simultaneously, e.g., "Not only am I a transition person as far as the changes that happened to me in the religious life, but I am in transition in myself."

6. A teacher who read an early draft of this chapter commented: "My principal did not go to the funeral of a teacher at our school who died of AIDS; he simply asked if we 'were well represented.'"

7. Some of the awkwardness of this terminology comes from my attempts to circumnavigate the strong ideological currents intrinsic to this word. To speak of a "literal" versus a "symbolic" family is to give precedence to a particular construction of family as more "real." I am trying to argue that all "families" are socially constructed realities, having moral and material dimensions.

8. By using the word "interpolation," I enter a particular part of the debate on the nature of subjectivity. I find the metaphor of "summoning" very useful, but I disagree with Althusser's characterization of agents as solely the creations of discourse. In my view, they are also its creators.

9. By using the word "habitus," I enter another part of the debate on the nature of subjectivity. Here again I find the metaphor extremely helpful, even though I am using it to describe the predispositions of a counterhegemonic, rather than the dominant ideology, as Bernstein does.

R E F E R E N C E S

Bellah, R., R. Madsen, W. Sullivan, A. Swidler, & S. Tipton. (1985). *Habits of the heart: Individualism and commitment in American life.* (New York: Harper and Row).

Christ, C. (1980). *Diving Deep and Surfacing : Women writers on spiritual quest.* (Boston: Beacon Press).

Fiorenza, E. S. (1985). *In memory of her: A Feminist theological reconstruction of Christian origins.* (New York: Crossroads).

Huebner, D. (1966). Curricular language and classroom meanings. Reprinted in W. Pinar, (Ed.), *Curriculum Theorizing: The Reconceptualists.* (Berkeley: McCutchan) 217-236.

Huebner, D. (1967). Curriculum as concern for man's temporality. Reprinted in W. Pinar, (Ed.), *Curriculum Theorizing: The Reconceptualists.* (Berkeley: McCutchan) 237-249.

Huebner, D. (1975a). The tasks of the curricular theorist. In W. Pinar, (Ed.), *Curriculum Theorizing: The Reconceptualists.* (Berkeley: McCutchan) 250-270.

Huebner, D. (1975b). Poetry and power; The politics of curricular development. In W. Pinar, (Ed.), *Curriculum Theorizing: The Reconceptualists.* (Berkeley: McCutchan) 271-280.

Huebner, D. (1984). The search for religious metaphors in the language of education. *Phenomenology and Pedagogy,* 2(2): 112-123.

Kolmer, Sr. E. (1980). Catholic women religious and women's history. In J.W. James, (Ed.), *Women in American Religion.* (Philadelphia: University of Pennsylvania Press).

West, C. (1982). *Prophesy deliverance! An Afro-American revolutionary Christianity.* (Philadelphia: Westminster Press).

CHAPTER FIFTEEN

Word Worlds

The Literary Reference for Curriculum Criticism

Madeleine R. Grumet
1989

Curriculum is both a producer and product of culture. If we understand culture to be a system of meanings available to actors situated in shared space, time, history, and possibility, then it is reasonable to think about curriculum development and criticism as hermeneutic activity, as acts of interpretation. The O.E.D. offers an analysis of "interpretation" that justifies our sense of its complexity. Its prefix "inter" means between, and the root is traced to its Sanskrit actecedent, prath—to spread abroad. Interpretation occurs at the junction of oppositions. The route that leads to the prefix "inter" (between) carries us into the unknown, the meaning between the lines of text, between the words of a foreign language, between the announced intentions of another's words.[1] The route that leads to the root "prath" (to spread about) carries us out into the world. Interpretation resonates with all the oppositions and tensions of education: the private and the public, the unknown and the known, the individual and the collective, conservation and transformation.

In *Bodyreading*, I explored the ceremony divination that constitutes the cultural history of reading, as the priest pores over the entrails of the cow (whose fourth stomach is called the read), looking for signs of how to live.[2] In that ritual reading retains the dialectic of internal, external, private, and public that we find in interpretation. But I think that we can argue, with regret, that our time reading has relinquished its public presence and retreated to a private domain of escape and fantasy. Happily, the public possibilities of interpretation have survived, for we still use that word to signify the act of making a meaning available to someone else.

THE POLITICS OF INTERPRETATION

The study of curriculum invites our study of the politics of interpretation, for it is through acts of interpretation that we constitute the disciplines of knowledge and spread what we know about. If we subscribe to Richard Rorty's position we agree that knowledge cannot be conceived as a mental mirror of the world.[3] He argues that knowledge is constituted by a continuous conversation that symbolizes and expresses our various experiences of the world, and that it achieves authority and dignity through consensus.

Now I admit that the notion that knowledge and curriculum are merely moments of conversation can be distressing to diligent scholars. The chatter of cocktail parties comes to mind, even though one hardly ever goes to such a thing these days. But this 1950s hangover emerges to taunt us with its casual triviality, linking conversation to tinkling glasses and office gossip. We have always been suspicious of conversation, denigrating it when it does not proceed according to the rules, regulations, interruptions, and eavesdropping of authorities.

Conversation is, nevertheless, a friendlier process for the generation and interpretation of those powerful and organizing ideas that we call knowledge than the process of assassination described by Wallace Stevens in this excerpt from "Extracts from Addresses to the Academy of Fine Ideas."

> The law of chaos is the law of ideas,
> Of improvisations and seasons of belief,
>
> Ideas are men. The mass of meaning and
> The mass of men are one. Chaos is not
>
> The mass of meaning, It is three or four
> Ideas or, say, five men or, possibly, six.
>
> In the end, these philosophic assassins pull
> Revolvers and shoot each other. One remains.
>
> The mass of meaning becomes composed again.
> He that remains plays on an instrument
>
> A good agreement between himself and night,
> A chord between the mass of men and himself.
>
> Far, far beyond the putative canzones
> Of love and summer. The assassin sings
>
> In chaos and his song is a consolation.
> It is the music of the mass of meaning.

And yet it is a singular romance,
This warmth in the blood-world of the pure idea,

This inability to find a sound,
That clings to the mind like that right sound, that song

Of the assassin that remains and sings
In the high imagination, triumphantly.[4]

Our choices are not easy. On one hand we have Rorty's easy sociability, which, though desirable, ignores the power of knowledge, the struggle for dominance, the dirty deals and desperate moves that, at least occasionally, motivate academic discourse. On the other we have Stevens' assassin, a cold-blooded imposter who pretends to have prevailed through inspiration but has merely killed off the competition.[5]

Now curriculum is not merely the presentation of knowledge. It is a process of interpretation. But, if we suspect that our idealized image of the philosophers and their students ambling along in profound and peripatetic conversation idealizes the politics of classical knowledge, we know that in our schools, classroom discourse, community politics, bureaucratic regulations, and publishing agendas determine the rules of that conversation, undermining its promise of open inquiry and democratic participation. If the poet's hyperbolic metaphor of assassination is too strong for us to acknowledge, we who are responsible for the lives of children, we may admit that the arrangements and categories of curriculum can kill the spirit they promise to nourish with neglect if not abuse.

L I T E R A R Y   C R I T I C I S M

I intend to proceed by examining the role of interpretation in writing and reading and criticizing texts, and then by comparing its process in literary discourse to its role in the production and criticism of curriculum discourse. This inquiry was initiated when my daughter, Jessica, then a high school junior, came home from school with *The Great Gatsby* and an assignment to write a critical essay about it. She, understandably, was under the impression that "critical" meant that she was to judge the novel, to say whether it was bad or good. Knowing that she had not the experience to make that judgment, not quite ready to become an assassin, and, understanding that the judgment was not identical to noting whether she had enjoyed the book or not, doubting that conversation would suffice, she was at a loss to know what to do in the name of a "critical essay." In order to help her to figure out what critics do, I started taking books of criticism off the shelf, to see what they did in the name of literary criticism. What appeared to be going on in all these "lit. crit." texts was a recontextualization of the content of the book. If writing was an act of abstraction that lifted phenomena out of the domain of daily existence and perception and built a discourse around it, then the critic's reading appeared to recontextualize the phenomena by returning it to a world the critic understood, enjoyed, cared about.

I advised Jessica to talk about Gatsby and his world from the vantage point of hers. Now this may seem too subjective to those who worry about theories of reading that collapse the meaning of the text into the reader's story. But Ricoeur has reminded us that the meaning of the text cannot be collapsed into the writer or the reader's world; that is, points, instead, to a third domain, one of possibility rather than the actualities within which reader and writer have formed their meanings, a third domain constituted by, but not identical to, their two worlds of meaning.[6] The meaning that might emerge from Jessica's "critical" essay would point to this third world, the place where her experience and F. Scott Fitzgerald's would converge. Jessica was called upon to enact a reading and to offer it as an interpretation.

O R D E R S   O F   C R I T I C I S M

Now the word "critical" is itself derived from the ancients' sense of the universal order of things. It comes from the word "crisis," which linked astrological and biological time together as it designated a moment when the motion and alignment of the planets would influence the process of a disease. Ancient metaphysics linked the health of the body, the character of the person, the order and prosperity of the state to the motion of the planets. This sense of continuity, reincarnated in the Renaissance notion of "The Great Chain of Being," promoted a comforting, if singular, coherence. Our sense of a critical issue as one that marks a decisive turn in some process is a meaning that we share with ancient thought. We differ from our forebears as we define the context of the issue as well as the route to its solution.

In contrast to the ancient reliance on a universal order, contemporary notions of the "critical" locate it not in a vast and intricate order of persons and things, but in the independent reasoning of an objective mind. This was the triumph of the Enlightenment as science emerged to tell us that rather than being the pawns of forces out of our control (such as the movements of the planets), human beings could isolate a phenomenon from its existential clutter, study its dynamics, and control it. Our ancient notions of the critical had left us utterly dominated by forces outside our control; our Enlightenment notions of the critical have left us isolated in a fiction of autonomy and control. We have had to invent the concept of ecology to return us, and knowledge, to the world.

Recent curriculum initiatives express the Enlightenment rather than the Classical version of this opposition. They have been promoting the notion of critical thinking in context-free cognitive processing schemas, which claim to develop a capacity for critical thinking that is independent of the forms and traditions of particular academic disciplines, let alone the moon and the stars.

A more useful sense of the critical may be found in works of literary criticism. If we consult a text by Harold Bloom or Barbara Johnson we find that its author is less concerned with gauging the value of a literary work than in providing a context to help us to make sense of it. Every work of art is a design drawn from the lived world of its artist. What the critic does is return the work to the world.[7]

It is in this transfer from one lived reality to another, from the writer's world to the world of the text, from the text's world to the world of the critic, that, Maurice Natanson argues, the dynamic and revelatory character of literature resides.

> The achievement of fictive consciousness is the revealing of the transcendental structure of daily life.... That transcendental structure consists of the horizon of daily life and the prioris which attend it: the metaphysical constants of our being. What we ordinarily take for granted in daily life is rendered explicitly by the constructive activity of fictive consciousness. Far from the literary microcosm reflecting the world, it reveals to us the experiential foundation of our world.[8]

What is rendered explicit is not encoded on any page. It appears in neither the writer nor the critic's text. It is rendered explicit only to consciousness. It appears in the spaces between both texts. It is the mysterious or internal part of the word "interpretation." And when it is spread about it cannot be traced as explicitly as utterances in the public discourse, but is intuited or intimated as a barely perceptible shift of enlargement of the horizon that demarcates our human possibilities. The influence of literature on our human condition rests on writing, reading, and interpretation.

There are other designations for this understanding. I believe it is the experience that Ricoeur has situated in his spatial metaphor of the third world to which the text ultimately refers.[9] It is what Susanne Langer has coded as the "virtual" in *Feeling and Form* when she argues that all art forms function to make us conscious of aspects of our lived worlds, that, while they undergird all of our mundane experience, escape our perception and reflection.[10]

Let me then propose an analogy between literature and curriculum by suggesting that the teacher like the writer creates a world around some phenomenon and that the literary or curriculum critic's interpretive task is to recontextualize that novel or classroom in the world that the critic knows and understands. What we need to discover is whether the critic is an assassin, or a conversationalist, or whether there is yet another relation, another politic for interpretation that we need for curriculum criticism.

A   C R I T I C I S M
O F   L I T E R A R Y   C R I T I C I S M

In the October 27, 1988, issue of the *New York Review of Books* there is a lengthy review of eight books of literary criticism in an essay by Frederick Crews entitled "Whose American Renaissance?" The essay shows us how the politics of interpretation have been waged in critical studies of American literature as Crews juxtaposes the approach taken in a new work, *The Cambridge History of American Literature,* to its predecessors.

The critics in the new text present themselves as "spokespersons for dissensus." Crews explains their epithet:

> They will dissent, that is, from the leading liberal myths about American history and the application of those myths to criticism of our alleged classics. And they will demystify "canonicity" itself—the notion that certain texts are so self-evidently superior that they form an indispensable set of touchstones. No one will have to wait twenty years to discern the figure in this carpet.[11]

Crews makes it clear that the dissensus critics are not chasing an endless chain of signifiers in endless deconstructionist conversation. Nevertheless they are determined not to function as assassins, disdaining foundational claims, methodological formalism, and ideological pieties. They counter the charge that their own commitment to social struggle and to bringing works of minority perspectives into the canon is ideological by claiming that it is less conservative than the ideologies that directed earlier schools: the chauvinism of Vernon Parrington's valorization of the nativism and progressivism of Whitman, Twain, Dreiser, and Lewis; the postwar defeatism of New Criticism's pleasure in irony; obscurity and symbolism. Nevertheless, Crews rebukes the dissensus critics whom he calls the "new Americanists" for the narrowness of their own readings and their allegiance to political correctness.

> It ought to be possible for critics who are politically unembarrassed by ambiguity and irony to leave "cold war" rationalizations behind, branch out from the canon, yet continue to affirm what radicals sometimes forget, that there is no simple correlation between political correctness and artistic power.[12]

To correct them he offers the example of Edmund Wilson's 1962 reading of *Uncle Tom's Cabin,* which celebrated the "nobility and urgency of Stowe's theme; the mortal peril that slavery was posing to the entire nation's soul. Her vision of a truly Christian Union not only fired her imagination, it also spared her from the sectionalism and scapegoating that had marred most abolitionist literature…. In Wilson," Crews declares "we had a model of the critic who can appreciate the historical reasons for a novel's power without needing to convert its politics into his own."[13] In praising Wilson, Crews reveals the order of his own criticism. He requires the literary critic to recontextualize the text within the lived world of the writer. He is not invoking the intentional fallacy that insists that we recover the writer's intention, but he is maintaining that we understand the power of a fictive world as it spoke to the existential world that it addressed. To the degree that the fictive world addresses the concerns of that world but manages to bring to them larger moral implications and possibilities it is powerful, significant literature. As Wilson praises the sense of Stowe's world. What is left out of this exemplar that Crews gives us, is the reference, if Wilson identified any to Wilson's world.

A   C r i t i c i s m   o f   C u r r i c u l a r   C r i t i c i s m

It is timely that we turn to the model of literary criticism for curriculum criticism because the last few years of school reports and critiques such as those generated by Hirsch and Bloom have turned the debates about schooling into texts and criticism has become a criticism of those texts. Ironically, we can condemn Hirsch and Bloom for the same narrowness that Crews laments in the dissensus critics, even though it is dissensus itself that distresses these conservatives.

Hirsch and Bloom fail to bring the reference of the world of teachers and their students into their critiques of curriculum. They do not manage to understand a context that is not their ow, as Wilson has. The reference of Bloom and Hirsch is to the world of their own aspiring youth. It is drenched in nostalgia, poignant with regret that the world that they put so much hope in has slipped away. For Bloom, it was a world of so much sense that he needn't worry about its reference. It was a world, he thought, of truths and values that would, as in the old idealist dream, escape from the change, the decay that marks us and all we make as mortal. Hirsch, on the other hand, acknowledges the dynamic of reference but subverts it. Insisting that the sense of the school curriculum can only be grasped by children who can grasp its reference, he would have the sense to stay constant and have us collapse reference into it. The ground of reference is no longer the province of the reader, or in this analogy, the student. It does not emerge from a live system of meanings but is a set of learned schemas that must be mastered because they justify what makes sense to Hirsch.

Whatever criticisms we may have of the various reports on schooling or the texts produced by Bloom and Hirsch and Bennett and Cheney, whether we engage them as conversationalists or spurn them as assassins, we may appreciate the fact that the debate about education is being waged in texts and not only in state regulations and lawsuits. Furthermore, the reports and critiques have provoked scholars and educators and their professional organizations to respond, as in the fine defense of humanities education prepared by the American Council of Learned Societies that appeared in a recent issue of *The Chronicle of Higher Education.*

We have eavesdropped on these conversations of literary critics and literate curriculum critics because we suspect that we, hiding here behind the arras, can pick up a point or two for our own work as teacher educators and curriculum theorists. We have for some time preferred the arras to the one way window. And while the arras that separates us from the social sciences prohibit us from jumping into those conversations, they also protect us from adopting all the assumptions of these discourses.

In many important ways curriculum is not text. Curriculum is an event. It happens and passes. Though the classroom is distinct from the mundane world as is the text, the border that separates it from the world permits crossing, not without papers, of course. In this way schooling takes place in the cultural space that anthropologists call liminal, for it is transitional, neither fictive nor real, neither here nor there. The teacher who creates the world of curriculum, situating its phenomenon in space and time, in the politics of discourse, shaping its sense and its reference, is more closely bound to convention than the writer because she invites other people's children to actually spend their days within the pages of her book. Less free to establish a wildly fictive world that the writer, that teacher is more legally and historically bound to an intricate history of conventions.

On the other hand, the teacher is not committed to the world she creates to the same extent of the writer whose fictive world, for all its imaginative possibility, is fixed in the object of the book. The revulsion that some writers feel for their work is caught in this reification when what was lively, fluttering gasping for life, becomes a thing. The lesson, the class, escape that solidification. There are some who would not have it so. Still wedded to an industrial rather than postindustrial capitalism, they try to make the class into a thing, giving it weight by demanding heavy tomes of objectives and competencies and manuals, giving it shape by demanding its standardization, giving it value by limiting the number of those who can associate the experience of the class with their identity.

Nevertheless, these attempts to turn teaching into the production of things never succeeds enough. The teacher is free to change the class as it transpires. "Oh, let's not do the vocabulary today," "You know, what you just said puts a whole new light on this;" "Tell me what you think about the Ayatolah's threat to murder the author of *The Satanic Verses*." We even have conversation about assassination.

The teacher is not exiled from the world that she creates as the writer is. The borders are open. She can pass back and forth between the mundane and the curricular world and does, while the author is banished from the fictive world she has created as soon as it becomes the book.

Finally, and most important for my purposes, is the difference in the relation of the teacher to her students and the writer to her readers, and as a consequence, the relation of these artists to their critics. The book is a monologue. Intertextual, intersubjective, influenced, even imitative, writing requires the author to go on at some length without a response. Unlike the teacher the writer does not have the opportunity to change her inflection, lower her voice, or find her reader with her eyes. Separated by time and space from immediate communication with her reader, the writer does not have the teacher's access to the criticism of the yawn, or worse, the spitball. The writer does not have the ability to incorporate the criticism of the world that she is making into that very world itself.

On a Sunday morning I find the language for the distinction between curriculum and text in the *Book Review* section of the New York Times, which has been delivered to my front step, slightly damp with snow. The text, which challenges us to think beyond text, is not the first feature of the section; that place of privilege is reserved for talk about texts. It is the essay that talks about that one finds now, featured at the bottom of the page, an essay that talks about talk about texts. We could say that if the featured review slides toward sense, its escort leans toward references.

So it is with the piece, "Whose Canon Is It, Anyway?" by Henry Louis Gates. Reminding us that "underemployment among black youth is 40 percent, (and) 44 percent of black Americans can't read the front page of a newspaper, Gates challenges academics to examine the reference of their struggles for equity, for pluralism on the lives of black Americans.

> As writers, teachers of intellectuals, most of us would like to claim greater efficacy for our labors than we're entitled to. These days, literary criticism likes to think of itself as "war by other means." But it should start to wonder: have its victories come too easily? The recent turn toward politics and history in literary studies has turned the analysis of texts into a marionette theater of the political, to which we bring all the passions of our real-world commitments. And that's why it is sometimes necessary to remind ourselves of the distance from the classroom to the streets. Academic critics write essays, "readings" of literature, where the bad guys (you know, racism or patriarchy) lose, where the forces of oppression are subverted by the boundless powers of irony and allegory that no prison can contain, and we glow with hard-won triumph. We pay homage to the marginalized and demonized, and it feels almost as if we've righted an actual injustice. (Academic battles are so fierce—the received wisdom has it—because so little is truly at stake.) I always think of the folk tale about the fellow who killed seven with one blow: flies, not giants.[14]

Gates raises the question and then confesses to his own involvement in that literary struggle. Gates is not giving us one of those only-struggle-in-the-streets matters talks. He argues for a recognition that the inclusion of black literature to the canon not work merely to incorporate it, but to reveal its relation to the white-male literature that dominates it: sense and reference. Black and white texts are written, he reminds us, in reference to each other. He addresses the challenge to reveal the dialectic between the "American" tradition and the specificity of the history and melody of the black experience.

What Gates is teaching us is that the sense of the text, its identity, so to speak, is constituted by its reference to the world. And he is reminding us that even that sense that seems utterly specific and contained has gained that coherence and clarity by the suppression of its own otherness. And then he makes the move that even Wilson cannot make and addresses his own excluded world. He tells us the extraordinary story of how he found his public voice through his mother's words.

> I remember my first public performance, which I gave at the age of 4 in the all-black Methodist church that my mother attended, and that her mother had attended for 50 years. It was a religious program, at which each of the children of the Sunday school was to deliver a "piece"—as the people in our church referred to a religious recitation. Mine was the couplet, "Jesus was a boy like me,/And like Him I want to be." "Not much of a recitation, but then I was only 4. So, after weeks of practice in elocution, hair pressed and greased down, shirt starched and pants pressed, I was ready to give my piece. I remember skipping along to the church with all of the other kids, driving everyone crazy, repeating that couplet over and over: "Jesus was a boy like me/And like Him I want to be."
>
> And then the worst happened: I completely forgot the words of my piece. Standing there, pressed and starched, just as clean as I could be, in front of just about everybody in our part of town, I could not for the life of me remember one word of that piece.
>
> After standing there I don't know how long, struck dumb and captivated by all of those staring eyes, I heard a voice from near the back of the church proclaim, "Jesus was a boy like me/And like Him I want to be."
>
> And my mother, having arisen to find my voice, smoothed her dress and sat down again. The congregation's applause lasted as long as its laughter as I crawled back to my seat.
>
> What this moment crystallizes for me is how much of my scholarly and critical work has been an attempt to learn how to speak in the strong, compelling cadences of my mother's voice. As the black feminist scholar Hortense Spillers has recently insisted, in moving words that first occasioned this very recollection, it is "the heritage of the mother that the African-American male must regain as an aspect of his own personhood – the power of 'yes' to the 'female' within."[15]

Let me close with interpretation, by shifting from the sense of Gates' memory, as he has done, to its reference to teaching. Whereas criticism and interpretation are seen as acts that are distinct from the text, teaching must incorporate those processes in the very heart of every curriculum and every lesson.[16] That is the lesson of Shirley Heath's important book, *Ways With Words*, as she shows us how to give students a grasp of language that will permit them to interpret its reference and to be skillful manipulators of it for the purposes of their own expression. It requires us to bring the reference of the students' worlds into the curriculum without collapsing into their specificity. It challenges us to keep the tension of sense and reference, what is common and particular, alive in every class. It reminds us that when we try to bring children into the world of knowledge by demanding that they repudiate what they know, all we will find is resistance, even if we misidentify their loyalty as ignorance.

The contribution of the writing, reading, and interpretation of autobiographical accounts of educational experience is significant in teacher education if it is used to reveal to those who would teach others the rich references to the world that their own ways of making sense have excluded. The teacher who can be the critic of her own assumptions can welcome the diversity in her students' experiences without defensiveness and denial.

I thank Crew, and Wilson and Gates, yes and Bloom and Hirsch (ah, the old urge to assassinate) for their good conversation and for teaching me once again to respect the difference between reference and deference.

N O T E S

1. *The Compact Edition of the Oxford English Dictionary*. Oxford University Pess, 1982, p. 1467.

2. Madeleine R. Grument, "Bodyreading" in *Bitter Milk: Women and Teaching* (Amherst: University of Massachusetts Press, 1988).

3. Richard Rorty, *Philosophy and the Mirror of Nature*. (Princeton, N.J.: Princeton University Press, 1982).

4. Wallace Stevens, "Extracts for Addresses to the Academy of Fine Ideas."

5. Jurgen Habermas' notion of ideal speech is an attempt to provide a vision of the politics of expression that would allow us to speak without fear and deception about our experiences of the world. He offers a model of an ideal discourse that permits "three or four ideas, or, say, five men or, possibly, six" to talk to each other instead of killing each other.

6. Paul Ricoeur, *Interpretation Theory*. (Fort Worth, Texas: Texas Christian University Press, 1976).

7. These paragraphs discussing the etymology and meanings of the word "critical" have been adapted from an earlier essay, "Parents and Teachers: A Critical Convergence," *The Elementary School Journal*, University of Alberta.

8. Maurice Natanson, Phenomenology and the Theory of Literature" in P. 97.

9. Ricoeur, *Interpretation Theory*.

10. Langer, Susanne, *Feeling and Form* (New York: Charles Scribner's Sons, 1953).

11. Frederick Crews, "Whose American Renaissance?" *New York Review of Books*, October 27, 1988, p. 68.

12. Crews, p. 79.

13. Crews, p. 81.

14. Henry Louis Gates, "Whose Canon Is It Anyway?" New York Times Book Review, February 26, 1989.

15. Gates, p. 45.

16. James Olney, in *Metaphors of Self* shows us how criticism and interpretation are bonded to the autobiographical accounts of some writers, like Jean-Paul Sartre, who is constantly working to identify the assumptions in the

paragraph he has just written so that he can wriggle out of them in the next paragraph. Olney calls this autobiography complex, as distinct from autobiography simplex, which just presents a logic for a life without challenging or revising it. Some of the novels of Henry James and Ford Maddox—Ford also works to portray this process, and one can find this double-take in the critical writing of Jane Gallop, and JoAnne Pagano as well. Nevertheless, unless these texts are written by some group process, the critique and revision, though it may be drawn from the writer's otherness, cannot comprehend another, as teaching does.

CHAPTER SIXTEEN

Ideology and
Methodological Attitude

Patti Lather
1989

There is no social practice outside of ideology (Hall, 1985: 103).

In 1983, Eisner wrote, "for 80 years educational research has been defined largely as a species of educational psychology...in turn...influenced largely by behaviorism" (p. 14). Just five years later, Eisner's words seem dated: the grip of psychologism on educational theory and practice has been loosened by an explosion that has transformed the landscape of what we do in the name of educational research. This explosion goes by many names: phenomenological, hermeneutic, naturalistic, critical, feminist, neo-marxist, constructivist. And now, of course, we have the proliferation of "post-conditions": postpositivism, postmodernism, poststructuralism, post-Marxism, and, my least favorite, postfeminism.[1] In spite of so many differences within each of these terms that they are better referred to in the plural, e.g., feminisms, postmodernisms, each questions the basic assumptions of what it means to do science. What we are faced with, in essence, is a transdisciplinary disarray regarding standards and canons where a proliferation of contending paradigms is causing some diffusion of legitimacy and authority (Marcus and Fischer, 1986; Clifford and Marcus, 1986).

As I said at the 1987 AERA conference,[2] all of this shifting, all of this de-centering and dis-establishing of fundamental categories, gets dizzying. It is not easy to sort out the seduction of "the glamour of high theory" (JanMohamed and Lloyd, 1987:7) from what is useful for those of us concerned with what it means to do educational research. This time of openness, however, seems ripe for making generative advances in the ways we conceptualize our purposes and practices.

What follows will look at three possible framings of the "uneasy social sciences" in what is generally referred to as "the postpositivist intellectual climate of our times" (Fiske and Shweder, 1986:16). I am naming my three frames post-Kuhnian, critical, and poststructuralist. I will sketch how each frames issues of ideology and methodology. What we have, then, is framings of framings.

> What is really happening, then, is itself a function of frames, which are a kind of fiction (Hassan, 1987:118).

FRAME 1: THE DISCOURSE OF PARADIGM SHIFTS

> Scientists firmly believe that as long as they are not *conscious* of any bias or political agenda, they are neutral and objective, when in fact they are only unconscious (Namenwirth, 1986:29)

Thomas Kuhn's 1962 *The Structure of Scientific Revolutions* has been appropriated by postpositivist philosophers of science as a canonical text. The concept of paradigm shift has permeated discourse across the disciplines now for over two decades. Educational research has not been impervious to the great ferment over what is seen as appropriate within the boundaries of the human sciences. With positivist hegemony broken, many see this as a time for exploring ways of knowing more appropriate for a complex world of interacting, reflexive subjects rather than the mute objects upon which is turned the gaze of methods developed in the natural sciences (Bakhtin, 1981). Kuhn wrote, "Rather than a single group conversion, what occurs (with a paradigm shift) is an increasing shift in the distribution of professional allegiances" as practitioners of the new paradigm "improve it, explore its possibilities, and show what it would be like to belong to the community guided by it" (1970:157-158).

Rather than an orderly succession of alternative paradigms, however, multiple emergent paradigms, especially paradigms of disclosure rather than paradigms of prescription, and advocacy paradigms versus "neutral" paradigms, are vying for legitimacy. Is what we have here Paul Diesing's (1971) framing of scientific growth as phases of precision/rigor and vagueness/suggestiveness, or is something more fundamental going on?[3] Is what we have here Kuhn's (1970) framing of the issue as the interspersal of periods of normal and revolutionary science, or, to use poststructural philosopher John Rajchman's (1985) words, "Are we living in some great irruptive moment in which all will be changed?" (p. 116)

Kuhn's model of scientific change is rooted in the history of the natural sciences. In his view, the social sciences are a preparadigmatic hodgepodge of techniques largely borrowed from the natural sciences, too unformed to support productive normal science (1970:160). This aspect of Kuhn's thought has not been much noted, however, by those in the human sciences who have appropriated his language of successive paradigms, anomalies, revolutions, and competing modes of scientific activity.

Within Kuhnian arguments, the central tension that causes a paradigm shift is internal to the discipline, technical breakdown brought on by the inability of the dominant paradigm to explain empirical anomalies. "Change comes from within and is formed by the limitations of what is already known. It is a closed system, constrained by the limited knowledge of the trained practitioners who are admitted to the club" (Gonzalvez, 1986:9).

Methodological variety is presented as assumedly politically neutral paradigm choices, all of which seek to capture, via language, the closest possible representation of what is "really going on." Ideology is framed either as a de-politicized sort of world view that shapes paradigmatic choice, or as bias to be controlled for in the name of objectivity. Method is seen as emergent but capable of increasing systematization (e.g., Lincoln and Guba, 1985; Miles and Huberman, 1984), and the descriptive adequacy of language as a transparent representation of the world is assumed. In terms of the relationship between researcher and researched, what Dreyfus and Rabin (1983) term, "The Great Interpreter who has privileged access to meaning" (p. 180) plays the role of adjudicator of what is "really" going on, while insisting that the truths uncovered lie outside of the sphere of power. Willis terms this claim of privileged externality, this assumedly politically neutral position, a "covert positivism" (1980:90) in its tendencies toward objectification, unitary analysis, and distanced relationships between subject and object. In Foucault's words, " 'Knowable man (becomes) the object-effect of this analytic-investment, of this domination-observation'" (quoted in Dreyfus and Rabinow, 1983:160).

Post-Kuhnian frameworks deemphasize the political content of theories and methodologies and deny the dissolving of the world as structured by referential notions of language. I will deal later with the poststructuralist argument that we must abandon efforts to represent the object of our investigation as it "really" is, independent of our representational apparatus, for a reflexive focus on how we construct that which we are investigating. I turn now to those concerned with the ways in which ideas about science serve particular political or economic interests, and to the discourse of feminists and neo-Marxists who raise the question, "in whose interest, by sex, race and class, has knowledge been generated?" (Gonzalvez, 1986:16).

FRAME 2: DISCOURSE TOWARD A CRITICAL SOCIAL SCIENCE

What counts is the further scientific development at such a theoretical and methodological level, and in terms of such problem constellations, that the distance of science from politics becomes unacceptable by its own standards (Dubiel, 1985:187).

Efforts toward a critical social science raise questions about the political nature of social research, about what it means to do empirical inquiry in an unjust world. Habermas' (1971) categories of human interest—the technical, the practical, and the emancipatory—give rise to three distinct inquiry paradigms: positivism, hermeneutic/interpretive, and critical/emancipatory (Berstein, 1976; Morgan, 1983; Fay, 1987). "Action science as a form of praxis" (Peters & Robinson 1984) aspires to paradigmatic status as a major alternative to other forms of social research (Lather, 1986a). Schubert (1986) summarizes the growing articulation of this position.

> Proponents of critical praxis purport to go beyond the hermeneutic by emphasizing more emancipatory political interests. They claim the search for meaning and virtue is impossible if not accompanied by a social organization that empowers human beings to transcend constraints imposed by socio-economic class and its controlling ideologies. Meaning and virtue desired by practical interests can only be pursued if pedagogy goes beyond interaction to provide for socio-economic equity and justice. Thus, critical praxis combines inquiry and action in an attempt to realize and expose that which is oppressive and dominating. (p. 182)

Based on Habermas' (1971) thesis in *Knowledge and Human Interests* that claims to value-free knowledge obscure the human interests inherent in all social knowledge, critical theorists hold that there is no end to ideology, no part of culture where ideology does not permeate. This most certainly includes the university and the production of social knowledge. Hesse (1980) terms the recognition of the pervasiveness of values and the openly emancipatory intent of a critical social science as "epistemological breaks" portending a more reflexive and, hence, valid human science (p. 196). Grounded in the reemergence of the Frankfurt School and its concern with questions of domination and resistance at the level of subjectivity, discourse toward a critical social science is primarily concerned with ways of generating knowledge that turn critical thought into emancipatory action.

T H E   P O L I T I C S   O F   M E T H O D :
M E T H O D O L O G Y   A S   I D E O L O G Y

Built upon Gramsci's (1971) thesis that ideology is the medium through which consciousness and meaningfulness operate in everyday life and Althusser's (1971) focus on the materiality of ideology, ideology is conceptualized as possessing both distorting, oppressive moments and moments of clarity and emancipation. Within post-Althusserean Marxism or cultural Marxism, ideology is viewed as something people *inhabit* in daily, material ways and which speaks to both progressive and determinant aspects of culture (Apple, 1982; Wexler, 1982; Giroux, 1983).

While ideology remains a much disputed term, with more orthodox marxists defining it as false consciousness and opposing it to the "true" knowledge of scientific marxism, methodology as ideology is the more contemporary enframing of this long-running issue in the human sciences. Methods are assumed to be permeated with what Gouldner (1970) terms "ideologically resonant assumptions about what the social world is, who the sociologist is, and what the nature of the relation between them is" (p. 51). Sederberg (1984) delineates shared characteristics of both ideology and methodology: each is concerned with the creation of consensus, of shared meaning within a particular community; each focuses on how to go about constructing and supporting explanations; each is prescriptive in terms of establishing a reliable foundation for our understanding of social reality; each is concerned with validation; each is enforced. Methods, then, are inescapably political "as they define, control, evaluate, manipulate and report" (Gouldner, 1970:50).

While the purpose of method has traditionally been to provide some standards of logic and evidence, the controls of logic and empirical validation are weakening (e.g., Harding, 1982). A variety of incompatible directions are available in the culture, all competing for allegiance. Within this context, methodology is seen as much more an inscription of legitimation than a process that helps us get closer to some "truth" capturable through conceptual adequation (Sederberg, 1984). The point is that "the role of ideology does not diminish as rigor increases and error is dissipated" (LeCourt, 1975:200). Ideology can only be understood, not escaped. Such a stance provides the grounds for both an "openly ideological" approach to critical inquiry (Lather, 1986b) and the necessity of self-reflexivity, of growing awareness of how researcher values permeate inquiry.

A D V O C A C Y ,   M E T H O D O L O G Y , A N D   R E F L E X I V I T Y

As part of the post-Althusserean rejection of economism and determinism, consciousness and subjectivity rise to the fore in critical inquiry as the juncture between human agency and structural constraint takes on theoretical urgency. The goal is a critical social science that alleviates oppression by spurring "the emergence of people who know who they are and are conscious of themselves as active and deciding beings, who bear responsibility for their choices and who are able to explain them in terms of their own freely adopted purposes and ideals" (Fay, 1987:74).

The subject of such a science is theorized as living in a crisis of legitimacy (Habermas, 1975); this crisis provides a material base for the hope that subordinated groups will arise to construct more democratic social forms. The ability of the oppressed to comprehend a reality that is "out there" waiting for representation is assumed (Flax, 1987; Fay, 1987), as is the central role to be played by "transformative intellectuals: (Aronowitz and Giroux, 1985) "critical pedagogues" who will serve as catalysts for the necessary empowering dialogue. Much of this goes on under the rubric of "critical ethnography" (Simon, 1986), where more standard neo-marxist ideology critique (e.g., Repo, 1987) is being supplanted by more linguistically informed ethnography. This emergent body of work combines phenomenology and semiotics to focus on the relationship between the conscious and unconscious dynamics embedded in social relations and cultural forms (e.g., Simon, 1987).

In terms of methodology, the central issue for a critical social science is how to bring political commitments to one's research in order to generate new ways of knowing that do not perpetuate power imbalances. The line between emancipatory inquiry and pedagogy blurs as critical researchers focus on developing interactive approaches to research (e.g., Lather, 1986a). Additionally, there is growing recognition that reflexivity is needed to guard against researchers imposing meanings on situations rather than constructing meaning through negotiation with research participants (e.g., Acker, Barry, & Esseveld, 1983). Self-reflexivity becomes essential in understanding how empirical work is selective, partial, positioned (Roman, 1987). To the extent that the critical inquirer's self perceived role is "interpreter of the world" (Reynolds, 1980-1981:87), exposer of false consciousness, the intent of such work to demystify the world for the dispossessed is confounded. Respondents become objects-targets, others to be acted upon, rather than empowered agents who understand and change their own situations. As a result, much advocacy inquiry falls prey to what Fay (1987) notes as the irony of domination and repression inherent in most of our efforts to free one another.

Science could develop into a progressive moment within the consciousness of the society it both studies and shapes, but it is not enough to be oriented toward the interests of underprivileged social groups. An emancipatory, critical social science will develop out of the social relations of the research process itself, out of the enactment of what in the Frankfurt School was only incipient: implementation in research praxis (Dubiel, 1985:185). Fay (1987) argues that such a critical social science must be limited in aspiration and see itself as a way that intellectual effort might help improve the political situation, as opposed to seeing itself as "the key to redeeming our social and political life" (p. ix).

As we shall see in the next section, however, poststructuralism argues that no discourse is innocent of the Nietzschean will to power; the discourse of emancipation is as much a part of Foucault's "regimes of truth" as not. Spivak (1987) cautions, "the desire to 'understand' and 'change' are as symptomatic as they are revolutionary" (p. 88). Whether the goal of one's work is prediction, understanding, or emancipation, all are, for Foucault, ways of "disciplining the body, normalizing behavior, administering the life of populations" (Rajchman, 1985:82). All are forms of knowledge and discourse that we have invented about ourselves; all define, categorize, and classify us. All elicit the Foucauldian question: how do practices to discover the truth about ourselves influence our lives?

FRAME 3: POSTSTRUCTURALISM: DISCOURSE ON DISCOURSE

> A good proportion of our intellectual effort now consists in casting suspicion on any statement by trying to uncover the disposition of its different levels. That disposition is infinite, and the abyss that we try to open up in every word, this madness of language (is an) abyss that has to be opened up first, and for tactical reasons: in order to break down the self-infatuation in our statements and to destroy the arrogance of our sciences (Barthes, quoted in Smith, 1988:99).

Poststructuralism is both a condition of life under advanced monopoly capitalism (Jameson, 1984) and a response across the disciplines to the contemporary crisis of representation (Marcus & Fischer, 1986). This unprecedented transdisciplinary diffusion of ideas and methods is grounded in the marxist renewal since Althusser coupled with recent French theory, especially the work of Foucault and Derrida (Dreyfus & Rabinow, 1983). The central issue for the cultural studies approach arising out of this conjunction is the formation of subjectivities and the processes by which theories and practices of meaning-making shape cultural life.

The recent linguistic turn in social theory focuses on the power of language to organize our thought and experience. Language is seen as both carrier and creator of a culture's epistemological codes. The ways we speak and write are held to influence our conceptual boundaries and to create areas of silence as language organizes meaning in terms of preestablished categories. Poststructuralism displaces both the post-Kuhnian view of language as transparent, and critical theorists' view of language as ideological struggle waged on the playing field of dialectics. Raising both the dangers of objectification and the inadequacies of dialectics, poststructuralism demands radical reflection on our interpretive frames. Reflexivity becomes "the new canon" (Rajchman, 1985) as we enter the Foucauldian shift from paradigm to discourse, from a focus on researcher ontology and epistemology in the shaping of paradigmatic choice, to a focus on the productivity of language in the construction of the objects of investigation.

The material ground of poststructuralism is the information age of complex and ever-unfolding knowledge in a world marked by gross maldistribution of power and resources. The postmodern world is one of multiple causes and effects interacting in complex and nonlinear ways, all of which are rooted in a limitless array of historical and cultural specificities. The intent of poststructuralism is to open the future to a new form of knowledge, to come up with ways of knowing appropriate for a new world, forced by the weight of the present horror to go beyond present constructions.

Poststructuralism holds that there is no final knowledge; "the contingency and historical moment of all readings" means that, whatever the object of our gaze, it "is contested, temporal and emergent" (Clifford & Marcus, 1986:18-19). Whether the reign of paradigms is over or merely suspended for a time, the argument is that "the play of ideas free of authoritative paradigms" (Marcus & Fischer, 1986:80-81) will move us further into some new way of producing and legitimating knowledge, into what Derrida (1978) calls "the as yet unnamable which is proclaiming itself" (p.293). "To still pose one paradigm against the other is to miss the essential character of the moment as an exhaustion with a paradigmatic style of discourse altogether" (Marcus & Fischer, 1986:X). What we are dealing with, then, is the argument for a Feyerabendian sort of "postparadigmatic diaspora" (Caputo, 1987:262).

From a poststructuralist perspective, ideology is viewed as a constitutive component of reality: "the production of meaning, the positioning of the subject, and the manufacture of desire" (McLaren, 1987:303). There is no meaning-making outside ideology. There is no false consciousness, for such a concept assumes a true consciousness accessible via "correct" theory and practice (Hall, 1985). As we attempt to make sense in a world of contradictory information, radical contingency, and indeterminacies, ideology becomes a strategy of containment for beings who, in spite of David Byrne's advice, cannot "Stop Making Sense."

Poststructuralism views research as an enactment of power relations. The focus is on the development of a mutual, dialogic production of a multichoice, multicentered discourse, a particular moment of textual production that says more about the relationship between researcher and researched than about some "object" capturable via language. Research discourse/practices are seen as primarily designed to generate authoritative knowledge (Cherryholmes, 1987) as attention turns to the productivity of language within what Bakhtin (1981) has termed "the framing authorial context" (p. 358). Objectivity, for example, is seen as a textual construction more fruitfully displaced by a deconstructive emphasis on writing and the social relations that produce the research itself. Rather than "objectivity," questions such as the following rise to the fore:

1. How do we address questions of narrative authority raised by poststructuralism in our empirical work?
2. How do we frame meaning possibilities rather than close them in working with empirical data?

3. How do we create multivoiced, multicentered texts from such data?

4. How do we deconstruct the ways our own desires as emancipatory inquirers shape the texts we create?

5. Why do we do our research: to use our privileges as academics to give voice to what Foucault terms "subjugated knowledges" as another version of writing the self?

6. What are the race, class, and gender relations that produce the research itself?[4]

Within the poststructural suspicion of the lust for authoritative accounts, a relational focus on how method patterns findings replaces the objectifying and dialectical methods of post-Kuhnian and critical approaches. What is sought is a reflexive process whereby science can continually demystify the realities it serves to create. By focusing on our too easy use of "imposed and provided forms" (Corrigan, 1987:33), we can learn to speak from "a decentered position of acknowledged, vested interest" that strips the authority of our own discourse in order to "interrupt dominant and alternative academic discourses that serve Eurocentric, sexist, racist, and classist power relations."[5]

While poststructuralism is dismissed by many as "the opiate of the intelligentsia (Dowling, 1984:85), my reading of recent cultural theory sees increasing attention paid to issues of usefulness, and to how poststructuralism might provide both the grounds and the means for developing theory based on the open-endedness of practice and struggle (Smith, 1988; Yeatman, 1987; Spivak, 1987; Weedon, 1987; Laclau & Mouffe, 1985; Ellsworth, 1987; Huyssan, 1987; Caputo, 1987; Hartsock, 1987; de lauretis, 1987). In some ways we are only beginning to understand, perhaps "the postmodern turn" (Hassan, 1987) is about more freely admitting politics, desires, belief into our discourse as we attempt to resolve the contradictions of theory and practice.

CONCLUSION

This paper is positioned somewhere in the midst of what Habermas (1975) refers to as a "legitimation crisis" of established paradigms in intellectual thought. The orthodox consensus has been displaced; postpositivist philosophies of science focus more and more on the interpretive turn, the linguistic turn in social theory. Social science is increasingly polarized as the political content of theories and methodologies becomes apparent. On the one hand, a sense of experimentation and breaking barriers pervades.[6]

On the other hand, well represented by D.C. Phillips (1987), self-termed "closet Popperian/Hempelian" (p. 111), are those who warn that the post-Kuhnian ship of science has run aground on the shoals of relativism (p. 22). In his recent book, Phillips asks, do "the apparent demise of positivism" (p. 80) and "the new philosophy of science run rampant" lead to "the end of social science as it is currently known" (p. 82)? While I suspect that my arguments may be seen by Phillips as one of the "startling flights of fancy" (p. 80) occasioned by the postpositivist era, the answer I put forward is "It already has."

N O T E S

1. Regarding "postfeminism," I am ready to entertain such a stance once we live in a postpatriarchal world. My present self-description is feminist poststructuralist or, in Gayatri Spivak's phrase, "feminist, marxist deconstructivist" (1987:117). As Haraway notes, "It has become difficult to name one's feminism by a single adjective" (1985:72).

2. Division B sponsored symposium, "The Implications of Critical Theory: Efforts Toward Emancipatory Research and Pedagogy." American Educational Research Association Conference, Washington, D.C., April 20-24, 1987.

3. The work of Guba and Lincoln (1981) and Lincoln and Guba (1985) was problematic in its collapsing of all alternative paradigms into one, the "naturalistic." That they are beginning to rethink this position is obvious in the framing of a conference in 1989 on new paradigm research where they moved from a one-paradigm model to conceptualizing three alternative paradigms to positivism: Positivist, critical and constructivist. This was in response to those concerned with what Guba terms the "parochialism" of the initial proposal for the conference (Feb. 8, 1988, correspondence with Egon Guba).

4. There questions grow out of my very fruitful collaboration over the last few years with Ann Berlak and Janet Miller.

5. Correspondence from Elizabeth Ellsworth, 3-1-88.

6. My favorite experimenters and barrier-breakers are the poststructuralist anthropologists, e.g., Clifford and Marcus (1986), Marcus and Fischer (1986). Other examples of my growing collection of what might be termed "deconstructivist empirical work" include Mulkay, 1985; Mishler, 1984, 1986a,b; Zeller, 1987.

7. For a critique of how issues of relativity get framed in the human sciences, see Lather, 1988 and 1991. At the heart of this critique is Bakhtin's (1984) argument that relationality is not relativism, that all thought is not equally arbitrary; positionality weighs heavily in what knowledge comes to count as legitimate in historically specific times and places. Relativity is an issue only within the context of foundationalist epistemologies which search for a privileged standpoint as the guarantee of certainty, a position increasingly called into question by radical hermeneutics and postmodernism.

R E F E R E N C E

Acker, J., Barry, K., & Esseveld, J. (1983). Objectivity and truth: Problems in doing feminist research. *Womens Studies International Forum*, 6 (4), 423-435.

Althusser, L. (1971). Ideology and ideological state apparatuses. In *Lenin and Philosophy and Other Essays*. (New York: New Left Books).

Apple, M. (1982). *Education and power*. (Boston: Routledge and Kegan Paul).

Aronowitz, S., & Giroux, H. (1985). Radical education and transformative intellectuals. *Canadian Journal of Political and Social Theory*, 9 (3), 48-63.

Bakhtin, M. (1981). *The dialogue imagination: Four Essays*. Translated by C. Emerson and M. Holquist. (Austin: University of Texas Press).

Bakhtin, M. (1984). *Problems of Dostoevsky's poetics*. Edited and translated by C. Emerson. (Minneapolis: University of Minnesota Press).

Bernstein, R. (1976). *The restructuring of social and political theory*. (New York: Harcourt, Brace and Jovanovich).

Caputo, J. D. (1987). *Radical hermeneutics: Repetition, deconstruction, and the hermeneutic project*. (Bloomington, IN: Indiana University Press).

Cherryholmes, C. (1987). Construct validity and the discourses of research. *American Journal of Education*.

Clifford, J. (1983). On ethnographic authority. *Representations*, 1, Spring, 118-146.

Clifford, J., & Marcus, G. (Eds.). *Writing culture: The poetics and politics of ethnography*. (Berkeley: University of California Press).

Corrigan, P. (1987). In/forming schooling. In David Livingstone (Ed.), *Critical Pedagogy and Cultural Power*. (South Hadley, MA: Bergin and Garvey) 17-40.

De Lauretis, T. (1987). *The technologies of power: Essays on theory, film, fiction*. (Bloomington, IN: Indiana University Press).

Derrida, J. (1978). Structure, sign and play in the discourse of the human sciences. In *Writing and Difference*. Translated by Alan Blass. (Chicago: University of Chicago Press).

Diesing, P. (1971). *Patterns of discovery in the social sciences*. (New York: Aldine-Atherton).

Dowling, W. C. (1984). *Jameson, Althusser, Marx: An introduction to the political unconsciousness*. (Ithaca: Cornell University Press).

Dreyfus, H., & Rabinow, P. (1983). *Michael Foucault: Beyond structuralism and hermeneutics*. (Chicago: University of Chicago Press).

Dubiel, H. (1985). *Theory and politics: Studies in the development of critical theory*. Translated by Benjamin Gregg. (Cambridge: MIT Press).

Eisner, E. (1983). Anastasis might be still alive, but the monarchy is dead. *Educational Researcher*, May, 13-24.

Ellsworth, E. (1987). The place of video in social change: At the edge of making sense. Unpublished manuscript.

Fay, B. (1987). *Critical and social science*. (Ithaca: Cornell University Press).

Fiske, D. W., & Shweder, R. A. (Eds). (1986). *Metatheory in social science: Pluralisms and subjectivities*. (Chicago: University of Chicago Press).

Flax, J. (1987). Postmodernism and gender relations in feminist theory. SIGNS, 12 (4), 621-643.

Giroux, H. *Theory and resistance in education: A pedagogy for the opposition*. (South Hadley, MA: Bergin and Garvey).

Gonzalvez, L. (1986). The new feminist scholarship: Epistemological issues for teacher education. Unpublished paper.

Gouldner, A. (1970). *The coming crisis of western sociology*. (New York: Basic Books).

Gramsci, A. (1971). *Selections from the prison notebooks of Antonio Gramsci*. Quintin Hoare and G. Smith (Eds. and translators). (New York: International Publishing).

Guba, E., & Lincoln, Y. (1981). *Effective evaluation*. (San Francisco: Jossey-Bass).

Habermas, J. (1971). *Knowledge and human interests*. Translated by Jeremy J. Shapiro. (Boston: Beacon Press).

Habermas, J. (1975). *Legitimation crisis*. (Boston: Beacon Press).

Hall, S. (1985). Signification, representation, ideology: Althusser and the post-structuralist debates. *Critical Studies in Mass Communication*, 2 (2), 91-114.

Haraway, D. (1985). A manifesto for cyborgs: Science, technology, and socialist feminism in the 1980's. *Socialist Review*, #80, 65-107.

Harding, S. (1982). Is gender a variable in conceptions of rationality? *Dialectica*, 1982, 36, 225-242.

Harding, S. (1986). *The science question in feminism*. (Ithaca: Cornell University Press).

Hartsock, N. (1987). *The postmodern turn: Essays in postmodern theory and culture*. (Ohio State University Press).

Hassan, I. (1987). *The postmodern turn: Essays in postmodern theory and culture.* (Columbus: Ohio State University Press).

Hesse, M. (1980). *Revolution and reconstruction in the philosophy of science.* (Bloomington, IN: Indiana University Press).

Huyssan, A. (1987). Introduction to *critique of cynical reason,* by Peter Sloterdijk. (Minneapolis: University of Minnesota Press).

Jameson, F. (1984). Postmodernism, or the cultural logic of late capitalism. *New Left Review,* #146, 53-92.

Jan M., Abdul R., & Lloyd, D. (1987). Introduction: Toward a theory of minority discourse. *Cultural Critique,* #6, 5-12.

Kroker, A., & Cook, D. (1986). *The postmodern scene: Excremental culture and hyper-aesthetics.* (New York: St. Martin's Press).

Kuhn, T. (1970). *The structure of scientific revolutions.* (Chicago: University of Chicago Press).

Laclau, E., & Mouffe, C. (1985). *Hegemony and socialist strategy: Towards a radical democrataic politics.* Translated by Winston Moore and Paul Cammack. Thetford, Norfolk.

Lather, P. (1986a). Research as praxis. *Harvard Educational Review,* 56 (3), 257-277.

Lather, P. (1986b). Issues of validity in openly ideological research: Between a rock and a soft place. *Interchange,* 17 (4), 63.84.

Lather, P. (1988). Educational research and practice in a postmodern era. Paper presented at the American Educational Research Association annual convention, April 5-9, New Orleans.

Lather, P. (1991). *Getting smart: Feminist research & pegagogy within the postmodern.* (New York: Routledge).

Lawson, H. (1985). *Reflexivity: The post-modern predicament.* (LaSalle, IL: Open Court.)

LeCourt, D. (1975). *Marxism and epistemology.* (London: N.L.B.).

Lincoln, Y., & Guba, E. (1985). *Naturalistic inquiry.* (Beverly Hills: Sage).

Lyotard, J. (1984). *The postmodern condition: A report on knowledge.* Translated by G. Bennington and B. Massumi. (Minneapolis, Minnesota: University of Minnesota Press).

Marcus, G. E., & Fischer, M. (1986). *Anthropology as cultural critique: An experimental moment in the human sciences.* (Chicago: University of Chicago Press).

McLaren, P. (1987). Ideology, science, and the politics of marxian orthodoxy: A response to Michael Dale. *Educational Theory*, 37 (3), 301-326.

Miles, M., & Huberman, M. (1984). *Qualitataive data analysisa: A sourcebook of new methods*. (Beverly Hills: Sage).

Mishler, E. G. (1984). *The discourse of medicine: Dialectics of medical interviews*. (Norwood, N.J.: Ablex).

Mishler, E. G. (1986a). *Research interviewing: Context and narrative*. (Cambridge, MA: Harvard University Press).

Mishler, E. G. (1986b.) The analysis of interview-narratives. In T.R. Sarbin (ed.), *Narrative Psychology: The Storied Nature of Human Conduct*. (New York: Praeger) 233-255.

Morgan, G. (ed.). (1983). *Beyond method: Strategies for social research*. (Beverly Hills: Sage).

Mulkay, M. (1985). *The word and the world: Explorations in the form of sociological analysis*. (London: George and Unwin).

Namenwirth, M. (1986). Science through a feminist prism, in *Feminist Approaches To Science*, edited by R. Bleir. (New York: Pergamon) 18-41.

Peters, M., & Robinson, V. (1984). The origins and status of action research. *The Journal of Applied Behavorial Science*, 20, 113-124.

Phillips, D.C. (1987). *Philosophy, science, and social inquiry: Contemporary methodological controversies in social science and related applied fields of research*. (New York: Pergamon Press).

Rajchman, J. (1985). *Michael Foucault: The freedom of philosophy*. (New York: Columbia University Press).

Reinharz, S. (1985). Feminist distrust: A response to misogyny and gynopia in sociological work. Unpublished paper. Expanded version of "Feminist distrust: Problems of context and content in sociological work," in *Clinical Demands of Social Research*, edited by D. Berg and K. Smith. (Beverly Hills: Sage).

Repo, S. (1987). Consciousness and popular media, in *Critical Pedagogy and Cultural Power*, edited by D. Livingstone. (S. Hadley, MA: Bergin and Garvey) 77-98.

Reynolds, D. (1980-1981). The naturalistic method and education and social research: A marxist critique. *Interchange*, 11 (4), 77-89.

Roman, L. (1987). Punk feminity. Unpublished dissertation. University of Wisconsin-Madison.

Schubert, W. (1986). *Curriculum: Perspectives, paradigm, and possibility*. (New York: MacMillan).

Sederberg, P. C. (1984). *The politics of meaning: Power and explanation in the construction of social reality*. (Tucson, AZ: The University of Arizona Press).

Simon, R. (1986). On critical ethnographic work. *Anthropology and Education Quarterly*, 17 (4), 195-202.

Simon, R. (1987). Work experience, in *Critical Pedagogy and Cultural Power*, edited by D. Livingstone. (S. Hadley, MA: Bergin and Garvey) 155-178.

Smith, P. (1988). *Discerning the subject*. (Minneapolis: University of Minnesota Press).

Spivak, G. (1987). *In other worlds: Essays in cultural politics*. (New York: Methuen).

Weedon, C. (1987). *Feminist practice and poststructuralist theory*. (Oxford, England: Basil Blackwell).

Wexler, P. (1982). Ideology and education: From critique to class action. *Interchange*, 13 (1), 53-78.

Willis, P. (1980). Notes on method. From *Culture, Media, Language*, Stuart Hall, et. al. (eds.). (London: Hutchinson).

Yeatman, A. (1987). A feminist theory of social differentiation. Paper presented at the American Sociological Association Annual Meeting, Chicago, Illinois.

Zeller, N. *A rhetoric for naturalist inquiry*. Unpublished dissertation, Indiana University, 1987.

CHAPTER SEVENTEEN

A Bell Ringing
in the Empty Sky

David W. Jardine
1992

I

> Whereas a church spire inspires me to lift up my eyes to the heavens above, entering a tea room inspires in me something different. The entrance to the ceremonial room, by the very way it is built, urges me to incline my body and to bow, bringing me closer to the earth those textured layers of humus allow buds of tea trees to leaf. The savoring of the tea allows me to touch again this earth that cradles and nourishes both my body and soul. During the tea ceremony, I come to respect the fullness of silence, and I become aware of how silently I participate in the constituting of that silence. And in that silence, I experience being-one-with-the-earth. (Aoki, 1987, p. 67)

The title of this paper is taken from a piece of Japanese music performed unaccompanied on a wooden flute called a shakuhachi, performed by Goro Yamaguichi. The piece, whose Japanese title is *Kohu Reibo*, was originally composed by Kyochiku, a Zen priest. It is said to have come to him in a dream during which he attained enlightenment—that moist, green, earthy enlightenment that dispiriting Western aspirations seem only to look down upon.

This piece of music and its evocative title call up a sense of openness and spaciousness; images of echoing and resonances; images of the time and the quiet needed for a conversation to go on; images of the space for the natural affections of speech, its kindness, its interweaving and living kinships or "family resemblances" to come forth.

I suspect that it is evocative partially as a response to the clangor in which many of us live—the urban, cluttered, and noisy abode out of which our curriculum theorizing often arises as a hurried response to our shortened breath. Our aspirations are strangulated into an unearthly discourse that must always have something new and notable to say at a moment's notice. We live, it seems, in a relentless proliferation of speech that leaves us neither time nor occasion nor place for a settling word, for quietly shepherding the mystery of our earthliness, which is no mystery at all, which is right at our fingertips no matter what. And, more horrifying, it is we *in education* who are so caught up in this senseless roar and rush. Silence has become stupidity; taking time or hesitating before you speak has become a sign of incompetence or a lack of mastery in certain specifiable "communication skills"; speaking has become self-declaration; failing to declare oneself has become weakness; speaking with one's own voice has become gastric self-reporting. The living Word and the silences and spaces it requires to hear its calling, is succumbing to the telegraphed stutters of televangelistic discourse.

What is so very horrifying is that, whether we intend it or not, we *are* what we deeply hope our children will become. Recently, a kindergarten teacher in the Rocky View School District in Alberta was fired by the parents advisory board because, at the end of kindergarten, not all of the children could read. And I find myself tongue-clicking at the pedagogical inappropriateness of such actions while rushing to meet publication schedules, requiring my student-teachers to compose hurried-yet-reflective journal entries about their teaching practice, and contemplating the need to write a book in order to secure career advancement. My son Eric, like any child, inhales my aspirations while breathing his own breath. This air, this atmosphere, is the real work (Snyder, 1980) I do no matter what I say.

This certainly veers too close to home—that we may be offering our children an Earth on which only such ever self-present exhaustion, noise, and hurry is not only *possible*, but rather widely desirable. Such offerings are full of the "sadness, absurdity and despair" (Merton, 1972, p. 297) that issues from being deeply "unearthed," deeply "unhuman," deeply out of touch with our humus. We have become schooled into aspirations that draw our eyes upward, or, more horrifying, inward into the seductive Cartesian allure of self-presence, self-stimulation, and self-annunciation (Smith, 1988, p. 247).

In *Nausea*, Jean-Paul Sartre's fingertips are no longer flesh of the same Earth as the tree he touches; they are no longer flesh at all. His fingertips are only his reflective self-awareness of that touching.

> Geneson: So when Sartre—goes to the tree, touches the tree trunk and says, "I feel in an absurd position—I cannot break through my skin to get in touch with this bark, which is outside me," the Japanese poet would say...?
> Snyder: Sartre is confessing the sickness of the West. At least he is honest. The (poet) will say, "But there are ways to do it, my friend. It's no big deal." It's

no big deal, especially if you get attuned to that possibility from early in life. (Snyder, 1980, p. 67)

Something is awakened here that is beyond the nightmare of self-presence and its ensuing exhaustion. It is a "call to be mindful of our rootedness in earthy experiences" (Aoki, 1987, p. 67). But more: such a call can best be heard "if you get attuned to that possibility from early in life." Attunement. But also pedagogy. The possibility of touching the Earth, this attunement, is rooted (perhaps also uprooted) early in life.

Mindfulness of our rootedness in earthy experiences is a breakthrough to the belonging—together of things that goes on without us, without our doing. It is a realization of the deep, earthy collectivity of things that is not of our own making, wanting, or doing. In one formulation, hermeneutics seems to verge near this: the hermeneutic project is concerned, "not what we do or what we ought to do, but what happens to us over and above our wanting and doing" (Gadamer, 1975, p. xvi). But this hermeneutic project still remains a matter of Eurocentric enculturation, lacking the scent and the fragrance and the fleshy intersections of an Earth that "happens" (even if it *doesn't* happen "to us") and to which we are indebted in silent ways that speak neither Greek nor German. In mindfulness of this silent collectivity of the Earth, there is an archaic debt at work, the debt of breath and blood and sun and soil and sky, and all those hopelessly naïve things the forgetting of which threatens to suddenly and violently trivialize our urbane theorizing with unspeakable ecological events that we, in all our earnestness, cannot outrun or sidestep. We pay homage to the grounds of our talk by evoking the thrilling names and concepts scattered over the history of phenomenology, hermeneutics, critical theory, deconstruction, and whatever is named as next with the loudest voice while forgetting the real ground right under our feet, the real breath we inhale to speak this homage, the real breath we hold in breathless anticipation for the latest news.

I I

A Bell Ringing in the Empty Sky: Both title and music bring out a sense both of the exquisite solitariness of nature, and of the vibrant and crawling interrelatedness and resonances of the Earth. It brings out "both of these"—both the interrelatedness and the solitariness, both the intertwining kinship of things and the uniqueness, individuality, and utter irreplaceability of everything. For this bell is in an empty sky, solitary and unsurrounded; and it is *ringing out*, echoing and resonating with all things. It strikes an image of interdependency and relatedness that *issues from* exquisiteness and is not at odds with it. It strikes against an old image, rooted in Aristotle and coined all too clearly by Descartes: "a substance is that which requires nothing but itself in order to exist" (1955, p.

275). This is a perfect segue into the unearthly loneliness we now are facing and are solemnly passing on to our children under the guise of education and the individual, manic pursuit of excellence-as-self-absorption—and with this, all the little built-in panics and terrors that come with the blind rush to be up-to-date, ahead of the game, or, as phallocentrism would have it, the potent desire to end up "on top."

A bell ringing in the empty sky says this: any thing requires *everything else* in order to exist. Each thing stands before us on behalf of all things, as the absolute center of all things, and, at the periphery of all things. It is an absolute, irreplaceable, exquisite existence because it is empty (Japanese, *Ku*; Sanskrit, *sunyata*) of self-existence. This essay from which you are reading does not simply announce itself, announce what it "is." It is not exquisitely this piece of paper because it requires nothing but itself in order to exist; it is not a *substance* in the scholastic sense. Rather, it is what it is because it is what it is not—it announces sun and sky and earth and water and trees and loggers and the meals they eat and chainsaws and gasoline and pulp and the dioxin produced by the bleaching of this paper and the effluent and the poisoned fish near pulp mills, and the cancer and the pain and the death and the sorrow and the tears and the Earth and the trees growing up out of it. It announces all things without exception, just as a bell echoes everywhere, even where it is unheard. This piece of paper, in all its uniqueness and irreplaceability, requires *everything else* in order to exist. Pulling out this piece of paper tugs at the fabric of all things without exception. Thus, to paraphrase Nishitani (1982, p. 156), the fact that this paper is this paper is a fact in such a way as to involve at the same time the deliverance of all things in their original, earthly countenance and interdependency (Sanskrit, *pratitya-samutpada*). This is why it makes a literally humiliating sort of sense to say that if this particular piece of paper did not exist, nothing would exist, for with the nonexistence of this paper, a constitutive element of all would be what they now are *with* the existence of this paper—without this piece of paper, *everything* would be changed. This is also why there is a peculiar disorientation involved in suddenly realizing that *any* object, even the most trivial of things, is in the center of this interdependency, with all things ordered around it. There is nothing special about this particular piece of paper *and* it is the absolute center of all things without exception. To push this disorientation further, "*the center is everywhere.*" Each and every thing becomes the center of all things and, in that sense, becomes an absolute center. This is the absolute uniqueness of things, their reality" (Nishitani, 1982, p. 146). And even further:

> That a thing *is*—its absolute autonomy—comes about only in unison with the subordination of all other things. It comes about only...where the being of all other things, while remaining to the very end the being that it is, is emptied out. Moreover, this means that the autonomy of this one thing is only constituted through a subordination to all other things. Its autonomy comes about only on a

standpoint from which it makes all other things to be what they are, and in so doing is emptied of its own being. (p. 148)

In short, and against the scholastic notion of "substance," we have a simple, ecologically sane insight: "all things in the world are linked together, one way or the other. Not a single thing comes into being without some relationship to every other thing: (Nishitani, p. 149).

Realizing this is not simply "knowing," it ushers the possibility of *our own* deliverance from self-presence, self-stimulation, and self-announcement, drawing our eyes downward to this precious Earth, silently announcing the *real* genealogy, the *real* generativity and interdependencies of things and of ourselves, not just the one that happens from the neck up with the aid of Husserl or Heidegger or Gadamer. Clearly, moving in this direction risks the possibility of a liberating, albeit painful humiliation of our unchecked desire to put our edifications and aspirations at the center of all things. We risk finding that it may be elevating of Hans-Georg Gadamer's WARHEIT UND METHODE to say that it has the integrity and fertility and unbetraying character of a handful of Earth.

I I I

The bell ringing in the empty sky is not interconnected with the entities that surround it through a filling of the intervening space with knick-knacks, like some Victorian parlor: a peculiarly appropriate image for British empiricism and the relentless proliferation of clutter from experimental designs, designed to fill the gap between one finding and the next through first methodically isolating some supposedly separate intervening variable—another knick-knack found between two others—and then summoning up doubtful, dusty, mathematized interconnectedness of our own making between what we have first rendered isolated by the demands of the logic of empiricism. Thus the interconnectedness of things becomes like cobwebs in the dark. Life becomes sadly episodic, momentary in place and time, reduced to divisible minutiae coupled with "a strange, almost occult yearning for the future" (Berry, 1986, p. 56) when things will finally be okay. And, in inverse proportion to a diminishing sense of time and place, our sense of our own potency and importance becomes distended: as time becomes more and more televised-episodic, the most meager remembrances become enormous and powerful in their resonances: as "personal space" holds sway as a sense of place, that things are all right can be confirmed by just looking around me—inside my house, inside my car, inside my head, everything is fine.

> The industrial conquistador, seated in his living room in the evening in front of the TV set, many miles from his work, can easily forget where he is and what he has done. He is everywhere and nowhere. Everything around him, everything

on TV, tells him of his success: *his* comfort is the redemption of the world. (Berry, 1986, p. 53-54)

I V

This bell ringing in the empty sky is interconnected with the entities around it; it can issue its resonance with all things, precisely because it is not crowded/surrounded/enclosed. The empty sky is not a vacuum to be filled. It is not filled with the sound of the bell. It doesn't long to be filled. It is not deserted or alone or lonely. It is empty in the sense that it is empty of self-existence (Sanskrit: *svabhava*): to be what it is, it empties out into all things without exception, it summons up an intimate, unenclosed indebtedness to the whole of the Earth.

This exquisite thing is part and apart, precisely the phrase used to elicit the paradoxical and irresolvable place of children in our lives (Smith, 1988a, p. 175). Part and apart; not quite the same, but not simply different. Children are our kin, our kind, and we are drawn out to them by a natural affection (a "kindness") in the same way that the bell rings out while remaining itself; in the same way that the bell can ring out only *because* it remains itself. Only because of the empty sky can it have the room to ring out. Only because our resonant, generative, and ambiguous kinship is not an identity or a difference can we be drawn to children with a natural affection. To sustain this natural affection, this kinship requires that we neither desire children to be us, nor abandon them to their difference. Children are what they are because they are what they are not—their existence summons up us and the whole of the earth as part of them, and apart from them. Akin.

Kin, kinship, kind, kindness, natural affection. And the parallel Sanskrit root is *gen*—generativity, regeneration, genesis, genealogy, generousness, that which is freely given. Affection, freely given. We should hesitate over this and imagine it as a way of calling attention to what grounds educational inquiry. Not isolatable substances, such that our work can speak of children as "that which needs nothing other than itself in order to exist" (which, with the advent of modern science, becomes "that which can be isolated as a variable that can be controlled, predicted, and manipulated such that its linear influences can be tracked"—note the relentless proliferation of stages and sub-stages in developmental theories of child development, their manic multiplication a sign of the desire to be close to children, to bridge the difference, to embrace them). Rather, what grounds education inquiry is affection, freely given; what grounds educational inquiry, what compels us to consider children *at all*, is that they are us, they are our kind, our kin, and we deeply desire to understand them and to understand ourselves in relation to them. Somehow, this makes madness of inquiry, which *begins* with methodical isolation and severance and fragmentation of our lives and children's lives into severed competencies; somehow this accounts for the despair and pain that both we and children are experiencing in these times, perhaps especially in the area of education.

> Not only is fragmentation a disease, but the diseases of the disconnected parts are similar or analogous to one another. Thus, they memorialize their lost unity, their relation persisting in their disconnection. Any severance produces two wounds that are, among other things, the record of how the severed parts once fitted together. (Berry, 1986, pp. 110-111)

Such fragmentation and isolation results in an image of inquiry as an out-of-control urban(e) sprawl that knows nothing of the moist earthly ground it travels, upon which it relies, and which it covers over with a lifeless veneer of its own making. (I cannot help thinking of the clear and well-lit overhead projector images of models and flow-charts, each line well-drawn and unequivocal, with all the difficult and generative resonances severed, it is hoped, once and for all.) Inquiry in education thus:

> becomes more and more organized, but less and less orderly. No longer is human life (understood as) rising from the earth like a pyramid, broadly and considerately founded upon its sources. Now it scatters itself out in a reckless horizontal sprawl, like a disorderly city whose suburbs and pavements destroy the fields." (Berry, 1986, p. 21)

V

Understood as a living, earthly relationship, this paradox of our lives with children—part and apart—is not struggling to resolve itself into well-drawn, unambiguous, unequivocal declarations. Rather, being mindful of this paradox and its generative irresolvability "makes meaningful and beautiful the primary paradoxes that human beings *have* to live with" (Snyder, 1980, pp. 29-30), the "original difficulty" (Caputo, 1987) that resides in the issuing forth of new life in our midst. Children are a reminder of archaic debts, reminders of a real genealogy and the interlacing of that genealogy with all things. Perhaps this is why Gary Snyder (1980) maintains that we should live in a place as if we and our children, and their children, will live there a thousand years. This genealogy, this generativity, and this deep natural affection—the question of "kind"—does not and cannot simply string along a chromosomal thread, but exhales outward into the whole of the Earth, into a sense of place and space, coupled with an attunement to what is needed for a livable future. The whole Earth is our "kind," our kin. We are human, full of humus, and our natural affection cannot begin with isolating humanity as "that which needs nothing but itself in order to exist." Our humanity is not a substance. We are empty of self-existence and only as such—only interlaced with all things—can we be what we deeply are.

With the interdependence of all things, cause and effect are no longer
perceived as linear, but as a net, not a two-dimensional one, but a system of
countless nets interwoven in all directions in a multidimensional space. (Hahn,
1988, p. 64)

    Even the very tiniest thing, to the extent that it "is," displays in its act of
being the whole web of circuminsessional interpenetration that links all things
together. (Nishitani, 1982, p. 149)

Whispering in this paradox of solitariness/exquisiteness and interrelation is a
sense of having a place that is not of my own making: it is granted a place, freely
given, and mindfulness of this gift is, in a deep sense, a finding (Heidegger,
1968). My being, even in my individuality, is an original blessing (Fox, 1983), a
gift—it is a *given*, and the most intimate and original response must be one of
thanks for the naturally affectionate generosity of the Earth. It is mere hubris to
consider ever finding ourselves out of debt, thinking a thought, living a life that
owes nothing, which is perfectly self-enclosed. Such was the poverty and
disaffection of Descartes' dream (Jardine, in press)—the unindebted thought
thinking itself, self-present, out of relation to all things. True thinking does not
and cannot repay this debt. True thinking simply heightens our sense of this
original debt, this original gift, this original blessing. In receiving, a giving.

V I

A Bell Ringing in the Empty Sky: This image cannot live with the bizarre and
convoluted horror pronounced so calmly in the mid-nineteenth century by
Arthur Schopenhauer.

"The world is my representation:" This is a truth valid with reference to every
living and knowing being, although man alone can bring it into reflective,
abstract consciousness. If he really does so, philosophical discernment has
dawned on him. It then becomes clear and certain to him that he does not
know a sun and an earth, but only an eye that sees a sun, a hand that feels an
earth; that the world around him is there only as representation, in other words,
only in reference to another thing, namely, that which represents, and this is
himself. (1966, p. 63)

At first glance, Schopenhauer's words might seem to foretell a sense of
interdependency, but, in the end, it is only a dependency. To understand the
sun, the Earth, requires only a reflective understanding of our powers to
represent. Between sun and earth there is an interdependency, but such
interdependency is a matter of our powers to represent. Between sun and earth
there is an interdependency, but such interdependency is a matter of our
representing, of our *bestowing* cosmos on chaos (as Jean Piaget so calmly defines
the young child's actions on the world) (1971, p. 15), such that interdependency

is rooted in a deeper dependency on the one who represents. The Earth is ours to envisage, to make in our own image. Thus "the sickness of the West" begins. In our envisaging of the Earth, all we can see is this façade, and this façade gains its integrity by being linked back to human being—suddenly we, as humans, have no place on the Earth but have become that place in which all other things, the whole Earth, comes forth.

> Man sets himself up as the setting in which whatever is must henceforth set itself forth, must present itself. Man becomes the representative of that which is. What is decisive is that man expressly takes up this position as one constituted by himself...and that he makes it secure as the solid footing for a possible development of humanity. There begins that way of being human which mans the realm of human capacity as a domain given over to measuring and executing, for the purposes of gaining mastery of what is as a whole. (Heidegger, 1971, p. 32)

Under the shadow of Western epistemology, "what is as a whole" possesses a singular center that dispenses the possibility of things and thus oversteps its own earthly possibility with unearthly, transcendental zeal. The human being becomes the condition for the possibility of all things. The world becomes our representation as we solemnly become the singular representatives of all things. We become, here, the grand colonizers. We become the ones that savage those whom we consider unorganized, uncivilized, illogical, immoral, immature, by rendering them in our own image. We don't allow them a face (difference, here, must be fixed, for to be different is to fail to be at the center); we give them a façade of our own making. Deep in our Western heritage, and threading lines into contemporary educational theory and practice, there is a pleasant, attractive name for this colonization—we wish to understand.

V I I

From Immanuel Kant's *Critique of Pure Reason* (1787), we have the fearful recoil from the decentering discoveries of Copernicus. Copernicus displaced the Earth as center and placed the sun at the center of the visible universe. The heavens no longer revolved around us. Kant's Copernican Revolution reclaimed what was lost in this movement.

> A light broke upon the students of nature. They learned that reason has insight only into that which it produces after a plan of its own, and that it must not allow itself to be kept, as it were, in nature's leading-strings, but must itself show the way with principles of judgement based on fixed laws, constraining nature to give answer to questions of reason's own determining. Reason...must approach nature in order to be taught by it. It must not, however, do so in the character of a pupil who listens to everything the teacher chooses to say, but of an appointed judge who compels the witnesses to answer questions which he had himself formulated. While reason must seek a nature, not fictitiously

ascribe to it, whatever has to be learnt, if learnt at all, only from nature, it must adopt as its guide, in so seeking, that which it has itself put into nature. (p. 20)

To understand the essence of the Earth, one must understand the essence of Reason, for it is from Reason that the synthetic unity of nature-as-experienced, its interrelatedness, arises. To understand the Earth, we must seek what we have put there. Here, once again, is the deep hubris and deep faith of European Enlightenment—*only Reason is exquisite*, untouched, unsurrounded, ringing forth with no equal, graciously *bestowing* its forms on all things through its resonating synthetic acts.

V I I I

The spirit of the Earth, its inner fire, its *logos*, has become ourselves. In this way, *eco logos* becomes *ego logos*, ecology becomes egology. Understanding ourselves need only refer to ourselves: to our skills and concepts, our mastery of requisite inner states of competence and performance, our skill at wielding methods and processes. We no longer need to rely on how our selves are reflected back to us from what surrounds us and houses us (*eco*), from what *things* have to say about *us*. The Earth has been silenced—we are the only resonance, the only and singular voice (see Habermas' [1973] characterization of scientific discourse as monologic).

Consider: eco, dwelling, abode. Consider Heidegger's definition:

Dwelling is not primarily inhabiting but taking care of and creating that space within which something comes into its own and flourishes. Dwelling is primarily saving, in the older sense of setting something free to become itself, what it essentially is...Dwelling is that which cares for things so that they essentially presence and come into their own. (cited in Sessions & Devall, 1985, p. 98-99)

And thus consider the legacy of Kant: the place where things are brought into their own and flourish in human consciousness and human articulation. Certainly, dwelling is that which cares for things, but since the integrity of things is a bestowal of Reason, caring for things, caring for this precious Earth, becomes a matter of Reason caring for and heeding itself. The care involved in dwelling becomes meticulous and methodical carefulness. Dwelling becomes equated with the caution and suspicion of logico-mathematical discourse. Dwelling becomes method. Or, consider the legacy of Nietzsche. Here, dwelling, the place where things are brought into their own, becomes self-declaration, self-announcement, desire, and will. Lost is any sense of something being worth saying: gained is an ascendancy of simply saying, the episodic scatter-shot of opinion and rapid-fire whole-language blabbering all at once. All at once, for it no longer matters if anyone really listens. Listeners are just raw meat; they provide only resistance and gutted nourishment that can increase my sense of power—I must consume the listener with my speech, demand attention, and all of this must be done quickly. I write this under the influence of practicum supervision, where many grade one classrooms have become filled with a panicky rush where there is so very much being done and so little time for anything. There is no time to *dwell* over anything, to take care and consideration and deep attention to what you are doing (teacher or child), to prolong the sensuous richness of things, or the sonorous richness of words and melodies, to let the resonances ring out fully. There is no time for silence, for space, for seasonality, for these are merely lack of will, lack of diligence and effort, failures to produce.

I X

The universe is a dynamic fabric of interdependent events in which none is the fundamental entity. (Hahn, 1988, p. 50)

But it is so difficult to actually believe this, to summon up the understanding of myself that allows this to come forward. I am not an exception to the interweaving, earthly indebtedness and interdependency, but an instance of it. Believing this requires a deep sort of "letting go" that is not commonplace in Western aspirations. It entails a sort of simple, reverential understanding of things and our reliances on them.

> The Red Wheelbarrow
> so much depends
> upon
>
> a red wheel
> barrow
>
> glazed with rain
> water
>
> beside the white
> chickens.
> William Carlos Williams (1985, p. 56)

But this also brings a realization of the fact that "the self in its original countenance" (Nishitani, 1982, p. 91) is an earthly self, full of the humus that interweaves with all things.

> The self is here at the home-ground of all things. It is itself a home-ground where everything becomes manifest as what it is, where all things are assembled together into a "world." This must be a standpoint where one's own self in all things, in living things, in hills and rivers and towns and hamlets, tiles and stones, and loves these things "as oneself." (Nishitani, 1982, p. 280-281)

There is a peculiar turn, here, that distinguishes this passage from those of Eurocentrism. Seeing oneself in all things is not a matter of the violent colonization of all things, as if to see oneself "in" all things is to have impregnated them, to have pissed on every tree, surveyed every acre. It is not a matter of enslaving all things and making them indebted to me. It is, rather, a matter of recognizing my indebtedness to *them*. Loving all things as oneself is a matter of *emptying out* that self, of *giving away* one's center(ed)ness. This means, at first twist, becoming " nothing." But it also means, at once, becoming all things:

> I gave up trying to carry on an intellectual interior life separate from the work, and I said the hell with it, I'll just work. And instead of losing something, I got something much greater. By just working, I found myself being completely there, having the whole mountain inside of me, and finally having the whole language inside of me that became one with the rocks and with the trees. (Snyder, 1980, p. 8)

This is so difficult to realize, even gazing out the window to these trees, this snow, that all things are not there for me. This is the sting of ecological insight. But in this insight is contained something precious. Once I deeply realize that all these things are not here for me, they begin, so to speak, to turn away; they no longer pay any special attention to me; they are not formed up and tarted up for my perusal. Suddenly, I am no longer the displaced, post-Copernican, questioning stranger, the colonizing interloper, the condescending intruder to whom attention must be paid and who can make demands without attention to where I actually am, without attention to what is *already at work without me*. Suddenly, I *belong* here. I *live* here. This Earth is my *home*. I can finally experience my being as resonant, indebted, and interwoven with these things. I am no longer the judge posing questions and demanding silence. I can begin, as ecology suggests, to become deeply conversant with things, listening, asking, responding, inhaling, and exhaling. Such conversation is only possible insofar as it issues up out of a sense of the integrity of my interlocutor—the Earth in all its wondrous articulations.

X

There are afoot forms of philosophical/educational discourse that speak on behalf of deconstructing the violent, retentive centrations that have ruled our lives—logocentrism, phallocentrism, Eurocentrism, anthropocentrism, adulto-centrism. And often, such language is disorienting, intentionally disruptive, disrespectful, unsettling, profane, sarcastic, destructive, negative.

Question: What is such work for? The danger we face is that we may come to believe, with the "post-modernist" disassembling of violent centrations, that nothing is the center, that all things are trivial and episodic and unconnected, and that only a vague, exhausted and, in its own way, violent licentiousness is possible.

A bell ringing in the empty sky: all things are at the center. All things are exquisite. What hopefully emerges from such disassembling of the clangor are those archaic sounds and resonances that were not of our own assembly in the first place. What hopefully emerges out from under the exhaustion is a deep love and compassion for all things.

X I

> The real work is what we really do. And what our lives really are. And if we can live the work we have to do, knowing that we are real, and that the world is real, then it becomes right. And that's the real work: to make the world as real as it is and to find ourselves as real as we are within it. (Snyder, 1980, p. 82)

How can our eyes be drawn back to Earth and to the real work of attending and attuning to the *humus* out of which our humanity has arisen? We cannot confront this epistemological legacy head on, for it already defines its foes. But neither will it do to fantasize about wide open spaces or escapes to elsewhere. For there is no "elsewhere." It is this place, this space that is at issue in drawing our eyes back to Earth. This is the juncture at which the real work becomes an economic and political matter. It is at this juncture that the real work becomes physically, spiritually, linguistically, culturally, and autobiographically bound in ways that no heavenward glance can surmount. The *real* critique does not fall from above; it issues up out of the Earth we actually walk, the life we actually *find* ourselves living. This school, this classroom, this moment with this child— these are the resonant moments that are full of our indebtedness and fully worthy of our attention. If a bell ringing in the empty sky becomes a woozy vision of Japanese exotica, the real work is lost and the talk is mere pornography and titillation with novelty items. Although the problem is "where do you put your feet down; where do you raise your children; what do you do with your hands?" (Snyder, 1980, p.66), the problem is also how we find ourselves enabled or disabled to respond to, to even *raise* these questions. The real work is right here.

So it will not do to deny that this paper is written by a male of European/Caucasian descent, someone economically well-off, living on an acreage far outside a city, with plenty of trees and sun and sky, with a reasonably secure job that has built-in luxuries, built-in time, and space for mindfulness and earthly tempos. I am one for whom these words are easy to pronounce, for they do not have to clamor up out of the deadly white-noise silencings that define and defile so many. "How can I, as an educator, fulfill my responsibility to my own people: my own people whom I love yet who, like I do, live under an economic and epistemological dispensation which is the *problem* for most of the world" (Smith, 1988c, p. 92)?

I hope my son can live a life that is not just a niche in the clutter (however, I see how cluttered his school life is *already*; I hear the ecological rumblings in the distance). I hope he finds the empty space required for the natural affections and kinships of speech and experience and understanding to come forth. I hope he becomes deeply conversant with this precious Earth. I hope someday that he will understand that he, in his good fortune, is indebted to all things without exception. I'm afraid that he'll *have* to see someday that his good fortune is the *problem* for most of the world and that some of those debts are coming due.

And I am frightened that I won't know what to say when he asks what I have actually *done* to live in the spirit of a loving and compassionate indebtedness to all things; what he will say if he discovers that it is some of *my* ignored debts that he must repay, perhaps with his life (after all, where exactly is the dioxin produced by the bleaching of these very pages?). *This* is the real work of my life as an educator, no matter what I say.

A bell ringing in the empty sky.

REFERENCES

Aoki, T. (1987). In receiving, a giving: A response to panelists gifts. *Journal of Curriculum Theorizing.* 7(3), p. 67.

Berry, W. (1986). *The Unsettling of America.* (San Francisco: Sierra Book Club).

Caputo, J. (1987). *Radical hermeneutics.* (Bloomington: Indiana University Press).

Descarates, R. (1955). *Selections.* (New York: Charles Scribner's Sons).

Fox, M. (1983). *Original blessing.* (San Francisco: Bear and Co.).

Gadamer, H.G. (1975). *Truth and method.* (New York: Seabury Press).

Hahn, T.N. (1988). *The sun in my heart.* (Berkeley: Parallax Press).

Heidegger, M. (1971). The age of the world-picture. In *The Question Concerning Technology.* (New York: Harper and Row).

Heidegger, M. (1973). *Time and being.* (New York: Harper and Row).

Hume, D. (1956). *Treatise on human understanding.* (Oxford: Oxford University Press).

Jardine, D. (in press) Awakening from Descartes' nightmare: On the origins of the love of ambiguity in phenomenological approaches to education. *Studies in Philosophy and Education.*

Kant, I. (1964). *Critique of pure reason.* (London: Macmillan).

Merton, T. (1972). *New seeds of contemplation.*)New York: New Directions Books).

Nietzsche, F. (1975). *The will to power.* (New York: Random House).

Nishitani, K. (1982). *Religion and nothingness.* (Berkeley: University of California Press).

Piaget, J. (1952). *Origins of intelligence in children.* (New York: International Universities Press).

Piaget, J. (1965). *Insights and illusions of philosophy.* (New York: Meridian Books).

Piaget, J. (1971). *The construction of reality in the child.* (New York: Ballantine Books).

Piaget, J. (1973). *Psychology of intelligence.* (Totowa: Littlefield, Adams and Co.).

Schopenhauer, A. (1966). *The world as will and representation.* Vol. 1. (New York: Dover Books).

Sessions, G., & Devall, B. (1985). *Deep ecology.* (Salt Lake City: Peregrine Books).

Smith, D.G. (1988a). Children and the gods of war. *Journal of Educational Thought*, 22A (2).

Smith, D.G. (1988b). On being critical about language: The critical theory tradition and implications for language education. *Reading-Canada-Lecture*. 6 (4), P. 247.

Smith, D.G. (1988c). The problem of the south is the north (but the problem of the north is the north). Forum of the *World Council on Curriculum and Instruction*. 2 (2).

Snyder, G. (1980). *The real work*. (New York: New Directions).

Williams, W.C. (1985). *Selected poems*. (New York: New Directions Books).

CHAPTER EIGHTEEN

Toward an Eschatological Curriculum Theory

Patrick Slattery
1992

> The impetus for choosing and becoming in us is not something that need be externally imposed; but it is rather a process of helping others see possibilities and helping them free themselves for going beyond this present state of embedded existence…. We must keep up our hope.
>
> —James B. Macdonald
> "Curriculum, Consciousness, and Social Change"
> in *Contemporary Curriculum Discourses* (1988, p. 163)

> Without hope, the capacity to imagine social alternatives is a head-game, lacking force and true self-engagement.
>
> —Philip Wexler
> "Body and Soul: Sources of Social Change and Strategies of Education"
> in *Contemporary Curriculum Discourses* (1988, p. 219)

I N T R O D U C T I O N

The protagonist in Walker Percy's novel *Love in the Ruins* is a psychiatrist named Tom More who is living in New Orleans in the "dread latter days of the old violent beloved U.S.A. and of the Christ-forgetting Christ-haunted death-dwelling Western World" (1971, p. 3). Tom More, in the midst of the desolation of modern decadence, awaits the final apocalyptic catastrophe. He concludes, "Two more hours should tell the story. One way or the other. Either I am right and the catastrophe will occur, or it won't and I'm crazy. In either case the outlook is not so good" (p. 3). In Percy's novel, More seeks to make sense out of his own human experience as a survivor in the latter days of modern society.

Decay is evident; the human spirit is weary. In a final effort to save humanity, Dr. Tom More produces 100 compact pocketsize machines of brushed chrome which he calls the "More Qualitative-Quantitative Ontological Lapsometer, the stethoscope of the spirit" (p. 62). In the end though, it is not the Lapsometer that saves society. Rather, Walker Percy's paradoxical humor finds hope as expressed in the theme that humanity must return to basic values and love if there is to be meaningful survival. The novel ends on Christmas Day. Tom More and his wife, reunited in the midst of the decay and ashes, go to bed "twined about each other as the ivy twineth" (p. 403). They make love in the ruins. And just as the wisteria vines are growing out of the ashes, a resurgence of nature, life, and hope occurs. Mardi Gras awakes to Ash Wednesday and awaits Easter Sunday. Percy's legacy to the future of the world is described by Mary K. Sweeney as an understanding that "with the blotting out of the corruptible creations of humanity, there will be new beginnings with the miraculous sprouting or organic life" (1987, p. 79). In the spirit of Walker Percy, contemporary eschatological theology and curriculum theory is combined with an examination of the concept of hope in a postmodern society in this project.

The current crisis in contemporary American education can be characterized as a struggle to control the direction of schools for the future. Some insist that American education should embrace the traditional Judeo-Christian canonical vision exemplified in the work of William Bennett in *The James Madison School* (Bennett, 1988), E.D. Hirsch in *Cultural Literacy* (Hirsch, 1987), and Allan Bloom in *The Closing of the American Mind* (Bloom, 1987). Others pretending to moral neutrality and scientific objectivity believe that the empirical-analytical paradigm should continue to dominate research methodology and classroom practice in hopes of eventually discovering the data and objectives that will cure the ills of the public schools (Hunter, 1982). Finally, there is a growing interest in a reconceptualization of education that will support a post modern emancipatory curriculum (Pinar, 1988).

All three positions presuppose serious deficiencies in education requiring immediate attention. The malaise and hopelessness of contemporary society identified by numerous cultural critics spell turmoil in the educational domain. Henry Giroux recognizes both hopelessness and turmoil, and issues a challenge to the educational community to move beyond the modern paradigm for understanding the crises. He writes, "Given the current mood of cynicism, despair, and defeatism, it is important for radical educators to move beyond theories of reproduction that do nothing more than either analyze the contradictions that exist in schools or point to the way in which schools are influenced by structural determinants in the wider society" (1981, p. 424). Michael Apple argues that educators must become committed to practices that promote emancipation. The neutrality of a detached intellectual is impossible, he argues (Apple, 1979). According to Apple, educators must "affiliate with cultural, political, and economic groups who are self-consciously working to alter the institutional arrangements that set limits on the lives and hopes of so many people in this society" (1979, p. 166). As affiliation with groups that challenge modern institutional arrangements grow, the concern for a postmodern curriculum will develop. If there is to be a renewed sense of hope in education and in society, it will be important to move from modernism to a postmodern vision rooted in emancipation and liberation. This journey will require us to use the maps provided by the advancements of the past to chart our course to liberatory practices. A reconceptualization in eschatological theology and in curriculum theory offers a means for moving toward this new vision.

In theology, reconceptualization suggests a reevaluation of the understanding of certain concepts: omnipotence and omniscience, grace and anthropology, the meaning of evil, and of the relationship of the present generation to the Parousia. An authentic ecumenical orientation and a proleptic vision of the goal of history will become dominant themes in the reconceptualization of eschatology. Hans Kung has recently proposed that theology is on the verge of an epochal threshold and Kuhnian paradigm shift with ecumenism as the focus (Kung, 1988). This is apparent despite the fact that some in church leadership cling to an outmoded paradigm. Kung writes,

> One is surprised only how the Roman Inquisition—now under Cardinal Joseph Ratzinger—after such a "chronique scandaleuse," still thinks it can impose its medieval paradigm, in the face of all the findings and results from the reformation and the modern period, in the midst of the transition to postmodernity, with the old methods. (pp.292-293)

The possibility of a paradigm shift and accompanying methodological transformation in eschatological theology is not without historical precedence. The early Christian church reevaluated the belief in the imminent return of Jesus by the end of the first century (C.E.) when it became apparent that the apocalyptic events would be delayed beyond the generation of the apostles and disciples. This reevaluation created the need for a radically new approach to evangelization and hermeneutic interpretation in the early Christian community.

In curriculum theory, the reconceptualization that has occurred reevaluates themes that parallel theological issues and reconsiders methodologies as well. Some of the themes include issues related to power and control, transformation and transmission, social scientific and humanistic methodologies, and race and gender studies. This reconceptualization in curriculum theory and in eschatological theology provides a framework for advancing renewed experiences of hope in schools and society. Only with this renewed sense of hope will it be possible to discover "love in the ruins" of modernity.

WHY ESCHATOLOGICAL THEOLOGY?

The importance of eschatology as a framework for developing and understanding contemporary curriculum is evident in the emerging literature in both the curriculum field and in philosophical theology. Philip Phenix writes that "without hope, there is no incentive for learning, for the impulse to learn presupposes confidence in the possibility of improving one's existence. The widespread loss of hope is one of the principal causes of educational problems that beset contemporary America" (1976, p. 329). Phenix articulates the concern of those who recognize the problems that are arising in education because of apathy and despair. Without a vision of future possibilities impinging on lived world experiences, individuals lose the incentive to contribute to community growth.

David Ray Griffin offers a concise view of the urgency of a new vision of improved existence. Offering insurance of global survival, Griffin proposes a spirituality that emphasizes internal relatedness rather than external and accidental relatedness. There is a concern and respect for the past in which the present moment of experience is seen to enfold within itself the entire past. The future is also related to the present, not in the sense that it is decided and complete but in the sense that it grows out of the present and utilizes the contributions of the present. "(This) postmodern perspective offers the more hopeful vision that, through the emergence of a new worldview and a concomitant spirituality, with new interests, new values, new approaches, and new practices, the course of our world can be radically changed without cataclysmic revolution" (Griffin, 1988, p. 14).

Rosemary Radford Ruether also proposes that a new understanding of eschatology is essential. She refutes the view that eschatology is either an end-point of history or a transcendence of death. Rather, redemptive hope is the constant quest for internal relatedness, which is the connecting point for all existences: past, present, and future. According to Ruether, "God's Shalom is the nexus of authentic creational life that has to be reincarnated again and again in new ways and new contexts in each new generation" (1983, p. 69). Social change for Ruether is found in the continual conversion back to an authentic creational life. She writes

> This concept of social change as conversion back to the centre, rather than to a beginning or end-point in history, seems to me a model of change that is more in keeping with temporal existence, rather than subjecting us to the tyranny of impossible expectations. (1983, p. 70)

Apocalyptic eschatology has conditioned humanity for this tyranny, and modern nihilism has provided a tyranny of meaninglessness. A postmodern eschatology can transform these experiences of despair and tyranny.

Another example in curriculum theorizing implying the importance of eschatological themes is found in a recent essay by David G. Smith. Smith records the events of one elementary social studies classroom and presents an analysis of the language used to describe school experiences. Paraphrasing Hans-Georg Gadamer, Smith writes that "language not only tells us what we are, it tells us what we were and what we hope to become" (1988, p. 422). Smith argues that curriculum research must reconcile the past, present, and future. He concludes, "An attention to the eidetic quality of our life together is an attempt to bring into the center of our research conversation everything that we are, as a way of reconciling in the present moment our ends with our beginnings" (1988, p. 435). Curriculum, like eschatology, seeks to overcome despair by providing an environment where relatedness stimulates growth.

The important themes emerging in contemporary curriculum discourses as well as in postmodern theological reflections recognize the urgent need for transformative processes that incorporate an understanding of the past and future as constitutive of present experience. The four authors cited above— Phenix, Griffin, Ruether, and Smith—provide a sample of the way that this emerging theme is permeating contemporary curriculum and theological literature. These themes point toward the development of an eschatological curriculum theory. Whether or not Hans Kung and others who link these themes to Kuhnian paradigm shifts and epochal thresholds are correct, it is certain that the emphasis in contemporary theology and curriculum studies on the process of transformation, emancipation, liberation, relatedness, and synthesis of time will have a significant impact on both fields of study. In curriculum and theology, the insistence on viewing past experiences and future possibilities for individuals and for society as an integral part of present reality is a dramatic shift away from the modern perspective. Modernity has accompanied the isolation of the individual, frozen in quantifiable time and space, unable to establish relationships and incapable of affecting the future course of events. In contrast, the postmodern vision of the individual person in relation to others and connected to a meaningful past and emerging future is essential for individual transformation, social change, and global survival. This emerging eschatological theme in curriculum theory and theology provides support for a new vision of education and society, suggested in the following section.

THEOLOGIANS AND CURRICULUM THEORISTS IN AN AGE OF HOPE

Popular culture envisions eschatological happiness in the attitude of Bobby McFerrin in the song, "Don't Worry, Be Happy" from the soundtrack of the movie Cocktail. Despite troubles with furniture thieves, demanding landlords, diminishing finances, lost relationships and personal depression, McFerrin still finds cause to smile, reduce his anxiety, and be happy. He even offers his telephone number to those who want to call him for his recipe for ontological bliss. Is McFerrin's happiness an anesthetic remedy designed to deaden the troubled human heart as a survival technique? If so, then Christopher Lasch was correct when he asserted that people have lost confidence in the future (Lasch, 1984). The arms race, terrorism, environmental deterioration, and long-term economic decline have taught people to prepare for the worst and retreat from commitments to community programs that promote an orderly and secure world. In the nuclear age, personal survival and happiness override efforts to overcome evil.

Even attempts to awaken the public to global concerns often enforce the same inertia that they seek to overcome. One author has concluded, "The great danger of an apocalyptic argument is that to the extent it persuades, it also immobilizes" (Falk, 1971). Richard Falk's argument succinctly clarifies why a reconceptualized curriculum will profit not only from dialogue but also from a theoretical engagement with postmodern theology, especially as this theology will provide a heuristic metaphor for proleptic hope. Education can no longer rely on traditional and apocalyptic eschatology to provide appropriate metaphors for the future. The reconceptualization of eschatology, where the future and transcendence become transformative for the individual and the global community, is an imminent necessity.

In crises and suffering, people seek survival. They do not look back, lest they become trapped in debilitating nostalgia. They do not look ahead because impending disasters are predicted at every turn. As a result, individuals under siege retreat into a protective womb for shelter against adversity. In education, the retreat is seen in the movement to objectify every dimension of the curriculum. Statistical jargon is used to persuade a skeptical public and a hostile government that disaster can be avoided. An "objective," back-to-the-"basics," "teacher proof" curriculum presumably provides the accountability demanded. Individual teachers and students become cogs in the educational wheel whose needs must be minimized for the sake of equilibrium. Lasch warns, "Emotional equilibrium demands a minimal self, not the imperial self of yesteryear" (Lasch, 1984, p. 15). In an effort to restore the imperial self, modern technological curricula have sought to promote the status of teachers and students through accountability movements, but ironically, by rejecting the uniqueness of individual students and limiting the autonomy of teachers, the modern movement has debilitated the very people it has sought to liberate. As an example, Stanley Aronowitz, in *Politics and Higher Education in the 1980s*, points out that current education policy seeks to persuade that the basics movement can solve the economic crisis for graduating students. Aronowitz disagrees and contends that "to combat inequality, students require knowledge and, most of all, hope in their collective powers to change the world so that democratic power replaces corporate control" (Aronowitz, 1981, p. 465).

Mark Taylor in *Erring: A Post-Modern A/Theology* describes a pattern similar to Aronowitz in modern humanist movements. The "Death of God" provided the ultimate philosophy for liberating individuals from enslavement to a deity. Modern industrial and technological advances would emancipate humanity and lift individuals to new heights of perfection in harmony with nature. However, like the technological solutions of modern education, the individual was destroyed in the process. Taylor says, "By denying God in the name of man, humanistic atheism inverts the Creator/creature relationship and transforms theology into anthropology. The humanist atheist fails to realize that the death of God is at the same time the death of self" (1984, p. 20). Contemporary education and theology have both failed to "liberate" the self. Individuals are beginning to recognize the limits of technological models in education, theology, and ecology. The goal of mastery and domination in all three has failed. It has become clear that "mastery, utility, consumption, ownership, propriety, property, colonialism, and totalitarianism for a seamless, though seamy web. In the shadow of the death of God, humanism tends to become inhuman…. The economy of domination carries within it the seeds of its own negation. Eventually consumption becomes all-consuming" (1984, p. 28). The limited usefulness of apocalyptic theology, traditional humanism, and technological educational movements requires that society turn to a new, postmodern metaphor. A reconceptualized eschatology represents one such metaphor that can bring hope without omnipotent domination and omniscient mastery.

What is the alternative proposed for a postmodern curriculum theory rooted in a reconceptualized eschatology? Lasch describes it as "a new culture—a postindustrial (postmodern) culture—based on a recognition of the contradictions in human experience, not on technology that tries to restore the illusion of self-sufficiency or, on the other hand, on a radical denial of selfhood that tries to restore the illusion of absolute unity with nature. Neither Prometheus nor Narcissus will lead us further down the road on which we have already traveled much too far" (1984, p. 20). The postmodern curriculum, therefore, must offer a recognition of competing values and contradictory experiences and not a recycled Tylerian program. Neither must the curriculum propose a rejection of the individual in an attempt to find an untenable harmony between past theories and present practices. A postmodern curriculum turn to eschatology helps us to understand the apparently irreconcilable contradictions between (1) omnipotence/evil (authority/error) and (2) omniscience/journey (order/chaos) in human experience and education. The integration of these apparent contradictions more profoundly explicates reality than modern technological and industrial solutions or radical illusions of perfect harmony and unity between nature and the individual. Process theology recognizes that the journey, simply the process, contains the best understanding of the focus of history (Cobb, 1976). Contemporary curriculum theory also recognizes that the process of running the race, *currere*, best explains the focus of education (Pinar and Grumet, 1976). William Schubert summarizes this position as follows.

> One of the most recent positions to emerge on the curriculum horizon is to emphasize the verb form of curriculum, namely, currere. Instead of taking its interpretation from the race course etymology of curriculum, currere refers to the running of the race and emphasizes the individual's own capacity to reconceptualize his or her autobiography. The individual seeks meaning amid the swirl of present events, moves historically into his or her own past to recover and reconstitute origins, and imagines and creates possible directions for his or her own future. Based on the sharing of autobiographical accounts with others who strive for similar understanding, the curriculum becomes a reconceiving of one's perspective on life. It also becomes a social process whereby individuals come to greater understanding of themselves, others, and the world through mutual reconceptualization. The curriculum is the interpretation of lived experiences." (1986, p. 33)

The future is not simply a historical goal to be reached; the curriculum is not simply an objective to be implemented. Rather, both at their best must prioritize relations, mutual interdependence, and creative transformation. The postmodern eschatological curriculum exists whenever the future is active in illuminating the past and transforming the present. In theology, it is said that "while the modern form of the death of God comes to expression in humanistic atheism, the postmodern form points to a posthumanistic a/theology. Posthumanistic a/theology maintains that the inversion (of the Creator/creature relationship), though it is necessary, does not go far enough" (Taylor, 1984, p. 28). Postmodern theology and curriculum must move beyond, not compete with, modern movements and see that the creative tension of the "already" and the "not yet" within the individual cannot be eradicated by imposing an external apocalyptic lesson plan of prepackaged knowledge or predetermined salvation. The tension itself produces growth; therefore, accountability movements that seek to eliminate uncertainty and tension also eliminate creative transformation.

Maybe Bobby McFerrin has something else in mind when he sings, "Don't Worry, Be Happy." Is McFerrin's happiness really a deep personal joy, rather than superficial resignation, because he has experienced a vision of reality other than psychic survival? Does this vision inspire his transformative hope, and is there really a reason not to worry and smile: Has McFerrin rejected the cataclysmic apocalyptic vision and interiorized the proleptic hope of process theology? Possibly Christopher Lasch's critics were not correct after all. Emotional equilibrium may depend more on a conscious acceptance of the creative tension between the "already" and the "not yet," rather than a reduction of the individual to a minimal self. Like Lasch, William Faulkner may have had an accurate eschatological insight when he accepted the Nobel Prize for literature in 1950. Faulkner began, like Richard Falk above, by admitting that "our tragedy today is a general and universal physical fear so long sustained by now that we can even bear it" (Faulkner, 1950). But Faulkner did not despair; he knew the role of the poet-educator in the process of establishing hope. He brings this argument to a conclusion that postmodern theologians and curriculum theorists would understand very well.

> I decline to accept the end of humanity. It is easy enough to say that humanity is immortal simply because it will endure; that when the last ding-dong of doom has clanged and faded from the last worthless rock hanging tideless in the red and dying evening, that even then there will still be one more sound: that of a puny inexhaustible voice still talking. I refuse to accept this. I believe that humanity will not merely endure: humanity will prevail. Men and women are immortal, not because they alone among creatures have an inexhaustible voice, but because they have a soul, a spirit capable of compassion and sacrifice and endurance. The poet's, the writer's, duty is to write about these things. It is the poet's privilege to help humanity endure by lifting the heart, by reminding humanity of the courage and honor and hope and pride and compassion and pity and sacrifice which have been the glory of the past (Faulkner, 1950).

In the spirit of Faulkner, the postmodern educator with a new eschatological metaphor will now have philosophical and theological support for encouraging students not merely to accept meaningless curriculum for some nebulous future good but to tap the spirit of compassion and sacrifice and endurance within their unique souls and prevail in the struggle to live meaningful and hopeful lives in the present. By tapping this resource rich in the traditions of courage, honor, and pride, the educational community lifts hearts and transforms lives. The future is full of hope, because, although it is "not yet" clear and complete, it is "already" present and active within the individual. Christa McAuliffe, in a statement made before the launch of the space shuttle Challenger, expresses this very succinctly when she concluded, "I teach, I touch the future." Educators should decline to design a curriculum that promotes domination of nature, mastery of external knowledge, preparation for a distant and predestined future, and mere endurance in a god-forsaken world. In the postmodern theological spirit, we should create an interdependent and emancipatory curriculum full of tension, question, struggle, grappling, and sharing, with a holistic process rather than a whole product as our goal. Let us reach back and beyond and create a milieu of hope. Let us touch the future, now.

R E F E R E N C E S

Apple, M.W. (1979). *Ideology and curriculum*. (London: Routledge and Kegan Paul). (See Boggs, C. (1976). *Gramsci's Marxism*. London: Pluto Press. Chapter 5.)

Aronowitz, S. (1981). Politics and higher education in the 1980s, in *Curriculum and Instruction*, edited by Giroux, Penna, and Pinar. (Berkeley: McCutchan) 455-465.

Bennett, W. (1988). *James Madison Elementary School: A curriculum for American students*. (Washington, D.C.: U.S. Department of Education).

Bloom, A. (1987). *The closing of the American mind: How higher education has failed democracy and impoverished the soul of American students*. (New York: Simon and Schuster).

Boff, L. (1985). *Church: Charism and Powe: Liberation theology and the institutional Church*. (New York: Crossroads).

Cobb, J.B., Jr. (1976). *Process theology: An introductory exposition*. (Philadelphia: The Westminster Press).

Falk. R. (1971). *The endangered plante*. (New York: Random House).

Faulkner, W. (1965). Speech of acceptance upon the award of the Nobel Prize for literature. In *Essays, Speeches, and Public Letters of William Faulkner*, edited by James B. Meriwether. (New York: Random House). (Quotation is paraphrased to eliminate sexist language.)

Freire, P. (1970). *Pedagogy of the oppressed*. Translated by M. B. Ramos. (New York: Seabury Press).

Giroux, H. (1981) Hegemony, resistance, and the paradox of educational reform, in *Curriculum and Instruction*. (Berkeley: McCutchan) 400-430.

Griffin, D.R. (1988). *Spirituality and society: Postmodern visions*. (Albany: State University of New York Press).

Habermas, J. (1971). *Knowledge and human interests*. (Boston: Beacon Press).

Hirsch, E.D., Jr. (1987). *Cultural literacy: What every American needs to know*. (Boston: Houghton Mifflin).

Hunter, M. (1982). *Mastery teaching*. (El Segundo, CA: TIP Publications).

Kung, H. (1988). *Theology for the third millennium: An ecumenical view*. (New York: Doubleday).

Lasch, C. (1984). *The minimal self: Psychic survival in troubled times*. (New York: W.W. Norton and Company).

MacDonald, J.B. (1988). Curriculum, consciousness, and social change, in *Contemporary Curriculum Discourses*, edited by William F. Pinar. (Scottsdale, AZ: Gorsuch, Scarsbrick) 163-171.

Moran, G. (1981). *Interplay: A Theory of religion and education*. (Minneapolis: Winston Press).

Percy, W. (1971). *Love in the ruins*. (New York: Farrar, Straux, and Giroux).

Phenix, P. (1976). Transcendence and the curriculum, in *Curriculum Theorizing*. (Berkeley: McCutchan) 323-340.

Pinar, W. F. (Ed.) (1988). *Contemporary curriculum discourses*. (Scottsdale, AZ: Gorsuch, Scarsbrick).

Ruether, R.R. (1983). *To change the world: Christology and culturalism criticism*. (New York: Crossroads).

Schubert, W.H. (1986). *Curriculum: Perspective, paradigm, and possibility*. (New York: Macmillan).

Smith, D.B. (1988). Experimental eidetics as a way of entering curriculum language from the ground up, in *Contemporary Curriculum Discourses*, edited by William F. Pinar. (Scottsdale, AZ: Gorsuch, Scarsbrick) 422-435.

Sweeney, M. (1987). *Walker Percy and the postmodern world*. (Chicago: Loyola University Press).

Taylor, M.C. (1984). *Erring: A post-modern a/theology*. (Chicago: University of Chicago Press).

Tyler, R. (1949). *Basic principles of curriculum and instruction*. (Chicago: University of Chicago Press).

Wexler, P. (1988). Body and soul: Sources of social change and strategies of education, in *Contemporary Curriculum Discourses*, edited by William F. Pinar. (Scottsdale, AZ: Gorsuch, Scarsbrick) 219.

CHAPTER NINETEEN

Of Seagulls and Glass Roses

Teachers' Relationships with Literary Texts as Transformational Space

Dennis J. Sumara
1993

Whatever may be the individual contents which come into the world through a work of art, there will always be something which is never given in the world and which only a work of art provides: It enables us to transcend that which we are otherwise so inextricably entangled in—our own lives in the midst of the real world.

Wolfgang Iser, *The Act of Reading* [1]

The myth of poetics deals with "why there is being rather than nothing," at the awe, wonder, and anxiety of this puzzle.

James MacDonald [2]

THE RELATIONALITY OF CLASSROOM SPACE

One of the most profound experiences I had as a student in public school took place in my grade ten math class. I was not overly fond of math and it was with some trepidation that I arrived on that first day of classes to a new teacher, Mr. Shields. As he entered the classroom I was surprised, for he did not look like most of my other male teachers. Instead of a suit he wore blue jeans and a loose knit sweater and sported a rather long, scruffy beard. But what I remember most was that on that first day of math class, Mr. Shields did not pass out textbooks, distribute a course outline, teach a math lesson, go over behavioral expectations, assign a seating plan or any of the expected things. Instead, he pulled from his back pocket a well-worn copy of a book entitled *Jonathan Livingston Seagull*,[3] which he told us was a very special book for him—a book he would like to share with us. And so, on that first day of math class we listened as Mr. Shields read the first few chapters of a novel.

I don't remember much about the story, except that the main character was a seagull named Jonathon Livingston who unlike other seagulls preferred to soar like an eagle rather than stay close to land. Most of the other details are lost to me now; however, what I do remember is the way I *felt* as Mr. Shields read the book, which he continued to do for the first fifteen minutes of math class each day until it was finished. As I heard about Jonathon Livingston, the ambitious, outcast seagull, I was learning about Mr. Shields; about what was important to him, the way that he saw life. And during that reading I came to understand that maybe I would be able to do some math after all; maybe there was something meaningful to be learned here. The oral reading of the novel provided a special space in which we could live in an experience together, an experience where there were no expectations, no threats, no grades, no recriminations, no judgements. That experience was profound for me, for it served to mediate my relationship with Mr. Shields and eventually my attitude and relation to the subject at hand. I did very well in math that year.

From this example we can see that like everything in the world, the classroom is relational. Understood in this way, the classroom cannot merely be seen as a place where subject matter is "mastered," where curriculum is "covered," or where learning is "tested." The classroom becomes a myriad of ever-evolving relationships: between teacher and students, students and each other, teacher and texts, students and texts. Moreover, these relationships overlap and intertwine; we are indeed entangled in them, and in no way can discern their beginnings or endings. As Merleau-Ponty reminds us, "we are ourselves this network of relationships."[4] Once we understand this, it becomes clear that the texts that are used in schools are not merely things that are transposed onto already existing relationships. Because they are inextricable from life itself, these texts influence, affect, and change the fabric of all of the relations in the classroom. Choosing *this* book over *that* is to choose one complete fabric of relations over another, for in pulling one thread of the relational fabric we alter the whole thing.

It can be seen, then, that bringing a text into the classroom mediates all experiences in that classroom. Although I did not know it then, my years of teaching in schools—my own years of bringing texts into classrooms—have helped me to understand that bringing *Jonathon Livingston Seagull* into the math classroom was more than just the reading of a story; it was the bringing forth of an invitation to join with the teacher in an already established relation with that story. By reading this novel, he brought forward himself. It was not the "public" Self of the mathematics teacher, but rather a more personal Self that had been developed in his out-of-classroom relational experience with this novel. By bringing forward his relationship with the text, this teacher brought forward what James Macdonald has called the *mytho-poetic*;[5] an ontological understanding emerging from the transactional relationship between reader and fictional text.

It is significant that the deep pedagogical relation that many of my classmates and I developed with this teacher was within the shared experience of the *literary* text and not the *mathematics* text, for although I am sure that we did work through a mathematics text it is not one that I remember. It is the experience that we shared with the novel that I remember. This raises the question of the quality of the relations between various texts. How is the relationship with the literary text different from the expository text? And, furthermore, how do these texts work to affect the human, pedagogical relations in the classroom?

T H E   M O V E   F R O M   G I V E N   T O   P O S S I B L E   W O R L D S

Real art has the capacity to make us nervous.

Susan Sontag, *Against Interpretation*[6]

John Fowles, author of the celebrated novel *The French Lieutenant's Woman*, suggests that there is an experiential difference between reading the expository text and reading the literary text.

> Our educational systems...confuse things by failing to teach the young to distinguish between the very different experiences of reading fiction and non-fiction. Their aims are diametrically opposed in may ways: learning to dream awake, against learning to absorb hard facts; almost, to be subjective, to learn to feel, to be oneself—or to be objective, become what society expects.[7]

Susanne Langer[8] helps us to understand that the experiential difference is connected to the communicative function of nonfiction and the formulative function of fiction. She explains that the former is a type of written discourse which is meant to tell, to explain; the latter is a reconfiguration of this discourse into a form that does not *give* the experience but rather invites the reader into a *potential* experience.[9] Literary critic and reading theorist Louise Rosenblatt explains this as the difference between the *efferent* and the *aesthetic* reading; the efferent is related to the instrumentally communicative function of language; the aesthetic to the experience of being drawn into language which fulfills a formulative function.[10] Whatever word we choose to name the distinction, those of us who read fiction understand that there is a difference between reading fiction and nonfiction, and although this essay is not the place to take up John Fowles' concern about whether or not we "teach" students how to experience fiction, it does seem significant that the literary text, as a school text, as well as all of the contextual relations to which this text is inextricably connected, is often more memorable than other texts of specific content like the mathematics text. The question here becomes one of why this should be so. Why is it that the literary text was able to enhance my relations with mathematics in a way that the mathematics text could not?

Perhaps part of the answer lies in the fact that within the mathematics textbook the words and symbols are meant to correspond to specific and exact meanings. When symbols are used in this way, they are meant to be transparent—their meanings embedded in the symbol for the reader, to extract. In a sense, the "telling" text, the text which serves to communicate particular facts, excludes the reader's experience, since s/he is expected to translate these symbolic tellings and directives into the "right answer." In the mathematics textbook the world is pre-given, and readers are meant to appropriate that word. Readers are subservient to the text; it tells them what to mean. The mathematics textbook, as it exists between the teacher and the student, becomes the space within which "correctness" is established. Like many other expository texts of particular content, it leaves little space for the reader, and further more, little space for interactive interpretation between various readers. As students work through algebraic algorithms, problems of probability and geometrical gyrations, they are not meant to reflect upon these in terms of their own relation to life. Although these text oriented activities have *meaning*, they are not *meaningful* in the same way as a literary text can be.[11] The move from meaning to meaningful is the move from the communicative to the formulative, for in the latter, the reader needs to immerse herself in meaning that emerges from the bringing of her own experience to the text. Like most texts in the public school classroom, the mathematics text is preoccupied with epistemology—with questions about *knowing* rather than ontological questions about *being*. Hence, the relations readers have with texts like these are not ones which show why they *are*, they show what they *know*. They experience the tyranny of enforced subscription to a generalized set of truths, which is purported to exist within the mathematics textbook.

In his book, *The Art of the Novel*, Milan Kundera suggests that "The novel is the imaginary paradise of individuals; the territory where no one possesses the truth."[12] Similarly, Susanne Langer suggests that although the literary text is comprised of elements of the material world, it does not have a real world correspondence. It is virtual.[13] Although there are seagulls in the world that communicate with each other, they are not the same as Jonathon Livingston. As the author constructs the literary work s/he appropriates elements of the real world and converts them—with the help of literary devices, textual stylings, and imaginative repositionings—into an artistic work that invites readers to participate in an experience. In the good literary text, readers must find a place for themselves among that which has been presented by the author.

Many readers have known the difficulty of "getting into" the experience of the literary text. "Getting into" implies that the reader, as Madeleine Grumet tells us, must "pore over the text, like the priest reading the entrails, seeking signs of how to live."[14] It is this poring over, this seeking signs of how to live, that signifies the shift from epistemology to ontology, for in the search to "get in" we are searching for a "place" for our Selves. Unlike the expository text which attempts to "tell" the reader how to understand, the literary text can only "invite" the reader to engage with the characters, the setting, the situations. Unlike the relation with the expository text, then, the literary text requires that the reader participate more actively in the experience of the text. When the initial work has been done by the reader, when s/he has crossed the boundary of the "difficulty" of "getting into" the text, the reader often finds that s/he is "lost" in the mutual understanding of a world created in the transaction between reader and text.[15]

It is significant that although at times we hear that readers of expository texts have become "absorbed" by the text, we seldom hear that they have been "lost" in it. Max van Manen explains that this feeling of "lostness" is characterized by a forgetting of the material structure of the text.

> During the first so many pages, we may be quite aware of an author's style, the peculiar way a story is structured, the feel or the tonal quality of the text. But then we "get into the book," as we say. And now the words, the pages, and textual structures become immaterial. As if we are looking at a picture in a certain way, no longer seeing the paint and canvas; but seeing through the surface, as it were.[16]

Many who read novels have had this feeling of being "lost." Paradoxically, it seems that it is only in being "lost" that we can become "found" in the text, for to be "lost" does not mean to give up one's Self, but rather to reposition oneself into a "possible" world—one which emerges from the transaction between the reader's own experience and the pre-given words and structure of the literary text.[17] The literary text does not diminish the reader or "subsume" the reader into the text; rather, it allows the reader to engage in a type of personal reflection within the experience of reading the text—a way for us to come to know ourselves. It appears, then, that the way in which we come to know ourselves in the literary work is not embedded in the work, but rather emerges from our own interaction with the work. It is in this interactive process, manifested in the feeling of being lost, that the reader of the novel is sometimes able to find feelings, ideas, possible worlds that s/he did not have prior to the reading. Gadamer equates this fusing of Self and literary text to a game where the player simultaneously plays and is played by the game. Although constrained by the rules of the game, these do not determine the meaning of the game—only the playing can do that.[18] Similarly, although the literary text is constrained by a set of linguistic conventions and stylistic structures as pre-given by the author, the meaning can only be realized in the evocation of the text by the reader. In a well constructed and evocative literary text we find ourselves immersed in the midst of the "performance" that is the text (the play), and if we read well (play well), we find ourselves being immersed in (played by) the game that is formed between ourselves and the text. Becoming "lost" in the literary text, then, can be seen as "finding oneself" for the "losing" means that the text and the reader have become ontologically fused; the text and the interpreter are one.[19]

Unlike many classroom texts of specific content the literary text becomes an invitation for students to engage in the fusion of literary text and Self. The fact that we remember and value these fusions years after their occurrence signifies their power. In many ways, when we speak of these relationships we equate them to another sort of personal relationship: that which we have with close friends. How is it that our relations with some literary texts can seem as personal as relations with friends? What constitutes the closeness that a reader feels for these texts?

D E V E L O P I N G   A N D   S H A R I N G P E R S O N A L   R E L A T I O N S H I P S

The real is a closely woven fabric.
Maurice Merleau-Ponty, *Phenomenology of Perception.*[20]

The relationship that readers have with favorite novels becomes a personal one. While reading, we sometimes develop strong feelings of attachment to the characters—their situations, their desires, their lived experiences. As readers, we position ourselves as the "dark other" in the text—as shadow amid the lives of characters whom we come to know intimately.[21] In discussing her strong attachment to Michael Ondaatje's novel *The English Patient,*[22] Rebecca explained that she felt strongly drawn to, and influenced, by her reading of it; so much so, that for weeks following the reading she used the experience of the reading as a reference point for real-life experiences. Over time, the initial feelings of attachment and attraction to the book became inextricable from her reflections on her own life. Because she felt profoundly affected by these feelings she felt compelled to revisit them by rereading the novel. Margaret Hunsberger suggests that rereading becomes a way to deepen an already established relation with a text.

> The essence of re-reading appears to be found in interaction and sharing. The reader interacts with the text and through it with the author in the pursuit of further questions and answers and of a familiar and secure world in which to dwell.[23]

Rereading seems to lead to a greater sense of intimacy between reader and text. As Rebecca reread *The English Patient* her involvement with the characters and their situations became exponentially stronger, for the rereading was not merely a revisiting of a text, but a revisiting of a text with which she was already relationally bound. Just as friends often become closer and more intimate, over time the personal relationship with the literary text often deepens with rereading. As these relationships develop further the reader begins to feel somewhat attached to not only the literary text, but to the relationship with it.

This feeling of attachment with some literary texts makes the personal relationship with it akin to personal relations that we have with some of our friends. Oftentimes we will meet strangers with whom we develop beginning friendships. Because we share something in common or feel in some way attracted to them, we want to deepen our relationship. Although it is not the same as "rereading" a work of literature, in that the "text" of a person is never static like that of the printed literary text, the deepening of the relationship does require a deliberate planning of events in which the two friends meet to engage in common activities. Through these events the feeling of comfort among two persons increases, at times becoming transformed into relations that are more personal and intimate than usual. When this begins to happen, we generally work harder to develop this relationship. We intensify our communicative encounters by telephoning each other more frequently, meeting for lunch, and going out together for the evening. Through these socially mediated circumstances our fondness and familiarity with our friend grows. The friend becomes an important part of our lives. If the relationship becomes strong enough, we find concrete ways in which to take care of it. We remember birthdays and anniversaries, buy gifts for the friend, go out of our way to "be there" for them. This caring is not merely an attentiveness to the friend, it is a maintenance of that which exists *between* friends: *the relationship*. It is not surprising that we find that when people talk about their friendship with another they speak not of the friend, but of the relationship, the *third thing*. "I really value our friendship, it means so much to me; I am deeply committed to our relationship, and wouldn't do anything to hurt it."

The relationship with a close friend, then, is something that we want to be committed to and responsible for. We want to *care* for it, to ensure that it survives and thrives. We are protective of it, and do not want others to infringe upon it, damage it, destroy it. Like other things that are important to us, we want the committed relations that we have with others to be validated by our friends, our peers. Part of the process of caring for the relationship, then, seems to be a deliberate effort to forge connections between various relationships that we have. Our responsibility shifts from the maintenance of the personal relation with the friend to a desire to make connections between these various friends.

One way of making these connections between important, but disparate friendship relations, is to arrange events in which our friends meet. In these situations the person who has choreographed this event becomes the most vulnerable if things do not go as planned. This was the case with Ruth, who several years after having moved to a new city, organized an evening dinner party that would serve as a gathering place for her new friends. As the evening progressed, however, Ruth found herself feeling uncomfortable because it seemed that not all of her friends were getting along or liking one another. At one point in the evening David told her that he found Leslie overly aggressive and opinionated. Although Ruth tried to ignore this comment, knowing that she could not be responsible for the relations others would form, she felt angry and hurt; angry because she felt that David was not trying hard enough to get to know Leslie; hurt because in judging Leslie, David was really judging her taste in friends.

It is not surprising that we are told that we are judged by the company we keep for it is understood that there is a collective consciousness, a way of "being" with friends, which is more than the sum of the parts: the friendship itself carries life. The desire for friends to merge their relationships, then, is the desire to enrich one's own being, one's own existence, and furthermore to enrich those of our friends. So it is that we weave and re-weave the complex relations that bind us to one another, and in the midst of this action find ourselves immersed in emotion. The emotional commitment that we feel toward others in our private, personal relations with them cannot help but become infused with our more public, communal relations.

Is this, then, what it is like to have, be committed to, and care for a personal relationship with a favorite literary work? As Rebecca reread *The English Patient*, she began to feel closer and more committed to not only the characters and the situation, but to the way in which this novel helped her to understand her real life. For although the novel had immersed her in a virtual world, her experience of that world was not virtual. Like all experiences it was real. In a sense, one might say that Rebecca's relationship with *The English Patient* represented a new way of seeing herself and her world. It is not surprising then, that Rebecca should want to be committed to that relationship, to take care of it, and, because she feels it is good, to share it with her friends. Just as we sometimes talk about our private "real lives" with some of our close friends, we sometimes talk about the relationship we have with literary texts with our close friends. In fact, we often speak of them as if they are our close friends. This is significant, for if we believe the adage *we are our own best friend*, the literary text might be even closer to us than we think.

As with our relationships with friends, the relationships we establish with literary texts can be ones which we cherish, of which we speak with fondness. As such, we sometimes want our friends to come to know and love books with which we have established relationships. This becomes most evident when we strongly recommend them to our friends: "You *must* read this book! I won't tell you any more about it until you have read it! I'm anxious to hear what you think about this book!" The desire for our friends to read books we love is fueled by our human desire to make connections in our life, to become intertextual. Additionally, the common reading of a loved book allows the relations with the book to mediate the relations among friends and acquaintances. Most significant, however, is that the offering of the literary text becomes an invitation to our friends into an experience they may not ordinarily have. Because we care for our friends and we care for our relations with books, we want our friends to take the invitation seriously. We want them to become committed and earnest about entering into those relations we have brought forth. More than this, we want them to enjoy the experience, to form their own personal relationship with the book that facilitates conversations about the experience of reading it. It is from this desire for the experience to be good and the relationship to be strong and positive that we sometimes feel hesitant or reluctant to offer the invitation to our friends. Hence, comments like "It takes a while to get into the book, but be patient, once you do, you'll love it!" or "I like this book because it's Science Fiction; anyone who likes science fiction will enjoy reading it!" Our qualifying comments become the way to tell our friends that we want them to make the commitment to giving the relationship an honest effort. After all, we do want this to be a good experience for them.

It is significant that we expect our friends to take the reading of a favorite book seriously. For as Gadamer has already suggested to us, the engagement with the work of art, including the literary work of art, is like a game which we play and which simultaneously plays us. In order to become wrapped up in the to-and-fro motion of the play of the game as organized by the "rules" of the text, we need to take the game seriously; we need to be earnest in our endeavor to play well. It is only through playing well, and allowing themselves to be "played" by the literary text, will our friends be able to establish a meaningful relation with the literary work we have recommended. If this in fact does occur we feel satisfied that not only have we made available a new relationship for our friends, but also that we will have something else in common. Our conversations about the book are generally animated: "What did you think of it? When did you figure out what was going on?" Our discussion about the personal relations which each of us has had with the text, as it evolves publicly in our conversation about it, becomes a mediating event in which we can come to more closely know ourselves and each other. Through discussing characters and events in the book we demonstrate our own feelings, our own desires, our own limitations. Our friends do the same. Although the characters and events as written by the author are not real, are virtual, our personal experience of reading the text and entering into relationship is real, as are the conversations about those relations.

The conversations become an event where the lived experience of the reading relationship becomes fused with the face-to-face human contact we have with our friends. These are ontological conversations, for in them, we do not merely work to understand the text, but to also come to an understanding of ourselves and each other.

If our friends are not willing or able to enter into relations with the book (experience) we have offered, we become disappointed. We feel as though they have missed an opportunity which they might have enjoyed, and even more so, we feel as though we have been cheated out of the chance to share something that is important and close to us. If the friend has actually read the book, and not liked it, we want to know why, we wonder how this can be so. We feel that they have neither "played" well nor have they allowed themselves to be "played" during their time in the game of the text. Similar to the disappointment that Ruth felt toward David when he was unable to initiate a relationship with Leslie, we wonder if the friend has really tried hard enough, whether s/he has been committed enough to forming a relationship with the book. We sometimes feel personally slighted when the book we have recommended is rejected. For as we have seen, our feelings about the book are not contained only in the book, but rather in the *relationship* that we have with the book. When someone suggests that the book is not good, that it is boring or poorly written, that person is not merely commenting on the book, but also on our taste in books, on our own relationship with that book.

This type of relationship with a literary text is still somewhat different than the personal relationship with friends. One of the major differences between these relationships is illuminated by Gagamer's explication of the quality of a good literary text, suggesting that, like any work of art, it has the character of being *repeatable*.[24] In other words, the experience of the text is not limited to any immediate temporal or spatial context, but is capable of being a repeated experience by various readers in various contexts. Good works of literature endure across generations and various readers because there is, embedded within its form, the potential for meaning which transcends the particularity of context. Human relations do not have this capacity, for the human Self is continuously evolving; it is not a "set" text like the literary work, and as such the personal relations among friends, although similar to the personal relations with texts, are different. Perhaps this is why books are often thought of as "lifetime" friends, for although the structure and meaning of the relationship evolves as the years go by, there is an essence of the literary work which remains constant, predictable, comforting. Hence, persons who value their personal relations with literary works will often never part with them, and no matter how strenuous the activity of moving them from place to place, will usually ensure that their books stay close to them, physically part of their world.

Understanding how the personal relationship with some literary works is similar to, yet often even deeper than, the relations among close friends can help us to see why the sharing of these relations with others becomes an emotionally charged event. If these are the experiences of sharing these relationships with our friends, what is the experience of inviting students in classrooms to share the teacher's already established relationship with favorite literary texts?

THE LITERARY TEXT AS SCHOOL TEXT

We teachers hide the work we care about in classrooms just as artists stack it in their attics.

Madeleine Grumet, *Bitter Milk* [25]

Each year, Marie brings her favorite short story, Alden Nowlen's "The Glass Roses,"[26] into her high school English classroom. She usually begins the class by telling the students that it is one of her favorite stories, and that she would like to spend the period reading it to them. She then sits on the side counter of the room facing the class and proceeds to read aloud the entire story. Because it is a story that she loves and knows very well, Marie reads with great animation, demonstrating for her students, by the way she reads, how much she cares about the story. While she is reading she looks up periodically and scans the class; she knows they are listening, she can tell by the intensity of the look, the way in which movement has all but ceased, the way energy has been focused toward the story. No one is looking around the room, noone is shifting around in her or his seat. Marie finds this deeply satisfying. She senses that the students are with her when she finishes reading, she closes her book and waits. She does not ask questions, put an assignment on the board, assign a response journal entry, or arrange students into discussion groups. She waits. The silence lasts for a minute or two. As students reemerge from the experience of the story, there is some movement, some stretching, some large breaths. Finally one of the students says "Wow, that was incredible!" and this starts a conversation about the personal experiences that students had with this story as Marie read it to them. During the conversation students talk about connections it has made in their real lives, abut how they felt as the story evolved, and in turn, respond to others' and Marie's own personal responses. As the class comes to an end it is clear to everyone, especially Marie, that this has been a class where incredible interpersonal, intertextual connections have been made. This was a class in which all of them had touched each other.

Although there are many short stories, novels, and poems with which Marie has formed a close relationship, this is one of the few that she uses as part of the curriculum for any of her English classes. She uses this one, more than others, because it seems to be the kind of story which facilitates the quality of shared experience which was just described. Marie, however, alters her usual approach when using this story. When the favorite story is brought into the classroom it is treated differently from others. It is typically not used as a vehicle through which "skills" are taught, but rather is brought forth as a work that is to be "experienced" rather than analyzed. Teachers who bring forward these favorite works do so with the same intentions as those of us who invite friends to read books we love. They want their students to love the story as they do and for a strong and deep relation to be formed.

It is important to understand why Marie is reluctant to use literary works with which she has formed close relations as classroom texts. Like relationships with good friends, the relationship with the literary text becomes the third thing that is cared for by Marie. It becomes an important mediating space in which she has come to think ontologically. The personal relationship between Marie and these tests has a life inextricably connected to hers; it has become part of the continual rewriting of her own subjectivity. When Marie brings this text, and her relationship with it, into the classroom, she becomes more vulnerable than usual. She brings more of her private Self to the surface.

To choose to bring the favored literary text into the classroom, then, is to choose to bring, in a more self-conscious manner, a personal relationship into the classroom. For Marie this entails a greater risk than usual. Because the personal relationship which Marie has with the text is inextricable from the text, the move from personal reading to public reading becomes more difficult than usual. It becomes a delicate undertaking in which Marie must take care to protect her own relationship with the literary work while simultaneously attempting to mediate a potential relationship between her students and this text. It is this desire to invite the Other (students) into her own relation with the literary text that make this move pedagogical, for with it, Marie is not merely inviting students into a learning experience, she is inviting them into a living experience. It is a vivid demonstration of James Macdonald"s depiction of the importance of incorporating the human relationship with poetics into "a more satisfying interpretation of what is."[27]

THE MOVE FROM KNOWING TO BEING

Tact converts incidence into significance.
                    Max van Manen, *The Tact of Teaching*[28]

It is significant that many teachers who bring favorite literary texts into the classroom choose to read them orally. Aside from the fact that the oral reading of the text by the teacher excludes the possibility for misreadings, ineffective readings, or nonreadings, it is important to understand that in choosing to "perform" a reading of the text, these teachers choose to come between their students, the author, and the text. Margaret Hunsberger reminds us that the oral reading becomes a "bonding together of reader and text so that they in combination can interact with the audience."[29] By performing an oral reading of the text, teachers choose to show more deliberately their relational connections to the text in this deliberate act of interpretation. For in reading orally, these teachers perform a first-order act of interpretation for the audience of students. The oral reading, then, transforms the engagement with text from a *private* one which students might have, to a *public* one.

In an important way this act of mediation—of interpretation—demonstrates the teachers' desire to protect their relationships with texts, while simultaneously attempting to "lead" students into the "game" of the text. By becoming one of the "players" in the performance of the text-game, the teacher helps to establish the tone of the "playing field," encouraging students to join with her in the to-and-fro action of the playing within the play of the performance (the "play"). It is within this curricular engagement that the pedagogical relation between teacher and students becomes strengthened, for it is during events such as these that concerns of learning content become inextricable from concerns about who the participants *are*.

Teachers who strive to achieve this sort of pedagogical relationship with students are exhibiting what Max van Manen has called *tactfulness* in teaching. In the forming of the pedagogical relation the tactful teacher learns to overcome the modern tendency to self-centered subjectivism and turns her energy instead to the Other, the students in her care. As a "mindful orientation in our being and acting with children,"[30] pedagogical tact requires that the teacher become open to the students' experiences—to bring those into the fold of the curriculum as planed. It might seem that the bringing in of the literary text in which the teacher is already relationally bound is a selfish act, but if one considers the risk that the teacher is taking in bringing forth her own vulnerability, it can be seen that it is not selfish, not thoughtless, but rather tactful and thoughtful. For in the bringing forward of the *third thing*—the relation between literary work and Self— the teacher issues forth an invitation for the students to join with her in an embodied experience of life. As situated within the event we call curriculum, this invitation places the teacher at greatest risk, for it is not merely the literary text which is held up for scrutiny, it is the relationship which she has with the text. Because Marie is a tactful, thoughtful teacher attuned to her students, she wishes to bring them into her experience, her relation with this text. She wishes to share with them something she feels is meaningful. She wishes to touch them. The literary text, and the relationship she has with it, becomes the mediating space in which these transformations occur.

This is not an ordinary event in the classroom, though. It is special, and as such needs to be approached in a special manner. Knowing this, we can understand why Marie avoids "schooling" the experience. She does not treat the story "The Glass Roses" as she might other stories that she teaches with which she does not have the same kind of relationship. These other stories are ones that are often used to teach skills; they are analyzed, picked apart, critiqued, discussed in terms of style, conventions, form, and content. When the teacher does not have a personal relationship with the literary text it lends itself more readily to these activities. The favorite text, however, must not be subject to this sort of abuse, for that might threaten the potential relationship that students might have within the reading experience of this text.

When Marie brings forward her own relationship with the text the moment becomes anxious and unpredictable. This is largely so because Marie wishes the students to become committed to establishing a relationship with the text she has brought forward. She desires this not only because she wants their experience to be positive and worthwhile, but also because she wants her own relationship with the text to be valued by the students. It is at this moment that the emotional and intellectual become embodied in the experience of sharing the literary text, for it is at this curricular intersection that deeper and more profound pedagogical relations have the potential to be formed. Because Marie simultaneously cares about the literary text, her own relationship with it, and for her own students, she deliberately plans ways to make the experience meaningful. Madeleine Grumet helps us to understand why Marie would choose the literary text for these purposes.

> Because art forms express knowledge about feeling, they provide a bridge between public and private readings. Because aesthetic activity requires the making of things, comprehension is made palpable and accessible to the perception and response of other readers. Every time a text is drawn into performance, it is the reading of the text and never the text itself that is performed.[31]

It is not surprising, then, that Marie should choose to read "The Glass Roses" aloud to her students. By reading aloud Marie can ensure that every word, every image of the text is lifted from the page. There is seldom much said before the reading other than the fact that it is a "favored text" and other prefatory comments that indicate to the students that they are being invited into a special relationship. Once the text is read there is a moment of anxiety on Marie's part: "Did they like it? Did they understand it? What are they thinking about?" By waiting for a response from the students, and focusing on the meaning-making that occurred for the students as they formed their personal relationship with the text, Marie brings forth the ontological. Each personal experience with the text is mediated, not by assignments that ask students to critically analyze the text, but rather with class conversation in which the personal relationship is made public. During the course of this conversation, Marie is able to share with students how she felt while reading certain sections and how these have affected her life. She is able to bring forward, in the event of curriculum, a personal relationship that she had previously formed with the text. In so doing, she invites her students to do the same, and further, to engage with her in the fusing of these personal relationships into the publicly constituted one of the English classroom. It is indeed a thoughtful, tactful act.

READING RELATIONSHIPS AS TRANSFORMATIONAL SPACE

> What a dangerous activity reading is; teaching is.
> Sylvia Ashton-Warner, *Teacher* [32]

We have already seen that the literary text is unlike other texts. Because of the potential that it holds for relationship with readers through which ontological questions can be asked, it moves from concerns about "Knowing" to concerns about "Being." When teachers bring their personal relations with favorite texts into the classroom three is an implicit invitation for students to move beyond the literary text, beyond themselves, beyond the desire of the teacher, into a relationship space where questions of Being can be pondered. In discussing their relation to "The Glass Roses" Marie's students enter into conversation which is attentive to the Other—to other students, to Marie, to others outside the classroom. In turn, by sharing her relationship with this story with her students Marie brings her whole Self forward; she is no longer just the teacher who *knows*, she is the teacher who *is*. In the move from the personal to the public Marie and her students learn about themselves and each other, a learning which is risky, fraught with ambiguity, but deeply satisfying.

Canadian author Margaret Atwood suggests that "Good writing takes place at intersections, at what you might call knots."[33] It seems that the kind of reading from which deep relationships between readers and texts emerge also occurs at knots, at places in one's life where new understanding is required. The bringing forth of these relations in the space that we call curriculum becomes productive, for as Madeleine Grumet tells us, "Knowledge evolves in human relationships."[34] If we consider this in light of Heidegger's belief that "ontology is only possible as phenomenology,"[35] we can come to a deeper understanding of the incredible importance of the way in which teaching can become Being in the classroom, where relationships with literature become the "knots" through which the pedagogical text is written and read. When Being is allowed to pervade the curricular space of the classroom through the relationship with the literary text it is hard to imagine that something is being "taught." For it is during the moments when the experience with a virtual text become transformed into shared relations with that text that the artificially imposed boundaries between the Self and the Other in the classroom disappear. Within these moments literature is not taught, literature does not teach about life, literature is not a vicarious experience; instead, literature becomes inextricable from the immediacy of life itself.

Furthermore, it is during these moments—these emotionally charged moments—that the teacher, as she brings forward the relation that she has with the text, engages in a kind of ontological pointing where questions of how she is in the world supercede questions of what the text is about. In so doing, the teacher creates an event of curriculum in which she is invested more deeplu than usual. The fact that students often react to these events with more than usual attention goes beyond the careful orchestration of the event by the teacher. It goes beyond the fact that students are "set up" to more fully appreciate the importance of this curricular moment. For although caring and commitment to the relations to this text have been shown to be vital in the preservation of it when it is brought to light publicly, these alone cannot account for the power of its effect in the daily curriculum of public schooling. Rather, the power emerges from the fact that when teachers bring forward a personal reading relationship for public scrutiny in the classroom they bring forth a more vulnerable Self. And when they do so, students notice the difference. It is during moments of noticing the difference that all of the relations in the classroom change; moments that are infused with a heightened awareness of what it is like to be human. But most of all, it becomes a moment of ontological pointing where all the participants of this public experience become aware of themselves in relation to each other and their world.

Finally, it is important for us to understand that overall significance of this point of relational connection, for as James Macdonald reminded us over 20 years ago:

> It is clear to me now that when we speak of education we speak in the context
> of a microscopic paradigm of a macroscopic human condition, a paradigm that
> holds all of the complexities in microcosm of the larger condition.[36]

Here Macdonald is pointing to the fractal nature of any relationship, which, as part of a complex fabric of interconnections, contains within it all aspects of the whole. To understand curriculum, then, is not to attempt to grasp "everything" in an attempt to predict and control what might be, but rather to become mindful of the easily missed details, for it is through this hermeneutic mindfulness that we will finally understand that like all life, curriculum begins and ends with an attentiveness to the truth of the particular. By focusing on the teacher's evolving relationship with the literary text, as these become transformational points in the school curriculum, we gain a greater understanding of, and appreciation for, the relational complexity of life itself.

> The text is material, it has texture, it is woven; we pull and tug at it, it winds around us, we are tangled up in it.
>
> Madeleine Grumet, *Bitter Milk*[37]

N O T E S

1. Wolfgang Iser, *The Act of Reading*, (Baltimore: John S. Hopkins University Press, 1978), p. 230.

2. James Macdonald, "Theory-Practice and the Hermeneutic Circle," in William Pinar's (Ed.) *Contemporary Curriculum Discourses*, (Scottsdale, AZ: Gorsuch Scarisbrick, 1988), pp. 101-113.

3. Robert Bach, *Jonathon Livingston Seagull*, (New York: The Macmillan Co., 1970). In the midst of writing this paper I found this book in the library and 20 years after my first encounter with it, reread it. Although this rereading was clearly a very different experience than the first one, I was amazed and delighted how close the rereading brought me to my experiences in Mr. Shield's math class. It demonstrated to me that the acts of reading and writing have no discernable beginning and end points in our lives; they become inextricably woven into the textuality that comprises the ever-evolving Self.

4. In the preface to his seminal work, *The Phenomenology of Perception* (London: Routledge and Kegan Paul, 1962), Maurice Merleau-Ponty explains that it is precisely because everything in the word, including ourselves, is relational that we must attend closely to the way in which the lived experience of this relationality becomes expressed in day-to-day phenomena.

5. In his essay "Theory-Practice and the Hermeneutic Circle," Macdonald describes the mytho-poetic as a third methodology situated between science and critical theory, which is "particularly related to the use of insight, visualization, and imagination" (p. 108). Macdonald was one of the first curriculum theorists to link notions of ambiguity, serendipity, intuition, and imagination with the so-called empirical sciences and critical social sciences. Recently, we have seen this idea coming to the forefront in areas such as cognitive theory (see Varela, Thompson, and Rosch, *The Embodied Mind*, [Cambridge, MA: MIT Press, 199]); in the recent philosophy of Richard Taylor (see *Sources of the Self* [Cambridge, MA: Harvard University Press, 1989]) and Anthony Kerry (see *Narrative and the Self*, [Bloomington, IN: Indiana University Press, 1991]); in cultural anthropology (see *Writing Culture: The Poetics and Politics of Ethnography*, James Clifford and George Marcus, Editors, (Los Angeles, CA: University of California Press, 1986]) to name a few.

6. Susan Sontag, *Against Interpretation*, (New York: Anchor Books, 1990), p. 8. With this phrase Sontag points to the way in which the artwork can speak ontologically. I use it here to signify the inherent ontological value that many of us who read and teach literature see in the literary work of art and its potential to cause us to see ourselves differently (perhaps nervously).

7. Cited in Antonia Fraser's (Ed.) *The Pleasure of Reading*, (New York: Alfred Knopf, 1992), p. 74.

8. Susanne Langer, *Problems of Art*, (New York: Charles Scribner's Sons, 1957).

9. Langer makes this distinction by suggesting that "It is the communicative office of language that makes the actual world's appearance public, and reasonably fixed. The formulative power of words is the source and support of our imagination; before there can be more than animal communication, there has to be envisagement, and a means of developing perception in keeping with conception" (*Problems of Art*, 1957, P. 149). She further suggests that this formulative (poetic) function of words is marginalized in schools where discourse is generally communicatively instrumental. Although "poetics" is derived from the same material as discursive speech, what is created is not actual discourse, but rather "a composed and shaped apparition of a new human experience" (p. 148).

10. Louise Rosenblatt, *Literature As Exploration*, (New York: Appleton-Century, 1938) and *The Reader, The Text, The Poem*, (Carbondale, IL: Southern Illinois University Press, 1978). Rosenblatt was the first literary critic and reading theorist to acknowledge the importance of the relationship which is developed between reader and literary text. Implicit within her theory is the importance of resymbolization on a variety of different levels. As the reader interacts with the literary text s/he goes through a transactive process of reresymbolizing his or her own thoughts with those presented in the text. In this sense, reading, for Rosenblatt, is a form of cultural rewriting, a purposeful construction and reconstruction of thoughts and ideas which emerge from the transaction between reader and text. Although she does not explicitly align herself with the hermeneutic phenomenology of Heidegger or Gadamer, it is clear that her theory of "coming to understanding" is compatible with Heidegger's *Dasein* and Gadamer's insistence that coming to an understanding of this being can only occur through a dialectical hermeneutic where understanding of Self and Other occurs through questions that present themselves in conversation, for it was through Rosenblatt that the "conversation" between text and reader gained priority and prominence.

11. This orientation to the learning of mathematics is, of course, not accidental. In his book *A Reading of Truth and Method* (New Haven and London: Yale University Press, 1985) Joel Weinsheimer maps out the terrain of modern mathematics, suggesting that "the reason for the invention of mathematical symbol-languages and their perfection in the last hundred years was that conventional language entangles us in pseudo-problems, ergo logic's claim to have rid us of this kind of error by perfecting an artificial system of signs (p. 42). He goes on to explain that for some mathematicians who were attempting to enact the Cartesian project, "the crucial problem of mathematics...was to demonstrate the internal consistency of nonreferential axiomatic systems, miniature languages that are both complete and unambiguous, because they refer to nothing but themselves" (p. 44). He further reminds us that modern calculus is founded upon a procedure called "axiomatization," which "involves emptying the primitive terms of all meaning and specifying how they may be combined" (p. 45) so that everything seems perfectly ordered, explained, and predictable. From this it is easy to understand how some forms of modern mathematics moved from a *meaningful* activity (i.e., one which is pregnant with possible meaning) to one which represented a correspondence theory of truth. Because these sorts of mathematical systems guarantee this particular brand of truth-telling they have become popular within public school mathematics curricula where the ranking and sorting of students is founded upon forms of accountability that are explicitly measurable across various contexts.

12. Milan Kundera, *The Art of the Novel*, (New York: Harper and Row, 1988), p. 159.

13. Susanne Langer equates the *virtual* in creative objects as a space created by the artist (or in this case the author) which "is new in the sense that it never existed before" (1957, p. 29). Wolfgang Iser, in his phenomenological account of reading (*The Act of Reading*, Baltimore: Johns Hopkins University Press, 1978), implies this use of virtuality within the fictional text itself when he says that "the meaning of a literary text is not a definable entity, but, if anything, a dynamic happening" (p. 22), and when he explains that "literary texts initiate 'performance of meaning' rather than actually formulating meaning themselves" (p. 22).

14. Madeleine Grumet, *Bitter Milk: Women and Teaching* (Amherst, MA: University of Massachusetts Press, 1988), p. 135.

15. There have been a number of books written which address the phenomenon of becoming "lost" in the literary text. Most notable are Wolfgang Iser's *The Act of Reading*, (Baltimore: Johns Hopkins University Press, 1978), Louise Rosenblatt's *The Reader, The Text, The Poem*, (Carbondale, IL: Southern Illinois University Press, 1978), Victor Nell's *Lost In A Book: The Psychology*

of Reading For Pleasure, (New Haven and London: Yale University Press, 1990), Norman Holland's *The Dynamics of Literary Response*, (New York: Columbia University Press, 1968), Peter Rabinowitz's *Before Reading: Narrative Conventions and the Politics of Interpretation*, (Ithaca and London: Cornell University Press, 1987), and J.A. Appleyard's *Becoming A Reader: The Experience of Fiction From Childhood To Adulthood*, (New York: Cambridge University Press, 1990).

16. Max van Manen, "Phenomenology of the Novel, or How do Novels Teach?" *Phenomenology + Pedagogy* 3, No. 3, (University of Alberta, 1958), p. 181.

17. The notion of "transaction" as popularized by literary theorists Louise Rosenblatt (1978, *The Reader, The Text, The Poem*) and Wolfgang Iser (1978, *The Act of Reading*) suggests that meaning does not reside within the text or the reader, but rather in the interactive work which takes place as the reader works through the structure of the pregiven literary text. Although guided by the text as given, the actual experiencing of the text by the reader becomes the site from which literary meaning is formulated. Neither of these theorists suggests that "any interpretation" of the literary work (any meaning) is possible, for the interpretation, although generated from the reading experience, depends on the structure of the pregiven text as a focal point.

18. Hans Georg Gadamer, *Truth and Method* (2nd Rev. Ed., J. Weinsheimer and D.G. Marshall, Translators, New York: Crossroad, 1990) pp. 106-107. Gadamer further explains that in order to play and become played by the text, the player (reader in the case of playing in the literary work) must take the "game" seriously, must enter with earnest intentions.

19. My use of the phrase "ontologically fused" is largely derived from Gadamer's notion of the *fusion of horizons* as the process of coming to understanding whereby the present moment is understood as post "horizons" or understanding become integral in the construction of the present (*Truth and Method*, 1989, p. 396). In texts this fusion of horizons becomes related to the questioning, for as Gadamer tells us, "we understand only when we understand the question to which something is the answer, but the intention of what is understood in this way does not remain foregrounded against our own intention. Rather, reconstructing the question to which the meaning of a text is understood as an answer merges with our own questioning. For the text must be understood as an answer to a real question" (ibid, p. 374). Literary and reading reception theorist Wolfgang Iser applies this notion to reading literary texts when he explains that "every moment of reading is a dialectic of protension and retention, conveying a future horizon yet to be occupied, along with a past (and continually fading) horizon already filled" (*The Act of Reading*, 1978, p. 112).

20. Maurice Merleau-Ponty, *The Phenomenology of Perception* (London: Routledge and Kegan Paul, 1962), p. x.

21. Geoff Fox, "Dark Watchers: Young Readers and their Fiction," *English In Education*, 13, No. 1 (1979). The concept of the "dark other" that Geoff Fox suggests emerged from interviews with one reader who in discussing her interaction with a novel, positioned herself as "stand[ing] apart, watching from the shadows" (p. 32). In his analysis of this, Fox theorizes that she is not merely incidental to the story, but rather "is the power, not the text: her sensitivities are playing upon the novel and without her the story could not develop" (p. 32). In my own discussions with adult readers, I have found that they frequently talk about "being in" the text, amid the circumstances of the characters as a "watcher" who "feels" what the characters are feeling at that moment.

22. Michael Ondaatje, *The English Patient*, (Toronto: McLelland and Stewart, 1992).

23. Margaret Hunsberger, "The Experience of Re-Reading," *Phenomenology + Pedagogy*, 3, No. 2, (University of Arizona, 1985), p. 166.

24. Gadamer names this quality **Gebilde** (*Truth and Method*, 1989, p. 110). In his book *A Reading of "Truth and Method"* (New Haven and London: Yale University Press, 1985), Joel Weinsheimer helps us to understand that **Gebilde** signifies the detachability of the meaning of a "game" (which Gadamer uses to help us to understand what it is like to participate aesthetically in a work of art) from any subject. This detachability becomes the metamorphosis into **Gebilde**—that is, structure, form (pp. 111-112).

25. Madeleine Grumet, *Bitter Milk*, p. 91.

26. Alden Nowlen, "The Glass Roses" in Laurence Perrien, Ed., *Story and Structure*, (Toronto: Harcourt, Brace, Javonovich, 1987).

27. "Theory-Practice and the Hermeneutic Circle", p. 109.

28. Max van Manen, *The Tact of Teaching*, (London, Ont.: The Althouse Press, 1991), p. 187.

29. Margaret Hunsberger, "The Experience of Re-Reading," 1985, p. 165.

30. Max van Manen, *The Tact of Teaching*, p. 149.

31. Madeleine Grumet, "Lost Places, Potential Spaces and Possible Worlds: Why We Read Books With Other People," *Margins* 1 (1991): 48.

32. Sylvia Aston-Warner, *Teacher*, (New York: Simon and Schuster, 1963), p. 14.

33. Cited in Donald Murray, *Shoptalk*, (Portsmouth, NH: Heinemann, 1990), p. 80.

34. *Bitter Milk*, p. xix.

35. Martin Heidegger, *Basic Writings*, (New York: Harper and Row, 1977), p. 84.

36. James Macdonald, Introduction to "Curriculum Theory," in William Pinar's (Ed.) *Curriculum Theorizing: The Reconceptualists*, (Berkeley, CA, 1975), p. 4.

37. *Bitter Milk*, p. 144.

CHAPTER TWENTY

Remembering Capital

On the Connections Between French Fries and Education

Michael W. Apple
1995

INTRODUCTION

Everyone stared at the department chair in amazement. Jaws simply dropped. Soon the room was filled with a nearly chaotic mixture of sounds of anger and disbelief. It wasn't the first time she had informed us about what was "coming down from on high." Similar things had occurred before. After all, this was just another brick that was being removed. Yet, to each and every one of us in that room it was clear from that moment on that for all of our struggles to protect education from being totally integrated into the rightist project of economic competitiveness and rationalization, we were losing.

It was hard to bring order to the meeting. But, slowly, we got our emotions under control long enough to hear what the State Department of Public Instruction and the Legislature had determined was best for all of the students in Wisconsin—from kindergarten to the university. Starting the next year, all undergraduate students who wished to become teachers would have to take a course on Education for Employment, in essence a course on the "benefits of the free enterprise system." At the same time, all school curricula at the elementary and secondary levels—from five year olds on up—would have to integrate within their teaching a coherent program of education for employment as well. After all, you can't start too young, can you? Education was simply the supplier of "human capital" for the private sector, after all.

I begin with this story because I think it is often better to start in our guts so to speak, to start with our experiences as teachers and students in this time of conservatism. I begin here as well because, even though the administration in Washington may attempt to rein in some of the excesses of the rightist social agenda—in largely ineffectual ways—the terms of debate and the existing economic and social conditions have been transformed remarkably in a conservative direction (Apple, 1993). We should not be romantic about what will happen at our schools and universities, especially given the fiscal crisis of the state and the acceptance of major aspects of the conservative social and economic agenda within both political parties. The story I told a moment ago can serve as a metaphor for what is happening to so much of educational life at universities and elsewhere.

Let me situate this story within the larger transformations in education and the wider society that the conservative alliance has attempted. Because of space limitations in an article of this size, my discussion here will by necessity be brief. A much more detailed analysis can be found in my newest book, *Cultural Politics and Education* (Apple, 1996).

BETWEEN NEO-CONSERVATISM AND NEO-LIBERALISM

Conservatism by its very name announces one interpretation of its agenda. It conserves. Other interpretations are possible of course. One could say, somewhat more wryly, that conservatism believes that nothing should be done for the first time (Honderich, 1990, p. 1). Yet in many ways, in the current situation, this is deceptive. For with the Right now in ascendancy in many nations, we are witnessing a much more activist project. Conservative politics now are very much the politics of alteration—not always, but clearly the idea of "Do nothing for the first time" is not a sufficient explanation of what is going on either in education or elsewhere (Honderich, 1990, p. 4). Conservatism has, in fact, meant different things at different times and places. At times, it will involve defensive actions; at other times, it will involve taking initiative against the status quo (Honderich, 1990, p. 15). Today, we are witnessing both.

Because of this, it is important that I set out the larger social context in which the current politics of official knowledge operates. There has been a breakdown in the accord that guided a good deal of educational policy since World War II. Powerful groups within government and the economy, and within "authoritarian populist" social movements, have been able to redefine—often in very retrogressive ways—the terms of debate in education, social welfare, and other areas of the common good. What education is for is being transformed (Apple, 1993). No longer is education seen as part of a social alliance, which combined many "minority" groups, women, teachers, community activists, progressive legislators and government officials, and others who acted together to propose (limited) social democratic policies for schools (e.g., expanding educational opportunities, limited attempts at equalizing outcomes, developing special programs in bilingual and multicultural education, and so on). A new alliance has been formed, one that has increasing power in educational and social policy. This power bloc combines business with the New Right and with neo-conservative intellectuals. Its interests are less in increasing the life chances of women, people of color, or labor. (These groups are obviously not mutually exclusive.) Rather it aims at providing the educational conditions believed necessary both for increasing international competitiveness, profit, and discipline and for returning us to a romanticized past of the "ideal" home, family, and school (Apple, 1993). There is no need to control the White House for this agenda to continue to have a major effect.

The power of this alliance can be seen in a number of educational policies and proposals. These include 1) programs for "choice," such as voucher plans and tax credits to make schools like the thoroughly idealized free-market economy; 2) the movement at national and state levels throughout the country to "raise standards" and mandate both teacher and student "competencies" and basic curricular goals and knowledge increasingly now through the implementation of statewide and national testing; 3) the increasingly effective attacks on the school curriculum for its anti-family and anti-free enterprise "bias," its secular humanism, its lack of patriotism, and its supposed neglect of the knowledge and values of the "western tradition" and of "real knowledge"; and 4) the growing pressure to make the perceived needs of business and industry into the primary goals of education at all levels (Apple, 1988; Apple, 1993; Apple, 1996). The effects of all this—the culture wars, the immensity of the fiscal crisis in education, the attacks on "political correctness," and so on— are being painfully felt in the university as well.

In essence, the new alliance in favor of the conservative restoration has integrated education into a wider set of ideological commitments. The objectives in education are the same as those which serve as a guide to its economic and social welfare goals. These include the expansion of the "free market," the drastic reduction of government responsibility for social needs (though the Clinton Administration will mediate this in not very extensive—and not very expensive—ways), the reinforcement of intensely competitive structures of mobility, the lowering of people's expectations for economic security, and the popularization of what is clearly a form of Social Darwinist thinking (Bastian, Fruchter, Gittell, Greer, & Haskins, 1986).

As I have argued at length elsewhere, the political right in the United States has been very successful in mobilizing support *against* the educational system and its employees, often exporting the crisis in the economy onto the schools. Thus, one of its major achievements has been to shift the blame for unemployment and underemployment, for the loss of economic competitiveness, and for the supposed breakdown of "traditional" values and standards in the family, education, and paid and unpaid workplaces *from* the economic, cultural, and social policies and effects of dominant groups *to* the school and other public agencies. "Public" now is the center of all evil; "private" is the center of all that is good (Apple, 1995).

In essence, then, four trends have characterized the conservative restoration both in the Unites States and Britain—privatization, centralization, vocational-ization, and differentiation (Green, 1991, p. 27). These are actually largely the results of differences within the most powerful wings of this tense alliance—neo-liberalism and neo-conservatism.

Neo-liberalism has a vision of the weak state. A society that lets the "invisible hand" of the free market guide *all* aspects of its forms of social interaction is seen as both efficient and democratic. On the other hand, neo-conservatism is guided by a vision of the strong state in certain areas, especially over the politics of the body and gender and race relations; over standards, values, and conduct; and over what knowledge should be passed on to future generations (Hunter, 1988).[1] While these are no more than ideal types, those two positions do not easily sit side-by-side in the conservative coalition.

Thus the rightist movement is contradictory. Is there not something paradoxical about linking all of the feelings of loss and nostalgia to the unpredictability of the market, "in replacing loss by sheer flux" (Johnson, 1991, p. 10)?

At the elementary and secondary school levels, the contradictions between neo-conservative and neo-liberal elements in the rightist coalition are "solved" through a policy of what Roger Dale has called *conservative modernization* (Dale, quoted in Edwards, Gewirtz & Whitty, in press, p. 22). Such a policy is engaged in

> simultaneously "freeing" individuals for economic purposes while controlling them for social purposes; indeed, in so far as economic "freedom" increases inequalities, it is likely to increase the need for social control. A "small, strong state" limits the range of its activities by transferring to the market, which it defends and legitimizes, as much welfare [and other activities] as possible. In education, the new reliance on competition and choice is not all pervasive; instead, "what is intended is a dual system, polarized between...market schools and minimum schools" (Dale quoted in Edwards, Gewirtz, & Whitty, in press, p. 22)

That is, there will be a relatively less regulated and increasingly privatized sector for the children of the better off. For the rest—and the economic status and racial composition in, say, our urban areas of the people who attend these minimum schools will be thoroughly predictable—the schools will be tightly controlled and policed and will continue to be underfunded and unlinked to decent paid employment.

One of the major effects of the combination of marketization and strong state is "to remove educational policies from public debate." That is, the choice is left up to individual parents and "the hidden hand of unintended consequences does the rest." In the process, the very idea of education being part of a *public* political sphere in which its means and ends are publicly debated atrophies (Education Group II, 1991, p. 268).

There are major differences between democratic attempts at enhancing people's rights over the policies and practices of schooling and the neo-liberal emphasis on marketization and privatization. The goal of the former is to *extend politics*, to "revivify democratic practice by devising ways of enhancing public discussion, debate, and negotiation." It is inherently based on a vision of democracy that sees it as an educative practice. The latter, on the other hand, seeks to *contain politics*. It wants to *reduce all politics to economics*, to an ethic of "choice" and "consumption" (Johnson, 1991, p. 68). The world, in essence, becomes a vast supermarket (Apple, 1993).

Enlarging the private sector so that buying and selling—in a word competition—is the dominant ethic of society involves a set of closely related propositions. It assumes that more individuals are motivated to work harder under these conditions. After all, we "already know" that public servants are inefficient and slothful while private enterprises are efficient and energetic. It assumes that self-interest and competitiveness are the engines of creativity. More knowledge, more experimentation, is created and used to alter what we have now. In the process, less waste is created. Supply and demand stay in a kind of equilibrium. A more efficient machine is thus created, one which minimizes administrative costs and ultimately distributes resources more widely (Honderich, 1990, p. 104).

This is, of course, not meant simply to privilege the few. However, it is the equivalent of saying that everyone has the right to climb the north face of the Eiger or scale Mount Everest without exception, providing of course that you are very good at mountain climbing and have the institutional and financial resources to do it (Honderich, 1990, pp. 99-100).

Thus, in a conservative society, access to a society's private resources (and, remember, the attempt is to make nearly *all* of society's resources private) is largely dependent on one's ability to pay. And this is dependent on one's being a person of an *entrepreneurial* or *efficiently acquisitive class type*. On the other hand, society's public resources (that rapidly decreasing segment) are dependent on need (Honderich, 1990, p. 89). In a conservative society, the former is to be maximized, the latter is to be minimized.

However, most forms of conservatism do not merely depend in a large portion of their arguments and policies on a particular view of human nature—a view of human nature as primarily self-interested. They have gone further; they have set out to degrade that human nature, to force all people to conform to what at first could only be pretended to be true. Unfortunately, in no small measure they have succeeded. Perhaps blinded by their own absolutist and reductive vision of what it means to be human, many of our political "leaders" do not seem to be capable of recognizing what they have done. They have set out, aggressively, to drag down the character of a people (Honderich, 1991, p. 810), while at the same time attacking the poor and the disenfranchised for their supposed lack of values and character.

But I digress here and some of my anger begins to show. You will forgive me I trust; but if we cannot allow ourselves to be angry about the lives of our children, what can we be angry about?

Unfortunately, major elements of this restructuring are hardly on the agenda of discussions of some of the groups within the critical and "progressive" communities within education itself, especially by *some* (not all) of those people who have turned uncritically to postmodernism.

L O S I N G   M E M O R Y

What I shall say here is still rather tentative, but it responds to some of my intuitions that a good deal of the storm and fury over the politics of one form of textual analysis over another or even over whether we should see the world as a text, as discursively constructed, for example, is at least partly beside the point and that "we" may be losing some of the most important insights generated by, say, the neo-marxist tradition in education and elsewhere.

In what I say here, I hope I do not sound like an unreconstructed Stalinist (after all I've spent all too much of my life writing and speaking about the reductive tendencies within the marxist traditions). I simply want us to remember the utterly essential—not essentialist—understandings of the relationships (admittedly very complex) between education and some of the relations of power we need to consider but seem to have forgotten a bit too readily.

The growth of the multiple positions associated with postmodernism and poststructuralism is indicative of the transformation of our discourse and understandings of the relationship between culture and power. The rejection of the comforting illusion that there can (and must) be one grand narrative under which all relations of domination can be subsumed, the focus on the "micro-level" as a site of the political, the illumination of the utter complexity of the power-knowledge nexus, the extension of our political concerns well beyond the "holy trinity" of class, gender, and race, the idea of the decentered subject where identity is both nonfixed and a site of political struggle, the focus on the politics and practices of consumption, not only production—all of this has been important, though not totally unproblematic to say the least (Clarke, 1991; Best & Kellner, 1991).

With the growth of postmodern and poststructural literature in critical educational and cultural studies, however, we have tended to move too quickly away from traditions that continue to be filled with vitality and provide essential insights into the nature of the curriculum and pedagogy that dominate schools at all levels. Thus, for example, the mere fact that class does not explain all can be used as an excuse to deny its power. This would be a serious error. Class is, of course, an analytic construct as well as a set of relations that have an existence outside of our minds. Thus, what we mean by it and how it is mobilized as a category needs to be continually deconstructed and rethought. Thus, we must be very careful when and how it is used, with due recognition of the multiple ways in which people are formed. Even given this, however, it would be wrong to assume that, since many people do not identify with or act on what we might expect from theories that link, say, identity and ideology with one's class position, this means that class has gone away (Apple, 1992).

The same must be said about the economy. Capitalism may be being transformed, but it still exists as a massive structuring force. Many people may not think and act in ways predicted by class essentializing theories, but this does *not* mean the racial, sexual, and class divisions of paid and unpaid labor have disappeared; nor does it mean that relations of production (both economic *and* cultural, since how we think about these two may be different) can be ignored if we do it in non-essentializing ways (Apple, 1996).

I say all this because of very real dangers that now exist in critical educational studies. One is our loss of collective memory. While there is currently great and necessary vitality at the "level" of theory, a considerable portion of critical research has often been faddish. It moves from theory to theory rapidly, often seemingly assuming that the harder something is to understand or the more it rests on European cultural theory (preferably French) the better it is. The rapidity of its movement and its partial capture by an upwardly mobile fraction of the new middle class within the academy—so intent on mobilizing its cultural resources within the status hierarchies of the university that it has often lost any but the most rhetorical connections with the multiple struggles against domination and subordination at the university and elsewhere—has as one of its effects the denial of gains that have been made in other traditions or restating them in new garb (Apple, 1992). Or it may actually move backwards, as in the reappropriation of, say, Foucault into just another (but somewhat more elegant) theorist of social control, a discredited and ahistorical concept that denies the power of social movements and historical agents. In our rush toward poststructuralism, we may have forgotten how very powerful the structural dynamics are in which we participate. In the process, we seem to be losing our capacity to be angry.

One of the major issues here is the tendency of all too many critical and oppositional educators to become overly theoretical. Sometimes, in this process, we fail to see things that are actually not that hard to understand. I want to tell a story here that I hope makes my arguments clear. It is a story that perhaps will be all too familiar to those of you who have opposed the North American Free Trade Agreement (NAFTA).

E A T I N G   F R E N C H   F R I E S

The sun glared off of the hood of the small car as we made our way along the two lane road. The heat and humidity made me wonder if I'd have any liquid left in my body at the end of the trip and led me to appreciate Wisconsin winters a bit more than one might expect. The idea of winter seemed more than a little remote in this Asian country for which I have a good deal of fondness. But the topic at hand was not the weather; rather, it was the struggles of educators and social activists to build an education that was considerably more democratic than what was in place in that country now. This was a dangerous topic. Discussing it in philosophical and formalistically academic terms was tolerated. Openly calling for it and situating it within a serious analysis of the economic, political, and military power structures that now exerted control over so much of this nation's daily life was another matter.

As we traveled along that rural road in the midst of one of the best conversations I had engaged in about the possibilities of educational transformations and the realities of the oppressive conditions so many people were facing in that land, my gaze somehow was drawn to the side of the road. In one of those nearly accidental happenings that clarify and crystallize what reality is *really* like, my gaze fell upon a seemingly inconsequential object. At regular intervals, there were small signs planted in the dirt a few yards from where the road met the fields. The sign was more than a little familiar. It bore the insignia of one of the most famous fast food restaurants in the United States. We drove for miles past seemingly deserted fields along a flat hot plain, passing sign after sign, each a replica of the previous one, each less than a foot high. These were not billboards. Such things hardly existed in this poor rural region. Rather, they looked exactly—exactly—like the small signs one finds next to farms in the American Midwest that signify the kinds of seed corn that each farmer had planted in her or his fields. This was a good guess it turned out.

I asked the driver—a close friend and former student of mine who had returned to this country to work for the social and educational reforms that were so necessary—what turned out to be a naïve but ultimately crucial question in my own education, "Why are those signs for ***** there? Is there a ***** restaurant nearby?" My friend looked at me in amazement. "Michael, don't you know what these signs signify? There's no western restaurant within fifty miles of where we are. These signs represent exactly what is wrong with education in this nation. Listen to this." And I listened.

The story is one that has left an indelible mark on me, for it condenses in one powerful set of historical experiences the connections between our struggles as educators and activists in so many countries and the ways differential power works in ordinary life. I cannot match the tensions and passions in my friend's voice as this story was told; nor can I convey exactly the almost eerie feelings one gets when looking at that vast, sometimes beautiful, sometimes scarred, and increasingly depopulated plain. Yet the story is crucial to hear. Listen to this.

The government of the nation has decided that the importation of foreign capital is critical to its own survival. Bringing in American, German, British, Japanese, and other investors and factories will ostensibly create jobs, will create capital for investment, and will enable the nation to speed into the twenty-first century. (This is, of course, elite group talk, but let us assume that all of this is indeed truly believed by dominant groups.) One of the ways the military dominated government has planned to do this is to focus part of its recruitment efforts on agribusiness. In pursuit of this aim, it has offered vast tracts of land to international agribusiness concerns at very low cost. Of particular importance to the plain we are driving through is the fact that much of this land has been given over to a large American fast food restaurant corporation for the growing of potatoes for the restaurant's French fries, one of the trademarks of its extensive success throughout the world.

The corporation was eager to jump at the opportunity to shift a good deal of its potato production from the U.S. to Asia. Since many of the farm workers in the United Sates were now unionized and were (correctly) asking for a livable wage, and since the government of that Asian nation officially frowned on unions of any kind, the cost of growing potatoes would be lower. Further, the land on that plain was perfect for the use of newly developed technology to plant and harvest the crop with considerably fewer workers. Machines would replace living human beings. Finally, the government was much less concerned about environmental regulations. All in all, this was a fine bargain for capital.

Of course, *people* lived on some of this land and farmed it for their own food and to sell what might be left over after their own—relatively minimal—needs were met. This deterred neither agribusiness nor the government. After all, people could be moved to make way for "progress." And after all, the villagers along that plain did not actually have deeds to the land. (They had lived there for perhaps hundreds of years, well before the invention of banks, and mortgages, and deeds—no paper, no ownership). It would not be too hard to move the people off of the plain to other areas to "free" it for intensive potato production and to "create jobs" by taking away the livelihood of thousands upon thousands of small scale farmers in the region.

I listened with rapt attention as the rest of the story unfolded and as we passed by the fields with their miniature corporate signs and the abandoned villages. The people whose land had been taken for so little moved, of course. As in so many other similar places throughout what dominant groups call the Third World, they trekked to the city. They took their meager possessions and moved into the ever expanding slums within and surrounding the one place that held out some hope of finding enough paid work (if *everyone*—including children—labored) so that they could survive.

The government and major segments of the business elite officially discouraged this, sometimes by hiring thugs to burn the shanty towns, other times by keeping conditions so horrible that no one would "want" to live there. But still the dispossessed came, by the tens of thousands. Poor people are not irrational, after all. The loss of arable land had to be compensated for somehow and if it took cramming into places that were deadly at times, well what were the other choices? There *were* factories being built in and around the cities, which paid incredibly low wages—sometimes less than enough money to buy sufficient food to replace the calories expended by workers in the production process—but at least there might be paid work if one was lucky.

So the giant machines harvested the potatoes and the people poured into the cities and international capital was happy. It's not a nice story, but what does it have to do with *education*? My friend continued my education.

The military dominated government had given all of these large international businesses 20 years of tax breaks to sweeten the conditions for their coming to that country. Thus, there was now very little money to supply the health care facilities, housing, running water, electricity, sewage disposal, and schools for the thousands upon thousands of people who had sought their future in or had literally been driven into the city. The mechanism for not building these necessities was quite clever. Take the lack of any formal educational institutions as a case in point. In order for the government to build schools it had to be shown that there was a "legitimate" need for such expenditure. Statistics had to be produced in a form that was *officially* accepted. This could only be done through the official determination of numbers of registered births. Yet, the very process of official registration made it impossible for thousands of children to be recognized as actually existing.

In order to register for school, a parent had to register the birth of the child at the local hospital or government office—none of which existed in these slum areas. And even if you could somehow find such an office, the government officially discouraged people who had originally come from outside the region of the city from moving there. It often refused to recognize the legitimacy of the move as a way of keeping displaced farmers from coming into the urban areas and thereby increasing the population. Births from people who had no "legitimate" right to be there did not count as births at all. It is a brilliant strategy in which the state creates categories of legitimacy that define social problems in quite interesting ways. (See, e.g., Curtis, 1992 and Fraser, 1989.) Foucault would have been proud, I am certain.

Thus, there are no schools, no teachers, no hospitals, no infrastructure. The root causes of this situation rest not in the immediate situation. They can only be illuminated if we focus on the chain of capital formation internationally and nationally, on the contradictory needs of the state, on the class relations, and the relations between country and city that organize and disorganize that country.

My friend and I had been driving for quite a while now. I had forgotten about the heat. The ending sentence of the story pulled no punches. It was said slowly and quietly, said in a way that made it even more compelling. "Michael, these fields are the reason there's no schools in my city. There's no schools because so many folks like cheap french fries."

I tell this story about the story told to me for a number of reasons. First, it is simply one of the most powerful ways I know of reminding myself and all of us of the utter importance of seeing schooling relationally, of seeing it as connected—fundamentally—to the relations of domination and exploitation of the larger society. Second, and equally as importantly, I tell this story to make a crucial theoretical and political point. Relations of power are indeed complex and we do need to take very seriously the postmodern focus on the local and on the multiplicity of the forms of struggle that need to be engaged in. It is important as well to recognize the changes that are occurring in many societies and to see the complexity of the "power/knowledge" nexus. Yet in our attempts to avoid the dangers that accompanied some aspects of previous "grand narratives," let us *not* act as if capitalism has somehow disappeared. Let us not act as if class relations don't count. Let us not act as if all of the things we learned about how the world might be understood politically have been somehow overthrown because our theories are now more complex.

The denial of basic human rights, the destruction of the environment, the deadly conditions under which people (barely) survive, the lack of a meaningful future for the thousands of children I noted in my story—all of this is not only or even primarily a "text" to be deciphered in our academic volumes as we pursue our postmodern themes. It is a reality that millions of people experience in their very bodies everyday. Educational work that is not connected deeply to a powerful understanding of these realities (and this understanding cannot evacuate a serious analysis of political economy and class relations without losing much of its power) is in danger of losing its soul. The lives of our children demand no less.

N O T E S

1. I put the word "minority" in inverted commas here to remind us that the vast majority of the world's population is composed of persons of color. It would be wholly salutary for our ideas about culture and education to remember this fact.

2. Neo-liberalism doesn't ignore the idea of a strong state, but it wants to limit it to specific areas (e.g., defense of markets).

R E F E R E N C E S

Apple, M. W. *Teachers and Texts: A Political Economy of Class and Gender Relations in Education.* New York: Routledge, 1988.

Apple, M. W. Education, Culture and Class Power. *Educational Theory* 42 (Spring 1992): 127-145.

Apple, M. W. *Official Knowledge: Democratic Education in A Conservative Age.* New York: Routledge, 1993.

Apple, M. W. *Education and Power,* second edition. New York: Routledge, 1995.

Apple, M. W. *Cultural Politics and Education.* New York: Teachers College Press, 1996.

Bastian, A., Fruchter, N., Gittell, M., Greer, C. & Haskins, K. *Choosing Equality.* Philadelphia: Temple University Press, 1986.

Best, S., & Kellner, D., *Postmodern Theory.* London: Macmillan, 1991.

Clarke, J. *New Times and Old Enemies.* London: Harper Collins, 1991.

Curtis, B. *True Government By Choice Men?* Toronto: University of Toronto Press, 1992.

Education Group II, Eds. *Education Limited.* London: Unwin Hyman, 1991.

Edwards, T., Gewirtz, S., & Whitty, G. Whose Choice of Schools. *Sociological Perspectives On Contemporary Educational Reforms.* Edited by M. Arnot and L. Barton. London: Triangle Books, in press.

Fraser, N. *Unruly Practices.* Minneapolis: University of Minnesota Press, 1989.

Green, A. The Peculiarities of English Education. *Education Limited.* Edited by Education Group II. London: Unwin Hyman, 1991.

Honderich, T. *Conservatism*. Boulder, CO: Westview Press, 1990.

Hunter, A. *Children in the Service of Conservatism*. Madison, WI: University of Wisconsin Law School, Institute for Legal Studies. 1988.

Johnson, R. A New Road to Serfdom. *Education Limited*. Edited by Education Group II. London: Unwin Hyman, 1991.

CHAPTER TWENTY-ONE

Thinking Otherwise and Hearing Differently

Enactivism and School Mathematics[*]

Brent Davis
1995

There's a certain debate-like quality to much of the current discussion among mathematics educators. To anyone familiar with the recent history of the field, this observation is not news. As with most branches of educational inquiry, those involved in mathematics education have run up against seeming contradictions and incompatible recommendations in their efforts to understand the implications of "new" and "radical" theories of knowing.

Although there are some critical differences among the current theoretical offerings, those espousing them tend to gather under the banner of "constructivism,"[1] seeing as their task the displacement of a battery of culturally privileged and historically entrenched perspectives and practices that have, until only recently, gone virtually unchallenged.

As far as the theoretical foundations of research in mathematics education go, the impact of the constructivist movement has been nothing short of revolutionary, with few if any current research reports failing to acknowledge some measure of allegiance to this epistemological orientation. Nevertheless, despite the apparent solidarity, there are profound disagreements among researchers, especially with regard to the notion of "constructivist teaching." While many struggle to define the term, others contend that such efforts are not only ill-informed, they are destined to failure. Von Glasersfeld (1992), for example, has suggested that constructivism, as a theory of learning and knowing, can at best make us more aware of what we, as teachers, *cannot do*. Indeed, since

---

❖   This paper was awarded the Annual Aoki Award at the October 1994 JCT Conference in Banff, Alberta.)

a key tenet of constructivism is that there can be no such thing as an "instructive act" (i.e., in the causal sense of the phrase), the teacher can only be considered in terms of a source of perturbations intended to prod learners toward certain prespecified understandings.

As such notions filter their way from the theorist through the researcher to the teacher, they inevitably and violently run up against established perspectives and methods which, when considered alongside institutional constraints, program demands, and public expectations, militate against any sort of significant reform(ul)ation of mathematics pedagogy. This situation is further complicated by developments both within the discipline of mathematics and, in particular, among philosophers of mathematics. As alternative research methods are developed and dynamic new topics are investigated, innovative perspectives on such issues as the criteria for truth and the nature of mathematical knowledge are posing serious challenges to long-held beliefs undergirding much of current educational practice.

Thus, in terms of defining the role of the teacher, a sort of impasse has been reached. In this article I argue two main points: first, our arrival at this critical juncture is only one of the consequences of a mode of dualistic thinking that permeates much of the current research in the field. The resulting binaries are tightly coupled to constructivists' tendencies to locate themselves in direct opposition to the realist/objectivist conceptions of truth (and the corresponding representationist perspectives on cognition) that continue to be dominant among teachers. As such, the discussions and debates still ignore the issue of what it means to educate: we hear virtually nothing about the actual experiences of negotiating a curriculum, of affecting the lives and identities of learners, of contributing to the shape of our world—in short, of teaching children. Rather than assisting us to overcome some of the fundamental problems within the field, then, the "constructivist revolution" has only served to exacerbate them.

My second point is that there is a way to resolve these tensions, but their resolution is not to be found in an elaboration of either a realist or a constructivist perspective, nor in some compromise between the two positions. Such efforts compel us to focus on differences rather than enabling us to question the taken-for-granted notions out of which such differences arise. In effect, I am arguing that we need to turn away from the defining and definitive frames that we have constructed to contain curriculum and pedagogy and to turn toward the complex and shifting phenomena that we call teaching, joining with other curriculum theorists as we seek to formulate a curriculum that is no longer founded on "the striated linear instrumentalism deeply inscribed into our [intellectual] landscape" (Aoki, 1993, p. 259).

I have chosen to approach these issues through an exploration of three of the most prominent topics of debate within the field of mathematics education. Specifically, I will be focusing on varied orientations toward (1) the nature of the subject matter, (2) the process of learning, and (3) the role of the teacher. For each of these issues, I characterize how current discussions seem to be unfolding, focusing on some of their points of tension in this effort to sketch out an alternative perspective on mathematics teaching. These discussions are preceded by a brief introduction to the theoretical framework I am using. Finally, basing my remarks on my work with different teachers, I attempt to describe how such ideas might help to inform the teaching of middle school mathematics.

ENACTIVISM

OUR MODERN HERITAGE

As has been discussed at length by many contemporary thinkers, the predominant epistemological perspective in this "modern era" was first announced by Descartes in the seventeenth century. Since it has been thoroughly developed elsewhere, I will focus more on the consequences of his *cogito* than on its formulation.

In constructing his philosophy on the foundation of the *cogito*, Descartes concluded that one comes to know the world through gradually honing one's inner representations of an outer reality. He thus articulated an essential distinction between mental and physical objects, giving priority to the former and, in the same stroke, setting the foundation for a series of separations, including mind from body, self from other, knower from known, organism from environment. This modern/Cartesian/subjectivist-objectivist/dualistic orientation also contributed to a view of the *self* as an autonomous entity: isolated from others, independently constituted, disembodied, coherent, stable, and objectively real.

Further consequences of this perspective include an emphasis on the trustworthiness of the methods used to develop and verify mental representations. As these methods were framed in increasingly technical and technological terms, the universe came to be understood as something mechanical (supplanting organismic metaphors and supernatural characterizations). Machine metaphors eventually served to define Western perspectives on the universe, the earth, nature, our bodies, and—ultimately, with the development of the computer—our thinking. With this technical mind set, the goal of inquiry gradually shifted from bettering our understanding to controlling the objects of our inquiry. It is this framework that has supported a model of teaching that tends to be cast in the language of control and management...both of learning and of learners.

And, perhaps most significantly, with thought being afforded priority over being in Descartes'*cogito*, epistemic issues began to overshadow ontological concerns. It is thus that the focus of teaching and education have come to be the imparting of knowledge rather than the development of character or identity. Conventional conceptions of teaching and formal education embody many of the oppositions, tensions, and separations that are identified as "modernist": knowledge is considered apart from knowers, learning continues to be thought of as an essentially mental activity, and students are treated as insulated, autonomous, and static entities. In brief, objectivist perspectives on teaching actually have far more in common with subjectivist models than one might think. In particular, the tendency of proponents of either position to frame their theories and conclusions in the rhetoric of rationalism—that is, in the mode or argumentation identified by Descartes as the sole route to unimpeachable knowledge—is a matter that should give us pause.

Middle Ways

As suggested, these modern assumptions are now being challenged, with perhaps the most popular commentaries being collected under the title "postmodernism." Unfortunately, while postmodern discourses have offered valuable critiques of Descartes' legacy, it seems that one of the precepts of postmodernism—that the quest for new groundings is doomed to failure—has been profoundly misinterpreted as suggesting that we can say very little about anything. Not surprisingly, this conclusion has prompted numerous and zealous attempts to destroy the foundations of existing structures—thus demonstrating the temporal and contextual nature of all knowledge—while offering in their place the unsteady (and unsatisfactory) ground of falllibilist, relativist, and individualist accounts of knowing.

The new challenge thus seems to be the development of alternatives that abandon such assumptions but which do not give in to the temptation of seeking new groundings. Fortunately, there appears to be some convergent streams of thought emerging from such disciplines as continental philosophy (e.g., Gadamer, 1990; Merleau-Ponty 1962; Rorty 1990), cognitive psychology (e.g., Bruner, 1986; Piaget & Inhelder 1969; Vygotsky, 1978), biology (e.g., Maturana & Varelt 1987; Varelt, Thompson, & Rosch, 1991), and ecology (e.g., Bateson, 1979; Berry, 1977; Lovelock, 1979). Growing numbers of theorists in these fields are starting from the evolutionary metaphors of Darwin rather than the analytic and reductionist model of Descartes. (I might also add that there seem to be general movements away from Western religious and philosophic traditions and toward more openminded explorations of Taoism, Buddhism, and other systems of Eastern thought.) Many discussions are thus coming to focus on interconnections between individual and environment rather than on their separations. Following Varela, et al. (1991), I will use the term "enactivism" to refer to this school of thought.

The aforementioned dichotomies—among which are included mind versus body, knower versus known, organism versus environment—are thus suggested to be both false and avoidable, although useful for some purposes. In endeavoring to sidestep such tensions, enactivist theorists and researchers have offered new definitions of knowledge and communication and new models of cognition and learning. In the next section I attempt to elaborate on these perspectives through an exploration of their implications for the teaching of mathematics, as announced earlier, focusing on three topics: the natures of knowledge, learning, and teaching.

CURRENT DISCUSSIONS

THE NATURE OF MATHEMATICAL KNOWLEDGE

It is no mere coincidence that Rene Descartes, the person whose name is most often associated with the emergence of the modern era, was a mathematician. Reacting to the current state of knowledge, which he perceived to be a mixture of fact and fancy, Descartes called for a firmer foundation for truth, citing mathematics as the only reliable means of attaining that goal. Faithful to his announcement, over the next few centuries, mathematics came to permeate almost all aspects of inquiry. As it supplanted other models of reasoning, mathematics rendered suspect the experiential, the phenomenal, the narrative, and the supernatural as legitimate bases of knowing.

This privileging of mathematical knowledge reached its apex at the turn of this century as leading mathematicians set out to reconstruct mathematics as a strictly formal system. In this conception, mathematics—although not rendered devoid of meaning—was deliberately divorced from associations with our expenses. The rationale underlying this project was that we could only realize the full power of mathematics if we could relive it of the burden of associated, experiential knowledge. While this purpose may have been justifiable in terms of, for example, the intention of facilitating mathematical inquiry), it has contributed to the pervasive (and quite mistaken) perspective that mathematical notions are actually independent of human experience. With regard to teaching, these "formalist" views have come to undergird much of current educational practice, as revealed in seating arrangements that militate against interaction, pedagogy that favors replication over inquiry, and an examination regime that is premised on competitiveness rather than mathematical understanding.

However, among mathematicians and philosophers of mathematics, this formalist perspective has been widely discounted.[2] As alternative research methods are developed and dynamic new topics are investigated, such matters as the nature of mathematical knowledge, the diverse processes of mathematical inquiry, and the "unreasonable effectiveness" of the subject matter have become topics of intense interest. In terms of the topics of discussion among mathematics education researchers, these issues tend to arise in the form of an ongoing debate over whether mathematical knowledge is discovered or created—that is, phrased in terms of a question. "Do mathematical objects have a prior objective (real) existence or is mathematics essentially a mental activity?" At the moment, the latter perspective seems to be favored by theorists and researchers (see Ernest 1991), among whom notions of "truth" and "objectivity" are coming to be seen in terms of intersubjective agreement rather than discovery of a pregiven world. Nevertheless, the issue is far from resolved among theorists, with many finding the "fallibilist" notion that mathematics is something we create and subsequently impose on a detached and inaccessible universe to be as untenable as the opposing "realist" perspective that mathematical truths are, quite literally, hiding in the bushes awaiting discovery. The question that tends to be raised at this point is: How can we account for the tremendous descriptive and predictive capacities of mathematical ideas if they are merely mental constructs? (Hamming, 1980).

Further, although a popular topic among theorists and researchers, the nature of mathematics seems to be virtually a nonissue among practicing teachers, with a realist perspective on knowledge tending to be both reflected in curriculum documents and enacted in the classroom. Overwhelmingly, mathematics is seen as a collection of "tools" to be acquired for later application.

In spite of these dissimilarities in terms of both their underlying assumptions and their implications for teaching, the two systems of thought share some substantial common ground. Both rest, for example, on the rationalist premise that humans are set apart from the rest of the universe, incapable of knowing with certainty the nature of the reality beyond ourselves. Implicit in this notion is another separation: knowledge —collective or individual—is cast as some thing apart from ourselves and independent of our (physical) actions.

Enactivism, as its name suggests, starts out by problematizing the "thing-ness"—the objectivity—that tends to be attached to knowledge, locating what we know in the dynamic space of what we do. Knowledge arises neither by uncovering nor by inventing; rather it emerges from—that is, it is *enacted* through—the history of human participation in a responsive and similarly dynamic world. Far from merely *representing* the universe (thus setting us apart), our mathematics *presents* the rhythms of the planet and the patterns that are repeated in all forms and at all levels of life. Mathematics provides not just a description of the world; it opens that world to us and places us in a dialogical relationship with it. It does not reduce, but hints at and enables us to engage in conversation with the complex orders and the tangled relationships that inevitably exceed our attempts to understand and surpass our efforts to control. In this way, the distinction between individual knowing and collective knowledge is also challenged: through the enactivist lens, these are seen not as two categories but in dynamic, co-specifying, and ecological unity.

In brief, enactivism prompts us to question the common assumption that our knowledge sets us apart from other species. What we have forgotten in this formulation is that, even while it distinguishes us, our knowledge simultaneously places us in communion with the world. This is to say that our body of knowledge, as a collective analog of our physical bodies, plays a dual role: it separates us from, while it places us in relationship to, our environment. This body is never absolute or ideal; it can never be fixed or completed. It is, rather, shaped by the world while it participates in shaping that world, discernible by its dynamic form rather than by any sort of static character. So it is with the patterns of acting that we refer to as our mathematics: dependent on situation, fluid, and elusive. There is no "single" mathematics toward which we are progressing. Rather, as many research mathematicians will confirm,[3] and as any teacher who has participated in the meandering of students' mathematical explorations will attest, systems of mathematics can be as divergent as each of our histories.

In essence, then, the enactivist challenge is not to offer a new answer to the question, "What is mathematics?" That issue, they argue, can never be fully resolved because we cannot extract our dynamic selves or worlds from our mathematics. The more important question is thus, "What are we that we might know mathematics?[4]" And herein lies an important difference between enactivist and modernist perspectives: in the move to embrace the complexities of existence, the focus shifts toward understanding *being*, and away from questions of knowledge and validity. Put differently, priority is given to ontological concerns rather than epistemological, thus reversing Descartes' *cogito*.

THE PROCESSES OF LEARNING

An important part of our Western intellectual heritage is the belief in a more-or-less stable *self* that precedes learning and which is able to maintain its integrity through learning. When combined with its complementary notion—the pregivenness of the universe—this belief quite logically leads to a model of cognition in which the given subject must come to know the given world, whether this is thought to occur via representation of a real universe or via the autonomous creation of a subjective reality.

Thus, traditional understandings of formal education are predicated on the assumption that there is an objectively knowable world. Curriculum goals ("objectives") that reflect that world are selected in advance and, in the process of meeting these objectives, students are expected to more accurately *represent* the world as it is.[5] It is this "acquisition" model of learning that defines most of current practice. The alternative offered by constructivism begins with a contrary assumption: the universe is not objectively knowable. Rather, the learner constructs a world. Cognition is thus understood to be a process of "meaning-making," as the individual makes sense of prior, sociallydeveloped knowledge.[6] It is not a matter of acquiring appropriate representations of the world, but of constructing personally and socially viable "theories" of the ways in which the world works. Such theories are constantly undergoing revision as necessitated by new, previously unaccounted for, experience. (It bears noting that one has to move beyond this interpretive framework in order to explore possible implications for teaching and curriculum development. Concerned as it is with subjective sense-making rather than cultural dynamics, constructivism does not provide much help in discussions of matters related to collective action.)

A uniting feature of these two conceptions of learning—that is, of the acquisition model and the constructivist alternative—is that the issue of the identity of the learner, if considered at all, tends to be treated as peripheral. The question of the *self* thus represents a critical point of divergence between these conceptions and the enactivist account of cognition. Moving away from the belief that the self is unified and stable—albeit something that undergoes continuous change—enactivism regards personal identity as the very process of change itself. That is, like knowledge, identity is conflated with—*enacted* through—doing or acting. Gadamer (1990), for example, uses the metaphor of "conversation" to illustrate how our identities are dynamic, relational, and situational. Varela et al. (1991) uses the notion of "mutual specification" to argue that neither the *self* nor the world is pregiven. Neither are they separate: self and world, and self and other, are objectively intertwined and intersubjectively entwined. They are coemergent; they come to form together, bringing forth one another in a choreography of mutual specification. Implicit in this conception is a sense of ecological embeddedness, whereby the universe changes as something so minuscule as a thought changes—for that thought, like the thinker, is part of the universe.

Learning and cognition, then, are argued to be better understood in terms of adequate functioning in an ongoing interactive world than in the terms offered by subjectivist or objectivist accounts. The implications of this shift are manifold, with perhaps the most important one having to do with the notion of *meaning*. Conventionally, "meaning" tends to be understood in terms of connections or associations. On the more objectivist side, the meaning of a concept has to do with its relationships to other concepts, its possible applications, its derivation, etc. In short, meaning is something that can be taught. More subjectively, meaning is understood in terms of personal associations to other ideas, and it is something to be either supported or contradicted, depending on its appropriateness. In both cases, meaning is understood in formalized or formulated terms: it is something that can be, and usually is, state-able.

In enactivist terms, however, the bulk of our meanings are not formulated, but lived through—*enacted*. For the purposes of illustration, we can turn to Putnam (1989) who offers two opposing conceptions of the meanings of words. In formal terms, to know a word's meaning is to be able to provide a definition without using that word. However, he argues, most of the time we are unable to readily offer such definitions, and yet we clearly *know* the meaning of the words we are using—simply by virtue of the fact that we are using them. Their meanings are thus *enacted*, and it is to this unseen (or unacknowledged) part of the iceberg that enactivist theorists invite us to focus our attentions in our discussions of education. The measure of learning is not what can be restated but what is performed. Put differently, thought and action are not precursors to, or consequences of, meaning; they *are* meaning—meaning that is caught up in, rather than being dissociated from, the affective, the physical, and the dynamic that are the self.[7] (It almost goes without saying that those who are sympathetic to an activist perspective tend to reject the defining metaphor of cognitive science: mind as computer.) In contrast to the conception of the self as a "thing" that undergoes change—a conception common to both objectivist and subjectivist—self is reinterpreted here as the process, the product, and the instigator of change. Learning, then, is not a matter of "adding to" what is already there. Our learning, rather, is entangled in our becoming.

A second important implication of the enactivist perspective has to do with the idea of authority in learning. As noted earlier, among mathematics education researchers, theories of learning have recently moved from objectivist (e.g., acquisition metaphors) to subjectivist (i.e., construction metaphors) accounts. In effect, we have moved from the privileging of an external authority to the privileging of an internal one—that is, from the belief that teaching is a matter of telling to a belief that nothing can be told.

The difficulty here is not the location of the authority but that both authorities are, to use Charles Taylor's (1991a) term, "monological." In the more traditional conceptions of education, the monologic authority is the assumed-to-be objectively knowable real world. In the more child-centered perspectives, the monologic authority is found in the child's own subjective conceptions. As Taylor demonstrates, there can be no such single authority. Rather, issues such as "what we know" and "who we are" are *dialogical*; they are constantly negotiated through our interactions with one another within the context of our culture. That culture is, in turn, negotiated within the wider context of history, civilization, and environment.

Returning to the notion of *self*, then: our identities are not pregiven, but are constantly evolving. (See, for example, Bruner 1990; Kerby 1991; Varela et al. 1991) This notion offers a serious challenge to the current educational practices of preselecting what is valuable to know and then attempting to predetermine how it might best be learned. The *self* is not a static entity that has an existence independent of learning. On the contrary, our identities are established relationally and experientially, and so schooling plays an important role in determining who we might be. Discussions of learning, then—whether with regard to the subject matter or to cognitive processes—are fundamentally and primarily ontological and they do not belong in the ostensibly morally neutral epistemological camp that many (and perhaps most) mathematics educators would have us believe.

THE ROLE OF THE TEACHER

Just as the self is constantly evolving, so is the culture in which selves are established and which is established of selves. Thus, those involved in formal education are actively engaged in the transformation of our culture—including those attempting its mere transmission—and so, within an enactivist framework, we are provided with a moral imperative to work toward cultural reform. To fail in this task is to be complicit in promoting what Taylor (1991b) calls the "malaise of modernity" and what Varela et al. (1991) describe as "the sense of nihilistic alienation in our culture." The role of education, then, is neither to impose an objective world nor to nurture subjective worlds. Rather, in Bruner's (1986) terms, it serves as a "forum for negotiating and re-negotiating meaning" (p. 123)—an agent of culture-making—and is, fundamentally, a moral undertaking.

Enactivism thus offers a starting place for mathematics educators to respond to many of the current critiques of traditional classroom approaches. Mathematics instruction, in particular, has been a principal target of those critics who argue that, far from enabling learners to overcome existing social and economic barriers, schooling has contributed to the maintenance of such structures. Once popularly believed to be value-,gender-, and racially neutral, mathematics is now more widely understood to be inherently biased. Correspondingly, the tendency within formal education to equate mathematical logic to sound reasoning has thus been strongly criticized—opening the door to other modes of thinking and of argumentation.

So what does enactivism have to offer teachers and teaching? Let me precede my response to that question by comparing traditional transmission models of teaching with more constructivist orientations. Running parallel to a realist view of knowledge and an acquisition model of learning is a transmission model of instruction: teaching as telling. So conceived, the teacher's task involves first selecting the bits of knowledge to be passed on and then representing them to learners in an efficient and effective manner. The constructivist challenge, as might be expected, is based on the conviction that one's dynamic and unique knowledge is the product of accumulated experience. Teaching, then, is not a matter of ensuring that preselected truths are acquired, but of *facilitating* the construction of knowledge through the creation of appropriate learning environments. In effect, teaching is a matter of *orchestrating* the learners' experiences rather than transmitting knowledge.

Just as the movement from objectivist accounts of learning have amounted to little more than a transference of monologic authority, the shift from teaching as telling to teaching as facilitating amounts to little more than a renewed attempt to prescribe or to control the learning that occurs. That is, in spite of the insights offered by constructivist theorists, recent developments have served to bolster the modern desire to dictate outcomes—even though the recommended means of achieving these ends are markedly different.

Enactivist theory invites us to consider a different orientation to teaching which, although still concerned with what is learned, is not limited by efforts to prescribe learning outcomes. Rather, learning is seen to be *proscribed* by the teacher who is an important interactive part of the learning context. The movement from prescription to proscription might be characterized as a shift from the perspective that "what is not allowed is forbidden" to "what is not forbidden is allowed" (Varela et al. 1991)—a shift which enables us to overcome the inability of conventional learning theories to inform teaching. For example, von Glasersfeld's contention that constructivism tells us only what teachers cannot do, when considered alongside the desire to predetermine outcomes, has the effect of crippling efforts to describe teaching because our attention is directed to "what is not allowed." If, however, we shift our focus to "what is not forbidden" and abandon attempts to control learning, then we are no longer compelled to base our current teaching actions on as yet unrealized outcomes—a practice which has forced us to privilege what we eventually want to achieve at the expense of what is currently happening.

In essence, then, we are urged by enactivist theorists to abandon our efforts to define teaching and to prescribe methods, recognizing that teaching exists and consists in the dynamic and complex spaces between self and other, past and future, actual and possible. As Aoki suggests, if we are to come to an understanding of what teaching truly is, the mechanistic and reductionist perspectives that permeate "educational" inquiry must be put aside as we "undertake to reorient ourselves so that we overcome mere correctness, so that we can see and hear our doings as teachers harbored within pedagogical being, so we can see and hear who we are as teachers" (Aoki, 1992, p. 27). We must seek to understand what it means to be a teacher, what it means to participate in children's learning, what it means to stand in the world as an educator.

Teaching and curriculum, then, from an enactivist point of view, can neither be defined nor predetermined. Rather, they emerge in the interaction of teachers and learners. In brief, instead of understanding teaching as an attempt to control learning outcomes, teaching is recast in terms of providing occasions for (inter)action, recognizing that the students' meanings and understandings are developed through and revealed in such action. Such "occasioning" of action might be seen as embracing happenstance, in contrast to the more general tendency of avoiding it.

Following Weinsheimer (1985), we might use the term "hap" to refer to these sorts of opportunities. "Hap" is an archaic word which is used to refer to an event—especially one which comes to be associated with good fortune. It is the root of many familiar words, including *happen, happy, mishap,* and *perhaps.* With regard to teaching, conventional approaches might be characterized as attempts to avoid haps by prespecifying desired understandings and laying our teaching actions in clear and unambiguous terms. This approach would be entirely unproblematic if the world (or even mathematics) were unambiguous. It is against such rigid, depersonalized, and hapless approaches to teaching that this paper is directed. In contrast to the foci of both traditional and more constructivism-informed models of teaching, the emphases from the enactivist perspective are on attending to situations, looking for opportunities, participating in the unfolding of events, being aware of the complex webs of relationships in which learning occurs, and recognizing one's complicity in personal and collective knowings. In short, teaching is largely a matter of embracing the hap.

In my own research, this foregrounding of happenstance has come to be expressed in the phrase, "teaching as listening," where listening is offered both figuratively and literally. Figuratively, listening offers a powerful alternative to metaphors for teaching that focus on the monological (such as "transmission," "telling," "voice," or "empowerment"). Listening is necessarily dialogical, involving at the very least the intermingling of another's words with the text of my own experience.[8] Similarly, as I have developed elsewhere through a phenomenology of listening (Davis, 1994, in press), a listening orientation denies the possibility for rigid subject-object distinctions, reminding us that the issue of who we are is not separate from where we are, what we are doing, who we are with, and what we know.

In literal terms, listening can serve as a basis for teaching action, an idea that has been recently confirmed by Carpenter and Fennema (1992) who, after investigating the relative effectiveness of particular teachers, concluded that "listening to their own students was the critical factor" (pp. 467-468). It is my contention that a listening orientation helps to liberate us from the desire to control outcomes while acknowledging the fundamental role of the teacher in affecting learning. Put differently, in suggesting that the teacher's role involves occasioning of students acting, I am not in any way arguing that the teacher must forego all hopes of promoting understandings on particular (i.e., mandated by curriculum) concepts. But I am saying that this is not as straightforward as it might look.

I N T O   T H E   C L A S S R O O M

In this section, I attempt to "bring to life" the preceding discussion through brief, but pointed, glimpses into two classrooms. First I will visit a more traditional setting and then I will drop in on a classroom in which the teacher has begun to enact enactivist notions. Unfortunately, in endeavoring to highlight particular features of these settings, the brief sketches I provide may more resemble caricatures than portraits.

Teaching as Telling

Some time ago, I was replaying an audio-taped recording of a mathematics lesson for the purposes of locating and transcribing salient teacher-student interactions. A colleague from English education entered my office and, after listening for only a moment, demanded that I turn it off. When I did so, he immediately assumed the role of the teacher and proceeded to "re-enact" the unheard remainder of the lesson—imitating the voice, the manner, and the actions of the teacher with an eerie accuracy.

The point here is that he was able to do this because he had considerable experience with what seems to be an almost universal structure of school mathematics classes. Reflecting the fragmented, hierarchical, abstract, and impersonal content of the textbooks and curriculum manuals, the learners are arranged in ways that militate against interaction and which place imposed structure over inherent fluidity. The format of the lesson also bears a certain resemblance to the enacted image of the subject matter: predictable, fragmented, self-contained; characterized by coordinated, but not rhythmic, action (Taylor, 1991a). My colleague had only to recite a sequence of directions, modulating his voice to imitate the unrelenting beat of a forced march, to accurately mimic a lesson he had never seen.

Claiming to be able to describe a "typical" lesson, then, is not as incredible as it might at first sound, for we more-than-likely share a broad familiarity with such lessons. Consider the following account.

> As the bell rings, those few students who were still standing race to their desks. Chris stands at the front of the room where he can see everyone and where everyone can see him. He waits for a few seconds until the class falls silent.
>
> "Here are the answers to yesterday's homework. You can mark your own today." Chris clicks on the overhead projector and all the answers, neatly arranged, appear on the screen behind him. Over the next five minutes we hear little. Some pens scratching. Some whispers.
>
> The silence is broken by his query, "Any questions on the homework?" There were none. "Okay, we're moving on to subtracting integers today."
>
> A ten-minute lesson ensues in which the rule for subtraction is presented along with a variety of examples. As the lesson moves along, students are given

a few "Do Now" exercises and, after a moment of hasty computation, are asked to give their answers. Notes are written on the board and copied into workbooks. The students ask few questions.

The assignment—a textbook exercise—is then identified and students are given the balance of the class for independent work. During this time, Chris moves from raised hand to raised hand—confirming answers, pointing out errors, and repeating fragments of his earlier explanation. A reminder that the "rest of the page" is to be completed for homework is given as the bell rings to end the class.

Even though the details of this account are specific to this one class on this one day, there is a familiar flavor to the mechanically timed events and the clearly demarcated relationships that are presented. The subject matter, for example, seems to be "about" neither the teacher nor the students. Rather, the mathematics is an object that stands between them, holding them apart rather than facilitating their relationships.

But an analysis of the class members *inter*actions is even more telling. They are coordinated, but independent; they lack a common rhythm. This is hardly surprising, since it seems that the particular students are of little consequence to the way the lesson is taught. For his part, it is clear that Chris has presented this hapless lesson before and will teach it again.

It would be a simple matter to argue that Chris is working from a realist perspective on knowledge, an acquisition model of learning, and a telling approach to teaching. But it would not be much more difficult to argue that his teaching is founded on constructivist principles. He may well be working from the premise that learners are constructing their own sense of what is going on and, hence, a highly structured environment is necessary to ensure that subjective interpretations do not stray so far from one another that they are no longer sufficiently compatible for learners to fare well on, say, a standardized examination.

Once again, then, constructivism—in spite of the impact it has had on research and theory—can help us little when it comes to teaching...or to interpreting teaching.

TEACHING AS LISTENING

Let us now turn to a setting where the teacher is enacting his understanding of enactivist principles.

Tom wanders among his grade 7 students as they "play" with their Fraction Kits,[9] sheets of paper cut into halves, thirds, fourths, and other fractional pieces. He has posed the question to the class: What can you say about three fourths?

The class members are noisy and active. Groups are huddled together, most of them using the kits to devise methods of covering three fourths of a piece of paper. As Tom moves about the room, he listens, he questions, he requests that students display their work on the chalkboard.

Not everyone is finished when he calls them to a discussion of what they've done. Interesting insights and possible avenues for further investigation are presented. Sarah asks a question: How many different ways can you make three fourths using pieces from the kits? It prompts particular interest among the students, and Tom suggests that this would be an appropriate question to pursue.

Activity resumes as groups produce five, six, nine, eleven answers. As Tom passes by one group, he notices that Marilyn is using the charts differently than her classmates, as a generative tool rather than a mere recording device. With it she can determine ALL the possibilities for three fourths and various other amounts quickly and efficiently.

Noting that Jake, Marilyn's partner, is copying her responses without really participating, Tom asks Marilyn to explain her reasoning. She complies, but it's apparent that Jake doesn't understand. Nevertheless, he stops copying and returns to the kit as Tom moves on.

Moments later, Tom feels a small poke in his back. He turns to see Jake who is holding up his chart. On it an interesting pattern of numbers has been recorded.

"I know everything about '1'" Jake announces proudly.

And so it continued.

As I sat in on this lesson, I was almost taken aback by an approach to teaching that was much in contrast to the methods and perspectives that dominated my own experience. Tom did not seem to be saying much in this lesson. Rather, he seemed to be teaching by listening.

Although it's difficult to provide a fair representation of this lesson's flow, I think this account does point to a very different sense of the rhythms and movements that might occur within the classroom. Like the conversation, the structure of these interactions are not predetermined, but emerge as the participants are "conducted" (Gadamer, 1990) by the subject matter. As such, it is neither important to begin the description at the first bell, nor to continue it to the lesson's end. It had no formal opening or closure. When the final bell did ring, it marked an interruption to the action—not an end to a particular topic.

Regarding "the lesson concept," it is important to note that these students were not investigating an isolated or fragmented idea. Rather, as they investigated Tom's questions, and as they devised questions of their own, learners made use of addition, subtraction, multiplication, and equivalence concepts at levels of complexity that far surpassed mandated curriculum recommendations. However, this is not to say that they were making use of formal mathematics. No algorithms had been discussed; none were being used. Although symbols were used to record events, they were not being manipulated for calculation purposes. Rather, the students' understandings, their knowledge, and their meanings were enacted—that is, they were implicit in their actions. As such, the indicator of the learners' understandings of various concepts was not a quiz score, but the appropriateness of their actions in the given setting.

The role of the teacher in such an enactivist classroom is clearly neither "telling" nor "facilitating"—although elements of both conventional and constructivist perspectives seem to be woven into Tom's actions. For example, his selection of questions for investigation was a very directive act. At the same time, he avoided attempting to predetermine what would be considered "appropriate action," inviting learners to explore within an environment that many would call "constructivist."

His role was thus to provide occasions that would provoke actions, which would in turn provoke other actions. In so facilitating action, Tom was opening the possibility of noticing and capturing the haps that might occur. In the fragment of the lesson provided, for example, Sarah's question, Marilyn's method, and Jake's insight are parts of a web of haps that could never have been deliberately provoked. But, with the prodding of an attentive and knowledgeable teacher, these events set up a chain reaction of possibilities.

Perhaps the most pleasing of these "possibilities," from the teacher's perspective, was Jake's claim to know "everything about '1'." With a history of difficulty in classroom mathematics, Jake was unable to cope with Marilyn's approach and (as later analysis would indicate) was having other troubles with the task at hand. He thus selected to create a question of his own, soon arriving at the insight that the chart could be both a generative and a recording tool. Marilyn, a very successful student, was the only other class member to achieve this mathematical insight.

The point, then, is that in moving from a *prescriptive* to a *proscriptive* orientation, in abandoning efforts to control learning outcomes, in privileging neither the "voice" of the learner nor the authority of established knowledge, this teacher had opened up the possibility for an *enacted curriculum*—a learning space wherein the players and the field are critical, but where the playing—not the players, nor the field, nor the rules—is what really makes the game. To my mind, the teacher's role in this space is not that of a coach or a referee standing outside of the play (i.e., "directing" or "facilitating" the players' actions), and this is why I am so taken by the notion of teaching as listening. By orienting ourselves to listening, we become part of the interactive setting—caught up in the intersubjectivity of play. We need not downplay our wider experience because it is precisely that experience that makes it possible to notice openings—to listen. At the same time, by listening, we can resist the temptation to impose the insights that emerge from the mass of our experiences onto the developing conceptualizations of learners, allowing them to explore and affect—to converse with—the world.

In sum, then, the *enacted* curriculum of this setting was not predetermined, but emerged as the teacher interpreted student actions and used these interpretations as the basis for further curriculum-making. At times the teacher's actions were deliberate (i.e., based on careful analysis and thoughtful decisions); at times his actions were simply a consequence of the way that he stood in the world. They were actions that arose from, perhaps, a genuine curiosity of the mathematics of the setting, a hermeneutic interest in the child's actions, or a pedagogical concern for their well-being. All of these qualities, I contend, are aspects of listening, for in listening we position ourselves amid the dynamic interplay of evolving meanings and understandings of 'self/other' in a curricular landscape that allows multiplicity to grow in the middle" (Aoki, 1993, p. 267). By listening we place ourselves in the dynamic space of teaching.

N O T E S

1. "Constructivism"—like "feminism," "relativism," "postmodernism," and a plethora of other "-isms,"—has been used as an umbrella term for a range of loosely related notions. As such, it has been subject to a variety of interpretations (see, for example, von Glasersfeld, 1984). Sweeping statements about "constructivist beliefs" are, therefore, inherently problematic. I thus use the term to refer more to the general movement than to specific perspectives. Where it is necessary to refer to particular versions or tenets, I make reference to the theorists from whose work I draw.

2. The formalist perspective hasn't, however, been completely discounted among mathematicians. Various schools are continuing their efforts to establish a new formalist ground for mathematical knowledge. Ernest (1991) provides a concise overview of some of these attempts.

3. See, for example, the work of Lakatos (1976) or of Davis and Hersh (1981, 1986).

4. This idea is adapted from Warren McCulloch (1965). I am indebted to Thomas E. Kieren for the adaptation.

5. Scruton (1981) suggests that an increasingly accurate representation of the universe was also seen by Descartes as the goal of learning and thinking. However, it would be stretching things to suggest that Descartes had a realist perspective on knowledge. (Quite the contrary, it was his frustration with the state of knowledge that led him to formulate his *cogito*.) I mention this point to highlight the fact that, in discussing objective-subjective dichotomies, I do not mean to create fast categories.

6. It is important to note that there is hardly consensus on the issue among constructivists. Some (e.g., Steffe, 1989) place far less emphasis on the role of socially developed knowledge, contending that the learner's mathematical actions—and not socially sanctioned truths—are the most important sources of knowledge.

7. Two notes. First, I believe that this is what many theorists have in mind when they use the phrase "embodied knowledge." Second, I suspect that further remarks on the *location of meaning* are in order. In the objectivist account, meanings are external and state-able. In contrast, from the subjectivist perspective, meaning is internal, and, therefore, more dynamic. Nonetheless, the prevailing opinion is that in spite of its internal locus, it too is (and some argue that it must be) articulate-able.

From the enactivist perspective, meaning is not so easily located. Since, for the most part, unformulated meanings are "performed" in specific contexts, they cannot be characterized as "internal" or "external" to the *actor*. Rather, they are implicit in the *acting*—a location that is so dynamic that we have a hard time grasping it at all. In thus situating meaning, enactivist theorists also draw attention to its contextual nature. Particular sorts of acting are more likely to occur in particular contexts. Put differently, meanings—like actions—are "occasioned."

8. This idea of the "intermingling of voices" can be carried further to include an attendance to the many social, historical, and contextual "voices" that contribute to our own "conversational" identities. In listening, as in every act of cognition, we are (re)enacting our own historical situatedness.

9. As I think is clear from the account of the lesson, the sort of activity that is used is fundamentally related to the sorts of interaction that might occur. For those interested in a fuller account of this particular activity, see Kieren, Davis, & Mason (in press).

R E F E R E N C E S

Aoki, T. Tetsuo. (1992). Layered voices of teaching: The uncannily correct and the elusively true. In W. F. Pinar and W. M. Reynolds (eds.), *Understanding Curriculum As Phenomenological And Deconstructed Text*. New York: Teachers College Press.

Aoki, T. Tetsuo. (1993). Legitimating lived curriculum: Towards a curricular landscape of multiplicity. *Journal of Curriculum And Supervision*, 8(3), 255-268.

Bateson, Gregory. (1979). *Mind And Nature*. New York: E. P. Dutton.

Berry, Wendell. (1977). *The Unsettling Of America : Culture And Agriculture*. San Francisco: Sierra Club Books.

Bruner, Jerome. (1986). *Actual Minds, Impossible Worlds*. Cambridge, MA: Harvard University Press.

Bruner, Jerome. (1990). *Acts Of Meaning*. Cambridge, MA: Harvard University Press.

Carpenter, Thomas & Fennema, Elizabeth. (1992). Cognitively guided instruction: Building on the knowledge of students and teachers. In W. Secada (ed.), *Researching Educational Reform: The Case Of School*

Mathematics In The United States (a special issue of *(International Journal of Educational Research)*.

Davis, Brent. (1994). Mathematics teaching: Moving from telling to listening. *Journal Of Curriculum And Supervision*, 9(3), 267-283.

Davis, Brent. (in press). *Teaching Mathematics: Toward A Sound Alternative*. New York: Garland Publishing.

Davis, Philip J. & Hersh, Reuben. (1981). *The Mathematical Experience*. Boston: Houghton Mifflin.

Davis, Philip J. & Hersh, Reuben. (1986). *Descartes' Dream: The World According To Mathematics*. Boston: Houghton Mifflin.

Ernest, Paul. (1991). *The Philosophy Of Mathematics Education*. London: Falmer Press.

Gadamer, Hans-Georg. (1990). *Truth And Method*. New York: Continuum.

Hamming, Richard W. (1980). The unreasonable effectiveness of mathematics. *American Mathematical Monthly*, 87 (February), 81-90.

Kerby, Anthony P. (1991). *Narrataive And The Self*. Bloomington, IN: Indiana University Press.

Kieren, Thomas, Davis, Brent, & Mason, Ralph. (in press). Fraction flags: Learning from children to help children learn. *Mathematics Teaching In The Middle School*.

Lakatos, Imre. (1976). *Proofs And Refutations*. Cambridge, U.K.: Cambridge University Press.

Maturana, Humberto & Varela, Francisco. (1987). *The Tree Of Knowledge*. Boston: Shambhala.

McCulloch, Warren. (1965). *Embodiments of Ming*. Cambridge, MA: MIT Press.

Merleau-Ponty, Maurice. (1962). *Phenomenology Of Perception*. London: Routledge.

Piaget, Jean & Inhelder, Barabel. (1969). *The Psychology Of The Child*. New York: Basic Books.

Putnam, Hilary. (1989). *Reality And Representation*. Cambridge, MA: MIT Press.

Rorty, Richard. (1990). *Objectivity, Relativism, And Truth*. Cambridge, U.K.: Cambridge University Press.

Scruton, Roger. (1981). *A Short History Of Modern Philosophy*. London: Routledge.

Steffe, Les P., ed. (1989). *Epistemological Foundations Of Mathematical Experience*. New York: Springer Verlag.

Taylor, Charles. (1991a). The dialogical self. In D. Hiley, J. Bohman, & R. Shusterman (eds.), The interpretive turn. Ithaca, N.Y.: Cornell University Press.

Taylor, Charles. (1991b). *The Malaise Of Modernity*. Concord, ON.: Anansi.

Varela, Francisco, Thompson, Evan, & Rosch, Eleanor. (1991). *The Embodied Mind*. Cambridge, MA: MIT Press.

von Glasersfeld, Ernst. (1984). An introduction to radical constructivism. In P. Watzlawick (ed.), *The Invented Reality*. New York: Norton.

von Glasersfeld, Ernst. (1992, August). *Radical Constructivism And The Philosophy Of Mathematics*. Paper presented at the 7th International Congress on Mathematics Education (Quebec, PQ, August).

Vygotsky, Lev. S. (1978). *Mind In Society: The Development Of Higher Psychological Processes*. Cambridge, MA: Harvard University Press.

Weinsheimer, Joel. (1985). *Gadamer's Hermeneutics: A Reading Of "Truth And Method."* New Haven: Yale University Press.

CHAPTER TWENTY-TWO

Schools Where Ronnie and Brandon Would Have Excelled

A Curriculum Theory of Academic and Vocational Integration

Joe L. Kincheloe
1995

Having recently completed a detailed study of Richard Herrnstein and Charles Murray's *The Bell Curve: Intelligence And Class Structure In American Life* (1994), I am acutely aware of elitist discourse in education and psychology. Few academic locales reveal a class-biased elitism more clearly than the conversation about intelligence in educational psychology. The dialogue becomes especially elitist and condescending when issues surrounding the intelligence of blue collar, low status workers are broached. My contention in this essay is that we must, as critical and democratic scholars, induce the academic community to rethink this elitism and restructure schools in light of that reconceptualization.

The elitism in *The Bell Curve* is omnipresent and oppressive, as the authors speak unabashedly about dysgenesis and the social havoc wrought by the poor (and nonwhite). Using what my coauthors (Shirley Steinberg and Aaron Gresson) label an "'us' verses 'them'" social theory, Herrnstein and Murray value abstract ways of knowing over hands-on, bodily modes of understanding. Schools, of course, reflect this tacit assumption in their privileging of the academic over the vocational curriculum. This elitist view of education inflicts immeasurable damage on economically and racially marginalized students. Every day, thousands of brilliant students are taught that they are stupid. My friends Ronnie and Brandon illustrate this point.

Ronnie and Brandon are carpenters who completed some renovation work on my house a couple of years ago. During that period they became good friends of mine who talked with me for hours about education—their own in particular. Like many individuals in the trades, they hated school. Convinced by their school experience that they were stupid, they sought vocations that ostensibly had little to do with the skills schools teach. In their everyday work, I watched them employ sophisticated geometric and algebraic abilities, solving unstructured problems with their improvisational math. When I pointed out the sophistication of their operations, they found my praise difficult to accept. "This is not really math—it's not like the math you do in school," Ronnie told me. As I explained to them how their math was in many ways more sophisticated then what is typically taught in high school, they were fascinated. Focusing on their facility with unstructured problems as opposed to school's structured problems, I began to argue that they were not as dumb as they thought.

As I explained critical conceptions of class-bias in education and the exclusionary, elitist discourse of education psychology's view of intelligence they began to understand the socially constructed nature of intelligence and how they had been victimized by the elitist viewpoint. The more we talked, the more excited they got. Initially reluctant to express their concerns about the elitism of schooling with a college professor who taught teachers, they began to share with me the anger and resentment they harbored toward formal education. In conversations with other men and women in the trades, I have encountered similar anger. Schooling has had little positive effect on their lives. It was a place of embarrassment and hurt feelings, a place where one's failures and inabilities took center stage. "I just kept my mouth shut and hoped the time would pass quickly," Ronnie told me. As long as we continue to demean manual forms of intelligence, a large percentage of students, like Ronnie, will suffer through an irrelevant and humiliating school experience.

What Ronnie and Brandon intuitively understood was their "place" in the elitism of the schools they attended and the lack of connection between schooling and everyday life. Even when they studied algebra and geometry, for example, they saw little relevance for their carpentry. "I had to learn it all over again when I started working," Brandon explained. The school Brandon and Ronnie attended operated under the logic that if students learn a body of general skills, these skills can be transferred to a variety of work situations when the need arises. The skills are taught as isolated subtasks and evaluated by a student's ability to successfully perform the task when called upon. The concept of employing skills in appropriate contexts appears irrelevant in most schools (Raizen, 1989). Brandon and Ronnie were put off by this decontextualized drill on fragmented little skills. Drawing upon their experiences, they quickly understood my explanation of the modernist cognitive illness with its privileging of mind over body and its fragmentation of knowledge in a way that separates schools from the world in which people live and work.

As I write this essay about a curriculum theory that addresses the elitism/class-bias that shapes the education of the poor and marginalized, I cannot help but personalize the ideas as they relate to Ronnie and Brandon. What kind of education would have spoken to them and addressed their needs? What curricular arrangements would have made schooling meaningful in their lives? As educators, how do we act upon our understandings of the elitism, class-bias, and fragmentation that undermine our democratic yearnings for meaningful change? These are the question that form the conceptual infrastructure for this essay—a piece that offers some concrete notions about critically grounded curricular reform. Critical scholars are often accused of not being sufficiently specific about their proposals for democratic school reform. While attempting to avoid an authoritarian blueprint for the reform of schools, the essay offers a tentative proposal for one way of acting on our critical and democratic imperative in a curricular context— the integration of academic and vocational education. I hope that Ronnie and Brandon and their colleagues in the trades would approve.

THINKING ABOUT CURRICULAR INTEGRATION FOR ALL STUDENTS

In the integrated programs that now exist, possibilities for profound educational reform abound. Teachers loosened from the chains of top-down bureaucratic management discover surprising connections between academic and vocational content. Academic teachers often realize for the first time the teaching methods and the unique forms of motivation offered by vocational teachers. Vocational teachers in their collaborations with academic teachers discover windows through which they can contextualize vocational skills with academic knowledge. Long standing barriers between vocational and academic teachers are hurdled and in many situations the routine and boredom of the traditional school is shattered by integrative innovation. As students study vocational paths in an integrated manner, they take field trips, listen to talks from business and (too infrequently) labor leaders, and work in internships. New interest is generated in future occupations and the vocational consequences of curricular choices. Teachers come to realize the negative effects of their isolation from one another and of the isolation of their students from the outside world of business and politics. So far, these experiments in academic and vocational integration have provided a veritable seminar in the educational imagination for teachers and students alike (Beck, 1991; Grubb et al., 1991).

Discussions of academic and vocational integration have typically revolved around the reform of vocational education. The way integration will be viewed here, however, will concern the reform of education in general, both vocational and academic programs. Proponents point out that integration forces schools to reduce class size, improve student counseling, provide coherent programs of courses, offer greater contact between teachers and students, and create closer relationships with social institutions outside of school. Teachers in integrated programs are forced to confront and act to remedy the liabilities of the traditional organization of school—including the fragmentations of curriculum from students' lives and of schooling from the world outside of school. With such understandings, teachers in integrated settings are more prone to consider methodological innovations. Academic teachers, for example, find that the vocational connection provides the context in which engaging student projects that connect academic theory with vocational practice naturally emerge. Work education takes on new meaning in such situations as it positions teachers and students in closer contact with life than they have ever \ experienced in school settings. As they gain an authentic connection to the lived world, teachers and students come to recognize far more clearly the academic, vocational, sociopolitical, and cognitive capacities that competent and morally courageous students and workers must possess. Such a recognition can serve to construct a revolutionary consciousness, a way of seeing that will not allow the world to remain the same (Grubb et al., 1991).

Integration will require special types of teachers with special insights and abilities. The fragility of such an innovation becomes apparent when one thinks of how easily the process can be destroyed by administrators and teachers without a vision of the larger purposes of integration. For example, vocational instructors who continue to teach narrow job skills without concern for student appreciation of the academic principles that contextualize them will undermine an integrated curriculum. Academic teachers who view vocational instruction condescendingly and refuse to grant credit for "applied academic classes" will destroy any chance for success. Teachers who enjoy their neat and tidy Madeline Hunter lesson plans and their coherent and orderly courses may pose a problem for integrated programs. In light of such threats, integration demands a reconceptualized form of teacher education. Academic teachers must become more familiar with work education issues such as production processes, the activity-based teaching methods of sophisticated vocational programs, and the vocational decisions that all students face. Vocational teachers will require greater involvement in the academic disciplines most relevant to their vocational fields, as well as more study of the social and political dimensions of work. All teachers will need more experience in cooperative curriculum development grounded in a multidimensional understanding of educational purpose (Copa & Tebbenhoss, 1990; Beck, 1991).

With teachers who possess a sense of purpose and a democratic vision of integration, a major offensive can be launched against the class-based and race-based segregation of students within existing schools. The bifurcation of vocational and academic students has resulted in a division between college-bound and work-bound students. Of course, vocational courses are heavily populated by students of the lower socioeconomic classes, highlighting the unconscionable class divisions within schools. The integration of academic and vocational education means that everyone take vocational education. No longer would vocation-based experiences carry a stigma of low status. Well-informed teachers could sophisticate vocation-based classes in such a way that students who thought of themselves as academic would be induced to take them. On the other hand, students who thought of themselves as vocational would be induced to take academic courses that were integrated with concrete vocational experiences in such a way that would make them attractive.

Thus, integration can offer a vision of what American education can become, a practical strategy to address the class-bias that cripples the opportunities of children not born into middle class homes. For example, savvy teachers in charge of an integrated program might be able to make positive use of business participation in school life. Previous participation of business in education has been trivial at best and repressive at worst, with corporations and industries attempting to open "untapped markets" in classrooms or to indoctrinate students into ideological positions uncritical of the social abuses of business. In thoughtful, well-designed programs business people (along with representatives of labor) can "put their resources where their mouths are" and provide summer jobs and future employment to worthy students. They can reinforce the need for students to learn both academic and vocational competencies and put in concrete terms the relationship between school learning and other aspects of life. In their collaboration with integrated programs, business people can make sure that vapid work placement programs characterized by repetitive job experiences and simple-minded academic experiences become mistakes of the past (Grubb et al., 1991).

D U A L I S M S :   W H A T   A N D   H O W

Integration addresses a number of regressive modernist dualisms that serve to fragment reality. One of the most basic issues here involves addressing the distinction between knowing *what* and knowing *how*. Conventional wisdom positions this distinction as the separation of the learning of canonical knowledge through formalized teaching that is grounded on textbooks, lectures, and other materials, from learning by doing through first-hand experience. Those who are deemed capable by school authorities of learning the *what* are placed in academic tracks; those deemed capable of learning the *how* are placed in vocational tracks. Caught within the gravitational pull of this distinction are several other false binarisms, including the separations of theory and practice, thinking and doing, and learning principles and devising applications. When Hume, in the seventeenth century, proclaimed that he was giving up philosophy so he could go play billiards, he was referring to yet another dualism within this orbit: separating the abstract from the concrete is ill-advised because we often learn more about an abstract notion by analyzing its concrete expression. Indeed, one of the categories of post-formal thinking (see Kincheloe, 1995; Kincheloe & Steinberg, 1993) involves the ability to connect generalization and particularity in a way that grants observers a far more textured view of reality (Raizen, 1989).

Focusing on the context of work education, this modernist tendency for dualism exposes itself in the distinction between education and training. "Low-ability" students, the argument goes, are trained for specific tasks, while *true* education is reserved for the academically talented. The student who is trained for his or her vocation is incapable of grasping theory or understanding the whole. The trained student employs rule-of-thumb procedures, while the educated student invokes theory as he or she solves problems and reflects upon the process (Feinberg & Horowitz, 1990). Little reason exists to worry about the training of these "dullards"—the conventional wisdom has decided that they cannot be educated. On the basis of such beliefs the school curriculum is separated into different ability tracks and the vocational school is even physically separated from the academic school. Such a physical separation makes integration quite difficult, as academic and vocational teachers find themselves isolated from one another. Often, in their isolation, "us-and-them" relations develop (Hillison & Camp, 1985; Douglas, 1992).

When learning *what* is separated from learning *how*, the decontextualization of learning is justified. School knowledge is abstracted from the context in which it is learned and used, rendering the cultivation of post-formal modes of thinking impossible. It requires little argument to justify the notions that vocational preparation should involve the contextualizing influence of occupational processes. Even so, few educators have grasped the manner in which the dualisms serve to exacerbate learning pathologies in American schools. The Norwegian root word of "crazy" is *krasa*, which means fragmented, the separation of a whole that belongs together. Indeed, the panoply of dualisms to which we have made reference is nothing if not crazy. A critical pedagogy of work that integrates academic and vocational education seeks to end the crazy injustice that designates the poor and nonwhite as vocational students who are subsequently trained to fit into a repressive workplace.

John Dewey contended that the integration of academic and vocational education in American schools was directly related to the question of what type of life humans would produce in a technological civilization. Dewey understood that the act of academic and vocational integration signified a number of important understandings, including an appreciation of the subtle ways injustice is perpetuated at a tacit institutional level—a realization that present understandings of cognition do not adequately account for manual expressions of intelligence, and a cognizance of the fact that teaching methodology must be revolutionized. Dewey's symbiotic view of knowledge (as opposed to the dualist epistemological tradition) laid the foundation for a democratic society that valued both hand and brain, learning *how* and learning *what*, and forms of knowing emerging from various subcultures, including the subjugated knowledge of the poor and dispossessed (Wirth, 1983).

Now that the Perkins Act has mandated that academic and vocational education be integrated, the concept has new appeal and possibility (Hudelson, 1992). Even mainstream educators are arguing that vocational education can make academics more concrete and understandable, and that academic education can point out the vocational ramifications of all forms of learning (Beck, 1991). In this context, for example, vocational students in agriculture study environmental science, gaining insights into the connections between farming and various forms of pollution. At the same time these students might study the politics of environmental damage, exploring the ways that powerful agriculture-related businesses keep government from interfering with their ecologically insensitive practices. Home economics students uncover personal insights, studying the family from both psychological and sociological perspectives. In the course of such a study, students might examine the politics of the debate over family values, analyzing the assumptions that shape the various political positions. Auto mechanics students find physics and mathematics to be more meaningful and even easier to learn when considered in relation to cars (Rehm, 1989). In this situation, students might also explore the interesting history of automobile safety from both a technical and political perspective, analyzing the way the power wielded by U.S. auto manufacturers delayed the implementation of safety features.

This curriculum theory of academic and vocational education brings together five features in the attempt to address the rupture between learning what and learning how: academic learning, vocational learning, critical social concerns, worksite placement, and post-formal thinking. Sensitive to the social and economic context in which it must operate, this critically grounded integration cultivates an awareness of the relationship between its goals and the existence of the postmodern hyperreality and the emerging post-Fordist economy. Dedicated to the critical goals of social and economic justice, good work, and the analysis of power relations, the integrated curriculum utilizes experiential knowledge gained from worksite placement of students to help produce workers and citizens of all varieties who are capable of sophisticated analysis. Figure 1 may help us understand this curriculum theory.

T H E   V A L U E
O F   V O C A T I O N A L   E D U C A T I O N

As we explore the various dimensions of this theory of integration, the traditional question concerning what academic education can do for its stepchild, vocational education, is turned on its head. The question of what vocational education can do for academic learning focuses our attention on the reform of high school for all students, whether they be college bound or work bound. Vocational education by its nature addresses the traditional criticisms of academic education—its aridity, boredom, teacher dominance, lecture-centeredness, and student passivity. At its best, vocational education requires more participatory instructional strategies, promotes activities that are intrinsically interesting, stimulates cooperative rather than competitive learning, and provides more possibility for student initiative.

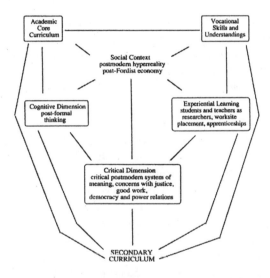

Figure 1: Critical Postmodern Integration of Academic and Vocational Education

Vocational education should not be seen as just another set of courses competing for a student's time. Such education should be carefully integrated with academic learning in a manner that facilitates young people's ability to understand and apply what they are learning in the academic core curriculum. Through this practical application of school knowledge, theoretical and conceptual ideas can gain new meaning for both students and teachers. Once integration takes place, teaching methods can never stay the same, as academic teachers begin to appropriate vocational strategies. Project-directed methods pursued in a specific context help academic teachers to transcend the decontextualized purposelessness that afflicts the high school. With this understanding, academic teachers begin to realize that the skills of general academic courses are not as transferable as educators have been comfortable thinking. Research seems to indicate that the degree to which academic or vocational experiences can be generalized depends on the resemblance between the conditions under which the learning takes place and the conditions under which it is to be applied. Of course, the point that once again emerges involves the context specificity of all learning (Copa &Tebbenhoff, 1990; Grub et al., 1991).

L E A R N I N G   A C A D E M I C   S K I L L S   I N   C O N T E X T

Students of cognition who examine learning in context (situated cognition) have criticized traditional cognitive science for its individualistic focus—that is, its exclusive concern with individual mental activity. In this isolation, traditional cognitive science has marginalized the wider social and material context in which thinking is implanted Such cognitive perspectives have led to schooling practices that involve the teacher as information deliverer, student as fact gatherer, and assessment as the testing of individual performance in a narrow setting. Utilizing anthropological and sociological ways of inquiring, students of situated cognition recognize the inadequacy of individualized and fragmented schooling. They realize that the world of the shop floor, hospital, or the family is a cosmos of constant change and ambiguity.

A critical postmodern pedagogy of work that integrates academic and vocational education understands that profound learning demands an education that takes place in a context that matters to the learner. Marginally literate adults enrolled in a workplace reading program experienced far greater improvement in job related reading than in general reading. Study after study indicates that learning which takes place in a meaningful context is more profound than decontextualized learning (Raizen, 1989). A critical curriculum of integration reorients schooling in a way that meaningfully contextualizes lessons in relation to work. Students learn academic skills in a vocational context where they can learn by doing with the freedom to profit from their mistakes (Harp, 1992; Schon, 1987). For example, a recent study analyzed a class attempting to teach students with weak math and reading skills to become electronics technicians. Traditional approaches provided remedial drills in math and reading before introducing students to the subject of electronics. In the program under analysis, Thomas Sticht, the instructor, began the course with what students already knew about flashlights, lamps, and radios. As students inspected the electrical devices, Sticht pointed out the systems-related and functional features of the equipment. Then in the *context* of these familiar devices, reading, writing, diagramming, mathematics, critical thinking, problem detection, and problem solving were integrated with the teaching of technical electronics (Raizen & Colvin, 1991).

The way individuals learn in the context of their jobs is very different from the form learning takes in the traditional school. Not only, of course, is most workplace learning group-based and cooperative, it relies on the use of simple and complex tools. In the work context, most workers, including even illiterate workers, acquire mathematical skills and formulate creative mechanisms to solve math problems. Studies of the computational skills of unschooled children who sell merchandise in the street markets of Recife, Brazil, indicate that they constantly make complex mathematical calculations in their businesses. When confronted with the same problems in a paper and pencil school-type test, they were lost. Indeed, their attempts to follow school-based math teaching methods disrupted the children's ability to compute. Such findings don't mean that we should scrap traditional methods of teaching math, but they do tell us that we should seriously reconsider them. The formal algorithms taught in schools need to be learned in context in a way that expands an individual's thought processes so that problems can be identified and solved. Such an approach would revolutionize the teaching of math as it provided meaning to math lessons. Academic and vocational integration offers the context needed to initiate such changes.

M A K I N G   A C A D E M I C   S K I L L S   U S A B L E

The integration of academic and vocational education requires curriculum developers to consider how academic skills can be understood and used by students and teachers. Such consideration necessitates a brief reference to modernist and postmodernist epistemologies—objectivism and constructivism. In subjectivism, facts are what they are, and truth can always be discerned by an appeal to the facts. A constructivist view of knowledge sees individuals constructing their meanings and interpretations of facts in light of their own experiences and contexts. The objectivist or modernist view of knowledge is a one-truth epistemology that has affected all aspects of Western life, education being no exception (Schon, 1987). Since objectivist knowledge (like a child's conception of pre-Columbian North America) is predefined and waiting to be discovered "out there," what use is it to teach speculative and interpretive strategies? Schools of the post-Enlightenment era emphasized not the production of knowledge but the learning of that which had already been defined as knowledge. Students of modernism's one-truth epistemology are treated like one-trick ponies, rewarded only for short-term retention of certified truths.

Teachers learn in their "educational science" courses that knowledge is acquired in a linear skill or subskill process. Pre-identified in the context of adult logic, the linear process is imposed on children in a manner that focuses teacher/parent attention away from the child's constructions of reality, away from the child's point of view. Thus, children's answers are often "wrong"; when actually given their point of view, the wrong answer may indicate ingenuity.

As a critical constructivist (see Kincheloe, 1993), I believe that learning is a form of "worldmaking." Engaging in thousands of acts of attention and inattention, naming, decoding, interpreting, and setting and transgressing borders, workers make their worlds and their know-how. Acting on this understanding, constructivist teachers avoid top-down curriculum designs where expert knowledge is transferred to students who memorize it. Instead, they teach for understanding and application, in the process researching students' original constructions of the subject at hand. A critical postmodern curriculum of integration takes student experience seriously, as its teachers attempt to discern the ways students give meaning to their lives and the role that schooling and work might play in that process.

The integration of academic and vocational education is connected to the core of this process, as it creates a context that allows schooling to connect with student interest. Operating in an integrated curriculum, a group of inner city high school students inquires into the forces that keep them out of the job market. In the process, they read literature on the relationships that connect work, racism, and class bias. Part of their inquiry involves conducting an ethnographic study of unemployed young people in their community, searching for patterns that grant insight into the origins, nature, and solutions to inner city unemployment. Not only are such students learning to read, write, communicate, and conduct research, their interest in school is piqued, and they are learning to think in a critical, a postformal manner. In addition, they begin to see that their lives are worthy of study, that they are intelligent, and that school learning could possibly play a role in improving the quality of their lives (MacLeod, 1987).

In harmony with advocates of situated learning, high school students scream for a real world context. Students studying physics in a critical, integrated curriculum might seek apprentice-like experiences with a mechanical engineer at a local factory. A deal could be worked out between the firm and the school, designating particular times for engineer volunteers to work with a few students. During the apprenticeship, students would shadow the engineer at work, learning specific ways that the professional incorporated various forms of knowledge into his or her practice. Close cooperation between the firm and the school would inform the engineer of the specifics of the high school curriculum so that he or she could tailor the apprenticeship to directly connect with the students' experiences.

Such an apprenticeship would be part of a curriculum of experience that connects the needs and concerns of students to conceptual/theoretical understandings and to the insights gained from a practical context. Such an education becomes indistinguishable from everyday life with little discontinuity between daily activities and the learning of work-related skills and sophisticated forms of cognition. Many of the work-related activities in this integrated curriculum situate learning as something that is undertaken for its immediate use and value, rather than as something required for a degree or for next year's class. The learning that takes place does not proceed in a linear order that is determined by a curriculum guide; indeed, outside authority has little to do with the activities of students and teachers. Stories are very important in the integrated curriculum, as they share experiences, exemplify and personalize learning, and interpret the relationship between school knowledge and the life experiences students and teachers bring with them. When apprenticeship-like activities are connected with a critical integrated curriculum, possibilities for cognitive growth are unparalleled.

A C T I V I T Y ,   C O N C E P T , A N D   C U L T U R E

Senta Raizen argues that in a vocational learning situation, the work activity being studied, the conceptual device being employed to study the activity, the cultural context formed by the dynamics of the workplace, and the ways of seeing characteristics of the people involved in such work must all be understood by a successful student. Activity, concept, and culture are, thus, interdependent, as students in a critical integrated program come to see the dynamic interaction of these components in all work situations. Learning conceived this way becomes, in a sense, a process of enculturation as students are introduced into a community with its own language, knowledge, ways of seeing, and conceptual tools (Raizen, 1989). A critical postmodern pedagogy of work disrupts the smooth functioning of such an enculturation, sensing that the term "enculturation" possesses a dangerous underside. Without a careful questioning, enculturation can come to mean adjustment to the world as it is. Such a vocational enculturation must always question the status quo in terms of a critical vision of a democratic, multicultural community.

Academic and vocational integration would allow for the construction of an educational situation that is aware of contextual factors in all learning. Students, for example, studying economic justice and democratic forms of work in an academically and vocationally integrated economics class would need to realize that, in the context of the existing American workplace, such an idea is viewed suspiciously. Understanding such a context, students would need to research the way workers deal with regressive management. In the process, students would develop strategies designed to address alienated workplaces in a way that is politically smart and contextually savvy. They could become agents of change who are aware of the fear their position engenders and of the conflict it could ignite.

At the same time, such students would come to understand the low regard this society holds for a curriculum that involves making a living. Detractors connect such studies with courses in underwater basket weaving, window cleaning, or mop jockeying. In their effort to ridicule the unfortunate tendency for "over-vocationalization," they over-generalize. To argue that concerns with making a living have no place in a liberal education is to contend that education has no connection to the larger social context. Traditional educational philosophy has often associated training for making a living with "dense" students (Beck, 1991). Education for the "less able" child included pottery, outdoor pursuits, weaving, woodworking, metalwork, domestic science and motherhood, and many other activities. Such activities have been thought to involve little or no reasoning and should be recommended for people with "limited intellect" (Carr, 1984). Students who study vocational topics will have to contend with these prejudices, not only in their education, but also in their work lives.

A critical integrated curriculum rejects these expressions of socioeconomic class prejudice. Respecting the intellectual and creative potential of *all* learners, the advocates of critical integration recognize that crafts and trades involve higher orders of intellect at both the perceptual and bodily levels. Such advocates refuse to validate the common assumption within the culture of formal education that the theoretical ways of knowing of the academic disciplines are innately superior to the practical ways of knowing of the vocations (Rehm, 1989, p. 110). When one knows how to perform a certain task, he or she is able to deploy strategies that help accomplish a particular purpose. Traditionally, psychologists and philosophers have not regarded such activity as manifestations of intellect. Any curriculum theory that fails to acknowledge the educational importance of the practical knowledge of the trades and crafts is guilty not only of pedagogical ignorance but of class bias as well.

When teachers make the attempt to cultivate practical knowledge, changes begin to occur in the everyday life of schools. For example, when reading teachers work with high school students with low reading skills, connecting reading improvement with the attempt to gain practical knowledge, they begin to reverse the failure of traditional remediation. Reading-to-do and reading-to-learn strategies make reading more enjoyable, in the process better developing general reading skills. Low-skill students fascinated with riding and repairing motorcycles can improve their reading dramatically when a teacher assigns material on this topic. The teacher's role does not end with the assignment, as he or she monitors progress and assigns students activities that expand their ability to conceptualize, interpret, apply, contextualize, and understand. Using postformal thinking (Kincheloe & Steinberg, 1993) as a benchmark, teachers connect reading improvement with cognitive development.

In this manner the curriculum of integration attempts to focus attention on the cognitive process—it attempts to induce teachers and students to think about their thinking, the connections between their academic knowledge and their practical knowledge. As students learn both *about* work and how to do it, they begin to concentrate on the transformative possibility of their experiences. Drawing upon critical democratic insights to analyze work and work education, critical students and teachers make explicit the types of thinking that ground repressive and antidemocratic perspectives. In this context students and teachers involved in a critical integrated curriculum studying home construction could analyze the political assumptions embedded in questions concerning shelter. Guided by their political concerns, they could analyze the politics of zoning laws in the local community, questions of homelessness, and problems with building codes. No aspect of work education would be studied in isolation, apart from questions of human values, power, and democracy (Simon, Dippo, & Schenke, 1991).

THE SPECIFICS OF INTEGRATION — THE NECESSITY OF TEACHER COLLABORATION

Integration, no matter what form it takes, should strengthen the teaching of all subjects. When adeptly executed, integration should make history, literature, and the social sciences come alive for previously unmotivated students. As long as such programs are grounded on a critical democratic understanding and are well-planned, locations such as an automobile garage can become places of unique and profound learning. Indeed, an integrated garage can become not merely a place to fix cars but a venue where physics, chemistry, and mathematics are studied in relation to cars. The physics of torque, the chemistry of gasoline as fuel, and mathematics of horsepower could provide compelling experiences for all students, especially ones never engaged by the traditional methods of schooling (Freeman, 1992; Feinberg & Horowitz, 1990).

One of the most important methodological features emerging in the integrated classroom involves the ability to move back and forth from the concrete to the abstract in the quest for deeper levels of understanding. Research seems to consistently show that students understand more quickly and more profoundly when they begin with concrete examples and then move to abstract theoretical principles. In one research study, a vocational teacher taught his electronics class to draw a graphic illustration of integrated circuits and then to perform the task in actual practice. Many students were not able to accomplish the exercise. When the teacher asked his class to begin with the concrete (the actual practice) and then move to the abstract (the graphic representation of what they had done), almost all of the students were able to successfully complete the task (Wirth, 1983; Packer, 1992; Mjelde, 1987).

The integration of academic and vocational education requires teacher collaboration. Teachers working together is a relatively rare sight in contemporary schools, as teachers retreat to their private domains. The benefits of collaboration become quickly apparent, as teachers better appreciate the relationships between courses, the common purpose that unites them with other professionals, the meaning of deeper levels of understanding, postformal thinking, and the relationship between good work and educational purpose. Collaboration does not mean that academic specialists would become interchangeable with vocational specialists, but it does mean that each would gain a far greater understanding of what the other does. With this understanding, and as they attend to the diverse aspects of a critical postmodern education and the synergisms created when one aspect is considered in relation to the others, their ability to turn out good students and smart workers will dramatically increase.

INTEGRATION SO FAR

With the passage of the Perkins Act, and with its mandate to integrate academic and vocational curricula, integration has gained momentum. Hopefully, the movement will avoid the fate of other progressive reforms that have lost their purposes and their critical edges in a sea of bureaucratic rules and regulations. Even in the early stages of the integration movement, we can identify unfortunate trends: schools rushing to meet the requirements of the Perkins Act by devising programs that are integrative in name only; the tendency for large industries and businesses to shift the emphasis of fledgling programs away from concerns with economic justice and democratic work toward more traditional attempts to adjust young workers to work as it presently exists; and the production of integrated curriculum materials that subvert the more critical and complex aspects of integration.

Nevertheless, promising examples of integration exist. In many schools vocational and academic instructors team-teach applied academic courses. Observers note that in the best of these classes, it is very difficult to differentiate the academic from the vocational teacher. Both instructors are familiar with the academic content and the vocational application and easily move back and forth between the concrete and the theoretically abstract. In such classes students are engaged and highly motivated, as teachers offer compelling reasons for attending to what is going on. Students are constantly moving between seatwork in academic classrooms to vocational applications in adjacent laboratories.

Teachers and students in field-based integration projects in construction have integrated their understandings of the world of work (including such domains as drafting, marketing, home economics, and horticulture) and their academic skills (for example, math, English, and science).

Critical dimensions of integrated programs seem to be more common in home economics than in other vocational areas. One program in family and technology, for example, examines the interrelationship between technological development and the work of the family. In such a context, students and teachers explore the ways that families construct meanings, develop values, and produce patterns of thinking. Another example of academic and vocational integration involves students learning the technology of filmmaking as they learn to perform research in various content areas. In one such program, high school students won several prizes in an international university-level film contest. In all of the examples of integration, there is one common thread: students and teachers were learning how to learn.

The possibilities for new curricula and methodological innovations are endless in programs that critically integrate academic and vocational education. Students and teachers have the possibility of opening new conversations about work and its role in their lives, and its relation to various aspects of physical and social reality. Students, especially those from economically disadvantaged homes, have a chance to escape the oppressive tracking system that delegates them to second class citizenship in America's schools. I envision a working class high school student deadened by eleven years of being labeled a failure entering an integrated auto mechanics/physics class. Fascinated by engines, he has become adept at auto repair and is excited about the new class. Entering a classroom of untracked, heterogeneous students, he is intimidated until he realizes that, for the first time since he started to school, he holds the valued knowledge—he is the student who understands the workings of the engine and its component parts. The instructors ask him to help his more economically privileged peers with their attempt to identify the parts of the engine. In this situation he is the smart one—for the first time he experiences school success. The effect is dramatic. His genius is recognized—Ronnie and Brandon's never was.

REFERENCES

Beck, R. (1991). *General education: Vocational and academic collaboration.* (Berkeley, CA: NCRVE).

Carr, H. (1984). We integrated the academics. *Vocational Education,* 59 (2), 34-36.

Copa, G. & Tebbenhoff, E. (1990). *Subject matter of vocational education: In pursuit of foundations.* (Berkeley, CA: NCRVE).

Douglas, A. (1992). Mending the rift between academic and vocational education. *Educational Leadership,* 49 (6), 42-43.

Feinberg, W. & Horowitz, B. (1990). Vocational education and the equality of opportunity. *Journal of Curriculum Studies,* 22 (2), 188-192.

Freeman, M. (1992). Food for thought. *Vocational Educational Journal,* 67 (8), 28-29, 71.

Grubb, N., Davis, G., Lum, J., Phihal, J., & Morgaine, C. (1991). *The cunning hand, the cultured mind: Models for integrating vocational and academic education.* (Berkeley, California: NCRVE).

Harp, L. (1992). Scuttled program's work, skill themes enjoying resurgence. *Education Week* (September 23), 1, 13.

Herrnstein, R., & Murray, C. (1994). *The bell curve: Intelligence and class structure in American life.* New York: The Free Press.

Hillison, J., & Camp, W. (1985). History and future of the dual school system for vocational education. *Journal of Vocational and Technical Education,* 2 (1), 48-56.

Hudelson, D. (1992). Roots of reform: Tracing the path of workforce education. *Vocational Education Journal,* 67 (7), 28-29, 69.

Kincheloe, J. (1993). *Toward a critical politics of teacher thinking: Mapping the postmodern.* (Westport, CT: Bergin and Garvey).

Kincheloe, J. (1995). *Toil and trouble: Good work, smart workers, and the integration of academic and vocational education.* (New York: Peter Lang).

Kincheloe, J., & Steinberg, S. (1993). A tentative description of post-formal thinking: The critical confrontation with cognitive theory. *Harvard Educational Review,* 63 (3), 296-320.

MacLeod, J. (1987). *Ain't no makin' it; Leveled aspirations in a low-income neighborhood.* (Boulder, CO: Westview Press).

Mjelde, L. (1987). From hand to mind. In D. Livingstone & contributors, *Critical pedagogy and cultural power*. (South Hadley, MA: Bergin and Garvey).

Packer, A. (1992). School to work: Helping students learn a living. *Education Week* (May 27), p. 28.

Raizen, S. (1989). *Reforming education for work: A cognitive science perspective*. (Berkeley, CA: NCRVE).

Raizen, S. & Colvin, R. (1991). Apprenticeships: A cognitive-science view. *Education Week* (December 11), p. 26.

Rehm, M. (1989). Emancipatory vocational education: Pedagogy for the work of individuals and society. *Journal of Education*, 171 (3), 109-123.

Schon, D. (1987). *Educating the reflective practitioner*. (San Francisco, CA: Jossey-Bass Publishers).

Simon, R., Dippo, D., & Schenke, A. (1991). *Learning work: A critical pedagogy of work education*. (New York: Bergin and Garvey).

Wirth, A. (1983). *Productive work in industry and schools*. (Lanham, MD: University Press of America).

CHAPTER TWENTY-THREE

The Palace of the Peacock

Wilson Harris and the Curriculum in Troubled Times❖

Cameron McCarthy
University of Illinois—Champaign
1996

INTRODUCTION

> Proof like Doubt must seek the hidden wound in orders of complacency that mask opportunist codes of hollow survival. (Wilson Harris, "A note on the Genesis of the Guyana Quartet." 1985, p. 7)

This essay looks at postcolonial literature as a space for the exploration of difference, not simply as a problem, but as an opportunity for a conversation about establishing a normative basis for communicative action in the curriculum. I wish to talk about a communicative action or dialogue that might get us beyond the implacable categories of Eurocentrism and the reductive forms of multiculturalism—beyond the quaint particularisms of the Wild West and the Rest. By invoking postcolonial literature, I am pointing toward a redeployment of the vocabulary of difference that might help us to humanize an increasingly commodified, instrumental, and deeply invaded curriculum field. I use as an exemplar of this new materialist humanism (what one postcolonial author calls "the visualization of community"—Gilkes, 1975) the work of the Guyanes, philosophical novelist, Wilson Harris. I look at his (1960) novel, *The Palace of the Peacock*.

❖ This paper was awarded the Annual Macdonald Prize at the September 1995 JCT Conference in Monteagle, Tennessee. The prize is offered in commemoration of James B. Macdonald's significant contributions to the curriculum field in the area of phenomenological and reflective inquiry

Harris' urgings to write began, interestingly, when as a young man, he worked for the Guyanese government as a land surveyor charting the interior of Guyana. Harris reports running around the forests of Guyana reading lots of Hegel and Heidegger. *The Palace of the Peacock* is a picaresque or quest novel, much like Herman Melville's *Moby Dick*, in which the main characters are pitted against nature in the journey of their lives. But in Harris' novel, nature is problematized. It is the fecund source of metaphors and allegories about the contested lives of human beings, their oppression of each other, and the open possibilities that reside within collective action and communal spirit and determination.

T H E   M O T I F   O F   P O S S I B I L I T Y

Our literatures did not passively accept the changing fortunes of their transplanted languages...Soon they ceased to be mere transatlantic reflections. At times they have been the negation of the literatures of Europe; more often they have been a reply. (Octavio Paz, *In Search of the Present*—Nobel Lecture, 1990, p. 5)

Some years ago I attempted to outline the possibilities of validating or proving the truths that may occupy certain twentieth century works of fiction that diverge, in peculiar degrees from canons of realism. I sought such proof or validation by bringing the fictions I had in mind into parallel with profound myth that lies apparently eclipsed in largely forgotten so-called savage cultures. (Wilson Harris, "A note on the Genesis of THE GUYANA QUARTET," 1985, p. 7)

I have come to the feeling that there are certain words, phrases, terms that I do not like, even when I am the one using them in my own writing: words and terms such as "origins," "center," "the best," "the brightest," "hierarchy," "pure," "Western," "civilization," even..."culture" (although I am sure to use the latter several times before this essay is finished). These words relay and circulate a certain kind of hypocrisy of completeness and self-sufficiency in curriculum theory and design and in the practical matters of everyday human life. Educational theorists and policymakers invested in these words—these lines of demarcation—now stand clumsily in the doorways of cultural commutation that link human groups to vast underground networks of feeling, sensibility, and promise. Words such as "origin," "Western," and "center" have led us to blocked visions, suspended horizons, and ineluctable retreats. They serve to repress interlocked histories and trestles of association. They paste over the fault lines that have, for sometime now, ruptured the undersides of imposed identities deep beneath the glistening surfaces of "Europe," "Africa," "Asia," the "Caribbean," the "Orient," and the "Occident."

So here we are, almost at the butt-end of the twentieth century, fighting old, stale atavistic internecine wars in the heart of the curriculum field and in the trenches of educational institutions. I guess it was Henry Kissinger who said that the battles in academic life are as vicious as they are because the stakes are so small. Maybe Old Henry is right, and it is partly our deep investment in words like "center" and "Western" that has gotten us in our present curriculum trouble—our present impasse between the Wild West and the rest of the world. In this new world order, each person grazes on his own grass, so to speak, and in a surrealist sense, turns the key on his own door. These lines of psychic tension and demarcation are powerfully registered in current debates over multiculturalism and curriculum reform. These debates radically oppose the literature and cultural production associated with the canon to the new literatures of postcolonial writers and indigenous minority novelists and poets. It is assumed by some of the more conservative thinkers, such as William Bennett (1984) and Dinesh D'Souza, that East is East and West is West and never should or must canonical and noncanonical literatures meet in the school curriculum. Some others, more reformist theorists, such as Molefi Asante (1993), assume that since the dominant curriculum thrives on the marginalization of the culture of minorities that minority identities can only be fully redeemed by replacing the Western and Eurocentric bias of the curriculum with non-Western minority literature.

Of course, when talking about this economy of oppositions, one cannot forget the rather unfortunate pronouncements of Fredric Jameson (1986) in an article he published in *Social Text* some years ago entitled "Third World Literature in the Era of Multinational Capitalism." In the article Jameson asserted that third world literary texts were "necessarily allegorical" and should be read as "national allegories." According to him, third world fiction lacks one critical historical variable that helps to establish the modern Western realist novel, namely

> a radical split between private and the public, between the poetic and the
> political, between what we have come to think of as the public world of classes,
> of the economic, and of secular political power: in other words, Freud versus
> Marx. (1986, p. 69)

Without this split, third world fiction can all be reduced to a single narrative paradigm: "the story of the private individual destiny is always an allegory of the embattled situation of the public third-world culture and society" (p. 65). You can see how far we have come here since Attila the Hun. This is not to say that Jameson's intuitions about third world fiction are entirely off the mark—Harris' work is after all deeply allegorical—but Jameson's problems begin when he takes a partial insight and recklessly presses it out into a totalizing usurping epiphany—filling up the periphery and the globe.

I must admit that I have reached a kind of exhaustion with a certain usage of the language of difference—a quiet weariness with the language of negation and fatalistic oppositions. This essay represents a new effort to articulate a motif of possibility – a pragmatics of curriculum that is socially extended, but at the same time deeply invested in the fictive worlds created in postcolonial writing. In these imperfect worlds of imagination, literature leads the way and sociology clumsily follows and, happily, without the burden of "controls." It is an attempt to, in Harris' words "visualize a community"—a community of lost or broken souls—the community of Donna Haraway's cyborgs, of Gloria Anzaldua's border people, of Gabriel Marquez' El Macondo, or the folk of Harris' Mariella, dwelling in the interior of Guyana—the mythical rain forests in which the *Cauda Pavonis* or *The Palace of the Peacock* might be glimpsed.[1]

I believe that the challenge of multiculturalism is the critical challenge of curriculum in postmodern times --it is the challenge of living with each other in a world of difference. I believe that postcolonial literature—even more so than postcolonial literary theory and criticism—has sought to foreground this challenge of living in a world of difference in late-century society, and as such presents us with fictive maps in which power and communication are conceived as operating horizontally, not vertically, not top down as in encoding-decoding, but rhizomatically in the sense that often cabalistic passageways link the mighty and the meek on shared and complex terrains. And some times the meek prevail. For example, in Wilson Harris' *The Palace of the Peacock*, tired of abuse, Mariella—Arawak woman and colony—shoots Donne, the colonial oppressor. Her actions are that of a Shaman of the folk. The landscape of power is altered in the twinkling of an eye. Donne, we later discover, is that part of the folk reproductive of the old colonial will to power—the colonizer in the colonized— that Mariella as Shaman and representative of the folk will redefine. It is within the context of these asymmetrical relations of colonizer and colonized that this literature takes on special significance, but the matter is never straightforward as we will see in the example of Harris' novel.

HISTORICAL FILIATION OF THE POSTCOLONIAL NOVEL

Of course, the implications of this literature for curriculum cannot be grasped without some attempt to follow its materialist filiations, distributed as they are in the histories of classical and modern colonialism, but even more recently, since the sixties, in the footprints scattered across the late-twentieth century megalopolis—London, Toronto, New York, Paris, Mexico City. These footprints register the presence of the daughters of the dust, the migratory waves of humanity now conquering the West. The state of exile is also the state of rupture of old paradigms, of lost selves, and new affiliations, the locus of emergent self-discovery. In its most compelling forms, postcolonial literature struggles to embrace the old and the new, multiple worlds, divided loyalties, and passionate desires of the Other. As the Sri Lankan writer, Michael Ondaatje (1992), puts it in *The English Patient*, this literature celebrates those "nationals...deformed by nation states [who]...wished to remove the clothing of our countries (pp. 138-139). These literary works document the other side of the postmodern—multicultural worlds from which there are no longer exits for retreat. Postcolonial writers are fabricating the new subjects of history and are seeking to install these new subjects within the folds of contemporary imagination. These new subjects are patched together and fitted out with leaky souls. They are flawed or broken human creatures—born in the crucible of cultural modernization, not at all, as some like Roger Kimbal (1990) or Dinesh D'Souza (1991) might argue, stilted prototypes of sociological tracts singing hollow histories of oppression and damnation. And they are not, for that matter, as Afrocentric writers like Mike Awkward (1989) might suggest, existing in some prelapsarian past standing up before Adam and Eve.

Emergent postcolonial literatures register a new structure of feeling, of overlapping and cascading epochs of time, of drifting space, of free associations, of the ample desires and insatiable appetites of the center and the periphery rolled into one. As such they offer a new late-twentieth century paradigm of curriculum, a poetics of a curriculum without borders. What we are witnessing at one level is the very transformation of the canons of English, French, and Spanish literatures, as Pico Iyer (1993) maintains in a recent TIME magazine article:

> Where not long ago a student of the modern English novel would probably have been weaned on Graham Greene, Evelyn Waugh and Aldous Huxley, now he will more likely be taught Rushdie and Okri and Mo—which is fitting in an England where many students' first language is Cantonese or Urdu. ...Thus the shelves of English bookstores are becoming as noisy and polyglot and many hued as the English streets. And the English language is being revolutionized from within. Abiku stalks us on the page, and triad gangs and "filmi" stars. Hot spices are entering English, and tropical birds and sorcerers; readers who are increasingly familiar with sushi and samosas are now learning to live with molue buses and manuku hedges. (Iyer, 1993, p. 70)

TRANSFORMING THE CANON, WILSON HARRIS AND THE NEW COMMUNITY

And I saw that Donne was aging in the most remarkable misty way. (Wilson Harris, *The Palace of the Peacock*, p. 49)

What might a community of lost or broken souls tell us about curriculum in late-century America? This is the question that Wilson Harris (1989) poses in his essay, "Literacy and the Imagination," where he suggests that solutions to the problem of literacy in the Americas must begin with the recognition of the inadequacy of programs of imposition such as agricultural extension programs and urban literacy projects that distrust the cultural resources that reside within the masses themselves. In other words, he argues that educators tend to have what he calls "illiterate imaginations." Harris' observations on literacy point us in the direction of the resources of the folk—of the popular—the kind of cultural resources of interpretation and action that Paulo Freire (1970) discovers in his literacy work with the Brazilian peasants in Pedagogy of the Oppressed. And in another way, this is what Gloria Ladson-Billings and Annette Henry (1990) have been calling for in their notion of a "curriculum of relevance."

Harris has provided an enfleshment of an answer to the problem of "illiterate imaginations" in books like The Palace of the Peacock (1960), Whole Armour (1962), Companions of the Day and Night (1975), Da Silva da Silva's Cultivated Wilderness (1977), and Genesis of the Clowns (1977). I want here to focus on The Palace of the Peacock as a meditation on a broken community and its set of propositions about a possible reintegration of this community of lost souls. I want to suggest that the way Harris negotiates canonical notions of literary genre, form, characterization, narrative, and social vision has a lot to teach us about the practice of curriculum in the world of difference that has overtaken our social institutions, if not our social consciences. I should say that I turn here to Wilson Harris' The Palace of the Peacock, but I could have turned to Gabriel Garcia Marquez' One Hundred Years of Solitude (1970), or Jamaica Kincaid's Lucy (1990), or Salman Rushdie's Midnight Children (1981), Ben Okri's The Famished Road (1992), Caryl Phillips' Cambridge (1992), Michael Ondaatje's The English Patient (1992), or Toni Morrison's Beloved (1987) or Jazz (1992), or, finally, Nawal El Saadawi's God Dies By the Nile (1985). All these novels follow broadly a path of deflation of classical realism of the nineteenth century novel and an implosion of an overmastering or ruling narrating subject. Instead, they put in place the angular points of view of a polyglot cast of new characters, protean personalities and kaleidoscopic visions, open-ended possibilities, and journeys from confinement to transformation.

The vast majority of these authors, as Pico Iyer (1993) notes:

> are writers not of Anglo-Saxon ancestry, born more or less after the war and choosing to write in English [or Spanish or French]. All are situated at the crossroads from which they can reflect, and reflect on new forms of Mississippi Massala of our increasingly small, increasingly mongrel, increasingly mobile global village. Indians writing of a London that is more like Bombay than Bombay, Japanese novelists who cannot read Japanese, Chinese women evoking a China they have seen only in their mothers' stories—all amphibians who do not have an old and a new home so much as two half-homes simultaneously. (Iyer, 1993, p. 70)

Where is Wilson Harris to be placed among this motley crew of writers? Well, in some ways, he is a precursor. Like the writers mentioned above he was "born after the War." But the war that is a point of reference for him is the war that fed the often bitingly satirical poetry of the British war poets—Wilfred Owen, Siegfried Sassoon, and Robert Graves. It is, of course, World War I. Harris was born in Guyana in1921. He is, as Robert Fraser (1988) tells it, a child of mixed Amerindian, Indian, African, and European blood. He began his professional life as a scientist, a land surveyor, working on the mapping of the often tricky interior of Guyana. "Guiana" (Guyana) interestingly is an Amerindian word meaning "land of many waters." Waterfalls abound and many, like the majestic roaring Kaiteur Falls, charge the interior with a sense of terror and sublimity. It is the awesome nature of this terrain that served as an initial inspiration for Harris. Wandering about in the interior of Guyana, Harris spent enormous amounts of time reading Heidegger and Hegel and meditating on time and the psychic dimensions of human life and the way in which the unpredictable and surprising topography of the Guyanese interior landscape seems almost to insinuate itself into the human personality. The rich unpredictability of the Guyana interior, in part, precipitated his early writings as an imagistic poet of the interior (Fraser, 1988). But most of Harris' work, like *The Palace of the Peacock*, would be written and published in London.

It is the manipulation of imagery, of metaphor, and symbol that constitutes the central activity in *The Palace of the Peacock*. The novel, written in 1960, serves a larger purpose of putting to melody a rendezvous with history—a re-encounter between the colonizer and the colonized, indifferent times and different places, in multiple personas, in real time, in dream and myth, in life and death. Together, the colonizer and the colonized must share a mutual responsibility for the future which, in *The Palace of the Peacock*, can only be glimpsed or constructed after an excruciating revisiting of the past. In the novel, Harris attempts to place twentieth century humanity in conversation with those who have been designated as the people of "savage cultures." But it is these same savage cultures of the interior of Guyana that support the weight of civilized existence in the coastal suburbs. To tell the story of this kind, in which multiple cultural systems of interpretations dialogue with each other, Harris must rent the fabric of the classical realist novel. Instead of the fiction of omniscience with its privileged narrator sitting on top of a hierarchy of discourses (see, for example, C.L.R. James' [1978] *Mariners, Renegades and Castaways*, in which James talks about the bureaucratic deployment of characterization in Herman Melville's *Moby Dick*), Harris produces a form of fiction that, in his own words, "seeks to consume its own biases through the many resurrections of paradoxical imagination and to generate foundations of care within the vessel of place" (1985, p. 9). *The Palace of the Peacock* is about the possibility of validating subaltern myths as opposed to colonial accounts of history. In some ways Harris is saying the folk may yet have the last laugh. For instance, the Caribs of Grenada, it is told, in one confrontation with the French, leaped off a mountain to their deaths rather than surrender to the colonizers. The Caribs record this event in myth and folktales in which their ancestors who plunged to their deaths in the seventeenth century ascend to heaven in a flock of stars. On earth the hill from which they jumped is called "la Morne des Sauteurs" or "Leaper's Hill." And at night, presumably, the stars continue to shine down in comment. The stars are in the Carib mythology and astrology the reconstitutions of their broken souls (EPICA Task Force, 1982, p. 9).

The extractable story of Harris' novel takes the form of a journey of reclamation, of rediscovery of the colony of Mariella. Mariella is the metaphor for alienated or hidden self—the living resources of the oral traditions of the folk—culture based on use value, outside the exchange relations of commodification. But on board the pontoon that sails up the Cuyuni River in the interior of Guyana are the polyglot broken souls of a subordinating history. Colonizer and colonized must journey, must reach deep into their own souls for new systems of communication that might settle old conflicts. Of course, the quest narrative goes back to the beginnings of the novel: Homer's *Odyssey*, Virgil's *Aeneid*, John Bunyan's *The Pilgrim's Progress*, the great stories of adventure of Geoffrey Chaucer's *Canterbury Tales*—"The Miller," "The Clerk," "Nunnes Priest," and the rest, the extended narrative improvisations and oral documentaries of the African griots—Amiri Baraka's original "Blues People." With the arrival of the modern novel, we have the founding myths of the mariners, renegades, and castaways, as C.L.R. James notes: Daniel Defoe's Crusoe in his *Robinson Crusoe*, Herman Melville's Ahab in *Moby Dick*, and the tormented protagonists of Joseph Conrad's travel fiction, Marlow of *Heart Of Darkness* and Nostromo of *Nostromo*.

But the crew that sets sail on the pontoon in *The Palace of the Peacock*, in a sense represents condensations and fragmentations of these prototypes. The new imaginary spaces which the characters in this novel inhabit are considerably deflated—bodies press sensuously against each other. Harris' characters embody the dialectical tensions of self and other, past and present. There is Donne, the tormented captain and leader. Named after the master of the literary technique of conceit—the metaphysical poet, John Donne. In *The Palace of the Peacock*, Donne is colonizer and agent of dominating instrumental reason, but it is his materialism that blocks his wholeness of being. His abuse of Mariella—Arawak, Shaman-woman, and colony—leads to one of his many deaths in the novel. Mariella takes revenge. Donne is also the colonizer mentality in the colonized who issues decrees: "Donne I suddenly felt in the quickest flash was in me" (p. 33). Vigilance is the ship's pilot, an Amerindian seer, on whom Donne and the crew must rely for his supersensitive vision to help them navigate and escape the perils lying in the bedrock of the river. There is Cameron, the Afro-Scot of "slow feet and fast hands" (pp. 25-26), in pursuit of deep materialist fantasies—the porknocker panning the river bed for ancestral gold and other precious metals. There is the musical Carroll, an Afro-Carib youth, and player of the Carib bone flute. In his hands, the oar becomes a fully tuned violin. There is Schomburgh, the German-Indian, fisherman and wise uncle to all. There are the Portuguese da Silva twins, at war with themselves and the world, constantly, self-contradictory. There is Wishrop, Amerindian (Chinese?), and Jennings the mechanic, Anglo-Saxon, married to the folk. And finally, there is Mariella, Shaman-woman ancient and yet youthful, as permanent as the stars. She appears in unexpected moments, everywhere, constantly altering the environment and chemistry of associations in the pontoon. Ultimately, Harris tells us this is one spiritual incestuous family that dreamed up their different origins:

> Cameron's great-grandfather had been a dour Scot, and his great-grandmother an African slave mistress. Cameron was related to Schomburgh (whom he addressed as Uncle with the other members of the crew) and it was well-known that Schomburgh's great-grandfather had come from Germany, and his great-grandmother was an Arawak American Indian. The whole crew was a spiritual family living and dying together in the common grave out of which they had sprung from again from the same soul and womb as it were. They were all knotted and bound together in the enormous bruised head of Cameron's ancestry and nature as in the white unshaved head of Schomburgh's age and presence (p. 39).

Unlike the nineteenth century realist novel of individual psychological inferiority, the specific emotions and dispositions of each character are distributed among the other characters in the novel. Donne's superciliousness can be found expressed in the da Silva twins. He is like the river boy, Carroll, filled with fear and wonder in the face of the majestic waterfall the crew must cross as they take their perilous journey up the river. His craven materialism is reproduced in the obsessed and self-commercial Cameron. These characters on board the shallow pontoon on the journey of their lives are peculiarly flat or hollow entities—broken individuals who need each other to be fully complete. There is no depth or latency to them. They flash on the surface of the novel. They are in some ways "parabolic" characters: to use the language of the West African critic, Emmanual Obiechina (1978), they introduce a symbolic motif that implicates themselves and the world. Their sharp edges fade and their personalities bleed into each other as the novel progresses. Harris is doing his best to suggest that they are in fact one subject of history, one community. We often find it impossible to tell these characters apart. At some point their individual characteristics are diffused throughout the crew. One gets the picture of a painter furiously experimenting with an expanding rainbow of colors in an infinite palette. One is reminded here of Peter Greenaway's strobic alternations of light and color in his film, *Prospero's Books* (1991). Unlike Captain Ahab's

Pequod, there is no deck in Harris' novel. These characters are anti-heroes fomented in the belly of the beast—clutching each other in fear and uncertainty as they struggle up river in their shallow dugout or pontoon. Nobody is traveling first class here. Their seven day journey is demarcated by seven deaths, seven dissolutions of the sovereign subject. This journey is, in part, Harris' great effort to recreate the Carib resurrection myth. In Carib mythological structures, human actors have no trouble traveling from life to death and back again, completing a mythical cycle of transformation. Of course this corridor from life to death is also opened up in Toni Morrison" *Beloved* (1987) and *Jazz* (1992), in the filmmaking of Julie Dash in *Daughters of the Dust* (1992), in Jorge Amado's *Dona Flor and Her Two Husbands* (1969), and in the dramatic fables of Derek Walcott such as those found in the collection of plays, *Dream On Monkey Mountain and Other Stories* (1972).

Harris also points us to the Renaissance fusion of art and science in the practice of alchemy (Harris, 1970). The seven day journey in *The Palace of the Peacock* may thus be compared to the seven stages of the alchemical process during which the *massa confusa* (the *nigredo* or chaos) is immersed (*ablutio*, a stage similar to Christian baptism or "death by water") and exposed to a series of chemical and physical changes—through to a stage of purification (*albedo*) to the final *aurum non vulgi* or *Cauda Pavonis* (the peacock colors), which represents a unity in diversity. (This is what the Guyanese critic, Michael Gilkes [1975] calls "the wedding of opposites.") In *The Palace of the Peacock*, the crew exists in the original state of *negrido* (chaos); their journey through the rapids (*ablutio*) leads to a creative life-in-death transformation, for which Carroll's role as Shaman is crucial: "Who and what was Carroll?...the living and dead folk, the embodiment of hate and love, the ambiguity of everyone and everything?" (p. 69). All this points to a process of inner transformation. Here, again, we see Harris' use of parallel or overlapping time. Carib Resurrection mythology and Renaissance, and Egyptian-derived alchemy come together to tell a story of the strange and the familiar in the "infinite rehearsal" of the folk and colonizer in the rivers and forests of the interior of Guyana. The journey up the river and toward the rendezvous with Mariella leads to a series of transformations of the crew in the old pontoon. Each member of the crew is not partially freed from the self-governing, materialistic and particularistic fantasies that dominated his relationships with his crew-mates. This sense of growth in knowledge and understanding is the effect of shared responsibility, mutual liability, and the washing away of implacable masks of sedimented identity and reason. The alchemical vision enlarges to contain the whole range of objects and persons in the novel. The action unfolds within a decentered and decentering sense of place and context. And the novel builds laterally but always furiously toward a final proliferation of images—fragments cobbled together in the Cauda Pavonis. This hollow but latent epiphany which Donne and his crew experience at the top of the rapids as they face their symbolic deaths is a reworking of Odysseus' enchantment, resistance, and partial surrender to the voice of the Sirens—his primitive self and other. Harris breaks through the conventional one-dimensional attitudes and responses to color, light, darkness, touch, smell, sound, and taste that inform our common sense encounters with each other and the world.

In his essay "On Culture and Creative Drama," Richard Courtney (1988) talks about a resurrection myth associated with the Amerindian peoples, the myth that is the creative foundation for Harris' novel:

> Each of these Indian peoples have a major myth which tells how a young hero (heroine) leaves the actual world (dies) and seeks his spirit from whom he obtains "power," returning with it to his village (resurrection) so that he can use this power on the people's behalf. (p. 6)

In *The Palace of the Peacock* this subaltern or revolutionary power derives from an unflinching self-critique and openness to contradiction, discontinuity, and difference. What Donne and his crew see and experience at the top of the rapid are the tenuous links that connect them to each other and to hidden moral resources within themselves:

> The crew was transformed by the awesome spectacle of a voiceless soundless motion, the purest appearance of vision in the chaos of emotional sense. Earthquake and volcanic water appeared to seize them and stop their ears dashing scales only from their eyes. They saw the naked unequivocal flowing peril and beauty and soul of the pursuer and the pursued all together, and they knew they would perish if they dreamed to turn back. (p. 62)

CONCLUSION:
MULTICULTURALISM, WORLD LITERATURES, AND THE FOUNDATIONS OF GLOBAL CONSCIOUSNESS

Current debates in multicultural education too easily oppose the literature associated with the canon to the new literatures of minority and indigenous groups, Western civilization to non-Western traditions, and so forth. It is assumed that since the dominant curriculum thrives on the marginalization of the culture of minorities that minority identities can only be fully redeemed by replacing the Western and Eurocentric bias of the curriculum with non-Western minority literature. The work of postcolonial writers such as Wilson Harris directly challenges the easy opposition of the canon to non-Western and third world literature and the curricular project of content addition and replacement that now guides some multicultural frameworks. My point of departure in this essay follows a theoretical and methodological line of thinking that draws on the historical and genealogical work of Michael Berube (1992), Gerald Graff (1987), and John Guillory (1990), who all in various ways argue for a noncanonical reading of the canon. In a strategy complementary to theirs, I have sought to uncover the deep philosophical preoccupations that animate third world writers like Harris in their encounter with master narratives of the West. There is, in, fact in the postcolonial literature a vast project of rewriting that is well on the way—a project that I wish to suggest that teachers and students in American schools cannot any longer remain blissfully ignorant of. Such a project of rewriting guides us toward reading literature both intertextually and contextually—reading literature "contrapuntally," as Edward Said (1993) suggests. That is to say, we might now read Joseph Conrad's *Heart of Darkenss* by the light of Chinua Achebe's *Things Fall Apart*; Daniel Defoe's *Robinson Crusoe* through the eyes of J.M . Coetzee's *foe* or Derek Walcott's *Pantomime*; Shakespeare's *Tempest* under the microscope of George Lamming's *The Pleasures of Exile*; Virginia Woolf's *A Room of One's Own* in concert with Jamaica Kincaid's *Annie John*; and Fyodor Dostoyevsky's *Notes From the Underground* within the knowing gaze of Ralph Ellison's *Invisible Man*.

What I am pointing toward is the need for educators to begin to let the sensibility of a complex, interdependent world into the lives of students. To challenge the tragic images of mainstream television and textbooks and to expand our own sensibilities in America by embracing the world. Postcolonial literature, it seems to me, works through a different set of propositions about human actors than the ones that seem to have taken hold in education lately: the origins claims, the centric claims, the West versus the rest, and so forth. These are all tired binarisms that have led to the regimentation of identities— each man turning the key on his own door. The great challenge of our time is to think beyond the paradox of identity and the other. This is a challenge to rejuvenate linkages of being and association among all peoples in these new times. It is also a challenge to follow the lost steps set in the cross-currents of history by those dwelling in the light of the *Cauda Pavonis* or the palace of the peacock—the final rendezvous with difference beyond the psychic interior of our human forests.

I believe books like Harris' *The Palace of the Peacock* open up this new terrain in which we find ourselves confronting the other in us. The lost and broken souls of history are asking for a parley that would lead to changing the truths and stabilities of the particularisms now overtaking educational life and the issue of curriculum change.

N O T E S

1. It might be helpful for the reader to take a look at some of the following
    articles and books in which these concepts of subaltern communities are
    discussed. Donna Haraway (1990) discusses the concept of "cyborg" (or the
    subaltern, feminist actor who attempts to build communities of resistance
    across "contradictory worlds" of interests, needs, and desires). Gloria
    Anzaldua (1987) talks about the people who exist between the colonizer
    and the colonized—people who inhabit the "third space" or, in her
    language, "inhabit both realities" of a colonizing United States and a
    colonized Mexico. Gabriel Garcia Marquez' (1970) people of "El Macondo"
    have to negotiate the ruptures generated in the transition from their peasant
    world to a highly industrialized and modernized context. And, finally,
    Wilson Harris' "Mariella" is both a site of colonial domination and the site
    of the new identities of the emergent peoples of Guyana and the Caribbean.
    Mariella is the colonial/postcolonial outpost that is at the center of the
    narrative of The Palace of the Peacock.

R E F E R E N C E S

Amado, J. (1969). Dona Flor and Her Two Husbands (trans. By H. Onis). New
    York: Knopf.

Anzaldua, G. (1987). Inspiriting Influences: Tradition, Revision and Afro-American
    Women's Novels. New York: Columbia.

Asante, M. (1993). Malcolm X As Cultural Hero and Other Afrocentric Essays.
    Trenton, NJ: Africa World Press.

Bennett, W. (1984). To reclaim a legacy: Text of the report of humanities in
    higher education. Chronicle of Higher Education, November 28, pp. 16-21.

Berube, M. (1992). Marginal Forces/Cultural Centers: Tolson, Pynchon, and The
    Politics of The Canon. Ithaca: Cornell University Press.

Courtney, R. (1988). On culture and creative drama. Youth Theatre Journal, vol.
    3, no. 1, pp. 3-9.

D'Souza, D. (1991). Illiberal Education: The Politics of Race and Sex On Campus.
    New York: Free Press.

El Saadawi, N. (1985). God Dies By The Nile (trans. S. Hetata). London:
    Atlantic Highland.

EPICA Task Force. (1982). *Grenada; The Peaceful Revolution.* Washington, D.C.: EPICA Task Force.

Fraser, R. (1988). Wilson Harris: *The Palace of the Peacock.* In D. Dabydeen (ed.), *Handbook For Teaching Caribbean Literature* (pp. 8-16). London: Heinemann

Freire, P. (1970). *Pedagogy of The Oppressed.* New York: Seabury.

Gilkes, M. (1975). *Wilson Harris and The Caribbean Novel.* London: Longman.

Graff, G. (1987). *Professing Literature: Institutional History.* Chicago: University of Chicago Press.

Guillory, J. (1990). Canon. In F. Lentricchia & T. McLaughlin (eds.), *Critical Terms For Literary Study* (pp. 233-249). Chicago, University of Chicago Press.

Haraway, D. (1990). A manifesto for cyborgs: Science, technology, and socialist feminism in the 1980s. In Linda Nicholson (ed.), *Feminism/Postmodernism* (pp. 190-233). New York: Routledge.

Harris, W. (1960). *The Palace of the Peacock.* London: Faber.

Harris, W. (1962). *The Whole Armour.* London: Faber.

Harris, W. (1970). History, fable and myth in the Caribbean and the Guianas. *Caribbean Quarterly,* vol. 16, no. 2, pp. 1-32.

Harris, W. (1975). *Companions of The Day and Night.* London: Faber.

Harris, W. (1977). *Da Silva da Silva's Cultivated Wilderness.* London: Faber.

Harris, W. (1977). *Genesis of The Clowns.* London: Faber.

Harris, W. (1985). A note on the genesis of *The Guyana Quartet. in* W. Harris' (Ed.), *The Guyana Quartet* (pp. 7-14). London: Faber.

Harris, W. (1989). Literacy and the imagination. In M. Gilkes (ed.), *The Literate Imagination* (pp. 13-30). London: McMillan

Iyer, P. (1993, February 8). The empire writes back. TIME, pp. 68-73.

James, C.L.R. (1978). *Mariners, Renegades and Castaways.* Detroit: Bewick/ed.

Jameson, F. (1986). Third-world literature in the era of multinational capitalism. *Social Text,* vol. 15, pp. 65-88.

Kimball, R. (1990). *Tenured Radicals: How Politics Has Corrupted Higher Education.* New York: Harper.

Kincaid, J. (1990). *Lucy.* New York: Farrar, Staus, Giroux.

Ladson-Billings, G., & Henry, A. (1990). Blurring the borders: Voices of African liberatory pedagogy in the United States and Canada. *Journal of Education*, vol. 172, no. 2, pp. 72-87.

Marquez, G.G. (1970). *One Hundred Years of Solitude* (trans. By G. Rabassa). New York: Harper & Row.

Morrison, T. (1987). *Beloved*. New York: Knopf.

Morrison, T. (1992). *Jazz*. New York: Knopf.

Obiechina, E. (1978). *Culture, Tradition and Society in The West African Novel*. London: Heinemann.

Okri, B. (1992). *The Famished Road*. New York: Anchor Books.

Ondaatje, M. (1992). *The English Patient*. New York: Vintage.

Phillips, C. (1991). *Cambridge*. New York: Knopf.

Rushdie, S. (1981). *Midnight's Children*. London: Penguin.

Said, E. (1993). *Culture and Imperialism*. New York: Knopf.

Walcott, D. (1972). *Dream On Monkey Mountain and Other Stories*. London: Jonathan Cape.

CHAPTER TWENTY-FOUR

On Becoming a "Little Sex Researcher"

Some Comments on a Polymorphously Perverse Curriculum[1]

Deborah P. Britzman
1996

Eve Sedgwick (1990) inaugurates her study *Epistemology of the Closet* with a grand narrative gesture she calls "risking the obvious" (p. 22). The phrasing is deceptive in its simplicity because, when it comes to the language of sex (and the closet, after all, is about that curious referentiality, that "open-secret" of sex), what is obvious for some becomes, for others, something to risk. When speaking about sex, there is that queer contradiction between the ambiguity of language itself and the dominant insistence upon the stability of meaning in sex practices. Cindy Patton (1991) wryly observes, "the language of sex is so imprecise, so polyvalent that it is 'hard' to know when we are talking about sex and when we are talking about business or politics or other weighty matters [like education]" (p. 374).

When thinking about the referentiality of sex, one comes up against a curious limit: the dominant insistence upon the stability of bodies, the body as fact and as transmitting obvious information. The insistence has to do with more than the fantasy that bodies say what they mean and mean what they say. In our context of education, the normal body must personify a stable meaning even as that meaning must be adjusted through developmental discourse. Now, while the problems with this sort of conceptualization are exponential, the little problem discussion engages is, "What becomes unthinkable when sexuality is thought to have a proper place?" This question is partly inspired by Cindy Patton's (1994) *Last Served? Gendering The HIV Pandemic*. There, Patton challenges the place of sexuality by positing the geopolitics of sexual space—that is, global migrations, global displacements and traveling, and how these movements produce sexuality. When bodies move, more than the scenery changes. Patton makes the significant point that travelers perform sexuality differently in different spaces. Her term "sexual landscapes," or the geographies of sex, signals something about the polyvalence of the traveler's body and something about the polyvalence of cultural meanings.

There are at least three early observations that can be made from thinking of sexuality as that which is other to boundaries. First, theories of sexuality as movement open very different conceptualizations of safer sex pedagogies, conceptualizations that begin with a notion of sexuality as dynamic. Here's what Patton has to say about educating the traveling body:

> Truly comprehensive approaches to safer sex will view all sexuality as the mingling of potentially different sexual cultures, requiring each of us to be educated and to educate others about the variety of possibilities for creating sexual identity and sexual practices which can stop the [HIV] epidemic. (p.48)

In this first practical observation, the sites of safer sex pedagogies are expanded to the travel agent, the barber, the cosmetic counter, the grocery store: all places where bodies travel, meet, and care for the self. They are also sites of desire and of accidental meetings. And, if the sites of safer sex pedagogies are brought into the everyday, the actual information to be had at these sites would begin with the consideration of bodies on the move in in-between spaces. The second observation is of a different order and concerns the idea that if sexuality is on the move, its moves are other to culture. We might insist that sexuality is otherness itself. The third observation concerns a domain of a different order, described by Driscilla Cornell (1995) as "the imaginary domain," that psychic space of proliferating design where "our sense of freedom is intimately tied to the renewal of the imagination as we come to terms with who we are and who we wish to be as sexuate beings" (p. 8). This brings the travel back to the body: one does not have to go far away to imagine something otherwise. In fact, all one has to do is imagine. Each of these observations, then, highlights the question of how sexuality might be imagined.

These movements and minglings of sexualities bear on my discussion because in the more progressive research on sexuality and adolescents, there is still a preoccupation with fixing the geography of sexuality to the narrowly constructed assignments of culture, gender, age, and neighborhood. These are the preoccupations I wish to disrupt, moving back and forth between the literature of AIDS activists, the theories of sex authored by Freud, Foucault, and Sedgwick, normative versions of sex education in compulsory education, and a few texts on adolescent sexuality.

In bringing such an odd juxtaposition of texts and theories—that is, in considering the discourses of sex and the discourses of the sexual body—we are left with the questions of what is imagined when sex is imagined and what is imagined when what is euphemistically called "sex education" is imagined. To return to Sedgwick's formulation, what can it mean to "risk the obvious" and to place the obvious at risk when the labile subject of sex is so conspicuously contested, masked, rated, counted, disavowed, and made synonymous with one's identity?

Our topic becomes even more complicated when one tries to plot the imaginative geography of sex as my beginning remarks might suggest, or when one tries to read sexuality through a favorite theory, instruction manual, or even the views of what can only be called an army of professionals. To muck up matters even more, when inserted into the school curriculum or the university classroom—when, say, education, sociology, or anthropology gets its hands on sexuality—the language of sex becomes explication-like and then...well...de-sexed. Even more, when the topic of sex becomes like a curriculum and stuck to the under-aged (and here, I mean the legal categories of children and youth) one can barely separate its objectives and fantasies from the historical bundles of anxieties, dangers, and predatory discourses that seem to render some sex intelligible and to relegate other sex to the unthinkable and the morally reprehensible. And, one might acknowledge the dreariness of even the "thinkable" version that makes sex into a danger and a duty to perform. There, sex becomes something that disturbs innocence and the everyday. It becomes indistinguishable from that strange economy of affects that Jonathan Silin (1995), Eve Sedgwick (1990), and Shoshana Felman (1987) all term "our passion for ignorance": the paradoxical desire not to know what one already knows, the passionate work of denial and disavowal.

With all of these lacuna in mind, Sedgwick persists in her willingness to place at risk the obviousness of sex. Structured as axioms, her first one states: "People are different from each other" (p. 23). There are all sorts of differences she plays while still managing to admit the impossibility of exhausting the possibilities and hence of finally accounting for all the differences between, within, and among individuals. And a certain geometric quality is allowed because she begins not with cultural universals but with a certain curiosity about polymorphous actions or the capacity for humans to be exponential in their strategies of meaning, their strategies of sex. Here are a few examples:

1. Even identical genital acts mean very different things to different people.

2. To some people, the nimbus of "the sexual" seems scarcely to extend beyond the boundaries of discrete genital acts; to others, it enfolds them loosely or floats virtually free of them.

3. For some people, it is important that sex be embedded in contexts resonant with meaning, narrative, and connection with other

aspects of their life; for other people, it is important that they not
be; to others it doesn't occur that they might be.

4.   Some people's sexual orientation is intensely marked by autoerotic
pleasures and histories—sometimes more so than by any aspect of
alloerotic object choice. For others the autoerotic possibility seems
secondary or fragile, if it exists at all. (pp. 25-26)

Sedgwick is interested in a sort of difference that "retains the unaccounted-for potential to disrupt many forms of the available thinking about sexuality" (p. 25). It is a project akin to what George Bataille (1986) calls "erotism," a certain subjective practice that allows for a question, for the self to be called into the play of the question. Something similar guides this present discussion, where I explore the contest of ambivalent discourses that endeavor to link sex with education. The ambivalence is structured like normative notions of sexuality, described by Anna Freud (1966; p. 157) as "the dual attitude of humans toward sexual life—constitutional aversion coupled with passionate desire—[that] Bleuler coined the term ambivalence." But sexuality is also structured by a mode of thought that refuses to secure itself and thus begins with the ascription of sexuality as difference. In this discussion, I am bringing a psychoanalytic curiosity to the conceptualization of sex: Neither biology nor anatomy, neither culture nor social role, neither object-choice nor aim are at stake. What is at stake is fantasy, eros, and the vicissitudes of life. Can pedagogy begin with these surprises?

Throughout, three versions of sex education are discussed: the normal, the critical, and the one not tolerated. It is the last form—the one that is not tolerated—that I am calling "the polymorphously perverse." The polymorphously perverse conceptualizes sexuality as movement and as otherness and, as such, as a part of the imaginary domain that means to refuse to stabilize sexuality through the consolation of place. In pedagogical literature on sexuality, it is often difficult to distinguish the normal from the critical version because even the critical version cannot exceed the moralism and the eugenic categories of the normal. And yet, in order to consider questions of implication, none must be willing to make an exploration of what it means to link together these two dynamics: sex and education. And, in thinking about what might constitute such an odd couple—that is, sex and education—we may as well raise difficult questions like: "Can sex be educated and can education be sexed?" "What might sex education be like if it could become indistinguishable from what Foucault (1988), in one of his last works, called "the care of the self" as a practice of freedom?"

Could such an exploration be what Freud (1968; p. 194) had in mind when, in his own inaugural study of sexuality, he termed children "little sex researchers?" The idea that there may be a relation between sexuality and curiosity—a relation Freud insisted upon in his study of the Little Hans case—allows us to question both the limits of sexuality, in what is euphemistically termed "sex education," and its beyond: the transgressions, pleasures, and inexhaustible sensualities, or in Foucault's often cited phrasing, the capacity to "produce pleasure with very odd things, very strange parts of our bodies, in very unusual situations" (cited in Halperin, 1955; p. 88). But what precisely is the insistence that there is a relation between curiosity and sexuality? Is the curiosity that Freud engages the same curiosity as the human sciences that mask power through their knowledge? And, if we can suggest a difference between little sex researchers and social science, then what can education learn from little sex researchers?

If sex is such a labile subject in its aims, knowledge, pleasures, and practices, then what exactly can be said of sex? Are its labile qualities the thing that has allowed educators to remain so keen on arguing for and against sex, on linking the construct of appropriate sex to the construct of age appropriateness, and on worrying over which knowledge holds in which bodies and in what circumstances? Are its labile qualities the thing that has allowed many educators to worry about whether sex education causes sexual activity—whether, say, discussions of homosexuality are the first step in the recruitment of sexuality? Does education cause sex? Why have educators been so persistent in their search for the origin of sexuality? And, to borrow an observation from Diana Fuss (1955), if schools were thought to be a site of sexual contagion and prevention, does that mean that early educators already had a sense of sexuality on the move?

These anxieties are not new and their history in North America seems caught in strange repetitions.[2] As early as 1895 debates over whether sexuality should be placed in the school curriculum were occurring in the United States (Hale, 1971)—even as, one might say, sex was already there. In Canada, the eugenicists pushed the school doors open to sex education for the normal by bringing sexual life under public scrutiny. By 1910, sex education was linked to the school curricular efforts at white racial improvement. Sex education was to become indistinguishable from white racial improvement and the State's concern for white Anglo-Saxon racial propagation (McLaren, 1990). In bringing to bear theories of racial degeneracy with those of sexual degeneracy, our eugenic educators could then shift from a preoccupation with defining deviancy to an occupation with constituting normalcy. Teachers were not immune from the effects of this discourse on degeneracy. Under the subheading "Abnormal Teachers," Maurice Bigelow's 1916 text, called *Sex-Education*, offers two kinds of warnings: Certain neurotic and hysterical men or women who lack thorough physiological training and whose own sexual disturbances have led them to devour omnivorously and unscientifically the psychopathological literature of sex by such authors as Havelock Ellis, Krafft-Ebing, and Freud, are probably unsafe teachers of sex-hygiene (p. 116).[3] Sex education, then, became the site for working on the bodies of children, adolescents, and teachers. The shift to a pedagogy for making normalcy and the idea that normalcy was an effect of proper pedagogy and not an *a priori* state, was essentially the grounds for the social hygiene movement called sex education. But as Bigelow perhaps unintentionally reminds, normalcy is so easily disturbed if left on its own.

To continue our little chronology of despair, we can go back to what might now be read as one of the first journals (dated around 1863) written by one student teacher, the hermaphrodite, Alexina Herculine Barbin. In this *Bildungsroman*, just at the moment when the question, "Do we truly need a true sex?" became answered with an emphatic "Yes!" (Foucault, in the Introduction to Barbin, 1980:vii), our student teacher sadly ponders a melancholy chronology that demands life be separated into a "before sex and after sex." Barbin laments what has been lost when what is lost is the freedom of being without a definitive sex—or, in Foucault's phrasing, "the happy limbo of a non-identity" (p. xiii). Perhaps one might learn from Alexina that sexuality is otherness.

Still, 30 years later it will come as no surprise to note, as Freud does note in his first essay on sexuality (published in 1905), that what characterizes the literature of psychological development is the contradiction between the paucity of materials on the sexuality of children and the proliferation of interdictions on their bodies. By paucity of materials, Freud suggests not so much that sexuality was not being discussed. The paucity had to do with how discussions of sex were anchored in discourses of pathology and racial eugenics. Against this eugenics of sexuality, Freud offers a counter version and a move against psychology. Sexuality, Freud argues, begins at the beginning of life and, therefore, is indistinguishable from any other experience because the body is all. More radical, the unconscious knows no gender. Further, he insists that sexual instinct is originally polymorphously perverse and hence not organized by object choice, true sex, and so on. And, in answering the question of why so many interdictions are stuck to the child's body, Freud attributes the adult's intolerance of children's sexuality to the adult's forgetting of its own infantile sexuality. The dynamic is termed "infantile amnesia," quite a curious category that suggests early infantile memories of eroticism are buried and, therefore, preserved in repression. Perhaps this might explain the ambivalence Freud offered in his terming the unconscious the "id" or the "it."

Before moving on, shall we accept the psychoanalytic insight that repression does not exactly mean throwing something away? Rather, in psychoanalytic discourse, repression is the work of turning away, the work of ignoring and forgetting an idea, or an attempt at undoing the affect from the idea. The movement of repression is dynamic and productive, one of turning and returning. What makes the return of the repressed so uncanny is that new ideas become attached to the old affects. Because of the process of substitution, displacement, and condensation, however, the new content still contains the kernel of the old dynamic or affect. Thus repression is a response to instinctual demand. I add this little footnote because of all the discourses offered to education, psychoanalysis, I believe, is one of the most helpful in its theories of learning and in its curiosity toward what is not learned. And given the turns and return of education, one could argue that education as a discourse and as a practice can be seen as staging the return of the repressed.

Education, then, organized as it is by adults, offers tribute to this burial, this forgetting, those "irruptions of the id" (Freud; 1966: p. 17), or again, this making of the "passion for ignorance." For remember, in Freud's view, there is nothing innocent about forgetting, slips of the tongue, jokes, indeed, all forms of parapraxes—those bungled actions that point elsewhere even as they can be observed daily in an out-of-classroom life. Indeed, there is nothing arbitrary when one considers the work of the educational unconscious. In thinking about this first form of forgetting, where children's sexuality slips between the fault lines of adult recall, Freud locates a second structure of forgetting: education. This allows for the psychoanalytic idea that the very grounds of education requires the disavowal of particular forms of sexual pleasure. But more than this. By imagining that sexuality is akin to normal development—indeed, by insisting that sex be inserted into developmental discourse—the cost of this wish for sex to be a *bildungsroman* is the necessary forgetting that perversity is the grounds of possibility for sexuality itself.[4] Here, my definition of perversity is simply "pleasure without utility." But in the insistence that pleasure be confined to utility, the work of the apparatuses of education, law, and medicine becomes preoccupied with normalizing sexuality to the confines of proper object choice and marital reproductive sex. In normative developmental models of education, sex education becomes preoccupied with posing, as a problem, the specification of the proper object and with rewarding those subjects who desire the interdictions of morality and the state apparatus.

Anna Freud (1979) would continue the psychoanalytic critique of education. Her lectures to teachers suggest three ways psychoanalysis could be useful to education: as offering criticism to educational methods, as extending teachers' knowledge of human vicissitudes, and, in Anna Freud's words, as "endeavoring to repair the injuries which are inflicted upon the child during the process of education" (p. 106). Anna Freud is even more specific: "it should be said that psychoanalysis, whenever it has come into contact with pedagogy, has always expressed the wish to limit education" (p. 96). This is because education, in the psychoanalytic sense, functions as the superego. Its work is to install the guilt that can berate the ego and have enough surplus guilt left over for the ego to berate others. We are left with another queer contradiction: If education demands the renunciation of instinct, how is sex education even possible? Or, what can be the aim of sex education of the object if education is in the renunciation of sex?

But Anna Freud (1966) offers another kind of advice in a later work, one perhaps more modest and urgent. It has to do with her distinction between psychology, a discourse that structures education, and psychoanalysis, a method that works against developmental progression. Remember, for psychoanalysis, sexuality does not begin with puberty. And children, forever curious about their own otherness, make their own theories of sexuality. While sexual curiosity is, in psychoanalytic terms, "the clearest manifestation of the child's intellectual activity," the sexual researches of children "hardly ever lead to a knowledge of the true facts of adult sexual life" (p. 165). Something more is required and it has to do with education's capacity for engaging and enlarging the ego's view of the world and of sexuality. Presently, the struggle between education and sexuality becomes crystallized in the following impossible demand: Renounce your instincts and educate your id. And, it is within these coarsened fault lines that little sex researchers come to a presumptive knowledge.

However, such ambivalence is also met by a different version of sexuality, one that passes psychic structure and stops, momentarily, to ponder the limits of sexuality as historicity. Now Michel Foucault teaches us how tricky are the actions of renunciation and education. And in specifying its tricks, Foucault (1990) offers another way to think about sex, one that emphasizes its invention, or what is commonly termed "construction," as opposed to the normalizing assertion that sex has "true nature." Foucault terms this latter wish "the repressive hypothesis," or the historical fantasy that there once was a time when sex was repressed and now it is time for discovering the secret of sex, of letting its true nature speak its truth. The repressive hypothesis structures critical models of sex education, models that link sex with emancipation, liberation, and mastery of one's destiny. Think of the 1960s discourse of sexual liberation or A.S. Neil's school, Summerville. While the proliferation of talk shows continues to work this fantasy of the truth of sex with great glee—providing, by the way, a stage for our army of professionals to extend the confessional into the living room and the studio audience—Foucault argues that sex is not the opposite of repression: as myth, desire, and representation, sex has a historicity. This historicity is implication of knowledge/power/pleasure.

In fact, for Foucault, if one cares to examine the genealogy of sex one is led not just to education but to the entire academic knowledge production apparatus, to various eugenic and racist movements, to such seemingly neutral categories of the state such as population, demographics, birth certificates—indeed, to bio-power itself. Foucault notes four "great strategic unities" that formed specific mechanisms of knowledge/power/pleasure: the rendering of women's bodies as hysterical, a pedagogization of children's sex, a socialization of procreative behavior, and a psychiatrization of perverse pleasure (1990; p. 105). We will return to these strategies of power and the cast of characters that spring from these strategies shortly. Foucault's interest is in how the surfaces of bodies have been inscribed by, and therefore have come to take on, new forms of intelligibility through the contradictory workings of modern knowledge, labor, and the state apparatus.

For Foucault, it is probably more accurate to speak of the historicity of sex as a burgeoning nineteenth century discourse. Its knowledge targets its own inventions or a series of imagined problem populations: "the masturbating child,"[5] "the hysterical woman," "the pervert," and "the Malthusian couple" (p. 105). These, for Foucault, are the great strategic unities of sex.

Now as a brief aside, the character of the masturbating child—say, an army of little Hans—is a crucial trope in the early discussions over the aims and goals of sex education in the United States. It can be said that the ghost of the masturbating child—that is, the return of the repressed—haunted the "resignation" of Surgeon General Joycelyn Elders. Remember when she said "yes" when asked the question of whether masturbation is a form of safer sex? Even earlier in this century, the development of Kellogg's Corn Flakes was originally promoted for their capacity to curb boys from masturbating. I leave it to your imagination as to how the Corn Flake works even as, to return to the writing of Bigelow, daydreams can also slip too easily into mental masturbation.

But let us return to our strange cast of affected characters. Such a strange cast of characters, made from the stuff of unspecified actions, becomes translated into knowable identities, lifelike examples of the value and the strategies of various eugenics movements. One could say that such a cast of characters becomes the poster people for eugenic campaigns. More specifically, such identities become the anchorage points and props for various forms of racism and colonized orders. How does this work? Again, Foucault considers the strategies of knowledge that produce such a cast: first there must be analysis or an installation of a problem. Then, that problem must be constituted as pathological. Finally, a cure must be offered to normalize the pathology. As with early forms of sex education—what I am calling "normal forms"—children must be constituted as a problem population in need of education or normalization.

But at the same time that bodies were becoming the targets of these new forms of knowledge, Foucault emphasizes yet another dynamic, perhaps one that leads us to a critical sex education. And here is where renunciation becomes tricky. It has to do with the fact that with the making of these new and knowable identities came the demands of those so identified, demands that structure such present social movements as feminism, gay, and lesbian civil rights, children's rights, and anti-racist education. Essentially, this proliferating geometric design is what Foucault means by power, or "manifold relations of force" (p. 94). What made such identity categories hold good, then as now, were the burgeoning social hygiene movements variously termed as pedagogy, criminal justice, psychology, anthropology, medicine, *and* sociology and the burgeoning movements that demand civil rights, decolonization, and self determination. The apparatuses that give sex meaning allow modern knowledge to take hold of the body and, of course, for the body to resist and recast modern knowledge. And while critical sex education begins with the demands of those identified, more often than not, this mode of education still depends upon the eugenic ideal that certain knowledge be affixed to certain identities.

Foucault offers us another way to think about sexuality, not as development or identity but as historicity and relation.

> Sexuality must not be thought of as a kind of natural given which power tries to hold in check, or as an obscure domain which knowledge tries gradually to uncover. It is the name that can be given to a historical construct: not a furtive reality that is difficult to grasp, but a great surface network in which the stimulations of bodies, the intensification of pleasures, the incitement to discourse, the formation of special knowledge, the strengthening of controls and resistances, are linked to one another, in accordance with a few major strategies of knowledge and power. (pp. 105-106)

As is historicity, sexuality is on the move. Sexuality may well be seen as both the limit and in excess of knowledge/power/pleasure, if one cares to tease out a tension glossed in the above quote. For if sexuality is historicity, it is one that produces the very subject Foucault (1983; p. 212) has in mind, subject to the control of others and subject to one's self knowledge. We may be closer to Freud than thought, for Freud was concerned with how people suffer from self knowledge and from helplessness.

To conceptualize sex as the "great surface network," however, allows one to ponder the specific relations made intelligible when sex becomes coupled with education. We might think how sex becomes subjected to larger questions that organize pedagogical efforts and that span relations between children and adults, between home and school, and between identity and its representation. Simon Watney (1991) makes similar points in his essay "School's Out." He offers a stunning inversion of "the usual question of what children supposedly want or need from education, and [instead] ask what it is that adults want or need of children in the name of education." The question is good, I think, because it requires adults to implicate themselves in how adult desire also structures educational imperatives and the construct of child development. But something more must be considered in our exploration, and this has to do with the limits of knowledge. We might also consider the possibility of knowledge itself as being insufficient because of our time in the pandemic known as AIDS.

It is this possibility—the insufficiency of knowledge—that I think the field of education ignores. But like the return of the repressed, that endless repetition of substitutions that seems so strangely familiar, the insufficiency of knowledge, and the incapacity to recognize its limits, returns in the form of a text. The question I am working with is how does a text on adolescent sexuality get caught in the fault lines of sex education in our time of AIDS? The text is edited by

Janice Irving, *Sexual Cultures and the Cultures of Adolescents*. Chapters engage the social effects (in terms of what must be excluded and rendered as deviant) of a sex education that can imagine sex as having a true nature only if it is white, middle class, and heterosexual. The volume is further focused by an emphasis on a prevention model of sex education: prevention of bodily harm (where sex education becomes a protective knowledge of various sexually transmitted infections and early pregnancy avoidance); protection against homophobia, racism, and sexism (where sex education critiques and corrects practices of bodily subordination); and prevention of stereotypes about femininity, disabilities, and perhaps masculinity (where sex education critiques representations of the body). In a certain way this prevention model might be relevant to all parts of the school curriculum, a kind of effective education, borrowing from Foucault's version of effective history, where the purpose of knowledge is to work against itself and not to affirm the order of things.

The unaccounted for problem becomes how to imagine which knowledge will allow for new practices of the self when the dominant knowledge of sexuality is so caught up in and constituted by discourses of moral panic, protection of innocent children, the eugenics of normalcy, and the dangers of explicit representations of sexuality. More pointedly, when sex gets into the hands of politicians, social policy makers, religious fundamentalists—all of whom bear down upon the ways education might imagine sexuality—what's a curriculum to do? If everything causes sexuality—or more interestingly, if anything can make sexuality (and therefore make sexuality perverse)—then what should be the subject of sex education?

But alas, the subject is dual. And this is signaled in the title of the text, "sexual cultures" and "adolescent identities." Writing within what might loosely be called poststructuralist theory, most authors maintain the necessity of considering both adolescents and culture as social constructions. They try to hold onto that difficult and slippery argument that constructions or representations, while imaginary and historical, take hold so well precisely because they are animated by their social effectivity. But positing a phenomenon as a construction, as opposed to an always-already-there-thing in a field of practice called education, seems to place at stake both education and its subjects.

In the field of education, the arguments against social construction have been with us for a while. For those who refuse discourse theory, the debate tends to stall between the contradictory assertions that either there are adolescents or there are no adolescents. Either there is culture or there is no culture. A different way of thinking about constructions or inventions might begin with another look at Foucault's deconstruction of the repressive hypothesis, for the repressive hypothesis is a sort of conceptual fortress that preserves the ground for such distinctions as those between innocence and guilt, normality and deviance, and nature and culture.

The repressive hypothesis would say of adolescents that there once was an unencumbered or true adolescence that became subject to all sorts of worries. First adolescents were care-free, now they are careless. The productive hypothesis would say that such worries produce what we call "the adolescent" or, as Irvine writes, that "recently invented life stage shaped by economic and political influences" (p. 7). In the productive hypothesis, what seems to be at stake is how the body is read (and not whether there is a body) when the body is assumed to stand in for adolescents. In the case of culture, the repressive hypothesis would posit culture as a trans-historical and unitary set of behaviors, customs, modes of address, and so on, passed down through generations. The seamless picture only becomes distorted when a culture becomes interfered with by an outside force. In this hypothesis, culture is the sacred object and becomes the sacred ruin through no fault of its own. Moreover, to return to one's culture becomes a journey back to *a priori* origins. The productive hypothesis reads suspiciously, positing culture as far more contentious and as requiring—as a condition of making and recognizing its members—internal processes of regulation and exclusion. And, even these processes of distinction would produce new cultural forms and new sorts of demands. From the vantage of the productive hypothesis, culture is never innocent.

From these sorts of assertions one can then question the fault lines of discourses on sex that advocate cultural appropriateness and age appropriateness. For if both of these terms are constructed terms, then along with the construction comes a target for appropriateness. This, after all, is the limit of appropriateness and where critical models of sex education may become indistinguishable from normative models. Should sex education even be coupled with appropriateness of any kind?[6] What is appropriate for whom if culture has that teleological talent for excluding its members on the basis of cultural appropriateness or, better, on the criteria of authenticity? Can a notion of appropriateness ever become uncoupled from developmental theory? Or, to exceed our present limit and, perhaps, begin with the perverse: What if sex education became a lifetime study of the vicissitudes of knowledge, power and pleasure?

Irvine signals some of these tensions when she states the text's problematic nature.

> Although effective research and education on adolescent sexuality can only proceed from a standpoint of strong cultural analysis, there is some complexity to this task… . In sexuality research…one must negotiate the tension between simplistic overgeneralization about culture and [in the words of Carol Vance] "the anarchy or sexual idiosyncrasy." (p. 9)

With Vance's phrasing, we are back to Sedgwick's axioms and the difficulty of pinning down our unruly subjects or even provisionally risking any form of cultural essentialism.

These are significant tensions because they point to the necessity of calling into question three dynamics: research, education, and culture. These dynamics can be seen as comparable to Foucault's operations of knowledge/power/ pleasure: analysis, problematization, and cure. Each dynamic or mode of intelligibility has become significantly troubled in our time of AIDS. As AIDS activists continue to teach, the dynamics of research, culture, and education have been constituted by their own passion for ignorance and by their incapacity to theorize beyond the repressive hypothesis. What is at stake when one faces the conditions youth and adults confront as they fashion their lives? What if what is at stake are the limits of our knowledge?

Here, then, are the fault lines of this text and perhaps of feminist, antiracist, and gay affirmative educational efforts. It has to do with a reliance on representation in perhaps its most naïve and anthropological sense. For in these critical pedagogies there is still the instance that only certain knowledge be affixed to certain populations and that knowledge itself be wrested from its own otherness and become a provision of anthropological information on cultural attributes. The problem of taking an anthropological approach is that attribution theory is grounded in a eugenics of the body. More often than not, the information models assume, on the one hand, a stability in language and bodies and thus cannot think the geopolitics of sexual spaces. On the other hand, the information model of sex education requires the mistaken assumption that information will be no problem to the learner or the teacher. What is completely unthought is that every learning is also an unlearning. What is yet to be made is a theory of learning that can tolerate its own implication in the passion for ignorance and in the apparatus Foucault called knowledge/power/pleasure. Shall we begin to admit that the passion for ignorance even structures critical learning?

This is not to say that youth should not consider cultural relations or that youth should not have access to accessible information. It is to insist, however, that cultural relations and information of any kind be taken as symptomatic rather than curative and final, and as subject to the work of those who engage its myriad meanings. Moreover, in the context of safer sex education, the matching of knowledge to identities cannot admit the crucial understanding that one's sexual conduct is a practice, not a window into one's true rational identity. Indeed, and to return to Foucault again, "We must conceive of sex without the law, and power without the king" (1990; p. 89). What seems to be at stake here is how one conceptualizes dynamics of cultural relations, specific information, and the discourses of sex. One might as well engage the problem of how sex can be culturally appropriate and, if it can be, what of perversity? One might consider culture not as a venerated sacred object to be protected and preserved, but as a highly contentious and contradictory site where discontentment and the discontent are produced and where the geopolitics of sexuality refuse the stability of cultural, national, gendered, and sexual boundaries.

It may be more useful to consider Jonathan Silin's (1995) notion of a socially relevant sex education—that is, curricular endeavors unafraid to consider children and youth as "little sex researchers" interested in the vicissitudes of life and death. Then, pedagogical efforts could become unsatisfied with the pinning of knowledge to specific identities and more restless—or better, polymorphous in its perversity—in what can be imagined when sex is imagined and in what can be acknowledged when the erotics of pedagogy and knowledge are acknowledged. For if we take seriously social theories about the historicity and contentiousness of constructions (as relations of power) then pedagogy might begin with the assumptions that identities are made and not received and the work of the curriculum is to incite identifications and critiques, not close them down.

Still, a socially relevant sex education can only offer more questions. What values, orientations, and ethics should a socially relevant sex education appeal to if culture is not a tidy safe house or if culture produces its own set of inequalities along the lines of gender, socioeconomic status, sexual practices, age, concepts of beauty, power, and body? If adolescents are a social construction as well—and hence have no universality except for the fact that, in North American contexts, the category takes the form of an extra legal status of citizenship and sexual consent, and is thus subject to the controls of parents and school supervision—and, if certain other constructions such as HIV, STDs, unplanned pregnancies, and various sexualized forms of violence place adolescent bodies—in whatever ways—at risk, then how are educators and students to engage ethically within a sex education viewed as indistinguishable from a practice of freedom and a care of selves? For these questions to be important, it will not be enough for educators to debate them, make a decision, and then serve up as an easy-bake sex education curriculum. Shall we admit there is nothing easy in sex education and if the concern is to make a curriculum that does not incite curiosity, then sex education will continue to signify "our passion for ignorance?"

Given such heteroglossic contexts, given the complexity of forces that imagine sexuality, and given our time of AIDS, perhaps part of what is needed is ongoing curricular endeavors that begin with antiracist, antisexist, and antihomophobic suppositions. But we must also begin to admit that such suppositions must be forced to cut through the affirmations of cultural appropriateness, age appropriateness, and indeed cultural relevancy itself, for it is these constructs that prohibit the thoughts that sexuality is movement and bodies travel. I am advocating for a curriculum that can bear to refuse the grounds of eugenics and social hygiene—and for an effort that can come to its own social relevancy because it is fashioned by those participating and because those who make the curriculum are making new interests capable of pushing the limits of critique and pleasure. But in making such a curriculum, can sex education exceed sociological categories and be more than a semester where bodies are subject to both the humanistic constructs of self-esteem and role models and the endless activities of voting on knowledge and the finding of stereotypes? More to the point, can sex be thought of as a practice of the self rather than a hypothetical rehearsal, as in preparation for the future? And if such questions can be thought about seriously, one might just as well consider *not* how sex can fit into the curriculum but how sex might allow the entire disciplinary enterprise of education to be invented as inciting ethical projects of caring for the self.

It is not as if such projects were not occurring. More often than not the sorts of projects I have in mind live in the outside of public education beyond the confines of disciplined knowledge and beyond the defensive mechanism of official school talk. The projects may be known for their contention, for their refusal to tidy categories, for the debates they allow, for the practices that become possible and impossible, and it is precisely these dynamics that education disavows. But one can still think of the poetry of Essex Hemphill and Marilyn Hacker; the dances of Bill T. Jones; the essays of Pat Califia and Joan Nestle; the films of Derek Jarmen, Maria Brumberg, and John Greyson; the novels of Toni Morrison, Samuel Delany, David Feinberg, and Henry Roth; and the collection of short essays and stories published by Plume called the *High Risk* series. And just as Sedgwick's list of axioms should invite the reader to produce one's own, so, too, with this present listing. For the thing in common in both "lists" is the invitation to think, the invitation to imagine as Foucault imagines, the capacity to "produce pleasure with very odd things, very strange parts of our bodies, in very unusual situations."

The sort of invitation I have in mind does not include a place of final destination. Rather, the exploration that is offered is one that can both tolerate the study of the vicissitudes of life and death and consider the surprises of the imaginary domain. The point of departure is conversation and a generous making of a sociality that refuses to justify itself through the consolation of fixing a proper place.

For such conversations to even become thinkable in relation to education, educators will be required to get curious about their own conceptualizations of sex and, in so doing, become civil libertarians for the explorations and curiosities of others, for the freedom of "the imaginary domain." For when one becomes a "little sex researcher," one is interested in the study of pleasures and the detours taken. When one can study the histories that sex provokes, the perversities it might imagine and perform, then one is likely to engage as well the study of where knowledge breaks down, becomes anxious, and is built again. The curriculum moves toward the polymorphously perverse and onto Bataille's notion of "erotism," when the problem becomes the making of questions that can unsettle the finitude education and the bodies that live there have become.

And if the question can tolerate its own perverse journey then maybe a certain curiosity can be made. But it will have to begin, as the first few lines of Essex Hemphill's (1992) poem "Now We Think" begins, with a practice of care for the self:

> Now we think
> As we fuck

N O T E S

1. I would like to acknowledge a much shorter version of this paper in *The Review of Education/Pedagogy/Cultural Studies*, titled "Towards a polymorphously perverse curriculum" (forthcoming).

2. Diana Fuss (1995; p. 108) offers a stunning literary exploration of "the highly-charged erotic climate of the single-sex school" in terms of its fears and desires for lesbian subjects. In positing the fault lines of a discourse on sexuality that worries about contagion, she offers insight into the more normative fear of sexuality as contagion. While this direction has been significant in tracing the persistent phobic discourse against gay and lesbian civil rights, this paper takes movement in a centrifugal (as in fugitive) direction.

3. I thank Kate Kaul for pointing out this text to me.

4. In its common usage, the term "perversion" connotes a moralistic judgement on transgressing social convention, nature, and what is accepted as "normal." This essay works with the term perversity in the psychoanalytic sense. There, perversity invokes any sexual activity that deviates from coitus with a person of the opposite sex for the purpose of reproduction. Essentially and regardless of object choice, perversity refers to every other practice of pleasure that has no other reason than pleasure. Laplanche and Pontalis (1988) offer the following observation.

   So-called normal sexuality cannot be seen as an a prior aspect of human nature [and citing Freud]: "the exclusive sexual interest felt by men for women is also a problem that needs elucidating and is not a self-evident fact." One could...define human sexuality itself as essentially "perverse" inasmuch as it never fully detaches itself from its [infantile] origins, where satisfaction was sought not in a specific activity but in the "pleasure gain" associated with functions or activities depending on other instincts. Even in the performance of the genital act itself, it suffices that the subject should develop an excessive attachment to forepleasure for him [or her] to slip toward perversion. (pp. 307-308)

   Throughout this essay, my use of perversion is meant to signify actions without utility rather than unfortunate moralistic usage that structures homophobic discourse.

5. For a long discussion of the relation between social hygiene movements and sex education, see Nathan Hale, Jr. (1971).

6. For the best discussions of how the construct of age appropriateness and its discourses of development deny the sexuality of children and produce the exclusion of gay and lesbian bodies, see Jonathan Silin's (1995) stunning critique of developmental psychology in his chapter 4, "Developmentalism and the Aims of Education," and Simon Watney's (1991) essay, "School's Out."

R E F E R E N C E S

Barbin, H. (1980). *Herculine Barbin: Being the recently discovered memoirs of a nineteenth-century French hermaphrodite*. Introduced by Michel Foucault. (New York: Pantheon Books).

Bataille, G. (1986). *Erotism; Death and sensuality*. (San Francisco: CA: City Lights Press).

Bigelow, M. (1916). *Sex education*. (New York: MacMillan).

Cornell, D. (1955). *The imaginary domain: Abortion, pornography and sexual harassment*. (New York: Routledge).

Felman, S. (1987). *Jacques Lacan and the adventure of insight; Psychoanalysis in contemporary culture*. (Cambridge, MA: Harvard University Press).

Foucault, M. (1983). The subject of power. In H. Dreyfus and P. Rabinow, *Michel Foucault: Beyond Structuralism an Dhermeneutics*, Second Edition, pp. 208-226. (Chicago: University of Chicago Press).

Foucault, M. (1988). *The care of the self*, Vol. 3 of the *History Of Sexuality*. (New York: Vintage Books).

Foucault, M. (1990). *The history of sexuality: An introduction*, Vol. 1. (New York: Vintage Books).

Freud, A. (1966). *The ego and the mechanisms of defense*. (Madison: International Universities Press).

Freud, A. (1979). *Psychoanalysis for teachers and parents*. (New York: Norton Press).

Freud, S. (1968). *The standard edition of the complete psychological works of Sigmund Freud*, Vol. VII (1901-1905). (London: Hogarth Press).

Fuss, D. (1995). *Identification papers*. (New York: Routledge).

Hale, N. (1971). *Freud and the Americans: The beginnings of psychoanalysis in the United States, 1876-1917*. (New York: Oxford University Press).

Halperin, D. (1995). *Saint Foucault: Towards a gay hagiography.* (New York: Oxford University Press).

Hemphill, E. (1992). *Ceremonies: Prose and poetry.* (New York: Plume Books).

Laplanche J. & Pontalis, J. B. (1988). *The language of psychoanalysis.* (London: Karnac Books and the Institute of PsychoAnalysis).

McLaren, A. (1990). *Our own master race: Eugenics in Canada,* 1885-1945. (Toronto: McClelland and Steward).

Patton, C. (1991). Visualizing safe sex: When pedagogy and pornography collide. In D. Fuss, ed., *Inside/Out: Lesbian Theories, Gay Theories,* pp. 373-386. (New York: Routledge).

Patton, C. (1994). *Last served? Gendering the hiv pandemic.* (London: Taylor and Francis).

Sedgwick, E. (1990). *Epistemology of the closet.* (Berkeley: CA: University of California Press).

Silin, J. (1995). *Sex, death and the education of children: Our passion for ignorance in the age of aids.* (New York: Teachers College Press).

Watney, S. (1991). School's out. In D. Fuss, ed., *Inside/Out: Lesbian Theories, Gay Theories,* pp. 387-404. (New York: Routledge).

CHAPTER TWENTY-FIVE

On Finding One's Place in the Text

Literacy as a Technology of Self-Formation[1]

Suzanne de Castell
1996

When classrooms are places of exile, texts can offer safe haven. This paper pursues questions of textual location in three different but interestingly related directions. First, there is the distinctive place of text within "post-literate" culture. Second, moving within that space, we encounter the *text itself as a kind of place*, a place Illich (1989) has termed "literate space." And finally, there is the question of what it is to *occupy* literate space, and what it takes to find a place for oneself within such a space.

A useful point of embarkation may be found in a rather minor remark about the fate of education in a postmodern world. This remark, a proclamation of sorts, is found in a smallish text commissioned by the Conseils des Universites of the Government of Quebec: Jean Francois Lyotard's (1984) *The Postmodern Condition; A Report on Knowledge*. Lyotard's by now often rehearsed proclamation is this: that with the computerization of information, education as we have come to know it is about to become, indeed is already becoming, obsolete.

"Our working hypothesis," writes Lyotard, "it that the status of knowledge is altered as societies enter what is known as the postindustrial age and cultures enter what is known as the post-modern age." This pronouncement heralds Lyotard's discussion of the transformation of knowledge in computerized societies. "The nature of knowledge," he goes on to say,

> cannot survive unchanged.... It can fit into new channels and become operational only if learning is translated into quantities of information. We can predict that anything...that is not translatable in this way will be abandoned. Along with the hegemony of computers comes a certain logic, and therefore a certain set of prescriptions determining which statements are accepted as "knowledge" statements.

Lyotard goes on to remark—and this is I think tremendously significant for us as educators because it addresses what for many of us here has been the heart and soul of our work:

> We may thus expect a thorough exteriorization of knowledge with respect to the "knower" at whatever point he or she may occupy in the knowledge process. *The old principle that the acquisition of knowledge is indissociable from the training (Bildung) of minds, or even of individuals, is becoming obsolete and will become ever more so.* [my emphasis]

Teachers, and especially, of course, teachers of children, whenever they feel free to actually confess it, will, I believe, generally report that their interest is far less in instilling quantities of information into young minds than in building hearts and souls and character. And it is this mission which, on Lyotard's analysis, is rendered obsolete by the reconfiguration of "knowledge" effected by new technologies, in general, and processes of the computerization of information, in particular.

What will today and in the future count as "knowledge," what will henceforth answer Spencer's question about "what knowledge is of most worth" is, says Lyotard, "whatever can be most fully exteriorized." The traditional educational project of what used to be called "character-formation" may perhaps then fall to the media or the marketplace or the streets, but "knowledge" in its postmodern incarnation will have no role to play in it.

"The relationship of the suppliers and users of knowledge to the knowledge they supply and use," says Lyotard, "is now tending, and will increasingly tend, to assume the form already taken by the relationship of commodity producers and consumers to the commodities they produce and consume—that is, the form of [exchange] value."

I want to examine here a connection I think is implicit in Lyotard's argument, a connection to which, however, he does not pay explicit attention: the connection between this traditional educational project of self-formation, and the traditional educational means for its accomplishment—the book.

Until just a few decades ago, the book was literate culture's central vehicle for self-preservation and self-renewal. Nowadays, the book is increasingly regarded as an obsolete technology, a technology that many feel has outlived its usefulness. We live today not in a literate, but in a *post-literate* culture—a culture that has been fundamentally and irreversibly defined and shaped by literacy, but in which new technologies and practices of representation and communication have largely superseded writing and the written word. It seems to be no mere coincidence that the demise of the educational project of self-formation is announced at the very same moment in the evolution of our culture that the book itself is being pronounced obsolete. And the connection is, I think, this: the book, that literacy—the reading and writing of literate texts—has been this culture's primary technology *for* the formation of the self.

Today, however, much that had been accomplished textually, whether in business, in culture, or in personal and social life, now relies increasingly on quite "un-bookish" information technologies—new media of representation and communication which, while they do rely on literate competence, make demands upon new logics and grammars and embedded ethical and epistemological conventions.

In education, accordingly, "computer literacy" and "media studies" threaten to supersede language and literature study, and "viewing and representing" have already assumed positions of prominence alongside "reading, writing, listening, and speaking" in the mandated curriculum guidelines—even though what's involved in "viewing and representing" remains largely unformulated in terms of actual educational theories and practices.

What, then, of the place of literacy in a postliterate culture?

To approach this question, we may adopt and extend some sentences from Foucault, for it is he who has perhaps most articulately construed the book as a "technology of the self." And it is Foucault who has most fully investigated and documented significant historical uses of literacy as a disciplined set of techniques for self-formation. I begin this journey in and through literate space, then, from Foucault's (1986) setting out of the uses of literacy as a technology for the project he calls the "care of the self," my destination is an argument for a socially responsible ethics of pedagogical salvage and recycling.

There are reasons to suggest that both of these obsolete forms—the book as an educational medium, and the formation of self as education's principle project—can and must be reclaimed, and as a matter of some urgency. But, this reclamation project requires, oddly enough, a radical and, some would doubtless say, a *reactionary* reversal of emancipatory classroom practices.

L I T E R A T E   S P A C E :
(W H A T   K I N D   O F   A   P L A C E ... ?)

To conceive of literacy as a means to both individual and, indeed, social identity development, is to understand reading and writing less in terms of communication, expression, information production and exchange, and "meaning-making," and much more as a means to the development of identity *as a "reader,"* that is to say, as an *occupant* of literate space. This fundamental shift in emphasis from "production" to "location" in conceptualizing literate values represents a transformation in what we might call the economics of literacy pedagogy, from *exchange* value to *use* value.

We may think of literate space as a kind of virtual reality, a place that we can occupy, whether as citizen or outsider, colonizer or colonized, a place in which we can work, or seek entertainment, or engage with others, and, most significantly, a place in which we can find and fashion and refashion the selves we would become. From such a conceptual standpoint, emphasis is placed less on making meaning from text than on finding, through the embodied discourses and material practices of reading and writing, one's *place* in the text. In a brilliant essay entitled "Our Homeland, The Text," George Steiner relates Jewish "bookishness" with a history of exile. Seeking to understand cultural tradition of reverence for scholarship, Steiner refers to the long history of physical dislocation, which made of the Jews a diasporic people, and speaks of the necessity to find a "home" in the text. Let us follow Steiner's illuminating perspective on literacy, then, and deemphasize the pursuit of meaning in order to highlight the pursuit of place—a literate space that has been construed historically in terms of two dominant metaphors: reading as a "journey" and the text as a kind of "mirror."

T E X T U A L   S U B J E C T S :
R E A D I N G   A N D   W R I T I N G   A S
" T E C H N O L O G I E S   O F   T H E   S E L F "

Although its verbal formulation is Michel Foucault's (Martin, Gutman, & Hutton, 1988), the conceptualization of literacy as a "technology of the self" is a familiar one. Classical scholar Eric Havelock (1986), a pioneer in the study of literacy, has written that "as language became separated from the person who uttered it, so also the person, the source of the language, came into sharper focus, and the concept of selfhood was born." The self, Havelock tells us, is an invention of literacy. And Ivan Illich (1989) argues in the same vein that "the idea of a self that continues to glimmer in thought or memory, occasionally retrieved and examined in the light of day, cannot exist without the text: and he continues: "The self is a cloth we have been weaving over centuries in confessions, journals, diaries, memories, and, in its most literate incarnation, the autobiography, to tailor the dress in which we see our first person singular" (p. 72).

Foucault's genealogy of ethics advances our understanding of the ways reading and writing have functioned historically as central among the practices by means of which a self constituted itself as a subject. In examining the textual practices by means of which a human being turns him/herself into a subject, Foucault distinguishes two uses of this technology of self-formation: the first is based in first-and second-century Graeco-Roman philosophy, and the second in fourth- and fifth-century Christian spirituality.

Central to Graeco-Roman practices, he tells us, were the *hypomnemata*—copy-books, account-books, and notebooks into which were entered "quotations, fragments of works, examples and actions to which one had been witness or of which one had read the accounts, reflections, or reasonings which one had heard or which had come to mind" (Martin, Gutman, & Hutton, 1988, p. 364). These notebooks, Foucault stresses, must not be mistaken for diaries because they were not a way of giving an account of oneself, but rather a way of taking the self "into account." Hypomnemata functioned as aids to memory for the purpose of guiding one's conduct, to assist one in actively developing "dominion" over the self, to suppress rebellion, to manage and administer, in short, to "govern" the self.

The book, in this instance, enables a species of self-formation which, while solitary, is yet intersubjective: the private formation of a social self by the disciplined application of external models as guides for the self. Important, here, is that the subject is the *agent* of self-formation, with dominion over itself.

Textual practice as a technology of the self underwent substantial and significant transformation in its progressive incorporation into Christian techniques. Foucault explains this movement away from a disciplined art of self-care as a gradual covering over of the aesthetics of existence with a concern for purity, for purification.

> In Christian asceticism the question of purity becomes more and more important; the reason why you have to take control of yourself is to keep yourself pure. This new Christian self had to be constantly examined because in this self were lodged concupiscence and desires of the flesh. From that moment on, the self was no longer something to be made, but something to be renounced and deciphered. (pp. 365-366)

This is the confessional mode—a detailed description and expression of the self, which is a disclosure intended to purify—an account of "temptations, struggles, falls, and victories" which reveals and makes public what was hidden. Here, now, is writing as spiritual combat, premised on the possibility of demonic possession, of the "devil inside" deceiving the self. The way to tell the difference between good and evil thoughts is that evil thoughts can't be expressed without difficulty; everything that can't be expressed becomes a sin (pp. 47-48). Here, says Foucault, "writing constitutes a test and something like a touchstone: in bringing to light the [inner] movements of thought, it dissipates the inner shadow where the enemy's plots are woven" (p. 367).

Foucault's account of the transformations from the classical self to the modern subject—from a self defined by its actions to a self defined by its thoughts—is invaluable in understanding the historical primacy of textual practices in the construction of subjectivity and to conceptions of the self, and in seeing the diversity of textual practices and the potential diversity of conceptions of the self thereby constituted. Foucault reminds us that people have been reading and writing about themselves for two thousand years, but he shows us that they have not all done it in the same way and not, therefore, to the same effect. Hence, it is not enough, he argues, simply to see in general terms *that* the subject is constituted through literacy; we also need to understand *how*, and in quite particular terms. Because Foucault reminds us, "it is not just in the play of symbols that the subject is constituted. It is constituted in real practices—historically analyzable practices. There is a technology of the constitution of the self which cuts across symbolic systems while using them" (p. 369). What is from this standpoint important to see are the various ways in which textual practices concerned with the emergence, the nature, and the cultivation of subjectivity differ under different circumstances and conditions, for different purposes, and with different effects. What, then, are the real practices and conditions under which, *in classroom contexts*, literacy and self-formation converge?

BAKHTIN AND THE QUESTION OF "SPEECH GENRES"

Mikhail Bakhtin's (1986) discussion of "speech genres," and Habermas' (1979) critique of institutional discourses as "systematically distorted communications" provide invaluable assistance in seeing how, in the context of classroom "speech genres," the dialogical practices of the "new literacy" operate as *confessional* discourses, such that the expression of subjectivity and its repressive normalization are one and the same—simultaneous. Amidst contemporary enthusiasm for Bakhtin's writings on the dialogic, for heteroglossia, polyphony, and carnival, often overlooked is his attention to the not-said. He distinguishes at one point between quietude and silence: "In silence," he says, "nobody speaks (or somebody does *not* speak)" (1986, p. 133). Like Foucault, Bakhtin asks us to attend as much to silence, to those voices which may not speak, as to polyphony, to the clamor of the many voices which may.

A Bakhtinian analysis of pedagogic discourse allows us to identify the distinctive speech styles and genres of the classroom, not in order to reify these, but to identify their boundaries and to challenge their limits, to reveal their ritualistic character and their constraining normativity, to see how the interpretations we are able to make in such contexts, and, therefore, the selves we are able to construct there, must be seen as inevitably limited, shaped by others, by conventions, by the "addressee" within all dialogic relations. "As we know," says Bakhtin:

> the role of the *others* for whom the utterance is constructed is extremely great...the role of these others, for whom my thought becomes actual thought for the first time (and thus also for my own self as well) is not that of passive listeners, but of active participants in speech communication. From the very beginning, the speaker expects a response from them, an active responsive understanding. The entire utterance is constructed, as it were, in anticipation of encountering this response. (p. 94)

In the context of classroom "dialogues" then, linguistic interaction is never "free and equal discussion." It is always institutionally framed within a system of "language games."

These institutionalized discourses and representational practices are part of what Foucault termed the "mechanics of power," and they, themselves, produce that subjectivity, that identity, which they simultaneously "express." Says Foucault (1972):

> In a society such as our own, we all know the rules of exclusion. The most obvious and familiar of these concerns what is prohibited. We know perfectly well that we are not free to say just anything…. In appearance, speech may well be of little account, but the prohibitions surrounding it soon reveal its link with desire and power…speech is no mere verbalization of conflicts and systems of domination…it is the very object of man's conflicts. (p. 216)

And, on this same point, from Edward Said (1983):

> Far from being a type of conversation between equals, the discursive situation is more usually like the unequal relation between colonizer and colonized, oppressor and oppressed. …The situation of discourse…hardly puts equals face to face. Rather, discourse often puts one interlocutor above another. (pp. 48-49)

Discourses are, for Foucault, practices that systematically form the objects of which they speak: "Discourses are not about objects; they do not identify objects, they constitute them and in the practice of doing so conceal their own invention" (1972, p. 49).

This way of looking at things calls radically into question the idea of "expressing one's subjectivity," and challenges the very possibility of such goals as "discursive freedom," of "empowering the voices of every student," and of "opening up the classroom for the expression of personal meaning and significance."

So, while the image of the absorbed reader "at home in the text" is widely espoused as a normative ideal for educators and their students, the extent to which such a possibility can be realized in fact seems very much to depend upon the discursive framing of student reading/interpretation, the ways in which, in classrooms, private reading becomes public discourse.

" T H E   N E W   L I T E R A C Y " : L I B E R A T O R Y   O R   L I B E R T A R I A N ?

With the rise of reader response theories, educational applications of constructivism, writing process and authorship theories and pedagogies, and the primacy of the monologic, authoritative text has been challenged, and a dialogical "new literacy" (Willinsky, 1990) commended to teachers as a suitably "postmodern" educational response to the conditions of postliterate culture. The death of the author heralds the birth of the reader—signaling an educational paradigm shift from passive consumption to entrepreneurial production. This is generally thought of as "a good thing," educationally speaking, and pleasingly harmonious with contemporary enthusiasm for rendering public education more "vocationally relevant."

Central to the theory and practice of this new literacy is its pedagogy of "coming to voice" through "dialogue"—the text itself is seen as a more or less inert corpus of potential meanings: it is discourse which brings it to life, realizes its performativity.

But, this purportedly liberatory pedagogy is, in its present incarnations, all too often more, and not less, repressive. Under such conditions, for many students and perhaps in a very fundamental sense, for all students, the strongest voice is silence. More often, of course, one is reduced to lying, to the positioning of oneself in discourse as its normatively sanctioned subject by means of complementary rituals of simulation, the enactment of a discursively legitimate subjectivity. Where discursive practices enacted in the name of "self-expression" actually function to silence, control, and render invisible, survival very often depends upon voluntarily making oneself as invisible as possible. But, in pedagogic contexts in which "self-expression" and "personal meaning" come to be increasingly central media of exchange, and in which discourses, both formal and informal, circulate about identity—particularly raced, classed, sexed, and gendered identities hitherto unrecognized—invisibility is scarcely a option. What replaces that aspiration is active simulation, a ritual enactment of institutionally sanctioned roles in the name of an empowering authenticity. As Pam Gilbert (1988) points out in relation to gendered subjectivity, "young women will speak from within the patriarchal discourses of literature, education, psychology, and adopt speaking postures which are necessarily involved in the construction of their own subordination and oppression" (p, 262). How much more is this the case for other, far more stigmatized, social groups?

For significant numbers of students, the fear of self-disclosure is so great that one is unable to demonstrate what, in fact, one has taken from and made out of one's reading. An "official" subjectivity must be constituted as the legitimate basis from which to speak, an acceptable persona from whose subject position "personal" meaning is being made: what is read is rendered "relevant" to one's "self." By such means a relation is *forged* in both senses, simultaneously made and made up, between reader and text.

Notwithstanding their avowed intents, however, "new literacy" pedagogical practices are not about opening up discourses to permit differences or a range of subjectivities. Rather, they function in a manner very much like the confessional—to repress, to foster self-censorship, to mirror for the self a rationally organized and homogenized subject of regulation. Foucault's use of the panopticon metaphor is relevant here. In that discussion, he argues that simply flattening out relations of power into a horizontal scheme, while providing the illusion of democratic order, serves only to push mechanisms of power underground. They become dispersed throughout a horizontal power structure and thereby obscured, all the more effectively to do their work of policing subjectivity. As Foucault asks: "Do you think it would be much better to have the prisoners operating the panoptic apparatus and sitting in the central tower, instead of the guards?" (1980, p. 164).

So far as classroom reading practices are concerned, what we confront is a kind of discursive panopticon. Individuals begin to construct their own ontological straightjackets within a public discourse on subjectivity in which confession becomes an obligatory practice of expunging aspects of the self, in which the purpose of enforced speech is to bring the self to light, not to illuminate and cultivate it, but to eradicate those parts that can thereby be seen by more discriminating eyes to be pollutant. This is not a practice of acknowledging multiple selves, it is a project of standardizing and censoring selves.

To require students to "speak the self," to find and make public one's "authentic voice" is, under prevailing institutional conditions, an act of treachery. The deceit here is the pretense that power does not circulate through these discourses, that discourse is not always already prestructured by unequal relations of power—and thence to presume and to promise, but not to produce in actual fact, the conditions of safety ("familiarity," "intimacy," in Bakhtin, 1986, p. 96) that might make it possible to try to challenge and to extend the existing discursive limits and boundaries on what may be spoken and on who may speak, indeed, more profoundly, on who may exist at all. This is the procedure so well described by Foucault, of simultaneously placing boundaries and concealing the fact of their placement so their existence cannot be named. Better by far, as Bakhtin, too, would argue, to name these boundaries, so at least we may know our place, if we may not always have the ability in actual fact to change it.[2]

A pedagogy of unrestrained dialogicality, for students already at risk of discrimination, can so far only amount to a reaffirmation, or worse yet an expansion of education's traditional discursive strategies of normalization because the voices and the "knowledges" of others that the new literacy proposes to bring prominently into the educational foreground are thus to be spoken in practice within a discursive frame in which they are prohibited, stigmatized, and punished. And where this is the case, to compel their expression is to enable and, indeed, to sanction their public eradication.

Unless and until educators are capable of effecting a kind of safety and respect for difference which is, at the present time, nowhere in sight, then it would seem far preferable to revert—albeit with explicit irony (Bakhtin, 1986, p. 148)—to traditions of uninterrogated subjectivity, to unmediated private reading, and to formally structured and clearly delineated public speech, leaving the "self" and its "meanings" and its "expression" out of classroom account.

RECYCLING "FORMAL"
EDUCATION

I would, in closing, draw your attention to the concluding chapter of Willinsky's *The New Literacy* (1990), a chapter entitled "Critical Futures," which asks about its "new possibilities for intellectual action in the classroom" (p. 241), about its "long term impact…on students," and which closes by asking: "What is it we are modeling for these New Literates: what is it we hope for their literacy" (p. 242). This chapter's introductory quite is from Virginia Woolf: "It should be our delight," she says, "to watch this turmoil, do battle with the ideas and visions of our own time, to seize what we can use, to kill what we consider worthless, and above all to be generous to the people that are giving shape as best they can to the ideas within them." The concluding paragraphs, liberally peppered with memorable and inspiring phrases from Woolf, exhort teachers to find in the programs and practices of the new literacy "their own happy place in the world as teachers of literacy. …Through the efforts of these programs," we are assured, literacy finds a lively home in the engaging and critical community of the classroom. It reaches out from the students' page in many directions, allowing these students, as they look up from their work, to see beyond the classroom to the entirety of the world-in-progress, while finding a place for themselves in the breadth of this redefinition (p. 243).

Through these new literacy programs, we learn, teachers find a home, literacy finds a home, and students find a place not in the text, but outside it in the classroom and beyond the classroom, to the "entirety of the world-in-progress."

But, interestingly, revealingly, where Virginia Woolf, who is responding to the suggestion that *everyone* can write, remarks that "at the heart of this immense volubility, this flood and foam of language, this irreticence and vulgarity and triviality, there lies the heat of some great passion which only needs that accident of a brain more happily turned than the rest to issue in a shape that will last from age to age"; Willinsky turns this remark on its head: "Yes," he concurs, "there may be that one work which rises out of all this writing, but the great passion of the new literacy—encouraging the flood and foam of language, risking the vulgar and trivial—is for the rest of these writers in the heat of engagement and the potential of empowerment" (p. 242). While Woolf here would turn our attention to the best, Willinsky would—and with Woolf's very own words, it should be noted—turn it to the rest. But, *at whose risk* is this lusty encouragement of the flood and foam of the vulgar and trivial? For let us not fail to notice that Woolf is writing here not of the foam and flood of language in the public space of the classroom, but of the solitary privacy of "Hours in a Library." Nor let us forget that is was Virginia Woolf who knew what it was to be a woman denied these hours, prevented from grappling with ideas, prevented from speaking, from writing; it was she who told us that what is needed, if one is to find one's voice, is not the "cut and thrust" of public dialogue, but, above all, a room of one's own.

Far from endorsing, then, an increased candor, intimacy, or familiarity in the speech genres that constitute classroom discourse, as I think the "new literacy" seeks to do, my own plea urges a re-formatization of pedagogic communications, a reinstatement of the objective style of discourse, of the disengagement of intelligent and informed critical analysis—not, as in current liberal parlance, a "pedagogy of the repressed," one which at least explicitly acknowledges the untrustworthiness, the lack of sympathy for, or sensitivity to, difference, which has from the start defined both the substance and the intent of institutionalized education. And it is probably worth remarking how often we seem to find that those very practices denounced as reactionary by the mainstream are advocated by those at the margins as not only in their educational interests, but, indeed, as essential to their very survival. My argument here is that for many forms of subjectivity to survive, it is essential that they not be spoken at all, except with the most extreme caution, and under carefully crafted conditions of protection—conditions that are far from being even understood, let alone secured within the discursive contexts of public schooling.

When teachers instruct students to "find their place in the text," they invariably refer not to the actual reader's own place, the place that only readers can find for themselves, but to the place in which the teacher, acting for the institution, seeks to position them.

But, there are those of us for whom precious little space exists in these institutions—in the classroom, the workplace, the family—for whom the virtual space of the always ambiguous text provides a sanctuary, a place for subversive readings, for readings "against the grain," readings that are not only against the grain of the text, but against the grain of the world—a sanctuary for identity formation which is both rare, then, and vital to our survival.

The fragile ambiguity upon which the preservation of this space depends cannot withstand the massed voices of the classroom "community," whose discursive rituals of debasement and exclusion are currently encouraged and esteemed in the name of "student voice" and "empowerment." For these make of the always ambiguous text, a literal text, and the literal text is a place no less policed and regulated than the physical spaces of public culture.

It is, finally, this place of ambiguity that must be our destination in all our journeys through literate space. For it is in virtue of its unique capacity to *refuse* the literal that the distinctive educational role of literacy still resides—this perfect indeterminacy of meaning that elevates the text above and beyond the as yet brutish and stubbornly literal character of postliterate technologies, making of literacy not the obsolescence predicted by Lyotard, but, indeed, *primacy* as a medium of humane educational practice—a practice in which nothing is produced, in which, conversely, everything is consumed in and by an active, engaged, *and private* practice of self-formation.

Paradoxically, it may be that the formulation of an "ethics and politics" of literacy will require our willingness to know less about our students in order that, in the end, our students might know more. My argument here is that, notwithstanding contemporary enthusiasm for "dialogue" and "self-expression," no better possibility exists for readers on the margins to make for themselves a home in the texts they read.

N O T E S

1. This paper needs a small explanation—it was written some time ago for a talk to English teachers, and then it was printed in a local journal for English teachers. But, people like it, and I thought it seemed well-suited to this particular issue of JCT.

2. "The better a person understands the degree to which he is externally determined...the closer he comes to understanding and exercising his real freedom" (Bakhtin, 1986, p. 137).

R E F E R E N C E S

Bakhtin, M.M. (1986). *Speech genres and other late essays.* V.W. McGee, trans. C. Emerson & M. Holquist, eds. (Austin: University of Texas Press).

Foucault, M. (1972). *The archeology of knowledge.* A.M. Sheridan Smith, trans. (New York: Pantheon Books).

Foucault, M. (1980). *Power/Knowledge: Selected interviews and other writings, 1972-1977.* C. Gordon, ed. & trans. (New York: Pantheon Books).

Foucault, M. (1986). *The care of the self.* R. Hurley, trans. (New York: Pantheon Books).

Gilbert, P. (1988). Text analysis and ideology. In S. de Castell, A. Luke, & C. Luke, eds., *Language, Authority, and Criticism: Readings on the School Textbook.* (New York: Falmer Press).

Habermas, J. (1979). *Communication and the evolution of society* T. McCarthy, trans. (Boston: MA: Beacon Press).

Havelock, E. (1986). *The muse learns to write: Reflections on orality and literacy from antiquity to the present.* (New Haven: Yale University Press).

Illich, I., & Sanders, B. (1989). ABC: *The alphabetization of the popular mind.* (New York: Vintage Press).

Lyotard, J. F. (1984). *The postmodern condition: A report on knowledge.* G. Bennington & B. Massumi, trans. (Minneapolis: University of Minnesota Press).

Martin, L. H., Gutman, H. & Hutton, P. (Eds.). (1988). *Technologies of the self: A seminar with Michel Foucault.* (Amherst, MA: University of Massachusetts Press).

Said, E. (1983). *The world, the text, and the critic.* (Cambridge, MA: Harvard University Press).

Steiner, G. (1996). Our homeland, the text. In R. Boyers & P. Boyars, eds., *The New Salmagundi Reader.* (New York: Syracuse University Press).

Willinsky, J. (1990). *The new literacy: Redefining reading and writing in the schools.* (New York: Routledge).

CHAPTER TWENTY-SIX

Toward a Ludic Pedagogy

An Uncertain Occasion

Marla Morris
1996

Alfred North Whitehead's claims in *Process and Reality* (1978) about who and what we are ontologically (a series of actual occasions or events) suggests that human beings are ambiguous, ambivalent, uncertain creatures. As a series of actual occasions we have what Whitehead terms a "subjective aim." A subjective aim is my freedom. But freedom is not radical or simple because I am embedded in my own complex past, my own personal history, and that past shapes my present, and writes and re-writes my future. At each and every moment I appropriate that past into my present and this affects my possibilities. This appropriation of my past is always uncertain—and even constrained. I am constrained internally by my particular psychic make up; I am constrained externally by my class, race, gender, sexuality, and socioeconomic position. The direction my life might take is riddled with uncertainty.

This profound sense of uncertainty in Whitehead resonates with many feelings about what some call the "postmodern condition." Lyotard, Derrida, Baudrillard, Kroker, Cook, and others seem to believe that we have arrived in a new historical epoch: the postmodern (Kellner, 1991). Have we arrived? I'm not so sure. The supposed break between the modern and the postmodern is not entirely clear. Nonetheless, I think postmodern theory has much to offer in this uncertain age. More specifically, postmodern theory in the ludicmode may offer some clues toward revisioning ideas such as agency, power, politics, and identity. As a feminist and as an educator I am particularly interested in the possibilities that ludic postmodern theory may bring to pedagogy. Through the looking glass of ludic theory educators might continually re-envision, and re-contextualize, re-interpret pedagogy.

The word "postmodernity" suggests that modernity has been surpassed. Of course, as I already mentioned, this point is suspect, debatable, problematic. Even though divisions such as the modern and the postmodern are simplistic namings of historical time, I would like to briefly examine what I think designates this broad division. I believe that the modern period, generally speaking, can be traced back to Descartes. Descartes lusted after an archimedean point from which he could view reality, the self, the world, God. Descartes lusted after what he termed indubitable principles. Although Descartes began his philosophical wanderings with doubt, he ended his wanderings in absolute certainty, embracing clear and distinct ideas. Certainty and clarity are some of the linchpins of modernity.

The dawning of postmodernity, if indeed there is such a historical epoch, also begins in doubt. Unlike modernity, unlike Descartes, I suggest that the postmodern condition generates not clear and distinct ideas, but only more doubt, *doubt ad absurdum, doubt ad nauseum*. "The hard die of rationalism we have inherited, once presented as the unique, progressive and symmetrical appropriation of reality, has been softened up, submerged, thwarted in an excess of sense, in a short-circuiting" (Chambers, 1990, p. 2). A postmodern sensibility is one that has short-circuited on clear and distinct ideas, on universal claims to truth, on the notion of progress, on fixed identities, on grand theories. Grand theories, or metanarratives tend toward "repression, homogeneity, and a totalitarian domination which has epistemological, sexual, political and cultural dimensions" (Kellner, 1991, p. 60). The totalitarian domination of homogeneity, in particular, is devastating for American culture and American schooling, as I will discuss later in this paper, as it annihilates difference, as it squashes out creativity.

Postmodernity begins not only with doubt and more doubt, but also with an awareness, a consciousness that something has gone wrong. Descartes' indubitable principles and the hope for finding, with certainty, the land of milk and honey, the promised land of certainty, is now demolished. Indubitable principles are now challenged by atomic bombs, holocausts, AIDS. A postmodern space is one of dis-content, dis-ease, dis-array. It is a space that is a tearing down. But also it is a space of building up, creating, dreaming, imagining. In this postmodern space "there is no archimedean view point, history and culture are texts, admitting an endless proliferation of readings, each of which is itself unstable" (Butler, 1990, p. 142). Nuclear proliferation and the proliferation of readings, as Butler suggests, are unstable, unsettling, uncertain. All the world is but a text and the text is slippery. The signifier has been snapped off from the signified; sliding signifiers are blowin' in the wind. The textual world is no easy read; in a difficult reading hour there is no "correct exegesis," no "correct interpretation. This text-of-a-world verges on de-scripted, script-less, not scriptured.

There are many types of postmodern theory. "Resistance postmodernism," for instance, attempts to grapple with large, macrostructural forms of oppression (e.g., the oppression of patriarchy). Teresa Ebert (1993) suggests that, in the face of this disturbing postmodern condition, it is necessary to resist structures of oppression. Ebert claims that a resistance postmodernism is "a collective practice through which existing social institutions are changed" (p. 6). One of the goals of resistance postmodernism, then, is to become emancipated from structures of oppression by uncovering "strategies of power" (p. 13) that set oppression in motion.

Deconstructionism and poststructuralism are other broad strands of postmodern theory. Derrida and Foucault might be considered representative figures of deconstructionism and poststructuralism respectively. "Derrida considered...collage/ montage as the primary form of postmodern discourse" (Harvey 1989, p. 51). Through reading Heidegger, Derrida discovered that language cannot so easily be interpreted. The text is constantly reinterpreted, the signified/signifier have no connection, meanings are ambiguous.

Foucault (1990) thought that the notion of power admits of much ambiguity. People do not possess power. Power is an ambivalent force that permeates culture in mysterious ways. Foucault suggests that power and knowledge are inextricably linked. This link makes the power equation even more difficult. If knowledge is bound up by language and language is continually reinterpreted, fragmented, it becomes very difficult to say that power, if oppressive, might be dismantled by locating it in large, macrostructural sites. Power is not that simple. It is diffuse, fragmented, and changeable.

Much ludic postmodern theory draws on deconstructionism and poststructuralism. Ludic postmodern theory deals with the problems of language and power. "Ludic postmodernism is best conceptualized as a crisis of representation, a crisis in which texts constituted by difference can no longer provide reliable knowledge because the real meaning itself is self-divided and undecidable" (Ebert, 1993, p. 15).

Readings of histories/herstories are many, infinite, perspectival. Texts, lives-as-texts, are, then, ambivalent, ambiguous, uncertain. Living is, as Whitehead suggested, an uncertain occasion. No longer am I certain about "what constitutes an adequate description of social reality" (Lather, 1991, p. 21). I suggest that an "adequate" description of social reality admits of multiple, particular, perspectival, positioned, situated viewings. What is "inadequate" is a totalizing description of social reality that pretends to know the whole story. I cannot know the whole story because I am situated in a particular place, space, life. I am not uncomfortable with the idea that there is "no unified representation of the world" (Beyer & Liston, 1990, p. 374).

Ludic postmodernism might sound like John Cage, Philip Glass, Laurie Anderson. In these sounds I hear playfulness, light-heartedness, and cynicism.

No trumpets of glory over the heavens here though, no easy resolutions, no resolve of sounds even. The sounds of ludic postmodernism are uneasy sounds.

Ludic postmodern images, too, may be uneasy. Consider this: Descartes is sitting in front of his fireplace working on *Meditations on First Philosophy*. He is nearly finished, certain that he is certain about certainty, when in walks a trickster, a hermes figure, a cyborg on roller skates. The cyborg on roller skates throws Descartes' manuscript into the fire. Descartes is sure he must be dreaming. Alas, he is dreaming. But when he wakes up he sees Aristotle's archer (from *The Nichomachean Ethics*) standing in front of him aiming toward a target near the fireplace. Just as the archer gets ready to shoot his arrow, a trickster, a hermes figure, Dante's Beatrice (from *The Inferno*), a cyborg on roller skates all march into Descartes' room and move the archer's target. The archer misses his target and accidentally hits Descartes in his right hand, his writing hand. Descartes never finished *Meditations on First Philosophy*. This ludic image, this parody, is not meant to only be funny, ludicrous. This image, this ludic image of Descartes is also meant to undermine Descartes' notion of certainty. Moreover, I raise this question: What if Descartes never finished *Meditations on First Philosophy*? Would others in the modern period still lust after clear and distinct ideas? Would modernism have taken the same twists and turns? I cannot answer these questions. I am uncertain.

Parody, as a satirical imitation, is a ludic postmodern strategy. Parody might serve to dis-mantle, dis-lodge, dis-locate what Simone de Beauvoir (1948) and Jean-Paul Sartre (1977) termed "the spirit of seriousness." The spirit of seriousness is that spirit which upholds universals, absolutes, objectivity. Parody is one vehicle that may serve to undermine the spirit of seriousness. Parody inverts the spirit of seriousness, it makes the serious silly and by doing so it may en-able one to uncover, dis-cover assumptions and presuppositions that tend toward totalizing, totalitarian knowing. Parody is not simply funny. I suggest that it may be, in some forms, also political. Parody may, in some instances, be an oppositional politic.

One such oppositional politic is drag. Drag may un-cover assumptions spectators might have about gender, sexuality. Judith Butler (1990) suggests that drag undermines "the notion of a true gender" (p. 337). A drag queen is usually a male dressed as a woman. Drag queens intend to confuse the spectator. And, in this confusion, drag can undermine one's assumptions about the supposed connection between sex and gender. An illustration: several years ago I lived in the French Quarter in New Orleans, one block away from Bourbon Street. My father lived around the corner from me on Burgundy Street. Burgundy Street is a haven for drag queens. This, my father did not realize. I did—since I lived in the Quarter for years and was familiar with the scene. The scene is this: If you meet a woman in a bar in the Quarter, especially on Burgundy Street, you may be surprised that that woman is not the person you thought *he* was. My father met a woman, or so he thought, in a bar on Burgundy Street. My father wanted me to meet this woman. I did. My father, you see, had fallen for a drag queen. I'm sure that when I broke the news to him he felt quite confused. Judith Butler (1990) claims that drag "suggests a dissonance not only between sex and performance but between sex and gender, gender and performance.... In imitating gender, drag implicitly reveals the imitative structure of gender itself" (p. 338). Drag, then, undermines assumptions that sex and gender are necessarily connected. What I wear doesn't necessarily determine who I am. Many drag queens that I have known are trans-gendered, not simply cross dressers. This further complicates our ideas about fixed genders. Some drag queens are transvestites and are heterosexual. Some drag queens call themselves transgendered lesbians. Drag is not simply ludic. I suggest it is an oppositional politic undermining assumptions about gender, sexuality.

Critics of postmodern theory claim that ludic strategies are not political, ludic strategies are simply cynical (Donovan, 1994; Ebert, 1993; Shapiro, 1995). Shapiro (1995), for instance, suggests that postmodern theory has created "a sensibility that is increasingly cynical and increasingly reluctant to articulate the values of human rights, liberty" (pp. 31-32). Therefore, Shapiro suggests that postmodern theory is apolitical. As I have suggested ludic postmodern theory is not apolitical; it can serve to undermine dangerous assumptions. Ludic theory simply approaches politics from a different angle, a ludic angle. This angle might even prove more powerful than talk of human rights and liberty. I feel that many are, as Shapiro points out, reluctant to talk of human rights and liberty because these ideas don't make much sense in the postmodern age. Briefly, the word "rights" suggests that I may have "entitlements." That is, I may be entitled to life, liberty, happiness. These are my rights. However, who decides that I have these rights? In whose interests are my rights taken away? What exactly is a "right"? What exactly is an "entitlement"? Entitlement theory in ethics is a tricky business. Everyone can't be entitled to everything; entitlement theory slips very easily into oppression, exclusion. Further, the term "human" in the equation of human rights is so broad that it tends to be empty of content. Who decides if I am human enough, or fully human, so as to be entitled to rights? If I am, for instance, nonheterosexual, in these United States, I am not entitled to the same rights as heterosexuals. Am I not fully human?

Shapiro is also disturbed that postmodern theorists do not address the problem of liberty. Again, what does that word "liberty" mean? It is so vague that it seems empty of content. Whose liberty? Is liberty the same for everyone? Does liberty mean noninterference (as in J.S. Mill's On Liberty)? If so, doesn't liberty create selfish people? If my liberty means don't interfere with me, how can I communicate with others at all? What kind of liberty is libertarianism? Is that what Shapiro means? If so, I'm not comfortable with that either. The terms "human rights" and "liberty" don't make much sense to me and that is why I would be reluctant to address them.

Shapiro says that this "Postmodern bizarre…is terrifying and repulsive" (pp. 31-32). What is repulsive to me are terms like "rights" and "liberty" because they can become oppressive. Ludic strategies, however, work to undo oppressive situations. And although I may be uncertain as to the consequence of a particular ludic performance, I am not terrified that it will completely demolish my ethical/political sensibilities. As Diane Elam (1994) points out, uncertainty "is neither an absolute obstacle to action nor a theoretical bar to praxis" (p. 31).

The ludic performance of drag as oppositional political praxis illuminates assumptions about dressing generally. Drag is a form of dressing that is free of constraints. Constrained dressing, for example, is the enforced uniform. When I am constrained in my dress I am also constrained in my psyche, in my being. A short autobiography: One of my memories of high school is the gym uniform. The gym uniform was blue and white striped, skin tight, ugly, embarrassing. Even though I graduated high school over fifteen years ago, this uniform still haunts me. There is something very insidious about that uniform. The image is this: I stand in a row with thirty other girls in blue and white striped, skin tight, ugly uniforms. Standing in this row, we wait to be counted by the gym coach. After the counting of heads, the rows of blue and white striped uniforms, skin tight, ugly, march off to the showers, strip down, shower, uniformly, and return to classrooms in the sunny Southern California space. A parallel image: Thirty girls in blue and white striped prison uniforms, lined up in rows on the concentration camp grounds, wait for the counting of heads by the SS leader. After the counting of heads, the rows are dismissed to the showers. The blue and white striped uniforms are undone, the rows of girls shower, but never return. This was the parallel image that always popped into my mind during gym class.

There is something sinister about uniforms. Uni-form = the American dream of uniformity, homogeneity, conformity. Stripped of my identity, my integrity, stuffed into the uni-form, forced to stand in a uni-form row, I felt sick during gym class. The gym coach said that she couldn't judge our performance "objectively" if we didn't wear uniforms. If we weren't dressed the same, the gym coach thought she couldn't judge fairly, she couldn't judge without bias. However, to judge "objectively" suggests judging objects. To object-ify is to turn subjects (human beings) into objects. This is exactly what the Nazis did in the death camps. The nazis forced everyone to wear uniforms, to be branded, to be turned into objects. To bake in ovens like objects.

The Village People, in the 1980s, wrote a song called "YMCA" parodying the whole notion of uniforms. This ludic performance, this dressing up as police officers and construction workers, illuminates the ridiculousness of having to wear uniforms. This parody undermines the social constructions of dress, dress codes. This parody undermines the seriousness of uniforms. The taken-for-granted assumption that goes along with my wearing a uniform—that is, that it must be worn because it somehow identifies me—has now been un-dressed, un-covered, dis-mantled.

Like the enforced uniform, the classroom space is uniformly constructed. I look around at the schools in which I have taught and I see the same things: desks in rows, podiums, clocks, chalkboards. This factory model classroom hasn't changed much over time. Professors are encouraged to produce efficient workers, to ready the students for the work force, enforced work. Students are forced to work, forced to memorize, recite, spit back the same things year after year. Students are to learn the same way, learn the same things: students = clones. This cloning process, however, is quite insidious. Orwell's dream.

In some classrooms there is a new uniform: the circle. No more rows, now there are circles. To my mind, this is only a new uni-formity. Merely taking off one uniform (e.g., rows of desks) and putting on another (e.g., circles) doesn't necessarily affect the dynamics of the classroom in significant ways. Students may still feel like factory workers—even if they feel freer to speak out, as the circle might create spaces for more open dialogue. However, I contend that the circle may create even more difficulties for students who feel marginalized. The circle might feel invasive to students who already feel vulnerable. Therefore, students who didn't speak in rows are even less likely to speak in circles. Pedagogically, the difference in classroom dynamics, I suggest, begins with the teacher, not with the configuration of the classroom.

Pedagogues should not be demagogues. Rather, pedagogues might be more like cyborgs, ludic cyborgs. I suggest that change for the better in the classroom begins with a cyborgian pedagogy. My cyborgian pedagogy is informed by Donna Haraway (1991) as she suggests that the "cyborg is resolutely committed to partiality, irony" (p. 151). The cyborgian pedagogues' knowings are perspectival, partial, situated. A cyborgian epistemology is always partial. When I walk into my classroom I tell my students that I am not an "expert." My knowings are partial, perspectival. I carry psychological baggage with me into my knowings too, and this baggage may be unconscious. Although I have worked very hard over the years to drop this baggage I may not have been completely successful. Some of that baggage is still hiding, waiting in the wings to pounce out as it were. Some of my students are not happy about my pronouncements as a cyborgian pedagogue. Some drop my classes because they are in search of the "experts." I wish them well.

Haraway suggests that partial knowings must be couched in "accountability" (p. 111). If partial knowings build on accountability, I must take responsibility for my knowings. But I cannot be accountable for every knowing or any knowing. How can I be accountable for anything? I cannot. An anything goes epistemology simply will not do. Further, Haraway suggests that "we must be hostile to...holisms" (p. 192). Holistic knowings are dangerous knowings because they presume to know all, to know the whole picture, to know the whole story. I cannot know all, I am not omniscient. I cannot pretend to know, say, the whole picture of social reality. But I can say that I know my social reality, with uncertainty, with ambiguity. My understanding is one that is unsure of what is standing under me; my understanding is partial, situated, even impure. Holistic knowings smack of too much purity. The cyborgian pedagogue's knowings are anything but pure. Sullied knowings are more to the point. Sullied knowings are uncertain, ambiguous, tainted with light and dark.

Haraway calls her epistemological position "feminist objectivity" (p. 188). I think Haraway uses the term objectivity to avoid problems associated with relativism. The debate about relativism is nothing new. One can trace the debate back to the pre-Socratics in Western philosophy. William James (1907), for instance, has been "accused" of committing the crime of rampant relativism in his essay *What Pragmatism Means*. In this work, James suggests that if it works for you do it. In a nutshell, that is James' version of pragmatism. But take the counter-example of Jeffrey Dahmer. Killing, cutting, and eating people worked for Jeffrey. The ethics of cannibalism are relative to Jeff's situation. The situation required dead men. Does that make cannibalism right? What's right for me may not be right for you, what works for me may not work for you. But if my situation is relative to me, how can I tell if I am doing something good? Haraway might suggest that Dahmer's knowings, eatings, were not "accountable."

Haraway attempts to avoid problems like these by calling her epistemology "objective." This "feminist objectivity" is

> the Alternative to relativism [which] is partial, locatable...the possibility of webs of connections, called solidarity in politics and shared conversations in epistemology. Relativism is a way of being nowhere while claiming to be everywhere equally. The "equality" of positioning is a denial of responsibility and critical inquiry. (p.191)

I don't think Haraway has moved out of a realistic position. A situated knowing is still relative to one's situation; a partial knowing is still relative to one's knowings. To me, Haraway is offering simply a more qualified form of relativism by suggesting that one is not "equally" positioned. Haraway's use of the term "objectivity" is, I find, misleading.

Feminist objectivity, as Haraway suggests, might lead to "shared conversations" (p. 191). A shared conversation is partial, locatable, positioned. Haraway also contends that partial knowings may lead to solidarity. But, I suggest, in the classroom, shared conversations may not lead to solidarity, even though they seem to be shared. Underneath the façade of sharing may be feelings of hostility. In some cases, situated knowings may lead to dissonance. Dissonance, though, may serve to unsettle a false sense of certainty that students bring with them into the classroom. Sometimes dissonance creates a very live space in the classroom. A shared conversation must allow for dissonance, even dismay. Epistemological *jouissance* is still possible even with/in dissonance. A deeper understanding about partial knowings, even if these partial knowings are painful knowings, may still lead to joy. Epistemological *jouissance* doesn't necessarily mean that shared conversations lead to unbounded solidarity.

If I cannot experience epistemological jouissance even in dis-chordant knowings—even in dis-chordant conversations—anger and embitterment might lead to what Worth (1933) terms an "epistemological shut down" (p. 9). An epistemological shut down barricades any conversation. I have experienced many of these epistemological shut downs in the classroom. They are not easy to break through. Once students become angry, or once I become angry or feel embittered, the class is over if I cannot move through the walls of the shut down. Movement through the walls is an uncertain occasion. Sometimes I can push down the walls, other times I fail. A strategy that I find very useful is autobiography.

Some consider autobiography a ludic strategy (Ebert, 1993). This particular strategy is a way of distancing the classroom from the present difficulties, whatever they may be, and illuminating the problem through an analogous life story. After I reflect on my life story, I ask my students to reflect upon their own life stories and to try to relate them to the present problem in the classroom. For instance, I once said to my students that schooling can ruin you, it can make you turn into a zombie through standardized testing, standardized curricula. My students looked absolutely bewildered. My students did not understand what I was talking about. Some even got mad. I experienced an epistemological shutdown. So I told my students about my own experiences in school and how I thought they related to Andy Warhol's art.

I told my students that last spring that I took a trip to the Andy Warhol museum in Pittsburgh, Pennsylvania—my home town. I was interested in Warhol because we both attended the same school: Carnegie-Mellon University. He became famous, I dropped out. At any rate, the Warhol museum houses about seven floors of art. Room after room, floor after floor, contains Warhol and more Warhol. I saw seemingly mindless repetitions of Campbell's Soup cans, mindless repetitions of Brillo pad boxes, mindless repetitions of Mao Tse-Tung's face, of Marilyn Monroe's face, of Andy Warhol's face. I saw boxes of cornflakes, bottles of Coca-Cola.

I told my students that I thought Warhol was parodying the mindlessness of American culture. Americans are bombarded with these images day after day and we don't stop to think how or why they affect us. These images serve to normalize Americans. A normal American eats Campbell's Soup, drinks Coca-Cola, uses Brillo pads, thinks about Marilyn Monroe (just think of Madonna): Warhol is poking fun at our normalization. In an interview with Gene R. Swenson (1963), Warhol said:

Someone said that Brecht wanted everybody to think alike. I want everybody to think alike. But Brecht wanted to do it through Communism, in a way. It's happening here all by itself without being under strict government. ...Everybody looks alike and acts alike and we're getting more and more that way. (p. 131)

This ludic statement that everyone should be more alike is clearly parodying the standardization of American culture. It's not only ludic but it is also "menacing" (Bourdon, 1993, p. 9). David Bourdon suggests that Warhol's work had a sinister side, a cynical side. It is menacing because it illuminates America's terrible tendency toward normalization, sanitation, homogeneity. Schooling, as part of American culture, is part of this terrible tendency toward normalization. Standardized testing, standardized curricula, standardized seating arrangements are very much like Warhol's vision.

Warhol is also parodying the world of so-called "high art"; Bourdon (1993) comments, "There was no shortage of observers who declared that the artist's brand-name subjects were too 'low,' 'vulgar,' and 'commercial' to be considered seriously as fine art" (p. 9). Paintings of Coke cans, Brillo pad boxes, and soup cans are not exactly the content of, say, a Rembrandt. Warhol's ludic art is clearly a statement against the elitism in the world of high art. Warhol is really asking what is fine art, what is high art? What is art? Who decides what art or high art is?

Like Warhol, educators might question why certain subjects are considered too "vulgar" for learning. Educators might question who it is that decides what is too vulgar for learning? Who decides what is unthinkable? Whose interests are being served? The things that get excluded form the curriculum may serve to only sanitize more, normalize more, oppress more. What tends to be excluded? The histories of women, the histories of African-Americans, the histories of gays, lesbians, transgendered, nonheterosexual peoples. Queer theory tries to grapple with these exclusions. Women's studies attempt to bridge the supposed gap between "high" and "low" culture. But still American education has a long way to go to heal the wounds of exclusion.

While at the Warhol museum, I nearly excluded a careful viewing of Warhol's (1978) "Oxidation" painting because I wasn't really impressed by the content or style. However, some mysterious force compelled me to look closer. As I read about the actual creation of the painting I became rather fascinated. Picture this: Warhol and other artists begin by covering their canvasses with copper paint. They then proceed to urinate onto them, causing the paint to oxidize. Painters pissing on canvas smacks of the in-your-face quality of ludic postmodernism. Warhol is saying, in essence, "piss on this, piss on high art, piss on art, here's your art, here's art for you." The Oxidation paintings are funny, yes; but there is also something menacing about them as David Bourdon (1993) suggests. This pissing in the face of high culture is an angry pissing. Warhol expresses an oppositional politic that I think is filled with rage.

This rage returns and re-turns me to the classroom. I told my students this story and broke through the epistemological shut down. The only way I could break through was by this sort of in-your-face ludic strategy. Through storytelling, autobiography, biography, memory and counter-memory, laughter, tears, and ludic moments the cyborgian pedagogue somehow breaks through the walls of epistemological shutdowns. Teaching becomes an oppositional politic.

Teaching a class on drag queens, gym uniforms, and Andy Warhol might suggest a skepticism and cultural critique of uniformity, homogeneity, conformity, standardization, and elitism. All of these things have been injected into American schooling and American curricula. As an educator I feel that it is crucial that I tell my students that I am opposed to homogeneity, conformity, standardization, and elitism. I am outraged by them, in fact. Pedagogy built on ludic examples and counter-examples may create a space for oppositional politics, a space for tearing down walls, and a space opened to creativity.

Ludic creativity is playful, fearless, awe-some. Teachers must not only tear down assumptions that may serve to oppress, but must also inject creativity back into the classroom. Standardization has suffocated our students' creativity. It is very difficult to teach students to stop repeating, to stop spitting back information, because it has been drilled into them forever. As educators we must find ways to encourage students to simply think for themselves as individuals. The classroom must become alive space for students and that comes through creativity. As Donna Haraway (1991) suggests, "I want to argue for a doctrine and practice...that privileges contestation, deconstruction, passionate construction" (p. 192). Passionate construction. This is what we must inject into the classroom as cyborgian pedagogues. But passionate construction only comes after passionate deconstruction. If I haven't deconstructed my own assumptions and presuppositions, I cannot passionately construct, re-construct, re-vision, re-envision.

Ludic strategies teach that pedagogues might walk a path without a path. As an educator I might carry on a shared conversation, a shared dialectic without resolution, without resolve. A cyborgian pedagogy is a monstrous space, an uncertain space, a funny, ludic space, a ludicrous space. This shape-shifting space is a place where teachers and students learn as they unlearn, discover as they uncover. A ludic pedagogy is also a place of resistance. A cyborgian pedagogue is resistant to uni-forms, uniformity, conformity, comfort, domestication, uniform knowings, standardized curricula, standardized testings, standardized knowings. A ludic pedagogy is an uncertain space, an occasion for uncertainty. A ludic pedagogy constantly re-interprets, re-contextualizes visions of an uncertain horizon.

R E F E R E N C E S

Beyer, L. & Liston, D.P. (1990). Discourse on moral action? A critique of postmodernism. *Educational Theory*, 42 (4), 371-393.

Bourdon, D. (1993). Andy Warhol and the American dream. In J. Baal-Teshuva (Ed.), *Andy Warhol: 1928-1987* (pp. 9-16). (Munich, Germany: Prestel-Verlag).

Butler, J. (1990). Gender trouble, feminist theory, and psychoanalytic discourse. In L.J. Nicholson (Ed.), *Feminism/Postmodernism*. pp. 324-340. (New York: Routledge).

Chambers, I. (1990). *Border dialogues: Journeys in postmodernism*. (New York: Routledge).

Descartes, R. (1641). *Meditations on first philosophy*. In T. V. Smith & M. Greene, eds. (1956), *Philosophers Speak for Themselves: From Descartes to Locke*. pp. 49-113. (Chicago: The University of Chicago Press).

Donovan, J. (1994). Feminist theory: The intellectual traditions of American feminism. (New York: Frederick Ungar).

Ebert, T.L. (1993). Ludic feminism, the body, performances and labor: Bringing materialism back into feminist cultural studies. *Cultural Critique*, 23, 5-50.

Elam, D. (1994). *Feminism and deconstruction: Ms. en abyme*. (New York: Routledge).

Foucault, M. (1990). *The history of sexuality: An introduction*, Volume 1. R. Hurley, trans. (New York: Vintage). (Original work published in 1978).

Haraway, D. (1991). *Simians, cyborgs, and women: The reinvention of nature*. (New York: Routledge).

Harvey, D. (1989). *The condition of postmodernity: An enquiry into the origins of cultural change*. (New York: Basil Blackwell).

James, W. (1907). What pragmatism means. In M.H. Fisch, ed. (1951), *Classic American Philosophers*, pp. 128-135. (Englewood Cliffs, NJ: Prentice Hall).

Kellner, D. (1991). Reading images critically: Toward a postmodern pedagogy. In H. Giroux (Ed.), *Postmodernism, Feminism and Cultural Politics: Redrawing Educational Boundaries*, pp. 60-82. (New York: State University of New York Press).

Lather, P. (1991). *Getting smart: Feminist research and pedagogy with/In the postmodern*. (New York: Routledge).

Sartre, J.P. (1977). *Being and nothingness*. H. Barnes, trans. (Secaucus, NJ: The Citadel Press). (Original Work published in 1956).

Shapiro, S. (1995). Educational change, the crisis of the left: Toward a postmodern educational discourse. In B. Kanpol & P. McLaren (Eds.), *Critical Multiculturalism: Uncommon Voices in a Common Struggle*, pp. 19-380. (Westport, CT: Bergin & Garvey).

Swenson, G.R. (1993). Interview with Andy Warhol. In J. Baal-Teshuva (Ed.), *Andy Warhol: 1928-1987*, pp. 131-132. (Munich, Germany: Prestel-Verlag).

Whitehead, A.N. (1987). *Process and reality* (corrected edition). (New York: The Free Press). (Original work published in 1929).

Worth, F. (1993). Postmodern pedagogy in the multicultural classroom: For the inappropriate teacher and imperfect spectators. *Cultural Critique*, 25, 5-32.

CHAPTER TWENTY-SEVEN

Resisting "Resistance"

Stories Women Teachers Tell

Petra Munro
1996

WHAT'S RESISTANCE GOT TO DO WITH IT?

I did not want to be a teacher. Teaching was women's work. The images of teachers—the spinster, schoolmarm, old maid, motherteacher—did not speak to my understandings of self. These scripts define a woman's role relative to the male plot in which a woman's relation to knowledge is restricted to her naturalized capacity for nurturance. Teachers facilitate knowledge but cannot become knowers themselves.[1] Thus, not only are the meanings women give to their work as teachers and the agency for the teaching act obscured, but women's subjectivity and agency are denied.

This paper explores the resistance to erasure in which "women are either absent or represented as the objects of knowledge, rarely its subjects" (Pagano, 1990; p. xvi). Women's experience of resistance must be first and foremost understood from their position as objects. As Bettina Aptheker (1989) suggests:

> Women's resistance comes out of women's subordinated status to men, institutionalized in society and lived through every day in countless personal ways. Women's resistance is not necessarily or intrinsically oppositional; it is not necessarily or intrinsically contesting for power. It does, however, have a profound impact on the fabric of social life because of its steady, cumulative effects. It is central to the making of history, and...it is the bedrock of social change. (p. 173)

Two points are central to my argument. Women have resisted. And, women's resistance is shaped primarily and fundamentally by our position as objects. Because women traditionally have been defined as objects, Nancy Miller (1989) maintains, women's relation to integrity and textuality, to desire and authority, and, thus, to resistance, displays structurally important differences from the universal position claimed by patriarchy.[2] It is from this standpoint, in which the very naming of ourselves as subjects is an act of resistance, that this paper explores how women teachers constitute their subjectivity through, and in, their life history narratives.

Interpreting the narratives of women teachers, I am situated in a paradoxical moment in which I simultaneously seek to create and to disrupt the notion of the subject. Listening to and interpreting women's lives has been central to the feminist reconstruction of the world (Personal Narratives Group, 1989). That "gender" is crucial to this understanding is the very contribution of feminism. Yet, the notion of woman, positioned within language as a "subject," is a masculinist construction of an essentialized self that feminists have sought to disrupt (Butler, 1990). If there is no such category as "woman," since gendered "identity" is construction of masculinist binary thought (Cixous, 1981; Irigary, 1985), what becomes of the subject traditionally thought necessary for resistance? If the subject is "indeterminate," "incoherent," and "contingent," what becomes of the categories "woman" and "resistance"? In a poststructuralist world "where points of resistance are everywhere and power is everywhere" (Young, 1990), is everything resistance? If, contrary to what is often assumed, it is the absence of resistance that is impossible, how do we speak of resistance? Does the rejection of the subject preclude the possibility of resistance (Hekman, 1990)?

For feminists, resistance is a slippery construct in which we grapple with the need to claim a position as a subject, resisting our erasure, while recognizing that the very appropriation of subjecthood reifies the category of subject that has been essential to patriarchy (Gilmore, 1994; Jacobs, Munro, & Adams, 1995). Within recent feminist, poststructuralist work the very category of the subject has been contested. Feminist critique challenges the humanist tradition, which depicts the subject as unitary, essential, and universal by shifting the terrain from asking "who" the subject is to revealing how individuals are continually being constituted through discourses as apparently unified subjects (Bloom & Monro, 1995; Britzman, 1995; Flax, 1990). The poststructuralist freeing of the "subject" in which subjectivity is seen as nonunitary, multiple, and constantly in flux is central to deconstructing the universal male subject of liberal, humanist as well as neo-Marxist, discourse. Yet, to what degree does the notion of subjectivity, in which individuals actively choose from multiple and often conflicting discourses, merely act as a new and more accurate "truth" claim. In what ways does the creation of a new subject, albeit nonunitary, perpetuate discursive practices that reify a universal reality central to modernist thought? The contradictory ways in which postmodern discourses can function speaks directly to the need to reconceptualize resistance.

For feminists, the postmodern "death of the subject" (Lather, 1991; p. 28) has been simultaneously emancipatory and cause for grave concern. Despite the postmodern emphasis on difference and polyvocality, feminists have been concerned with the potential relativism of the postmodern subject (Alcoff, 1989; Benhabibv, 1995; Harding, 1987; Mascia-Lees, Sharpe, & Cohen, 1989). Feminist critics suggest that it is, perhaps, no accident that at the very time feminists and others obtained a subject, the subject became nonunitary. As Nancy Hartstock (1990) asks: "Why is it that just at the moment when so many of us who have been silenced begin to demand the right to name ourselves, as subjects, rather than as objects of history, that just then the concept of subjecthood becomes problematic?" (p. 163).[3] What becomes of the politics of resistance when there is no subject? Positioning resistance within these larger ideological, political struggles in which feminists struggle to account for the specificity of gender/subjectivity without falling either into an essentialized discourse or lapsing into relativism highlights the insidious hegemony of binary modernist discourse (Whitson, 1991).[4]

Accordingly, I am reluctant to reduce current feminist theorizing to the dualistic tension reproduced in the essentialism/relativism debate. In fact, this simplistic dichotomy merely recreates the binary view of the world that I, as a feminist, seek to disrupt. Like Patti Lather (1991; p. 30), I maintain that feminism "becomes not a veering between the passive, dispersed subject of deconstruction on the one hand, and, on the other hand, the transcendent subject of most emancipatory discourse, but the site of the systematic fighting-out of that instability" (quoted in Riley, 1989[5]). It is in the site of the "fighting-out" that new considerations of resistance must be explored.

R E R E A D I N G   P A S S I V I T Y   A N D   R E S I S T A N C E

> Girls are conditioned into passivity, the story often goes; this is why they do so badly at school: implicitly femininity is seen as a series of roles, often imposed by agents of socialization, of whom the worst offenders are taken to be women: mothers and female teachers. (Walkerdine, 1990; p. 133)

For women teachers, the site of this "fighting-out" takes place in the daily negotiation of the incompatibility of being a teacher (subject) and a woman (object). Teaching is a site in which gender norms become inscribed through discourses like "women's true profession," and the all too familiar stereotypes of teachers as "motherteacher," "old maid," or "spinster." These controlling images and ideologies are designed to make sexism "appear to be natural, normal and an inevitable part of everyday life" (Collins, 1990; p. 68) and the patriarchal control of the profession normative (Apple, 1985). These essentialist gender roles inscribed in cultural myths like "teaching as women's true profession" have functioned to mask the agency of women teachers' lives. Yet, women teachers have not simply been acted upon but have negotiated, resisted, and created meanings of their own (Casey, 1993; Hoffman, 1981; Kaufman, 1984; Weiler, 1994). It is the everyday resistance of teachers to this objectification that this paper explores as a site of "fighting-out."

How women teachers "struggle to write the moving and multiple feminine subjects against the stereotyped woman" (Wexler, 1987; p. 96) attunes us not only to the sites of conflicting gender norms inscribed in teaching, and thus the "micropractices" (Foucault, 1980) of power and resistance, but how these stereotypes function as a form of gender regulation. What becomes essential to rethinking resistance is a focus on the "politics of the everyday" in which certain discursive practices are refused or "taken-up" and new ones created. How women teachers negotiate the tensions between dominant stereotypes of women's nature and social role and the meanings they give to their work is central not only to rethinking resistance but fundamental to rethinking pedagogy and curriculum from the women's standpoint.

In retrospect, my desire to collect the life histories of women teachers was certainly a response to my need to understand my own decision to go into teaching, a profession in which women are valorized for their nurturance and, thus, simultaneously situated for oppression. I hoped, like others (Grumet, 1989; Lewis, 1993; Middleton, 1993; Pinar, 1983), to rewrite the traditional script in which the female teacher submissively ushers girls and boys into the world of patriarchy. My interest in how other women teachers resisted and negotiated dominant stereotypes led to my study of the life histories of six women teachers (Munro, 1991). In collecting their life histories, I initially wanted to "give" voice to women teachers' stories of resistance. Taking for granted that women's resistance would be covert (and thus previously undiscovered and untheorized), lest they risk the very positions from which they could enact change, I sought to recover the stories of women teachers who identified themselves as political subversives and thus felt confident that I would be able to rewrite the traditional familial plot.[5] I had hoped to hear stories of subversion to reveal subversive acts of teachers like those described by Madeleine Grumet (1989).

> Docile, self-effacing, we [women teachers] hand in our lesson plans, replete with objectives and echoes of the current rationale, and then, safe behind the doors of our self-enclosed classrooms, subvert those schemes, secure in their theoretical wisdom, intuitive rather than logical, responsive rather than initiating, nameless yet pervasive. (p. 24)

This focus on women teachers as "activists" came from my desire to dispel the myth of teachers as passive, docile, and submissive and portray them as active agents struggling against hegemonic constraints. Yet, despite my desire that the women name their resistance by calling themselves activists, it was the many, and often contradictory, ways in which they named their experiences that illuminated new understandings of resistance.

Ironically, it was the "life historians" resistance to the naming of themselves as activists (or feminists), and often their denial of gender oppression, either as women or teachers, despite the historical conditions and cultural norms which prescribed gender norms, that prompted me to rethink the concept of resistance.[6] I now understand their refusal to "name" themselves activists as a form of resistance through which they contested the dominant masculinist narrative that defines power from a phallocentric world view—where power is understood to be monolithic and a possession to be seized and acquired. As women in a patriarchal society, their refusal to acknowledge dominant power relations signified their understanding of their exclusion from these power relations and represented an attempt to subvert their reproduction. In refusing to name themselves as "activists," they deconstruct the dichotomies of active/passive, male/female, which reify dominant gender discourses. Naming, the usual right of the patriarch, proffers the right to determine identity and fate (Mackethan, 1990). Refusal to "take up identities" (Riley, 1989), in this case as resistors, not only conveys a form of resistance through which they become subjects, but highlights forms of resistance usually obscured when resistance is understood as reactive acts of opposition that operate outside the forces of power.

I now question whether the very naming of myself as "activist" is yet another example of the way in which patriarchy actually functions to reproduce existing structures and relations of power. Did my initial resistance to dominant gender roles in the naming of myself as "activist," in fact, function to reinforce the patriarchal mapping of the world? Embracing the term "activist," do I collude with the division of the world into "active" and "passive," male and female, public and private?[7] Perhaps it is the case, as Gilbert and Gubar (1979) suggest, that women find it necessary to act out male metaphors, as if trying to understand their implication. The "trying on" of masculinist narratives such as "activist" speaks to the disruption of a stable coherent self while simultaneously serving to warn us that because narrative conventions work as unconscious ideologies on individual subjects, patriarchal and other harmful ideologies are often represented, produced, and reworked in the texts and stories women write and tell, thus causing them to participate in their own oppression (Bloom & Munro, 1995).

What had not been initially apparent to me was that my idealization of resistance reproduced the masculinist narrative of the autonomous individual and, in effect, reproduced those modes of oppression which I sought to critique. In fact, my romanticized view of resistance, as embedded in the individual, actually served to reify a unitary, stable, and coherent subject. Understanding women's forms of resistance necessitates rejecting, or at least putting to the side, traditionally exclusive notions of power as opposition, subjectivity as unitary, and resistance as public and oppositional to power.

So, in the end I did not "give" voice to stories of resistance as I originally understood that term. Instead, by focusing on the personal narratives in the life histories of women teachers, how they tell their stories, as well as what they tell, becomes significant in understanding forms of resistance. It was the life historians' resistance to traditional notions of power that attuned me to the complex and contradictory ways in which they revised the standard cultural plot. This article explores three different forms of resistance I came to recognize in their accounts: the displacement of hegemonic gender ideologies through engaging them; women's narrative construction of subjectivity as nonunitary through the use of metaphors like the "drifter"; and the naming of self in their narratives, which subverts traditional patriarchal understandings of teaching. Interpreting these narratives necessitates understanding how dominant ideologies of resistance have shaped our conceptions of power, knowledge, and subjectivity. It is to this that I will turn briefly in the next section.

R E T H I N K I N G   R E S I S T A N C E

So, how can we rethink resistance? In light of the poststructuralist assertion that "where there is power, there is resistance" (Foucault, 1978; pp. 95-96), is resistance an obsolete notion? "Resisting" dominant understandings of resistance reflects my concern with not wanting to reproduce notions of the individual and change based on a masculinist narrative that romanticizes women's lives by merely recounting great deeds performed by women. Such exemplary narratives cloak the often silent and hidden operations of gender and leave untouched traditional assumptions about the very nature and categories of resistance and gender—rather than asking us to reconceive of these.

Two notions seem to me to be central to the traditional concept of resistance. Resistance is defined in terms of opposition and power. Opposition implies force, and this, as Bettina Aptheker (1989; p. 170) suggests, is counterposed to accommodation or collaboration. Traditional understandings of resistance also assume that power is defined as political power which can be acquired, seized, or shared. These universalized definitions of resistance as political/public and oppositional are firmly grounded in patriarchal understandings of power as identifiable and, thus, contestable. The corollary assumption that change is linear and incremental has similarly functioned to exclude women's forms of resistance.

These traditional understandings of power differ markedly from under-standings in which "meaning can be political only when it does not let itself be easily stabilized and when it does not rely on any single source of authority, but rather, empties it, or decentralizes it" (Trinh, 1991; p. 42). An understanding of resistance based on positionality (Alcoff, 1989) acknowledges subjectivity as nonunitary and continually in flux, yet does not exclude the agency of the subject. For women, the decentering of the subject has in fact served as a primary form of resistance. I understand Maxine Greene (1992) when she suggests that women's understanding of subjectivity as nonunitary signifies a resistance to phallocentric reification and a form of subversion to patriarchy.

My own seduction by resistance theory has its origins in Marxist and reproduction theories which locate the structures of oppression, and consequently, change, in economic relations of power.[8] The location of power in macrostructures situates resistance in a binary world in which the oppressed (powerless) struggle against the oppressor (powerful). Despite the allure of this neat metanarrative, in which power resides solely in the state or economy, as a feminist I was concerned with the overly deterministic and reductionist nature of Marxism's tendency to overlook the individual subject as an agent of change capable of conscious, critical thinking (Anyon, 1983; Apple, 1979; Gramsci, 1971; Wexler, 1976; Willis, 1977). Unfortunately, the Marxist division of the world into the powerless and powerful, the oppressor and oppressed, the emancipator and those needing emancipation, reproduced the very binaries that were central to patriarchy and which I, as a feminist, sought to disrupt.

Despite the radical nature of Marxism as a theory of social change, it is deeply embedded in humanist notions of subjectivity, power, and change. Progress, in this sense, is defined in terms of modernity in which change is linear, incremental, and progressive rather than recursive and transformative (Doll, 1993). The dichotomy between liberation or oppression set up in Marxist theories of social change has traditionally functioned, according to Bettina Aptheker (1989),

> "to situate women, if they have been seen at all, as objects of oppression: either as victims of circumstances to be rescued, educated, and brought into productive and public life; or as the backward and misguided pawns of reactionary (or counterrevolutionary) forces to be won over to progressive and revolutionary movements. In neither case are women seen as an autonomous, purposeful, active force in history." (p. 171)

The hegemony of Marxism as a radical discourse was interrupted by a number of sociopolitical movements, including feminism, as well as interpretivist and phenomenological movements (Greene, 1975; Pinar, 1975), which opened up new possibilities for understandings of subjectivity and resistance. A phenomenological framework highlighted the social individual by acknowledging that humans act in a world of meaning which they encounter and help to create, renegotiate, and sustain. In focusing on the "lived experience" and "agency" of social actors, the role of the individual in negotiating and resisting hegemonic forces is highlighted. By placing the individual and her interpretive and negotiating capacities at the center of analysis, those engaged in the phenomenological critique rejected the reduction of the subject to passivity, notions of false consciousness, and economic determinism.[9] What remains problematic is that by focusing on the subject, interpretivists potentially romanticize the individual and reinforce traditional notions of an autonomous individual free from the material forces of social structures.

As a feminist, this romanticization of the individual is unsettling because it deflects the role of social structures such as patriarchy. Seeking some resolution (yes, I still thought I could achieve one), I turned to the work of neo-Marxists or production theorists such as Adorno (1973), Althusser (1971), and Habermas (1976), who rejected the notion of a single, central apparatus of control (Bourdieu, 1977). They rejected the binary, which situated power either as property of the individual (phenomenologists) or macrostructures (Marxists) by focusing on how ideology and culture (as well as economic hegemony) reproduce existing power relations through the production and distribution of a dominant culture that tacitly confirms what it means to be educated (Giroux, 1983). In particular, the work of Gramsci (1971) suggested how structural determinants were not static but were continually being reimposed and thus capable of being resisted by historical subjects. Work on resistance influenced by Gramsci (Williams, 1977) recognized the importance of ideological practice in power and resistance and worked to undermine distinctions between cultural, social, and political processes (Abu-Lughod, 1990). Thus, resistance took its shape in the alternative cultural and political institutions created by the oppressed as a means of understanding, opposing, and changing their position. Neo-Marxists charged that it was the distribution of knowledge and its legitimation, rather than the acquisition of specific values and behaviors, that was central to understanding reproduction (Apple, 1979; Bernstein, 1975).

Influenced by Gramsci (1971) and Freire (1973), who stressed the power of individuals to come to a critical consciousness of their own world, production theorists, also sometimes known as new sociologists (Apple, 1979; Giroux, 1983; Wexler, 1976), stressed the dialectic between individual consciousness and structural determinants. Mechanisms of reproduction are never complete and always meet with opposition. Central to critical theorists' understanding of the complex interaction between agency and structure was this concept of resistance. Critical educational theorists adopted a concept of resistance to highlight the complexity of the relationship of individual consciousness and structural determinants. The work of critical, neo-Marxists (Anyon, 1983; Willis, 1977) further highlighted the complexities of resistance by suggesting that what might appear to be genuine instances of resistance have had the long-term effect of reproducing, at a deeper level, the dominant order (Stanley, 1992). This focus on the complex forms of resistance interrupted static and bound understandings of resistance by acknowledging the fluid and contradictory ways in which resistance could function.

The impact of production theory or the "new sociology" on education emerged in its practical sub-discourse of "critical pedagogy," whose advocates are dedicated to producing emancipatory knowledge, which has as its goal the "conscious empowerment" of the oppressed to change their exploitative situations (Apple, 1978, 1979; Comstock, 1982; Freire, 1973; Giroux, 1986; McLaren, 1989). Central to a critical perspective is the assumption that oppressed persons are not "empowered," or "conscious," and that only those championing a critical perspective have the inside track. Although a critical perspective is attractive because it focuses on resistance and emancipation, thereby addressing the feminist goal of ending oppression, the question of who determines what knowledge and action is necessary to eliminate oppression remains unresolved.

Although knowledge is no longer understood in a positivist sense as neutral or objective, the concept of knowledge as resistance/emancipation still assumes an inherently human essence waiting to be liberated from an unjust, imposed power structure. As Valerie Walkerdine (1990) points out, central to these theories is the notion of the individual as a "real and essential kernel of phenomenological Marxism, whose outer skins are just a series of roles which can be cast off to reveal the true and revolutionary self" (p. 9). As a feminist, this understanding of resistance is particularly problematic due specifically to the romanticism of the individual, which is allied to an ideology of the heroic and consequently understood as male. The very agency of individuals to resist, claimed by feminists and critical theorists, seems undermined by talk of the need to "empower" and "emancipate" (Ellsworth, 1989; Gore, 1993; Orner, 1992). Angela McRobbie (1982) asks: "How can we assume that they need anything done for them in the first place? Or conversely, that we have anything real to offer them?" (p. 52). The liberatory discourse of both critical theorists and feminists, which suggests the "conscious empowerment" of the oppressed, again divides the world into tidy categories of "oppressed" and "non-oppressed."

Other studies on resistance highlighted the shortcomings of resistance theory as conceived by Willis and others in the 1970s. Bullough, Gitlin, and Goldstein (1984) suggest that resistance theory has been overly simplified and confused with opposition to authority. They argue that resistance can develop only when there is a conscious intention to bring about change. Similarly, Weiler (1988) warns against the potential of any act of opposition being labeled as resistance without considering the quality of that resistance. Ethnographic studies by Connell, Ashedon, Kesler, and Dowsett (1982) and Simon (1983) suggest that an understanding of resistance, as opposed to deviancy, can be achieved only by looking at the broader context within which schools exist. They are critical of the decontextualized, abstract nature of many studies that neglect the interaction of family, school, and work in the constitution of subjectivity. Despite these critiques, as a feminist, I was disturbed by what I perceived as the continued understanding of resistance as a concept that was both unitary and universal.

Feminists working from a cross-cultural/poststructuralist perspective (Anzaldua, 1990; Christian, 1988; Hooks, 1989; Narayan, 1988; Spelman, 1988; Spivak, 1987; Trinh, 1987) have been particularly critical of the oppressive and impositional nature of "universal" theorizing by highlighting that ways of perceiving oppression and liberation are inherently culture bound and, thus, function to dismiss alternative forms of resistance. This critique of critical discourses has highlighted its tendency to remain grounded in a liberal., humanist tradition that assumes a common experience emerging from rational and reasoned thought. Rejecting univocal interpretations of experience, feminist poststructuralists maintain that the subject is no longer universal (Smith, 1993). The focus on how discourses create subjects as well as how women resist the constitution of their subjectivity suggests that the subject is constantly in flux. Subjects do not hold power. Power is not a single possession, nor is it located in a unitary, static sense. Power is shifting and fragmentary, relating to positionings given in the apparatuses of regulation themselves (Walkerdine, 1990; p. 42). It is everywhere and nowhere. There is no archimedean point or privileged site of power.

According to Davis and Fisher (1993), power is a "capillary" circulating through the social body and exerting its authority through self-surveillance and everyday, disciplinary micropractices. Power is dispersed, like a web, with no beginning or end. Frank Pignatelli (1993) suggests that in expanding the surface on which power operates, this should lead not to despair, but in fact permits an increase in the amount of power exerted. Although Foucault's dispersal of power and the subject appear to negate the possibility of resistance and political agency, Pignatelli suggests that, quite to the contrary, Foucault's reconceptualization of power increases the potential for agency through creating sites in which new forms of identity and subjectivity can continually be invented. By linking power to knowledge through discourse, Davis and Fisher (1993), in fact, argue that the focus shifts from the repressive to the productive features of power. Accordingly, "power produces all social categories, including women, constituting them as both objects and subjects of knowledge" (Davis & Fisher 1993; p. 9). The subject does not vaporize but in fact has a plethora of modes in which to constitute acts of agency. According to Allen Feldman (1991), "political agency is manifold and formed by a mosaic of subject positions that can be both discontinuous and contradictory" (p. 5). Because power is decentered and plural, so, in turn, are forms of political struggle. This understanding of power is attractive because, as Nancy Fraser (1989) suggests, it widens the arena within which people confront and seek to change their lives.

For many feminist poststructuralists it is precisely the loss of the unitary subject which is necessary for re-envisioning resistance and agency. The loss of agency to a kind of discourse determinism, in which individuals are agents who playfully manipulate identities (Mahoney & Yngvesson, 1992) or in which individuals resist decoding because of the potential multiplicities of meanings, is rejected by reconceiving of gender as so complex that the fragmentation of the subject provides new ways to imagine concepts like agency and resistance.

This decentering of the subject necessitates the eradication of "gender" as a binary model of domination proposed by earlier feminist theories in which gender was theorized as either a complex network of identity formations produced in power relations or as an ideological system in which patriarchy required difference in order to assert male dominance (Braidotti, 1994). Gender, the category until recently central to feminist theorizing, has become increasingly unreliable and suspicious (Nicholson, 1994). Gender identity is both material and symbolic and functions as a complex way to regulate normative male and female identities. Creating multiple stories of gender and the subject, Sarah Westphal (1994) posits that

> thinking in terms of fragments means thinking in terms of choice and accountability within a vast range of possibilities, which enables the feminist thinker to sustain ambivalence in the face of inherently conflicted situations, rather than resorting to premature closure. (p. 161)

Rather than suggesting that the subject is passively constructed by discourses, thus denying the possibility of agency, de Lauretis (1987) describes a feminist subject whose awareness of the contradictions of gender identity becomes "a critical vantage point" providing the creative potential for resistance.

How, then, do teaching and resistance intersect? Valerie Walkerdine (1990; p. 3) maintains "teachers are not unitary subjects uniquely positioned but are produced as a nexus of subjectivities in relations of power which are constantly shifting, rendering them at one moment powerful and at another powerless." For Walkerdine, resistance is not just struggle against oppression of a static power; relations of power and resistance are continually reproduced, in continual struggle and constantly shifting. This focus on the social practices that constitute everyday life is, as Foucault (1980) suggests, more fundamental than belief systems when it comes to understanding the hold that power has on us. Seeking the positions in the "politics of everyday life" from which women teachers construct and are constructed attunes us not only to the forms of resistance women enact but also to how these forms of resistance can reveal, as Abu-Lughod (1990) suggests, historically changing relations of power. Abu-Lughod suggests the question we need to ask is not "What is resistance?" but "How does resistance make tangible the locations of power and dominant relations?" How does a richer understanding of resistance help us to re-envision the site of women's everyday "fighting out"?

CHOOSING A METHOD OR DID IT CHOOSE ME?

Because narrative is the fundamental way in which humans make sense of their experience (Polinghorne, 1988), women's telling of their stories provides a way to grasp human behavior through the use humans make of language (Holquist, 1988; p. 23). And, for women, the authoring of the self (Casey, 1993; Munro, 1995) is in itself the fundamental form of resistance.

My choice of life history method was thus implicitly grounded in my feminist and poststructuralist perspective. Although not without its problematics (Jipson, Munro, Victor, Froude Jounes, & Freed-Rowland, 1995; Munro, 1993), the focus of life history on understanding how women constitute their subjectivity is central to understanding women's experiencing of the world. Four major concerns have been central to my choice of a research method. Traditionally, knowledge, truth, and reality have been constructed as if men's experiences were normative, as if being human meant being male (Personal Narratives Group, 1989). Consequently, my first concern was the need for a method that allowed women to discuss their lives in their own voices. In avoiding an essentialist/universal tendency in favor of discontinuity/difference, I hoped to subvert the notion of an absolute truth or reality which has functioned to exclude women's stories. Second, I needed a method that would allow me to convey the contradictory, partial, and subjective nature of a life. As Jo Anne Pagano (1990) suggests, "there is more than one way to tell a story and more than one story" (p. 197). Similarly, according to William Tierney (1992), the "task of the researcher is not to discover the 'true' interpretation, for none exists, instead the challenge is to uncover the multiple voices in society that have been silenced." Acknowledging subjectivity and working toward the demystification of a stable, coherent self, Denise Riley (1989) suggests that the "political problem isn't so much of identities but of when women take on the identities of 'women' and how" (p. 136). Consequently, my goal became illuminating the complexities, contradictions, and tensions in women's stories rather than getting "the right story." Thirdly, I wished to employ a method that was collaborative in order to minimize the potential for exploitation inherent in any research relationship (Munro, 1993). Lastly, I required a methodology that would allow me to practice the self-reflexivity necessary for revealing my biases as well as the emergent nature of my understandings.

Six life histories were conducted over a period of eight months. My choice of life historians was serendipitous. Most I came to know through word-of-mouth as I described my research interests to friends and colleagues. I did not look for women who "named" themselves activists or feminists. What I did seek was women who considered themselves "career teachers"—which meant that they described themselves as having a lifelong commitment to education. The oldest of the life historians, Agnes, was born in 1897; the youngest, Bonnie, was born in 1945. Their experiences ranged from rural one-room school houses to urban schools in inner cities. In addition to multiple interviews with the primary informants, there were several other sources of data. Supplementary interviews with former students, colleagues, and administrators were conducted; the life historians' own writings (published as well as personal) and documents (curriculum plans, pictures, vitas) were analyzed. Historical research investigating the school and community histories in which the life historians worked was also conducted. Archival work, in this case at the University of Chicago and National College of Education, also contributed to establishing a historical context for understanding the narratives of one of the life historians. The emphasis on supplementary data collection was not intended to undermine or check the validity of the women's own narratives. Instead, the thick supplementary data was sought in order to enrich understandings of the historical complexities of these women's lives. My goal was not just a valorization of individual stories but an understanding of the complex relations of power regulated through changing notions of subjectivity and gender. Again, it is in the nexus of these subjectivities that resistance, the site of daily "fighting out," becomes visible.

BECOMING A TEACHER: "I COULD HAVE LIVED ANOTHER LIFE"

A central theme of the life history narratives was the stories of "becoming teachers." As women who described themselves as committed to education, I assumed I would hear stories about women who entered teaching consciously so as to bring about change. I did not expect to hear the stories of resistance they told about entering teaching. Yet, each of the life historians struggled in some way with her decision to enter the teaching profession despite the gendered norm that teaching was "women's true profession." As I sought to understand what I perceived as a contradiction in their lifelong commitment to education and their resistance to entering teaching, I recognized that this not only represented a site of gender conflict, but that in coming up against gender ideologies that conflicted with their own understandings of self, this was a site of resistance.

At our first meeting Cleo, one of the life historians with whom I worked for over six months, announced to me, "I could have lived another life and been just as happy." I was taken aback that someone who had committed more than 30 years of her life to teaching, administration, and social studies curriculum reform could so easily have "lived another life." Was this what she thought I wanted to hear? Where was the committed activist I sought? This was not the oppositional resistance I was seeking! In retrospect her statement seems consistent with her own conception of herself as someone who did not "follow the norms" and rebelled against them "so that I could be myself." Her ambivalence toward teaching not only mirrored my own resistance to becoming a teacher, in which I saw women valorized as "nurturers" and consequently positioned for oppression by an essentialist discourse, but highlighted the complex ways in which we construct our lives despite the gender myths regarding women's natural nurturing desires.

Born and raised in the South in the 1920s, Cleo characterized her childhood as one in which she learned that "it was clear that you just did certain things, like wearing white gloves and a hat, even if it was just to the corner store." As a young woman, she rebelled against the "marriage plot" (Aisenberg & Harrison, 1988) and sought to "live her own life" by taking flight from societal and familial norms through travel and education. In the early 1940s, she traveled to Panama and eventually to the Pacific Northwest where she pursued her intellectual interests in economics and history (in which she was always "one of the boys) at the University of Washington. Her story of rebellion, adventure, and flight took up a traditional masculinist narrative of separation and autonomy. Although I was initially intrigued with the agency of her story, her use of a traditional masculinist narrative, as I understood it, threatened to erase her very subjectivity. Linda Brodkey and Michelle Fine (1991) suggest that women are presumably attracted to discourses that promise to represent us to ourselves and others as empowered subjects. Yet, her decision to become a teacher, a traditionally female profession (disempowered), seemed in conflict with her own self representation as rebel and intellectual (male, empowered). Rather than interpret this as a contradiction, I saw this as a "critical vantage point" in which the negotiation of conflicting subjectivities provided a site of resistance.

How was I to understand her decision to become a teacher? Like Cleo, who wanted to be a government economist, I preferred a profession not associated with "women's work." Yet, we both became teachers. Why then teaching? Had we given in to the plot of teaching as "women's true profession?" On the contrary, I sensed that in some form teaching became a site for rebellion and escape where Cleo could fulfill her intellectual interests. What other profession provided women a place to express and pursue their love of books and ideas and be taken at least somewhat seriously? Again, I could identify with this part of Cleo's story: her rebelliousness, her choice to be a secondary social studies teacher because it provided the opportunity to pursue intellectual interests while cloaked in the acceptability of a woman's profession.

Hiding behind the guise of the "good" teacher, I, like Cleo, would not be suspect. Behind closed doors, I could pursue not only my love of ideas, but also encourage this in my students as a means of bringing about social change. Or, could it be that we were resisting our resistance to patriarchy's script for women by entering teaching as a way of coming to terms with being women, something which we had stalwartly denied in our efforts to be accepted in the patriarchal world?

I also wondered what role Cleo's family's strong disapproval of her choice of teaching played in her decision. She reflected:

> No one in my family was a school teacher. When I first mentioned it to my family, I remember that my aunt objected strenuously. She said, "Cleo you don't know what you're talking about." "What was her objection?" I inquired. "Well, I'm not sure actually that I even know. It just wasn't something that we did." I was intrigued. I asked, "If it wasn't what you did, why did you do it?" "A lot of my friends were doing that," she responds.

Cleo simultaneously resists what I interpreted as her family's class bias toward teaching as a middle class profession. By claiming that all her friends were doing it, Cleo resolves her conflicting feelings about becoming a teacher, and by minimizing her own agency, she does not consciously submit to the patriarchal script written for women teachers. In effect, this deft maneuver permits her to still write her own story as "teacher-as-intellectual."

Cleo's invoking of the dominant ideology of teaching as "women's true profession" contrasted strongly with my own deeply embedded notions regarding resistance and change in which the rejection of hegemonic ideologies is central to bringing about change. From a critical and neo-Marxist conception of resistance, I initially interpreted Cleo's engaging of teaching as "women's true profession" as giving in to the male plot, as a form of "false consciousness." Yet, for Cleo, invoking dominant ideologies allowed her to defer her family's disapproval and thus created the conditions through which she felt she could justify her decision to become a teacher while redefining "teacher" to fit her identity as teacher-intellectual. Trinh Minh-ha (1991) has suggested that, in engaging dominant ideologies while simultaneously disrupting them, women "narrate a displacement" as they "relentlessly shuttle between the center (patriarchal norms) and the margins (their own understandings)" (p. 17).

Bonnie's story of teaching also revealed how engaging hegemonic ideologies functioned as a form of resistance, despite my understanding of resistance as a word that implied opposition. Although currently a high school social studies teacher and department chair in the Pacific Northwest, Bonnie framed her story of entering teaching within the context of her work as a union organizer and as a Vista volunteer in the South during the Civil Rights Movement. Captured by the agency of her story, which I initially interpreted as subverting the patriarchal narrative for women, I was surprised when she recalled her decision to enter teaching in the early 1970s: "There weren't many alternatives and it was the beginning of the baby boom and lots of us were graduating in teaching." Like Cleo, she defers her decision to others, and invokes the dominant ideology that teaching is women's true profession by suggesting that "there weren't many alternatives." I wondered what role telling this fiction played? I imagined that engaging the ideology of teaching as "women's true profession" allowed Bonnie to reconcile conflicting images of herself as activist with dominant images of teachers as passively enacting women's natural nurturing capacity.

Bonnie's initial ambivalence about teaching is reflected in her continual negotiation between her own self image as political activist and "do gooder," and the roles prescribed by patriarchy, which suggest women should not have an authoritative, public voice. For Bonnie, her understanding of herself as political activist was reflected in her commitment to protecting teachers' rights and acknowledging teachers' agency through association work. She recalled:

> The teachers' association was important to me. It was my high priority. Kids and marriage were my low priority. Men want women to fit into their lives. I was trying to create something separate and distinct, not fit into someone else's life. I chose not to have children. I could never envision myself with children. I always had all these other things to do.

For Bonnie, stepping outside, creating "something separate," not fitting into "someone else's life," allowed her to move "out of one's place," as bell hooks (1990; p. 145) describes it, and into a space where "we confront the realities of choice and location." By reinscribing teaching with her understanding of herself as activist she "displaces" patriarchal norms inscribed in teaching. Trinh Minh-ha (1991) suggests "displacing is a way of surviving," for in displacing ourselves, "we never allow this classifying world to exert its classificatory power" (p. 21).

Despite my desires to hear tales of resistance, I was surprised when Agnes, aged 94 (born in 1897), the oldest of the life historians whom I interviewed, also revealed that she had not always wanted to teach. She embodied for me the dedication and commitment to teaching that common stereotypes of teaching as a transient or a semiprofession dismiss. I was captivated by the story she told of beginning her teaching career in 1915 in a one- room school house in central Kansas, receiving her bachelor's degree in education at the University of Chicago in 1924 (her primary mentor and professor was Dr. Alice Temple, one of Dewey's students), working for 41 years as a teacher-educator at the National College of Education (originally a women's college founded by Elizabeth Harrison in the 1890s), and, then, upon her retirement from National, marrying for the first time at age 68. She recalled her decision to go into teaching:

> At first, I didn't think of teaching at all, and then I had two aunts who were teachers and an uncle who was a professor so it was rather natural that I should get into teaching. Girls in our community rarely went into anything but teaching. I can't think of them going into anything but teaching.

Like Cleo and Bonnie, Agnes partially attributes her decision to go into teaching to the fact that "girls rarely went into anything else." The juxtaposition of her characterization of teaching as "natural" and her own recounting that "I didn't think of teaching at all" highlighted again the tensions and contradictions in women's lives as we negotiate patriarchal norms.

Central to each of these tales was telling the story that "teaching is the only profession open to women," when, in fact, the clerical and nursing professions were also open to women. I wondered what prompted them to construct this fictionalized tale. Jo Anne Pagano (1990; p. 195) suggests that the fictionalized self is not a lie or masquerade but, in itself, a theoretical construct. Their stories become a form of agency through which they "dispense with boundaries" (Jagla, 1992; p. 62) to create and recreate a reality more consistent with their images of themselves as intellectual, activist, or teacher-educator. Thus, the fictions they tell both enable them to write against the patriarchal script and function as a form of resistance.

I do not want to romanticize women's resistance to teaching. Not all the teachers I interviewed were as ambivalent as Cleo, Bonnie, and Agnes about their decision to go into teaching. Evelyn, born in Chicago in1907, recalled that she always wanted to be a teacher. Her struggle to become a teacher centered on gaining her family's acceptance of her decision to teach. She recalled:

> From the time I can remember, I wanted to teach. In those days, people thought girls got married and didn't really need to go to school. We were not a wealthy family and an education beyond high school was not really considered necessary. Well, I started high school and I did start a four year course, not a two year, but a business course, which my mother's family wanted.

Her family's lack of support and societal norms suggesting that women did not need an education did not make Evelyn's choice to be a teacher an easy one. Finally, with her mother's support, and after two years of teacher training at the Chicago Normal School, at age 18, Evelyn began her career in education as an elementary teacher, then as principal at Dusable High School, and finally as Assistant Superintendent for the Chicago School District. For Evelyn, the dominant ideology of "teaching as women's true profession" was engaged as a form of resistance in which she contested societal and family norms that "an education was not really necessary." Again, it is not a simple matter of either totally accepting or rejecting hegemonic discourses, but, instead, of making sense of them in multiple and often contradictory ways.

Beginning with their decisions to enter their "chosen" profession, teaching was a space in which these women continually had to define themselves by reconciling conflicting images of self with societal expectations of the gendered nature of teaching. Their narratives reveal not only the gendered constructions of teaching but their resistance to these. Ironically, central to their resistance was the embracing of the hegemonic ideologies of teaching as "women's true profession." Likewise the stories or "fictions" they tell suggesting that no other professions were open to women create realities that allow them to enter teaching without erasing their agency. Their struggles, as represented in their narratives, suggest the complex ways in which women construct their stories as active subjects.

If we could not imagine our roles as teachers beyond the dominant stereotypes written of women, what desire would there be for many women to become teachers? In recalling our lives, redefining and recreating them through our stories, real and imagined, I believe we resist the naming of our experiences by others' definitions of what reality should or ought to be. In contesting the patriarchal scripts written for women, we reconstruct history to fit our understandings of our experiences, despite dominant assumptions that teaching is a natural, not an active, extension of our lives. Thus, our constructions, our fictions, express the visions we hope or wish to enact. Trinh Minh-ha (1991) suggests that "our very existence consists in our imagination of ourselves" (p. 8). The fictions that women write about teaching, the engagement of imagination to write and rewrite our lives, consequently become one source of resistance in enacting our own lives.

T H E   D R I F T E R

The stories that I heard spoke not only of resisting teaching but also resisting moves into administration. Women administrators continually negotiate conflicting gender ideologies because they must function in a culture in which power and authority are defined by patriarchal and masculinist norms. More importantly, our understandings of terms like power and authority are located in, and dependent on, gendered understandings in which male behavior is constituted in opposition to female behavior (Butler, 1990). For women, to be female is to not have authority. Thus, to be a female administrator is necessarily a contradiction.

Originally, my goal had been to work with women teachers. I had no intention of exploring women in administration. Although all six of the life historians I worked with were introduced to me as "teachers," it turned out that four of the six had also been administrators. Initially, I interpreted their moves into administration as a form of resistance on two levels. First, moving into administration contested dominant understandings of women teachers as having a low work commitment. Second, I saw their moves into administration as their taking on positions of power from which they could enact change. In hindsight, my original interpretations were embedded within understandings of change as consolidation of power and as a progressive series of incremental moves within a hierarchy of power. Again, what I interpreted as resistance, the life historians named something else.

In light of their successful careers and what I perceived as an orderly progression, in most cases from teacher to chairperson to administrator, I was surprised at the manner in which Agnes, Cleo, and Evelyn described their careers as "not planned." In speaking about their work, they described moves in their careers as "just happening" or it was by "accident" or "I was lucky." Cleo recalled moving into administration: "I just sort of fell into it." I struggled to understand why they "resisted" conceptualizing themselves as active agents. Had they internalized patriarchal norms so well that they were merely acting out their roles as "dutiful and appropriately meek daughters?" (Jacobs, 1992).

Again, it was Cleo's story that intrigued me because of what I perceived as the apparent contradictions between her role as district administrator and her persistent claims that "she never wanted to be the top Joe." Cleo reflected on her career: "It wasn't conscious. I didn't plan ahead. I was a drifter." Her description of herself as a drifter contrasted strongly with my own perception of Cleo as actively pursuing a career despite societal norms, which Cleo described as "I think you were expected to get married and have a family." I wondered why, despite her success, she persisted throughout our interviews to attribute her success to others or to chance. I wondered, did her image of herself as a "drifter" allow her to construct a self which fit more readily with social expectations of women as powerless and without authoritative roles? Or was it, as Carolyn Heilbrun (1988) has pointed out, that women have difficulty taking credit for their accomplishments because they see these as grounded in relation to others, not as individual, autonomous accomplishments.

Again, resistance—in this case to acknowledging their own agency in becoming administrators—was in opposition to my search for resistance as counter-hegemonic. I struggled to understand what I saw as a contradiction. In reading other works on women's lives (Aisenberg &Harrison, 1988; Hancock, 1989), I was surprised to find that, in their analysis of the case studies of women, the term "drifter" also appeared in accounts of women's descriptions of their lives. The term was used not in the negative sense of aimless or unmotivated, but as a way to describe stepping outside the norms as a means of creating their own concepts of themselves and their work which reflected their understandings.

At first, I did not interpret Cleo's story of the "drifter" as a form of resistance. Again, my understandings of resistance and change, which assumed that change results from deliberate and active resistance to the structures perpetuating oppression, seemed to get in the way. Yet, paradoxically, Cleo's lack of intentionality, through the naming of herself as a drifter, becomes transformed into an expression of agency. By seeing herself outside societal norms, she deflects and decenters these and does not have to be defined by them. In this sense, the drifter can write her own script. In "refusing the hierarchical construction of the relationship between male and female…analyzing the way any binary opposition operates, reversing and displacing its hierarchical construction, rather than accepting it as real or self-evident or in the nature of things" (Scott, 1898; p. 92), the drifter embodied for me the process of deconstructing the scripts written for women.

Bettina Aptheker (1989) maintains that traditional understandings of resistance assume that change is "social rather than individual, political rather than personal, and that resistance implies a movement embracing large numbers of people in conscious alliance for a common goal" (p. 171). In listening to these women's stories, new understandings of resistance were emerging that highlighted the complex interactions of women's struggle to make their lives real. Reconceptualizing resistance as grounded in women's ability to displace traditional norms through metaphors like the "drifter" and to disrupt dominant ideologies through engaging them seemed to capture my understanding of poststructuralist conceptions of power.

Yet, despite my understanding of poststructuralist (Foucault, 1979) perspectives, acknowledging power relations as situated, shifting, and fragmented, I wondered why I had such difficulty in recognizing and naming these forms of resistance that now seemed so clear. The life historians' understandings of themselves as drifters, as outsiders, highlighted the fact that women are situated differently within power relations (Bartky, 1990; Hartstock, 1990). As Cleo often commented, "I really didn't fight it; a fight with no chance of winning is not a real good fight." As Sandra Bartky (1990) suggests, Foucault's understanding of social relations neglects the fact that women are situated differently within power relations. Excluded from the construction of dominant social theories, as well as the resultant norms, women function as outsiders in the system of relations as Foucault describes them. For women who explicitly or implicitly understand their "otherness" and who seek to maintain their identity, survival depends on displacing dominant social relations.

These women's constructions of knowledge of themselves is a reflection of power relations. In envisioning themselves outside dominant social relations as drifters (or as activists or intellectuals), their constructions of themselves become a form of empowerment. I agree with Carolyn Heilbrun (1988) that power is the ability to take one's place in whatever discourse is essential to action. For some women, this has been in the margins (hooks, 1990). I am reminded of Charlotte Perkins Gilman's (1989) conclusion in The Yellow Wallpaper, her fictionalized autobiographical account of her struggle to stay real as she peels back the layers of wallpaper in the room where she has been confined by her husband. At the end of the story, she declares, "I've got out at last…and I've pulled off most of the paper, so you can't put me back." Escaping the roles prescribed for women (even through madness), the metaphorical use of wallpaper for the patriarchal scripts written to contain women, identity and thus survival, becomes embodied in the continual peeling back or traversing of these boundaries. By resisting a stable, coherent self, the metaphor of the drifter provides a continual displacement through which these women resist the naming of their realities by others. The displacement of the unitary subject, thus, becomes a form of resistance in which power is dispersed rather than consolidated.

R E W R I T I N G   T E A C H I N G :
T E A C H I N G   A S   A   L I F E ' S   W O R K

Re-envisioning her life as that of a "drifter," Cleo displaced patriarchal norms, allowing her to write her own story. Bell hooks (1990) suggests that it is from the margins that we can "envision new alternatives, oppositional aesthetic acts" (p. 145). This was nowhere more apparent to me than in the stories Cleo, Evelyn, and Bonnie told regarding their decisions to become administrators. I originally interpreted their moves up the "career ladder" into administration as a form of resistance in which they located themselves in positions of power usually reserved for males and, more importantly, from which they could enact change. I was intrigued by their stories of becoming administrators because it disrupted the stereotype of women teachers as lacking motivation and career aspirations and spoke to my understanding of teachers as activists.

Again, what I interpreted as resistance, they named something else. Evelyn, who had struggled to become a teacher despite her family's objections, recalled her move into administration.

> I wasn't too sure that I was going to enjoy being a principal. And, I really didn't go into it with great fervor. I don't think I would ever have taken the exam except the principal for whom I was working just almost insisted, and I was weak enough to go ahead and take it, and I passed it. Well, then you get into it.

Evelyn's reference to being weak seems to imply that she compromised her commitment to teaching. This reluctance to leave the classroom was echoed in the stories of others as well. For example, Cleo reflected on her position as District Coordinator of Curriculum: "It was something I did; it wasn't that I wanted to move to some other plateau.... I wasn't trying to reach the top in either teaching or administration; I had no desire to be the top Joe." Cleo's and Evelyn's attributing their career achievements to others, as well as their consistent stories of discomfort in becoming administrators, seemed again to highlight the tension between my reading of their stories as willing "daughters" to patriarchy's desired subservience and their decentering of traditional norms through resisting "moves up" the career ladder.

Despite career norms that suggest moving into administration is a step up the ladder, as well as a measure of one's success, the women not only deferred their moves into administration to others but, in some cases, actually resisted becoming administrators. In response to my question if she had ever considered becoming an administrator, Bess simply responded, "No, I never wanted to leave the kids." Minnie recalled that she was never interested in being an administrator, "I was perfectly happy in the classroom. ...I wanted to be a teacher, not a boss." Their sense of agency, in staying teachers, acts as a form of resistance against hierarchical, patriarchal notions of success. In fact, like other teachers (Biklen, 1983), these women saw moving "up" into administration as diminishing the quality of their work as educators. While others (Lortie, 1975) suggest that women's "flat career lines" reflect a lack of agency and are evidence of women's lack of commitment to work, Bess and Minnie interpret their decision to stay in the classroom as a commitment to a different set of values.

> Teachers were always good to me. I had very few situations where they were out to get me, which is not too abnormal with administrators. I'm still with teacher groups. I am not with administrators. I'm with the same group of women as when we started and most of us were teaching. Now we're all retired. But they're all teachers. Classroom teachers. Once a month we all have dinner or something.

Evelyn recalls her responsibilities as principal in chaperoning the basketball team on away games as "when you teach and are away, you are the parent." Naming themselves teachers, despite the fact that they worked as administrators, functions as resistance on two levels. First, women reject the shaping of their lives according to male norms and expectations by speaking in the language of teaching, which subverts hierarchy. The women administrators use the naming of themselves as teachers as a way to assert the intentionality that teachers have. They reinvest the authority usually given to administrators, a traditionally male domain, back into teachers, whose authority is often questioned by administrators. By refusing to call themselves administrators, they resist a notion of control and power that does not conform to their understandings of change as embedded in relationships rather than imposed from an authority position. Secondly, in refusing to name themselves administrators and in reconceptualizing their careers so that they are not bracketed by the usual career norms of the corporate model, these women rewrite their lives to fit their experiences. In essence, women teachers resist traditional notions of career, success, and commitment which separate, dichotomize, and establish hierarchical levels. By naming themselves teachers, these women deflect career norms based on men's understandings, which do not reflect the meanings they give to their work.

By subverting the system, by speaking in a language which is not acknowledged and rarely understood, these women deflected patriarchal career norms and definitions of teaching. For women whose use of the master's language would result only in their being trapped in the master's game (Lorde,

1984), women have created alternatives to standard forms of language that serve as a resistance.

R E S I S T A N C E   R E D E F I N E D

I do not mean to romanticize the lives of women teachers or to suggest a monolithic view of women teachers as resistors. Yet, in today's postmodern world I walk a fine line. For as women, if we explore our agency or claim our own voices, we are reminded of the potential totalizing tendencies of asserting a stable and coherent identity. Yet, if we abandon our search, we risk complying with patriarchy's aim to name our desires.

In gaining a deeper understanding of the role of resistance in making sense of the often contradictory and multiple dimensions of our lives, I believe the life history process also enhances our understanding of curriculum. The collection of life histories did not lead to a neat and tidy understanding of a life, nor is curriculum a neatly wrapped package of knowledge that we pass from teacher to student.

If curriculum is our "lived experience," it seems that the content of a life or of a curriculum becomes meaningful in understanding how we construct, make meaning, or use it to piece together our lives (Showalter, 1986). It is not just the story, but also how we tell it and retell it, that reveals the process of "becoming" (Aoki, 1992). In continually "becoming," in naming and renaming, in moving back and forth into the margins, women actively subvert and decenter dominant relations. When curricular practice is seen and remembered as fluid and embedded in lived experience, women not only subvert traditional norms but deflect the standardization of curriculum that has traditionally functioned as a form of control. Resistance becomes a never ending dance in these spaces of contradiction.

In listening to these women speak about their lives, I found embedded in their stories the struggle to name their own realities, to acknowledge the meanings they give to their experiences, in spite of predominant assumptions regarding the nature and roles of women. Displacing dominant gender ideologies by engaging them, constructing the "drifter" as a from of deconstruction and creating a language to subvert traditional norms in the naming of themselves as teachers, each of these movements served as forms of resistance to the prescribed norms women struggle against in writing their own stories. Consequently, resistance is not an "act" but a movement, a continual displacement of others' attempts to name our realities. This is a resistance born out of survival, an attempt to stay real and claim the realities of our lives as women, as teachers, and as women who choose to be teachers.[10]

N O T E S

1. Exploring the relationship between women's identity and the teaching profession has been the focus of many feminist theorists in education (Clifford, 1989; Grumet, 1989; Jipson & Munro, 1992; Martusewicz, 1992; Miller, 1988; Pagano, 1990; Walkerdine, 1990). Central to this research has been the point that teaching and curriculum cannot be adequately theorized without an understanding of the intersections of gender ideologies and teaching as a profession. How gender ideologies become inscribed as natural in teaching and how gender ideologies are used in conflicting and contradictory ways to control the profession is central to understanding the larger cultural, economic, social framework within which women teachers negotiate understandings of self.

2. Not only have women been excluded from or marginalized from the centers of power, but because women have not set the ground rules for social existence they have not had the power to name what constitutes power, resistance, or social change. For women, the position from which they experience power is fundamentally different from that of men. First they have been excluded from shaping dominant social relations and their naming; second, the very notion of experience as the legitimate indicator of what is right or wrong with the world, or even what the world is like, can be called into question by men since being a woman in a patriarchal society means being someone whose experience of the world is systematically discounted as trivial or irrevalent (Leck, 1987).

3. Sandra Harding (1987) suggests that relativism is fundamentally a sexist response that attempts to preserve the legitimacy of androcentric claims in the face of contrary evidence.

4. Feminists grappling with the tension between postmodernism/feminism with the most compelling discussion are those who also situate the dilemma within the larger structures of power relations of a postcapitalist/late twentieth century society (Alcoff, 1989; Flax, 1989; Lather, 1991; Spivak, 1987).

5. My focus on teachers as activists took up the claim made by others (Hoffman, 1981; Kaufman, 1984) that teachers entered and pursued teaching for a variety of reasons, including bringing about social change. My research in educational/curricular history had led me to discover a strong network of women teacher activists at the turn of the century. Women educators like Margaret Haley, Ella Flagg Young, and Grace Strachan were

not only involved in "equal pay for equal work," but resisted the "factoryizing" and deskilling of teachers through the imposition of standardization of methods and curriculum and involvement of business in education.

I questioned not only why these women's stories had been excluded from the curricular canon, but how the complicated relationship between cultural representations of women's prescribed place and the nature of teaching as described in education and curricular discourses has in essence functioned to marginalize and distort this history. For example, David Tyack (1974) describes Ella Flagg Young as "one of Dewey's strongest advocates...a woman of great courage, intelligence, and compassion, she taught teachers about Dewey's 'new education' when she served as instructor at the Normal School from 1905 to 1909" (p. 178). Recently, Mary Jo Deegan (1990) has argued that Ella Flagg Young was not only an advocate of Dewey's thought but a central contributor to his emerging educational philosophies. Thus I was concerned that the relationship sketched by Tyack (1974) seemed to have more to do with the expectations produced by gender discourses (women as helpers and facilitators of knowledge rather than creators of knowledge) than with the factual evidence about women teachers. In part, my original project (Munro, 1991) sought to understand women's experience from their standpoint, not the distorted view of women teachers' lives produced by a universal masculinist discourse.

6. The term "life historians" is suggested by Marjorie Mbilinyi (1989) as an alternative to the objectifying labels of "informant" and "subject."

7. I would like to acknowledge Geraldine Clifford for pointing this out to me in the course of our correspondence.

8. Reproduction theory, most notably articulated by Bowles and Gintis (1976), attributed the reproductive role of schooling in maintaining a capitalist society to a "correspondence principle" in which schools function to mirror and reproduce a stratified class structure and dominant social practices.

9. As Joan Cocks (1989,) in her discussion of Gramsci's, Williams', Said's, and Foucault's notions of power and resistance suggests, their critique of macrostructures as dominative power is based on the fact that there are always experiences to which "fixed forms" do not speak, aspects of actual consciousness diverging from "official consciousness" (p. 64). The existence of experience not entirely vanquished by dominating systems is how we know they are dominating, after all.

10. I would like to thank Leslie Bloom, Mary Ellen Jacobs, Michelle Masse, and Anne Trousdale for their thoughtful comments on earlier drafts and

ongoing conversations regarding issues of resistance. A special thanks to
Douglas McKnight for his assistance in the final editing.

R E F E R E N C E S

Abu-Lughod, L. (1990). The romance of resistance: Tracing transformations of
power through Bedouin women. *American Ethnologist*, 17 (1), 41-55.

Adorno, T. (1973). *Negative dialectics*. (London: Routledge).

Aisenberg, N. &Harrison, M. (1988). *Woman of academe: Outsiders in the sacred
grove*. (Amherst: The University of Massachusetts Press).

Alcoff, L. (1989). Cultural feminism versus poststructuralism: The identity crisis
in feminist theory. In M.R. Malson, J.F. O'Barr, S. Westphal-Wihl, & M.
Wyer (Eds.), *Feminist Theory in Practice and Process*, pp. 295-327. (Chicago:
University of Chicago Press).

Althusser, L. (1971). *Lenin and philosophy and other essays*. (New York: Monthly
Review Press).

Anyon, J. (1983). Intersections of gender and class; Accommodation and
resistance by working class and affluent females to contradictory sex-role
ideologies. In S. Walker & L. Barton (Eds.), *Gender, Class and Education*, pp.
19-37. (Sussex, UK: Falmer Press).

Anzaldua, G. (1990). *Making face, making soul*. (San Francisco: Aunt Lute
Foundation Books).

Aoki, T. (1992). Layered voices of teaching: The uncannily correct and the
elusively true. In W. Pinar & W.M. Reynolds (Eds.), *Understandings
Curriculum As Phenomenological and Deconstructed Text*, pp. 17-27. (New
York: Teachers College Press).

Apple, M. (1978). The new sociology of education: Analyzing cultural and
economic reproduction. *Harvard Educational Review*, 48 (1), 495-503.

Apple, M. (1979). *Ideology and curriculum*. (London: Routledge & Kegan Paul).

Apple, M. (1985). Teaching and "women's work": A comparative historical and
ideological analysis. *Journal of Education*, 86 (3), 455-473.

Aptheker, B. (1989). *Tapestries of life*. (Amherst: University of Massachusetts
Press).

Bakhtin, M. (1981). *The dialogic imagination*. (Austin: University of Texas Press).

Bartky, S. (1990). *Femininity and domination: Studies in the phenomenology of oppression*. (New York: Routledge).

Benhabib, S. (1995). Feminism and postmodernism: An uneasy alliance. In S. Benhabib, J. Butler, D. Cornell, & N. Fraser (Eds.), *Feminist Contentions: A Philosophical Exchange*, pp. 17-34. (New York: Routledge).

Bernstein, B. (1975). *Class, codes and control : Towards a theory of educational transmissions*. (London: Routledge & Kegan Paul).

Biklen, S. (1983). Women in American elementary school teaching. In P. Schmuck (Ed.), *Women Educators*, pp. 223-243. (Albany: State University of New York Press).

Bloom, L. & Munro, P. (1995). Conflicts of selves: Non-unitary subjectivity in women administrators' life history narratives. In A. Hatch & R. Wisniewski (Eds.), *Life History and Narrative*, pp. 99-112. (London: Falmer Press).

Bourdieu, P. (1977). *Outline of a theory of practice*. (New York: Cambridge University Press).

Bowles, S. & Gintis, H. (1976). *Schooling in capitalist America*. (New York: Basic Books).

Braidotti, R. (1994). Theories of gender. In C. McDonald & G. Wihl (Eds.), *Transformations in Personhood and Culture After Theory: The Languages of History, Aesthetics and Ethics*, pp. 133-152. (University Park: Pennsylvania State University Press).

Britzman, D. (1995). Is there a queer theory? Or, stop thinking straight. *Educational Theory*, 45 (2), 151-165.

Brodkey, L. & Fine, M. (1991). Presence of mind in the absence of body. In H. Giroux (ed.), *Postmodernism, Feminism and Cultural Politics*. (Albany: State University of New York Press).

Bullough, R.V., Gitlin, A., & Goldstein, S. (1984). Ideology, teacher role, and resistance. *Teachers College Record*, 86, 339-358.

Butler, J. (1990). *Gender trouble: Feminism and the subversion of identity*. (London: Routledge).

Casey, K. (1993). *I answer with my life: Life histories of women teachers working for social change*. (New York: Routledge).

Christ, C. (1986). *Diving deep and surfacing: Women writers on spiritual quest*. (Boston: Beacon Press).

Christian, B. (1988). The race for theory. *Feminist Studies*, 14 (1), 67-69.

Cixous, H. (1981). Castration or decapitation? *Signs: Journal of Women in Culture*, 7 (1), 41-55.

Clifford, G. (1989). Man/woman/teacher: Gender, family and career in American educational history. In D. Warren (Ed.), *American Teachers: Histories of A Profession At Work*, pp. 293-343. (New York: Macmillan).

Cocks, J. (1989). *The oppositional imagination: Feminism, critique and political theory*. (New York: Routledge).

Collins, P.H. (1990). *Black feminist thought: Knowledge, consciousness and the politics of empowerment*. (New York: Routledge).

Comstock, D. (1982). A method for critical research. In E. Bredo & W. Feinberg (Eds.), *Knowledge and Values in Social and Educational Research*, pp. 370-390. (Philadelphia: Temple University Press).

Connell, R.W., Ashedon, D., Kessler, S., & Dowsett, G. (1982). *Making the difference: Schools, families and social division*. (North Sydney: George Allen & Unwin).

Davis, K. & Fisher, S. (1993). Power and the female subject. In S. Fisher and K. Davis (Eds.), *Negotiating the Margins: The Gendered Discourses of Power and Resistance*, pp. 3-22. (New Brunswick, N.J.: Rutgers University Press).

de Lauretis, T. (1987). *Technologies of gender: Essays on theory, film and fiction*. (Bloomington: Indiana University Press).

Deegan, M. (1990). *Jane Addams and the men of the Chicago school, 1892-1918*. (New Brunswick: Transaction Books).

Doll, W. (1993). *A post-modern perspective on curriculum*. (New York: Teachers College Press).

Ellsworth, E. (1989). Why doesn't this feel empowering? Working through the repressive myths of critical pedagogy. *Harvard Educational Review*, 59 (3), 297-324.

Feldman, A. (1991). *Formations of violence: The narrative of the body and political terror in Northern Ireland*. (Chicago: University of Chicago Press).

Flax, J. (1989). Postmodernism and gender relations in feminist theory. In M.R. Malson, J.F. O'Barr, S. Westphal-Wihl, & M. Wyer (Eds.), *Feminist Theory in Practice and Process*, pp. 51-74. (Chicago: University of Chicago Press).

Flax, J. (1990). *Thinking fragments: Psychoanalysis, feminism & postmodernism in the contemporary west*. (Berkeley: University of California Press).

Foucault, M. (1978). *The history of sexuality. Vol. 1: An introduction*. (New York: Random House).

Foucault, M. (1979). *Discipline and punish: The birth of prison*. (New York: Vintage Books).

Foucault, M. (1980). *Power/knowledge: Selected interviews and other writings, 1972-1977.* (Sussex, UK: Harvester Press).

Fraser, N. (1989). *Unruly practices: Power, discourse and gender in contemporary social theory.* (Minneapolis: University of Minnesota Press).

Freire, P. (1973). *Pedagogy of the oppressed.* (New York: Seabury Press).

Gilbert, S. & Gubar, S. (1979). *The madwoman in the attic: The woman writer and the nineteenth-century literary imagination.* (New Haven: Yale University Press).

Gilman, C. P. (1989). *The yellow wallpaper.* (New York: Bantam Books).

Gilmore, L. (1994). *Autobiographics: A feminist theory of women's self-representation.* (Ithaca: Cornell University Press).

Giroux, H. A. (1983). *Theory and resistance in education.* (MA: Bergin & Garvey).

Giroux, H. A. (1986). Curriculum, teaching and the resisting intellectual. *Curriculum & Teaching,* 1 (1, 2), 33-42.

Gore, J. (1993). *The struggle for pedagogies.* (New York: Routledge).

Gramsci, A. (1971). *Selections from the prison notebooks.* (New York: International).

Greene, M. (1975). Curriculum and cultural transformation: A humanistic view. *Cross Currents,* 25 (2), 175-186.

Greene, J. (1992, April). *There's No Identity Like No Identity: Poststructuralist Perspectives.* Paper presented at the annual meeting of the American Educational Research Association, San Francisco.

Grumet, M. (1989). *Bitter milk: Women and teaching.* (Amherst: University of Massachusetts Press).

Habermas, J. (1976). *Communication and the evolution of society.* (Boston: Beacon Press).

Hancock, E. (1989). *The girl within.* (New York: Fawcett Columbine).

Harding, S. (1987). Introduction: Is there a feminist method? In S. Harding (Ed.), *Feminism and Methodology.* (Bloomington: Indiana University Press).

Hartstock, N. (1990). Foucault on power: A theory for women? In L. Nicholson (Ed.), *Feminism/Postmodernism,* pp. 157-175. (New York: Routledge).

Heilbrun, C. G. (1988). *Writing a woman's life.* (New York: Ballantine Books).

Hekman, J. (1990). *Gender and knowledge: Elements of a postmodern feminism.* (Boston: Northeastern University Press).

Hoffman, N. (1981). *Women's true profession: Voices for the history of teaching.* (New York: McGraw-Hill).

Holquist, M. (1988). *Dialogism: Bakhtin and his world.* (New York: Routledge).

Hooks, b. (1989). *Talking back: Thinking feminist, thinking black.* (Boston: South End Press).

Hooks, b. (1990). *Yearning: Race, gender and cultural politics.* (Boston: South End Press).

Irigary, L. (1985). *Speculum of the other woman* (G. Gill, Trans.) (Paris: Editions de Minuit). (Original work published in 1974.) Jacobs, M. (1992). Personal communication.

Jacobs, M., Munro, P., & Adams, N. (1995). Palimpsest: Re/reading women's lives. *Qualitative Inquiry,* 1 (3), 327-345.

Jagla, V.M. (1992). Teachers everyday imagination and intuition. In W. Schubert & W. Ayers (Eds.), *Teacher Lore,* pp. 61-80. (New York: Longman).

Jipson, J. & Munro, P. (1992). What's real: Fictions of the maternal. *JCT: An Interdisciplinary Journal of Curriculum Studies,* 10 (2), 7-28.

Jipson, J., Munro, P., Victor, S., Froude Jones, K., & Freed-Rowland, G. (1995). *Repositioning feminism and education: Perspectives on educating for social change.* (Westport, CT: Bergin & Garvey).

Kaufman, P. (1984). *Women teachers on the frontier.* (New Haven: CT: Yale University Press).

Lather, P. (1991). *Getting smart: Feminist research and pedagogy within the postmodern.* (New York: Routledge).

Leck, G. (1987). Review article: Feminist pedagogy, liberation theory and the traditional schooling paradigm. *Educational Theory,* 37 (30), 343-354.

Lewis, M. (1993). *without a word: teaching beyond women's silence.* (New York: Routledge).

Lorde, A. (1984). *Sister outsider.* (Trumansburgh, NY: Crossing Press).

Lortie, D. (1975). *Schoolteacher.* (Chicago: University of Chicago Press).

Mackethan, L. (1990). *Daughters of time: Creating woman's voice in southern story.* (Athens: The University of Georgia Press).

Mahoney, M. & Yngvesson, B. (1992). The constitution of subjectivity and the paradox of resistance: Reintegrating feminist anthropology and psychology. *Signs: Journal of Women in Culture and Society,* 18 (11), 44-73.

Martusewicz, R.A. (1992). Mapping the terrain of the postmodern subject. In W. Pinar & W. Reynolds (Eds.), *Understanding Curriculum As Phenomenological and Deconstructed Text*, pp. 131-158. (New York: Teachers College Press).

Mascia-Lees, F.E., Sharpe, P., &Cohen, C. (1989). The postmodern turn in anthropology: Cautions from a feminist perspective. *Signs: Journal of Women in Culture and Society*, 15 (1), 7-34.

Mbilinyi, M. (1989). I'd have been a man. In Personal Narratives Group (Eds.), *Interpreting Women's Lives*, pp. 204-207. (Bloomington: Indiana University Press).

McLaren, P. (1989). *Life in schools*. (New York: Longman).

McRobbie, A. (1982). The politics of feminist research: Between text, talk and action. *Feminist Review*, 12, 46-57.

Middleton, S. (1993). *Educating feminists: Life histories and pedagogy*. (New York: Teachers College Press).

Miller, J. (1988). The resistance of women academics: An autobiographical account. In W.F. Pinar (Ed.), *Contemporary Curriculum Discourses*, pp. 486-494. Scottsdale, AZ: Gorsuch Scarisbrick, Publishers).

Miller, N. (1989). Changing the subject. In E. Weed (Ed.), *Coming To Terms: Feminism, Theory, Politics*, pp. 3-16. (New York: Routledge).

Munro, P. (1991). *A life of work: Stories women teachers tell*. Unpublished doctoral dissertation. (Eugene: University of Oregon).

Munro, P. (1993). Continuing dilemmas of life history research: A reflexive account of feminist qualitative inquiry. In D. Flinders & G. Mills (Eds.), *Theory and Concepts in Qualitative Research: Perspectives From the Field*, pp. 163-178. (New York: Teachers College Press).

Munro, P. (1995). Speculations: Negotiating a feminist supervision identity. In J. Jipson, P. Munro, S. Victor, K. Froude Jones, & G. Feed-Rowland, *Repositioning Feminism and Education: Perspectives On Educating For Social Change*, pp. 97-114. (Westport, CT: Bergin & Garvey).

Narayan, U. (1988). Working together across difference: Some considerations on emotions and political practice. *Hypatia*, 3, 31-47.

Nicholson, L. (1994). Interpreting gender. *Signs: Journal of Women in Culture and Society*, 20, 79-103.

Orner, M. (1992). Interrupting the calls for student voice in "liberatory" education: A feminist poststructuralist perspective. In C. Luke & J. Gore (Eds.), *Feminism and Critical Pedagogy*, pp. 74-89. (New York: Routledge).

Pagano, J. (1990). *Exiles and communities: Teaching in the patriarchal wilderness.* (Albany: State University of New York Press).

Personal Narratives Group. (1998). *Interpreting women's lives: Feminist theory and personal narratives.* (Bloomington: Indiana University Press).

Pignatelli, F. (1993). What can I do? Foucault on freedom and the question of teacher agency. *Educational Theory,* 43 (4), pp. 411-432.

Pinar, W. (1975). *Curriculum theorizing: The reconceptualists* (Berkeley: McCutcheon).

Pinar, W. (1983). Curriculum as gender text: Notes on reproduction, resistance and male-male relations. *Journal of Curriculum Theorizing,* 5 (1).

Polkinghorne, D. (1988). *Narrative knowing and the human sciences.* (Albany: State University of New York Press).

Riley, D. (1989). Feminism and the consolidation of "women" in history. In E. Weed (Ed.), *Coming To Terms,* pp. 134-142. (New York: Routledge).

Schultz, E. (1990). *Dialogue at the margins: Whorf, Bakhtin and linguistic relativity.* (Madison: University of Wisconsin Press).

Scott, J. (1989). Gender: A useful category of historical analysis. In E. Weed (Ed.), *Coming To Terms,* pp. 81-100. (New York: Routledge).

Showalter, E. (1986). Piecing and writing. In N. Miller (Ed.), *The Poetics of Gender.* (New York: Columbia University Press).

Simon, R.I. (1983). But who will let you do it? Counter-hegemonic possibilities for work education. *Journal of Education,* 165, 235-256.

Smith, S. (1993). Who's talking/Who's talking back? The subject of personal narrative. *Signs: Journal of Women in Culture and Society,* 18 (2), 329-407.

Spelman, E. (1988). *Inessential women.* (Boston: Beacon Press).

Spivak, G. (1987). *In other worlds: Essays in cultural politics.* New York: Methuen.

Stanley, W. (1992). *Curriculum for utopia.* (Albany: State University of New York Press).

Tierney, W. (1992, April). *On Method and Hope.* Paper presented at the annual meeting of the American Educational Research Conference, San Francisco.

Trinh Minh-ha (1987). Difference: "A special third word women issue." *Feminist Review,* 25, 5-22.

Trinh Minh-ha (1991). *When the moon waxes red.* (New York: Routledge).

Tyack, D. (1974). *The one best system.* (Cambridge: Harvard University Press).

Walkerdine, V. (1990). *Schoolgirl fictions.* (London: Verso).

Weiler, K. (1988). *Women teaching for social change.* (Boston: Bergin & Garvey).

Weiler, K. (1994). The lives of teachers: Feminism and life history narratives. *Eductional Researcher,* 23 (4), 30-33.

Westphal, S. (1994). Stories of gender. In C. McDonald & G. Wihl (Eds.), *Transformations in Personhood and Culture After Theory: The Languages of History, Aesthetics, and Ethics,* pp. 153-164. (University Park: The Pennsylvania Sate University Press).

Wexler, P. (1976). *The sociology of education: Beyond equality.* (Indianapolis: Bobbs-Merrill).

Wexler, P. (1987). *Social analysis of education.* (New York: Routledge).

Whitson, J.A. (1991). Post-structuralist pedagogy as counter-hegemonic discourse. *Education and Society,* 9 (1), 73-86.

Williams, R. (1977). *Marxism and literature.* (London: Oxford University Press).

Willis, P. (1977). *Learning to labor: How working class kids get working class jobs.* (Westmead, UK: Saxon House).

Young, I. (1990). The ideal of community and the politics of difference. In L. Nicholson (Ed.), *Feminism/Postmodernism,* pp. 300-324. (New York: Routledge).

CHAPTER TWENTY-EIGHT

Identity, Self, and Other in the Conduct of Pedagogical Action:

An East/West Inquiry

David Geoffrey Smith
1996

I

Identity is problematic at the heart of almost all debates in the contemporary Western tradition. In this paper I wish to examine the notion of identity as both a Western preoccupation and, differently, as a central theme in Eastern wisdom traditions. In the process, I will also relate the discussion to questions about the conduct of pedagogical action. By pedagogical, I mean an interest in how both the implicit and explicit values of a people get mediated through relations with the young. It is in this sense that an interest in identity is also an interest in action, namely that any form of action, pedagogical or otherwise, implies a theory of identity. As a teacher, the question of "what is to be done" with respect to others (a particular child, or group) depends on who I think the Other is, and who I think I am in relation that person.

I also write as a person formed by both Eastern and Western traditions, born in China during the Maoist revolution, but formally educated in the British liberal tradition. So in a way I write from middle space, neither east nor west, looking for a way through the kinds of intellectual and cultural binaries that seem to so hopelessly ensnare creative thinking in the contemporary context. My argument will be that the West is currently at a kind of intellectual and cultural impasse, even a state of exhaustion, precisely because of being stuck in a particular kind of desire with respect to identity. Only through an abandonment of that desire, along the lines, say, of ancient Ch'an master Huang-po's "great relinquishment" may it be possible to enter the broader ocean of wisdom that can enlighten our lived burdens as parents, teachers, colleagues, friends, and especially enemies. Matisse once said of his paintings: I never finish them, I just abandon them." Such abandonment may be the only means through which what is genuinely new can find its life, but it requires very careful understanding. Certainly abandonment cannot mean a giving up of our deepest human responsibilities.

I I

As a field of discourse in the Western tradition today, *identity* is talked about in many different ways. "Identity politics," for example, is allied to the "politics of representation" and the question of how my identity, especially as a racial, sexual being gets constructed and defined within the overall configurations of culture. The topics of Self and subjectivity, with their complementary labor of (auto)biography, story, and narration are driven by a belief that one's identity is somehow knowable in itself if only one could find the right way to it.

In pedagogical terms, identity is stubbornly entrenched as the theoretical axis around which virtually all the defining concerns revolve. This is true whether one is speaking of child development (presuming progression from one identity [child] to another [adult]—the myth of adultomorphism, as David Kennedy describes it[1]), the psychology of individuation, aimed at cultivating a strong sense of "self-esteem"; curricular judgements about the degree to which school texts accurately reflect a presumed state of actual affairs; or, teacher education models driven by standards of achievement and excellence determined to be normative.

These examples all reflect fairly recent history, however, and are in a sense symptomatic of the endpoint of a long chain of cultural experience and reflection.[2] The belief that there is an essential, irreducible *I* that is knowable, stable, and discussible may be largely an inheritance from Aristotle, particularly his Theory of Substance, which covered three different aspects: substance; being possessing attributes (the subject); and that of which one precdicts qualities. Aristotle's theory was borrowed by the early Christian church for its description of the nature of God as being of one substance but three personal expressions— the doctrine of the Trinity.

Current interests in autobiography have a serious precedent in Saint Augustine of the fourth century. His *Confessions* were an experiment in the art of introspection, with introspection being the means by which to unravel and describe all of the ways the human soul could be devious in the search for its true, divinely inspired identity.

The contemporary split in Western academies between philosophy and psychology first arose in the eighteenth century through the work of Immanuel Kant, who proposed that every person's Self was actually composed of two aspects: a transcendental subject or ego, which is the ground of all knowledge and perception, and an empirical ego, which is what we observe when we undertake introspection, or the thing we impute to other people, with qualities, attributes, etc. The former became the domain of the philosophers, the latter of psychologists. Actually Kant's formulation of the split subject was very reminiscent of the ancient Etruscan understanding of "person," which comes from the Latin word "mask" (L. *persona*). Certainly I am the person you see, but there is another person, too, behind the mask of the public self.

If the theme of identity seems to dominate so many fields in the West today, this may be largely due to two factors, the first identified by German sociologist Max Weber at the turn of the century,[3] and the second by writers in the area of postmodern and postcolonial theory.[4] Weber argued that industrial, technical cultures are publicly dominated by excessive rationalization, intellectualization, and especially by a certain "disenchantment of the world." This drives people inward to try to reclaim personal values deemed to be under threat by the increasing specialization and compartmentalization of knowledge, and the widespread impersonal controls over how the average citizen lives. Capitalism is the quintessence of such rationalization, whereby the ends (making money and profit) completely dominate the means of personal expression and creative outlet. The Self thus becomes the last haven for any sense of individual possibility

By far the most important influence in current debates about identity is that developed through the literature on postmodernism and postcolonialism. In brief, the suggestion is made that the identity "West" can no longer be accepted as a pure thing because it depends on a refusal to recognize and honor its own dependencies. Since the Renaissance Western ascendance in the geopolitical sphere, in terms of economic and political power, depended upon the subjugation, enslavement, and even obliteration of Others, Others now claiming their place within the new configurations of world order. The West is now having to "face" itself in the faces of those it once defaced, and the challenge is very unsettling, particularly for those who have a lot to lose in any new equation of, say, redistributed wealth. In this sense, the new crisis of identity in the West is not so much an intellectual issue as a concrete practical one of how to re-think a world in which the West and all of its prized assumptions about nature, man, and truth, are literally "relativized."

Today, then, the Western subject has been "decentered," to use the term of Michel Foucault. In the field of education, and especially curriculum studies, the decentering of the West has meant widespread reevaluation of the central canons and oeuvres that have defined school and university programs to this point, with a bringing forward of what has been systematically excluded in the "standard" works of the tradition as taught. Where are the voices of women, blacks, aboriginals, and the colonized in the triumphalist male, white, European imperial males? This has been a guiding question in currirular discussions for the last 15 years, or so.

It is the condition of feeling decentered, which is, according to literary critic Terry Eagleton,[5] "the true aporia, impasse or undecidabiliy of a transitional epoch"; the epoch in which, as Western people, we now find ourselves. At the heart of this undecidability is, as Eagleton describes it, "an increasingly clapped-out discreditable, historically superannuated ideology [sic] of autonomous Man." Eagleton's argument is that the fiction of autonomy is the anchor myth of liberal capitalism whereby people are educated to believe that they can discover themselves through their various accumulations and achievements. In fact, however, the success of consumer culture depends precisely on the Self not being a reducible concept, with a consequent need to sustain people's generalized anxiety about such a condition. As David Hume said in the eighteenth century, "The Self is a justifiable but unprovable concept."[6] Consumerism is sustained precisely by the feelings of lack that people have about themselves, and the (false) promise of satisfying that lack with an endless array of material goods, circulating ideas about psychological fulfillment, etc. Capitalist pedagogy exhausts itself with endless busyiness, predicated on an assumption that student or teacher agitations are the consequence of allowing feelings of lack to rear their ugly heads, with the remedy being to labor even more intensively to fill any empty spaces with variations-on-a-theme activities.

The collapse of Autonomous Man has produced a fierce competition to redefine the character of the human project. It is, however, a curious but perhaps inevitable feature of the new identity politics that while the configuration of identities has been changing, to be more inclusive, more pluralistic, the consequences still seem full of pathos because somehow the social grammar has remained the same. Step one may involve the overthrow of old stereotypes, alliances, identities; step two, the formation of new ones. But has anything really changed? No longer a Yugoslavian, now I am a Croat, and as such now I fight Serbs instead of the KGB. No longer a dysfunctional heterosexual, now I am positively gay or lesbian, yet still I find myself entangled in the same jealousies and bitternesses of hetero intimacy. No longer a slave without a vote, now I am an African American determined to participate in democratic process, but still I have to confront myself within the limits of democracy, manipulated as it is by big business and conservative government. No longer exclusionary high school English literature texts, now texts that attempt to include stories about everyone, everything, as if such could be possible. What is a fully representational textbook anyway?

The point is that within this new identity politics, identity is still linked to a profound *desire* for identity, and there is something neurotic, something of the nature of tail-chasing, at work in the whole enterprise. It all still depends on an assumption of the possibility of identity, that somehow if only I could change my circumstances the real me would have a chance to flourish, to find itself. But perhaps it is this assumption that must bear scrutiny, with the fiction of identity being precisely what sets up the possibility of persons being set against each other, or in collaboration to serve a common purpose at someone else's expense.

So what is left? A neo-Nietzschean inversion into cynical nihilism? A swirling postmodern dance of surfaces that leaves everyone burned out and suicidal? A collapse into market-sponsored media inventions of personhood, with an endless fashion file of consuming souls drained of all ethical substance and psychic inferiority?

| | |

There have been several recent attempts by notable Western scholars to rethink the notion of identity away from the usual, basically Aristotelian, typifications of a stable unified subject. Joanna Macy, for example, working from a systems-theory model influenced heavily by Indian Buddhism, proposes that we should understand persons to be much more fluid and impermanent in their respective manifestations. Persons must be seen in terms of "their relations rather than substance": so that "personal identity appears as emergent and contingent, defining and defined by interactions with the surrounding medium."[7] A person doesn't so much *have* experiences, in the manner of Descartes' ego, as exist inseparably from those experiences.

Such a formulation, however, while solving the problem of the irreducibility of the Self by pointing to its necessary relations, still is in a sense atomistic. The Self is sustained through its relations, but the relations, in turn, are sustained by the participation of the same Self. There is no one without the other, yet still they exist together as a self-sustaining entity.

In pedagogical terms, collaborative learning and classrooms organized around principles of ecology reflect this kind of systems theory view, and for that very reason can be very depressing, heavy places for children to be. "Whew! Now I am actually *tied* to you, whether I like it or not. We *have* to collaborate, because independent thinking is now somehow shown philosophically to be false thinking." I may be tied to my field of relations and influence, but whether this is burdensome or emancipatory requires further consideration.

In *Self as Other*, Paul Ricoeur[8] similarly suggests that any attempt to define the Self exclusively as a question of who or what "I am" should be abandoned in favor of realizing that identifying our own selves depends on the presence of, and our interaction with, "others," as necessary context. The narrative self is a kind of storytelling ego who identifies him or herself as the center around which is constellated a series of Others who provide the necessary conditions out of which the drama of the Self can be revealed. There is an inextricability of Self and Other, with the Other maintained as a kind of Other-for-the Self.

Pedagogically it can be seen how this view sponsors a certain requirement of friendliness with others, a new kind of ethical foundation for social relations. If I harm you, somehow my own self requirements are diminished, or at least the context of my life is‍ harmed. One can see, though, how the kind of self-conscious interdependency at the heart of this orientation might easily produce a certain hypocrisy in human relations, insofar as ultimate self interest inevitably overshadows any genuine interest-free concern for another's welfare, or love of another purely for that person's sake. Others simply provide the backdrop for that autobiography in which inevitably I am the hero.

In what follows, I wish to work through the issue of "identity" from a kind of "third space,"[9] a move which relegates the whole identity question to a different kind of frame, and invites certain reconsiderations of our Western prejudices over the matter.

I V

"You should know that Buddha-dharma is to be studied by giving up the view of self and other."[10] This statement by thirteenth century Japanese Zen master Dogen is easily de-exoticized for Western readers by pointing out that *buddha*, in the original Sanskrit simply means "one who is awake," and *dharma*, again in Sanskrit, means literally, "carrying" or "holding." Studying the buddha-dharma, then, refers to the action of being awake to, or attending to what carries, upholds, or sustains us as human beings.

Typical responses in the Western tradition to the question of what sustains us include, for example, positing the god(s) concept, whereby everything that is unexplainable by my received rationality is dumped into a cosmic cargo container for "explanation later," producing a phenomenology of postponement in the now, a kind of intellectual and moral torpor with respect to current problems. Teaching requires a kind of amnesiating Subject who deflects students' hard questions with responses like: "Don't worry, when you grow up you will understand." A teacher formed by the god concept inevitably plays the god role in the classroom.

Another response D.T. Suzuki has called "the homocentric fallacy,"[11] the idea that the whole of creation is focused intentionally around the human species, and that survival or fall depends exclusively on what human beings do or neglect to do. This theory has iterations in Marx, for example, who established the theory of subjectivity on the basis of the historically materially productive activities of humankind. The social-construction-of-reality myth that dominates contemporary social science in the West arises from this. The pedagogical analog might be found in blind encouragements of students to "be whatever you want to be," as if to be human means being free at all times to shape and mold oneself according to will.

Then there is the response of what can be called one-turn negation, an adolescent protest against meaning and the refusal to take any creative responsibility for human difficulty, except perhaps for one's own. The refusal to see the question of what sustains us as a matter of public concern, with a lapse instead into private visions, undergirds most of our secular systems of education. Teaching becomes a kind of "informatics," a condition that celebrates decontextualized "bites" of information. Here, so-called facts, in isolation, are privileged over their interrelated meaning, and the hard task of interpretation is left to specialized others—philosophers, priests, witches. The closest a teacher gets to being "philosophical" is to declare everything a matter of point-of-view, the curse of perspectivism that haunts most of today's classrooms.

Why should it be important to consider the question of what sustains us, as Dogen urges? In grand terms, the answer might be: in order to discover the world more clearly as our true home; or to find ourselves in the world in terms of the world itself, rather than fighting against it, or demanding that it be hammered into the template of our concepts of it. More clearly, it is a matter of having all our work and action ever more finely tuned to the realities of the world, according to the world's own nature. In speaking this way, we are not just talking of the world as the planet Earth, with New York, Teheran, Soweto, etc. all vying for attention on the present world's stage. Instead, the appeal is to the world as in the Old English w(e)orold, meaning "age," from the Greek Aeon. In this sense of world, time and space intersect, or are inseparable, even identical. It is the sense one gains by staring into the sky on a clear night and seeing the stars and planets, asteroids, comets, gas clouds, and so on, all in continuous motion, all in a state of the most intimate intermingling, interfusion, and co-origination, all so big and far away, yet so near. One's meditation inspires the feeling of being part of an ongoing drama, one without beginning or end. One is unequivocally in it, even though as a human being one feels so small, so insignificant in the face of it. One thinks of the forces that are at work constantly, as the universe undergoes its endless transformations, out of which the earth has momentarily appeared, and into which eventually it will disappear to be reworked into new forms in new ages. This "I," this Self which meditates on these things, is sustained, shaped, molded, carried, and upheld both by, and in the midst of, these transformations, but only in a certain sense, and it is one that offends our common sense because it is a condition not of lively, self-conscious affirmation in the spirit of the Happy Face of good liberal capitalism. Instead it is the primordial condition of both creation and destruction, to be awake to, which means that whether I live or die really seems quite beside the point. To truly live, then, in the way this world shows its way to be, I must embrace without equivocation the truth of my mortality as part of my vitality. As the contemporary Vietnamese Zen Master Thich Naht Hanh has put it, "Birth and death are fictions, and not very deep,"[12] by which he means that even when I die, I continue living, in the plants and insects that consume me for their nourishment and life, and in the memories of those with whom I have lived for a brief span, and who themselves go on living. Similarly, as I live by the grace of the animals, plants, and insects that give me life, so too am I dying, eventually to be taken in again for other purposes. Every identifiable "thing" is itself in a condition of constant mutation, completely infused with everything else, never "this" for more than a moment; soon to be "that," or "this-and-that." In spite of everything, the whole remains whole, teeming with fluid ambiguity, but never without integrity.

If we are to get closer to the sense of what sustains or upholds us, these last examples, of how dying and living are themselves concepts that require deep meditation, may point to how that very meditation can lead us to a healthy abandonment of the concepts of Self and Other. It is not that there is no Self and Other, as in the one-turn negation, but rather that the formulation puts the emphasis in the wrong place. There is a place where Self and Other cannot be identified separately because the moment one is identified, so too in that very instant is the other named or brought forward. The game of trying to separate them is one, not just of futility, but worse, of utter violence, because they are always everywhere co-emergent, with a denial of one being a denial of the other. In the third century, Indian philosopher Nagarjuna declared that in the life of true liberty, "there is neither yes nor no, nor no-yes or no-no."[13] He was trying to point to the futility of dualistic thinking, drawing attention instead to the pre-existent unity by which all dualisms are already held together. Here we might say, "Not Self and Other, and not *not* Self and Other." In other words, Self and Other should not be held as independent entities, yet too, neither should we deny that Self and Other exist. After all, common sense tells us that I am me and You are you, and these separations are required for simple functioning, for example, within the space limitations of our homes, schools, and other institutions. What Nagarjuna is saying, though, is that we should not rest in our commonsense perceptions, complacency with which provides all the ammunition one needs to set oneself against the other should the "I" be threatened. As Peter Hershock has put it, "the gathering with which we identify ourselves is actually a learned process of simply divorcing that over which 'I' cannot exercise direct control."[14]

Living in the pre-existent unity of the world, or rather, living in such a way as to put the awareness of that unity in front of the desire for the usual discriminations that inevitably emerge from language, tribe, and nation, is a form of life-practice that is "to be realized and not sought," as Chih Tung, disciple of Hui Neng, founder of the Ch'an (Zen) school in the seventh century, has put it.[15] One cannot seek it, because that would put it "over there" somewhere, while it is already "here," inherent in every present moment. Also, to posit it over there, means it would have to be apprehended by some pre-existent Ego that somehow lies outside of the whole process. So the truth of living awake to the way that sustains us requires a different manner of proceeding, a manner not dependent on language, rationality, or culture; it requires a simple openness to that which meets us at every turn, in every thing, every thought, feeling, idea, person. Everything is a reminder of who and what we are, a kind of calling back to our more essential truth. Becoming awake to what sustains us is a form of realization of what it is we already are. Indeed, as David Loy has put it, "What you seek, you already are."[16] Sometimes this is spoken of as the process of finding one's "Original Face."[17]

Being in the presence of someone who is truly awake can be very unnerving, especially for those who have not "faced" themselves. The person seems like a mirror in which one sees oneself for the first time and is aghast. There is an uncanny stillness present, reminding us of our constant agitation, our frenetic searching for that which we cannot name but feel we should be able to if only one more turn be taken with this or that. The stillness of one who is awake does not arise out of passivity, quietism, or simple resignation but rather from deep attunement to the coherence and integrity of everything that is already and everywhere at work in the world as it is. The face of one who has found their Original Face seems to contain everything and nothing all at once. It is as if the face could burst forth with joy at any moment, or register the most profound anger. It is the Face of complete potentiality because indeed it is has seen everything. It has seen human misery in its most abject expressions, joy in its most robust celebrations. In the presence of one who has faced himself, one feels understood, found, unconditionally accepted, but this acceptance does not necessarily induce pleasure. It does not mean an endorsement or condoning of bad things, things that hurt others, for example. Rather, in facing one who has faced himself, one has the feeling of being seen, deeply, and in that very instant one begins to see the foolishness of one's own ways, perhaps for the first time, ways that arise precisely out of the desire to arbitrate the boundaries of Self and Other, to secure or justify the Self against the Other. And in seeing one's actions as, in a sense, arising out of ignorance, one is filled with desire to live differently, with greater awareness.

What would be the face of teaching for a teacher who is awake to what sustains us? In Sanskrit, there is a word, *upaya*, used precisely to describe the teaching style of an Awakened One.[18] Literally, it refers to "skill in means, or method." It also has the connotation of "appropriateness," of knowing exactly what is required in any specific instance. Students under the tutelage of one who is awake often find the teacher to be a bundle of contradictions, because what is said to one may be completely reversed in instructions to another. This is because the teacher understands the unique needs and capabilities of each, honoring differences, and knowing what is best for each.

In terms of contemporary pedagogy, we can see the way *upaya* refutes any systematic approach to instructional conduct, making possible an opening of a much fuller range of expression both on the part of the teacher as well as the student. The interest of the teacher is not to teach, in the usual sense of imparting well-formulated epistemologies, but to protect the conditions under which students in their own way can find their way. One of the key conditions for this effort is to be vigilant of students' motives. Is the learning simply for personal aggrandizement, careerism, a way by which to assert the Self over the Other? Or is it oriented to an ever deepening humility (literally, "groundedness">L. *humus*) that arises from seeing the interconnectedness of everything and the essential humor of our co-origination. In such circumstances, one student may need severe discipline, another strong encouragement; always the concern is for each one to discover a sense of what upholds him or her, and the original face that bears their hope for a new originality in the present.

There is a likeness here to the practice in many aboriginal cultures in North America of appointing elders gifted with discernment to the post of "child watcher." Their job is to keep watch over the children, at play, in community activities, and so on, to see what the particular gift of each child might be, as it arises naturally in the context of everyday life, and then to guide each child into efforts that can bring the gift to its fullest expression. Such a practice holds up for criticism all those pressures in modern capitalist culture that encourage students to fit themselves to the requirements of the corporate agenda, taking a narrow, time-bound characterization of success to be of universal application.

As far as classroom management is concerned, pedagogy that faces itself may elaborate the suggestion of Thich Nhat Hanh: "We need to look at a conflict the way a mother would who is watching her two children fighting. She seeks only their reconciliation."[19] From the point of view of full compassion, war arises precisely out of Self and Other, with attempts to name the virtue of one at the other's expense. Wisdom, however, desires the loss of neither, seeing their essential mutual necessity within the integrity of what sustains us.

If facing oneself as a teacher is a task to be realized and not sought, that is, attended to as an already inherent potentiality rather than something to be obtained and validated by external certification, what are the safeguards to ensure that one's teaching practices are not simply the manifestation of a new blind narcissism or a celebration of a newly realized subjectivity? Again, those who have gone before have understood the problem. In the ancient Pali language, there are two terms that identify stages along the way of finding one's way as a teacher who is awake. In the first stage, *jhana*, the aim is to achieve a kind of stillness of heart and mind through ritual stopping of intellectual and cognitive habits.[20] It is the process of emptying the mind of thoughts, worries, fantasies, etc. by accepting their unresolvability. They cannot be resolved in any final sense because they are themselves simply products of the mind, that jumping monkey which tries so hard to not let us rest.

In the condition of stillness, it becomes possible to hear new sounds, or old sounds in a new way, appreciate tastes once numbed out by old habits of taste, see a child, spouse, partner, parent, in a way that honors them more fully, instead of constrained by the usual fears, desires, and projections. One begins to understand how pedagogical confidences learned in one's teacher training may have only limited application in the face of any classroom's true complexity; and that dealing with that complexity requires not yet another recipe for control, but precisely the opposite, namely a radical openness to what is actually happening therein, in the lives and experiences of both students and oneself, and an ability to deal with all of it somehow on its own unique terms. Again, such an ability requires first and foremost a true facing of oneself and others as sharing in a reality that at its deepest level is something held in common, something that upholds one and all together in a kind of symphony.

At the age of fifty-one, Confucius had not yet faced himself, and was therefore not yet a teacher. One day he went to his Master Lao Tan (Lao Tzu), who asked him how he had been spending his time. Confucius replied that he had been studying mathematics for five years, light and darkness for twelve years, and memorizing perfectly the six *Great Books*, called *The Odes*, *History*, *Poetry*, *Music*, *The Changes*, and *The Seasons Spring and Autumn*. Lao Tan then began to talk to Confucius about the way which upholds us, sustains us, and carries us. Confucius retired to his hut for three months, and then returned to his teacher, saying, "I have understood now. The crows and magpies incubate their eggs, and fish plan their spawning; the locust engenders itself by metamorphosis; the birth of the younger brother makes the older cry. For a long time now I haven't participated in these transformations." *The person who does not participate in transformation, how could such a person transform others?*[21]

Confucius' last remark signifies the second major turning point on the way to waking up as a person, on the way to becoming a teacher, and that is taking up the hard challenge of self-transformation. The meaning is carried in the Pali word *upacara*. The task is chiefly one of beginning to pierce through all of the social, political, and cultural illusions by which one's identity has been created and has sustained itself to the present point. Without doubt, therefore, it involves culture criticism, criticism of bad economic practices that destroy the common realm for the greed of the few; criticism of social structures and attitudes that demean others of different race, class, or gender in order to affirm only one type as the "real" thing. More than anything else, however, it forces a recognition of how one is oneself always and everywhere complicit in such ignorance, and that the hardest work, the work that provides the only true authority for teaching others about social transformation, is by addressing the condition of one's own ignorance. Rwanda does not just exist in Africa, Rwanda also exists in my own heart-mind, to deny which is to deny, and hence not face, the vicious fantasies I am quite happy to entertain, even maintain, about the family across the backlane, for example, whose barking dog keeps me awake at night and who refuse to discipline the same, in spite of my mock-friendly overtures. I have to face the fact that I myself am really not so distantly removed from committing a vile atrocity; that though I have a naturally smiling face, it can hide feelings of hatred. I know that I am capable of the most calumnious and vituperative delusions. These Other sides of my face I must face too, if I want to be a teacher, or more accurately if pedagogic authority is to flow out of me in the manner of the world's upholding, in a way that reveals the deepest truth about the world rather than acting against it. I may have a teaching certificate, a civil license to teach, but whether I am a teacher, really, depends on something else. It depends on the ability to "be still, and to know God,"[22] as an ancient Hebrew poet has expressed it, which means the ability to dwell openly in that which cannot be named but within which we live and move and have our being. Without attention to this which contains both this and that, self and other, you and me, life becomes nothing but a half-life, a kind of fake optimism about the Now that is fundamentally conservative because it refuses to love the Other as Itself, to see them as one, instead banishing the Other as enemy, or potential enemy, of the "I."

"Your enemy is your teacher," says Song-chol, head of the Chogye Order in Korea.[23] "Adversity is the only teacher," said Aeschylus, the early Greek dramaturge.[24] "When you have eaten the bread of suffering, and drunk the water of distress, then you will see your Teacher face to face" said the Hebrew prophet Isaiiah.[25] All of these examples imply the truth well understood by Freud that what we keep at bay, what we hate, what we demonize, is most typically what we fear. What we fear, we repress, and what we repress comes back over and over to haunt us in our dreams, in our compensatory actions, until the day comes when we can no longer run away from it and have to make friends with it and embrace it as part of what sustains us. Isaiah understood this seeming contradiction well: suffering and distress are like bread and water, forms of nourishment. To accept this, however, requires a discerning of how they act together within a deeper truth of things, a truth that is deeper than any pain I might feel when I have lost my beloved, my job, my country. In fact it is precisely such experiences of loss that can divest us of the illusion of trying to secure ourselves, yet in that very divestment we can see more clearly the security already manifest in the world, the world which is already carried, upheld and sustained in spite of our most advanced management systems, comprehensive insurance policies and hyper-developed health care products—those monuments to human cowardice that reveal our reluctance to be taught the things of greatest importance.

To be a teacher, then, requires that I face my teacher, which is the world as it comes to meet me in all of its variegation, complexity, and simplicity. When I do this, I face myself, and see myself reflected in the faces of my brothers and sisters everywhere. If I look to see myself only in the faces of those portrayed in glamour magazines, or in *Fortune 500's* "Top Ten CEOs," I suffer a fundamental double impoverishment. Not only will I be disappointed in myself, but also I will miss the point that such people represent only a small dot on the mirror of reality, and to try to copy them is to force myself to become equally small. By facing too those whose faces have been seared by the fires of life, seeing myself in them, I become more fully human, more open and generous, more representative of the real thing we call Life.

CONCLUSION

Western critics of Eastern philosophy often suggest that the latter sponsors only quiescence and pacifism, and does not take full enough responsibility for dealing with the hard, concrete problems of existence on this side of the river. Such a remark, of course, only points to the privilege the West gives to action and activism, and does not face all of the negative consequences that Western activism has inflicted on the world. Even in the field of medicine, for example, the rush to interventional practices too often gets in the way of natural healing, and a true pedagogy of suffering. Ashis Nandy has eloquently drawn attention to the phenomenon of "iatrogenesis,"[26] whereby acts of treatment themselves often cause different kinds of disease. In Western medicine, the patient is no longer allowed to be patient, the clinical vultures always hovering overhead waiting to dive in with the latest "procedure."

Certainly the most profound disease in Western pedagogy is activism, or action for its own sake. Children in today's classrooms have virtually no time to simply dream, wait, think, ponder, or learn to be still. There is so little opportunity to find one's original face, because every space is seen to require some sort of instructional intervention. Indeed, using the language of this paper, Western pedagogy is too often precisely an act of de-facement, for both teachers and students, as they struggle mercilessly to fit themselves in to codes and agendas that maim and scar the soul. Ironically, such maiming arises precisely out of good intention and great earnestness. But that very earnestness itself gets in the way of self-understanding, because the Self cannot understand itself until it loses itself in the work of great relinquishment, of being born again in the ocean of wisdom wherein Self and Other have no time to negotiate their differences. In the ocean of wisdom, the moment Self and Other have been identified they have disappeared, or been transformed or mutated into yet another unfolding of the drama in which all things, all people regardless of race, gender, or class, participate. Whether that participation is creative or destructive depends on whether one clings to or relinquishes old identities that have already passed anyway. To find one's original face as a teacher means to stand before one's students as the embodiment of true liberty, known everywhere by its mark of deep humor, which arises from the awareness that at the heart of life is a contradiction. To find myself I have to lose myself, otherwise death comes in the most vainglorious guise, death by a thousand Self achievements that leave me isolated in the cage of my own subjectivity, bereft of the companionship of the world, bereft indeed of pedagogy, which means, basically, companionship (Gk. *Paedagogos*, one who accompanies children).

We might note in closing the profound engagement between one who is awake and children, or, as it might be described, the universal attractiveness of Wisdom to children. Ryokan-osho, an eighth century enlightened hermit, was described in the following terms:

> Hair unkempt, ears sticking out,
> His tattered robes
> Swirling like smoke,
> He walks home
> With hordes of children
> Swarming all around.[27]

The image has a mirror in the Christian story of the children "coming to Jesus."[28] As teachers and teacher educators we might ask what is it that makes genuine enlightenment attractive to children. I think it has something to do with the way the teacher who is awake has recovered from the snares and entrapments of Self and Other thinking, now accepting all others in the way a very young child does, trusting the world as being the only world there is, engaging it without fear. Fear comes later.

N O T E S

1. See David Kennedy, *Young Children's Thinking: An Interpretation From Phenomenology* (unpublished Ph.D. dissertation, University of Kentucky, 1984).

2. For this discussion on historical developments in the lineage of identity, I have been very much served by John Forrester, "A brief history of the subject," in *Identity: The Real Me*, ICA Document #6 (London: Free Association Books, 1987), 13-16.

3. For an extended discussion of Weber's argument, see David Loy, "Preparing for something that never happens: The means/ends problem in modern culture," *International Studies in Philosophy* 26, No. 4 (1994), 49ff.

4. See, for example, Patrick Williams and Laura Chrisman, *Colonial Discourse and Postcolonial Theory: A Reader.* (New York: Columbia University Press, 1995).

5. Terry Eagleton, "The politics of subjectivity," in *Identity: The Real Me.* ICA Document #6. (London: Free Association Books), 1987, 47.

6. In Forrester, "A brief history of the subject," 14.

7. Joanna Macy, *Mutual Causality in Buddhism and General Systems Theory.* (Albany: State University of New York Press), 1991.

8. Paul Ricoeur, *Self As Other.* (Chicago: University of Chicago Press), 1992.

9. The concept of "Third Space" I borrow from Homi Bhabha but develop differently here. See Homi Bhabha, "The third space," in *Identity: Community, Culture, Cifference*, edited by Jonathan Rutherford (London: Lawrence and Wishart, 1990).

10. Kazuaki Tanahashi, editor, *Moon in A Dewdrop: Writings of Zen Master Dogen.* (San Francisco: North Point Press), 1985, 157.

11. D.T. Suzuki, *Living By Zen.* London: Rider, 1990.

12. Thich Nhat Hanh, "Look into your hand, my child!" *The Acorn: A Gandhian Review* 3, No. 1 (March 1988), 10.

13. Vincente Fatone, *The Philosophy of Nagarjuna.* (Delhi: Motilal Banarsidass), 1981.

14. Peter Hershock, "Person as narration: The dissolution of 'Self' and 'Other' in Ch'an Buddhism," *Philosophy East and West* 44, No. 4, (1994), 691.

15. In *The Diamond Sutra and the Sutra of Hui Neng*, translated by A.F. Price and Wong Mou-Lam. (Boston: MA: Shambhala Press), (1969), 69.

16. David Loy, "Indra's postmodern net," *Philosophy East and West 43*, No. 3 (1993), 485.

17. For a discussion of this concept, see Achaan Chah, *A Still Forest Pool*. (London: The Theosophical Publishing House), 1989.

18. This is discussed more fully in Donald S. Lopez, Jr., *Buddhist Hermeneutics*. (Honolulu: University of Hawaii Press), 1988.

19. Thich Nhat Hanh, *The Sun My Heart*. (Berkeley: Parallax Press), (1988), 42.

20. In Chinese, the one word *hsin* means mind-heart, in recognition that the work of mind and heart cannot be separated.

21. This story is recorded in Tchouang-Tseu, *Oeuvres Completes*. (Paris: Gillimard), (1969), 47. Emphasis mine.

22. Psalms 46:10.

23. Ven. Song-chol, *Echoes From Mt. Kaya*, ed. Ven. Won-tek. (Seoul, Korea: Lotus Lantern International Buddhist Centre), (1988), 81.

24. In Richard Palmer, *Hermeneutics*. (Chicago: Northwestern University Press), (1969), 43.

25. Isaiah 30:20.

26. Ashis Nandy, "Modern medicine and its nonmodern critics: A study in discourse," in *The Savage Freud and Other Essays on Possible and Retrievable Selves*. (Princeton, N.J.: Princeton University Press), (1995), 145-195.

27. In Koji Sato, *The Zen Life*. (Kyoto: Tankosha), (1984), 177.

28. Mark 10:13.

CHAPTER TWENTY-NINE

Early Education
as a Gendered Construction

Shirley R. Steinberg
1996

Resting at the basis of a patriarchal system is the marginalization of women's work—and early childhood education, of course, is women's work. Various scholars have used such phrases as "the ideology of domesticity" and "the culture of romance" to refer to women's responsibility for unpaid work at home and their acquisition of status by way of their relationships with males. In the ideology of domesticity and the culture of romance, women's work revolves around the home and family, both in and outside the home. In such a context, women's work outside the home reflects women's assumed-to-be innate ability to nurture, to care for children, and to cultivate a homelike atmosphere. Obviously, there is nothing wrong with this culturally sanctioned ethic of caring—indeed, such an ethic can be used to humanize workplaces, schools, and society in general. Problems emerge, however, when such caring is viewed as an essential essence of womanhood and the sole quality needed to achieve success as an early childhood educator (Lutrell, 1993; Rubin, 1994; Sidel, 1992).

Without the contextualization provided by an understanding of the asymmetrical power relations between women and men, this ethic of caring can contribute to the exploitation of women and the subversion of a critical vision of professionalism among early childhood educators. When women operating on the basis of the ethic of caring subordinate their own concerns and needs, they reinforce patriarchal power relations between their husbands, male principals, bureaucratic supervisors, and themselves. Operating on the assumptions underlying the ideology of domesticity and the culture of romance, many women are led to careers that reflect these nurturing and maternal concerns—careers like early education. The key dynamic in a critical reconceptualization of the role of the early childhood teacher involves the analysis of the relationship between "woman as caregiver" and "educational professional as analyst of the social contexts, the discursive constructions, and the power relations that shape childhood and schooling for children."

One important dimension of the asymmetrical power relations between women and men that relates directly to the professional aspirations of women in "traditional, nurturing" roles involves feminine knowledge claims. In patriarchal societies, men's claim to knowledge, its production, and its validation carries more weight than women's. While different socioeconomic classes and racial and ethnic groups hold differing perspectives on this social dynamic, men's knowledge about work, teaching, and other "technical" domains garners more status and legitimacy.

This power dimension is illustrated daily on the individual level with men in board meetings interrupting and speaking over women or appropriating authority over what women have said (with, for example, such seemingly supportive remarks as, "What Connie meant was that..."). The same pattern is discernible on TV when an advertisement promotes a household product for women (e.g., dishwashing detergent). While the video depicts a woman using and enjoying the product ("My hands are softer after washing the dishes..."), a male voice-over provides the technical information, a la Mr. Tidy Bowl as expert ("Three out of four dermatologists conclude that new, improved..."), and the trappings of authority. The woman, alone with her "inferior" form of knowledge, is an inadequate authority in a patriarchal society. Bring in the man with the deep voice. Bring in the male scholars with their objective and detached child observations and scientific judgments. Male research rigor constructed a developmental psychology and grounded on rational, hierarchical theories that work to legitimate the practice of early childhood education. It is no surprise that the resulting methods of measurement and comparison that have come to dominate early childhood education have supported existing power hierarchies, privileging male over female, European over non-European, adult over child, and so forth. Early childhood teaching practice in this paradigm is women's work— labor long on nurturance and short on complexity and intellectual demand. Such a work form easily fits the categorization of glorified babysitting with its attending low wages and low status (Aronowitz & Di Fazio, 1994; Meissner, 1988).

Woman's jobs have always been more vulnerable to "proletarianization" than men's. Women's work has been rationalized, and we have witnessed a major expansion in positions with minimal autonomy and control. Teaching, of course, has been increasingly rationalized, with more and more teacher-proof materials and supervisory control. The decrease in jobs with autonomy cannot be separated from the sexual division of labor: Women in jobs with minimal autonomy (but amid substantial bureaucracy) make more concerted attempts to shape both the content of the position and the manner in which it is to be performed. Early childhood teachers, of course, often find themselves trapped in these discursive and material chains. They are expected to "cover" the curricular material provided to them by administrators. As pink collar assembly-line workers who move children along a conveyor belt of a prescribed course of study, teachers follow the directions of absentee experts—of *Goals 2000* authors who decree that all children should enter school "ready to learn" (Banfield, 1991; Fine, 1993; Johnson, 1991).

These epistemological and political dynamics constitute a part of the larger justification for critical, empowered early childhood educators who conduct their own research and produce their own knowledge. This vision of the early childhood professional fights the "maternal model" of the early childhood teacher with its essentialized view of woman as nurturer. The critical childhood educator develops an understanding of educational purpose—preferably one that is aware of its dependence upon an awareness of larger social purpose. As a teacher researcher, the critical childhood educator continually attempts to evaluate her or his strategies for implementing those educational values deemed of worth. In this context such teachers fight with mainstream texts and rewrite them as a form of critical research; they resist the demands of the official curriculum that they defer to the experts, as they expose the assumptions the experts make about the submissive role of early childhood teachers and the compliant role of women. What is not being overtly stated here, they ask? Do the goals of the experts conflict with our critical curriculum? If so, why does the conflict exist? The answers to such questions may lead early childhood teachers to develop ties to various women's organizations and other democratic social groups. Collaboration with such groups may provide teachers with ways of examining their work never before imagined (Butler, 1990; Pagano, 1990). Using women's resource centers and on-line World Wide Web resources, collaboration can be personal or electronic as early childhood teachers communicate their ideas and talk about their teaching.

Images of early childhood education have haunted our popular culture consciousness: memories of *Romper Room's* syrupy voiced Miss Diane (always a Miss) gathering unusually large preschoolers around her to instruct them in absurd and rote games, never asking for thoughtful input from the kids. Children were middle class, well-groomed, and obedient. Never did we view misbehavior or mutiny as the rompers roamed to the beat of their drummer. From Miss Diane our image of early childhood caretaker faced to *Mary Poppins*. Disney educated us that the nanny could manage "bad" children as long as she was bestowed with magical powers. Mary was also unattached (little time to dance with Bert, the chimney sweep), her raison d'etre was exclusively to nurture her charges. This image of the single female caretaker implies that a good early childhood educator should be single in order to fulfill her own mothering needs: a partner could possibly divert her energies. Sacrifice being essential in the ideology of domesticity, Mary's pride in her vocation seemed to lie in the fact that she was supercalifradulisticexpeladocious through her magic, thus the "lowly" vocation was at least palatable.

Mrs. Doubtfire was also successful, funny, and heartwarming. The fact that this lovable "old battle-ax" was indeed a *male* ensured her success with difficult children. As the children ran previous female nannies ragged, Mrs. Doubtfire knew how to solve problems, how to make learning exciting, and how to engage the children in fulfilling activities. No "normal" female caretaker could work with the two difficult children, daddy in drag come in to save the day—neither mommy nor nanny could cope with the little heathens. Many movie viewers watched in amused disbelief as Arnold (Conan/Terminator) Schwarzenegger tamed a difficult gaggle of girls and boys in *Kindergarten Cop*. With the validation of a male superstar, the low-status profession of a male early childhood educator became respectable. Still, the humor of the movie revolved around a brave, highly skilled male confronted with the mundane trials of this low-skill, "female" job.

Males in television have been portrayed in a positive, heroic manner through class and education as they deal with early childhood nurturing. Mr. French (*A Family Affair*) and Mr. Belvedere each portrayed a male's role as early childhood nurturer. With stiffened British accents and demeanors, these "nannies" rose above the usual job to add class and stability to the children they nurtured. Not only did they competently take care of the children, but the entire house goose-stepped to their march. Their maleness commanded deferential treatment, as even their employers addressed them as "Mister." The homes were ruled with "an iron hand," and no "monkey business" was detected. Problems were solved with logic and discussion; calculation, deceit, or manipulation was not a part of these quasi-noblemen's agendas.

The network sticom situates a female nurturer in a role such as that of Fran in *The Nanny*. This show reveals a popular image of women in early childhood professions in an entirely different light from the highly esteemed Mr. French and Mr. Belvedere. Anti-Semitic images aside, *The Nanny* depicts a single, mini-skirted, fashion fiend who takes a job as a governess for a wealthy Englishman. Once again, class comes into play as we are constantly reminded of the aristocratic status of the father and Fran's Brooklyn-bred lack therof. Fran is the only one who can work with the children—utilizing manipulation, deceit, and her sexuality to accomplish her vocational and romantic objectives. We never expect Fran to manage, through intellect, to encourage thoughtfulness and problem solving abilities in her charges; we simply watch as she bumbles through childcare with absolutely no consciousness of what she or her children need. As Mr. Belvedere spouts an epithet from John Locke to make a cogent point, Fran is capable of instructing the children only through such quips as "get what you can," "it is worth it for a free meal," and "you don't have to like him to go out with him."

These white and middle-class examples of early childhood education and care show up again and again in popular culture, reinforcing the early childhood, single female teacher as one who can neither get a "real" job nor a "real" man. In contrast, Arnold the kindergarten terminator never had trouble juggling females *and* his job as a kindergarten teacher. However, female images reflect the notion that early childhood education is for "old maids." Teaching preschool is the bottom of the barrel, nursery school is a step up, and kindergarten is only a notch above. As we deconstruct a school's hierarchy, we see that the lower the grade, the less important the teacher. Why is it that the male elementary school teacher always teaches fifth and sixth grades? Women's work is reserved for women. Can men be expected to tie shoes, wipe noses, and button coats? Only if a British accent, coat and tails, and knowledge of Shakespeare accompanies these acts. Once appropriated from the female early childhood caretaker, issues of class emerge, or machismo, as in the *Kindergarten Cop*; axis of power *a la* patriarchy and classism are created in order to present a male in a plebeian profession acceptable to viewers.

It is no surprise that toys reinforce the feminization of the early childhood teacher. Mattel's *Dr. Barbie* is depicted only as a pediatrician, complete with a pink office; the new *Teacher Barbie* is an instructor of a preschool, and the *Love to Read Barbie* is given four-year-old charges to whom she reads *Mother Goose*. Each of the new Barbie collections in which she is placed in a professional role locates her as working exclusively with young children. There has never been a Barbie high-school teacher, drama coach, or basketball coach. Other than cheerleading and ballet, Barbie's pedagogical knowledge is restricted to working with pre-five-year-olds. The blonde bimbo's penchant for easy living and cute, fluffy little pink jobs is thus reinforced (Steinberg, 1993). Kindergarten G.I. Joe? X-Man pre-school? Nursery Ken? I don't think so.

In the early 1980s, English-royalty junkies watched in horror as the Prince of Wales began to romance a shy, nineteen-year-old nursery teacher. Referred to in the media as "only" a preschool teacher—a woman without a profession, a vocational worker—no one was impressed with the possibility that the future kind of England could marry a person of such low social-vocational status. The difficulties of viewing early childhood education as a position of status—that of an educator and a researcher—must be reinvented. Through a reinvention of early childhood educator, women and men who hold the position are empowered to do what they have always done, yet with recognition and respect.

As critical teacher researchers, early childhood teachers may formulate an inquiry project revolving around the status of women teachers of young children in a particular school or a specific school district. As part of the research project, early childhood teachers would study the theoretical dynamics of women's relation to education. Having some insight into the ways women have been historically marginalized as teachers and as students, critical teachers would trace the ways such roles have been socially constructed. In the process they would uncover the hidden ways that prevailing norms of school achievement may distort the skills and unique perspectives brought to the classroom by girls and other students who are in some way different. When teachers comprehend the parameters of behavior, schools allow different kinds of students; teachers and students alike are empowered to better appreciate the ways that forces of patriarchy and education interact to shape the future socioeconomic roles of girls and boys. For example, do gender, race, and socioeconomic class intersect in ways that help determine assessments of which children are merely "too frisky" or which children are "bad" and have a so-called attention deficit disorder? Such determinations drastically influence the quality of a young child's vocational future. Beginning with these theoretical notions, early childhood teacher-researchers are equipped to analyze tacit gender policies in their schools and districts. Based on their findings, action can be taken to establish gender equity for both teachers and students.

Maxine Greene argues that while feminine notions of caring and connecting are indeed valuable, they are not, in themselves, enough to change schools (Greene, 1988). In addition to caring and connecting, we must develop new forms of analysis, new definitions of higher orders of thinking that expose the deep structures and discursive formations that covertly shape both our consciousness and our socio-educational institutions. In this context we can begin to replace the masculinist discourse that negates body and feeling with a new female expressiveness that draws upon the nonverbal communication forms of the body and emotion; early childhood teachers begin to move to what Joe Kincheloe and I (Kincheloe & Steinberg, 1993) describe as postformal thinking. Such a cognitive form negates truncated communication that excludes body and feeling as it embraces Cartesian-Newtonian logocentrism (Darder, 1991; Lather, 1991; Leeks, 1988; May & Zimpher, 1986; Reinharz, 1992; Walkerdine, 1988, 1990; Wertsch, 1991).

This truncated masculinist thinking tends to undermine our understanding of difference as it confuses divergence with deficiency. Such a view is grounded upon the innate rigidity of modernist notions of intelligence as a specter emerging from innate inner structures. The early Piaget, in particular, supported the notion that the appropriate pedagogical direction was to take the students' developmental processes away from emotions—thus the logical could control the child's mental progress. Consequently, stages were created around this science based upon logic—this logocentrism—these stages would become essential footings in the mainstream discourse about intelligence. However, feminist theory would eventually call attention to this grand narrative, arguing that the understanding of the social construction of individuals (according to class and issues of gender) and the impossibility of separating both logic and emotion will force us to ask questions of essentializing human development. Feminist theory demands that we examine the difference between different ways of knowing: between masculine and feminine, between black and white, between rich and poor—all ways of knowing unique to each individual. For example, we see that the masculine would represent the "correct" path for the development of human cognition. Feminists teach us that intelligence must be reconceptualized in manners that consider the plethora of ways of knowing and thinking of which human beings are capable. We are taught that intelligence is not a feature of a certain person, but it is related to the weaving of thoughts, ideas, behaviors, situation, context, and outcomes (Bozik, 1987; Kincheloe, 1993; Lawler, 1975; Walkerdine, 1984).

Such analysis is dangerous to the status quo of early childhood education. Not only does it challenge the way we teach and assess young learners, but it sends a wake-up call to those who would marginalize the predominately female core of early childhood teachers. No longer content to lounge in the male elementary school principal's harem, early childhood teachers expose the ideological forces that shape their views of themselves as teachers and citizens in the community. How do ideological forces define women teachers' relationship with the teaching workplace and their superiors in the bureaucratic hierarchy? As critical researchers, early childhood teachers deconstruct the gender context that has insidiously shaped the field—in the process reconceptualizing the most basic assumptions of early childhood education.

R E F E R E N C E S

Aronowitz, S. & Di Fazio, W. (1994). *The jobless future: Sci-tech and the dogma of work.* (Minneapolis: University of Wisconsin Press).

Banfield, B. (1991). Honoring cultural diversity and building on its strengths: A case for national action. In *Women, Work, and School: Occupational Segregation and the Role Of Education*, edited by L. Wolfe. (Boulder, CO: Westview Press).

Bozik, J. (1990). *Gender trouble.* (London: Routledge).

Darder, A. (1991). *Culture and power in the classroom: A critical foundation for bicultural education.* (Westport, CT: Bergin and Garvey).

Fine, M. (1993). Sexuality, schooling, and adolescent females: The missing discourse of desire. In *Beyond Silenced Voices: Class, Race, and Gender in United States Schools*, edited by M. Fine and L. Weis. (Albany, NY: State University of New York Press).

Greene, M. (1988). *The dialectic of freedom.* (New York: Teachers College Press).

Johnson, W. (1991). Model programs prepare women for skilled trades. In *Women, Work, and School: Occupational Segregation and the Role of Education*, edited by L. Wolfe. (Boulder, CO: Westview Press).

Kincheloe, J. (1993). *Toward a critical politics of teacher thinking: Mapping the postmodern.* (Westport, CT: Bergin and Garvey).

Kincheloe, J. & Steinberg, S. (1993). A tentative description of post-formal thinking: The critical confrontation with cognitive theory. *Harvard Educational Review*, 63, Fall, 296-320.

Lather, P. (1991). *Getting Smart: Feminist research and pedagogy with/In the postmodern.* (New York: Routledge).

Lawler, J. (1975). Dialectical philosophy and developmental psychology: Hegel and Piaget on contradiction. *Human Development*, 18, 1-17.

Lesko, N. (1988). *Symbolizing society: Stories, rites, and structure in a catholic high school.* (New York: Falmer Press).

Luttrell, W. (1993). Working class women's ways of knowing: Effects of gender, race and class. In *Understanding Curriculum as a Racial Text: Representations of Identity and Difference in Education*, edited by L. Castenell and W.F. Pinar. (Albany, NY: State University of New York Press).

May, W. & Zimpher, N. (1986). An examination of three theoretical perspectives on supervision: Perceptions of preservice field supervision. *Journal of Curriculum and Supervision*, 1, 2, 83-99.

Meisner, M. (1988). The reproduction of women's domination in organizational communication. In *Organization Communication*, edited by L. Thayer. (Norwood, NJ: Ablex Publishing).

Pagano, J. (1990). *Exiles and communities: Teaching in the patriarchal wilderness.* (Albany, NY: State University of New York Press).

Reinharz, S. (1992). Feminist methods in social research. (New York: Oxford University Press).

Rubin, L. (1994). *Families on the faultline: American's working class speaks about the family, the economy, race, and ethnicity.* (New York: HarperCollins).

Sidel, R. (1992). *Women and children last: The plight of poor women in affluent America.* (New York: Penguin Books).

Steinberg, S. (1993). A doll's house. In *Kinderculture: The Corporate Construction of Childhood*, edited by S. Steinberg and J. Kincheloe. (Boulder, CO: Westview Press).

Walkerdine, V. (1984). Developmental psychology and the child-centered pedagogy: The insertion of Piaget into early education. In *Changing the Subject*, edited by J. Henriques, W. Hollway, C. Urwin, C. Venn, and V. Walkerdine. (New York: Methuen).

Walkerdine, V. (1988). *The mastery of reason: Cognitive development and the production of rationality.* (London: Routledge).

Walkerdine, V. (1990). *Schoolgirl fictions.* (New York: Verso).

Wertsch, J. (1991). *Voices of the mind: A sociocultural approach to mediated action.* (Cambridge, MA: Harvard University Press).

I

The Reconceptualization of Curriculum Studies

William F. Pinar
1988

As established curriculum scholars will recall, the Reconceptualists were a group of iconoclastic curricularists whom Daniel and Laurel Tanner made famous. For students of the field of curriculum who are perhaps unsure of the meaning of the term, I will recount the history of the Reconceptualists, an exercise that will not only introduce the Reconceptualists, but also the curriculum discourses presented in this volume.

While my reference to the Tanners is intended to amuse established scholars and tease my colleagues Daniel and Laurel Tanner, it is true that their 1979 "The Reconceptualists: Emancipation from Research" which appeared in the *Educational Researcher*[1], did focus a growing controversy within the field, a controversy intensified but not I feel provoked by the Reconceptualists. Philip Jackson's[2] critique a year later, published in *Curriculum Inquiry* in 1980, turned out to be an aftershock. The term and the controversy have all but disappeared, as the field has incorporated the critique of the Reconceptualists, as evidenced in William Schubert's[3] treatment of the topic in his widely read *Curriculum: Perspective, Paradigm, Possibility*. This incorporation, signaling a significant reduction in the field's resistance to the Reconceptualists, ended this interesting "event."

Who were the Reconceptualists? What was the Reconceptualization? What was Reconceptualism? Many of those whose work appears in this volume have been identified as Reconceptualists. Their work, termed both Reconceptualism and the Reconceptualization, challenged the dominant tradition in the field, a tradition characterized by behavioral objectives, planning, and evaluation. Curriculum studies had begun in the 1920s as a subfield of educational administration. The main function of this emerging discipline was to develop and manage curricula for a public school system in a period of rapid expansion. Consequently the early texts of the field addressed issues of development, including curriculum planning and evaluation. The term *Reconceptualists* described individuals whose scholarship challenged this tradition—that is, suggested that the function of curriculum studies was not the development and management but the scholarly and disciplined understanding of educational experience, particularly in its political, cultural, gender, and historical dimensions. During the past two decades the field of curriculum has been reconceptualized from an exclusively practice-oriented field to a more theoretical, historical, research-oriented field. The essays in this text, representing the primary curriculum discourses today, would have been unthinkable just 20 years ago.

While curricularists may disagree over why and when the American Curriculum field became vulnerable to a reconceptualization, I suggest 1957 as a usable date. Sputnik launched the U.S. into one of its periodic anxiety attacks over its schools and their performance[4]. The Kennedy administration replied to this anxiety by initiating the "curriculum reform movement." To lead this movement, specialists in the academic disciplines were chosen. Curriculum specialists (those holding advanced degrees in curriculum studies) were overlooked, thus undermining the field's status and its legitimacy within educational scholarship. Also by the late 1950s, the decades-old expansion of the nation's school population was ending, and the population of graduate students studying curriculum, as well as the population of schoolchildren stabilized and then began to decline. Of course, there were regional differences, but in general by the late 1960s curriculum as a field, weakened by being overlooked by federal curriculum reform efforts and affected by declining enrollments, was vulnerable to attack.

The first volley was fired by Joseph Schwab[5] in 1969, in "The Practical: A Language for Curriculum." He identified the field's apparent demise in its "flight from the practical." (The Schwabian critique has been pursued by Ian Westbury[6] at Illinois, William Reid[7] at Birmingham, and by Michael Connelly[8] at OSIE, among others.) Herbert Kliebard[9] shared Schwab's sense of crisis; however, his diagnosis suggested that the field had been atheoretical and ahistorical. In 1975, in his "The Curriculum Field: Its Wake and Our Work," Dwayne Huebner[10] proclaimed the field dead, not due to either theoreticism or its opposite, but rather from excessive diversity of purpose and an attendant lack of focus and unity. In 1978, when giving the first invited "state of the art" address to the Curriculum division of AERA with John McNeil[11], I declared the field arrested and suggested that Habermas' notion of emancipatory knowledge might stimulate the movement. Philip Jackson's[12] 1980 "Curriculum and its Discontents" ended the decade of attacks. To this point, no subsequent critique has followed.

Long before the attacks began (and quite apart from the reverberations of Sputnik, the curriculum reform movement, and declining enrollments) several lone individuals, critical of Tylerian[13] mainstream of the field, worked to legitimize conceptions of curriculum devised from philosophy, aesthetics, and theology. Dwayne Huebner[14] and James Macdonald[15] worked respectively at Columbia and at Wisconsin (and later North Carolina) to strengthen curriculum's theoretical base, but in ways that were allied with the humanities rather than the behavioral sciences (and educational psychology in particular). As a graduate at Ohio State student in 1969 I was introduced to their work by Paul Klohr[16], and to the work of Maxine Greene,[17] who had considerable interest in curriculum. I also read the work of Elliot Eisner[18], a theorist whose curriculum and evaluation scholarship inspired strands of the Reconceptualists' work, but who, like Greene, declined to be affiliated with the movement. After leaving Columbus that year to teach English at a suburban New York City School, I studied with Huebner at Columbia.

In 1973 I invited Huebner, Macdonald, Greene, and others to Rochester, New York, in hope that these dissidents might find common cause. I linked the conference to the notions of "cultural revolution" and "heightened consciousness," dated terms that make one wince today[19]. Yet, it was an effort to link the ideas of curriculum theorists to development in the political and cultural spheres, and those efforts continued, indeed became one of the major themes of the Reconceptualist movement. Approximately 150 individuals from across the U.S. attended. Paul Klohr helped plan the conference and James Doi (then Dean at the University of Rochester and now dean of Education at the University of Washington in Seattle) funded it. The proceedings, published by McCutchan, still sell steadily, if modestly, today.

The 1973 Rochester conference was the first in a series of conferences which punctuated the intensified interest in curriculum studies. Yearly conferences are still held, now under the supervision of the *Journal of Curriculum Theorizing*[20] and the sponsorship of the University of Dayton[21]. The sequence and sites of the conferences of the 1970s illustrate the tensions and divisions within the movement.

Almost as soon as the conferences began, internal divisions appeared. These struck me at the time at least partly a function of differences in personalities, but as I reflect now I realize that the ideological differences were quite real and perhaps paramount. These were, in the broadest terms, between Marxists of various orientations and interests, and those who were interested less in macro-order issues and more interested in the individual. Institutional rivalry also played a part, albeit a minor one. Generally speaking, the rivalry was between

Columbia and Wisconsin on one hand and band Ohio State and Rochester on the other.

For instance, the 1974 conference, sponsored and held at Xavier University of Cincinnati, was chaired by Professor Timothy Riordan, an Ohio State Ph.D. The 1975 conference at the University of Virginia was chaired by Professor Charles W. Beegle, also an Ohio State graduate. Humanistic themes, often focusing on the individual, predominated at these meetings, although political themes were just barely secondary. By 1976, tensions between the two broad groups discernibly increased, partly in response to the book I edited and misentitled *Curriculum Theorizing: The Reconceptualists*[22]. In that volume I differentiated between *critical* and *postcritical* theorists, placing the Marxists in the former and those of us interested in the individual and related concerns in the later. Of course, it was implicit that postcritical theorists were somehow more advanced, psychologically if not theoretically, and it takes little imagination to conjure up the response of Mike Apple and the growing ranks of Wisconsin—and Columbia—trained Marxists. In 1976, Alex Molnar a University of Wisconsin Ph.D., chaired the meeting at Wisconsin in Milwaukee, (ASCD later published selected proceedings),[23] and political themes dominated. Indeed, a number of presenters in the ill-conceived postcritical category did not manage to get on the program at all. My only position, for instance, was respondent to a major address by Professor Elliot Eisner.[24] In 1977 the politically oriented curriculum scholars, took charge of the meeting at Kent State University in Ohio. In spite of the proximity, this was not Ohio State territory. Richard Hawthorne, a University of Wisconsin Ph.D., chaired the meeting. While the postcritical group was more adequately represented on the program than in 1976, the politically oriented group again dominated the conference program and discussions. A 1978 meeting was held at Georgia State University, chaired by professors Dorothy Huenecke and G. W. Stansburg, at which political analyses were emphasized.

After that meeting I was determined to regain control of the conferences. To whatever extent these conferences were a movement that would reshape curriculum studies theoretically and methodologically, they could not, if they were to survive, be viewed as completely or even primarily identified with Marxist orientations, however crucial these were to the theoretical development of the field. Of course, Apple's contribution was large and growing, Giroux was yet to appear (both of these I will discuss momentarily), and clearly one of the major contributions of so-called reconceptualist thought (though Apple also rejected the term) was a political critique of curriculum development, evaluation, and other curriculum domains. My concern was just how much "space" (to borrow a poststructuralist term) these analyses ought to occupy, at least on the conference programs.

In 1978 Ronald E. Padgham, a Rochester Ed.D., chaired the meeting at the Rochester Institute of Technology. That same year I started *The Journal of Curriculum Theorizing*, and the editors of that periodical also undertook the yearly sponsorship of a curricular conference. From 1979 to 1982, the journal-sponsored meetings were held at the Airlie Conference Center in northern Virginia. In 1983 they were moved to their present site, the Bergamo Conference Center in Dayton, Ohio, where it is supported by the University of Dayton.

What is the status of the "Reconceptualists" in 1987? Before I answer that question, let me note that the term as applied to the scholars themselves, implying a unified effort derived from a common base, is a misnomer. I have tried to clarify this important point on several occasions over the years, but to little effect. My argument in the 1975 volume, which has this term in its subtitle, was that the *work* of these individuals, though originating in quite different and often opposing traditions, functioned to reconceptualize the field of curriculum studies. After the events of the 1960s, and the critiques of the 1970s, the field was vulnerable to reconceptualization, and the work of Huebner, Macdonald, Apple, Kliebard, and others such as Eisner and Greene addressed the atheoretical and ahistorical character of the traditional curriculum field. A more accurate subtitle would have referred to the work of these scholars—simply "The Reconceptualization"[25]—rather than to the individuals themselves.

Nevertheless, in that volume a self-divided movement was christened, or at least conceptualized. What happened to it, in answer to the question I posed a paragraph back, is that to some extent it has succeeded, and to a considerable extent the American field has indeed been reconceptualized.

I suppose the most striking evidence of the reconceptualization having occurred is visible in the programs of the annual meetings of the American Educational Research Association. There the work of many of the individuals whose names are synonymous with the movement is read and discussed. Division B must prove more consternating to some of the AERA leadership since many of the reconceptualist themes litter the Division B landscape, in particular, political, feminist, poststructuralist, phenomenological, and autobiographical themes. Some of the historical work such as Selden's[26] has a political or critical dimension. AERA being an "empirical" social science organization, it is a significant piece of evidence for reconceptualization having occurred that Division B-sponsored work often overlaps with the Bergamo conference program. Conversely, the reconceptualist conferences sponsor non-reconceptualist work. That has to do partly with the success of reconceptualiztion and with internal developments in the movement, and to these I now turn.

During the early years, approximately 1973–1976, the sense of opposition to the mainstream of curriculum theory defined the movement, but as the literature of reconceptualization grew in size, attention shifted from critique of the

Tylerian tradition to Reconceptualist themes themselves. (Examples of these themes comprise this text.)

Certainly the major theme, in number of publications and in complexity of articulation, became politically and economically oriented scholarship. The primary scholar in this area was Michael W. Apple[27]. The scope of his achievement is difficult to assess, but it is clear that it is immense. Both in volume and complexity of his scholarship, and through the work of many students, Apple's contribution to curriculum studies is perhaps greater than any other single individual's associated with reconceptualization. His elaboration of concepts like "hidden curriculum," "hegemony," "reproduction or correspondence theory," and "resistance theory" now form a major constituent element of contemporary curriculum study. Apple himself, and through the work of his students (among them Landon Beyer[28], Nancy King[29], Joel Taxel[30], Linda Christian-Smith[31], Andrew Gitlin[32], Kenneth Teitelbaum[33], Jose Rosario[34], Leslie Roman[35], and others[36]), has produced a significant body of research and theory.

Second to Apple, and perhaps second due only to the fact that he has not trained as many Ph.D. students, is Henry A. Giroux[37], who has been remarkably prolific. His work is complex and appeals to some scholars who find Apple excessively deterministic. Giroux appears to be more influenced by, and his work illustrative of, the dynamism of the work of the Frankfurt School. His elucidations of ideology, culture, resistance, and most recently, with political theorist Stanley Aronowitz[38], educational reform, have become fundamental, perhaps central theoretical statements from the field.

Also in this general category are Jean Anyon[39], whose study of working class and suburban classrooms is well known, and Philip Wexler[40]. Wexler's work is often placed in sociology and social psychology, but those elements that address curriculum are important. His student, James A. Whitson[41], promises to make an original contribution to this field.

The feminist perspective, or perspectives, probably ranks next in importance to the political one, and of course the two have considerable areas of intersection. I would argue (not neutrally, given that she was my student) that Madeleine Grumet[42] is making the major contribution in this sphere. Her new book, *Bitter Milk: Women and Teaching*, may prove as influential as did Apple's *Ideology and Curriculum* in 1979, or Giroux's *Ideology, Culture and the Process of Schooling* in 1981. First, working with autobiography, then phenomenology and psychoanalysis, Grumet's work details several different dimensions of curriculum experience, specifying the particular configurations that constitute women's experience. Janet Miller[43], another former student of mine, began in autobiography, and her current work preserves an autobiographical aspect as she amplifies women's voices in her studies of teaching and learning. Jo Anne Pagano's[44] recent feminist work portends much, as does Patti Lather's[45].

Florence Krall's autobiographical work[46] sometimes evokes feminist themes. The many voices here, often intersecting with more exclusively political ones, run close to the "cutting edge" of contemporary curriculum discourse.

The third major theme might well be phenomenology, epitomized by the important work of Ted Aoki[47], now retired from the University of Alberta. His work depicts both theoretical and curriculum development project issues from the phenomenological perspectives, and his students, working in Canada, the U.S., and Australia, are extending this unique and valuable perspective. Also in this phenomenological category is the work of Max van Manen[48], editor of the Alberta journal *Pedagogy and Phenomenology*, as well as David G. Smith[49] at Letherbridge and Margaret Hunsberger[50] at Calgary.

Much work published in JCT and presented at Bergamo each autumn falls outside these categories. William Doll's work[51], first on Piaget, now on Schoen and Prigogine, has extended our understanding of epistemological and theory-practice issues, respectively. My own work[52], spanning autobiography, gender, literary theory, as well as periodic commentaries on the field, fits in no one category easily. Richard Butt[53], at Letherbridge, has worked on theory-practice issues and is now working in the area of biography, as have Bonnie Meath-Lang and John Albertini (although their specific interest is in dialogue journals)[54]. The general biographical category of work overlaps, I think, with that done by F. Michael Connelly at OSIE and his students, perhaps most notably Jean Clandinin[55] at Calgary. Edmund C. Short's[56] work includes analyses of the field. There is as well a continuing and developing historical opus, contributed by Kliebard[57], Franklin[58], Selden[59], Kridel[60], and O. L. Davis[61]. William Reynolds[62] has combined the interests in hermeneutics and politics in his critique of literature. James T. Sears[63] articulates important issues of gender, but his work also investigates aspects of teacher preparation and qualitative inquiry in curriculum. There are poststructuralist critiques, advanced most dramatically by Jacques Daignault[64] and Clermont Gauthier at the University of Quebec. There is mytho-poetical work, such as that of Ronald E. Padgham[65] and Nelson Haggerson[66], and related work in other specializations, such as supervision, typified by Noreen Garman[67] at Pittsburgh. William Schubert[68] has advanced our historical knowledge of the field, notably by his useful and important bibliography as well as his (with George Posner[69]) genealogical work, now being updated. He has made theoretical contributions in the area of teaching and curriculum, but his most far-reaching impact is his achievement in *Curriculum: Perspective, Paradigm, and Possibility*. This synoptic text is the first to adequately represent the changing landscape of curriculum study and responsible scholars will make it, I suspect, their main text in introductory courses.

So what started as an opposition to the mainstream and tradition of the field has become the field, although complicated, with several centers of focus. There is no "Reconceptualist" point of view, or even points of view. Perhaps that sort of formulation made sense when such varied scholarship appeared to have more in common than it did with the Tylerian tradition which had dominated the traditional field. As shown by AREA Division B conference programs, by the volume of work those termed Reconceptualists, by the appearance of that work in non-Reconceptualist journals such as *Curriculum Inquiry*, *Journal of Curriculum Studies*, *Curriculum Perspectives*, and the *Journal of Curriculum and Supervision*, and its appearance in ASCD yearbooks[70], by the support of non-Reconceptualist work at the Bergamo conference, the Tylerian dominance has passed. Like a disappearing star in another galaxy, however, it takes some years for everyone, depending upon his or her location, to see this. The fact is that to a remarkable extent reconceptualization has occurred[71].

N O T E S

1. D. Tanner and L. Tanner, "Emancipation From Research: The Reconception Prescription," *Educational Research* 8, no. 6 (June 1976): 8–12.

2. P. Jackson, "Curriculum and Its Discontents, " Curriculum Inquiry 10, no. 2 (Summer 1980): 159–172.

3. W. H. Schubert, Curriculum: Perspective, Paradigm, Possibility (New York: Macmillan, 1986).

4. For a more detailed version of this view, see W.F. Pinar and M. Grumet, "Theory and Practice and the Reconceptualization of Curriculum Studies," in *Rethinking Curriculum Studies*, edited by M. Law and L. Barton (London: Croom, Helm, 1981), 20–44.

5. J. J. Schwab, *The Practical: A Language for Curriculum* (Washington D.C.: National Education Association, 1970).

6. I. Westbury and N.J. Wilkof (eds.), *Science Curriculum and Liberal Education* (Chicago: University of Chicago Press, 1978). Many of Schwab's essays are collected in this volume.

7. W. Reid, Thinking About The Curriculum (London: Routledge and Kegan Paul, 1978).

8. Connelly's earlier work, which anticipates his current research, is available in F. M. Connelly, A. S. Dukay, and F. Quinlan (eds.) *Curriculum Planning for the Classroom* (Toronto: Toronto/OSIE Press, 1980). See also D. J. Clandinin, "Teachers Knowledge: What Counts as Personal in Studies of the personal," *Journal of Curriculum Studies*, 1987, in press; also D. J. Clandidin, "On Narrative Method, Biography and Narrative Unities in the Study of Teaching, " *Journal of Educational Thought*, 1987 (in press); and F. M. Connelly and D. J. Clandinin, *Narratives of Experience*, New York: Teachers College Press (in press).

9. H. M. Kliebard, "Persistent Curriculum Issues in the Historical Perspective, " in *Curriculum Theorizing*, ed. W. F. Pinar (Berkeley: McCutchan, 1975), 39–50.

10. D. Huebner, "The Moribund Curriculum Field" Its Wake and Our work, " *Curriculum Inquiry* 6, no. 2 (1976).

11. W. F. Pinar, "Notes on the Curriculum Field 1978," Educational Researcher 7, no. 8 (September 1978): 5–12.

12. Jackson's essay also appears in H. Giroux, A. Penna, and W. Pinar (eds.), *Curriculum and Instruction* (Berkeley: McCutchan, 1981), 367–381.

13. William Schubert suggested that Tyler's work has been criticized out of historical context, and is thus unfair. This point is an important one and needs to be developed.

14. See, for instance, D. E. Huebner, "Curriculum as a Concern for Man's Temporality, " in *Curriculum Theorizing*, ed. W. F. Pinar (Berkeley: McCutchan, 1975), 237–249.

15. See, for instance, James B. Macdonald, "A Transcendental Development Ideology of Education," in *Heightened Consciousness, Cultural Revolution, and Curriculum Theory*, ed. W. F. Pinar (Berkeley: McCutchan, 1974): 86–116. For a commemoration of Macdonald's contribution to curriculum studies, see *The Journal of Curriculum Theorizing*, 6 no. 3.

16. Klohr invited Huebner and Macdonald to Ohio State for a 1967 Conference, the proceedings are publish in *Theory Into Practice*, 6, no. 4 (October 1967), for which Klohr was the guest editor. The issue entitled "Curriculum Theory Development: Work in Progress" anticipates the reconceptualization of the 1970s, of which Klohr was a major if unacknowledged architect. For instance, Klohr and I together drew up the speakers' list for the 1973 Rochester conference. We were coeditors of *Curriculum Theorizing* (Berkeley: McCutchan, 1975) until the final few months before publication. A study of Klohr's pedagogical and theoretical influence is overdue.

17. See, for instance, her "Curriculum and Consciousness," in *Curriculum Theorizing*, ed. W. F. Pinar (Berkeley: McCutchan, 1975), 299–322.

18. In addition to his widely read and influential work, *The Educational Imagination* (New York: Macmillan, 1985), Eisner collected the papers of the 1969 Cubberly Curriculum Conference (which he chaired), publishing them in *Confronting Curriculum Reform* (Boston: Little, Brown, 1971). This collection contains jams B. Macdonald's "Responsible Curriculum Development, " (pp. 120–133) among other noteworthy essays.

19. W. F. Pinar (ed.), *Heightened Consciousness, Cultural Revolution, And Curriculum Theory: The Proceedings Of The 1973 Rochester Conference* (Berkeley: McCutchan, 1975).

20. JCT is published by the not-for-profit Corporation for Curriculum Research, 53 Falstaff Road, Rochester, New York 14609.

21. Ellis Joseph, Dean of the University of Dayton's College of Education, is the key benefactor. Professor Joseph Watras, Assistant Editor, plays an

important role in both JCT and the annual Bergamo conferences. As of this writing (1987), other institutions supporting JCT include Louisiana State University, St. John's University, University of Wisconsin-Stout, University of Alberta, University of Lethbridge, Bowling Green State University, and the National Technical Institute for the Deaf of the Rochester Institute of Technology.

22. W. F. Pinar (ed.), *Curriculum Theorizing: The Reconceptualists* (Berkeley: McCutchan, 1975).

23. A. Molnar and J. A. Zahorik (eds.), *Curriculum Theory* (Washington D.C.: Association for Supervision and Curriculum Development, 1977).

24. E. W. Eisner, "The Curriculum Field Today: Where We Are, Where We Were, and Where we Are Going," which was not included in Molnar and Zahorik's Curriculum Theory. The essay did not serve as the introductory chapter of Eisner's *The Educational Imagination* (New York: Macmillan, 1985), 1–24. Why the essay did not appear in Molnar/Zahorik volume is uncertain. (personal communications from Eisner, May 11, 1987, and from Molnar, May 1987).

25. The term *Reconceptualists* implied a degree of ideological unity that never existed. The Reconceptualization was a fragile, diverse coalition of individuals, many of whose interests intersected. The sense in which the term was accurate was that it conveyed a shared purpose among ideologically diverse individuals in redoing curriculum studies. After the publication *of Curriculum Theorizing: The Reconceptualists*, I critiqued the subtitle in two essays, W. F. Pinar, "The Reconceptualization of Curriculum Studies," *Journal of Curriculum Studies* 10, no. 3 (1978): 205–214, and "What is the Reconceptualization?" *The Journal of Curriculum Theorizing* 1, no. 1, 93–104, but the term persisted. The issue of the accuracy of the term aside, its currency and resiliency had mixed consequences. Positively, it helped to create a sense of unity and purpose among those who had been isolated in the respective institutions. Negatively, the term allowed the mainstream to marginalize the work of the Reconceptualists, alleging that they were merely a radical group, ungrounded in and uncommitted to curriculum studies. The Tanner's 1979 statement expressed the views of many mainstream curricularists.

26. See S. Selden, "Biological determinism and the Normal School Curriculum: Helen Putnam and the N.E.A. Committee on Racial Well-Being, 1910–1922," *The Journal of Curriculum Theorizing* 1, no. 1, 252–258, reprinted in Part I.

27. Among his many publications are *Ideology and Curriculum* (London: Routledge and Kegan Paul, 1979); and most recently, *Teachers and Texts*

(London: Routledge and Kegan Paul, 1986). See his "The Culture and Commerce of the Textbook," in Part I.

28. See, for instance, L. E. Beyer "Art and Society," *Journal of Curriculum Theorizing*, no. 2 2:72–98, reprinted here in Part VI.

29. N. W. King, "Play in the Workplace," in *Ideology and Practicing Education*, eds., M. W. Apple and L. Weiss (Philadelphia: Temple University Press, 1983), 262–280.

30. J. Taxel, "The American Revolution in Children's Fiction: An Analysis of Literary Content, Form, and Ideology," *Ibid*, 61–88.

31. L. Christian-Smith and L. Roman (eds.), *Becoming Feminine: The Politics of Popular Culture* (London: Flamer Press, forthcoming. 1988).

32. A. Gitlin, "School Structure and Teacher's Work," in *Ideology and Practicing Education*, eds. M. W. Apple and L. Weiss (1983), 193–212.

33. K. Teitelbaum, "Contestation and Curriculum: The Efforts of American Socialists, 1900–1920," in Landon E. Beyer and Michael W. Apple, eds., *The Curriculum: Problems, Politics, and Possibilities* (New York: State University of New York Press, forthcoming); "Outside the Selective Tradition: Socialist Curriculum for Children in the United States, 1900–1920," in Thomas F. Popkewitz, ed., *The Formation of the School Subjects: The Struggle for Creating and American Institution* (Philadelphia: Falmer Press, forthcoming).

34. J. Rosairo, "Harold Rugg and How We Come to Know, " *The Journal of Curriculum Theorizing* 2, no. 1:165–177, reprinted in Part IV.

35. See, for instance, L. Roman and L. Christian-Smith (eds.), *Feminism and the Politics of Popular Culture* (London: Falmer Press, 1987).

36. See, for instance, Cameron McCarthy, "Marxist Theories of Education and the Challenge of Politics of Non-Synchrony" in *Becoming Feminine and the Politics of Popular Culture*, eds., L. Roman and L. Christian-Smith (London: Falmer Press, 1987); Daniel Liston, "On Facts and Values: An Analysis of Radical Curriculum Studies, " *Educational Theory* 36, no. 2 (Spring 1986): 137–152.

37. Among his books are H. A. Giroux, A. N. Penna, and W. F. Pinar (eds.) *Curriculum and Instruction* (Berkeley: McCutchan, 1981); and most recently, *Schooling for Democracy: Critical Pedagogy in the Public Sphere* (Minneapolis: University of Minnesota, 1988).

38. See S. Aronowitz and H. A. Giroux, "Ideologies about Schooling: Rethinking the Nature of Educational Reform," *Journal of Curriculum Theorizing* 7, no. 1: 7–38.

39. See also J. Anyon, "Schools as Agencies of Social Legitimation, " *The Journal of Curriculum Theorizing* 3, no. 2: 86–103, reprinted in Part III of this volume.

40. See, for instance, P. Wexler, "Body and Soul," *The Journal of Curriculum Theorizing* 4, no. 2: 166–180, reprinted in Part III of this volume.

41. See, for instance, J. A. Whitson, "The Politics of the Non-political Curriculum, " printed in Part III of this volume.

42. See M. R. Grumet and W. F. Pinar, "Socratic Caesura and the Theory-Practice Relationship," in Part II; M. R. Grumet, "Bodyreading," part V; and M. R. Grumet, "Women and Teaching, "Part VI.

43. See, for instance, J. L. Miller, "The Resistance of Woman Academics: An Autobiographical Account, "Part VI.

44. See J. A. Pagano, "The Claim of Philia," in Part VI.

45. P. Lather, "The Invisible Presence: The Absence in Gender Analysis in Research on Teaching," paper presented at the Bergamo Conference on Curriculum Theory and Classroom Practice, October 17, 1985.

46. F. R. Krall, "Behind the Chairperson's Door: Reconceptualizing Women's Work," *The Journal of Curriculum Theorizing* 5, no. 4: 68–91, reprinted in Part VI of this volume.

47. See, for instance, T. Aoki, "Towards a Dialectic Between the Conceptual World and the Lived World: Transcending Instrumentalism in Curricular Orientation," *The Journal of Curriculum Theorizing* 5, no 3: 4–21, reprinted in Part V. Also see his "Interests, Knowledge, and Evaluation: Alternative Approaches to Curriculum Evaluation, "*The Journal of Curriculum Theorizing* 6, no. 4: 27–44, and his "Toward Understanding Computer Applications," *Journal of Curriculum Theorizing* 7, no. 61–71.

48. See, for instance, M. van Manen, "The Relation Between Research and Pedagogy," reprinted in Part V. Van Manen is editor of the journal *Phenomenology + Pedagogy*, published at the University of Alberta, and the editor of University of Alberta publications entitled *Texts of Childhood, Texts of teaching, Texts of the Body*, and *Texts of Human Relations*. For more information, write to Professor Max van Manen, Department of Secondary Education, Faculty of Education, University of Alberta, Edmonton, Alberta, Canada T6G 2G5. For a related and significant effort in the area of Mathematics Education, see Linda Brandau, "On Disturbing Persistence of

Estrangement From Mathematics and How It Can Be Disturbed," in *Journal of Educational Thought*.

49. [1]D. G. Smith, "Experimental Eidetics as A Way on Entering Curriculum Language from the Ground Up," *The Journal of Curriculum Theorizing* 5, no. 3: 74–95, reprinted in Part V.

50. See, for instance, M. Hunsberger, "The Experience of Re-reading," in *Texts and Teaching*, ed. M. van Manen (Edmonton: University of Alberta, n.d.)

51. See, for instance, W. E. Doll, Jr., "Curriculum Beyond Stability," in Part II.

52. See, for instance, W. F. Pinar (ed.), *Heightened Consciousness, Cultural Revolution, and Curriculum Theory: The Proceedings of the Rochester Conference* (Berkeley: McCutchan, 1974); W. F. Pinar (ed.), *Curriculum Theorizing: The Reconceptualists* (Berkeley: McCutchan, 1981); and the present volume.

53. See, for instance, R. Butt and D. Raymond, "Arguments for Using Qualitative Approaches in Understanding Teacher Thinking: The Case for Biography," *The Journal of Curriculum Theorizing* 7, no. 1: 62–93.

54. J. Albertini and B. Lang, "Analysis of Student/Teacher Exchanges in Dialogue Journal Writing," The Journal of Curriculum Theorizing 7, no. 1: 153–201.

55. D. J. Clandinin, *Classroom Practice* (London: Flamer, 1986).

56. See, for instance, E. C. Short, "Knowledge Production and Utilization in Curriculum," *Review of Educational Research* 43, no. 3 (Summer 1973); R. E. Richard and E. C. Short, "Curriculum Inquiry from a Religious Perspective: Two Views," *Journal of Curriculum Theorizing* 3, no. 2: 209–222; W. H. Schubert, G. H. Willis, and E. C. Short, "Curriculum Theorizing," *Curriculum Perspectives* 4 (May 1984): 69–74.

57. H. M. Kliebard, *The Struggle for the American Curriculum 1893–1958* (London and Boston: Routledge and Kegan Paul, 1986).

58. B. M. Franklin, *Building the American Community* (London: Falmer, 1986); see also his "Self-Control and the Psychology of School Discipline," *The Journal of Curriculum Theorizing* 1, no. 2: 238–254, and his "Whatever Happened to Social Control: The Muting of Coercive Authority in Curriculum Discourse," *The Journal of Curriculum Theorizing* 3, no. 1: 252–258. Both are reprinted here in Part I.

59. S. Selden, "Biological Determinism and the Normal School Curriculum," reprinted here in Part I.

60. See C. Kridel, "Castiglione and Elyot: Early Curriculum Theorists," *Journal of Curriculum Theorizing* 1, no. 2: 89–99.

61. Davis has collected a series of recorded interviews with curriculum scholars. For information, write him at the University of Texas, Austin, TX 78112.

62. W. M. Reynolds, "Freedom From Control," *Journal of Curriculum Theorizing*, forthcoming.

63. See James T. Sears, "Peering into the Well of Loneliness: The Responsibility of Educators to Gay and Lesbian Youth," in *Social Issues and Education*, ed. A. Molnar (Alexandria, VA: ASCD, 1987), 79–100. See also J. T. Sears, "Rethinking Teacher Education: dare Teach Educators Work Toward a New Social Order?" *Journal of Curriculum Theorizing* 6 (Fall 1985): 24–79.

64. See J. Daignault and C. Gauthier, "The Indecent Curriculum Machine,: Who is Afraid of Sisyphus?" *Journal of Curriculum Theorizing* 4, no. 1, 177–196.

65. Padgham's work has moved from the aesthetic (see his essay in Part IV) to the mythic, much of the latter under the influence of Jean Houston. See his "Education on the Edges Creating New Myths for Education," paper presented at the Bergamo Conference, October 18, 1985.

66. See, for instance, N. Haggerson, "Reconceptualizing Professional Literature: An Aesthetic Self-Study," *The Journal of Curriculum Theorizing* 6, no. 4: 56–73

67. See N. Garman, "Reflection, The Heart of Supervision," *Journal of Curriculum and Supervision* 2, no. 1 (Fall 1986): 1–24.

68. W. Schubert, *Curriculum: Perspective, Paradigm, Possibility* (New York: Macmillan, 1986). For a somewhat negative review of the book, see B. M. Franklin in *Educational Studies* 18, no. 1 (Spring 1987): 119–124.

69. W. H. Schubert and G. J. Posner, "Origins of the Curriculum Field Based on a Study of Mentor Student Relationships," *Journal of Curriculum Theorizing* 2, no. 2: 37–67. See also G. J. Posner and A. N. Rudnitsky, *Course Design* (New York: Longman, 1986).

70. J. B. Macdonald and E. Zaret (eds.), *Schools in Search of Meaning* (Washington D. C.: ASCD, 1975), and most recently, A. Molnar (ed.), *Social Issue and Education* (Alexandria, VA: ASCD, 1987).

71. While the academic field of curriculum studies has been reconceived, the major ideas that constitute the contemporary field of study have yet to make their way to colleagues in elementary and secondary schools. If there is a "second wave," such schools will be its site.

I I

Curriculum Reconceptualized:
A Personal and Partial History

Janet L. Miller
1998

I have my own version of a history of the U.S. curriculum theory movement, known as the reconceptualization, and of JCT: *Journal of Curriculum Theorizing* and the annual conference it sponsors. It's a history that emerges through my work as managing editor of JCT from its inception in 1978 through 1998. And it's a history saturated with my memories of particular individuals, places, and ideas as well as with my own interpretations of their intersections. For this version, I embellish my earlier chroniclings (1978; 1996) of the reconceptualization through a focus on the primary manifestations of the movement—the journal and its conferences.

Of course, as I construct this version, I also must acknowledge that in all remembering, there is forgetting. Thus, this is a very partial history, partial in terms of preference and commitments as well as gaps and silences.

To write about 25 years of what still is termed by many as "reconceptualist" work also compels me to acknowledge that there are those in the curriculum field, writ large, who have little or no knowledge of this curriculum movement. There are those who do not know about or who ignore or marginalize work that JCT publishes and supports through its annual conference, colloquially known and referred to here as "Bergamo."[1] There are those who are unaware of extensive documentation and analysis of the reconceptualization in master's theses, doctoral dissertations, journal articles, books, and synoptic curriculum texts.[2]

On the other hand, many in graduate and undergraduate curriculum programs have studied the reconceptualization, even as Bill Pinar has explained that there was no methodologically or ideologically unified "Reconceptualist" point of view or even points of view. Still the term persists, even as "the reconceptualization" of the curriculum field has been accomplished in terms of incorporating theory, history, and research orientations into what heretofore had been an exclusively practice-oriented endeavor (Pinar, 1988).

Whether acknowledged in broad curriculum circles or not, many associated with the reconceptualizing of the curriculum field have worked, for more than 20 years, to move the field away from its long-standing managerial, technocratic, and positivist orientation, and toward multivocal, multiperspectival theorizings of curriculum. Contemporary curriculum theorists have moved from either neo-Marxist or phenomenological orientations that characterized early reconceptualist inquiry into a riotous array of theoretical perspectives that point to expansive and complex conceptions of curriculum reconceptualized. Yet, at the same time, I believe that this work still is loosely united by a commitment to examine what Patricia Williams, among others, asserts: "That life is complicated is a fact of great analytic importance" (1991, p. 10).

PRECURSORS OF THE RECONCEPTUALIZATION

From my perspective, a history of the reconceptualization, of *JCT*, and of Bergamo begins in the 1960s. Paul Klohr, in 1967, helped to organize a conference entitled "Curriculum Theory Frontiers" at Ohio State University. Presenters included Elsie Alberty, Kelly Duncan, Alexander Frazier, Jack Frymier, Charles Galloway, Dwayne Huebner, Paul Klohr, and Jim Macdonald. This 1967 conference marked a gathering of individuals who were honoring the 20-year anniversary of the first U. S. curriculum theory conference. That 1947 conference, held at University of Chicago, was entitled "Toward Improved Curriculum Theory," and participants included Hollis Caswell, Virgil Herrick, B. Othanel Smith, and Ralph Tyler.

The 1967 conference not only marked a break from the dominant technocratic emphases on curriculum design and development that had characterized the field. It also foreshadowed Jim Macdonald's article, "Curriculum Theory" (1971). In that important article, Macdonald noted disagreement among "theorizers" about the purpose of curriculum theorizing. He identified three major camps: (1) those who see theory as a guiding framework for applied curriculum development and a tool for its evaluation; (2) those who are committed to a conventional concept of scientific theory and who see the purpose of theory as primarily conceptual in nature; and (3) those who see theory as a creative intellectual task that should be used neither as a basis for prescription nor as an empirically testable set of principles and relationships.

Soon after the 1967 conference, in the late 1960s, Bill Pinar began his doctoral studies in earnest at Ohio State, with Paul Klohr and Donald Bateman serving as his mentors. (During the time that he taught high school English on Long Island, Bill also had studied with Dwayne Huebner at Teachers College, Columbia University). As Bill studied curriculum theory with Paul, their discussions necessarily included analyses of the 1947 and 1967 curriculum theory conferences, Macdonald's 1971 article, and their subsequent influences on the field.

I N I T I A L   A S P E C T S   O F   T H E
R E C O N C E P T U A L I Z A T I O N

The 1967 conference, Macdonald's delineation of varied perspectives on the purpose of curriculum theorizing, and Paul Klohr's encouragement and visions for the field—all provided incentives for Bill to organize a curriculum theory conference in 1973 at the University of Rochester. That conference was entitled "Heightened Consciousness, Cultural Revolution, and Curriculum Theory" and its proceedings were published the following year (Pinar, 1974).

Macdonald's 1971 article also provided an initial framework that Bill elaborated and extended in his organizational structure for the collection entitled *Curriculum Theorizing: The Reconceptualists* (Pinar, 1975). Drawing from Macdonald's "three major camps," Bill distinguished among traditionalists, conceptual-empiricists, and reconceptualists. And among the "reconceptualists," who attempt to understand the nature of educational experience, Bill posited the work of those whom he termed "postcritical" as shifting from criticism of the old to creation of the new. Existentialism and phenomenology provided conceptual tools by which to "create the new." Modes of inquiry were literary, historical, and philosophical, and Bill's work, especially, demonstrated the strong influence of psychoanalytic theory.

But some, after the publication of the 1975 reconceptualist text, took issue with Bill's definition of "postcritical" as separate from and apparently, from the arrangement of the book, of greater importance than reconceptual political and methodological criticism of "the old," e.g., the traditionalists and the conceptual-empiricists. Pinar's critics claimed that a concern with transcendence and consciousness, and a moving away from the criticism of the old into a creation of the new, obscured and minimized the importance and necessity for political criticism and action. Reliance upon existential-phenomenological methodology, they asserted, mystified the issues and could only lead to yet another version of a moribund curriculum field. Bill's reply at that time was that all acts must begin with self, and that recognition of self and of one's place in the world could become ultimately political, for one is free to act once one has understanding; one's experience may then be placed within its political, social, and psycho-social dimensions.

These initial conflicts between what I will reductionistically call "the political" and "the personal" characterized the early years of the reconceptualization and its journal and conference. In retrospect, these conflicts, situated in binary and oppositional terms, only begin to suggest the tensions (as well as the intersections) among a multitude of perspectives, and theoretical orientations and discourses, including historical, poststructural, hermeneutic, constructivist, neo-Marxist, feminist, psychoanalytic, cultural, queer, and phenomenological, from which contemporary curriculum theorists work. At the same time, those initial orientations hinted at what now has become the necessarily interdisciplinary and intertextual bases for curriculum theorizing.

A PERSONAL HISTORY OF JCT
AND ITS CONFERENCES

There is a reason, of course, that I identified the beginnings of curriculum reconceptual history with a conference organized by Paul Klohr at Ohio State University. I learned about the 1967 conference because of Paul's presence at the 1973 conference at the University of Rochester, where Madeleine Grumet and I were master's students studying with Bill.

I had just begun my graduate degree in English education a few months before the 1973 conference and I didn't yet know much about curriculum theory. But in the one day that I attended the conference, I heard Jim Macdonald, Dwayne Huebner, Don Bateman, Paul Klohr, and Maxine Greene, all major figures in the field and all, as it would turn out, major influences in my life and work.

By 1974, I was a doctoral student at Ohio State, studying with Paul Klohr in curriculum theory and Don Bateman in English education. Following the 1973 conference, Bill had encouraged others to sponsor a curriculum theory conference. So in my first year as a doctoral student, I traveled, as did fellow doctoral students Bob Bullough, Craig Kridel, Leigh Chiarelott, and Paul Shaker, to Xavier University in Cincinnati, Ohio, for the 1974 conference. At that conference, Paul Klohr presented a paper in which he presented guidelines for viewing the work of the reconceptualists within the third category of Macdonald's 1971 analysis: those who are engaging in fresh modes of inquiry in order to create the new. According to Klohr, conflicting ideas concerning ways and means of such creation were inherent within initial stages of the reconceptualization, and yet some common elements already could be traced among this emerging work. These included the individual as culture creator as well as culture bearer, and the celebration of diversity and pluralism in both social ends and the proposals projected to move toward those ends (Klohr, 1974).

Other conferences, organized by individuals associated with the reconceptualization, followed the one at Xavier University: 1975 at the University of Virginia, 1976 at University of Wisconsin-Milwaukee, 1977 at Kent State, and 1978 at both Georgia State University and Rochester Institute of Technology. I attended all of these.

In 1974, I was introduced to Maxine Greene at the Xavier University conference in Cincinnati, sat with her and a few others at breakfast one morning, and listened in amazement. Maxine talked about the latest novels and essays that she had read, the latest plays as well as musical and dance performances that she had seen, the art that she had viewed, and what all of these had to do with curriculum. In particular, she talked of her increasing interest in the work of women in education and of challenging gender-biased conceptions of curriculum and research. In that one breakfast conversation, Maxine touched on a number of my own developing academic interests. And she did so in ways that resounded with my English major and teacher background and experiences.

Given that I was quite interested in ways that I might study the influences on, and manifestations of, the gendered aspects of myself as teacher, I was determined to hear more, to hear Maxine in her gravelly Brooklyn voice talk about Sartre, literature, the arts, imagination, women, education, and praxis. Those determinations, sparked at both the 1973 and 1974 conferences, led to my dissertation work at Ohio State on Maxine's curriculum theorizing, even as she rejected any designation of reconceptualist in her own work.

THE JOURNAL

Throughout Bill's and then my doctoral studies at Ohio State, Paul Klohr had been encouraging the establishment of a journal devoted to what Paul called "fresh" approaches to the conceptualization of curriculum studies and work. And what had become clear to many of us involved in the curriculum theory conferences from 1973 through 1978 was that there were few journals and fewer spots on AERA's program, in the mid and late 1970s, that were open to work that incorporated political, and phenomenological and/or autobiographical theorizing. Thus, in 1978, Bill Pinar, with the royalties from his 1975 book, established *The Journal of Curriculum Theorizing*, now known to most as *JCT*. He invited me to serve as managing editor, a position I held through 1998.

During that first journal organizing year of 1978, on an old manual typewriter, I haltingly composed letters to Maxine Greene, Dwayne Huebner, Paul Klohr, and Jim Macdonald, among others, asking for their support in terms of serving on our editorial board or presenting at the conferences that the journal officially started to sponsor in 1979. Although Greene and Huebner declined board of editors membership, our original board of editors included distinguished established scholars as well as newer scholars in the field. This mix has continued to characterize the *JCT* Board of Editors even as its membership, of course, has rotated and changed through the years under the editorship first of Bill Pinar, then Bill Reynolds, Jo Anne Pagano, and Co-Editors Brent Davis and Dennis Sumara.

Our first journal issues were compiled on electric typewriters—in fact, our whole effort to establish the journal had a grassroots feel to it. For example, we initially rejected, and have continued to reject, possibilities of journal publication under the aegis of a large publishing house so that we might retain our commitment to the publishing of avant-garde work. And for the first decade of the journal's existence, we were attempting to publish a journal with international circulation without the benefits of desktop computer production.

The journal purchased a "composer," a typewriter-styled machine that could produce typeset copy. First Bill, then Margaret Zaccone (whose organizational and managerial leadership continues to support *JCT* and the Corporation for Curriculum Research in substantial and amazing ways), and then Eileen Duffy, my secretary at St. John's University, typed issues of the journal on the "composer." Not until the end of the 1980s were we finally able to enjoy the advantages of desktop publishing.

The first issues of *JCT* were eight and a half by eleven sized, with plain white covers and black binding. But the simplicity of our journal design and production belied the excitement that Bill and I and the board of editors felt as we forged a new space in the curriculum field for what many still call "alternative" voices, discourses, and perspectives.

As the journal moved into libraries and into graduate curriculum studies classrooms, we began to receive a substantial number of manuscripts submitted for publication consideration. Fully aware of the risks of establishing a new journal, I was elated by these submissions, for they indicated that curriculum scholars were viewing the journal as a viable publication arena as well as a welcoming venue for avant-garde work. Paul Klohr's push for, and Bill Pinar's commitments to, establishing a journal that would welcome "fresh" perspectives and forms of inquiries in the curriculum field were indeed visionary.

THE CONFERENCES

The *JCT*-sponsored curriculum theory conferences began in 1979. Still a relatively small group, we met at the Airlie Conference Center, outside Washington, D.C. from 1979 through 1982. I have vivid early Airlie memories: Bill and I assembled the first program into what we hoped were viable session combinations from proposals strewn about on my living room floor. Jim Macdonald helped us distribute name tags to participants at the makeshift registration table. Bill and I waited on Airlie's green manicured front lawn to greet all the conference participants arriving on the two buses that I had scheduled from Dulles Airport. I stood at the podium in Airlie's main meeting room and announced, just before each set of concurrent sessions, the room assignment for each participant. And I cannot forget a masked Gail McCutcheon delivering her paper on Halloween night. Madeleine Grumet presented the first version of her "Conception, Contradiction, and Curriculum" paper, Bill Pinar elaborated his psychoanalytic and autobiographical inquiries, and Jacques Daignault and Clermont Gauthier introduced poststructuralism into our conference as well as curriculum theory discourses—all at Airlie.

As the JCT conference grew both in number and reputation, we moved to the larger Bergamo Center, associated with the University of Dayton in Ohio. We made this move in order to avoid ideological conflicts not only over the plantation-with-slave quarters origins of Airlie House but also with various groups that met simultaneously with us at Airlie, not the least of which was the CIA.

During the Bergamo-site years (1983-1993), the JCT conference became known outside curriculum theory circles, and grew to include participants from a variety of fields in education. Presentation modes grew more diverse as participants began to include performance, exhibition, and media representations. And there was always drama, no matter what the topic.

A profound moment at Bergamo was when many gathered to mourn the death of James B. Macdonald and, at the same time, to celebrate and commemorate his vastly influential curriculum theorizing. One vivid image among many—Dwayne Huebner's hands grasping both sides of the podium as he struggled to complete his tribute to Jim.

I always will recall Bergamo as a dramatic as well as dizzying confluence of people and ideas: the emergence of feminist theorizing; debates about difference and its representations; poetry and ecology, peace, and aesthetic education mixed together with Ron Padgham and a giant bubble-maker; Tom Kelly and his "best titles of Bergamo" contest; the annual Saturday night formal entertainment in the chapel, culminating in the presentations of the Macdonald Prize and the Aoki Award (I distinctly remember squeals of excitement from the audience as Bill and I announced Sue Stinson, University of North Carolina-Greensboro, as the recipient of JCT's first annual Macdonald Prize); and the informal entertainment in the lounge area every night of the conference.

After many years of meeting at Bergamo, a reduction in that site's accommodations motivated the move for the 1995 and 1996 conference to the DuBose Center in Monteagle, Tennessee. The 1997 and 1998 conference locale was Four-Winds Conference Center, just outside Bloomington, Indiana. We plan to return to Bergamo in 1999, if lodging arrangements can accommodate all conference participants. The conference center in Banff had provided a spectacular setting for the 1994 conference, and serves as the conference site in the year 2000.

CONTINUING HISTORIES

In recalling the establishment and development of both the journal and its conferences, then, I have returned in my rememberings to those exciting first years of JCT's existence. And I returned to the conceptual and methodological perspectives that undergirded our attempts to establish the journal and its annual conference as viable spaces in which to pursue work that, at the time, was considered outside the curriculum mainstream. Given that some of this work still is regarded by many as fringe, and given that technocratic and linear constructions of curriculum still dominate, especially in elementary and secondary schools, the commitments and goals described in the very first announcement of JCT's existence seem pertinent still. That announcement claimed that the work of the reconceptualization was, in one essential sense, "the work of developing alternatives. It is more ambitious however; we aspire to a fundamental reconceiving of current ideas of curriculum.... The journal will not be afraid to publish work of writers who are not well known, including work by graduate students. We are especially interested in work that is intellectually experimental. We are willing to take risks, publishing material more conservative journals would reject. Some of these articles will be controversial—at least we hope so."

We intend to print pieces that speak to school teachers and administrators, to interested laymen, as well as to our colleagues in colleges and universities. On occasion, we will print articles written with the often powerful simplicity of the autobiographical voice. At the same time, we remain conscious that the journal is responsible to the field as presently constituted. Our primary commitment is to assisting the field to take its "next step," but we recognize that such a step can only finally be taken by us all, by traditionalists, and conceptual-empiricists as well as by reconceptualists. We want to minimize the rigidifying effect ("here I stand, there you stand") such categories often have. We want exchange, including criticism (1979).

I think that it is important to historically situate the original intentions of JCT and its conferences in order to contextualize how and why initial reconceptualizing work erupted within a field that had been called moribund just a few years earlier. To historically situate these beginnings is to necessarily call attention to particular aspects of the field during the 1960s and 1970s as well as to their historical antecedents. It is to call attention to particular theoretical orientations that emerged in response to technocratic and controlling conceptions of curriculum. It is to note that curriculum as only predetermined "content and facts" to be "covered and memorized" seemed, in light of the Viet Nam war especially, to be devoid of human relevance, to use the word of the times.

At the same time, I urge ongoing contextualization of current work represented in the journal and its conferences; such contextualization can illuminate the continuing need to challenge managerial approaches to, and technocratic, apolitical, and ahistorical constructions of, curriculum.

Thus, to continue to historically situate JCT and Bergamo is also to call attention to the ways in which conceptions of curriculum as only predetermined "content and facts"—conceptions that spawned the journal and its conferences and underlined the urgency of that "reconceptual" work—still often attend in our classrooms, in our work with students, teachers, principals, and superintendents, parents and community members. Therefore, those of us who still are concerned about mechanistic and behaviorally oriented manifestations of curriculum work in schools must continue to interrogate curriculum constructions that deny any and all aspects of the reconceptualization. Our work to theorize, to question, to constantly rewrite ourselves with, and in, curriculum "reconceptualized" is not finished.

I agree, then, that what identifies 25 years of curriculum theorizing is not the term reconceptualist, per se, but rather collective although diverse approaches to resisting technologies of education that try to separate content, pedagogy, and learning into discrete, measurable, and observable units of behavior and product. One ongoing characteristic of JCT and its conferences is a commitment among its participants to reveal and to challenge traditional conceptions that insist on a static definition of curriculum as a predetermined, linear, depersonalized, apolitical, and discrete body of knowledge. Such a definition completely misses the analytic importance of those complications of life that cannot be predicted or controlled.

Many of us enact this commitment with, through, and in the multiple discourses, experiences, concerns, and interpretations of students, teachers, parents, and school administrators. We can be heard now not just at Bergamo but also at AERA conference presentations, in the pages of diverse education journals, and in the classrooms of those with and for whom we work. Those of us who have participated and continue to participate in the work that has become known as reconceptualist in nature are necessarily grounding that work in our own daily educational practices while, at the same time, always questioning and always theorizing what it means "to educate, what it means to be educated" (Pinar, Reynolds, Slattery, & Taubman, 1995, p. 8).

So—my rememberings as well as my obvious commitments to the journal and its conferences of course reflect my investments in the work and theorizing of all those associated with JCT and the reconceptualization. My memories here attempt to honor the connectedness that informs and impels my own work as well as the work of others long involved in this project called the reconceptualization. At the same time, a curriculum field reconceptualized in fact requires this final acknowledgment: the brief history I've reviewed here speaks of, as well as constantly questions, my partiality in terms of remembering, interpretation, and attachment.

N O T E S

1. The journal's original title was *The Journal of Curriculum Theorizing*. During
    Jo Anne Pagano's term as editor, the Board of Advising Editors voted to
    change the title to *JCT: An Interdisciplinary Journal of Curriculum Studies* to
    recognize the acceptance of *JCT* as an identifying acronym as well as the
    expanded dimensions of work appearing in the journal. During Brent Davis
    and Dennis Sumara's co-editorship, the title was changed once again to
    JCT: Journal of Curriculum Theorizing to acknowledge the journal's historical
    roots.

    Throughout this article, I will refer to *JCT's* collective conferences as
    "Bergamo." Here, I follow Craig Kridel's (1996) lead.

    > After considerable discussion on the matter of an appropriate
    > "working title" for the *JCT* Conference on Curriculum Theory and
    > Classroom Practice, I have decided to use the term "Bergamo" to
    > represent all avant-garde curriculum theory conferences that have
    > been held in the autumn since 1974. The term offers as much (and as
    > little) clarity as such titles as "Baroque" and "Renaissance" offer their
    > respective eras, and using a common term is easier than trying to
    > distinguish Airlie, Bergamo, DuBose, [Four-Winds] or Banff
    > Conferences (p. 41).

2. Space does not permit me to document the proliferation of references that
    address the reconceptualization. See Pinar, Reynolds, Slattery, and
    Taubman's 1995 text, *Understanding Curriculum*, for full documentation of
    these writings.

R E F E R E N C E S

"Announcing." (1979) *The Journal of Curriculum Theorizing*, 1:1.

Klohr, P. R. (1974). Curriculum theory: The state of the field. Paper presented
    at the Curriculum Theory Conference, Xavier University, Cincinnati, OH,
    October.

Kridel, C. (1996). Hermeneutic portraits: Section editor's notes. *JCT: Journal of
    Curriculum Theorizing*, 12:4, 41.

Macdonald, J. B. (1971). Curriculum theory. *Journal of Educational Research*,
    64:5, 196-200.

Miller, J. L. (1978). Curriculum theory: The recent history. *The Journal of Curriculum Theorizing*, 1:1, 28-43.

Miller, J. L. (1996). Curriculum and the reconceptualization: Another brief history. *JCT: Journal of Curriculum Theorizing*, 12:1, 6-8.

Pinar, W. F. (Ed.). (1974). *Heightened consciousness, cultural revolution, and curriculum theory*. Berkeley: McCutchan.

Pinar, W. F. (Ed.). (1975). *Curriculum theorizing: The reconceptualists*. Berkeley: McCutchan.

Pinar, W. F. (Ed.). (1988). *Contemporary curriculum discourses*. Scottsdale, AZ: Gorsuch Scarisbrick.

Pinar, W. F., Reynolds, W. M., Slattery, P., & Taubman, P. M. (1995). *Understanding curriculum*. New York: Peter Lang.

Williams, P. J. (1991). *The alchemy of race and rights: Diary of a law professor*. Cambridge: Harvard University Press.

The Bergamo Conferences, 1973-1997:

Reconceptualization and the Curriculum Theory Conferences

Craig Kridel
1998

The Reconceptualist conferences and subsequent curriculum theory meetings will always prove difficult to discuss even though many participants could provide hour-upon-hour of interviews. Such information is welcomed by oral historians; however, one will be hard-pressed to ascertain the membership and impact of what became a loosely conceived group. As William Pinar stated in his essay, "There is no 'Reconceptualist' point of view, or even points of view" (1988, p. 7). Moreover, the "act of reconceptualization"—now transformed to "understanding curriculum"—is equally difficult to determine and made somewhat more troublesome since the term "Reconceptualist" was rarely a self-proclaimed moniker and more often used by critics: "the term allowed the mainstream to marginalize the work of reconceptualists, alleging that they were merely a radical group, ungrounded in and uncommitted to curriculum studies" (Pinar, 1988, p. 11). Yet, avant-garde curriculum theorists met then and continue to meet to this day—for what can be traced as an unbroken period of 25 years. Their presence is as furtive and illusive as those "education movements" from the late nineteenth and early twentieth century; however, their impact upon the field of education is evident and calls for further examination.

While other essays in this section discuss the history of the reconceptualists and the formation of *The Journal of Curriculum Theorizing*, I wish to explore the work of individuals who have met annually since 1973; once called reconceptualists, presently they work in the area of curriculum and cultural studies, broadly conceived. My analysis, however, is quite specific since I do not address publications per se but, instead, examine presentations that occurred during this 25-year-period at a series of curriculum theory conferences. These meetings were held at 12 different locations and include 1915 titled presentations. While certain conferences may have maintained a unique identity, distinct from the preceding and subsequent meetings, the array of conference discourse throughout this period clearly displays connection and focus among the gatherings and among the participants. I refer to the meetings collectively as "Bergamo Conferences" and, while they portray a somewhat idiosyncratic approach to curriculum studies, the presentations and presenters most certainly display a far-reaching and not-fully-recognized impact upon the field of education.

What becomes quite evident, however, is that the gatherings of the reconceptualists and subsequent curriculum theory conferences are oddly portrayed in the professional literature. I do not allude to the critiques of "reconceptualism" that occurred through the 1970s and early 1980s (Tanner & Tanner, 1979, 1980; Pinar, 1979; Finkelstein, 1979; Greene, 1979; Jackson, 1980). Instead, I refer to the Reconceptualist Movement as it has been presented in the synoptic curriculum textbooks of the 1970s through 1990s. By examining conference programs and assorted conference themes and by placing this information in juxtaposition with synoptic textbook descriptions, many interesting and somewhat unacknowledged dimensions emerge.

Listed below are the individual citations for each conference, identified by year, conference title, place, program organizer, number of presentations, and the number of presenters.[1]

1973   Heightened Consciousness, Cultural Revolution, and Curriculum Theory; The Rochester Conference; William Pinar; 14 presentations; 14 presenters

1974   Reconceptualizing Curriculum Theory; The Xavier Conference; Timothy M. Riordan; 11 presentations; 11 presenters

1975   Reconceptualizing Curriculum Theory; The Charlottesville Conference; Charles Beegle; 19 presentations; 26 presenters

1976   The Milwaukee Curriculum Theory Conference; University of Wisconsin, Milwaukee ; Alex Molnar and John Zahorik ; 38 presentations; 61 presenters

1977   Kent Curriculum Theory Conference; Kent State University; Richard Hawthorne; 31 presentations; 46 presenters

1978a   The R.I.T. Curriculum Theory Conference; Rochester Institute of Technology; Ronald E. Padgham; 27 presentations; 27 presenters

1978b   The Curriculum Theory Conference; George State University; Wayne Urban and Dorothy Huenecke; 19 presentations; 33 presenters

1979   A Curriculum Theory Conference; Airlie House, VA; JCT; 27 presentations; 38 presenters

1980   A Curriculum Theory Conference; Airlie House, VA; JCT; 54 presentations; 65 presenters

1981   A Curriculum Theory Conference; Airlie House, VA; JCT; 50 presentations; 61 presenters

1982   A Curriculum Theory Conference; Airlie House, VA; JCT; 59 presentations; 68 presenters

1983   Curriculum Theory and Classroom Practice; The Bergamo Conference, Dayton, OH; JCT; 136 presentations; 160 presenters

1984   Curriculum Theory and Classroom Practice; The Bergamo Conference, Dayton, OH; JCT; 100 presentations; 124 presenters

1985   Curriculum Theory and Classroom Practice; The Bergamo Conference, Dayton, OH; JCT; 139 presentations; 189 presenters

1986   Curriculum Theory and Classroom Practice; The Bergamo Conference, Dayton, OH; JCT; 166 presentations; 222 presenters

1987   Curriculum Theory and Classroom Practice; The Bergamo Conference, Dayton, OH; JCT; 113 presentations; 172 presenters

1988   Curriculum Theory and Classroom Practice; The Bergamo Conference, Dayton, OH; JCT; 126 presentations; 175 presenters

1989   Curriculum Theory and Classroom Practice; The Bergamo Conference, Dayton, OH; JCT; 179 presentations; 328 presenters

1990   Curriculum Theory and Classroom Practice; The Bergamo Conference, Dayton, OH; JCT; 235 presentations; 365 presenters

1991   Curriculum Theory and Classroom Practice; The Bergamo Conference, Dayton, OH; JCT; 208 presentations; 404 presenters

1992   Curriculum Theory and Classroom Practice; The Bergamo Conference, Dayton, OH; JCT; 188 presentations; 421 presenters

1993   Curriculum Theory and Classroom Practice; The Bergamo Conference, Dayton, OH; JCT; 207 presentations; 431 presenters

1994   Curriculum Theory and Classroom Practice; Banff; JCT; 219 presentations; 358 presenters

1995   Curriculum Theory and Classroom Practice; Monteagle, TN; JCT; 223 presentations; 399 presenters

1996   Curriculum Theory and Classroom Practice; Monteagle, TN; JCT; 136 presentations; 265 presenters

1997   Curriculum Theory and Classroom Practice; Bloomington; JCT; 191 presentations; 388 presenters

THE RECONCEPTUALISTS AND PRE-AIRLIE/AIRLIE
HOUSE CONFERENCES, 1973-1982, 349
PRESENTATIONS; 450 PRESENTERS

The beginnings of the reconceptualists have been described by William Pinar in this appendix (the Introduction to *Curriculum Discourses*, 1988, see this volume, appendix) as well as in *Understanding Curriculum* (Pinar, et al., 1995). Comments need not be summarized or repeated here; one point, however, needs to be underscored—namely, much reconceptualist work took place before the first "reconceptualist" conference. I mention this as a way to underscore the importance of the conferences for academics to come together and explore the reconceptualization of curriculum. The gatherings proved a significant factor in determining a distinct group identity—one stronger than if community was established merely through publications.

Pinar readily acknowledges that many individuals in the late 1960s and early 1970s were re-examining the field and the role of the curriculum theorist prior to the 1973 Rochester Conference. For example, the 1967 Ohio State University Conference focused presentations around this very theme—"the curriculum theorist at work," and James Macdonald's often cited essay, "Curriculum Theory," was published in January 1971. Macdonald refers to "a third group of individuals (who) look upon the task of theorizing as a creative intellectual task." This unnamed group appeared in various conventional forums. ASCD sponsored a radical caucus in the late 1960s and 1970s. While the most tangible work of this group was published as the 1975 ASCD yearbook, *Schools in Search of Meaning* (Macdonald, et al., 1975), individuals also appeared regularly on ASCD programs in the early 1970s. AERA, not viewed as an organization of radical and normative thought in the early 1970s, similarly programmed sessions by this "third group." The 1972 AERA conference included "Oppression and School" with the participants Michael Apple, Richard Kunkle, Steven Mann, and William Pilder (James Macdonald served as Vice-President of Division B). And perhaps the distinguishing publication, the 1975 reconceptualist compendium, *Curriculum Theorizing: the Reconceptualists*, consisted mostly of items published primarily between the years 1967-1972.

My point is only to underscore that much substantive work was published prior to 1973, the first conference. Yet, the reconceptualists emerged not necessarily from publications; the coalescence of a group occurred, as one would assume, at the conferences. Many publications were being released, yet the conference setting—with its occasions for community and controversy, for praise and ad hominem attacks— afforded the time and opportunity to forge a place, a venue, for theoretical exploration and discourse. This must not be taken-for-granted in any treatment of the history of these curriculum theory conferences. The term reconceptualist "helped to create a sense of unity and purpose among those who had been isolated in their respective institutions" (Pinar, 1988, p. 11). The annual meeting and the building of a collective memory—the recognition that a common group of individuals have attended consecutive meetings for more than two decades—this must not be underestimated.

The "fugitive" conferences, those between 1973 and 1978, were not commonly directed gatherings; in fact, the organizer of the next year's conference typically volunteered the final day of the current meeting. The Rochester conference was titled, "Heightened Consciousness, Cultural Revolution, and Curriculum Theory" and displayed work in the broadly conceived areas of curriculum theory. The next two conferences, 1974 Xavier conference and the 1975 Virginia conference, were titled "Reconceptualizing Curriculum" and sought to embody tenants described in the 1974 general session by Paul Klohr (what has been described as the "reconceptualist articles of faith"; Pinar, et al., 1995, p. 224). The themes of heightened consciousness and cultural revolution were prevalent in the presentations by participants including Ross Mooney, Maxine Greene, Dwayne Huebner, Macdonald, Pinar, and Apple in Xavier and, in 1975, at Virginia by Greene, Pinar, Madeleine Grumet, Louise Berman, and Jessie Roderick. The emergence of concurrent sessions at Virginia broadened dramatically the discourse of the "reconceptualization" into various areas including the fields of curriculum development, instruction, and teacher education.

The 1976 Milwaukee conference sought more to represent the entire "field" and included general sessions by those not regularly attending past conferences, most notably Ralph Tyler ("Desirable Content for a Curriculum Development Syllabus Today"), and Elliot Eisner ("The Curriculum Field Today: Where We are, Where We Were, and Where We are Going"), along with then-perennial presenters: Apple ("What Do School Teach?"), Mann ("Class Analysis and Curriculum Development"), Macdonald ("Value Based Curriculum Theory"), and Huebner ("Toward a Political Economy of Human Development and Curriculum"). The Milwaukee Conference's sectionals represented the typical crosssection of avant-garde theorizing: "Life History and Curriculum" by Pinar; "Deceptive Arts in Pedagogy" by Francine Shuchat-Shaw & Janet Miller, "Epistemological Concepts of the Language of the Practical" by Max van Manen; "Dramatic Interpretation of Poetic Events: Limitations of Curriculum Theory" by Timothy Riordan; "Multiple Paradigms for Curriculum Research" by George Posner; and "On the Ideological Uses of Curriculum" by Wayne Urban.

The next meeting, the 1977 Kent State Curriculum Theory Conference, continued Milwaukee's effort to schedule general sessions by those not typically viewed as reconceptualists— Joseph Schwab, Decker Walker and Robert Zais— along with regulars Apple, Molnar, Macdonald (with the noted absence of Pinar). Similarly, the sectionals included regular presenters: Shuchat-Shaw's "In Search of Congruence"; Grumet's "Dual Organization and School Change";

Timothy Leonard's "Common-Sense, Critical Reflection and Theory"; Robert V. Bullough's "Thoughts on Teacher Education and the Problems of Coming to see Self Differently"; Elinor Scheirer's "Beyond Frustration: A Search for a Classroom-Based Curriculum Theory"; all displayed the miscellaneous assortment of work in curriculum, foundations, and teacher education. In addition, the beginning of self-examination and the recognizing of the reconceptualists began to occur, as displayed in three sessions: van Manen's "Reconceptualism in the Curriculum"; Miller's "Curriculum Theory of Maxine Greene: A Reconceptualization of Foundation in English Education"; and B. J. Benham's "Curriculum Theory in the 1970's: The Reconceptualist Movement."

The next year—1978—contained a spring conference at Rochester Institute of Technology and an autumn conference at Georgia State University. The R.I.T. Curriculum Theory Conference continued to balance presentations between what has been identified as the split between neo-Marxist and phenomenological theorizing; "regular conference presenters" were represented, including Pinar, Apple, Miller, Shuchat-Shaw, Bullough, Grumet, Posner, Steven Seldon, and Barry Franklin. The Georgia State Conference broadened its invitations with first time presentations by Herbert Kliebard and Harry Broudy, and regular presenters, including Urban, Pinar, Hawthorne, Berman, Macdonald; yet, the orientation seemed to focus less on theory and more on foundations of education and curriculum development. The conferences could have ended at this time, as then reported by certain organizers; *The Journal of Curriculum Theorizing* emerged, however, to provide continual administrative leadership.

Emphasis during these pre-Airlie House conferences focused upon the justification of theory as well as the exploration of political and phenomenological critique. When one views conferences not just by general/keynote sessions but, instead, by including all presentations from the concurrent sessions, a relatively even balance emerges between the then-opposing political and phenomenological groups. Yet, other topics arose as many conference presentations sought to relate theory to the "world of practice." The initial configuration of presentations, loosely tabulated, included substantive representation in the areas of state-of-the-field, curriculum theory, political critique, and phenomenology; also represented were presentations in the area of school practice, research, and teacher education.

The new-formed *Journal of Curriculum Theorizing* established itself as the conference coordinator, and between 1979 and 1982 meetings were held at Airlie House, a conference center outside of Washington, DC. The 190 presentations during the Airlie years configure somewhat similarly to the 159 sessions between 1973-1978 with increases in the areas of general curriculum development, research/evaluation, and teacher education. What is noteworthy, however, is the emergence of presentations in the areas of gender and autobiographical discourse: Janet Miller's "The Sound of Silence Breaking: Feminist Pedagogy" and "Feminism and Curriculum Theory"; Patti Lather's "Feminization vs. Feminizing: Female Empowerment and the Restructuring of Teaching"; Florence Krall's "Indwellings: Reconceiving Pan" and "Behind the Chairperson's Door: Reconceptualizing Women's Work."

While Pinar acknowledges a reconceptualization occurring by 1988 and suggests an ongoing and never-ending quest to reexamine and reconceptualize curriculum, by 1982 the reconceptualists were a defined topic for synoptic textbook writers. The "movement" appears in John McNeil's 1977 synoptic, *Curriculum: A Comprehensive Introduction*. (The 1976 synoptic texts by Tanner & Tanner and by Zais, a participant in the 1977 and 1978 conferences, do not refer to the group.) McNeil uses the term reconceptualists, yet describes the group—Huebner, Donald Bateman, MacDonald (*sic*)—as "soft curricularists" (in contrast to hard curricularists) who "do not study change in behavior or decision-making in the classroom, but the meaning of temporality, transcendence, consciousness, and politics" (1977, p. 314); Pinar's *Heightened Consciousness* and *Curriculum Theorizing* is also cited. Saylor, Alexander, and Lewis' 1981 synoptic, *Curriculum Planning for Better Teaching and Learning*, notes "a small but able group known as reconceptualists" (1981, p. 267), including Huebner, Macdonald, Greene, Pinar, and Apple and cites publications from 1975 to 1978. In one of the few encouraging comments made by textbook writers, the authors state the "reconceptualists are to be encouraged in their work" (1981, p. 267). Subsequent descriptions by other authors underscore the theoretical aspect of this group with little or no involvement in actual school practice.

McNeil's 1981 second edition of *Curriculum* devotes several pages to the reconceptualists (within the configuration of traditionalists, conceptualist empiricist, and reconceptualist, an organizational scheme substantiated in *Curriculum & Instruction: Alternatives in Education* by Giroux, Penna, & Pinar, 1981); moreover, he includes a discussion of the exchanges among the Tanners, Pinar, Finkelstein, and Greene. Yet, McNeil voices what became a common criticism—of the reconceptualists as well as of all theorists—the lack of involvement in curriculum development and school practice. This dart would be thrown continuously and displays itself to this day in comments directed at those who attend Bergamo gatherings.

Toward the end of the Airlie House Conferences the reconceptualists were active and vibrant to textbook writers; however, few self-proclaimed reconceptualists were present at the conferences. A group of reconceptualists had been identified by synoptic authors to include Pinar, Apple, Macdonald, Huebner, and Greene; the actual participation of all but two was over.[2] Moreover, as early as the 1980s, presentations were beginning to reflect on the past work of the reconceptualists as noted in Robert Donmoyer's general session,

"The Reconceptualists Revisited" (1981). Even today, synoptic text discuss the reconceptualists in present tense, much beyond a time when one could find such an individual. Quite clearly, further disjunctures existed between conference activities and those period textbook accounts, yet an active and vital group of individuals continued to meet annually at Airlie House, many nearing a decade's worth of attendance.

CURRICULUM THEORISTS AND THE BERGAMO CONFERENCES, 1983-1993 (1,797 PRESENTATIONS, 2,891 PRESENTERS) AND THE POST-BERGAMO CONFERENCES 1994-1997 (769 PRESENTATIONS; 1,410 PRESENTERS)

By the time the conference moved to Ohio, fewer reconceptualists could be found. The term arose periodically in conference sessions as historical critique or reflections, yet self-proclaimed reconceptualists seemed not to attend what had been called the reconceptualist's conference. Synoptic textbook authors saw otherwise and continued to portray the reconceptualists as an active current group. As Ornstein and Hunkins state in *Curriculum: Foundations, Principles, and Issues:* "They (the reconceptualists) feel that true understanding will come from aesthetic, humanistic, and existential postures. Focusing on understanding oneself will lead to truly heightened consciousness" (1988, pp. 292-293) While not all citations in these synoptic treatments stem from the 1970s, their perspectives ultimately result from 1970s literature or from other synoptic texts. Unruh and Unruh's 1984 textbook notes a current group of critics "from among the curriculum theorists who are known as reconceptualists" (p. 4). While noting a 1982 JCT article, this discussion of the reconceptualists is framed by a 1974 Apple quote; leading writers are noted as Macdonald, Pinar, Huebner, Apple, and Greene. By this time, only Pinar and Macdonald were still attending gatherings; the other three had not attended a conference in six years.

Please know that my intention is not to criticize those individuals who attempt the difficult task of providing an up-to-date overview of the field of curriculum. I wish merely to underscore that the awareness of the reconceptualists no longer represented what had emerged as a vital and substantial gathering of academics at the Bergamo Center in Dayton, Ohio, each autumn. The conference presentations had expanded quite substantially and the meeting itself was attracting large groups of individuals from a variety of fields. "Heightened consciousness" was no longer the quest of conference participants.

The move to the Bergamo Conference Center actually saw a dramatic increase in the number of presentations—from 50 presentations and 61 presenters at the 1981 Airlie House conference to 208 presentations and 404 presenters at the 1991 Bergamo conference. Pinar described six types of discourses that then reflected the work in curriculum studies: political analysis; historical studies; feminist studies; phenomenological studies; aesthetic criticism; studies in theory, practice, and the field (1988). While all areas were represented, not all were represented equally. Historical studies, noted for its importance in past years, was on the decline. The "state-of-the-field" presentations of earlier years had all but vanished, and the many efforts to justify the role of theorizing—common in the 1970s—had diminished by the Bergamo years. Political, feminist, phenomenological, and aesthetic presentations were well represented with continual increases in autobiographical narrative. In addition, the sessions embodied innovative staging and acts of presentation— from conventional paper sessions to dance, music, readers' theatre, spiritual ceremonies, and other representational forms of inquiry.

Thus far I have randomly selected conference presentations as a way to portray the flavor of conference presentations. I cannot identify all themes nor is it appropriate to select titles most representative or significant. Bergamo sessions are quite unique, however, and as a way to suggest the array of inquiry, I have identified select titles of those individuals with the highest number of conference presentations.[3]

Janet L. Miller (42 presentations from 1975 until 1997): "Women as Teachers: Reflections and Rejections" (83); "Researching Teachers: The Problems and Potentials of Collaborative Studies" (86); "Expanding Contexts of Discovery" (88); "Creating Spaces and Finding Voices: Teachers/ Researchers' Reflections on Collaborative Inquiry" (89); "Curriculum as an Autobiographical and Biographical Text" (91); "Rewriting Gender Equity in Teacher Research" (93).

William Pinar (32 presentations from 1973 until 1995): "Political-Spiritual Dimension of Currere" (75); "The Abstract and the Concrete in Curriculum Theorizing" (79); "Curriculum as Gender Text: Notes on Reproduction, Resistance, and Male-Male Relations" (82); "Educational Theory and Social Action" (84); "Cries and Whispers" (88); "Curriculum as an Autobiographical and Biographical Text" (91).

Jo Anne Pagano (29 presentations from 1979 until 1995): "Getting Oughts from Is's: The Role of Criticism in Educational Theory and Practice" (1980); "The Nature and Sources of Teacher Authority" (82); "The Myth of Cultural Reproduction" (84); "Household Language and Feminist Pedagogy" (88); "The Desire to Desire: Subjectivity in Educational Narratives" (90); "Critical Pedagogy: Back into the Future" (92); "Critical Educational Theorizing in Unsettling Times" (93).

Jessie Goodman (27 presentations from 1983 until 1997): "A Thematic Alternative to Technocratic Curriculum Design: A Curriculum Case Study" (83); "Feminist Pedagogy: Issues Confronting the Male Feminist Elementary School Teacher" (85); Teaching Strategies, Political Tactics, and the

Socialization of Potentially Empowered Preservice Teachers" (86); "A Team Approach to Elementary Teacher Education" (90); "Dancing with the Devil: Establishing a Progressive Educational Institute during the Conservative Restoration" (91); "The Democratic Ethos of Harmony and Community Schools: How Can Public Schools Benefit?" (93).

David Jardine *(24 presentations from 1985 until 1995):* "Beyond Competence: Play in the Lives of Children" (85); "Family Stories: Developmental and Hermeneutic-Analogic Images of Adult and Child" (86); "Computers and Being-in-the-World" (88); "Divided by Little Songs, These Silences" (90); "Healing the Wounds: De-pathologizing the Agonies of Pedagogic Interpretation" (91); "The Profession Needs New Blood: Interpretation, Rite of Renewal and the Case of Student-Teaching" (93).

James Henderson *(24 presentations from 1983 until 1997):* "The Use of Qualitative Distinctions as a Basis for Curriculum Design" (83); "Craft and Artistry in Teaching" (85); "The Hermeneutics of Pedagogical Virtue" (87); "Living Praxis at the University: From Study Group to Interpretive Community" (89); "Discursive Democracy in Preservice Teacher Education" (91); "Transformative Curriculum Leadership: Theory and Practice" (93).

William Reynolds *(23 presentations from 1982 until 1997):* "Reading Curriculum Theory: A New Hermeneutic" (84); "Critical Pedagogy Within the Walls of a Technological Institution" (87); "Does a Philosophy of Education make a Difference in Elementary and Secondary Schools?" (89); "Paths of Least Resistance: Schooling as Popular Culture" (90); "Curriculum as Popular Culture" (91); "Order and Chaos: Teachers, Curriculum, and Changes in the Postmodern World" (93).

William Schubert *(22 presentations from 1979 until 1997):* "Teaching Curriculum Theory" (80); "Parental Theorizing and the Literature that Facilitates It" (83); "Autobiographical Responses to a Progressive Education Study Group in a University Setting" (85); "Teacher Lore Project" (88); "On Theorizing in Different Places" (91); "Stories from the Lives of Inner City Children and Teachers" (92).

William Doll *(22 presentations from 1976 until 1996):* "Post-Industrialization and Education" (77); "Curriculum, Order, and the Concept of Change" (80); "Curricular Foundations: Oswego's New Approach to Teacher Education" (83); "Curriculum Beyond Stability: Schon, Prigogine, Piaget" (86); "Chaos Theory as Paradigmatic Metaphor for Education" (88); "Constructing an Unstable Curriculum: An Alternative to the Tyler Rationale" (90).

Landon Beyer *(21 presentations from 1982 until 1997):* "The Ethical Potency of a Materialist Aesthetic" (82); "Critical Theory and the Art of Teaching" (84); "Educational Studies and Other Liberal Field of Study: A Response to the Holmes Group" (86); "The Liberal Arts, Education Studies, and Professionalism" (87); "The Arts as a Basis for Understanding Curriculum and

Teaching" (89); "Educational Change: 'School-Mart' or Social Responsibility" (92).

Dennis Carlson *(21 presentations from 1981 until 1996)*: "Learning to 'Be': Curriculum and the Ontological Sociology of the Self" (81); "Teachers, Class, Culture, and the Schooling Process" (84); "The 'Effective Schools' Movement, the Curriculum and Schooling" (87); "Neo-Marxism, Post-Structuralism and the Curriculum" (91); "New Directions in Multicultural Education" (92); "New Social Movements and the Curriculum" (93).

Patti Lather *(20 presentations from 1982 until 1997)*: "Issues of Validity in Openly Ideological Research" (83); "Empowering Pedagogy" (85); "The Theory and Practice of Liberating Research and Pedagogy" (87); "Breaking Forms: (Re)Writing (Re)Reading Power & Authority in Academic & Feminist Discourse (90); "Ethics, Language and Politics: Feminist Research (92); "Writing Data Stories in the Crisis of Representation" (93).

Many other individuals have made significant contributions to the collective memory of the Bergamo conferences through their participation, either from single paper presentations, continual participation as presenter and/or inquisitive member of the audience, or from subsequent postconference publications. Their involvement and participation has been identified by Pinar (1988, 1995) and can also be found throughout the pages of the *JCT*.

While the flavor of group interaction cannot be portrayed by a mere listing of titles and names; similarly, the meaning of Bergamo cannot be described by archival research. Efforts are underway to preserve the collective memory of the conferences through the JCT's column, Hermeneutic Portraits. The sense of exploration and innovation was readily apparent during the Reconceptualist conferences and continues through the Bergamo years. Janet Miller's "Curriculum Reconceptualized" (this volume, appendix) portrays this demeanor. As part of the Hermeneutic Portraits series, Leigh Chiarelott describes his conference participation: "I realized that I had been part of a special period in the history of curriculum theory and that these conferences, for better or worse, had profoundly influenced me as a teacher and scholar. I had observed, participated in, or heard some of the most original, most creative, most influential ideas and presentations in the field of curriculum theory over the past 20 years. More importantly, I was able to share many of those experiences with my students and colleagues, either directly or through papers presented at the conference" (Chiarelott, 1997, p. 49). Continuing with Hermeneutic Portraits statements, Landon Beyer comments: "the Bergamo conference has tended on the whole to be shaped by one central and widely shared commitment: the creation of an open, supportive, collegial environment in which people could explore possible new directions, speculate on new initiatives, or begin to put forward new and complex ideas. In short, the Bergamo conference has been a place where participants could take risks or suggest possibilities or explore tentative, only partly formed directions" (Beyer, 1998, in press).

By 1995, Pinar et al., expanded the conception of curriculum studies and "understanding curriculum" to include nine forms of texts: political text; racial text; gender text; phenomenological text; post structural, deconstruction, post-modern text; autobiographical/biographical text; aesthetic text; theological text; institutionalize text. I have sorted 2,915 conference titles within these conceptions of text; in fact, I have done this on three occasions and, as would be expected, the configuration displays a variety of presentations in all areas. Certain years prove a greater representation of one text over another, yet a general consistency displays proportions related more to conference attendance than to academic interest. Clearly, gender, political, poststructuralism, autobiography, and race texts began to increase in the late 1980s and guided the orientation of the conference. A consistent presence of school practice/curriculum development sessions appear as has been the case since the origins of the conference. Nonetheless, synoptic textbook authors continued to underscore a self-acclaimed split between theory and practice and seemingly to "set"—or "fossilize"— with an alarming commonality a group of theorists with references and quotes from the early 1970s.

John McNeil's 1985 third edition of *Curriculum* refers to reconceptualists in the present tense and states: "*Reconceptualists.* Their fundamental view is that an intellectual and cultural distance from curriculum practice is required for the present in order to develop more useful comprehensive critiques and theoretical programs" (McNeil, 1981, 1985, p. 362, p. 353). He goes on to describe the group: "Currently, reconceptualists are preoccupied with a critique of the field— a field they believe is too [much] immersed in practical, technical modes of understanding and action" (McNeil, 1981, 1985, p. 362, p. 353).

Oliva's 1988 second edition of *Developing the Curriculum* finds the reconceptualists currently active and draws upon the 1985 third edition of McNeil's *Curriculum* as a way to describe the term and Pinar's 1975 work to describe the intent and popularity of the theorists. Similarly, Ornstein and Hunkins' 1988 textbook, *Curriculum: Foundations, Principles, and Issues*, notes the current work of the reconceptualists from this earlier "fossilized" perspective: "Presently, the reconceptualists are focusing on a critique of the field, which they believe is too immersed in the practical, technologically oriented approaches to understanding and action" (Ornstein and Hunkins, 1988, p. 292). Ornstein and Hunkins' portrayal of the reconceptualists in this first edition and their 1993 second edition continues in a "pre-established" way: "Reconceptualists. Curricularists who are in this camp view that intellectual and scientific distance from curriculum practice are required if those in charge of education are to effectively critique and theorize about existing programs" (Ornstein and Hunkins, 1988, p. 292; 1993, p. 197).

While the fact that the reconceptualists are even portrayed in synoptic texts at all is commendable and on no occasion would I wish to be viewed as criticizing those authors attempting to provide an overview of an unmanageable field. Unfortunately, however, the sense of evolution and exploration of the Bergamo Conferences, as clearly displayed in presentations and the ambiance of the group, is overlooked or not acknowledged in the 1980s synoptics. Ironically, if any group of the 1980s most represented a reluctance to confine itself, to limit possibilities, and to be defined from 1970s publications, it would be those who participated in the Bergamo conferences.

BERGAMO CONFERENCES AND CURRICULUM DEVELOPMENT

The most startling aspect of the title-sorting and configurations is not the representation of the various discourses or the different forms of text. While general indications and trends can be perceived, I will be the first to admit that certain conference presentations fell among four (if not more) distinct forms of text and could not be attributable to any one area. The forms of discourses and their arising interplay only goes to display the richness and interdisciplinary, exploratory aspect of work that was and is presented at Bergamo. What becomes somewhat startling, however, is configuring the conference presentations in relation to the venue and audience, i.e., by whom is this presentation directed and to whom should this session be heard. This is when feminist/gender studies or aesthetic and political texts begin to take on new meanings.

First, however, I wish to underscore an ongoing criticism of the Reconceptualists. Textbook authors and critics often cite their lack of interest and involvement in curriculum development.

> Most reconceptualists have not provided specific advice on creating objectives. However, they do seem to have at least acknowledged that we can take a blended approach to writing objectives, perhaps using behavioral objectives for specific parts of a lesson and more global, open-ended objectives for the macro emphasis on the lesson (Ornstein & Hunkins, 1993, p. 227).

I posed this complaint earlier—the distancing from practice and the noninvolvement in curriculum development and classroom activities—and indeed its portrayal appears regularly in the synoptic textbooks.[4] My review of conference presentations suggests otherwise. The Reconceptualists and those individuals who continue to attend Bergamo Conferences have been quite active in curriculum development if one is as creative with the term "development" as the reconceptualists have been with the term "curriculum theory." With conventional K-12 perspectives of curriculum development, conference presentations represent, loosely figured, 16% of conference presentation. Yet, critics and textbook authors assume that curriculum development for curriculum theorists must occur in a K-12 setting. Cannot curriculum development occur at the postsecondary level? And, of course, one assessable venue for postsecondary curriculum development is in the area of teacher education.

Even as the meetings have been viewed as curriculum theory conferences, a reliable and loyal following of bonafide teacher educators has existed since the origins of the reconceptualists. Regular presenters whose work often addresses the development of teacher education programs have included Alan Tom, Jessie Goodman, Landon Beyer, Elinor Schemer, James Henderson, Paul Shaker, Leigh Chiarelott, Robert Bullough, Gary Knowles, Andrew Gitlin, Tom Lasley, Joseph Watras, William Ayers, Mara Sapon-Shevin, James Sears, J. Dan Marshall, William Armiline, Kathy Farber, and many others. *The Journal of Teacher Education*, under the editorship of Tom Lasley, devoted a theme issue to the reconceptualists, and *Teaching Education* was conceived, originated, and to this day, edited by individuals directly aligned with the Bergamo Conferences. Even with the most conventional conception of teacher education, the presentations represent, loosely figured, 11% of conference sessions. This is in contrast to an equal amount in autobiography/biography text, one of my other 19 categories, and in relation to 1% for the number of theological text presentations throughout the past 25 years. My point is only to state that teacher education has been well represented throughout the years and compares in number to other areas that have come to represent Bergamo, curriculum inquiry, and cultural studies.

However, if one reconceptualizes teacher education to include areas of feminist pedagogy, critical pedagogy, liberatory pedagogy, teacher lore, student lore, collaborative research/inquiry with teachers—all groundbreaking and legitimate forms of teacher education practice—then many more Bergamo presenters fall into the area of teacher education. With this broader conception of curriculum theory and curriculum studies, an astounding 57% of the presentations fall within a reconceptualized notion of teacher education/program development. What the synoptic textbook authors have overlooked in their treatment of the reconceptualists is that curriculum development can occur in places other than elementary and secondary schools (albeit, the market for their texts is not postsecondary education). The alterations of teacher education programs at a variety of institutions, including Mount Union College, University of Utah, Knox College; University of Illinois, Chicago; Slippery Rock University, Indiana University, University of Dayton, Bowling Green University, National Louis University, Brooklyn College, Louisiana State University, and many others, all have "Bergamo fingerprints"—touches of the reconceptualization of teacher education programs. Such work is curriculum development and attends quite directly to the full title of Bergamo conferences, Curriculum Theory and Classroom Practice. Classroom practice was not the difficult-to-access elementary and secondary schools but, instead, the classrooms of the professoriate, the curriculum theorist, and the many Bergamo participants who have devoted their careers to preserve teacher education.

C L O S I N G   C O M M E N T S

[T]he term "reconceptualist" ... was widely used in the 1970s and early 1980s to describe new forms of theorizing that were then emerging. It is still used occasionally, but its use has created some at least partially avoidable confusion. (Marsh & Willis, 1995, p. 104)

Avoidable confusion, indeed, even in the midst of such recent and contemporary activities. Our oral historians will have their hands full as they attempt to sort out these discrepancies. I am left, however, with many varying stacks of 2,915 notecards, an archival collection of all Bergamo conference programs[5], and an extensive array of curriculum synoptic texts. I sense that few Xavier and Virginia conferences participants suspected in 1974 and 1975 that they were involved in a group that would later appear in curriculum textbooks. Similarly, I sense that all of these participants would be surprised to learn in 1997 that this group still exists—at least, in the estimation of certain synoptic textbook authors. The reconceptualists have been described and categorized; however, the act of reconceptualization and efforts "to understand curriculum"—what has proven to be a transformation of curriculum theory, teacher education, and cultural studies— continues to distinguish and divide members of our academic field. The term "reconceptualist" meant something—even with the *unavoidable* confusion that it elicited. The power of community, the act of coming together for 25 years, and the term "Bergamo" now mean something—even though the construction of context and deconstruction of meaning will occur from many contemporary and retrospective perspectives. In 1978, Bill Pinar addressed the question, "what is the reconceptualization?" to the R.I.T. Conference participants.

The "prerequisite" for appreciating the term is illustrated by remarks overheard during the Milwaukee meeting. One listener thought the word meaningless. His companion replied: "No, it's not meaningless. While I'm unable to state precisely what it means, it does mean something. I attend AERA and ASCD meetings regularly, and I've attended three of these. Compare these meetings with those of AERA and ASCD and immediately it's obvious that there is something, however ill-defined, that is the reconceptualization." Such remarks I have overheard several times; perhaps you have too. The point is that however vague the term seems to us who attend these meetings, it is not meaningless; it does refer to something. What I am asking tonight is that you and others join me in identifying exactly what this "something" is. (1978, p. 2)

Twenty years later the same call can be made as we attempt to identify what this something is.

N O T E S

1. The number of presentations represents individually prepared paper presentations; a symposia with four papers would be counted as four presentations while a session with a single title and four participants would be counted as one. For this reason, I have also included the number of conference presenters since, at times, the number of individual sessions decreased as more symposia with numerous respondents were added to the program. The number of presenters does not accurately represent conference attendance since certain participants presented more than once and since not all conference attendees presented papers.

2. This group became the regularly cited list of reconceptualists. While few ever embraced this descriptor, their attendance at conferences was consistent from 1973 to 1976. Conference participation is as follows from 1973 through 1982, the end of the Airlie House years: Apple 74, 76, 77, 78a; Greene 73, 74, 75; Huebner 73, 74, 76; Mann 74, 76; Macdonald 73, 74, 75, 76, 77, 78b, 80, 81; Pinar 73, 74, 75, 76, 78a, 78b, 79, 80, 82.

3. I list randomly selected conference presentations. Since readers of this volume may have attended recent Bergamo meetings, I have selected from pre-1994 presentations.

4. I acknowledge that not all conventional synoptic textbooks "misportray" the reconceptualists; see Schubert (1986).

5. The Reconceptualist Collection, The Museum of Education, University of South Carolina. SP/sp1590.

R E F E R E N C E S

Beyer, L. (1998). Community, identity, and a sense of hope. JCT: Journal of Curriculum Theorizing, 13:4, in press.

Chiarelott, L. (1997). Bergamo, Banff, & beyond: Thoughts on the JCT conference. JCT: Journal of Curriculum Theorizing, 13:2, 48-49.

Finkelstein, J. (1979). Letter to the Editor. Educational Researcher, 8:9, 24-25.

Giroux, H., Penna, A., Pinar, W. (1981). Curriculum & instruction: Alternatives in education. (Berkeley: McCutchan).

Greene, M. (1979). Letter to the Editor. *Educational Researcher*, 8:9, 25.

Jackson, P. (198). Curriculum and its discontents. *Curriculum Inquiry*, 10:2, 159-172.

Marsh, C. & Willis, G. (1995). *Curriculum: Alternative approaches, ongoing issues.* (Englewood Cliffs, NJ: Merrill).

Macdonald, J. (1971). Curriculum theory. *Journal of Educational Research*, 64:5, 196-200.

McNeil, J. (1977; 1981; 1985) *Curriculum: A comprehensive introduction.* (Boston: Little, Brown).

Oliva, P. (1988). *Developing the curriculum.* (Glenview, IL: Scott, Foresman).

Ornstein, A. & Hunkins, F. (1988; 1993). *Curriculum: Foundations, principles, and issues.* Boston: Allyn and Bacon.

Pinar, W. (Ed.). (1974). *Heightened consciousness, cultural revolution, and curriculum theory.* (Berkeley: McCutchan).

Pinar, W. (Ed.). (1975). *Curriculum theorizing: The Reconceptualists.* (Berkeley: McCutchan).

Pinar, W. (1978). What is the reconceptualization? *The Rochester Institute of Technology Curriculum Theory Conference.* The Reconceptualist Collection, The Museum of Education, University of South Carolina.

Pinar, W. (1979). Letter to the Editor. *Educational Researcher*, 8:9, 6, 24.

Pinar, W. (Ed.). (1988). *Contemporary curriculum discourses.* (Scottsdale, AZ: Gorsuch Scarisbrick).

Pinar, W., Reynolds, W., Slattery, P., & Taubman, P. (1995) *Understanding curriculum.* (New York: Peter Lang).

Saylor, J.G., Alexander, W., Lewis, A. (1981). *Curriculum planning for better teaching and learning.* (New York: Holt, Rinehart and Winston).

Schubert, W. (1986). *Curriculum: Perspective, paradigm, and possibility.* (New York: Macmillan).

Tanner, D. & Tanner, L. (1975). *Curriculum development: Theory into practice.* (New York: Macmillan).

Tanner, D. & Tanner, L. (1979). Emancipation from research: The Reconceptualist prescription. *Educational Research*, 8:6, 8-12.

Unruh, G., & Unruh, A. (1984). *Curriculum development: Problems, processes, and progress.* (Berkeley: McCutchan).

Zais, R. (1976). *Curriculum: Principles and foundations.* (New York: Thomas Cromwell).

I V

JCT
Comprehensive Index
1998

E S S A Y S

Airini. (1997). Climbing Up to Check the Sky: Culture and Curriculum. 13:3, 22-27.

Albertini, John & Bonnie Meath-Lang. (1987). An Analysis of Student-Teacher Exchanges in Dialogue Writing Journals. 7:1, 153-201.

Alcazar, Al. (1995). The Journey "Now". 11:2, 35-38.

Anyon, Jean. (1981). Schools as Agencies of Social Legitimation. 3:2, 86-104.

Aoki, Ted Tetsuo. (1983). Towards a Dialectic Between the Conceptual World and the Lived World: Transcending Instrumentalism in Curriculum Orientation. 5:4, 4-21.

_____. (1986). Interests, Knowledge and Evaluation: Alternative Approaches to Curriculum Evaluation. 6:4, 27-44.

_____. (1987). Toward Understanding 'Computer Application'. 7:2, 61-71.

_____. (1987). In Receiving, A Giving: A Response to the Panelists' Gifts. 7:3, 67-88.

Apple, Michael W. (1979). On Analyzing Hegemony. 1:1, 10-27.

_____. (1981). Some Aspects of the Relationship Between Economic and Cultural Reproduction. 3:1, 130-142.

_____. (1985). There Is A River: James B. Macdonald and Curricular Tradition. 6:3, 9-18.

_____. (1988). The Politics of Pedagogy and the Building of Community. 8:4, 7-22.

_____. (1995). Remembering Capital: On the Connections Between French Fries and Education. 11:1, 113-128.

Aronowitz, Stanley & Henry Giroux. (1987). Ideologies about Schooling: Rethinking the Nature of Educational Reform. 7:1, 7-38.

Asanuma, Shiegeru. (1986). The Autobiographical Method in Japanese Education: The Writing Project and Its Application to Social Studies. 6:4, 5-26.

Atkins, Elaine S. (1988). The Relationship of Metatheoretical Principles in the Philosophy of Science to Metatheoretical Explorations in Curriculum. 8:4, 69-86.

Balcaen, Philip L. (1997). Practicing Conversation. 13:3, 37-42.

Barber, Elizabeth. See Nespor, Jan & Elizabeth Barber. (1992).

Baron, Daniel. (1979). A Case Study of Praxis. 1:2, 46-53.

Barone, Thomas E. (1982). The Meadowhurst Experience: Phases in the Process of Educational Criticism. 4:1, 156-170.

_____. (1992). Acquiring a Public Voice: Curriculum Specialists, Critical Storytelling, and Educational Reform. 10:1, 139-152.

Barton, Len. See Lawn, Martin & Len Barton. (1980).

Bash, James H. See Beegle, Charles W., Michael L. Bentley, & James H. Bash. (1987).

Bath, Stephen. (1987). Emancipatory Evaluation: Themes of Ted Aoki's Orientation to Curricular Evaluation. 7:3, 51-66.

Bazin, Nancy T. (1982). Feminism and Curriculum Theory, Part Two: Emerging from Women's Studies. (Part 1 by Janet L. Miller.) 4:1, 187-192.

_____. (1985). Women's Studies Today: An Assessment. 6:2, 117-121.

Beauchamp, Larry & Jim Parsons. (1989). The Curriculum of Student Teacher Evaluation. 9:1, 125-174.

Beattie, Catherine. (1986). The Case for Teacher Directed Curriculum Evaluation. 6:4, 56-73.

Beck, Dahlia & Mary Sheridan. (1996). For Such a Time as This: The Story of Esther and the Perplexed Curriculum. 12:2, 28-32.

Beegle, Charles W., Michael L. Bentley, & James H. Bash. (1987). Beyond 1986: Education for Survival. 7:2, 126-146.

Benham, Barbara J. (1981). Curriculum Theory in the 1970s: The Reconceptualist Movement. 3:1, 162-170.

Bennison, Anne, Susan Jungck, Ken Kantor, and Dan Marshall. (1989). Teachers' Voices in Curriculum Inquiry: A Conversation Among Teacher Educators. 9:1, 71-106.

Bentley, Michael L. See Beegle, Charles W., Michael L. Bentley, & James H. Bash. (1987).

Berk, Leonard. (1980). Education in Lives: Biographic Narrative in the Study of Educational Outcomes. 2:2, 88-154.

Berman, David M. (1993). The Road to Knowledge: Anthropology, the Social Studies, and the Public Schools. 10:3, 33-60.

Beyer, Landon E. (1983). Philosophical Work, Practical Theorizing, and the Nature of Schooling. 5:1, 73-91.

_____. (1987). Art and Society: Toward New Directions in Aesthetic Education. 7:2, 72-98.

_____. (1992). Transformation Tensions: Of the Inside and the Outside. 10:2, 101-122.

Blades, David W. (1995). Procedures of Power in a Curriculum-Discourse: Conversations from Home. 11:4, 125-155.

Block, Alan A. (1988). The Answer is Blowin' in the Wind: A Deconstructive Reading of the School Text. 8:4, 23-52.

_____. (1997). Finding Lost Articles: The Return of Curriculum. 13:3, 5-12.

Blumenfeld-Dones, Donald S. (1995). Curriculum Control and Creativity: An Examination of Curricular Language and Educational Values. 11:1, 73-96.

_____. (1996). "Teacher as Authority": A Model for Curriculum and Pedagogy, 12:3, 36-43.

Bolin, Frances. (1985). Dialogue or Anti-Dialougue? William Torrey Harris As Seen Through Paulo Freire's Theory of Dialogical and Anti-Dialogical Action. 6:2, 80-116.

Brantlinger, Ellen. (1989). Instructional Barriers to Teacher and Student Empowerment and Successful Education of Students in Mainstream Classrooms. 9:2, 39-54.

Briton, Derek. (1995). The Decentered Subject: Pedagogical Implications. 11:4, 57-76.

Britzman, Deborah P. (1992). The Terrible Problem of Knowing Thyself: Toward a Poststructural Acocunt of Teacher Identity. 9:3, 23-46.

_____. (1996). On Becoming a "Little Sex Researcher": Some Comments on a Polymorphously Perverse Curriculum. 12:2, 4-11.

Brouby, Harry S. (1981). Aesthetics and the Curriculum. 3:1, 124-129.

Brown, Theodore M. (1981). How Fields Change: A Critique of the "Kuhnian" View. 3:1, 5-13.

Bruckerhoff, Charles. (1988). Escape from the Classroom Routine: How Collegial Relations Sponsor Relief for Teachers. 8:2, 43-60.

Brunner, Diane DuBose. (1996). Silent Bodies: Miming those Killing Norms of Gender. 12:1, 9-15.

Bullough, Robert V. (1979). Persons-Centered History and the Field of Curriculum. 123-135.

_____. (1982). Teachers and Teaching in the Ninetheenth Century: St. George, Utah. 4:2, 199-206.

Bullough, Robert V., Stanley L. Goldstein, & Ladd Holt. (1982). Rational Curriculum: Teachers and Alienation. 4:2, 132-143.

Burke, Melva M. (1985). The Personal and Professional Journey of James B. Macdonald. 6:3, 84-120.

Butt, Richard. (1980). Against the Flight from Theory: But Towards the Practical. 2:2, 5-11.

_____. (1985). Curriculum: Metatheoretical Horizons and Emancipatory Action. 6:2, 7-23.

_____. (1995). Autobiographic Praxis and Self Education: From Alienation to Authenticity—Version One. 11:1, 7-48.

Butt, Richard & Danielle Raymond. (1987). Arguments for Using Qualitative Approaches in Understanding Teacher Thinking: The Case for Biography. 7:1, 62-93.

Butt, Richard, Danielle Raymond, & Lloyd Yamagishi. (1987). Autobiographic Praxis: Studying the Formation of Teachers' Knowledge. 7:4, 87-164.

Caplan, Alan. See Oberg, Antoinette, Daniel Scott, & Alan Caplan. (1996).

Carlson, Dennis. (1982). An Ontological Grounding for Curriculum. 4:2, 207-215.

_____. (1983). Of Capital, Labor and Teachers. 5:3, 148-158.

Carson, Terrance R. (1987). Teaching as Curriculum Scholarship: Honoring Professor Ted Tetsuo Aoki. 7:3, 7-10.

_____. (1992). Questioning Curriculum Implementation: Scenes from a Conversation. 9:3, 71-96.

Casey, Kathleen. (1989). Teachers and Values: The Progressive Use of Religion in Education. 9:1, 23-70.

Chambers, Cynthia. See Yamagishi, Rochelle, Tweela Houtekamer, Evelyn Goodstriker, & Cynthia Chambers. (1995).

Chambers, Cynthia M., Antoinette Oberg, Arlena Dodd, & Mary Moore. (1993). Seeking Authenticity: Women Reflect on Their Lives as Daughters, Mothers, and Teachers. 10:3, 73-108.

Chiarelott, Leigh. (1983). The Role of Experience in the Curriculum: An Analysis of Dewey's Theory of Experience. 5:3, 29-40.

_____. (1983). The Role of Experience in the Curriculum: An Application of Dewey's Theory of Experience. 5:4, 22-37.

_____. (1997). Bergamo, Banff, and Beyond: Thoughts on the JCT Conference. 13:2, 48-49.

Cobb, Paul. (1983). Critique of Currriculum and Change. 5:2, 62-74.

Daignault, Jacques & Clermont Gauthier. (1982). The Indecent Curriculum Machine. 4:1, 177-196.

_____. (1983). Curriculum and Action-Research: An Artistic Activity in a Perverse Way. 5:3, 4-28.

Darlington, Sonja. (1995). Reframing Education's Conversation: Politicizing the First-Year Student Environment. 11:3, 85-104.

Davis, Brent. (1995). Thinking Otherwise and Hearing Differently: Enactivism and School Mathematics. 11:4, 31-58.

de Castell, Suzanne. (1996). On Finding One's Place in the Text: Literacy as a Technology of Self-Formation. 12:4, 27-31.

Deutelbaum, Wendy & Adalaide Morris. (1983). The Anti-Pedagogical Pedagogues. 5:3, 143-147.

Dippo, Don. See Simon, Roger & Don Dippo. (1980).

Dixon, George. (1980). Taking Moral Education Seriously. 2:1, 203-208.

Dobson, Judith E. See Dobson, Russell L., Judith E. Dobson, & J. Randall Koetting. (1987).

Dobson, Russell L., Judith E. Dobson, & J. Randall Koetting. (1987). Looking At, Talking About, and Living With Children. 7:2, 111-125.

Dodd, Arlena. See Chambers, Cynthia M., Antoinette Oberg, Arlena Dodd, & Mary Moore. (1993).

Dolby, Nadine. (1997). The Flow of Values in History: A Tale of Two Teachers. 13:1, 6-14.

Doll, Mary Aswell. (1982). Beyond the Window: Dreams and Learning. 4:1, 197-201.

_____. (1988). The Monster in Children's Dreams: Its Metaphoric Awe. 8:4, 87-100.

_____. (1995). Teaching as an Erotic Art. 11:3, 131-146.

_____. (1997). Winging It. 13:1, 41-44.

Doll, Jr., William E. (1980). Play and Mastery: A Structuralist View. 2:1, 209-226.

_____. (1983). Curriculum and Change. 5:2, 4-61.

_____. (1983). Practicalizing Piaget: A Response to My Critics. 5:4, 92-110.

Donmoyer, Robert. (1980). The Evaluator as Artist. 2:2, 12-26.

Eisner, Eliot. (1997). Educational Challenges in the 21st Century. 13:3, 36.

Elbaz, Freema & Robert Elbaz. (1988). Curriculum and Textuality. 8:2, 107-132.

Elbaz, Robert. See Elbaz, Freema & Robert Elbaz. (1988).

Elliott, John. See Schubert, William H., George Willis, Helen Simons, Beverley Labbett, John Elliot, Barry MacDonald, Ralph W. Tyler, and Ernest R. House. (1995).

Emoungu, Paul-Albert. (1981). On the Radical Critique of Liberal Educational Reforms: Some Theoretical Issues. 3:2, 104-114.

Epstein, Irving. (1989). Critical Pedagogy and Chinese Education. 9:2, 69-98.

Ezeomah, Chimah. (1985). The Development of a Special Type of Curriculum for the Nomads of Nigeria. 6:4, 45-65.

Fawns, Roderick. (1980). The Rough Theatre of Science Teaching. 2:2, 213-222.

Feinberg, Paul R. (1985). Four Curriculum Theorists: A Critique in the Light of Martin Buber's Philosophy of Education. 6:1, 5-164.

Fisher, Barbara. (1980). Probing Inward: Reflections on Writing. 2:1, 135-164.

Franklin, Barry M. (1979). Self Control and the Psychology of School Discipline. 1:2, 238-254.

_____. (1981). Whatever Happened to Social Control? The Muting of Coercive Authority in Curriculum Discourses? 3:1. 252-258.

Franklin, Elizabeth A. (1989). Thinking and Feeling in Art: Developing Aesthetic Perspectives of Preservice Teachers. 9:2, 55-68.

Friesen, Carla. See Haig-Brown, Celia, Annette Le Box, & Carla Friesen. (1995).

Fry, Pamela. (1995). The Creation of Curriculum Reality: A Study of Metaphors in Education. 11:1, 97-112.

Fuller, Laurie. (1996). If Only They Knew: White Dyke Disclosures in Lecture. 12:3, 19-25.

Gabbard, David A. (1996). Of Authors, Intellectuals, and Social Inertia: Poststructuralist Reflections on Havel's "Largo Desolato". 12:2, 12-18.

Garman, Noreen P. See Holland, Patricia E. & Noreen P. Garman.

Gauthier, Clermont. See Daignault, Jacques & Clermont Gauthier. (1982).

Gauthier, Clermont & Maurice Tardif. (1995). Pedagogy and the Emergence of an Academic Order in the Seventeenth Century. 11:3, 7-43.

Gershman, Kathleen. See Oliver, Donald W. & Kathleen Gershman. (1992).

Giroux, Henry A. (1980). Beyond the Limits of Radical Educational Reform: Toward a Critical Theory of Education. 2:1, 20-46.

_____. (1980). Dilectics of Curriculum Theory. 2:2, 27-36.

_____. See Aronowitz, Stanley & Henry Giroux. (1987).

Goldman-Segall, Ricki. (1997). Looking Through Layers: Reflecting Upon Digital Ethnography. 13:1, 23-29.

Goldstein, Stanley L. See Bullough, Robert V., Stanley L. Goldstein, & Ladd Holt. (1982).

Goodman, Jesse. (1987). Masculinity, Feminism, and the Male Elementary School Teacher: A Case Study of Preservice Teachers' Perspectives. 7:2, 30-60.

Goodson, Ivor. (1993). From the Personal to Political: Developing Sociologies of Curriculum. 10:3, 9-32.

Goodstriker, Evelyn. See Yamagishi, Rochelle, Tweela Houtekamer, Evelyn Goodstriker, & Cynthia Chambers. (1995).

Gordon, Marshall & Ira Marc Weingarten. (1979). Communication or Communique: Towards a Theory of Practice. 1:2, 65-77.

Grabiner, Eugene. (1983). Juridical Subjectivism and Juridical Equivocation in the Bakke Decision. 5:3, 55-73.

Grabiner, Gene & Virginia Grabiner. (1987). The Self-Determined Educator and the Expansion of the "Labor-Education Thesis". 7:1, 39-61.

Grabiner, Virginia. See Grabiner, Gene & Virginia Grabiner. (1987).

Greenburg, Selma. (1982). The Women's Movement. 4:2, 193-198.

_____. (1983). The Resurrection of the Feminine Mystique. 5:2, 134-142.

Grumet, Madeleine R. (1979). Supervision and Situation: A Methodology of Self Report for Teacher Education. 1:1, 191-257.

_____. (1980). Autobiography and Reconceptualization. 2:2, 155-157.

_____. (1981). Conception, Contradiction and Curriculum. 3:1, 287-298.

_____. (1983). Response to Reid and Wankowski. 5:2, 124-127.

_____. (1985). The Work of James B. Macdonald: Theory Fierce With Reality. 6:3, 19-27.

_____. (1989). Word Worlds: The Literary Reference for Curriculum Criticism. 9:1, 7-22.

Haggerson, Nelson L. (1986). Reconceptualizing Professional Literature: An Aesthetic Self-Study. 6:4, 74-97.

_____. (1988). Reconceptualizing Inquiry in Curriculum: Using Multiple Research Paradigms to Enhance the Study of Curriculum. 8:1, 81-102.

Haig-Brown, Celia, Annette Le Box, & Carla Friesen. (1995). Power, Powerlessness, and Professional Development: The Possibility (?) of Polyphony. 11:4, 101-124.

Hamann, Donald L. (1981). A Curriculum Theory for Education Based on Transcendental Learning Theory: Centering. 3:2, 115-129.

Hammer, Rhonda. See McClaren, Peter & Rhonda Hammer. (1992).

Harper, Helen. (1996). Reading, Identity, and Desire: High School Girls and Feminist Avant-Garde Literature. 12:4, 6-13.

Henderson, James G. (1988). A Comprehensive Hermeneutic of Professional Growth: Normative Referent and Reflective Interplay. 8:3 147-167.

_____. (1992). A Thematic Analysis of Preservice Praxis: The Problem of Curriculum Text and University Context. 10:1, 117-138.

Herzog, Leslie. See Schubert, William, Ann Lynn Lopez Schubert, Leslie Herzog, George Posner, & Craig Kridel. (1988).

Hlynka, Denis. (1989). Making Waves with Educational Technology: A Deconstructionist Reading of Ted Aoki. 9:2, 27-38.

Holland, Patricia E. & Noreen P. Garman. (1992). Macdonald and the Mythopoetic. 9:4, 45-72.

Holt, Ladd. See Bullough, Robert V., Stanley L. Goldstein, & Ladd Holt. (1982).

House, Ernest R. See Schubert, William H., George Willis, Helen Simons, Beverley Labbett, John Elliott, Barry MacDonald, Ralph W. Tyler, and Ernest R. House. (1995).

Houtekamer, Tweela. See Yamagishi, Rochelle, Tweela Houtekamer, Evelyn Goodstriker, & Cynthia Chambers. (1995).

Huber, Margaret Ann. (1981). The Renewal of Curriculum Theory in the 1970s: An Historical Study. 3:1, 14-84.

Huebner, Dwayne. (1985). The Redemption of Schooling: The Work of James B. Macdonald. 6:3, 28-34.

_____. (1995). Education and Spirituality. 11:2, 13-34.

Huenecke, Dorothy. (Editor). (1981). The Kent State-Georgia Proceedings. 3:1, 85-90.

Itzkoff, Seymour W. (1983). Reductionism, Intelligence, and the Process Curriculum. 5:2, 75-83.

Iverson, Barbara & Hersholt C Waxman. (1981). Perspectives on Mentorship. 3:1, 193-201.

Jacknicke, Ken G. (1987). Educational Administration as a Praxiological Act. 7:3, 34-42.

Jagodzinski, Jan. (1996). The Unsaid in Educational Nattatology: Power and Seduction of Pedagogical Authority. 12:3, 26-35.

Jardine, David W. (1988). Play and Hermeneutics: An Exploration of the Bi-Polarities of Mutual Understanding. 8:2, 23-42.

_____. (1992). A Bell Ringing in the Empty Sky. 10:1, 17-38.

_____. (1995). "The Profession Needs New Blood." 11:3, 105-130.

_____. (1997). The Surroundings. 13:3, 18-21.

Jarrett, James L. (1980). Another Kind of Bias in Moral Education. 2:1, 227-237.

Jipson, Janice. (1992). Midwife and Mother: Multiple Reflections on Curriculum, Connections, and Change. 10:1, 89-116.

Jipson, Janice & Petra Munro. (1992). What's Real? Fictions of the Maternal. 10:2, 7-28.

Johnson, Kenneth E. (1993). Teaching the Postmodern. 10:3, 61-72.

Jones, Byrd L. & Robert B. Maloy. (1992). Schools for an Information Age. 10:1, 39-70.

Jones, Robert M. & John E. Steinbrink. (1988). Confluent Curriculum Development: A Logical Proposal. 8:1, 185-200.

Joseph, Ellis A. (1983). On the Separation of the Humanities and Technology From Each Other: A Triadic Explanation. 5:4, 58-67.

_____. (1988). Contributions of Theology to Theory in Educational Administration. 8:1, 37-54.

Jungck, Susan. See Bennison, Anne, Susan Jungck, Ken Kantor, and Dan Marshall. (1989).

Jurkowitz, Carolyn M. (1981). Shaping the High School Curriculum: The Case of Regional Accreditation. 3:1, 103-113.

Kantor, Ken. See Bennison, Anne, Susan Jungck, Ken Kantor, and Dan Marshall. (1989).

Kaufman, Barry A. & Gail M. Kaufman. (1980). Reconstructing Child Development for Curriculum Studies: Critical and Feminist Perspectives. 2:2, 245-268.

Kesson, Kathleen. (1995). Eco-Logos: Postmodern Revelations and the Recovery of Archic Wisdoms. 11:4, 11-30.

Kickbursh, Kenneth W. (1986). Curricul-In-Use and the Emergence of Practical Ideology: A Comparative Study of Secondary Classrooms. 6:4, 98-143.

Kincheloe, Joe L. (1995). Schools Where Ronnie and Brandon Would Have Excelled: A Curriculum Theory of Academic and Vocational Integration. 11:3, 61-84.

Kinlicheeney, Sr. Jeanette. (1995). Spirituality and Curriculum: A Native American View. 11:2, 39-48.

Kliebard, Herbert M. (1981). Dewey and the Herbartians: The Genesis of a Theory of Curriculum. 3:1, 154-161.

Koetting, J. Randall. See Dobson, Russell L., Judith E. Dobson, & J. Randall Koetting. (1987).

_____. See Yellin, David & J. Randall Koetting. (1988).

Korn, Carol. (1997). Children's Narrative and Pedagogical Listening. 13:2, 11-18.

Krall, Florence R. (1979). Living Metaphors: The Real Curriculum in Environmental Education. 1:1, 180-185.

_____. (1981). Navajo Tapestry: A Continuum for Ethno-Ecological Perspectives. 3:2, 165-208.

_____. (1982). Indwellings: Reconceptualizing Pan. 4:1, 217-249.

_____. (1983). Behind the Chairperson's Door: Reconceptualizing Women's Work. 5:4, 68-91.

_____. (1988). Flesh of the Earth, Voice of the Earth: Educational Perspectives on "Deep Ecology". 8:1, 55-80.

Kridel, Craig. (1979). Castiglione and Elyot: Early Curriculum Theorists. 1:2, 89-99.

_____. (1983). A Way of Life Revisited. 5:1, 92-95.

_____. See Schubert, William, Ann Lynn Lopez Schubert, Leslie Herzog, George Posner, & Craig Kridel. (1988).

_____. (1996). James Macdonald, Dwayne E. Huebner, & Paul Klohr. 12:1, 43-44.

_____. (1996). Hilda Taba and Alice Miel. 12:2, 37-38.

_____. (1996). Ronald E. Padgham and Francine Shuchat-Shaw. 12:3, 44-15.

_____. (1996). Janet L. Miller. 12:4, 41.

_____. (1997). Wilford Aikin. 13:1, 38-40.

_____. (1997). Leigh Chiarelott. 13:2, 47.

_____. (1997). Archival Repositories and the Preservation of the Present. 13:3, 35-35.

Labbett, Beverley. See Schubert, William H., George Willis, Helen Simons, Beverley Labbett, John Elliott, Barry MacDonald, Ralph W. Tyler, and Ernest R. House. (1995).

Laidlaw, Linda. (1996). Dangerous Writing: Life, Death, and Curriculum. 12:44, 44-46.

Lather, Patti. (1989). Ideology and Methodological Attitude. 9:2, 7-26.

Lawn, Martin & Len Barton. (1980). Curriculum Studies: Reconceptualization or Reconstruction? 2:1 47-56.

Le Box, Annette. See Haig-Brown, Celia, Annette Le Box, & Carla Friesen. (1995).

Lee, Yonghwan. (1995). Foucault, Lyotard, and Local Curriculum. 10:4, 83-113.

Leonard, J. Timothy. (1983). Mystery and Myth: Curriculum as the Illumination of Lived Experience. 5:1, 17-25.

Levine, Mary Anne. (1981). The Problem of the Learner in Curriculum Building. 3:1, 114-116.

Levy, Phyllis Saltzman. (1983). Creative Problem Solving in the Classroom. 5:1, 53-62.

Littleford, Michael S. (1979). Vico and Curriculum Studies. 1:2, 54-64.

_____. (1980). Vico and Dewey: Toward a Humanistic Foundation for Curriculum Studies. 2:1, 57-70.

_____. (1981). Social Action, Self Reflection, and Curriculum Theory: Part Two. 3:1, 211-221. (Part One by James R. Whitt.)

_____. (1982). Curriculum Theorizing and the Possibilities and Conditions for Social Action Toward Democratic Community and Education. 4:2, 144-152.

_____. (1983). Censorship, Academic Freedom and the Public School Teacher. 5:3, 98-131.

Luce-Kapler, Rebecca & Susan Walsh. (1996). Holographing the Page. 12: 19-27.

Lydon, Angela. (1995). An Ecozoic Cosmology of Curriculum and Spirituality. 11:2, 67-86.

Macagnoni, Virginia M. (1981). Zones of Potentiality Contributing to Consciousness: Thrust for Curriculum Design. 3:1, 222-231.

MacDonald, Barry. See Schubert, William H., George Willis, Helen Simons, Beverley Labbett, John Elliott, Barry MacDonald, Ralph W. Tyler, and Ernest R. House. (1995).

Macdonald, James B. (1981). Curriculum, Consciousness and Social Change. 3:1, 143-153.

_____. Theory, Practice and the Hermeneutic Circle. 3:2, 130-138.

Macdonald, James B. & Susan Colbert Macdonald. (1981). Gender, Values, and Curriculum. (1981). 3:1, 299-304.

Macdonald, Susan Colbert. See Macdonald, James B. & Susan Colbert Macdonald. (1981).

MacPherson, Sonia. (1997). Desire in the Margins: A Medieval Love Story and the Hidden Curriculum of Desire. 13:2, 19-26.

Maloy, Robert B. See Jones, Byrd L. & Robert B. Maloy. (1992).

Marsh, Colin J. (1987). Curriculum Theorizing in Australia. 7:2, 7-29.

Marshall, Dan. See Bennison, Anne, Susan Jungck, Ken Kantor, and Dan Marshall. (1989).

Martel, Angeline. (1987). Ethnicity, Language, and Culture in the Teachings of Professor Ted Aoki: Or, the celebration of a double vision. 7:3, 43-50.

Martel, Angeline & Linda Peterat. (1988). A Hope for Helplessness: Womanness at the Margin in Schools. 8:1, 103-136.

Martin, Kathleen. (1996). Side-By-Side Learning: Changing Habits of Thought. 12:3, 46-49.

Martusewicz, Rebecca. (1997). Leaving Home: Curriculum as Translation. 13:3, 13-17.

Mazza, Karen A. (1982). Reconceptual Inquiry as an Alternative Mode of Curriculum Theory and Practice: A Critical Study. 4:2, 5-89.

McCarthy, Cameron R. (1988). Slowly, Slowly, Slowly, the Dumb Speaks: Third World Popular Culture and the Sociology for the Third World. 8:2, 7-22.

_____. (1995). The Palace of the Peacock: Wilson Harris and the Curriculum in Troubled Times. 11:3, 43-60.

McClaren, Peter & Rhonda Hammer. (1992). Media Knowledges, Warrior Citizenry, and Postmodern Literacies. 10:2, 29-68.

McCrory, David L. (1981). A Map of the Concept of Curriculum Theory. 3:1, 91-102.

McCutcheon, Gail. (1979). Educational Criticism: Methods and Applications. 1:2, 5-25.

_____. (1982). Educational Criticism: Reflections and Reconsiderations. 4:1, 171-176.

Meath-Lang, Bonnie. (1981). "All the things I might not be ...": Issues in Communication for Curricularists. 3:1, 232-238.

_____. (1982). The Curriculum and the Search for Meaning: A Discussion of the Applications of Logotherapy to Education. 4:1, 202-207.

_____. See Albertini, John & Bonnie Meath-Lang. (1987).

Miller, Janet L. (1979). Curriculum Theory: A Recent History. 1:1, 28-43.

_____. (1980). Women: The Evoloving Educational Consciousness. 2:1, 238-247.

_____. (1982). The Sound of Silence Breaking: Feminist Pedagogy and Curriculum Theory. 4:1, 5-11.

_____. (1982). Feminism and Curriculum Theory, Part One: The Breaking of Attachments. (Part 2 by Nancy T. Bazin.) 4:1, 181-186.

_____. (1996). Curriculum and the Reconceptualization: Another Brief History. 12:1, 6-8.

_____. (1996). The Human Histories.... 12:4, 42-43.

Miller, John P. (1987). Transformation as an Aim for Education. 7:1, 94-152.

Milner, Joseph. (1987). Transvestite's Return: The Syntax Exchange of the Visual and Verbal Arts. 7:2, 99-110.

Mitrano, Barbara. (1981). Feminism and Curriculum Theory: Implications for Teacher Education. 3:2, 5-85.

Molnar, Alex. (1985). Tomorrow the Shadow on the Wall Will Be That of Another. 6:3, 35-42.

Moore, Mary. See Chambers, Cynthia M., Antoinette Oberg, Arlena Dodd, & Mary Moore. (1993).

Morris, Adalaide. See Deutelbaum, Wendy & Adalaide Morris. (1983).

Morris, Marla. (1996). Toward a Ludic Pedagogy: An Uncertain Occasion. 12:1, 29-33.

Munby, Hugh. (1983). Change in the Curriculum Concept. 5:2, 112-123.

Munro, Petra. See Jipson, Janice & Petra Munro. (1992).

_____. (1996). Resisting "Resistance": Stories Women Teachers Tell. 12:1, 16-28.

Nespor, Jan & Elizabeth Barber. (1992). Building an Educational Fact. 10:1, 71-88.

Nixon, Greg. (1997). Autobiography and the Quest for Nothing. 13:1, 30-37.

Noddings, Nel. (1981). Caring. 3:2, 139-148.

_____. (1983). Why is Piaget So Hard to Apply in the Classroom? 5:2, 84-103.

Oberg, Antoinette. See Chambers, Cynthia M., Antoinette Oberg, Arlena Dodd, & Mary Moore. (1993).

Oberg, Antoinette, Daniel Scott, & Alan Caplan. (1996). trialogue: preparation, repetition and .... 12:1, 34-42.

Oliver, Donald W. & Kathleen Gershman. (1992). Knowing as Participation. 10:2, 69-100.

Olson, John K. (1982). Three Approaches to Curriculum Change: Balancing the Accounts. 4:2, 90-96.

Osajima, Keith. (1992). Speaking of Silence. 9:4, 89-96.

Osborn, Robert L. (1979). The Validation of Private-Subjective Knowledge Claims. 1:2, 26-36.

Padgham, Ronald E. (1979). Twentieth Century Art and Contemporary Curriculum Theory. 1:1, 155-179.

_____. (1983). The Holographic Paradigm and Postcritical Reconceptualist Curriculum Theory. 5:3, 132-142.

_____. (1988). Thoughts about the Implications of Archetypal Psychology for Curriculum Theory. 8:3, 123-146.

Pagano, Jo Anne. (1981). The Curriculum Field: Emergence of a Discipline. 3:1, 171-184.

_____. (1987). The Nature of Sources of Teacher Authority. 7:4, 7-26.

Parrett, William. (1983). Alaska's Rural Schools: A Unique Challenge for Responsible Curricular Development. 5:3, 41-54.

Parsons, Jim. See Beauchamp, Larry & Jim Parsons. (1989).

Peterat, Linda. See Martel, Angeline & Linda Peterat. (1988).

Pinar, William F. (1979). What is the Reconceptualization? 1:1, 93-104.

_____. (1980). Notes on the Relationship between a Field and Its Journals. 2:1, 7-11.

_____. (1980). The Voyage Out: Curriculum as the Relationship between the Knower and the Known. 2:1, 71-92.

_____. (1980). Life History and Educational Experience. 2:2, 159-212.

_____. (1981). Life History and Educational Experience, Part Two. 3:1, 259-286.

_____. (1981). Caring: Gender Considerations, A Response to Nel Noddings' "Caring". 3:2, 149-151.

_____. (1983). Curriculum as Gender Text: Notes on Reproduction, Resistance, and Male-Male Relations. 5:1, 26-52.

_____. (1985). A Prayerful Act: The Work of James B. Macdonald. 6:3, 43-53.

_____. (1987). "Unwanted Strangers in Our Homeland": Notes on the Work of T. Aoki. 7:3, 11-21.

_____. (1988). Autobiography and the Architecture of Self. 8:1, 7-36.

Pines, A. Leon. (1982). Curriculum Development and Instructional Planning Within an Epistemological-Psychological Framework: A Theoretical Synthesis. 4:1, 88-105.

Piper, David. (1997). Lacan, Heidegger, and the Future Anterior of Teaching and Learning. 13:3, 28-33.

Pitt, Alice J. (1996). Fantasizing Women in the Women's Studies Classroom: Toward a Symptomatic Reading of Negation. 12:4, 32-40.

Posner, George J. (1979). Curriculum Research: Domains of the Field. 1:1, 80-92.

_____. See Schubert, William H. & George J. Posner. (1980).

_____. (1982). Cognitive Science and a Conceptual Change Epistemology: A New Approach to Curricular Research. 4:1, 106-126.

_____. See Schubert, William, Ann Lynn Lopez Schubert, Leslie Herzog, George Posner, & Craig Kridel. (1988).

Pritscher, Conrad. (1982). A Demonstration of Making Existence Explicit and Simultaneously Monitoring It. 4:1, 250-256.

_____. (1982). Time as a Horizon for a Curriculum. 4:2, 228-235.

_____. (1988). Creating New Concepts to Clarify What is Worthy of the Name "Education". 8:2, 61-76.

Rankin, John M. (1992). Objects on the Shelf: Transitional Objects in a Secondary School Curriculum. 9:4, 29-44.

Raymond, Danielle. See Butt, Richard & Danielle Raymond. (1987); Butt, Richard, Danielle Raymond, & Lloyd Yamagishi. (1987).

Raywid, Mary Anne. (1981). Up From Agape: Response to "Caring" by Nel Noddings. 3:2, 152-156.

Reid, Willian A. (1980). A Curriculum Journal and Its Field: A Question of Genre. 2:1, 12-19.

_____. (1980). Rationalism or Humanism? The Future of Curriculum Studies. 2:1, 93-108.

_____. See Wankowski, Kanek & William Reid. (1982).

Reiniger, Meredith Elizabeth. (1988). Autobiographical Search for Gyn/Ecology: Traces of Misogyny in Women's Schooling. 8:3, 7-88.

Reynolds, William M. (1987). Freedom from Control: Toward an Abolition of Teacher Materials and Minimum Competency Tests. 7:4, 65-86.

Richards, Robert E. & Edmund Short. (1981). Curriculum Inquiry from a Religious Perspective: Two Views. 3:2, 209-222.

Romer, Nancy. (1992). Building Campus Community to Challenge Bigotry and Support Multi-Culturalism. 9:4, 97-104.

Rosario, Jose. (1979). Aesthetics and the Curriculum: Persistency, Traditional Modes, and a Different Perspective. 1:1, 126-154.

_____. (1980). Harold Rugg on How We Come to Know: A View of His Aesthetics. 2:1, 165-177.

Saccalis, Nicolae. (1981). Education and How Ulysses Defeated the Cyclops. 3:2, 223-227.

Schnell, R.L. (1980). Reconstructing the Introductory History of Education Course. 2:2, 223-234.

Schubert, Ann Lynn Lopez. See Schubert, William H. & Ann Lynn Lopez Schubert. (1981).

_____. See Schubert, William H. & Ann Lynn Lopez Schubert. (1982).

_____. See Schubert, William H., Ann Lynn Lopez Schubert, Leslie Herzog, George Posner, & Craig Kridel. (1988).

Schubert, William H. (1992). On Mentorship: Examples from J. Harlan Shores and Others through Lenses Provided by James B. Macdonald. 9:3, 47-70.

Schubert, William H. & Ann Lynn Lopez Schubert. (1981). Toward Curricula That Are Of, By, and Therefore For Students. 3:1, 239-251.

_____. (1982). Teaching Curriculum Theory. 4:2, 97-111.

Schubert, William H., Ann Lynn Lopez Schubert, Leslie Herzog, George Posner, & Craig Kridel. (1988). A Geneology of Curriculum Researchers. 8:1, 137-184.

Schubert, William H. & George J. Posner. (1980). Origins of the Curriculum Field Based on a Study of Mentor-Student Relationships. 2:2, 37-67.

Schubert, William H., George Willis, Helen Simons, Beverley Labbett, John Elliott, Barry MacDonald, Ralph W. Tyler, and Ernest R. House. (1995). The Impact of Major Curriculum Reforms: A Cross-Cultural Comparison of the Eight Year Study in the U.S. and the Humanities Curriculum Project in the U.K. 10:4, 7-60.

Shuchat Shaw, Francine. (1980). The Meanings of Congruence. 2:1, 178-202.

Schwartz, Jr., John J. (1979). The World of Harold Rugg and the Question of Objectivity. 1:2, 100-228.

Scott, Daniel. See Oberg, Antoinette, Daniel Scott, & Alan Caplan. (1996).

Scott, Jeanette MacArthur. (1996). Complicating the Two-STEP: A teacher educator's re/entangling of theory and practice. 12:3, 13-18.

Sears, James T. (1985). Rethinking Teacher Education: Dare We Work Toward a New Social Order? 6:2, 24-79.

_____. (1993). Credibility in Teacher Education: Dilemmas of Faculty, Students, and Administrators at Indiana University. 10:3, 109-152.

Searles, W.E. (1982). A Substantiation of Macdonald's Models in Science Curriculum Development. 4:1, 127-155.

Seldon, Steven. (1979). Biological Determinism and the Normal School Curriculum: Helen Putnam and the N.E.A Committee on Racial Well-Being, 1910-1922. 1:1, 105-122.

Serafini, Anthony. (1981). Academic Publishing: Mammouth in the Morass. 3:1, 305-309.

Sernak, Kathleen. (1997). From the Individual to the Collective: An Ethic of Caring in the Organization of Schools. 13:2, 36-45.

Shapiro, Sherry & Svi Shapiro. (1995). Silent Voices, Bodies of Knowledge: Towards a Critical Pedagogy of the Body. 11:1, 49-72.

Shapiro, Svi. (1982). Shaping Educational Imagination: Class, Culture and the Contradictions. 4:2, 153-165.

_____. (1988). Education and Democracy: Constituting a Counter-Hegemonic Discourse of Educational Change. 8:3, 89-122.

_____. See Shapiro, Sheery & Svi Shapiro. (1995).

Sheridan, Mary. See Beck, Dahlia & Mary Sheridan. (1996).

Short, Edmund. See Richards, Robert E. & Edmund Short. (1981).

Simon, Roger & Don Dippo. (1980). Dramatic Analysis: Interpretive Inquiry for the Transformation of Social Settings. 2:1, 109-134.

Simons, Helen. See Schubert, William H., George Willis, Helen Simons, Beverley Labbett, John Elliott, Barry MacDonald, Ralph W. Tyler, and Ernest R. House. (1995).

Slattery, Patrick. (1992). Toward an Eschatological Curriculum Theory. 9:3, 7-22.

Smith, David G. (1983). The Erosion of Childhood: Good News or Bad News? 5:2, 128-133.

_____. (1983). Entering Curriculum Language From the Ground Up. 5:3, 74-97.

_____. (1996). Identity, Self, and Other in the Conduct of Pedagogical Action: An East/West Inquiry. 12:3, 6-12.

Smith, Richard & Anna Zantiotis. (1988). Practical Teacher Education and the Avant Garde. 8:2, 77-106.

Smits, Hans. (1997). Hermeneutically-Inspired Action Research: Living with the Difficulties of Understanding. 13:1, 15-22.

Spodek, Bernard. (1985). Reflections in Early Childhood Education. 6:3, 54-64.

Steinberg, Shirley. (1996). Early Education as a Gendered Construction. 12:2, 33-36.

Stinson, Susan W. (1985). Curriculum and the Morality of Aesthetics. 6:3, 66-83.

Stone, Joan B. (1979). Structures and Systems. 1:2, 37-45.

Stout, O. Hugh. (1995). African-American Spirituality. 11:2, 49-68.

Sturges, A.W. (1981). Assessing Ideologies. 3:1, 117-123.

Sumara, Dennis J. (1993). Of Seagulls and Glass Roses: Teachers' Relationships with Literary Texts as Transformational Space. 10:3, 153-182.

Swartz, Ellen. (1992). Cultural Diversity and the School Curriculum: Content and Practice. 9:4, 73-88.

Tardif, Maurice. See Gauthier, Clermont & Maurice Tardif. (1995).

Taubman, Peter M. (1982). Gender and Curriculum: Discourse and the Politics of Sexuality. 4:1, 12-87.

_____. (1992). Canonical Sins. 9:4, 7-28.

Taylor, Philip H. (1982). Metaphor and Meaning in the Curriculum: On Opening Windows on the Not Yet Seen. 4:1, 209-216.

Thayer-Bacon, Barbara. (1995). Wait a Minute, Please! or Why People Have Children. 11:1, 129-142.

Tucker, Mary Evelyn. (1995). Educating Eco-logically. 10:4, 67-82.

Tyler, Ralph W. See Schubert, William H., George Willis, Helen Simons, Beverley Labbett, John Elliott, Barry MacDonald, Ralph W. Tyler, and Ernest R. House. (1995).

Uhrmacher, P. Bruce. (1989). Visions and Versions of Life in Classrooms. 9:1, 107-116.

Vandenberg, Brian. (1979). Play as Curriculum. 1:2, 229-237.

van Manen, Max. (1979). Objective Inquiry into the Structures of Subjectivity. 1:1, 44-64.

_____. (1980). An Interview with a Dutch Pedagogue. 2:2, 68-72.

Vinz, Ruth. (1996). Horrorscapes (In)forming Adolescent Identity and Desire. 12:4, 14-26.

Wallenstein, Sandra. (1979). Notes Toward a Feminist Curriculum Theory. 1:1, 186-190.

_____. (1980). Images of the Evolving Curriculum. 2:2, 269-273.

Wallerstein, Nina. (1988). Interdisciplinary Approaches to Paulo Freire's Educational Theory. 8:4, 53-68.

Walsh, Susan. See Luce-Kapler, Rebecca & Susan Walsh. (1996).

Wankowski, Kanek & William Reid. (1982). The Psychology of Curriculum Theorizing: A Conversation. 4:2, 112-131.

Watras, Joseph. (1983). Problems in Multi-Cultural Education: The Textbook Controversy in Kanawha County, West Virginia. 5:1, 4-16.

Waxman, Hersholt C. See Iverson, Barbara & Hersholt C Waxman. (1981).

Wear, Delese. (1997). On Making Spectacles of Ourselves: Resisting the Medicalized Body. 4:2, 27-31.

Weill, Lawrence V. (1992). The Primacy of the Bachelardian Image in the Arts and Humanities. 9:3, 97-121.

_____. (1995). Images in the Arts and Humanities: Ontology and Higher Education. 10:1, 7-16.

Weingarten, Ira Marc. See Gordon, Marshall & Ira Marc Weingarten. (1979).

Werner, Walt. (1987). The Text and Tradition of an Interpretive Pedagogy. 7:3, 22-33.

Wexler, Philip. (1981). Change: Social, Cultural and Educational. 3:2, 157-164.

_____. (1982). Body and Soul: Sources of Social Change and Strategies of Education. 4:2, 166-180.

White, Kirke. (1980). The Work of Dwayne Huebner: A Summary and Response. 2:2, 73-84.

Whitt, James R. (1981). Social Action, Self Reflection, and Curriculum Theory: Part One. 3:1, 202-210. (Part Two by Michael S. Littleford.)

Williams, Terry Tempest. (1983). Earth and Story: A Revival of Relationships As Shown Through the Navajo Way. 5:4. 38-57.

Willis, George. (1979). Phenomenological Methodologies in Curriculum. 1:1, 65-79.

_____. (1981). A Reconceptualist Perspective on Curriculum Evaluation. 3:1, 185-192.

_____. (1989). Reflections of Performance, Pedagogy, and Parenting. 9:1, 117-124.

_____. See Schubert, William H., George Willis, Helen Simons, Beverley Labbett, John Elliott, Barry MacDonald, Ralph W. Tyler, and Ernest R. House. (1995).

Wolfson, Bernice J. (1985). Preface to a Special Issue of JCT Honoring the Work of James B. Macdonald. 6:3, 3-8.

_____. Closing Remarks. 6:3, 65.

Wood, Diane. (1996). An Inquiry into North American Dream(s). 12:2, 39-43.

Wood, George H. (1987). Education in Appalachia: Power, Powerlessness, and the School Curriculum. 7:4, 27-64.

Wood, James G. (1980). Number and Mathematical Thinking. 2:2, 235-244.

_____. (1983). Curriculum and Change: A Response. 5:2, 104-111.

Yamagishi, Lloyd. See Butt, Richard, Danielle Raymond, & Lloyd Yamagishi. (1987).

Yamagishi, Rochelle, Tweela Houtekamer, Evelyn Goodstriker, & Cynthia Chambers. (1995). Mitakuye Oyasin: Stories of Sacred Relations. 11:4, 75-100.

Yellin, David & J. Randall Koetting. (1988). Literacy Instruction and Children Raised in Poverty: A Theoretical Discussion. 8:4, 101-114.

Yeoman, Elizabeth. (1997). A Critical Incident in Teaching: Racist Discourse and Pedagogical Response. 13:2, 32-35.

Young, Delton W. (1979). Notes toward a Phenomenology of Non-Verbal Communication. 1:2, 78-88.

Zantiotis, Anna. See Smith, Richard & Anna Zantiotis. (1988).

R E V I E W S

Alexander, Kathryn. (1996). Memewars, by Adeena Karasick. 12:2, 46-47.

Anyon, Jean. (1980). Ideology and the Curriculum, by Micael W. Apple. 2:2, 280-282.

Athey, Irene J., Nancy E. Kossan, & Sherri L. Oden. (1979). Human Growth and Development: Wolfson College Lectures. by Bruner and Garton. 1:2, 255-261.

Atwell, Wendy. (1980). Subjective Criticism, by David Bleich. 2:1, 248-251.

Atwell-Vasey, Wendy. (1992). Bitter Milk: Women and Teaching, by Madeleine R. Grumet. 9:4, 105-112.

Bernier, Normand R. (1980). Ideology and the Curriculum, by Micael W. Apple. 2:2, 275-279.

Britzman, Deborah. (1987). Schooling as a Ritual Performance, by Peter McLaren. 7:3, 109-116.

Carlson, Kenneth. (1985). Critical Social Psychology, by Philip Wexler. 6:1. 171-178.

Cherryhomes, Cleo H. (1989). A response to reviews of Power and Criticism: Poststructural Investigations in Education, by Cleo H. Cherryholmes. 9:1, 205-218.

Clandinin, D. Jean. (1985). Terms for Inquiry into Teacher Thinking: The Place for Practical Knowledge and The Elbaz Case. 6:2, 131-149.

Cornbleth, Catherine. (1987). Compelling Belief: The Culture of American Schooling, by Stephen Arons. 7:3, 93-100.

Daspit, Toby. (1997). Curriculum Development in the Postmodern Era, by Patrick Slattery. 13:2, 44-46.

Dolan, Lawrence J. (1982). Evaluating with Validity, by Ernest R. House; Toward Reform of Program Evaluation, by Lee Cronbach and Associates. 4:1, 260-263.

Edelsberg, Chip. (1988). Curriculum Projects & Reports. 8:4, 143-155.

Eisner, Elliot W. (1981). Author's Reply. The Educational Imagination. 3:1, 324-326.

England, David A. (1988). Storm in the Mountains: A Case Study of Censorship, Conflict, and Consciousness, by James Moffett. 8:3, 205-211.

Eraut, Michael. (1981). School-Based Curriculum Development in Britain: A Collection of Case Studies, edited by John Eggleston. 3:2, 232-233.

Falk, Cliff. (1997). "That's funny, you don't look like a teacher", by Sandra Webber and Claudia Mitchell. 13:1, 48-52.

Gajewski, Thomas. (1997). The Brain Opera: Deweyan Occupations for the 21st Century? 13:3, 47-47

Henderson, James. (1988). Power and Criticism: Poststructural Investigations in Education, by Cleo H. Cherryholmes. 8:4, 135-141.

Holly, Grant I. (1980). Subjective Criticism, by David Bleich. 2:1, 252-255.

Johnston, D. Kay. (1992). Bitter Milk: Women and Teaching, by Madeleine R. Grumet. 9:4, 113-118.

King, Nancy R. (1982). Toward Wholeness: Rudolf Steiner Education in America, by M.C. Richards. 4:1, 257-259.

Klohr, Paul R. (1981). Curriculum Books: The First Eighty Years, by William Henry Schubert. 3:2, 229-231.

Kossan, Nancy E. See Athey, Irene J., Nancy E. Kossan, & Sherri L. Oden. (1979).

Lacey, Catherine A. (1992). Bitter Milk: Women and Teaching, by Madeleine R. Grumet. 9:4, 119-128.

Lankowski, Carl. (1982). The Poverty of Theory and Other Essays, by E.P. Thompson; Arguments with English Marxism, by Perry Anderson; Marx's 'Capital' and Capitalism Today, by Anthony Cutler, Barry Hindess, Paul Hirst, & Athar Hussain. 4:1, 264-272.

Lather, Patti. (1988). Power and Criticism: Poststructural Investigations in Education, by Cleo H. Cherryholmes. 8:4, 127-134.

Levin, Malcolm A. (1980). The Educational Imagination, by Elliot Eisner. 2:2, 286-288.

Linn, Max. (1996). The Cat in the Hat, by Dr. Seuss. 12:3, 52.

Littleford, Michael S. (1982). Soldiers of Light and Love, by Jacqueline Jones. 4:2, 236-241.

Miller, Janet L. (1980). Landscapes of Learning, by Maxine Greene. 2:1, 271-272.

Molnar, Alex. (1981). Thinking about Curriculum, by William A. Reid. 3:1, 321-323.

O'Brien, Mary. (1986). Is Mother Love Morality? 6:4, 177-182.

Oden, Sherri L. See Athey, Irene J., Nancy E. Kossan, & Sherri L. Oden. (1979).

Pagano, Jo Anne. (1980). Landscapes of Learning, by Maxine Greene. 2:1, 273-277.

Purpel, David E. (1980). Subjective Criticism, by David Bleich. 2:1, 265-270.

Rasberry, Gary. (1996). Wildmind, by Natalie Goldberg. 12:1, 52-54.

Scanlon, Patrick. (1986). Beating the Man with Words. 6:4, 172-176.

Schwartz, Jr., John J. (1979). The Social and Educational Thought of Harold Rugg, by Carbone. 1:1, 258-261.

Simon, Roger. (1980). Subjective Criticism, by David Bleich. 2:1, 256-264.

Stone, Joan. (1980). The Educational Imagination, by Elliot Eisner. 2:2, 283-285.

Sullivan, Edmund V. (1985). Critical Social Psychology, by Philip Wexler. 6:1, 165-170.

Swoboda, Debra. (1985). Critical Social Psychology, by Philip Wexler. 6:1, 179-183.

Taubman, Peter M. (1996). To the Lighthouse and Back: Writings on Teaching and Living, by Mary Aswell Doll. 12:4, 52-55.

Teitelbaum, Kenneth. (1981). Critical Teaching and Everyday Life, by Ira Shor. 3:1, 313-317.

Thornton, Stephen J. (1987). The Shopping Mall High School, by Powell, Farrar, & Cohen. 7:1, 222-228.

Watras, Joseph. (1988). Storm in the Mountains: A Case Study of Censorship, Conflict, and Consciousness, by James Moffett. 8:3, 212-217.

Whitson, James Anthony. (1987). Compelling Belief: The Culture of American Schooling, by Stephen Arons. 7:3, 101-108.

Willis, George. (1981). Thinking about Curriculum, by William A. Reid. 3:1, 318-320.

Yates, Lyn. (1985). Case Study and Problems of the Practical. 6:2, 122-130.

Zaret, Esther. (1981). Critical Teaching and Everyday Life, by Ira Shor. 3:1, 310-312.

P O E T R Y   A N D   L I T E R A R Y
A N T H R O P O L O G I E S

Alexander, Kathryn. (1997). Every Autumn. 13:3, 43.

_____. (1997). Pacific Currents Carry Aggie. 13:3, 44.

_____. (1997). Your Wedding Ring. 13:3, 44.

Almon, Bert. (1996). Covered with a While Cloth the Grail Enters the Chapel Perilous. 12:2, 44.

_____. (1996). The King George Hotel. 12:2, 45.

_____. (1996). Seven Learn Years Eat Seven Fat. 12:2, 45.

_____. (1996). Talking about Poetry at the Provincial Jail. 12:2, 44.

Hood, Marian R. (1996). Sarah. 12:3, 51.

_____. (1996). Thinking. 12:3, 50.

_____. (1996). When You Begin to Write. 12:3, 50.

Luce-Kapler, Rebecca. (1997). Fields of Poetry: Approaching the Poem (Part 1 of 2). 13:1, 45-47.

Milner, Edward W. (1980). Airlie: Sacrality, Paradigms and the AXIS MUNDI. 2:2, 274.

_____. (1981). Airlie: The Ontological Bridge. 3:2, 228.

_____. (1982). Airlie, 1981. 4:1, 208.

_____. (1982). A Full Curriculum for the Gifted Handicapped. 4:2, 216-227.

Norman, Renee. (1997). Spectrum. 13:3, 45.

_____. Healing the Split Subject. 13:3, 46.

Perreault, George. (1996). Going Home from the Clinic. 12:4. 51.

_____. (1996). Gypsies. 12:4, 50.

_____. (1996). Learning to Drive. 12:4, 50.

_____. (1996). The Words We Use. 12:4, 51.

Sobat, Gail Sidonie. (1996). The Cunning Linguist. 12:1, 51.

_____. (1996). right angles. 12:1, 50.

_____. (1996). Tubercular Desire. 12:1, 51.

_____. (1996). womanfruit. 12:1, 50.

Sterling, Colin. (1997) Graceland. 13:2, 5-10.

Swartz, Ronald. (1987). Johnny Dodd Rides Again. 7:3, 120-121.
Walsh, Susan. (1996). Waiting spaces for words. 12:4, 48-49.

V

Members of the Board of Advising Editors
Past and Present

Ted Aoki (1981-1990)
Mary Aswell Doll (1996-1999)
Robin Barrow (1995-1998)
Leonard Berk (1980-1988)
Alan Block (1996-1999)
Deborah Britzman (1992-1998)
Eric Burt (1985-1988)
Dennis Carlson (1992-2000)
Lewis Castenell, Jr. (1989-1990)
Cleo Cherryholmes (1989-1994)
Russell H. Coward, Jr. (1979-1981)
Jacques Daignault (1983-1990)
James DiGiambattista (1980-1981)
Lawrence J. Dolan (1980-1981)
Elizabeth Ellsworth (1989-1998)
Clermont Gauthier (1983-1989)
Marshall Gordon (1979)
Brenda Hatfield (1989-1994)
Dorothy Huenecke (1980-1989)
Ken Jacknicke (1985-1991)
Kay Johnston (1989-1994)
Thomas Kelly (1985-1991)
Kathleen Kesson (1996-1999)
Paul R. Klohr (1979-1989)
Craig Kridel (1979-1992)
Nancy Lesko (1993-2000)
Michael Littleford (1980-1985)
Cameron McCarthy (1989-1994)
Anthony Molina (1989-1994)
Joe Norris (1995-1997)
Robert L. Osborne (1980)
Jo Anne Pagano (1987-1992)
Frances Rains (1996-1999)

Michael W. Apple (1979-1990)
Judith Morris Ayers (1980-1983)
Charles W. Beegle (1979-1989)
Landon E. Beyer
(1985-1990, 1992-2000)
Leslie Bloom (1996-1999)
Robert V. Bullough, Jr. (1979-1990)
Richard Butt (1981-1983)
Terrance Carson (1989-1997)
Cynthia Chambers (1995-1998)
Leigh Chiarelott (1983)
Warren Crichlow (1989-1994)
Sonja Darlington (1996-1999)
George Dixon (1980-1981)
William E. Doll Jr. (1980-1990)
Barry M. Franklin (1980-1983)
Henry A. Giroux (1980-1989)
Madeleine R. Grumet
(1979, 1988-1991, 1995-1998)
Richard Hawthorne (1979-1981)
Wen Song Hwu (1995-1997)
David Jardine (1995-1997)
Ellis Joseph (1995-1997)
June Kern (1987-1988)
Joe L. Kincheloe (1995-1998)
Florence R. Krall (1980-1991)
Eleanore E. Larson (1980-1983)
Magda Lewis (1997-2000)
James B. Macdonald (1979-1983)
Bonnie Meath-Lang (1985-1992)
Alex Molnar (1979-1981)
Donald Oliver (1989-1994)
Ronald E. Padgham (1979-1988)

Meredith Reiniger (1983-1992)
Jose Rosario (1979-1983)
William H. Schubert (1988-1993)
Paul Shaker (1979-1993)
Patrick Slattery (1989-1994)
G.W. Stansbury (1980-1989)
Joan Stone (1983-1996)
Peter M. Taubman
(1980-1983, 1989-1994)
Max van Manen (1979-1989)
Joseph Watras (1983)
Philip Wexler (1980-1989)
David C. Williams (1979-1981)
George Willis (1979-1983)
John Willinsky (1995-1998)

George J. Posner (1979-1983)
William A. Reid (1980-1983)
Timothy Riordan (1979)
Paula Salvio (1995-1997)
James Sears (1985-1993)
Francine Shuchat-Shaw
(1979-1981, 1983)
David G. Smith (1995-1997)
Shirley Steinberg (1995-1998)
Jeanne Sullivan (1988-1993)
Wayne J. Urban (1979-1981)
Sandra Wallenstein (1979-1989)
Delese Wear (1996-1999)
James Anthony Whitson (1992-1996)
Jim Wood (1992-1993)

V I

Editors, Guest Editors, and Editors' Notes

Carson, Terrance R. (1995). A Teacher of Influence (Guest Introduction to the Special Issue: Recent Recipients of The JCT Annual Aoki Award). 11:4, 7-10.

Doll, William. (1995). The Loyola Spirituality Conference (Guest Editor's Notes to the special issue, Essays from "The Loyola Spirituality Conference"). 11:2, 7-12.

Pagano, Jo Anne. (1989). Editor's Note. 9:1, 6.

_____. (1989). Editor's Note. 9:2, 6.

_____. (1992). Editor's Note: Visions and Revisions. 9:3, 3-4.

_____. (1992). Editor's Note. 9:4, 3-4.

_____. (1992). Editor's Note. 10:1, 3-4.

_____. (1992). Editor's Note. 10:2, 3-4.

_____. (1993). Editor's Notes. 10:3, 3-6.

Pinar, William F. (1979). Editor's Note. 1:1, 5.

_____. (1979). Editorial Statement. 1:1, 6-9.

_____. (1979). Editor's Note. 1:2, 4.

_____. (1980). Editor's Note. 2:1, 6.

_____. (1980). Editor's Note. 2:2, 4.

_____. (1981). Editor's Note. 3:1, 4.

_____. (1982). Editor's Note. 4:1, 4.

_____. (1982). Editor's Note. 4:2, 4.

_____. (1983). Editor's Note. 5:1, 3.

_____. (1995). Editor's Note. 11:1, 6.

Reynolds, William M. (1987). Editor's Note. 7:1, 6.

_____. Editor's Note. 7:2, 6.

_____. Editor's Note. 7:3, 6.

_____. Editor's Note. 7:4, 6.

_____. (1988). Editor's Note. 8:1, 6.

_____. (1988). Editor's Note. 8:2, 6.

_____. (1988). Editor's Note. 8:3, 6.

_____. (1988). Editor's Note. 8:4, 6.

Salvio, Paula. (1996). Guest Editor's Notes: Reading and the Politics of Identity. 12:4, 2-6.

Smith, David Geoffrey. (1997). Guest Editor's Notes: The Geography of Theory and the Pedagogy of Place. 13:3, 2-4.

Sumara, Dennis J. & Brent Davis. (1996). Editors' Notes. 12:1. 2-5.

_____. (1996). Editors' Notes. 12:2, 2-3.

_____. (1996). Editors' Notes: Pedagogies of Worry/Worries of Pedagogy. 12:3, 2-5.

_____. (1997). Editors' Notes: The Work of Interpretation. 13:1, 2-5.

_____. (1997). Editors' Notes: History, Memory, Curriculum. 13:2, 2-4.

V I I

Editors

Volume 1 (1979)
  Editor: William F. Pinar
  Managing Editor: Janet L. Miller

Volume 2 (1980)
  Editor: William F. Pinar
  Managing Editor: Janet L. Miller
  Book Review Editor: Madeleine R. Grumet
  Editorial Assistant: Peter M. Taubman

Volume 3 (1981)
  Editor: William F. Pinar
  Managing Editor: Janet L. Miller
  Book Review Editor: Madeleine R. Grumet
  Editorial Assitants: Nancy A. Fruchtman, Emily J. Moskowitz

Volume 4 (1982)
  Editor: William F. Pinar
  Managing Editor: Janet L. Miller
  Book Review Editor: Madeleine R. Grumet
  Associate Editor: Francine Shuchat Shaw

Volume 5 (1983)
  Editor: William F. Pinar
  Managing Editor: Janet L. Miller
  Book Review Editor: Madeleine R. Grumet
  Associate Editor: Francine Shuchat Shaw (5:1 & 5:2)
  Assistant Editors: William Reynolds (5:3 & 5:4),
              Joseph Watras (5:3 & 5:4)

Volume 6 (1985-1986)
  Editor: William F. Pinar (6:1 & 6:3), Janet L. Miller (6:2),
      William Reynolds (6:4)
  Managing Editor: Janet L. Miller
  Book Review Editor: Madeleine R. Grumet

Associate Editors: June Kern (6:2, 6:3, & 6:4), Benjamin
    Troutman (6:2, 6:3, & 6:4)
Assistant Editors: Richard Butt,   Leigh Chiarelott, William
    Reynolds (6:1, 6:2, & 6:3),   Joseph Watras

Volume 7 (1987)
Founding Editor: William F. Pinar
Editor: William M. Reynolds
Managing Editor: Janet L. Miller
Book Review Editor: Madeleine R. Grumet
Associate Editor: Benjamin Troutman
Assistant Editors: Richard Butt, Leigh Chiarelott, Joseph
Watras

Volume 8 (1988)
Founding Editor: William F. Pinar
Editor: William M. Reynolds
Managing Editor: Janet L. Miller
Book Review Editor: James Anthony Whitson
Associate Editor: John T. Holton
Assistant Editors: Richard Butt, Leigh Chiarelott, Joseph
    Watras

Volume 9 (1989-1992)
Founding Editor: William F. Pinar
Editor-in-Chief: Jo Anne Pagano
Editor: William M. Reynolds
Managing Editor: Janet L. Miller
Book Review Editor: James Anthony Whitson
Associate Editor: John T. Holton
Assistant Editors: Richard Butt, Leigh Chiarelott, Joseph
    Watras, Alan A. Block

Volume 10 (1992-1995)
Founding Editor: William F. Pinar
Editor-in-Chief: Jo Anne Pagano
Editor:William M. Reynolds (for 10:1)
Managing Editor: Janet L. Miller
Book Review Editor: James Anthony Whitson (for 10:1—10:3)
Associate Editor: John T. Holton (for 10:1—10:3)
Assistant Editors: Alan A. Block (for 10:1), Richard Butt
    (for 10:1—10:3), Leigh Chiarelott (for 10:1—10:3), Joseph Watras
    (for 10:1—10:3)

Volume 11 (1995)
  Founding Editor: William F. Pinar
  Editors: Dennis J. Sumara, Brent Davis
  Guest Editor: William E. Doll, Jr. (11:2)
  Managing Editor: Janet L. Miller

Volume 12 (1996)
  Founding Editor: William F. Pinar
  Editors: Dennis J. Sumara, Brent Davis
  Guest Editor: Paula Salvio (12:4)
  Managing Editor: Janet L. Miller
  Cultural Product Reviews Editors: Mimi Orner (12:1, 12:2)
      Marla Morris (12:3, 12:4)
  Curriculum Forms Editor: Paula Salvio
  Hermeneutic Portraits Editor: Craig Kridel
  Literary Anthropologies Editor: Rebecca Luce-Kapler

Volume 13 (1997)
  Founding Editor: William F. Pinar
  Editors: Dennis J. Sumara, Brent Davis
  Guest Editor: David G. Smith (13:3)
  Managing Editor: Janet L. Miller
  Cultural Product Reviews Editor: Marla Morris
  Curriculum Forms Editor: Paula Salvio
  Hermeneutic Portraits Editor: Craig Kridel
  Literary Anthropologies Editor: Rebecca Luce-Kapler

SUBJECT INDEX

AUTHOR INDEX

W9-CSG-934

LAKOTA HONOR

Book 1 in the Branded Trilogy

KAT FLANNERY

LAKOTA HONOR
Book 1 in the Branded Trilogy

Copyright © 2013 by Kat Flannery. All Rights Reserved.

No part of this publication may be reproduced, stored in a retrieval system, or transmitted, in any form or by any means, electronic, mechanical, photocopying, recording, or otherwise, without prior written permission from the author.

This is a work of fiction. Names, characters, places and incidents either are the product of the author's imagination or are used fictitiously. And any resemblance to actual persons, living, dead (or in any other form), business establishments, events, or locales is entirely coincidental.

http://www.katflannery-author.com

FIRST EDITION TRADE PAPERBACK

Imajin Books—www.imajinbooks.com

May 30, 2013

ISBN: 978-1-927792-00-1

Cover designed by Ryan Doan - www.ryandoan.com

Praise for LAKOTA HONOR

"For something different, transport back to the old west with this paranormal historical, and its alpha hero, and a heroine hiding her secret talents." —Shannon Donnelly, author of the Mackenzie Solomon Urban Fantasy series

"Ms. Flannery doesn't shy away from writing gritty scenes or about unpleasant topics. In this book, she deals with child labor and abuse, as well as animal abuse, and I simply wanted to reach through the computer screen and kill the awful villain myself, I got so angry. That's what good writing is all about—bringing out strong emotions in a reader. Congratulations on a job well done!" —Peggy L. Henderson, bestselling author of the Yellowstone Romance Series

"Talented, Kat Flannery knows her Native American history and those who relish the conflict of a heroic half-breed trapped between the white man's world and the Indian will fall in love with *LAKOTA HONOR*." —Cindy Nord, award-winning author of *No Greater Glory*

"Kat Flannery's, *LAKOTA HONOR*, weaves a fast paced and beautiful prose that lures you through every chapter and leaves you wanting more. The struggles of the main characters break your heart and leave you rooting for them, for their struggles—although different—are similar at the core." —Erika Knudsen, paranormal author of *Monarchy of Blood*

"*LAKOTA HONOR* by Kat Flannery will hold your attention from beginning to end. Her ability to intertwine good and evil within the confines of the Indian and white worlds is nothing less than inspired. Nora and Hawk come together in a very different, magical way; she as a healer and he as a killer. The ancillary characters are well drawn. You either like them or hate them. You might also wonder about some of them as the story progresses." —Katherine Boyer, romance reviewer

"*LAKOTA HONOR* is a book that leads readers back in time and then invites them to question just how much has really changed. Get comfortable—you're not going to want to put this one down." —Leanne Myggland-Carter, operations manager at Canadian Authors Association-Alberta

For my brother, Joe.

"Each man is good in the sight of the Great Spirit" —Chief Sitting Bull

Acknowledgements

Writing this book was so much fun. I'd like to thank my publisher and friend Cheryl Tardif for planting the seed of a paranormal western in my head. I never would've thought to go there.

Rhonda, my editor, bless you for your patience. Carrie, for the millions of titles you shot my way until we decided on one. Mom and Dad, for letting me bounce ideas around and being my sounding board.

My husband and three sons for again allowing me to work many hours researching and writing this book; I love you.

To my readers, thank you for all your support.

Love,

Kat

PROLOGUE

Colorado Mountains, 1880

The blade slicing his throat made no sound, but the dead body hitting the ground did. With no time to stop, he hurried through the dark tunnel until he reached the ladder leading out of the shaft.

He'd been two hundred feet below ground for ten days, with no food and little water. Weak and woozy, he stared up the ladder. He'd have to climb it and it wasn't going to be easy. He wiped the bloody blade on his torn pants and placed it between his teeth. Scraped knuckles and unwashed hands gripped the wooden rung.

The earth swayed. He closed his eyes and forced the spinning in his head to cease. One thin bronzed leg lifted and came down wobbly. He waited until his leg stopped shaking before he climbed another rung. Each step caused pain, but was paired with determination. He made it to the top faster than he'd thought he would. The sky was black and the air was cool, but fresh. Thank goodness it was fresh.

He took two long breaths before he emerged from the hole. The smell from below ground still lingered in his nostrils; unwashed bodies, feces and mangy rats. His stomach pitched. He tugged at the rope around his hands. There had been no time to chew the thick bands around his wrists when he'd planned his escape. It was better to run than crawl, and he chewed through the strips that bound his feet instead. There would be time to free his wrists later.

He pressed his body against the mountain and inched toward the shack. He frowned. A guard stood at the entrance to where they were. The blade from the knife pinched his lip, cutting the thin skin and he tasted blood. He needed to get in there. He needed to say goodbye. He needed to make a promise.

The tower bell rang mercilessly. There was no time left. He pushed away from the rocky wall, dropped the knife from his mouth into his bound hands, aimed and threw it. The dagger dug into the man's chest. He ran over, pulled the blade from the guard and quickly slid it across his throat. The guard bled out in seconds.

He tapped the barred window on the north side of the dilapidated shack. The time seemed to stretch. He glanced at the large house not fifty yards from where he stood. He would come back, and he would kill the bastard inside.

He tapped again, harder this time, and heard the weak steps of those like him shuffling from inside. The window slid open, and a small hand slipped out.

"Toksha ake—I shall see you again," he whispered in Lakota.

The hand squeezed his once, twice and on the third time held tight before it let go and disappeared inside the room.

A tear slipped from his dark eyes, and his hand, still on the window sill, balled into a fist. He swallowed past the sob and felt the burn in his throat. His chest ached for what he was leaving behind. He would survive, and he would return.

Men shouted to his right, and he crouched down low. He took one last look around and fled into the cover of the forest.

CHAPTER ONE

1888, Willow Creek, Colorado

Nora Rushton scanned the hillside before glancing back at the woman on the ground. She could be dead, or worse yet, someone from town. She flexed her hands. The woman's blue skirt ruffled in the wind, and a tattered brown Stetson sat beside her head. Nora assessed the rest of her attire. A faded yellow blouse stained from the grass and dirt, leather gloves and a red bandana tied loosely around her neck. She resembled a ranch hand in a skirt.

There was no one else around, and the woman needed her help. She chewed on her lip, and her fingers twitched. *I have to help her.* She sucked in a deep breath, held it, and walked the remaining few feet that stood between her and the injured woman.

The woman's horse picked up Nora's scent, trotted over and pushed his nose into her chest.

"It's okay, boy," she said, smoothing back the red-brown mane. "Why don't you let me have a look at your owner?"

She knelt down beside the woman and realized she was old enough to be her grandmother. Gray hair with subtle blonde streaks lay messed and pulled from the bun she was wearing. Why was she on a horse in the middle of the valley without a chaperone?

She licked her finger and placed it under the woman's nose. A cool sensation skittered across her wet finger, and she sighed.

The woman's left leg bent inward and laid uncomfortably to the side. She lifted the skirt for a closer look. Her stomach rolled, and bile crawled up the back of her throat. The thigh bone protruded, stretching the skin bright white, but didn't break through. Nora's hands grew warm, the sensation she felt so many times before.

The woman moaned and reached for her leg.

"No, please don't touch your leg. It's broken." She held the woman's hand.

Ice blue eyes stared back at her, showing pain mingled with relief.

"My name is Nora," she said with a smile. "I am going to get help."

The wrinkled hand squeezed hers, and the woman shook her head. "No, child, my heart can't take the pain much longer." Creased lips pressed together as she closed her eyes and took two deep breaths. "Please, just sit here with me." Her voice was husky and weak.

She scanned the rolling hills for any sign of help, but there was no one. She studied the woman again. Her skin had a blue tinge to it, and her breathing became forced. *I promised Pa.* But how was she supposed to walk away from this woman who so desperately needed her help? She took another look around. Green grass waved in the wind. *Please, someone, anyone come over the hill.*

White daisies mingled within the grass, and had the woman not been injured, she would've plucked a few for her hair. She waited a few minutes longer. No one came. Her hands started their restless shaking. She clasped them together, trying to stop the tremors. *It would only take a few minutes. I can help her. No one would see.* She stared at the old woman, *except her.* If she helped her, would she tell everyone about Nora's secret? Would she ask any questions? *There were always questions.*

Nora's resolve was weakening. She ran her hot hands along the woman's body to see if anything else was broken. Only the leg, thank goodness. Lifting the skirt once again, she laid her warm palms gently on the broken thigh bone. Her hands, bright red, itched with anticipation. The leg seemed worse without the cover of the skirt. One move and the bone would surely break through the skin. She inhaled groaning at the same time as she placed her hands on either side of the limb. In one swift movement, she squeezed the bone together.

The woman shot up from the grass yelling out in agony.

Nora squeezed harder until she felt the bone shift back into place. Jolts of pain raced up and down her arms as the woman's leg began to heal. Nora's own thigh burned and ached, as her bones and flesh cried out in distress. She held on until the pain seeped from her own body into nothingness, vanishing as if it were never there.

She removed her hands, now shaking and cold from the woman's healed limb, unaware of the blue eyes staring up at her. Her stomach lurched, like she knew it would—like it always did afterward. She rose on trembling legs and walked as far away as she could before vomiting onto the bright green grass. Not once, but twice. She waited until her strength returned before she stood and let the wind cool her heated cheeks. The bitter taste stayed in her mouth. If the woman hadn't been there she'd have spit the lingering bile onto the grass. She needed water and searched the area for a stream.

Her mouth felt full of cotton, and she smacked her tongue off of her dry lips. She was desperate for some water. Had she not wandered so far from the forest to set the baby hawk free, she'd know where she was now and which direction would take her home. She gasped. She'd lost track of time and needed to get home before Pa did. Jack Rushton had a temper and she didn't want to witness it tonight.

"Are you an angel?"

She turned to face the woman and grinned. "No, Ma'am. I am not an angel, although I like to think God gave me this gift."

The woman pulled her skirt down, recovered from her shock and said in a rough voice, "Well if you ain't no angel, than what in hell are ya?"

Taken aback at the woman's gruffness, she knelt down beside her. *Here we go, either she understands or she runs away delusional and screaming.* "I...I am a healer." She waited.

The woman said nothing instead she narrowed her eyes and stared. "A witch?"

Nora winced.

"No, not a witch. I need you to promise you won't tell anyone what happened here today." Her stomach in knots, she waited for the old woman's reply.

"You think I'm some kind of fool?" She stood and stretched her leg. She stared at the healed limb before she hopped on it a few times. "People already think I'm crazy. Why would I add more crap to their already heaping pile of shit?"

Oh my. The woman's vocabulary was nothing short of colorful, and she liked it.

She smiled and stuck out her hand. "I'm Nora Rushton. It's nice to meet you."

The woman stared at her for a few seconds before her thin mouth turned up and she smiled. "Jess Chandler." She gripped Nora's hand with such force she had to refrain from yelling out in pain. "Thanks for your help, girly."

"I don't think we've ever met. Do you live in Willow Creek?"

"I own a farm west of here."

"How come I've never seen you?" *I never see anyone, Pa's rules.*

The wind picked up whipping Jess's hat through the air. "Max," she called over her shoulder, "fetch my hat."

The horse's ears spiked and he trotted off toward the hat. She watched in awe as the animal retrieved the Stetson with his mouth and brought it back to his master.

"I've never seen such a thing," Nora giggled and patted Max's rump.

Jess took the hat and slapped it on top of her head.

"Yup, ol'Max here, he's pretty damn smart."

"I'd say he is." She remembered the companionship she'd enjoyed with the baby hawk she'd rescued a few weeks ago. She'd miss the little guy. His feedings had kept her busy during the long boring days at home. "Miss Jess, I'm sorry to be short, but I have to head on home."

"Hell, girly, I can take you." She climbed up onto Max and wound the reins around her gloved hands. "Hop on. He's strong enough for two."

"Are you sure?"

"It's the least I can do."

She clasped Jess's hand and pulled herself up behind her. "Thank you, Jess, for keeping my secret." Placing her arms around the woman's waist, she gave her a light squeeze.

"Darlin," Jess patted Nora's hand, "you can rest assured I will take this secret to my grave." She whistled, and Max started toward town.

Otakatay sat tall on his horse as he gazed at the lush green valley below. The town of Willow Creek was nestled at the edge of the green hills. He'd been gone four round moons, traveling to Wyoming and back. The rough terrain of the Rocky Mountains had almost killed him and his horse. The steep cliffs and forests were untouched by man.

On the first day in the Rockies, he'd come up against a mountain lion, a grizzly and bush thick enough to strangle him. He used his knife to carve into the dense brush, and his shotgun to defend himself. When he could, he stuck to the deer trails, and in the evening built large fires to keep the animals at bay.

He glanced behind him at the brown sack tied to his saddle. Inside, there were three. This time he'd ask for more money. His bronzed jaw flexed. He would demand it.

The sky was bright blue with smudges of gray smoke wafting upward from the homes and businesses. The weather would warm as the day progressed and the sun rose higher into the sky. His eyes wandered past the hills to the mountains behind them, and his insides burned.

He clicked his tongue, and his mustang sauntered down the hill. Wakina was agile and strong. Otakatay knew he could count on him always. Over the years Wakina had kept pace with his schedule and relentless hunting. The emerald stocks swayed and danced before him as he rode through. The grass brushed the bottoms of his moccasins, and he dunked his hand into the velvety green weed. He'd make camp in the forest outside of the mining town.

Wakina shook his head and whinnied. Otakatay brushed his hand along the length of his silver mane.

"Soon my friend, soon," he whispered.

The animal wanted to run down into the valley, but resigned himself to the lethargic pace his master ordered. Wakina tossed his head.

Otakatay slapped Wakina's sides with the loose ends of the reins, and the horse took off down the hill clearing a path through the grass.

The rolling blanket of emerald parted as Wakina's long legs cantered toward the forest. Otakatay's shoulder-length black hair whipped his face and tickled his neck as his heart pounded lively inside his chest. It was rare that he felt so alive. His days consisted of planning and plotting until he knew every detail by heart. The eagle feather tied to his hair lifted in the wind and soared high above his head. For a moment he allowed himself to close his eyes and enjoy the smells of wildflowers and wood smoke. The sun kissed his cheeks and he tried to hold onto the moment, savoring the last bit of calm before rotten flesh and wet fur filled his nostrils.

His eyes sprung open. He pulled on the reins, and rubbed his nose to rid the smell, to push out the visions that saturated his mind. The scent clung to him burrowing deep into his soul and he mentally fought to purge it from his consciousness. He shook his head and concentrated on the fields, trying to push the memories away. He didn't want to do this, not now. He didn't want to see, feel, smell, or taste the memory again.

The rhythmic clanking echoed inside his head, and he squeezed his eyes closed. Sweat trickled down his temples. He clenched every muscle in his body. His hands skimmed the jagged walls of the damp tunnel. He stumbled and fell onto the rough walls, burning his torn flesh. He moaned. Every bit of him ached with such pain, he was sure he'd die. His thin body shook with fever. He reeked of blood, sweat and fear.

With each step he took, he struggled to stay upright and almost collapsed onto the ground. The agony of his wounds blinded him, and he didn't know if it was a combination of the sweat dripping into his eyes, or if he was crying from the intense pain. His back burned and pulsed with powerful beats, the skin became tight around his ribs as the flesh swelled.

He tripped on a large rock and fell to the ground. The skin on his knees tore open, but he didn't care. Nothing could ease the screaming in his back. Nothing could take away the hell he lived every day. He laid his head against the dirt covered floor. Dust stuck to his cheeks and lips while he prayed for Wakan Tanka to end his life.

CHAPTER TWO

The full moon brightened Otakatay's path into town. He'd been to Willow Creek before and knew the streets well. He stretched and accidently kicked the brown sack hanging from his saddle. He never looked inside the bag. Even when he'd shoved the contents inside, he closed his eyes.

He pulled his duster back around him. Although half Sioux, he chose to wear the white man's clothing. It allowed him to move about towns and be discreet. But he never took the eagle feather from his hair and he always wore it down, acting as a mask of sorts it shadowed his features from any prying eyes.

He tugged on the left rein and rode past the jailhouse. Inside the barred windows, a musty office displayed wanted posters for murderers, men who killed for greed and lust. Men like Gabe Fowler, wanted for the slaughter of three children and their parents outside of Rapid City, and Leroy Black, a bank robber who killed anyone that stood in his way. Men he'd hunted and destroyed.

It didn't matter to him if they were wanted dead or alive. Most times he brought them in slung over Wakina's back. It was easier that way. He'd learned long ago never to turn his back on the men he sought. A dead outlaw was better than a wounded one. He helped capture the worst kind of men—men like him.

He was a slayer of men and women—ruthless and unforgiving. He was Otakatay, one who kills many. A bounty hunter that killed men that needed killing. He received good money for the lives he stole. He had a purpose, a reason for ending their lives and nothing would stand in his way. Killing was what he did, and it had never bothered him until two years ago when he took this job. Now he preyed on something else. Now he killed innocent women.

He went from being a bounty hunter to a murderer. No better than the criminals he'd dumped at the sheriff's feet. The bitter taste of his transgressions tainted his mouth, making it hard to swallow. He spat, remembered his promise and justified his actions. There was no time for pity. No time to remember the way he was. He would never be those things again. He was evil. He was a nightmare come to life. He was death.

His horse trotted down the street. All the stores were locked up for the evening. Houses black, their residents fast asleep. He glared at the homes of the white eyes. He despised them. A half breed, he wasn't given the same rights as the wasichu.

He was not wanted in the white or red race. His village long ago disowned his family casting them from their tribe. Two years ago, the government had ordered all natives onto reserved land. He didn't even know where his people were and he didn't care. They'd shunned them, cast them into the world of the white man to be ridiculed and treated no better than a dog.

He was alone. He depended on no one and he liked it that way.

He led Wakina into the forest to the clearing by the river. There he dismounted and waited for the wasichu to arrive. A half hour later he heard branches cracking. He leaned against his horse's side and waited for the white man to appear.

"You're early," the wasichu said. "Did anyone see you?"

"No one saw me."

The man lit a cigar, and the sweet aroma puffed in a cloud above his head. "Well, did you bring them?"

He grabbed the bag and flung it at the wasichu.

"There are only three in here. You've been gone almost four months and you only found three?"

"I have other jobs."

"I don't care if you have fifty jobs, you do mine first." He held up the bag. "This comes before anything else."

"You got what you wanted."

"There should be more in here."

Otakatay shrugged.

"No more jobs until you've killed them all."

"I take orders from no one," he growled.

"You work for me, and I want my job done first. Do you hear me, breed?"

It was the name he'd been called since he was young. The name that separated him from any other race. He gnashed his teeth, and stepped forward, ready to kill the bastard with the tailored vest and pressed pants. Otakatay's hand pressed into the man's throat, squeezing he lifted him until his toes touched the ground.

"You will call me Otakatay," he snarled and squeezed some more.

"Or you will call me nothing at all."

The wasichu's face turned red. His mouth opened and closed, trying to suck in air.

Otakatay released him and watched as he fell to the ground gasping. His knife, sheathed to his side, poked his hip. The wasichu would die, but not until he had all he needed from him.

"Where's my money?"

The man stood, while rubbing his neck. He reached inside the pocket of his dress shirt and pulled out a roll of bills.

Otakatay ripped the greenbacks from his hand and counted them. "You owe more."

"Are you absurd? I've already given you way more than you're worth."

"No, white man, you owe more."

"I've given what is owed."

The arrogant fool wasn't backing down. But that would change. Otakatay would get what was owed to him.

"The price went up."

The wasichu swung the sack against his pant leg. The rhythmic sound brought back memories of his Ina as she'd sit around their cooking fire, tanning and raking the hide of a deer. He shook his head.

"You charged more last time."

"I kill women." He stepped forward, towering over the man.

"You've always killed women." He held up the bag. "*They* are all women."

He hung his head. He battled with the guilt over what he'd done. He never looked into their eyes. Never heard their voices—never saw their faces. From behind he slit their throats and took their lives.

"More."

"No!"

Otakatay stepped forward glaring. "You will pay."

"And if I don't?"

"You will die."

The wasichu's brow furrowed and his lips formed a thin line.

He waited.

The wasichu pulled out a twenty dollar bill and slapped it against Otakatay's hard chest. "You better find me more than three next time. They must be repopulating. What about children?"

He tore the money from the man's hand and gave him a shove.

"I do not kill children." He would kill this man and enjoy doing it. "The numbers have dwindled. There are few left."

"I don't give a damn if there's one left. You will find her and you will kill her."

He placed the money in the waistband of his denims. He'd been doing business with this jack ass for two years, and he was getting tired of the white eyes. Tired of the nightmares his duties caused. But he needed the money, and he'd made a promise.

"When will you return?"

"I will stay around here for a while."

He strode up to Otakatay. "No. You will leave. I can't chance someone seeing you."

He smiled. A toxic smirk with no sincerity attached to it. "I do what I want."

"No. You do what I damned well tell you."

He pulled the knife so fast the wasichu didn't know what was happening until it pinched his throat. "I'm beginning to think you have no brains, white man. No one tells me what to do."

He gulped and nodded.

I should kill this ass right now. As much as he longed to drive his knife into the wasichu's heart, he needed him for a little while longer. He put his knife back in its sheath.

The man walked to the river and dumped the bag's contents. "Contact me when there are more."

Otakatay watched him leave. By the next round moon, he would slide his knife across the wasichu's throat.

CHAPTER THREE

Nora waited an hour after lunch before slipping out her bedroom window. Father hadn't come home for the now dried and unappealing sandwiches she'd made. She knew she had time to sneak into the forest. She followed the path behind the stores so no one would see her. The day was hot for the beginning of May. Flies buzzed in front of her and she sidestepped so she didn't run smack into them.

The back door to the Mercantile was open, and she heard the owners, Willimena and Fred Sutherland, bickering. She didn't know them well, but from the few times she'd been allowed to go inside the clean, organized store, that's all they seemed to do.

Willimena, everyone called her Willy, was a large woman with a boisterous voice. Fred was short and slight with a bald spot on top of his head. It was clear to Nora from the first day she went into the store that Willy made all the rules. There was no credit allowed, except for the doctor of course. However, Fred was known to give candy sticks to the children who came into the establishment.

She picked up her pace, longing for the cover of the forest. She felt safe there. She loved to listen to the birds and watch the deer while she sat and reflected on her life, which would be easier if she didn't heal anyone. She knew this, but she couldn't turn a blind eye to those in need. God had given her the gift to heal wounds and save lives. To waste such a gift was immoral.

On the other hand, Pa might trust her, and she'd be like everyone else. She frowned. But how was she supposed to walk away from someone who was injured? How could she stare into the eyes of a person in pain, knowing she could help? *I can't.*

Jess Chandler had been hurt. The old woman would've died had Nora not healed her. Yet, her father refused to understand this. He saw the danger her gift caused and kept her locked up in the house all day.

She was like a bird in a cage, longing to spread her wings and fly. To be free.

Pa had become distant and spent most of his free time at the saloon. She feared he'd begun to resent her for the life they lived. She couldn't blame him. It wasn't easy moving all of the time, or the constant worry he felt when she'd used her power to heal someone. She closed her eyes.

Pa's tirades were justified. He'd stomp around and yell at her for putting her life in danger while throwing their meager belongings into bags. It was a scene she'd witnessed many times. Even though she wanted to argue, she always went along with him. She could never leave him, not after everything he'd done for her.

The long days on dirt roads, sometimes not even on a road, had worn on pa. She could see that now. Once a handsome man, his face now bore creases and sharp edges. His dark blue eyes seldom reflected the happiness she used to see in them as a child, instead they were bloodshot from the horrible habit he'd formed. When he looked at her, all she saw was anger and bitterness.

She sighed. She loved him. He'd always been there for her. Even though he was over bearing and demanded she live confined to his rules, her love for him would never change.

The elm trees rustled their leaves, welcoming her as she entered the thick woods. *I will make him see he can trust me.* She walked with a spring in her step, determined to work on this problem with Pa.

She made her way to the clearing by the river, her favorite spot. Water swished as it rushed by. Crickets chirped in the distance, and the birds whistled up above. She sat on a large rock and inhaled the air around her. Dirt, water, the musky scent of the spruce trees and the pungent smell of fish surrounded her.

She slipped off her boots and peeled off her stockings. She dipped a toe into the cold water, scrunched her face and dunked her whole foot in. Hands clenched at her sides, she waited for the shock to wear off and her muscles to relax before she put the other foot in. She giggled as the water rushed between her toes. Nora kicked her feet and splashed water onto her skirt. She could sit here all day.

A horse whinnied nearby, and she glanced across the river to try and catch a glimpse of the animal. She held her breath, when she saw a man standing amongst the trees. Branches rested on his wide shoulders. He was tall. A black duster hung to his shins. She squinted against the sun's rays to try and see his face. The Stetson he wore was pulled down low so she could only make out a square jaw and long black hair.

Nora slowly released the breath she'd been holding without taking her eyes from him. She pulled her feet from the water and sat up taller to get a better look. If she didn't know any better, she'd say he was glaring at her from across the river. She shivered. He didn't seem friendly that was sure. In fact he looked like an outlaw. Determined to stay where she was and not scare off, Nora held her position.

Her bottom slipped down the back of the rock, and she reached out to stop herself from falling onto the ground. Minutes passed while she righted herself, when she looked up, he was gone.

She searched the outline of the trees for the stranger and saw nothing. The hair on her neck stood, and she touched her feet to the mossy ground.

The sound of breaking branches startled her and she froze. *The stranger.* She stared straight ahead. Her hands balled into tight fists as she waited for whoever stood behind her to make themselves known.

"Afternoon, Miss Rushton."

The voice seemed pleasant and somehow familiar. She searched her mind for anyone with the clipped tone and southern drawl. One face came to mind, Doctor Spencer's. She listened to his long strides as he came closer and stood beside her.

She glanced up at him from her log. "Hello, Doctor."

"Miss Rushton." He tipped his round hat. "You shouldn't be in the forest alone. With the mine nearby, you never know who might be passing through Willow Creek."

She thought of the stranger. Doctor Spencer was right. She'd seen the men that sauntered in from the mountain. One man in particular disgusted her. Elwood Calhoun owned the mine and had taken an interest in Nora. He'd come to call several times, even though Pa or she had turned him down.

"Come on, I'll walk you home," Doctor Spencer said and offered her his hand.

On the few occasions she'd seen the doctor, the elderly man had always been kind to her. She sighed. She didn't want to leave the forest, she'd just gotten here, but rather than tell the doctor about her troubles, she put her stockings and boots back on and took his hand.

"Thank you, but I can find my way home, Sir."

He chuckled.

"Well, that may be, but I'm headed into town so we may as well keep each other company."

Even though she liked the doctor, she wanted to walk home alone. She was a strong individual but, fighting with Pa was a losing battle.

She scanned the countryside as they made their way out of the forest. Colors melted into one another as brown, green and orange smeared across a canvas of swaying stalks. She'd give anything to be able to run through them right now. She wanted to live without restraints. She wanted to stomp her foot and demand her father see her for the woman she was.

The doctor's long strides had her taking two steps to his one to keep up. He smiled as they walked into the street. Nora froze. She always went around back and crawled in her bedroom window.

He stopped also and gazed at her with kind brown eyes.

"Everything okay, dear?"

"Yes, yes. Everything is fine."

She smiled.

"I have to attend to some business at the Mcaffery home. Seems little Billy has broken his arm and I need to check on it. You'll be okay?"

"Of course. Thank you for accompanying me into town."

He nodded while taking out his pocket watch. "Very well." He glanced at the time. "Good day, Miss Rushton."

"Good day, Doctor."

She scooted toward home the back way, passing by Sheriff Reid.

She tipped her head and continued walking. She liked the Sheriff, but couldn't afford to stop and talk. Pa could venture out for a walk and see her. She glanced back into the forest. She'd never seen the stranger in the woods before, and her curiosity was champing at the bit to find out who he was. Why was he in Willow Creek, and why had he stared at her for so long?

"Miss Rushton." Sheriff Reid tipped his hat. "How are you this fine day?"

Damn it. "I am well, Sheriff." She took a step but he blocked her path.

She craned her neck to stare up at him. He had a square chin with a dimple in its center and was clean shaven. The sheriff was Pa's age, but that didn't stop her from thinking he was handsome. She'd bet in his younger years he'd broken a few hearts.

She inhaled and could smell the hint of cigar on him. She felt sorry for the lawman. His wife had died a year ago of pneumonia. They'd had no children, and she wondered if he regretted it now that he was all alone. She liked him, even if the town gossips thought he drank too much. She never took to gossip, and in her judgment he was a good man.

She fidgeted with her hands.

"Are you all right, Miss Rushton?"

He missed nothing. "Yes, yes I'm fine. Anxious to get home is all." Her insides tightened, and she pivoted on her heel. "Good day, Sheriff."

He didn't move.

She tapped her foot and peered around him toward the blacksmiths.

"I know you moved here last year, and Willow Creek is pretty quiet but you shouldn't wander into the forest by yourself."

Odd, first the doctor and now the sheriff was warning her to be careful? Did this have something to do with the man she'd seen earlier? Maybe he was an outlaw. His attire did fit the bill if the dime novels she'd been reading held any truth to them.

"I'd been thinking on talking to Jack about it, too."

Nora's breath caught in her throat. She pulled her gaze from the blacksmiths to stare up at the sheriff. She didn't know what to say without giving away that she wasn't allowed anywhere past the yard. If he told Pa she'd be in hot water.

"I'll do right to remember that. Thank you, Sheriff." She smiled and willed him to step aside so she could get home.

"If it's just the same, I'll walk you home and speak with Jack." He headed in the direction of the blacksmiths.

He was relentless. *Damn it. What in hell am I going to do now?*

Father wasn't going to be happy. She frowned. She didn't want to move again and that was always the outcome when Pa felt like things were beyond his control. Her shoulders slumped. She had to figure a way out of this. She had to stop the sheriff.

"Um, Sheriff Reid." She paused, unsure what to say next. "Thank you for your concern, however I am an adult and my father has no say over where I go during the day." *Seem convincing. This is my one shot.*

"Is that so?" he said and gave her a long look.

She tipped her chin up and nodded.

Their pleasant conversation had shifted to an uncomfortable silence, and she knew it was now or never.

"Thank you again, Sheriff, but I think I will walk the rest of the way on my own."

He stopped and glanced down at her. His eyes held a hint of sadness while they gazed into Nora's. "Good day to you," he said. His gun belt sat low on his hips and hugged his backside as he walked away.

He missed his wife. She'd seen the loneliness in his eyes. Understanding settled like a rock in her stomach. She knew what it was like to be alone and wish for someone to talk to—someone to confide in. She turned toward home and came within inches of being trampled by two horses pulling a fancy black wagon.

Would this day ever end?

She jumped out of the way, lost her balance and landed face first in a puddle. Mud caked the front of her dress and hung from the skirt. She pulled herself up and smacked her hands on the ruined dress. She licked her lips and regretted it the instant she tasted the mud. Nora ran her arm along her mouth. *I just want to go home.* She lifted her head to apologize to the driver for getting in his way. When she recognized him and cringed.

The wagon stopped.

"Miss Rushton." Clean white teeth smiled down at her. "You should be more careful. I'd hate to hit a pretty little thing like yourself."

She didn't want to talk to Elwood Calhoun. She didn't want to be anywhere near him. The black wolf dog tied to the wagon growled, and she stepped back. The mud-soaked dress clung to her legs making it difficult for her to move.

"Sorry," she called and turned from the mangy dog and his owner. *Keep walking.*

"Miss Nora, Miss Nora." The voice stopped her. *Joe.*

Elwood came into town once a month. Always clean shaven and dressed in the latest fashion, he boasted of the coal he got from the mountain. He was very well-to-do and flaunted his money in the saloon while gambling. His son Joe was what folks called simple. Born a cripple, he got around with thick wooden sticks that he leaned into and used as legs. Nora had seen him a few months back waiting outside the bank for his father. She was drawn to the kind boy and every time he was in town she'd made an effort to talk with him.

"Hi Joe," she said.

"I brought my cards. I brought my cards." He held up a stack of blue playing cards. "We can play old man, old man."

She smiled up at him.

"It's Old Maid, Joe," Elwood corrected and leered at Nora.

On his last visit to town she'd told him about the card game. "I'd like that, Joe, but right now I have to get home. I'm all wet."

Disappointment clouded his blue eyes, and he fidgeted with his sticks. Nora's heart ached. She couldn't let him think she didn't like his company, when in fact it was his father's she despised. Elwood had come to call each time he'd been in town. He wanted to court her and thank goodness Pa said no, shutting the door on the fancy dressed miner. He was getting irritated with the constant no's, and she wondered if or when he'd give up.

"How about tomorrow?" she asked. "I'll come by after lunch."

His face lit with joy and he tossed his head from side to side. "Okay, okay," he shouted.

She couldn't keep the smile from her face when he clapped his hands.

"Well, that's right kind of you," Elwood interrupted. "I'll make sure I'm there and we can all dine together. My treat."

Nora's smile disappeared. That was the last thing she wanted. He had a tendency to touch her, a hand on the shoulder or the back and she didn't like it one bit. She didn't want to owe him anything either and dinner with him was sure to have its obligations. "That won't be necessary," she said.

The sun reflected off of his gold tooth as he smiled down at her.

She stood stiff trying not to show her disgust.

"Dinner will be at five. We'll see you tomorrow," he said.

Unsure of what to say, she waved at Joe and spun around to head home. Her arms spiked with goose bumps and she shivered. The last time Elwood was in town he'd caught her behind the livery and tried to kiss her. The thought of his hands on her caused her stomach to revolt. She shook her head. Thank goodness for Seth the stable boy. He'd come around the corner while Elwood had her pinned up against the barn wall. If Seth hadn't shown up, she hated to think what would've happened.

Elwood had made it no secret that he wanted to marry her, and he seemed insulted that she wanted nothing to do with him. Other women gushed over his good looks, fancy clothes and wealth. But it was the cold look in his eyes, and the sense of entitlement to anything and anyone that had her running in the other direction.

Look what I've gotten myself into now. Mud ran down her ankles and into her boots as she walked. She couldn't let Joe down. The boy had a soft wit about him, and she wished she could heal his legs without any repercussions from his father. But she knew without a doubt, Elwood would use her for his own benefit. He did the same with his own son.

She listened to him brag to the townspeople about what a loving father he was to his simple son. He brought Joe to town for the sympathy and free wares the business owners would give him. She despised the shifty miner for using his own flesh and blood as a pawn.

Joe's wide smile stayed in her mind as she stepped over manure and continued on her way. He was a wonderful boy, and she couldn't figure out how someone so pure and kind came from something so arrogant and scary. It must be from the boy's mother, whoever she was.

How on earth was she going to avoid Elwood tomorrow? The man repulsed her. Every time she saw him, she could feel his eyes undressing her. *I will be in the dining room, he won't try anything there.*

She sighed.

She rounded the corner, relieved to be home. The acrid smell from the blacksmiths filled the air around her. She recognized the aroma from the town often aiding in telling her what time of day it was and when to get home. The morning's air tossed hints of baked bread, afternoon's sweet peas, honeysuckle and grain, and in the evening's wood smoke permeated the air with its spicy scent.

She hesitated at the gate. Pa wasn't home yet. She eyed the livery and then her muddy dress. She scrunched her toes and they squished against soft mud. She really should go home. *A few minutes won't hurt.* The door to the livery let out a sorrowful moan as she pushed it open and went inside. She came here almost every day to see the horses, and after her encounter with Elwood she needed something to calm her nerves.

The strong majestic animals fascinated her. The doctor owned the livery, but Seth Holmes ran it. The boy was no older than sixteen and

Nora liked him. He let her come into the barn anytime to feed and groom the horses. Best of all, he sensed that it was to be a secret and never mentioned it to Pa.

She unlatched the palomino's stall. He was the most beautiful animal she'd ever seen. The white mane and tail stood out against his honeyed hair. It was the animal's regal posture that drew her to him. She didn't know who he belonged to, but he was always here when she came.

She glanced behind her at Seth cleaning an empty stall. She wanted to ask him who owned the animal and why they didn't ride him, but she decided not to bother him with her nosey questions. It didn't matter to her who he belonged to, as long as he was here when she came to visit. She'd give anything to climb on his back and let him run through the valley. *I'd probably break my neck.* A risk worth taking to feel the wind in her hair. To feel fear. Exhilaration. A pulse inside her chest.

Her life wasn't filled with much excitement. The one thing that got her heart racing was sneaking around town. But now, after doing it for so long, she almost wanted Pa to catch her so she could yell and scream and fight with him. So she'd feel something other than the dull, repetitive, ho-hum emotions blended into the tasteless broth that was her life.

She grabbed the brush from the bucket and she nuzzled her face to his.

"Hello, Ghost."

CHAPTER FOUR

Elwood drove the wagon toward the white-washed hotel at the edge of town. He couldn't get the image of Nora Rushton out of his head. She was beautiful, and he'd love nothing more than to have her for his wife. When would she come to her senses and marry him? He was tired of waiting. She was a prize. A delicate little morsel he could nibble on whenever he needed.

Her long black hair and striking blue eyes held a hint of what lay beneath her dress. He was as sure as the money in the bank, under the frills and lace there was more to take his breath away. Hell, everywhere he'd go people would be jealous with her on his arm. He could show her off when he wanted to and keep her locked up until their children were born.

He snickered.

Joe hummed beside him. It was annoying and he glared at him.

"Stop that hummin' boy, or you'll be sorry."

"How come, Pa? How come?"

The invalid often repeated himself, and it drove Elwood crazy. Joe's brain didn't work like everyone else's. He was a burden, but he had value. People felt sorry for him, Nora in particular, and Elwood used that to his advantage by bringing Joe to town.

June waited outside the hotel for them, and he was glad the hotel maid had finished her errands in time to take Joe off his hands. He tipped his hat to two ladies walking past. Most of the people in town liked him, but it was his money and his business they liked more.

He didn't give a damn about the good people of Willow Creek, or any others for that matter. All he cared about was how much coal came out of his mountain and how fat his wallet was.

Five years ago he'd sold a few hundred acres of land near the mine at two dollars an acre above the price it was worth. He'd loaned the farmers money when the banks wouldn't. His plan had worked great. He charged high interest rates and collected regularly. And if he wasn't paid on time, he'd take the land and whatever was on it.

He'd raked in some good cash and was one of the wealthiest men in the area. Women threw themselves at his feet begging for a taste of his attention, and he'd obliged of course, using them for what he wanted and then discarding them. But Nora had never glanced his way. She never batted her lashes or pushed her breasts up at him.

He hunched over to set the brake. There were a few things that money couldn't buy and he'd made his living on taking whatever he wanted. He wanted Nora and damn it he'd get her.

"C'mon, Joe. We're here." Elwood jumped down from the seat and got their bags. The boy shimmied his way to the edge, and Elwood helped him down. At sixteen, Joe acted more like he was five. His head bobbed from side to side, and he started humming again.

"Joe," Elwood growled.

"Is June-bug here? Is she? Is she?" Joe propped one thick stick under each arm and hunched into them. Over the last two years, his back had curved and he'd grown a bump behind his neck. The Doc said it couldn't be corrected and Elwood didn't care. The more pitiful Joe appeared the more sympathy his loving father got. He took hold of Joe's arm and helped him along the walk. The bags were heavy and the boy was slow. He squeezed Joe's arm.

"Hurry up, Son," he whispered through a fake smile.

"Yes, Pa. Yes. Yes."

Joe's legs shook and Elwood held him upright. Once inside the doors of the hotel, Elwood handed Joe over to June.

"Mr. Calhoun," June greeted him. The older woman had worked at the hotel for years, and Elwood paid her a handsome amount to watch over Joe while he was in town. Lucky for him, she'd taken to Joe right away.

"Afternoon, June." Elwood moved around her to drop his bags onto the polished floor of the hotel lobby.

"Mr. Calhoun, glad to see you back in town, sir," Milton Smith, the owner, said. He picked up Elwood's bags. "Your room is ready. This way, sir."

He followed Milton to a room on the second floor, and headed straight for the bottle of whiskey he always demanded be there when he came to town. He poured himself a drink from the heavy glass decanter while June helped Joe up the stairs.

Elwood shrugged and took another swig.

The kid was more of a pain in the ass than anything. He poured himself another drink. But Joe's friendship with Nora served a purpose.

"I'm hungry. I'm hungry," Joe said as he hobbled into the room. His crutches scraped on the wooden floor and made Elwood wince.

"Pick those damn things up." He pointed at the boy's sticks.

Joe did as he was told and lost his balance. He would've fallen over if June hadn't caught him.

"Joe, darling you go ahead and scrape those sticks all you want to. It doesn't bother me none." June glared at Elwood.

Joe's blue eyes began to tear and his bottom lip trembled. He shook his head from side to side.

"Elwood, you tell this boy he can use his sticks the way he did before."

June was angry, and Elwood knew if he didn't say something to Joe, the whole damn town would know what he'd done. June sat on all the town committees. His horrible manner toward the boy would spread like wildfire and he'd be shunned.

"Go on." He waved his hand. "Walk with 'em the way ya were." He emptied the glass in one gulp leaving a trail of fire down his throat.

"Come now, dear, I made cookies today in hopes you'd stop by. They're in the kitchen."

"Mmmm. Cookies. I love cookies. I love cookies."

The maid giggled. "I know, dear. I baked them for you, and once you're settled we'll go down and get a few."

"Thank you, thank you, June-bug." His eyelids fluttered like butterfly wings.

Elwood rolled his eyes at the way people fawned all over the crippled kid. If June knew how he treated the boy back home, she'd shoot him for sure. Hell, he couldn't be expected to care for a simple minded kid. He didn't even like him. But he was his ticket to getting what he wanted.

He filled his glass again and swirled the gold liquid around before bringing it to his lips. The heady scent filled his nostrils and he inhaled. Yes, he'd have what he wanted. All of it. And no one would stand in his way.

CHAPTER FIVE

He saw the shadow on the stone wall. The long black snake snapped and buckled in the air behind him. The crisp crack echoed throughout the damp chamber. His hands were bound to a thick wooden pole, the same one he and two other boys had pounded into the ground a month ago—for this purpose. For pain. For torture. For fear.

He braced himself, closed his eyes and took a deep breath holding it within his lungs until they ached with the need for air. He pictured his Ina. Crack. The pain was instant. His flesh burned, and he could feel his skin as it hung in ripped pieces from his body. Crack. Again the long snake wielded its coiled end and bit into his back. Blood splattered onto the dirt floor. He tried to focus on the tiny dots that melted into the ground and disappeared at his feet, but his vision blurred.

Crack. He couldn't take anymore. He gasped as his body screamed in agony while his flesh was forever branded. The pain sliced through his ribs and into his very soul, filling him with hatred for the wasichu. His stomach rolled. Yellow bile spewed from his mouth and ran down his chest. Crack. The weight of the whip buckled his knees and he hung from the leather band tied around his wrists. The wounds on his back oozed and throbbed. His head lulled to the side, and he closed his eyes.

Otakatay woke from the dream panting. His heart thundered in his chest, and his body was moist with sweat. The moon was still high in the sky. He lay motionless on his sleeping mat and listened to the crickets sing, as the light breeze clapped the leaves together. The nightmare still vivid in his mind, he tried to abandon the awful memories and think of something else—something peaceful.

Had he been anyone else, peace might've come easy. But for him, a slayer of women and men, there was no such thing. He hunted with purpose, for a promise made. And he'd do whatever was necessary to fulfill it.

He thought of the man who hired him to kill the *witkowin*, the crazy woman and his lips thinned. The wasichu was evil, like his father. They both had the empty stare but one still walked this earth.

He sat up and struggled for a breath that wasn't paired with a sharp pain in his ribs. As he stretched his strong arms above his head, his back seized and spasms shook his whole body. The muscles didn't recuperate after the last time. The wounds had healed, but the flesh was a mangled, deformed mess. Rigid and raised the scars drew a grotesque pattern on his back and sides.

He traced a long, bevelled scar down his forearm. He would never forget the pain he'd endured. It intoxicated him and afterward he felt delusional. Full of angst and fear wondering if he was ever going to escape the dreadful memories of the life he'd been thrust into. He grabbed his shirt. Within the vacant eyes of the forest he went without one. When living among the wasichu, he never took it off.

He ran his fingers through his shoulder-length hair to untangle it. A fingertip caressed the eagle feather tied on the side, and his chest seized. *I promise.*

Wakina neighed and stomped a hoof, and Otakatay came alert. He grabbed his knife, rolled to the side and in two quick, soundless strides was behind a tree, waiting. He heard a branch snap, and then another and another. He raised his blade.

A deer pranced through the campsite and stopped at the bushes on the other side. The large buck stared straight at him.

He lowered his knife.

The deer bolted, disappearing into the trees.

"You should've known it was a helpless deer," he said to Wakina.

The horse turned his head, ignoring him.

He smiled and dug into his saddle bag for an apple. He sliced the shiny red globe in half, gave one piece to Wakina and took a bite out of the other.

The horse didn't even chew it, but swallowed the fruit whole.

"You, my friend, are a glutton."

Wakina bowed his gray head and nudged Otakatay's hand for more of the apple.

"I don't think so." He held up the fruit. "This is mine."

After he finished his half of the apple, he picked up a few dry branches and brought them to the pile of ash near his bed roll. Once he had the wood smoking he blew on it to fuel the fire. Satisfied with the height of the flames, he gutted and cooked the fish he'd caught yesterday.

Leaning against his saddle, he picked at the trout on his plate. The moon made its descent. The sky changed to orange and yellow as the first rays of dawn shone down.

Nora woke early and prepared some coffee. She added two more tablespoons of the grounds to make it extra strong. Pa had been out late the night before and lay slumped over the sofa. One arm dangled to the floor, while the other was tucked under his chest. She checked the tin in the cupboard above the stove. The money was gone. There had been thirty dollars in there. He'd taken it to gamble and drink, again.

Her face heated as anger raced through her veins. They were never going to have their own place if he continued on like this. Now with all their money gone, how would they survive until the end of the month?

She checked the cupboards, cornmeal, yeast, baking soda, one jar of fruit, one jar of meat and nothing more. She was thankful for her garden, but that wouldn't feed them for long. The garden was planted for the purpose of supplementing their meals. With no meat and no money the garden would feed them for another week.

Oh Pa, why? Why did you do this? She poured coffee into two cups.

"Pa, it's time to get up," she sang. "You don't want to be late for work."

She sat at the table and watched through half-closed eyes as her father dislodged his arm from under his chest. He groaned. The front of his shirt was stained brown, and an overwhelming odor invaded her nostrils. She covered her mouth and nose. He'd thrown up all over himself and the sofa.

Pa's face lost all color, and she knew he smelled the vomit, too.

She stood. "Here, Pa, let me help you."

He waved his arm at her. "No."

"But, Pa."

He swayed and almost fell from the sofa.

"Leave me be."

Tears formed in her eyes. What was happening to him? He was no longer the man she knew. She went to him and placed her hand on his shoulder.

He pushed her hand away, and ripped the soiled shirt off tossing it onto the floor. "I don't need your damn help."

She stepped back toward the table.

His pale face contrasted with swollen red eyes that glared up at her. "You left the yard. Jed said he saw you walking toward the forest yesterday."

Oh dear.

"I didn't go far, just enough to set the hawk free, that's all."

He swayed. "You know the rules. You've disobeyed me."

She held her tongue. Pa was provoking her. She'd seen this many times before when he'd had too much to drink and wanted to put the blame on her. If she took the bait, he'd be packing up their things and they'd be gone within the hour.

"I'm sorry, Pa. It won't happen again."

He tried to stand, and swayed to the side falling onto the sofa and into the mess there.

She grabbed the wet cloth on the counter and brought it to him.

"Here, let me help you."

"Get away from me." He swung at the cloth in her hand missing it by a foot.

She dropped the cloth onto the table and fled to her room closing the door behind her. She could hear him trying to get up off the sofa. The table shifted and something banged against the far wall. She cringed.

Pa went to work feeling the effects of his drinking almost every day, but this morning was different. He was still drunk.

She gnawed on her bottom lip while she waited for him to wash his face, dress and leave for work. Wanting to escape, she glanced at the window. She'd just promised Pa she'd stay in the cabin but a walk in the forest would do her some good. He wasn't going to check on her or say goodbye. She'd clean the mess when she got back. She braided her hair and crawled out the window. The morning air smelled much better than the awful stench inside the cabin.

Pa's drinking had always been a problem. When she was younger she'd find him in an alley curled up in his own vomit and urine sobbing about how he couldn't save her mother. Not strong enough to carry him home she'd sit and console him. He drank to forget and Nora was the reminder of what he'd lost. When he found out she could heal, he drank even more, distancing himself from his only child. He spent every night at the saloon gambling and drinking. She hadn't seen a glimpse of happiness in him in years.

She shook her head. Was their life that bad? Sure, she'd complained and argued with him for freedom; she'd do anything for him to loosen the rope tied around her neck. But was this life terrible enough to become inebriated every night? She pursed her lips.

She passed the Mercantile, and her shoulders slumped. They had no money. He'd gambled everything. How was she supposed to fix this? She couldn't get a job.

"Oh, damn it."

She shoved her hands inside her apron pockets. The hotel stood at the north end of Main Street and backed onto the forest. She had no problem walking past it except when Elwood was in town. She shivered and pulled her hands from the apron to rub along her arms.

When the mine owner was in Willow Creek she stayed close to home, but this time she'd have to see him. She promised Joe a game of cards this afternoon, and she couldn't let the boy down because his father was no good. She was determined to visit with him over a card game and not let Elwood intimidate her.

Lush moss blanketed the forest floor. She untied her boots and slipped them off. A squirrel ran along a branch above her, hesitated and then jumped to another. She giggled. Animals always had a way of calming her. Life never seemed awful in the thick of the forest.

Roots burst from the ground mangled and barbaric, and she stepped over them. She inhaled and her mind filled with the fresh, balsamic scent of pinecones. She skimmed the prickly pine leaf. She always loved the spruce trees. They never lost their glorious greenery in the winter like the others. Tall and magnificent, they stood like proud soldiers within the dense forest. They looked beautiful at Christmas time decorated with ribbons and candles, too.

A branch broke to her left, and a hand clamped over her mouth. She tried to scream, but nothing came out. Her heart hammered inside her chest. She struggled for air. She squirmed, trying to wiggle loose, but her arms were held tight to her sides. Cold steel pushed into her throat, and she froze.

"Quiet wasicun winyan—white woman," a low voice said from behind her.

She could see from the corner of her eyes, a dark hand across her mouth. *Indian!* She was going to be taken captive. She would be a slave for the rest of her life. Visions of wild Indians tearing at her clothes invaded her mind. Their filthy hands pawed at her virginal skin, taking from her what she fought to keep. She tried again to move, but his hand tightened around her mouth and he pushed the blade closer.

The forest floor swayed before her as the truth of what her future would be slammed into her chest. She pushed forward vomiting into his hand and all over her cheeks and chin.

A loud growl erupted from behind her, and she was thrown to the ground.

"Ahh, shit." His back was to her as he knelt down and washed his hand in the river.

She saw the glint of the knife in the shallow water. She needed to run, to scream, to get the hell out of there. She tried to move her legs, but the limbs proved useless.

"Clean your face." He stood over her now.

Afraid to make eye contact, she examined his moccasins. She'd never seen a pair this beautiful and wondered if his wife had made them. She'd heard of Indians taking more than one wife, and she drew back. *Oh, God. Please don't let that be his plan.*

"Go!"

She crawled to the river, cupped her hand in the cold water and splashed her face. She swished water in her mouth and spat it onto the ground.

"Get up."

She struggled to her feet, and her stomach rolled. She tucked a loose strand of hair behind her ear.

Nora's eyes met his. Her breath caught, and she took an unconscious step back. It was him. The stranger she'd seen the other day. Long, black hair framed his face. Dark stubble covered a strong jaw and high cheekbones. He wore black pants and a shirt opened halfway down his chest. She could see the muscles bunched there.

A scar peeked out of his collar and ran up his neck disappearing behind his hair. He stood at least a foot and half taller than her. Almond shaped charcoal eyes bore down upon her. If he meant to intimidate her, he had succeeded. He resembled evil, hatred and death all rolled into one. She shivered. The urge to run consumed her.

She tried to speak, but a lump had lodged inside her throat and nothing came out.

He stepped toward her.

She squeezed her eyes shut and waited.

He grabbed her braid and pulled her head back, exposing her throat. This was it, she was going to die. A tear slid down her cheek. Her heart hammered inside her chest. She had to calm down. She felt the Indians chest rub against her shoulder as he exhaled beside her. Leaves scrunched under his moccasins. The frigid blade bit into her flesh.

He pushed her away and growled, "Go home, little girl."

She almost tripped and fell, but grabbed onto a tree to catch herself. She stared at him. Had he told her to go home? He wasn't going to kill her?

He slid the knife into the leather sheath strapped to his pant leg, and she saw more scars around his wrists. Nora's hands heated and before she knew what was happening, she took a step toward him.

His head shot up and he glared at her.

"I'm Nora." What the hell was she thinking? The man almost killed her. *But he didn't and he'd been hurt badly one time in his life.*

He continued to glare at her. "Go home."

His voice reminded her of sand paper run along a block of wood and the low baritone key on the church organ.

"Are…are you passing through Willow Creek?" *Do as he says. Go home. What am I thinking?*

"Are you deaf? I said leave." He pointed behind her. "Go home."

He spoke English well. She assessed his face, his clothes, his skin tone. He wasn't only native, he was white, too.

He hadn't moved his arm from the stiff position.

She glanced in the direction he'd pointed with no intentions of leaving. Something about him fascinated her. At first she was scared to death and now she wanted to know something—anything—about him.

"I'm quite capable of finding my way home, mister."

He spoke in his language, and she knew by the way his face twisted with fury he was angry. He pulled the wide blade from its sheath, and sinister eyes glared into hers. His full lips lifted up at the corners, but not in a kind way and he ran the tip of the knife along his cheek.

She retreated. He advanced until they stood so close she could smell campfire on his skin.

He grabbed her braid and weaved the knife through it. "What a nice trophy this would make."

He is going to scalp me! She closed her eyes and enlisted any courage she had left deep inside her. She wasn't going down without a fight. She stood taller and lifted her chin. Inside she was panicking, but she'd rather die than allow him to take her beautiful hair.

He laughed, but there was nothing merry about it. He pulled a clump of hair from her braid and sliced it from her head.

She gasped and felt her head where he'd cut the hair.

He pointed the blade, the tip pricking her throat. "Go. Before I change my mind and take it all."

Without so much as a second thought, she rushed through the forest she loved, leaving behind the birds and the eerie stranger who scared and excited her at the same time.

CHAPTER SIX

Nora ran as fast as she could over the uneven ground. Branches slapped her face and pulled at her hair as she went by. She didn't look back until she stepped onto the path behind the hotel. Her heart thumped, and she wheezed low moans from her throat. She slumped against a tall spruce, put her hand on her chest and shivered as she glanced behind her into the dense forest. The dark trees were no longer welcoming. But she was more concerned with the stranger that lurked among them.

She turned and almost collided with Elwood's dog, Savage. The black half-wolf was wild and mean. Savage's fur was matted and dirty. An ugly looking scar that pulled the skin sat above his left eye and deformed the face. The hair on top of his head stood up, and his ears lay back and pointed. He hunched low as a deep threatening growl rumbled toward her. She glanced up at the street beyond the buildings. Where had he come from?

"Savage," she said in a commanding voice.

The dog's lip curled, large fangs dripped with saliva. The dog had chewed through the rope that tied him to the fancy wagon, and she doubted Elwood even knew he was missing.

Savage growled.

If she weren't in danger of losing a limb, she would've thought his growl sounded more like a giant cat's purr, a roll of the tongue making the sound rippled. Her toes scrunched, and she realized while running for her life in the forest, she had forgotten her boots. *Great.*

Savage crouched lower. The hair on his neck stood and his tongue dashed out to lick his fangs.

Oh, this isn't going to be good. All animals could smell fear and she stunk of it. Sweat trickled down her neck. She didn't dare move her hands from her sides, for fear the deranged animal would see her shaking and lunge for her throat.

She spotted the mercantile and the blacksmiths next door. She was so close to home. If she screamed would there be enough time for someone to come running and stop the animal from ripping her to shreds? *I doubt it. Besides, Elwood may be the one running and he's the last person I want to see.*

Another growl and this time a large paw stepped toward her.

Oh dear. She loved all animals, but this one was different. He was mean and wouldn't think twice about ripping her arm off. She thought of the stranger in the woods. He was similar to the wolf-dog. He, too, was a mixed breed, who would hurt, or even kill if the opportunity arose. After all, he was going to scalp her. *But he didn't. Yes, yes, he didn't but his dark eyes said he would.* And she knew without a doubt he was capable of anything.

His presence exuded arrogance—it reeked of danger, need and hunger. By taking his knife to her hair he'd accomplish scaring her to death, and making her run away terrified. She glanced at the dog, now two feet from her. She inched back into the tree, trying to melt into the trunk.

Savage growled.

"Savage, you go home." Her voice trembled. "You heard me. Now get going, right now."

The filthy animal barked and showed his teeth.

I'm dead.

"Nora, Nora," Joe yelled from between two buildings. He leaned into his walking sticks and waved.

She didn't dare move. The dog was so close now she could feel his breath on her hand. Joe's feet shuffled in the grass. She wanted to yell at him to go home, but didn't move for fear Savage would strike. She watched as Joe struggled to get to her. How she'd love to heal his mangled legs. Her hands grew hot and tingled. *I can't help him. If Elwood found out, he'd never stop pursuing me.*

Joe came up beside her. "Why ya way out here? Out here?"

She watched as his beautiful blue eyes rolled; something she'd seen him do many times.

Savage growled again.

"Oh, puppy, stop it. Stop it. " Joe reached for the dog.

Savage twisted his head and dug his teeth into Joe's hand.

Joe screamed and clutched his bleeding hand to his chest. He shook his head from side to side and opened and closed his eyes repeatedly.

Nora kicked the dog's snout with her bare foot and felt the jab of sharp teeth against her toes. She kicked him again, this time in the side. The horrible beast lunged at her and she kicked him harder. She knew the dog wouldn't stop now that he'd tasted blood.

She picked up the crutch Joe had dropped and swung at the dog catching him in the neck. He rolled backward and shook his head before he came at her again. This time she was ready. She'd never played baseball, but she watched a few games out on the church lawn. She positioned the crutch like a bat. Joe screamed in the background as Savage leapt toward her. She squeezed her eyes and swung. The wooden stick vibrated in her hands. The dog yelped and began to whimper.

She opened her eyes. Joe was crying and Savage lay on the grass, whining. *What have I done?* She dropped the crutch and knelt in front of him, but he got up and limped away. She stood and watched Savage until he disappeared into the trees behind them. Joe's crying became louder. She went to him and took his hand. The boy was beyond sobbing now, he gasped as fat tears messed his face. There was blood everywhere, and Nora's stomach rolled.

"I will fix it, Joe. I promise."

The boy's body rocked back and forth, and he almost lost his balance.

"Joe, you need to sit down."

He shook his head again, and she didn't know if he was answering her or if this was one of his odd behaviours. She slid the stick out from under Joe's arm and leaned him against her. She lowered them both to the ground. With Joe positioned against the tree, she took his hand once more.

Oh my. The tip of Joe's thumb hung by a few pieces of flesh. She couldn't see the rest of his hand, there was too much blood. Nora's hands shook with the need to heal him. Red blotches covered her palms, and the tips of her fingers were the color of Joe's bloodstained ones. She wondered if he would tell anyone, or what his reaction may be once she made this right. There was no time to debate the outcome. She needed to heal him.

Joe continued to cry, rocking back and forth.

"Here we go." She placed her hands on his to bring the thumb into place with the torn bone and flesh. The heat in her palms intensified and she squeezed.

Joe tried to pull away, but she held him to her. The boy's pain shot down her arms to nestle back into her own thumb. She swayed. The earth spun around her. She dug her knees into the grass and closed her eyes. She absorbed the wound until she felt the thumb was no longer dislodged.

The boy was silent when she released his hand.

She walked a few feet away into the forest where she threw up all over the bushes. She waited and vomited a second time. Still light-headed, she wiped her mouth with her apron and faced Joe.

The boy held his hand in front of his face. The thumb no longer bloody and looking horrid.

"How's your hand, Joe?" She knelt in front of him.

"It's all better. Look, Nora. Look." He shoved his hand into her face.

She giggled. "I see that. Are you okay now?"

The boy smiled and his eyes lit up. "You made me better. You. You. You," he shouted.

She smiled.

"Yes, Joe, I did. But you mustn't tell anyone."

"I know. I know. Like a secret."

"Like a secret,' she confirmed and squeezed his hand.

He tilted his head and scrutinized her for a long time before asking, "Are you a witch?"

The word sobered her. All of Pa's fears echoed in her mind. "No, Joe, I am not a witch."

"They're real you know. Pa says. Pa says."

"I'm sure they are, but I am not one of them." She eyed him. Did he believe her? She didn't need him telling folks she was a witch. People didn't like someone different, and if word of her gift got out they'd lynch her for sure.

"What are you? What are you?"

Nora sat a moment. She'd done this enough times to know the right answers. But she'd never healed someone like Joe, someone with a simple mind.

"Well, I'm—

"I know. You're a good witch." He smiled.

Oh dear. "No. No I'm not a bad, or a good witch, Joe. I'm just a girl with a gift."

"Like a present? A present?"

"Yes, like a present." She could work with this. "You know on Christmas morning how all the gifts are wrapped and under the tree?"

He shook his head and glanced at the ground.

She wondered why he didn't know. Elwood must buy his son gifts at Christmas. She put her hand on his shoulder.

"Well, they are wrapped up so you don't see what's inside. Like me. I'm wrapped up so no one sees my gift."

"Oh, you're a special present."

"That's right." She smiled and ruffled his hair.

"Nora, Nora I won't tell anyone you're a present," he whispered.

"Thank you, Joe. You're a good friend." She hugged him. "Now, let's get you cleaned up."

She took his hand and wiped the blood as best she could onto her apron. She looked like she'd slaughtered a chicken, but there were no signs of trauma on Joe.

"I'm going to head home and get cleaned up. Then I'll come back to the hotel and play a game of cards with you in the dining room."

She stood, helped him up and handed him his crutches.

"Okay. Okay!"

They walked to the street and before she left him, Nora brought her index finger to her lips. "Shhh."

Joe smiled and limped toward the hotel door.

Nora's feet were sore and her big toe was cut from Savage's teeth when she'd kicked him. She needed her boots. They were the only pair she had. She'd go home first and change then head into the forest to find them, before going to see Joe.

As she got closer to home, the morning altercation with her father came rushing back. Was he home? She doubted it. He'd go to work, because he didn't want to see her. Nora's eyes misted. She'd never felt so alone. Pa didn't want anything to do with her, other than to tell her where she could go and what she could do. There were no conversations about her day, no card games, no moments filled with laughter. They didn't talk to each other anymore. She was isolated in the tiny shack, forbidden friends, enemies and love.

She hiked up her skirt and climbed through the window. The smell of vomit filled her nostrils. Pa hadn't cleaned up the mess. She glanced at her bloodied, muddy apron and decided not to remove it until everything was tidied. She placed her ear to the door to listen, in case he was still home. Silence.

In the kitchen, she stood back and assessed the situation. Pa had left his clothes, dirty and smelling to high heaven, in a pile on the floor. The cushions on the sofa were still wet from his vomit. *Oh pa. What am I going to do with you?* She tossed the clothes out onto the porch to be washed. She filled two buckets, threw pa's clothes into one and carried the other one back inside.

From her knees she scrubbed the fabric on the sofa as best she could and sprinkled baking soda on top to rid it of the awful smell. Next she opened all the windows to air out the house and washed the floors. Nora's hair hung from her braid in damp wisps that stuck to her cheeks. The hammering and clanking from the shop echoed into the kitchen, and she wondered if she should go and see how her father was faring. The gesture would anger him. She'd be better off fetching her boots.

She peeked at the clock on the mantel. It was ten minutes past noon, and Pa wasn't coming home for lunch. He wouldn't be able to keep anything down anyway. Knowing it was safe to escape for a while, she went out the window.

Otakatay packed up his bedroll and tied it behind his saddle. He didn't like being this close to town. He inspected the place he'd slept for three nights. All evidence that he'd slept there had disappeared under the thick blanket of branches and leaves.

He mounted Wakina and guided the animal through the trees. Noise from town pushed through the swaying leaves to swirl around him. Horses pulled wagons, boots heels clicked on the wooden walk and children's laughter eased into his mind. He set his jaw against the reminders of a life he hadn't been allowed to enter. The streets he'd never walked along without being stared at or judged. The homes he'd never been invited into.

His eyes narrowed and his rugged features hardened. He grabbed the reins once more. He hated the wasichu. He hated their towns and their homes and the very ground they walked on. He hated that he had to mingle within their communities and buy goods from their establishments.

He tightened his hold on the reins until his knuckles paled. The white man took what he wanted without thinking of the consequences. They held themselves higher than any other creation while they pranced around like kings in this rough, uncivilized land.

His father was white, the first wasichu he learned to hate. Buck Morgan had been a useless piece of shit, mean to the very core and Otakatay despised him. He wished that instead of killing the snake so quickly he'd have prolonged his suffering. The son of a bitch hadn't deserved to live as long as he did. Otakatay ground his teeth until his jaw ached.

He could see the mountains through the tree tops. He'd return soon and claim what was stolen from him years ago. He patted his thigh where he'd sewn an extra piece into the pant leg for his money. He needed more. One more kill. The man will pay triple next time. One more victim and he'd have the amount he'd need to fulfill his promise. He caressed the feather in his hair.

He no longer wanted to kill the witch women. The softness of their skin, the smell of their hair—he'd never forget. He open and closed his hands. He could still feel their blood run down his arm after he sliced their throats. He could hear the quiet moan that seeped from supple lips as life wafted from their lungs. Sweat bubbled on his forehead and his stomach roiled. He bowed his head and inhaled until he collected himself. He scowled and hid behind the evil mask he'd perfected.

He sat up tall in the saddle. *I am Otakatay, one who kills many.*

He was vile and grim. He sat for a long moment listening to the squirrels rustle in the trees. Branches cracked as a fox bolted into his den. The muggy air filled his lungs leaving the familiar taste of pinecones, horse and earth on his tongue. Here, within the depth of the forest he felt welcome.

He clicked his tongue, urging Wakina on.

The river was quiet, and the chickadees chirping in the trees indicated it was safe to stop for a drink. He dismounted and released Wakina and watched as he made his way toward the rushing water. The horse trotted toward him with a black boot protruding from his mouth.

He pulled it from Wakina's strong teeth. The boot was old, the leather creased and soft from wear. He flipped it upside down. Two holes the size of his baby finger dripped water. The heel was worn down, smooth and shiny.

He thought of the crazy girl with the braid. This must be her boot. He scanned the area for the other one and spotted it by a rock. Both boots were wet and in need of repair. He often wondered why the wasichu didn't wear moccasins. The soft leather moulded the feet and kept them warm. He hung the boots on a branch to dry out. The girl would come back for them.

She was feisty, that one. He didn't understand why she wasn't afraid of him. Why hadn't she run the first time he'd told her to go? Most people never hung around long enough to be told to leave, but she did. And she even wanted to know his name.

His features softened for a moment before he tightened his mouth and narrowed his eyes. He pushed any warm thoughts from his mind. The notion of even one kind thought toward a wasichu was enough to make him sick. He swatted at the boots hanging from the tree, until they tumbled to the ground.

Wakina snorted.

"I will not help a wasichu," he said to him.

Wakina snorted louder and bared his teeth.

He glared at his horse. There was no pity left within him. No remorse for the things he'd done. He couldn't be the soft, timid boy who would sit on his Ina's lap and listen to stories. That person was no more. He was gone and would never return.

Wakina walked over, picked up one of the boots and placed it gently on a rock sitting in the sun.

"Do not touch the other boot, Wakina."

The horse snuffed at him, picked up the other boot and placed it next to its partner.

Otakatay strode toward the rock.

Wakina blocked his path.

He grabbed the reins, and looked straight into his eyes. "You, Wakina, I will eat one day if you keep this up."

He left the boots where they were and went back into the forest in search of a new camp.

CHAPTER SEVEN

Elwood paced the length of the dining room. He pulled out his pocket watch. Two o'clock.

"Damn it, Nora should've been here an hour ago to play cards with Joe."

She'd said after lunch. He clicked the watch closed and shoved it into his pocket. He glanced out the window, but there was still no sign of the dark-haired girl.

He eyed the liquor cabinet in the corner. Wine, whiskey and bourbon called to him. He hadn't had a drink since this morning and he'd been hankering for one the last hour. His stomach lurched. He'd been up half the night drinking and thinking about Nora and what it would be like to have her as his wife.

He'd grown restless at the mine, and he was bored with the women at the saloon. He wanted a wife and Nora was the one. She'd add immeasurably to the wealth he'd already obtained. The best part about his plan was he'd be able to take her whenever the need arose, and she wouldn't be able to do a damn thing about it.

He pulled on the collar of his shirt and undid the top button. Red and Levi were due back from the saloon any minute. The two men went everywhere with him. They were an extra pair of guns when he needed them and they helped keep order at the mine. He needed to collect on a few homesteads, and he'd be taking them with him.

Jess Chandler owed him more than the rest of the farmers he'd sold to. The crazy crow was a good shot and damn near put a bullet in him last time he'd been out to her place. He'd set her straight today. He'd bring old Savage and the boys. The mutt would attack anyone Elwood commanded him to, and Red could clip a whiskey bottle a hundred yards away. Elwood would love to see that devil woman thrashing on the ground with a chunk of her throat missing or a bullet in her chest.

He peered out the window once more and groaned. There was still no sign of Nora.

"Joe," he hollered. "Joe, come on in here."

The boy had been sitting in the lobby, waiting for Nora.

The shuffle of Joe's feet grew louder as he got closer.

"Yes, Pa. Yes, Pa."

Joe stood in the doorway wearing a blue shirt buttoned wrong and tucked into his denims. His rounded back was more prominent today, and the sadly buttoned shirt did nothing to hide it. His dirty-blonde hair stuck out in all directions, while crumbs from the cookie he'd been eating gathered at the sides of his mouth.

"Look at you." He motioned with his chin. "You're a mess."

He walked toward him.

"Damn it, boy, why can't you clean yourself up?" He raised his hand and the boy flinched.

He chuckled. The kid was afraid him. A rush of excitement bolted through his veins, and he brought his arm back down to his side. Some days he had to show the kid who was in charge. He'd done enough damage that it didn't much matter what he did to him anymore. Joe usually followed the rules, but when he didn't, Elwood had a way of reminding him.

He loved seeing the fear in Joe's blue eyes and the way he'd withdraw whenever Elwood was mad. The kid was useless around the mine, and most days he was locked in his room.

"Do you remember when Miss Rushton said she was stopping by?"

"I like Nora. I like Nora." He swayed his head.

"Yeah, I get that." Elwood went back to glance out the window. Why wasn't she here? He wanted to make sure they had dinner together. "Damn woman."

"Nora's not a damn woman. Damn woman. She isn't a witch, a witch either." Joe stopped, a loud moan came from his wet lips and his eyes rolled back.

Elwood turned from the window. "Ah, hell."

He grabbed Joe's arm, brought him to a chair and shoved him into the rose-colored fabric. He was getting mighty tired of these episodes and considered leaving the kid in the middle of nowhere. Be rid of the invalid for good. Spit dripped from Joe's mouth, and his whole body twitched. Elwood took his time removing his expensive suit coat which he placed neatly on a chair.

"I need a drink." He rummaged through the liquor cabinet.

Joe's arms were rigid, and his fingernails dug into his palms. The front of his shirt was wet, and a high pitched sound hummed from his lips. His boots tapped on the floor and grated on Elwood's nerves so that he knocked over a bottle of Champagne.

"Where's the damn whiskey?" He pulled out a dusty bottle of scotch and decided that would do.

Joe was still in the full effects of his fit.

Not bothered by it at all, Elwood uncorked the scotch, smelled the bottle and poured himself a drink.

The boys crippled legs bounced up and down in perfect cadence. Damn, this was taking forever. When this happened at the mine, he'd make sure he was nowhere near the kid. He downed the alcohol, poured himself another glass and walked toward Joe. He glared at him and gave his leg a little kick. The boy continued to shake, his body stiff.

He'd had enough. Elwood brought his leg back to kick him again, a little harder this time when he heard voices coming into the dining room.

He swallowed the remaining scotch and knelt in front of Joe when a man and woman entered the room.

"Son, come out of it. Daddy's here," Elwood crooned.

"Oh, dear." The woman rushed toward them. "Is your boy okay?"

"He suffers from fits." Elwood frowned and made his eyes water. "I hope he comes out of it soon."

"Oh, you poor thing."

June came into the room, a bag in each hand. She dropped them when she saw Joe. "How long has he been like this?"

"He just started. I've been trying to make him comfortable." Elwood feigned concern.

"Did you call for Doctor Spencer?" June asked.

Elwood hadn't even thought to call for the doctor. He masked his irritation. "No, I didn't have time. I didn't want to leave my boy."

June glared at him before she focused on Joe. "Dear, can you hear me?" She rubbed his shaking arms and started singing Mary had a Little Lamb, with compassion showing in her old eyes.

Elwood wanted to leave. He had better things to do than sit with the damn kid, especially after that episode. He wanted nothing to do with cleaning Joe up either. He eyed the scotch on the mantel. He could use another drink.

When he thought it couldn't get any worse, a crowd gathered. He had to keep from pressing his fingers into Joe's arm. The kid did this stuff all the time back at the mine. Hell, he was a constant nuisance and most times Elwood left him alone to deal with the aftermath by himself.

A bystander brought a chair for June to sit on.

"Try to make him comfortable," another person said and a woman wearing a black skirt covered with an apron brought in a blanket and laid it across Joe's restless legs.

Elwood eyed the liquor cabinet.

Joe's legs stopped twitching and his body gradually relaxed. He opened his eyes, glassy and dazed.

"Joe, can you hear me?" June rubbed his hand. "Are you all right?"

The boys eyes filled with tears, and it took all the strength Elwood had in him not to slap the kid across the face.

"Could someone get the boy a glass of lemonade, please?" June asked.

"My head hurts, my head hurts," Joe slurred.

"Would you like me to go for the doctor?" A young man asked.

"He'll be right as rain in a few minutes. Happens all the time," Elwood said as he ignored June's glare and grabbed the Scotch. He downed two glasses before the woman came back with Joe's lemonade.

The crowd disbursed after wishing Joe well. Elwood couldn't stand to be near the kid any longer.

"Seein' as how the boy's come out of it, I've got business to attend to." He left June and Joe in the dining room.

He walked around the back of the hotel to check on Savage. He picked up the chewed piece of rope. Savage was gone.

"Damn mutt. I should've shot him years ago." He whistled for Savage to come. "But the bastard does come in handy now and then."

He wanted to take him along while he collected payment from certain farmers, especially that crotchety Jess Chandler. She had a way of ruffling his feathers. Her and that damn shotgun. She won't mess with Savage, that's for sure. The vicious dog was feared by most men. He whistled again.

"Savage, where in hell are you?"

He scanned the edge of the forest and the street out front. There was no sign of him and he didn't have time to wait. His palm itched for some cash and his throat needed some whiskey. He'd take care of the dog when he got back. He'd make sure the son of a bitch never ran off again.

He glanced back one more time before he headed to the saloon to round up his men. The bloody dog would feel his whip when he found him. He laughed and weaved his way through the people on the boardwalk.

CHAPTER EIGHT

Nora's boots were placed on a rock beside the river. The one she'd sat on while dipping her feet into the cool water earlier. Hands on her hips, she scrutinized the area. She'd tossed her boots to the side, close to the water's edge, but not onto the rock.

Wondering how her boots got there, she pivoted on her heel and searched the area around her. She spotted a large footprint in the mud. *The Indian!* She ran her fingertips along the edge of the print and thought about the stranger she'd met this morning.

He had scared her half to death, coming up behind her the way he did. Goodness, he even made her vomit. Her cheeks glowed, embarrassed by how easily she'd spooked, but it wasn't until she looked at him that she was truly shaken. He was huge. A beast of a man—wide, jagged, rough and mean. Someone she didn't want to remember that was for sure, or run into twice.

She quickly searched the trees around her. Shades of green and brown blurred as she scanned the outlining area of the forest. Thinking of the Indian made her nervous. She swore she could feel his dark eyes upon her even now, and the hair on her arms rose. In his presence, she sensed danger and, worse yet, death. But there was something else. She could feel it, deep within her soul. Curiosity pushed her to find out more.

I'm crazy. He's dangerous. People didn't behave horrible for no reason. She thought of Savage, Elwood's dog. The signs were all over the animal that someone had mistreated him and she'd bet it was the rich miner. The black fur was matted, bald in places and his snout was deformed. She figured he'd been kicked or beaten with a stick and that was why he was so mean. The dog was born an innocent pup, as the stranger was once an innocent baby, but through circumstances beyond their control both of their paths had turned in the wrong direction.

What in the stranger's life had caused him to become so hateful?

What pushed him to be cruel enough to threaten an innocent woman?

Determined to find out, she made a vow to look for the man tomorrow. If he was still around she'd do her best to befriend him, if he didn't kill her first.

She picked up her boots, still damp and sat down on the rock. While tying them, she listened to the rushing water and wondered where the river was going in such a hurry. If she had a boat she'd ride out the currents to see where they'd take her. She'd never been on a boat, but she imagined the wind in her hair. Not a care would enter her mind. There would be no running, no hiding and no disappointing her father.

If I had a friend, we'd go together. A tear formed in the corner of her eye and she blinked it away. Friends weren't going to be popping up anytime soon. Willow Creek's women had long ago given up on befriending the blacksmith's daughter, thanks to Pa. Because of his selfishness, most of the women would rather talk behind her back than to her face. She cringed. During the first few months after moving here, the women came to call bringing pies and scones, but sadly she'd turned them all away. Even though she'd done so with a smile and a polite thank you, they never returned.

She shrugged.

"Yes, well it's not meant to be, and I can't sit around feeling sorry for myself, now can I?"

There was no answer, but she didn't expect one. She stood and straightened her skirt. Her shoulders slumped as the bereft feeling she'd known so well eased within her soul to nestle there, familiar and warm.

Nora walked down the boardwalk from the hotel. Poor Joe. The boy was resting after a bad fit this afternoon. Her chest constricted. She couldn't ease the seizures, or the mind, but she wished she could heal his legs. She battled with herself each time she saw his deformed limbs, wanting to help him. The boy didn't deserve to have so many problems.

When she asked, Elwood told her Joe had been born that way, but Nora wasn't too sure. Joe's legs were knurled and his calves pointed outward when he stood. But it was the hunch on his back that made her second-guess his father. If Joe had been born crippled, his hump would be much larger than it was now.

She shook her head. She shouldn't be thinking such horrible thoughts, but Joe had planted himself inside her heart, and she wanted to protect him. She considered him a friend. *Friend.* The word stuck in her mind and a smile spread across her face.

Joe was the one person who hadn't judged her. He allowed her to be who she really was, not someone she was told to be. Not a girl locked in a cabin with hopes and dreams, and a gift. She accepted him for his differences as he accepted Nora for hers.

She'd mended his thumb earlier and he never questioned her. He may have thought she was a witch, she grimaced, but when she explained things to him, he understood and promised to keep her secret. Even though Joe had a simple mind, she knew without a doubt the boy wouldn't tell a soul about the episode behind the hotel.

She glanced back at the building. If she'd come earlier, Joe might not have had the fit and they'd be sitting on the porch playing Old Maid. Nora felt terrible for making him wait. She would come back tomorrow and hope he'd be well enough to see her.

She took the path behind the stores home. The aroma of coal stoves heating up dinners wafted toward her. Smoke filtered up from the chimneys and dissolved into the gray sky. Her pace quickened. Pa would be home soon.

What was she going to make for dinner? There wasn't much in the tiny cupboards to cook and Pa had drunk away all their money. She sighed. He needed help, and she had to make him see that he was destroying his life as well as hers.

She climbed through the window and closed it quietly behind her. In the kitchen, she skimmed through their meager supplies, not bothering to take down the box that held her mother's jewelry. No, she wouldn't sell the few things she had left of her.

There was one jar of peaches and one jar of pork left, and she placed them on the counter. The bag of cornmeal was the last thing left on the shelf. She'd use that in the morning for their breakfast. They would make do.

She looked out the window at her garden. A handful of carrots and two hills of potatoes remained. They could get by for most of the week, if she were careful. She could make potato soup. The meal would last them a few days. She opened the icebox. Her shoulders sagged and her bottom lip trembled. No milk. She glanced back to the counter. A teaspoon of flour was left in the jar, and she'd used all the baking soda on the sofa earlier.

Inside the cupboard, two empty shelves stared back at her. She squeezed her eyes shut to stop the tears from flowing and pressed her forehead to the wood.

What will we do? Oh Pa, what will we do?

The door swung open and her father came in, harried, filthy and stinking of stale alcohol. How did Jed work with him all day and not be sick?

She planted a smile on her face. "Good evening, Pa. How was work?"

Pa's eyes narrowed. "It was work." He pulled a chair out and slumped down into it.

She fidgeted with her hands, twisting her fingers until they hurt. She opened the jars and put the meat in the frying pan. She needed to talk with him, but she didn't know how. Every time she confronted him about going out or having friends, he'd fly off the handle and spend the rest of the night drinking at the saloon. But she had to say something now. She had to. There was no food left.

He hunched over in his chair half asleep. He was drinking himself to death.

She cleared her throat. "Um, Pa?"

The meat in the pan sizzled and she flipped it with a fork.

He angled his head toward her, but didn't say anything.

She chewed on her bottom lip while wiping her hands up and down on her apron. *Quit being a ninny.*

"Pa?" she started again. "We need to talk about...about your drinking." She braced herself for what was to come. From head to toe her muscles tensed.

He was silent.

She took two plates of peaches and fried pork to the table. She watched, as he moved the rubbery meat from one end of the plate to the other, never bringing the fork to his mouth. She couldn't blame him because it didn't look appealing.

She stared at him. Was he going to say anything? Taking his silence as a sign that he was willing to listen, she put her fork down and said quickly, "Pa, you have to stop going to the saloon. You have to stop gambling."

He stared at his plate for what seemed an eternity.

She inhaled and waited for him to speak.

He placed his elbows on the table and folded his hands. His blue eyes penetrated right through her. "No daughter of mine will tell me what to do," he growled, deep and low.

"But, Pa, you've spent all our money again. You gambled and drank it all away."

He slammed his fist onto the table. Plates rattled against their forks.

She jumped.

"The money you talk of is mine. I work for it. I hammer every day for hours to put food on the table, and this is the thanks I get?"

"No, no I appreciate all of those things, I do." She knelt in front of him. "But, Pa, you're drinking more and more every time."

"Sheriff Reid mentioned that he spoke with you yesterday."

The damn lawman was a boot-licker.

"I...I went for a walk. I wandered a little too far. It was nothing." She fidgeted with her skirt.

"You broke the rules, Nora, and at the end of the month we will be moving."

"No, Pa. I thought it best to get some fresh air, that's all." She stood and walked to the counter.

"What do you know about what's best? You're still a child."

"That is not true, Pa. I am almost nineteen. Most women my age are married with children to care for." When he rolled his eyes and threw his fork onto his plate she knew this conversation wasn't going to go well. *I'm in it now, no sense turning back.*

"Marriage will never be in your future, Nora. I've told you that time and time again. You are different, and you need to accept that."

"I know I'm different. But I can still have a normal life—I can still be a normal girl."

"No, Nora, you can't."

"Mama could heal, and she married you." Bringing her mother into the conversation was a sure fire way to anger her father. Prepared for battle, she waited for him to say something.

"Your mother didn't tell me until it was too late, until I found her hanging from a tree with a rope around her neck." He pushed his plate away.

Tears filled her eyes, as she leaned against the counter. She knew how her mother died. Accused of being a witch, the townspeople broke into their home while her father was away and hung Hannah Rushton on the tree in their yard. Nora was a baby. Her father found her hours later nestled in the trunk in their bedroom. Afraid the angry posse would come for Nora, Pa took her and they fled in the middle of the night.

"I am not Mother. No one here knows about my gift."

"Gift?" he sneered. "You call what you have a *gift*? It's a damn curse."

"I can't change who I am."

"No, you can't. That's why you must obey the rules I have set for you." He tapped his fingertips on the table, a sign he was frustrated and needed a drink.

"But I—

"I know, Nora. You want to be normal. But you're not," his voice grew louder. "You are different, not by choice, but different just the same."

Desperation pulled at her sanity. She needed him to understand. "I have no friends. I want to get married some day. How can I do any of those things if you keep me locked up in the house?"

He stood and raised his voice, "Are you not hearing me, daughter? You will never have those things. There will never be anyone who can be trusted enough to know. They will kill you." He ran his hand along his red face. "Do you understand? They will kill you." He slumped into his chair and murmured, "I could not bear finding you hanged from a tree, too."

She went to him. "Please, Pa, I've been good. I promise. Let me have a little freedom."

"No."

Nora's cheeks flushed and she frowned. "I've met your end of the bargain. I stayed in the house," she yelled. "But you haven't kept yours. We have no money. You've gambled and drank it away."

His face twisted and he glared at her.

Nora stood her ground. She would not back down.

"I'm the head of this house. I say where the money is spent." He grabbed her arms and leaned in so close she thought he would fall on top of her. "Do you hear me?" He shook her. "I am tired of you accusing me of not giving a damn. If I didn't, I'd let you roam the hills using your *curse* on who ever needed it."

She looked into bloodshot eyes. There was no way to make him see. He was sick, and there was nothing she could do to help him. "I understand," she whispered.

"I don't think you do." He wrenched her closer. "You want to have friends, and go out, and get a job. But you're too stupid to understand what will happen when they find out you're cursed."

"I am not cursed," she shouted.

"Yes, you are." He tossed her to the ground as he stood. "You're the very reason I've had to move all over this damn country. You're the reason we've been chased down by people you've healed." He pointed a finger at her and his voice rose. "You are why there is nothing left of what we once had."

The words sliced through her and piece by piece he tore her down. Her soul begged for a kind word from him. Nothing but blame came from his lips. Blame, blame and more blame.

He hated her.

I will not cry. She blinked back the tears, and stood tall while he hurled insults at her.

"I'm sorry."

"Sorry?" He knelt down beside her and lifted her chin. "I love you, Nora." His eyes watered. "But some days I wish you were never born." With those words he left, shutting the door behind him.

Nora's heart broke. The one person she'd ever relied on, ever cared for, ripped the heart from her chest. The pain was almost too much to take. She brought her knees up and hugged them to her. How could he be so cruel? How could he say he loved her but then say those words? She wiped at a tear. Over the years, Pa's disposition had faded from joyful and light to ugly and dark. He resented her for the life they had to lead. He accused her for the alcohol he consumed.

She brought her forehead to her knees. *When did he begin to hate me so much?* She held out her hands. They had caused this—her gift. Maybe he was right. Maybe her hands were cursed after all. But how was she to stop helping those in need?

She shook her head. *If someone is hurt I need to help them.* She thought of Joe. If she hadn't healed him, he'd have no thumb. If she hadn't helped Jess Chandler, she might've died. And what of the animals that she found shot, in traps or wounded? She couldn't walk away from them either.

She couldn't do what Pa asked of her. She squeezed her hands together. She'd sacrificed her relationship with her father to save lives. Why couldn't he see the good she'd done? Instead, all he saw was a curse that had taken everything away from him.

She blew out a ragged breath

If she received nothing else from her ability to help those in need but to see their joy, then it was worth it to her. She couldn't change who she was, even though Pa would love nothing more. If she didn't use her gift at all and walked away from those in need, would he love her again? Would he take back the awful words he said? Acceptance weighed heavy upon her soul. Without saying the words, she knew the answer.

Nora gathered the dishes and pushed the untouched food onto one plate to be saved in the icebox for tomorrow. Her stomach lurched. The thought of eating the tasteless meat tomorrow night was enough to make her sick.

After she cleaned the kitchen, she heated water in the pot. A cup of tea would ease the tension in her neck and the headache she felt coming on. She took yesterday's leaves and dumped them into her cup.

She went to the window. The kerosene lamps lit the street. There was no sign of father. She knew where he'd gone. The water boiled and she poured some into her cup. She stirred the leaves and took a sip. The hot minty taste wasn't as strong as when she first used the leaves a couple of days ago, but it did the trick. And she didn't have a choice, there was no more left.

CHAPTER NINE

He lay awake listening to the sounds of a night he knew would end badly. He leaned over and placed his hand on his younger brother's chest. Little Eagle's soft breaths feathered his skin. Good, he was still asleep. A crash echoed through the tiny cabin.

He removed the thin blanket covering him and his brother. The straw-filled bed crunched under his weight as he shifted to roll off and touch his bare feet to the dirt floor. The fireplace on the far wall gave little light to the one room home, but he could still make out the table flipped on its side, two wooden chairs and a makeshift counter—a plank on top of three tree stumps.

Another bang followed by a pleading moan. Ina! He crawled around the bed to try and see what was going on, even though he already knew.

The warm glow from the fire cast the room in welcoming shadows, but the beast standing over his mother turned it into a nightmare. A meaty fist raised high in the air and rushed toward her as she lay on her side, bleeding from the temple. The thud of flesh meeting flesh sent his stomach rolling. He squeezed his eyes shut, tucked his head into his chest and prayed it would stop.

The dull sound continued. He covered his ears, tried to shut it out. If he were taller, stronger he'd be able to help her. Guilt consumed him, and a tear slipped past his black lashes.

A low whimper came from his Ina, and he wanted nothing more than to go to her. He needed to hold her in his skinny arms and tell her he loved her.

Tears wet his face, but he didn't bother to wipe them. More punches came. When would it end? How much more could she take? His chest heavy, the air seized within his lungs, as he muffled a sob into the straw-filled bed. His fingers gathered the blanket, gripping it tightly.

He needed to help her. He rubbed his cheek against the mattress, the straw poked through, cutting his skin. He searched the room for something—anything that he could use as a weapon. There was nothing. No gun, no knife, no magical spell to cast like in the stories he'd been told.

Silence. The room held an eerie stillness, and he strained to hear any sign his Ina was alive. He opened his eyes. The swine still stood above her, a bottle of brown liquid in his hand. He took a long drink and spat it all over her. She didn't move. The brute nudged her with his boot. Still nothing.

Rage bubbled hot and feral inside of him. Ina lay beaten and bloodied on the dirt floor while the monster, the beast—his father kicked her! He dug his hands into the dirt floor and squeezed, feeling the black residue filter through his clenched fingers.

A warrior's cry burst from his mouth as he bolted toward his father. Arms flailing, he punched and kicked trying to kill the wasichu. A large hand clipped his chin, dazing him, but he wouldn't give up, he couldn't. He had to save her.

He scratched and bit puncturing the skin, on his father's arms. Another backhand across the head sent him sprawling into the counter, breaking dishes and toppling it over. His arm was cut, and the side of his head pulsed with pain. A knife bounced to the floor and he grabbed it.

Arm held high he charged at his father. With one swing the knife was knocked from his hand, and thick fingers dug into his throat. He struggled for air as his feet left the ground. He kicked at the space around them, his vision blurred.

When he came to, it was still dark outside and his father was gone. His throat sore and swollen, he winced as he swallowed. He crawled toward Ina. Each move he took sent spasms throughout his scrawny body. By morning he'd be covered in bruises.

He would never forget these moments. The punches, smacks, kicks permeated his mind and stole to the very depths of his soul. His brother was awake. Three winters old, Little Eagle clutched the tattered blanket close to his mouth and stood over Ina. Little Eagle's round face was damp with tears.

He struggled to get closer. His tongue fatter in his mouth, he tasted blood when he licked his lips. He knelt beside them and held his little brother's hand.

"Misu, iyunke—Brother, lay," he said and guided him down to lie beside their mother.

"Ina, Ina?" Little Eagle whimpered.

His breaths came in quick puffs as his heart pounded in his throat. He placed their mother's head onto his lap. How was he going to fix her? Old bruises mingled with new ones coloring her face. A nasty scrape bled from the side of her head and into her blue-black hair. He ran his hand along the soft tresses, something he'd done since he was little. The motion had calmed him and helped him sleep.

He slowly got up, dunked a dirty cloth into the bucket and tenderly cleaned her wounds. Her deerskin dress was ripped at the neck and arms, traces of too many times their father had abused her. He ran the cloth along the cut on her head, trying to pull the dry blood from her hair. He'd cared for her several times in his twelve winters, and each time she grew weaker and weaker. He'd watched his Ina change from a strong, lively woman to a shell, a whisper of who she once was.

He turned a hate-filled glare toward the door where the man who called himself a husband, a father had left. He had no feelings but those of disgust, at the vile wasichu who stole from them a life filled of happiness and love.

He kissed her cheek and rested his face against hers.

"Ina, Ina, please wake up."

He lay like that for half hour, until he realized he could feel no breath touch his cheek. He sat up and watched her chest. He shook her.

"Ina, you've got to wake up."

His mother didn't move, and he gasped unable to accept what might be. He glanced at Little Eagle, nestled close to their mother on the floor.

"Wanbli Cikala—Little Eagle. Ina needs to stay warm. Go fetch some firewood."

The boy shook his head. "No, no," he cried clutching Ina's hand.

"Go. You must be big. You must help."

Little Eagle nodded and laid his blanket over Ina.

"Two logs," he said and his brother ran outside.

Hands shaking, he placed his finger into his mouth and held it in front of her nose. There was nothing. No air flowed from her lungs! He scanned the room searching for something or someone to help him. He shook her, once, twice a third time. No air. No air!

"Ina? Ina?"

He watched as her dark head lolled to the side, and he knew there was no life within her.

"Ku, ku, ku—come back, come back, come back."

Tears spewed from his eyes onto her face as he sobbed, clutching her body to his. He inhaled the wood smoke, the pine, the fresh scent that was her alone. He didn't want to forget. He didn't want to let go. He couldn't. He couldn't. He couldn't!

Wrenching sobs wracked his body in uncontrolled shakes. The pain inside his soul pricked and pierced at his sanity. He rocked her back and forth, clutching—grasping at what he once had. He pulled her closer and wept for the mother he'd lost, for the stories he'd not hear, for the love *he'd never see in her eyes again. He wept for the brother he'd have to tell, and the life they'd live without her.*

He stumbled to his feet and searched for something to ease his pain. Something to take away the fire from his insides, the weight of hopelessness, anguish and fear bore down upon him and buckled his knees.

Ina, Ina, Ina. His mother was gone.

His hands shook as he gripped the knife he'd tried to kill his father with. He sliced his chest four times. The misery, the torment poured out from inside of him. He howled, and as the blood ran from his chest, so did the tears from his eyes.

He rubbed his bleeding flesh, smearing two lines along his cheeks. He fell to his knees before his mother and gathered her into his arms. A low humming floated from his lips in between moments where his body broke down and trembled. He took Ina's hand and sliced her palm, before slicing his own and bringing them together.

"You will be with me forever, my Ina."

Otakatay tossed back the bed roll and sat up, panting. His lungs burned with the intensity of the dream and the vivid memory of his last moments with his Ina. His bronzed flesh glistened. Four scars stood out among the others. He closed his eyes. The ache in his heart radiated, encompassing his whole back. *Ina.* Oh, how he missed her. How he wished for that day back. He let her down. He didn't protect her. He didn't save her.

I couldn't. Years passed before he'd avenged that day and all the others that led up to it. But no matter what he did, no matter who he killed, the hurt stayed with him, a constant sickness that crippled him.

He remembered the suffering Ina went through, the anguish that followed afterward, the life they were thrown into. He touched the feather in his hair, a constant reminder of a promise he would fulfill at all costs.

There was no way to make it right. No way to change what had happened. He wiped at the tears that wanted to fall. He would not cry. He showed no weakness.

But he was so sorry he'd let Ina down. He'd let them all down. He studied the scar on his palm. *I will never forget.* He was no longer the happy boy who loved stories and whittling wood, or who had taught his brother to shoot an arrow. He was a killer, a violent, deadly man who with the skilled swipe of his blade had ended many lives.

I am Otakatay, one who kills many.

A chill swept over him and he pulled the deerskin shirt from his saddle bag. The leather was smooth and warm against his damp flesh. He rubbed the faded yellow skin between his fore finger and thumb taking comfort in the texture of the shirt and the rhythm of his fingers. A night owl hooted. The day was going to be long.

He placed the shirt back into the bag and threw his arms into the black cotton one he wore every day. He was restless, sleep eluded him. He gathered wood to stoke the fire.

Now warm and comfortable, he felt the feather tied in his hair. It was becoming dense and falling from the quill. He would need to get a new one.

He didn't think he'd find any witkowan in town, but it didn't hurt to have a look around. He needed one more kill. One more scalp to bring to the wasichu who hired him. Then he could take back what was his. He didn't have to kill anymore.

In a few hours he would put his black duster on and head into town. A nervous tension settled inside of him. No welcoming party would greet him. Instead, people would stare, point and run. Doors would be locked, windows closed and shutters brought down. Children herded indoors by fearful women and men with rifles.

He shook his head. His presence among the wasichu had disaster written all over it. He learned long ago to read the white eyes. He knew their actions before they surfaced in their own minds. Which gun they'd use to draw on him and where his bullet would strike, killing them instantly. He could spot the cowards that would attack from behind and the sensible men that didn't want any trouble at all.

He pulled the knife from his pant leg and sharpened the blade on his whetstone. If he had to venture among the wasichu, he'd go prepared. He was never without two knives and a rifle. Sparks flew from the blade as it scraped along the smooth stone. The owl's voice blending with the swipe of the blade played an earthy song that he embraced, allowing the melody to become a part of him.

CHAPTER TEN

Elwood pushed himself back into the wooden chair. A thick fog of cigarette and cigar smoke along with the scent of lustful women filled the saloon. He squinted through the haze and scrutinized the players around the table.

Ted Blair, the banker, sat stiffly in the chair across from him, his pointy nose buried in his cards. Levi and Red passed a bottle of whiskey between them and laid their cards on the table face down. They were here to fix the odds. Jack Rushton flopped close on his right and swayed back the other way again.

He glanced at his hand, a pair of kings and three ten's, a full house. Red had slipped him the winning card, and because of the ruse he'd won almost every hand. Dollar bills, coins and even a ladies watch piled high in the middle of the round table.

"You sure on that, Jack?" asked Ed Morgan, the dealer.

The gold watch was dainty, a pretty piece with clean lines and a round face. Elwood knew it was worth more than money.

"I'm fine with it. Nows let's play cards." Jack was well into the bottle before he sat down at the table and started tossing jewelry into the pot. He'd lost the gold wedding ring he wore in the last hand and threw in the watch so he could continue playing. The blacksmith was a tall man with a slight build and Elwood figured not worth a damn. He'd heard the man spent more time in the saloon drinking and gambling than at home with his pretty daughter.

He eyed Jack. Gambling with precious jewelry was a sign of bad things to come.

"I can give you a loan if that's what you need, Jack." Elwood pointed to the table and the loot awaiting his pocket.

Jack slumped toward him, and the smell of sour mash liquor followed.

He inched back.

Jack was so intoxicated he didn't even know what he'd said. Elwood didn't give a damn if he understood him or not. Hell, he didn't need anything from him other than control. He wanted what Jack had the pleasure of seeing every night.

He dug into his pocket and pulled out a handful of bills. "How much do you need?"

Jack swatted at his hand. "I ain't needin' yer money."

He balled his hands into tight fists until the urge to strangle the blacksmith left. He picked up the watch and cradled it in his manicured hands.

"Don't sell the pretty watch. You've already lost your ring. What will Nora think?"

Jack's bottom lip quivered and he blinked. Elwood knew he'd struck a chord.

"You don't talk about Nora. Sh...she is never going to marry you." He pointed at Elwood while swaying and almost falling from the chair.

"I've come to accept that."

"Leave her be. I won't condone it," he slurred.

Elwood had to refrain from kicking the chair out from under the drunken ass. He didn't give a damn if the old man condoned his marrying Nora or not, it was going to happen one way or the other.

"I can lend you the money." He held the watch in front of Jack.

"Leave it there," he stammered and tried to grab it from Elwood's hand.

Elwood persuaded people with his money in order to get what he wanted. He'd done the same thing with his land, and the best part was he could kick the farmers off if they were a dime short. The power he held over them made him giddy. He ran the mine the same way. He lorded over those brats for years, and he loved that they feared him. He paid them nothing and got labor in return.

Pretending to be kind was something he was good at, and Jack Rushton would fall for it like all the rest. Jack had the one thing Elwood wanted. Nora.

"How about I loan you the money for the watch?" He dangled the yellow band on his finger. "I will give it back once you've paid me." A lie of course, he'd use the watch to entice Nora.

"Hurry it up, Jack. We have a game to play," Ed growled.

Jack looked from the watch Elwood held, to the money on the table and back again. He peered out the window for a long while. "You'll leave Nora alone?"

He nodded a dark smile upon his lips.

"All right, you have a deal."

Elwood had to conceal his excitement. Soon Nora would be his. He dropped the watch in his pocket, counted out twenty dollars and handed the green backs to Jack. He'd given more than the watch was worth, but that would all come back to him tenfold when he had Nora in his arms and in his bed.

The game continued and within a half hour Jack had lost the twenty dollars, his pride and according to Elwood, his daughter. He watched as the man stumbled out of the saloon, falling over his feet a few times on the way. He stretched across the table and scooped up his winnings.

"Good dealing tonight, Ed," he said and slipped the dealer five dollars before following Jack outside.

CHAPTER ELEVEN

Nora stood at the window and watched Pa walk across the lawn to go to work. She didn't come out of her room until she heard the front door close. After last night's argument a conversation wasn't what either of them wanted. She ran the brush through her long hair, listening as it crackled.

She loved pa, but she didn't want to be a burden any longer. She had no control over why she'd received such a gift. Why her mother and grandmother bore the mark, or why they died.

She didn't know much about her mother, only what Pa wanted to tell her. Hannah Rushton was a healer, a woman with a curse, according to father. Whenever she'd ask about her mother, he usually held his lips firmly together and never said a word. On the rare occasion he mentioned her, she sucked in his words and buried them deep within her heart.

No matter what she did, or where she went, she knew she'd never change. People wouldn't expect Doctor Spencer to walk away from a sick child without giving him some medicine. If it came down to saving someone's life, she'd risk losing hers to save another's.

She braided her hair and tied the end with the same piece of leather she'd used since she was a girl. She held the tail of the braid close and examined the tanned leather strip. She often fantasized that her mother had worn it.

She opened the cupboard, stood on tiptoes, and grabbed the box. Her shoulders sagged at what she was about to do. *I have no choice.*

Faded blue flowers graced the sides of the box, and she skimmed her finger along the edge. Pa had given it to her for her tenth birthday. The only gift she'd ever received. She didn't want to take the treasures inside. They were the last things she had left of her mother. The hinges creaked in dismay as she lifted the lid. She blinked. *It can't be.* She placed her hand over her chest to ease the dull ache. The watch was gone. The beautiful gold watch that had rested on her mother's wrist wasn't there. Her eyes filled with tears. She pushed aside the silver brooch and gold ring with a ruby. The watch was gone. Pa had done this.

All for another drink and a game of cards.

She picked up the ring and placed it on her finger, turning the band. Pa had stayed out late last night. Now she knew where he'd gotten the money to do it.

She lowered her head. The watch was gone. He'd sold it for a bottle of whiskey, a damn bottle of whiskey. She slammed her hand onto the counter. Anger packed around her heart and fueled her irritation. She placed the brooch in her pocket, and went out the door, heading straight for the blacksmiths.

Inside, her nose burned with the heavy scent of ash, sweat and smoldering wood. She straightened and walked around a barrel full of water. Tools she'd never seen before leaned inside the tub, cooling off. The clanking and tapping reminded her of when she was little, sitting on a stump watching Pa work. Happier days assaulted her mind, forcing her anger out.

When she spotted him, her resolve faltered. She watched as he hunched over a large fire, heating a long piece of metal. Sweat dripped down his forehead, and his eyes squinted. He was tired—worn. She saw the wrinkles on his face, and the thought of tearing a strip off of him didn't seem to have the same effect anymore.

He glanced up.

Sadness reflected in his blue eyes and spread across his face. She stood still, waiting for him to say something. But when she saw a tear drop from his eye, all her anger left and she went to him.

"Oh, Pa." She placed her arms around his neck and hugged him.

Strong arms wrapped around her waist. "I'm sorry, Daughter."

The embrace didn't last long, but it was enough for her. He smelled of stale liquor, but she didn't care. For this moment he was her pa, the one who raised her. The father she missed very much.

"We will get through this," she whispered.

He nodded.

She wished she could take him home and feed him a warm meal. He needed to rest. His skin held a yellow tint, and the black circles under his eyes belied the late nights filled with drinking. He wasn't well.

"Pa, let me take you home. You should rest."

"No, I must work." His eyes shifted toward the ground, "I need to make up for the mistakes I've made."

"We'll make do. We always have."

He tensed, and she knew she'd touched a nerve.

"I don't need you telling me what to do, Nora." There was an edge to his voice, a warning.

"Yes, sir."

She kissed his forehead, and without glancing back, she went out the double doors and into the street. She was challenging him, and she waited for the shout, the hand on the arm to stop her but nothing happened. No fight. No argument. No admonition to go home and stay there.

She should've been relieved to have some freedom, to no longer be hidden from the world. Instead she felt horrible, incomplete, a puzzle in which Pa was the missing piece. He didn't care. He didn't love her. She stepped out onto the street.

She could come and go as she pleased, and yet it didn't please her one bit. The sun shone brightly in the clear blue sky, and she closed her eyes feeling the warmth on her face. The freedom should be exhilarating. She should be jumping for joy, but all she could think about was the distance he had placed between them, and she didn't know how to fix it.

She stopped before the boardwalk and swallowed thickly. She fingered the broach in her apron pocket. The bell over the door jingled a warm welcome as she entered the Mercantile. Doctor Spencer was leaving, so she held the door for him.

"Thank you, Miss Rushton," he said supplies in his hands.

"You're most welcome, Doctor." She couldn't hide the sadness in her voice and prayed the doctor didn't notice.

A quick look around told her no one else was in the store.

"Good morning, Miss Rushton," Fred said, with a bright smile.

"Good morning, Mr. Sutherland." She pulled the brooch from her pocket and laid it on the counter. "How much will I be able to buy with this?"

The shop owner glanced at her over his wire rimmed glasses, before he picked up the brooch to examine it. She saw a glimpse of pity in his wrinkle-framed eyes, but ignored it and waited patiently for his answer.

"I can give you three dollars for it." He placed the broach on the counter.

Three dollars wasn't much. She'd only be able to get a few things and they needed more. She caressed the ring on her right hand, slipped it off and laid it next to the broach. Her cheeks heated and she swallowed past the lump in her throat.

The shop owner picked up the ring. "This is nice. This is nice indeed."

She dipped her head to hide the tears threatening to fall. Hands folded in front of her, and she concentrated on squeezing them together.

"I will give you seven dollars for this one," Fred beamed.

Unable to find her voice, she nodded and waited while he counted out the money from his register. With a shaky hand, she scooped up the green bills, not knowing if he'd given her the correct amount or not.

She walked aimlessly around the store, the tins, boxes and fabrics all became a blur. She pulled the handkerchief from her pocket, tipped her head and blotted her eyes. She no longer cared about buying food. All thoughts of surviving left her, replaced with a mourning she'd never felt before. Her chest tightened as sharp pains spread to her back. She wrapped her arms around her to keep from crumpling on the floor and bawling like a baby. The brooch, the ring, the watch—they were all gone.

Mr. Sutherland held her mother's ring up to the light shining through the window. A bright smile creased his face. She needed to get out of the store before she ran over and took the ring back.

Head down, she pulled the door open, heard the faint jingle and stepped outside. A strong force sent her flying onto her butt. Before she realized what had happened, two large hands cupped under her arms and yanked her up.

Flustered, she flipped the hair that had fallen in her eyes to the side and stared up at—him. It was the Indian, the one who threatened to kill her. He was right here in front of her. She couldn't see his eyes because of the black Stetson low on his forehead, but there was no mistaking the square jaw and the feather peeking out from behind his ear. Nor was there any mistaking the smell of danger that seemed to surround him.

"Thank you," she said and smiled.

A low grunt was all she heard and then she was staring at his backside as he walked away. Children and their mothers hurried out of his way, panic and fear on their faces. She could see why they were scared. He was a frightful person. The black attire he wore didn't help, but she guessed it had more to do with his Indian blood than anything.

He walked with lethal prowess, a hunter seeking his prey. He held his shoulders straight and flexed his hands at his sides, ready to pull the knife he'd used on her the other day. There was no mistaking his aura; he was not someone you tangled with. She'd bet ten to one he'd come out the winner every time.

As people shuffled to the other side of the street and hastily went into shops, she knew he wasn't here to harm any of them. If he wanted to, he'd have done so by now. He was simply walking down the boardwalk, scaring the hell out of them instead.

Not bothering to right her skirt or apron, she trailed after him, curious about who he was and why he was here. He was heading out of town in the direction of the forest, and she was determined to follow.

She waited until he disappeared into the thick of the trees before going in after him. The smell of pine and moss tickled her nose as she took soft steps. Sun light burst through the trees and lit up the forest floor. She continued on, before she figured out he was no longer a few yards in front of her. She picked up her pace and scanned the trees around her, but there was still no sign of him. He'd vanished.

Where did he go?

She stopped, did a full circle looking into the dense bushes around her, but he was gone.

She glanced back toward town. She didn't want to go home. She had hoped to find the stranger and talk with him. She continued on her way deciding to sit by the river and collect her thoughts. After selling the last of her mother's jewelry, she didn't have it in her to go back to the mercantile.

They needed food and she'd buy it, but not right now. Not when her insides ached with such despair and guilt. She wondered if Mr. Sutherland would consider holding the items for her until she could get enough money to buy them back. The brooch maybe, but she doubted he'd give up the ring. For all she knew it could be on Wilimena's chubby finger by now.

She walked along the water's edge and watched while it receded in and out, leaving a trail of twigs and leaves. She rounded a bend and spotted a horse standing next to a tall oak. The lean creature stood still. The color of his coat was beautiful and resembled a storm filled sky. She inched forward and held out her hand. The horse didn't move.

"You're beautiful." She stepped closer.

A saddle was cinched around the animal's middle and a bedroll tied to his back.

The horse stepped toward her and placed his snout into her palm.

She smiled.

"You're a friendly one, aren't you?" She ran her hand between his eyes and down the length of his nose.

"You should not touch other people's belongings."

She spun around as the Indian made his way through the trees toward her. Where had he come from?

"I...I was walking and saw him."

"You were following me." He came closer, and instinct told her to run.

"My name is—

"I don't care who you are."

He took the horse's reins and pulled the animal away from Nora. The horse yanked his head back toward her.

"Wakina," he growled and tugged the reins again.

"What a beautiful name. What does it mean?" She examined him, trying to make out if he was frowning or if his lips were always pursed together.

Reins in hand, he turned and walked away.

She fell into step beside him. "What does your horse's name mean?" She wanted to know something—anything about the man. He was a mystery to her, and she could see he needed a friend or maybe it was her in need. She shrugged, it didn't really matter, and she was too darn curious to let this go. She saw the scars on his right forearm and her fingers pulsed.

"Sir, what does Wakina mean?"

"Go away."

He stared straight ahead, hat still on his head, he worked his jaw. She was annoying him, but he intrigued her so much she didn't care. "Sir."

He spun around almost knocking her to the ground a second time and leaned into her face. "Leave."

He's going to kill me. And judging by the gleam in his eyes, he was envisioning the way to do it. She shuddered. Something quick and effortless was probably the way he'd go. The knife across her throat or right into her heart. She wouldn't feel a thing. She pushed all thoughts of the consequences aside, tipped her chin up and stepped forward so her breasts brushed his chest.

"No. I think I'd like to stay."

"You do not get a choice," he uttered through clenched teeth.

He smelled of leather, smoke and a spice she couldn't quite put her finger on. She refrained from touching the feather in his hair, and instead stared into his troubled eyes. Sadness, anger and purpose melded together in the dark depths.

She smiled.

She never heard the sound of the blade until the tip pricked her throat. Black eyes, lethal and wicked, bore into hers. Tanned features tightened to conceal any hint of kindness and were replaced with evil and disgust. It was fascinating how he changed. How he masked any emotion other than hate and punched it forward onto his enemy, onto her.

She gasped. The enormity of his revulsion smashed into her, heavy and compressed. She felt dirty. Had her people done this to him? Had they mistreated him, pulling the hate from him, so anger was the sole emotion he displayed? Oh, if this was so, she needed to fix it. She needed him to see that not all white people were the same.

She closed her eyes. She had no idea where the courage came from to place her hand lightly over his. She felt the cool metal blade on the tip of her thumb but did not move her hand away. *If he is going to kill me, let it be quick.* She opened her eyes and watched as curiosity, anger and hate flickered across his face.

"Go," he rasped.

"No."

"I will kill you."

She gulped.

"Then do your best, because I'm not leaving."

He flexed his jaw, pushed the knife into her throat. The skin broke and she could feel the blood trickle down her neck. *Here we go. Please let Pa know how much I loved him.*

She held her breath and met his eyes.

Time stretched. His broad chest rose and fell as he exhaled onto her face.

She refused to look away.

He growled, flung her to the side and threw his knife. The wood split as the blade struck the tree. She checked to make sure he hadn't sliced her throat before he threw the knife. Blood smeared her fingers, and she pulled a handkerchief from her apron.

CHAPTER TWELVE

Otakatay pulled the knife from the tree. What in hell had the wasicun winyan been thinking? He glanced back at her. She sat on a tree stump blotting a white cloth to her neck. He'd cut her. Not enough to kill her, a nick from the tip of his blade to scare her. But it hadn't worked. Instead she'd challenged him with her blue eyes, pushed him to harm her.

He threw his knife again. Every muscle vibrated, wanting to release the energy alive and coursing rampantly through his veins. He should've smacked her. She'd be running away in fear then.

He shook his head. He didn't hit women. *No, I only kill them.* His stomach pitched. He looked at her again. He murdered women like her, women with kind smiles and bright eyes—women who haunted his dreams. He massaged his chest. He didn't want to think of them.

He grabbed his knife and slid it into the leather sheath strapped under the coat on his back.

"What do you want?" he barked.

She stopped dabbing her neck. "To be your friend."

He had no friends and didn't want any either. "I don't need a friend."

Without missing a beat she piped up, "Everyone needs a friend."

He saw sadness flicker across her face, and he stiffened. She was the one in need. He didn't give a shit what she needed. He wasn't it. There were plenty of wasichu in town she could mingle with. He went to Wakina, wrapped the leather reins around his hand and walked away. He heard her steps beside him. *Why won't she go away?* She was like a fly, a nuisance that hung around until you swatted it away or killed it.

He grunted. He'd tried that, and it didn't work.

He glanced at her through his lashes. He couldn't kill her. He didn't kill without reason, and as irritating as she was, it wasn't a good enough excuse to end her life.

"Sir, where are you from?" She skipped beside him.

He walked faster. A hand touched his arm and he pushed it away.

"Wakina means *Thunder* in Lakota," he said, still feeling the heat from her hand on his arm.

"Well, that makes perfect sense," she puffed.

He didn't know why he'd told her Wakina's Lakota name, or why he hadn't jumped on the horse's back leaving her far behind him. He scowled at her and an innocence he'd witnessed before surrounded her. *Ina*.

There had been nothing soft, nothing warm in his life for years and he didn't know what to do with it—with her. She had an aura that illuminated a goodness he'd thought forgotten within the wasichu.

She was different.

"He is the color of thunder clouds, dark gray. I see why you named him that." She ran her hand along Wakina's mane.

He ignored her.

"Where are you from?"

He avoided the question the first time. He didn't know, didn't want to remember. "I've lived all over."

She nodded, satisfied with his answer. "Do you belong to a tribe?"

"No." *I belong to no one.*

"Oh." She was silent for a long time, and he thought she was done asking questions until her full lips opened again. "Are you white, too?"

Not by choice. "Yes."

She stopped. He didn't, and soon he heard the rustling of the leaves as she caught up.

"You're a—

"Half breed." He didn't know what she was going to say and he didn't give a damn. Half breeds were outcasts. He'd been reminded every day of his life what he was.

"I wasn't about to say that," she whispered.

"It is what I am."

"It is cruel."

He tripped on a root but continued walking. "Why would you think it is cruel when your people continue to use it?"

"My people may use it, but it doesn't mean I do."

He'd brought her to his camp. *Damn it.* What the hell had he been thinking? He'd let his guard down for five minutes and this is what happens. *Why won't she go away?* Hell, even men feared him, yet this little minx walked beside him as if he were a preacher giving the Sunday Sermon.

He frowned.

She lifted her skirt, and he spied the white of her calves. His pulse quickened.

She plopped down onto the ground and crossed her legs. "You enjoy sleeping under the stars?"

He'd enjoy it if she'd leave.

"What is your name?"

"Otakatay."

He smiled, knowing what would come next.

"What does it mean?"

"One who kills many."

He watched amused as her mouth opened and closed a few times. White delicate hands fidgeted on her lap. "Why would your mother name you that?"

Ina. He made a fist, constricting the muscles within his arms. He could not change the past. He couldn't make things right. He touched the feather in his hair.

"Have you killed many?"

Her words seemed far away. "Yes." There was nothing more to say. He'd killed more than he could remember, more than he should have. More than he wanted.

"Are you a bounty hunter?"

Why was she asking so many damn questions and why in hell was he answering them? He left Wakina to wander and sat down across from her. He threw her a menacing glare, but the little nit didn't even flinch. He pulled the knife from his back and with brisk movements, sharpened it.

"Is that what you do?"

"I kill for money."

She chewed on the inside of her cheek.

She was troubled, he could tell. He hoped she'd get up and leave, now that she knew what he was.

"Have you ever killed someone who was innocent?"

He held the blade of his knife up to his cheek. "I kill those who are deadly and those who I'm paid to kill."

"Even if they are innocent?"

"It doesn't matter to me what they are as long as I get paid."

"Even...even women and children?" She folded her hands together, twisting them until the knuckles were white.

His face hardened. "No children."

"But, but you've killed women."

He remained silent.

"Oh my."

He'd had enough of the questions and decided it was time for her to leave. It was time for her to see what she was sitting across from.

"I am a killer." He dragged his blade slowly across the whetstone. "I've gutted, sliced and pitted bodies for greenbacks. I'm a shadow lurking in the corner, waiting to." He threw the knife, missing the side of her face by less than an inch, into the tree behind her.

She lifted a shaky hand up to her head and patted her hair. When her eyes met his there was no malice or hate within them. No trace of fear. He blinked. Why wasn't she scared? Why didn't she curse at him, yelling savage, lowlife, breed? *Why is she still here?*

She was not like any other wasichu he'd come across in his twenty-six winters. She was familiar in a peculiar way. He stomped down any gesture that might lead her to believe he was a good person. He wasn't.

He stood, and so did she. Dainty hands ran along the front of her skirt. The fabric should be burned, the edges frayed, the brown color faded and worn. He analysed her features. She was pretty, in a different sort of way. Pale skin, blue eyes and black hair were an odd combination, but one that seemed to compliment her. She was fine-boned, with dainty hands and short legs. Underneath the rags and braided hair, she was strong, a fighter. His previous attempts to scare her told him that. There was also kindness within her, and he'd seen it with his horse.

He shifted from one foot to the other, curled his fingers into fists. He wanted nothing to do with the wasicun winyan.

"I have to go," she said.

He watched as her eyes darted from him to Wakina. She went to the horse, placed her cheek against his and whispered something he couldn't hear.

"Goodbye, Otakatay."

He remained silent and watched her walk into the forest. When he couldn't see her anymore he let his shoulders fall, and kicked dirt over the ashes left from his fire last night. He broke branches throwing them onto the ground. He was moving camp. He didn't want her coming back with more questions. Shit, he'd rather face a den of rattlesnakes.

A terrifying scream carried over the trees and slammed into him. He pushed his feet into the ground, planting himself so he wouldn't move. She was fine, probably saw a snake.

Another scream echoed throughout the camp.

Wakina tossed his head and bared his teeth.

"No."

Two hoofs sprung into the air and landed with a puff of dirt onto the ground.

"Wakina."

The horse raised one leg, bared his teeth again and took off into the forest.

"Son of a bitch."

Otakatay pulled his knife from the tree and sprinted after Wakina. His moccasins allowed him to run with silent steps. A gift he'd acquired after much practice. He swatted at the branches, as he followed the sound of Wakina's hooves. He spotted the girl through the trees. She sat on a rotted stump by the river, holding something in her hands. Wakina stood next to her, his snout resting on her shoulder. *I will eat the animal yet.*

He set his jaw and pushed through the last tree in front of him. He saw the black fur on her lap. "Why are you holding a dead animal?"

Nora's tear-streaked face looked up at him, and he realized it wasn't an animal. It was a scalp. He ground his teeth together.

"It's a...a...a"

He yanked the wet hair from her lap and threw it into the river, making sure it was within the rapids.

Her hands shook. He didn't know what to do. He didn't want to help her, he couldn't.

"I will walk you to the end of the forest."

She didn't move, instead continued to shake worse than before.

"It was a scalp, Otakatay. It was a woman's scalp." More tears burst from her eyes, making the blue within them shine.

He didn't answer. He knew what it was. Remorse, grave and intense, weighed on his shoulders. He swallowed. He had nothing to offer her. He placed his hand upon her shoulder for a mere second, before snapping it back to his side. He was a killer. A low-life half-breed that belonged nowhere. There was nothing gentle within him.

He left her and went to stand by a tree. The distance helped to bring back his senses and the overwhelming urge to help the girl. Wakina stayed by her side and he glared at the horse.

She wiped her eyes with the back of her hand and gave Wakina a shaky smile. He scanned the river for more floating scalps and exhaled when he saw none.

She wrapped her arms around the horse's neck.

He'd never seen a wasichu show affection for an animal. He waited until she twisted toward him before ushering her out of the forest.

"Why, Otakatay, would someone scalp a woman?"

He clamped his lips together so he didn't confess.

She caught her foot and stumbled.

He grabbed her before she fell onto her face. He turned her in his arms and gazed into her eyes. They reminded him of a stormy sky, sapphire with a dark ring around the outside. A jolt of lightning shot through him, and he couldn't look away. He couldn't see anything but her.

He leaned forward, hovering above her pink lips. She smelled of roses, dirt and horse, and before he could control himself, before he could talk some sense into his thick skull, he grazed his lips over hers.

Softly, he melded them together, branding this moment into his mind forever. The sun's rays filtered through the trees and onto her hair, transforming the dull color to a shimmering shade of dark blue. She brought her arms up, wrapped them around his neck and tilted her head to deepen the kiss. He stilled, and his arms fell listlessly at his sides.

She dropped onto the ground with a thud and gaped up at him confused.

I have to be sure. He yanked her up and cushioned her back against his chest. He kissed her neck and pushed the hair to the side. Delicately, so he didn't startle her, he moved his lips up to her ear.

Amidst her braided hair, nestled so it wasn't easily seen sat his destiny. He hugged her to him as a wave of nausea bloated his stomach. Beads of sweat formed on his forehead. *One more. I need one more.* The demon inside him whispered, *slit her throat.* He squeezed his eyes shut. *Do it. Kill her.*

He fought with the hunter he'd become, and the promise he'd set out to fulfill. *One more. One more. One more.* He shoved her from him and watched as she hit the ground.

He took a step back.

"What?"

"Go." He pointed in the direction they'd been walking.

"But…"

"Get the hell away from me, witkowan," he growled. *She'd be the last one.* He stretched behind him, his fingers tightened on the handle of the blade.

She got up and wiped the mud smeared on the front of her dress. Confusion and hurt swarmed in her eyes. She walked away.

He pushed his heels into the ground as the words screamed in his head, *she has the mark.*

CHAPTER THIRTEEN

Nora walked through the last of the trees and onto the street. She'd refused to go back, or even turn around after he'd cast her out. She swiped at the hair falling into her eyes. The air was muggy and she fanned her face with her hand. *I kissed a bounty hunter.* She groaned and wiped her forehead.

Why had Otakatay told her to go? What had she done wrong? She thought he wanted to kiss her. *For heaven's sake, he started it.* She'd been so caught up in the moment she didn't know what to do.

It all happened so suddenly, first he was kissing her and then she was on the ground. She'd seen his face change from serene to disturbed within seconds, but there was no reason why. Not one she could see. She made a face. She never should've allowed him to kiss her at all.

"Damn it."

He was a killer, a bounty hunter. Her stomach turned. But she was drawn to him, determined to be his friend, even though it was clear he didn't want to be hers. In his eyes she saw sorrow, a yearning for acceptance, for peace. She'd never seen such misery, so instead of running from him, she'd taken a giant leap toward him.

She knew it was unsafe to be around him. *He threatened to kill me twice.* But no matter what he'd shown her or how badly he scared her, she was compelled to prove that not all white people were as cruel as he thought them to be.

She brushed her fingers across her lips. She could still feel his kiss—still taste him on her tongue. *Was it the kiss?* Was that the reason he wanted nothing to do with her? She paused. He'd changed after their embrace. His brown eyes hardened, and his features grew jagged and firm. *It had to be.* She must've done something wrong. She'd never been kissed like that before.

I've never been kissed at all.

She was inexperienced and was shocked when his lips met hers. She followed his lead, and look where that got her. She glanced back into the forest.

Not forty-eight hours before, he'd threatened to kill her and then he was kissing her. When his lips touched hers, excitement stirred within her and she instinctively kissed him back. She didn't think of the consequences, or why he'd kissed her at all. Nora's desire pushed all thoughts from her mind.

She was sure he found her amusing, a white girl easily seduced. He played a game, one she didn't want to be a part of. She wanted to be his friend, but he used and humiliated her. Nora kicked at the rocks on the road.

She'd never seen Otakatay before. Why was he here, in Willow Creek? *A bounty.* She froze. *But who?* She searched the street, wondering who Otakatay's next victim would be. Outlaws hid all over the territory and they could hide in Willow Creek without difficulty. Fear crawled up her spine, making the hairs on her neck spike. She'd pay more attention to who roamed the streets and to her flippant emotions when it came to the bounty hunter. She didn't want to be caught off guard if things went awry with either of them.

She shoved her hands into the pockets on her apron and felt the money. They needed food. She glanced at the mercantile. She needed to gather a few staples. She chewed on the inside of her cheek. After her encounter with Otakatay she didn't feel like eating lunch at all, and after Pa's night of drinking she doubted he would either. But there was always breakfast in the morning and a possible dinner tonight. She glanced down at the dried mud on her dress. She was a mess and she couldn't go into the store looking like a ragamuffin. But they needed food.

"Oh, hell." She hiked up her skirts and headed toward the store.

The bell jingled when she opened the door, and after the day she'd had, she found the bell to be more irritating than welcoming.

"Afternoon, Miss Rushton," Fred said merrily.

She nodded a polite hello and continued to the back of the store. She stacked flour, sugar, cornmeal, yeast and Willimena's raspberry jam in her arms. She placed them all on the counter. She'd worry about meat and eggs later. Right now she needed enough to make a few loaves of bread and the jam to spread it on.

"Will this be all?" Fred asked.

"A half pound of coffee, please."

The door to the back room swung open and a robust Willimena Sutherland sauntered through. A pale blue dress pulled tight over her plump hips and even larger breasts. "Miss Rushton," she said and her chubby hand swept across her forehead.

Nora saw it right away. There was no missing the ring on Willimena's pinky finger. She was sure the woman had shown it to her on purpose. She probably had no clue it was Nora's, and one look at Fred's uneasy stance told her he hadn't said a word about who the ring belonged to before he gave it to his wife. The ruby seemed quite a bit smaller than she remembered on Willimena's fat finger. Eyes downcast, she forced air into her lungs.

The ring didn't belong on anyone's finger except hers. Nora's cheeks flushed, and she bit her tongue to keep from shouting at them both. She balled the fabric on either side of her skirt into her hands and squeezed. She loved that ring. She loved the brooch and the watch wherever it was, whatever Pa had done with it, she loved that, too.

She focused on the counter. Nine brown and black smudges marked the wooden plank. She couldn't contain the hurt any longer. She handed Fred his money, scooped up the packages, and ran out of the store. She moaned, a strangled sound, and one by one the tears ran from her eyes. *I will not cry.*

The watch was gone, she'd sold all her mother's jewelry and she'd let Otakatay kiss her. She'd never been anything to anyone, and for a mere moment she'd allowed herself to get caught up in the affection of having someone other than her father care about her. What a fool she'd been. She sniffled, wiped her face on her sleeve, tilted her chin and carried on.

She unlatched the wooden gate on the short fence, glad to be home. Voices came from around back, and she went to investigate.

Elwood and two men she didn't recognize stood with her father in the yard in a heated discussion.

"I will pay you back. We settled that last night," Pa said in an even baritone. He used the no-nonsense voice whenever she was in trouble, and she knew something wasn't right.

"I am aware of what the agreement was, and I've come to collect," Elwood said.

He wore navy pants and a white shirt open at the collar. Had he not been so shady, or tried to accost her every time he was in town, she'd of thought he was handsome. But his attitude and forceful nature made him one of the ugliest men she'd ever seen.

His eyes roamed the length of her, and he smiled.

Goosebumps covered her arms and she shivered. The man repulsed her. Why would Pa have anything to do with him? He knew as well as she did that Elwood was a devious business man, ruthless to the core. He'd strike an old woman down to get what he wanted. A head taller than her father, Elwood was wide and powerful, which didn't bode well for people who could be intimidated. Plus he had two men with him, the odds didn't favor them.

"Pa, is everything okay?" She eyed Elwood while she put the packages down.

Pa faced her. The lines on his forehead more prominent then the day before matched the deep frown on his face. "Nora, go into the house."

She didn't want to leave. She wanted to stay right here and see what this was all about. Back rigid, she walked past Elwood when he grabbed her hand and brought it to his lips.

"I'd be obliged if you'd accompany me to dinner tonight, Nora."

"Elwood," Pa warned his face beet red.

She swallowed and forced herself not to shiver in disgust. "I'm sorry but I am not allowed to take suitors."

Elwood's beady brown eyes squinted, and he squeezed her hand. "I say you are, and so does the money your father owes me." He tossed his head back and laughed.

Nora stared at her father. "What is he talking about?"

"Never mind," Pa said.

"I loaned your father money to gamble and now he owes it back," Elwood said. "However, I'm kind enough to waive the loan for a night out with you."

"No." Pa grabbed Nora's other arm and pulled her toward him.

She didn't move. Elwood had a firm grip on her wrist. Pa wasn't going to answer her, so she decided to take matters into her own hands.

"I'm sorry, Mr. Calhoun, but your money issues are with my father, not me. So kindly let go of my arm."

She glared at him, and when she felt his grip loosen, she yanked her arm away and stepped behind her father. She watched the two men on either side of Elwood and wondered if they'd killed anyone like Otakatay had. Their clothes were dirty and by the look of them they hadn't been washed in weeks. But it wasn't their attire that had her heart in her throat; it was the soulless eyes that glared back at her. She concentrated on Pa's back, praying they'd all leave soon.

Elwood took the watch from his pocket and held it up. "You will not even think about it, Nora dear?"

He smiled when he heard her gasp.

No.

Of all the people Pa could've sold the watch to, it was Elwood, the filthy bastard. She clenched her jaw.

"One night with me and you can have the watch back."

Nora couldn't take it anymore. She went to step around Pa, when he pulled her back behind him. She glanced at the watch in Elwood's hand. She could do it, one night with him, for the watch. She had nothing left of her mother, and the watch was so special to her.

"Pa—

"No, Nora."

She watched from behind Pa's shoulder as Elwood shook his head and dropped the watch onto the ground. She took another step, but Pa's hand held her still. She wanted nothing more than to grab it and clutch it to her chest.

"Dinner with your daughter?" he asked Jack one more time.

There was a long pause, and Nora wondered if Pa had changed his mind, but he shook his head.

"No."

Elwood motioned to the tall red-headed man on his left. She watched horrified as he raised his large black boot and smashed the watch into bits.

The sound of the gold being crushed turned her stomach and bile rushed up her throat. She swallowed the bitter taste, and pushed the scream that wanted to burst from her lips back down. She tried to focus on anything but the watch. She refused to make a scene, when all she wanted to do was fall at his feet and cling to the bits and pieces lying on the ground.

Elwood would not see how this affected her. She blinked back the tears hovering within her lashes. She glanced at her father and saw his chin quiver.

"You'll pay your debt one way or another, Jack," Elwood said and winked at Nora. "And it will be *my* way. It always is."

They both sighed when he left the yard.

"It's okay, Pa." She placed her hand on his shoulder.

Pa stared straight ahead, lost within his own thoughts, and she wished she knew how to reach him. He shrugged her hand away and left without saying a word. She stepped back, stunned as he walked in the direction of the saloon. Thick tears fell from her eyes and soaked her face. Her arms hung frozen at her sides, she didn't have the energy to wipe them.

She knew he felt horrible for selling the watch, and as much as she didn't want to resent him for it, she didn't understand why it had to be to Elwood. She picked up the pieces. Holding them in the palm of her hand, she examined the broken heirloom—the shattered glass face, the deformed gold links. It would never look the same again.

She closed her hand and brought it to her chest. There were no memories of her mother to pull from her mind whenever she needed to. No lullabies, no stories, no kisses when she was sick. All she had were the fantasies built in her mind, and the pieces of jewelry Pa had given to her. She squeezed her hand until the knuckles went white. Now all that was left were broken bits, like her heart.

A low whine caught her attention, and she glanced out onto the street. Two more long moans floated toward her. She stood, dropped the pieces of the watch into her apron pocket and walked down the path behind the buildings.

The whine grew louder, and she peered into the woods. A brown burlap sack was tossed over something moving underneath. Curious, she pulled the rough fabric slowly away. She covered her mouth to conceal the loud gasp. Savage, Elwood's dog, lay beaten and bloody on the ground.

"Oh, no."

She eased past the branches and crawled toward him. A low growl met her as she came closer.

"Shush. It's okay, boy."

She inched her hand toward him. Savage bared his teeth and his head snapped to the side, almost taking her hand off.

How was she going to help him if he was going to bite her? She observed the street through the trees, glad no one could see them. Elwood could come back anytime, and she didn't want to be caught in the forest alone, with no one to protect her. She took a deep breath, held it and stepped closer again. Savage growled, but she laid her hand on the dog's side. In a flash he lunged and nipped her finger.

"Damn it." She clutched her finger close. Nora's hand throbbed as blood ran from her finger down her arm. He'd bit her good. The wound stung and by the way the skin was torn, she was sure a few stitches would be needed.

She shook her head and focused on the task at hand. She forced her hand back to Savage's fur, moving it soothingly over his coat. A growl rumbled from his chest, but he didn't move, and she exhaled.

"Okay, boy, I'm going to wrap the sack around you and lift."

Savage gave a high pitched whine, and Nora's heart broke. He was in pain and until she got him into the cabin to examine his wounds there was nothing she could do to help him. She wiggled the fingers on her uninjured hand. The need was there, both hands pulsed and heated.

The process of lifting the dog so she could slide the sack underneath him took forever, and she was sweating by the time she was finished. Blood flowed from wounds she couldn't see because of his fur. She didn't know where to place her hands so she wouldn't hurt him. Her finger hurt like hell and she needed to stop the bleeding. She ripped a piece of the fabric from the hem of her apron and bound the finger, using her teeth to tie it tight. She winced as the last knot was made and her finger was bandaged.

She peeked at the dog. "Here we go."

She shoved her hands underneath his belly before lifting him from the ground. She hadn't realized how heavy he was, and she took two quick breaths before hastily walking toward the cabin.

She laid Savage on her bedroom floor. The animal whimpered. She struck a match and lit the lamp on the table. When she lifted the sack from him, she couldn't believe what she saw. He'd been beaten with a stick or a leather rope. Pieces of his fur were missing from where he'd been cut. Slash marks sprawled across his back and under to his belly. She swallowed. The poor thing, he'd never had a chance.

Damn you, Elwood. She'd always known the man was cruel, but this was far too disgusting for any human to do. Savage had always been mean and it was as she'd suspected, someone made him that way.

The shaking began in her hands, relentless and unstoppable. She didn't know where to start, there were so many cuts. The white cotton wrapped around her finger stuck out as she laid her hand over Savage's black fur.

"Okay, boy, let's start slow."

One hot hand crept with ease over the longest cut. She closed her eyes, allowing his pain to encompass her body as the aching in her ribs and right side intensified. She drew in a quivering breath as she dragged her hand along the rest of the wound.

Savage moaned.

She was able to heal two more gashes before her stomach rolled and she puked in the bucket beside her. She wiped her mouth with her forearm and swept the braid back over her shoulder. The poor pup. While healing his wounds, she'd felt his pain. She rubbed her right side and inspected him. There were still so many.

A lock of hair fell in her face and she tucked it behind her ear. She'd heal the deep cuts first and then make a poultice for the others. She thought of Otakatay. The scars she'd seen on his neck and arms appeared similar to the ones Savage bore. *He'd been beaten.*

"Oh, dear God."

What had he been through? Who would do such a thing? Elwood's face shot across her mind and she scowled. He'd beaten his dog. She always knew he was a louse and this confirmed it. After a few long minutes of inspecting Savage's wounds, she knew which ones needed healing fast and which ones could be bandaged. She laid her hands over the cut feeling the skin close underneath. A burning sensation sliced across her back and around to her stomach. She arched and sucked in a hissing breath.

She healed four more wounds, but before she was done the last one, her stomach heaved and she threw up all over herself. It seemed like an eternity before she was able to bring her head up from the bucket. Spasms sliced through her middle, and damp hair clung to her temples. Her finger throbbed. She was so weak that instead of emptying the bucket or gathering bandages, she laid her head on the floor and closed her eyes. Savage placed his nose beside hers and they fell asleep.

CHAPTER FOURTEEN

Otakatay heard the branches break, and listened to the uneven melody hum throughout the forest. He patted the knife tied to his leg and flexed his back, feeling the leather casing shift slightly. The wasichu didn't care about their heavy feet. They didn't care about anyone other than themselves. Their arrogance and ignorance was what he hated most about them. He ground his teeth together and leaned against a tall pine to wait.

The wasichu stepped through the trees and came toward him. He didn't bother to conceal his disgust for the man who had hired him. They both had a purpose for using the other and once he was done, he'd kill the white eyes.

One more kill. He shook his head. The reminder called to him, taunting and sinful, while evil fingers pressed along his consciousness squeezing out the last of his reason. Would the nightmares cease after he killed the last one? Would he forget the softness of their skin while he clutched them close, or the sound of his blade cutting their throats? He tensed. Visions of thick scarlet covered his hand, hot and sticky. No cry. No whimper. Silence—a quiet he will always hear—a stillness that will haunt him for the rest of his life.

The killer inside of him mocked him for letting the girl go. He heard the sneer, the laughter, the growl for blood. And he'd saved her, even if for one day. He pushed her from him. The need to finish what he'd started to fulfill his promise crawled over him, biting at his reason. When he closed his eyes, he saw the mark and the face that went with it.

"Have you found any more?" The wasichu's voice brought him back to the conversation and the task at hand.

Tall and lean, the wasichu stood a few feet from Otakatay and he wondered why the white man hired him to kill these women. He never believed they were witches, as he'd been told. But for some reason unbeknownst to him, the man was obsessed. The women consumed him, and each time they met he pressed Otakatay for more.

"There are none." He thought of the girl, Nora, and decided to keep the information to himself.

The wasichu eyed him and murmured, "I have someone I want you to follow."

"I do not follow anyone."

"She may have the mark. I need you to be sure." He smiled. "And then I need you to kill her."

There was someone else? Why he felt relief that it wasn't the girl, that it wasn't Nora, he didn't know, and he brushed the reprieve aside.

"Where is this one?"

"She lives behind the blacksmith's shop in a cabin with her drunk of a father."

He froze. *Ina.* He struggled to stay with their conversation as a rush of emotions crashed down upon him. He couldn't draw air into his lungs. His chest ached. Ina—mangled and bloody, his brother, broken and frail and he could do nothing. He dropped his head, and inhaled slow and steady before he said in a low growl, "Fifty dollars is the price for this scalp." He was done. No more killing. He would fulfill his promise.

"Damn it. That's too much." The wasichu took out a handkerchief and wiped his face. "I will pay the regular fee."

"No." Otakatay pulled his knife from his back and took a step toward him. "You pay what I want. Nothing less."

"Are you going to kill me, Savage? Out here in broad daylight?"

Otakatay sprung forward, pushing the wasichu up against a tree. With his forearm against the man's throat, he dragged the blade of the knife along the whiskers on his cheek.

"Today I am feeling generous." He smiled. "How do you prefer to die? A slice across the neck so you bleed out slowly, or punctured in the stomach and gutted?" He pressed the blade into the wasichu's flesh, cutting him.

Blood dripped down his cheek and the wasichu's Adam's apple worked up and down. "Fine, fine. I will pay the fifty."

He reached into the man's front pocket and pulled out two bills. "I will take half now." He shoved the weasel from him and walked toward Wakina.

"You will kill her, if she has the mark, right?" he asked, while rubbing his neck.

"It will be done."

CHAPTER FIFTEEN

A knock at the door woke Nora. She'd fallen asleep on the floor, and the uneven boards did nothing for her aching muscles. She rolled over, feeling the ridges of the wood dig into her skin. Every joint screamed in agony.

She wanted to crawl into bed and sink into the covers for the rest of the day. Savage was still where she'd left him last night, resting on the blood-stained burlap sack. She could tell by the even rise and fall of his chest, he was out. Slowly, and with great care for her sore back, she stood and stretched before going to see who was at the door.

She'd look at Savage's wounds this afternoon. They needed to stay clean, lest infection set in. The sun peeked through the window, bright and welcome. She didn't hear father come home last night and wondered if he'd gone to work this morning. The rumpled cushions on the sofa and the pale blue blanket piled in the corner told her he'd been here, but there was no sign of him now.

Even after they reconciled yesterday, he still wanted nothing to do with her. A razor sharp spasm slashed across her middle. She bent over and tried to draw in air that wasn't paired with pain. She was helpless to the way her body dealt with pa's rejection. Another knock. She tucked her mangled insides away and opened the door.

"Mornin'," Jess said, "Damn, girl, you look like hell." A worn Stetson sat lopsided on her head, and a broad smile spread across her face.

Nora hadn't realized how terrible she looked until Jess had mentioned it. She glanced down, shocked to see the blood from last night still smeared across her apron and along her arms and hands. She'd fallen asleep and forgot to change. She lifted a hand to try and fix the stray hairs that had fallen from her braid, but she gave up and stepped aside.

"Please, come in."

Jess smiled and sauntered past to plop down in one of the two chairs at the table.

"Shit. Were you butchering a pig? Why in hell are ya covered in blood?"

The older woman's crassness was something she wasn't used to, but for all the spit and fire she was, Jess Chandler was indeed a kind hearted soul.

Nora sat across from her. "I rescued Elwood's dog, Savage. The bastard beat the animal just short of killing him."

Savage still had a long way to go until he recovered, but Nora had healed the worst of his wounds, the ones that would've killed him. She stretched her hands out on top of the table. The sleep had helped her to recuperate after healing the deep cuts, but it made her violently ill and very weak. Even now she still didn't feel up to grade.

Jess's eyes narrowed. "You be careful around that damn mutt. He's vicious and will kill if provoked."

She shook her head. "He's been mistreated."

Jess pointed to Nora's bandaged finger. "Where did ya get that?"

"He was scared and hurt. The animal was protecting himself. He's fine now."

The woman raised her thick eyebrows.

"Honest, he won't hurt me."

Jess took off her hat and placed it on the table. Her silver blonde hair was in a neat bun, and Nora noticed for the first time how pretty she was.

"Well, you better let me have a look." She held out her hand, and Nora laid her finger on the table. "That no good scalawag Elwood Calhoun is pure evil." She pointed her finger at Nora. "Probably could use a few stitches."

She winced.

"Pour a little whiskey on it and bandage it good. You don't want an infection."

She nodded.

"Listen here, girl. You'd be wise to stay away from Elwood."

"Oh, I can assure you that I plan to stay far away." She glanced at the doorway where Savage lay. "But he insists on courting me, even though I've refused several times."

"Well, to hell with him." Jess swatted the air and pulled a gun from the holster around her waist. "You point this in his direction, and I'll damn well guarantee that louse will be a runnin'." She slid the Colt .45 across the table and winked.

Nora didn't like guns. They scared her something fierce. But she saw her friend's point. If Elwood came by, she needed to protect herself and there was no better way than with a loaded gun. She ran her hand along the cool barrel and wrapped her fingers around the ivory handle. The gun was heavier than she expected, and she laid it back down on the table with a loud thud.

"Is it loaded?"

"Sure as hell is. Doesn't hold much use if'n it ain't." Jess paused. "You ever shoot one before?"

She shook her head.

Within the confines of the cabin, she learned how to load, cock and fire the gun. Nora placed the loaded weapon up in the cupboard.

"Time's a wastin' with that finger of yours. Get on over here so I can clean it up."

Nora sat across from her and watched Jess pull a silver flask from her pocket.

"What's that?"

"Whiskey."

Without another word, Jess poured the potent stuff all over Nora's finger.

"Hell and tarnation." She placed her head on the table and groaned.

"Ah shit, girl, you're tougher than that. I'm afraid you're in need of some sewin'." She doused the needle and thread with whiskey before taking Nora's hand and poking the skin.

Nora bit her lower lip and hummed. The sharp needle pricked her skin again, and she tensed.

"Almost done."

She hissed as the last stitch went through.

"Good as gold." Jess patted her hand.

Relieved the finger was bandaged and she'd never have to feel the fire from the whiskey on it again, she excused herself to change into a clean dress and apron.

"How long have you lived here, Jess?" she asked while pouring two cups of coffee.

"My husband Marcus and I bought our land ten years ago."

She saw the far off look in Jess's eyes and knew the woman was thinking of the past. Unsure if she should pry, she waited patiently for her friend to continue.

"Marcus wanted to be a farmer. And he was good at it, too. We had a few hundred acres back in Wyoming but lost everything from years of drought. We packed up and traveled around the country for a while. We buried two babies on those trails."

Nora placed her hand over Jess's. "I am so sorry."

"Ahh hell, it's in the past. Ain't nothin' nobody can do. After the disappointment and heartbreak, we decided not to try for any more children." She smiled sadly.

"We found Willow Creek and liked it here. I wanted to stay in town and work until we had enough of our own money to buy land, but Marcus was dead set on finding land first. And once Elwood had sunk his rotten teeth in, offering land and the money to loan us, Marcus signed the papers without even asking me." She took a long drink of coffee before she continued. "Four years later, my husband is shot out in the field and no one knows who did it."

"Why would someone kill, Marcus?"

"Money brings people to do things, horrible things."

Nora couldn't imagine losing a husband. The pain, the anguish Jess must have felt tore at her heart.

"Marcus found oil, and within two days of hearing it, Elwood was there willing to forget the money we owed him if we gave back the land. Marcus refused, and the next day he was found shot up in the east quarter of our spread. A week after I buried him, Elwood brought in his men to drain the oil. They didn't leave a drop. He's determined there's more on the land, but I won't let him near it. Between myself and the few cowhands I have left we protect what Marcus fought hard to keep."

"Oh, Jess, that's terrible."

"I get by. Marcus wouldn't want me to lie around and weep. I'm tougher than that. Hell, I'm made out of nails and I'll fight for what's mine."

"Your Marcus sounds like a fine fellow."

"He was, dear. He was."

She poured more coffee and enjoyed their conversation. The woman she'd come upon in the field weeks before had become her friend and she was thankful.

After Jess left, Nora went to check on Savage. The name irritated her, and every time it left her mouth she felt dirty. She thought of Otakatay and how he'd been mistreated. How he'd been called names and shunned by his people. It didn't matter to them that he was half white, when they stared at him all they saw was red. She was disgusted and ashamed to be a part of a race that was so cruel.

She ran her hand along Savage's black coat.

"Savage is for something wild or ferocious, and you, dear friend, are neither. I will call you Pal."

She smiled, satisfied with the name and the meaning it held. Nora inspected his wounds, a yellow crust had formed around the cuts. She needed to draw out the puss. She hurried into the garden and rummaged through the sparse rows. She scooped up the last cabbage, went into the house and boiled it.

On her knees, she placed the warm cabbage over Pal's cuts, breaking off bits to feed to him as well. There was no trace of meanness in him now. He put his head on her lap and nuzzled his nose into her hand. He was a good dog, part wolf, which made him intimidating, but she knew he'd never harm her again.

It was late afternoon when she'd gotten around to making bread, and she could now smell the mouth watering aroma throughout her kitchen. Pal had limped out of her bedroom to lay by the warm stove. She smiled and ruffled his fur when she heard Joe call her name from outside.

She opened the door and was greeted by a very happy Joe and the hotel's maid, June.

"Good afternoon, Miss Rushton," June spoke with clipped English in which every word was enunciated.

"Hello, Nora. Hello," Joe called from beside June.

"Hello, Joe." Nora laughed.

"Miss Rushton, I promised Joe I'd walk him over to visit with you. He's been wanting to see you for some time now."

"I'd love to visit with him. I can walk him to the hotel before supper." She moved to the side so Joe could shuffle in.

"That is most kind of you. His father sits down to dinner at six."

"Very well. He will be there by then."

June nodded and turned to leave. "Miss Rushton," she called, before Nora closed the door.

"Please, call me Nora."

"Nora, you can bring Joe to the back door by the kitchen. Mr. Calhoun never comes that way."

She eyed the maid. She'd never really talked to her, but June was aware of Elwood's infatuation with her and Nora was glad for the suggestion.

"Thank you."

She closed the door, turned and bumped right into Joe. His wide eyes gaped at the dog. Fear etched across his face, and his eyelids started to flutter.

"Joe." She touched his arm. "Joe, Savage is a good dog. He won't hurt you."

He shook his head from side to side and his bangs blew from his forehead.

"Let's sit you down." She walked him to a chair and eased him into it. "Savage was hurt real bad, and I brought him back here to help him get better."

"He's a bad dog. Bad dog."

"No, Joe, he's a scared dog. Someone mistreated him."

He peered into her eyes, and she saw something familiar within the blue depths. "Pa is mean to him. Mean to him."

"Yes, I know. I've fixed him up and he's on the mend."

Joe stood and went to the dog. He slid down the wooden sticks he used to walk, and sat beside the animal. "Poor puppy, poor puppy."

She knelt beside him. "Yes, he's been through a lot."

"Savage, Savage," he sang while playing with his fur.

"Joe, he's not a mean dog anymore, and therefore he needs a nice name, don't you think?"

"Yes, yes." He clapped his hands.

"I like the name, *Pal*."

She'd already named him, but she wanted Joe to take part.

Joe mouthed the words a few times before he said, "Pal, Pal. I like it!"

Nora laughed. The boy had nestled himself deep within her heart, and she cared for him like the little brother she never had.

CHAPTER SIXTEEN

Nora woke to the sound of a gunshot. The moon shone through her bedroom window allowing her to see without lighting the lamp. She grabbed her robe at the end of the bed and slipped it on. Pal got up slowly and moved to her side. Injured, the dog must've sensed her concern and she exhaled relieved to have him there. She hurried out into the kitchen to check on Pa.

He wasn't there. The blanket still folded nice and neat on the end of the sofa. A dreadful sensation stirred in her stomach and she shivered. She didn't know why, but she needed to find him. Without thinking, she went outside and headed in the direction of the saloon. Half way across the yard, she saw a crowd of people gathered around. She picked up her pace.

"Miss Rushton, you may want to wait until..." Fred said holding both her arms.

She didn't bother to stop, but instead yanked herself from him and pushed her way through the crowd.

"Pa!" she screamed and fell to her knees beside him.

He'd been shot. She frantically scanned his body as another muffled scream burst from her lips. The bullet went into his chest, and without thinking of the consequences she laid her shaking hands over the open wound, when her father grabbed them.

He didn't say anything. The look he gave her was enough. The white shirt he wore had absorbed the blood, and it clung to his skin. She searched the faces around her, the people who would hang her if they knew of her gift. Pa was right not here, not in front of them.

"I will get you home," she whispered, close to his ear as her tears fell onto his face.

Pale blue eyes stared up at her as he struggled to take a breath. Nora's head spun and she reached out, pressing her hands into the dirt road to steady herself. *This can't be happening. Pa can't be dying.*

He gasped, and she pulled at the rocks beneath her shaking hands.

"I need to get him home. I need to get him home," she said to the people huddled around her.

"Someone's gone for the Doc," Sheriff Reid said, and she smelled the liquor on his breath.

Nora glanced up at him, irritation melded with anger. *Damn it.* The need to fire away at the sheriff filled her, but she clamped her mouth shut instead. Starting a fight wouldn't get Pa home faster.

"Sheriff Reid, carry my father home."

He wobbled to the side and almost fell on top of her. She ground her teeth and glared at him. There was no time to wait for the intolerable sheriff to get it together. She searched the faces around her, but before she could ask anyone else, Seth came forward and without saying a word lifted Pa and carried him toward their cabin.

Nora followed on shaky legs. She needed to see how badly he was hurt. *I have to heal him.*

Seth laid Pa on her bed as the sheriff walked in. Pal growled from the mat in the corner, and Nora shushed him.

"What in hell?" Sheriff Reid said when he noticed Elwood's dog.

She didn't know he followed them into the cabin, and she didn't want him here once she started healing Pa.

"Thank you Sheriff, but I can take it from here." She ushered him outside with Seth and shut the door before he could utter another word. She ran to the bedroom. Hands hot and sweating, she ripped opened Pa's shirt. The bullet had gone into the center of the chest. How was he still alive? How did it not pierce his heart? It made no sense, but she was thankful he was still here. Her hands hovered over the wound, about to draw out the bullet, when he pulled them to the side.

"No, Nora, no," he rasped as blood formed at the corners of his lips and trickled down his cheek.

She wiped it away with her hand.

I have to help him. She had to make it right. She had to fix him. His skin had turned pasty and gray. Time was running out. Her heart raced and an overwhelming pressure filled her lungs. She couldn't breathe. Panic set in, eager to destroy the life she'd so easily taken for granted. She pressed her hands back over the wound.

"NO."

He was stronger than she thought, and he gripped her hands in his.

"Please, Nora. Let me go."

"No, Pa. No." What was he thinking? Why did he want to die? *God, please help me.* "I can't do that Pa, I can't." She tried again to pull her hands from his, but they didn't budge. Tears fell from her eyes and dripped from her chin.

"You can't fix this, Nora," he wheezed.

"Yes, I can." She tried again to pull free.

"I don't want you to."

She didn't want to hear it. She had no control and she stomped her feet. He was slipping away right before her and she couldn't do a damn thing. She struggled against his grip, trying to free her hands, but he held her still.

"Pa, let go," she sobbed. "Please, please let me help you."

She watched helpless as his eyes focused on her and a tear slid down his cheek. "I love you." He exhaled, and his hands fell to the side.

"No." She shook him. "No, no, no, Pa!"

She pressed her hands onto the hole in his chest and willed the skin to close—to somehow put the life back in him. Her hands no longer hot, she pressed harder, his blood covered them as she demanded the wound to heal.

"Please, please, please."

Nora screamed through clenched teeth and pounded her fists onto his chest.

"Please, Pa. Please come back."

She fell across him and wailed. The pain rolled over her, picking and pulling at the reality she didn't want to face. She shook him once more.

"Wake up, Pa. Wake up."

Blood soaked the front of her dress, and she shuddered. She ran her hands down his face and closed his eyes. Memories of their life together flashed across her mind, and she shook her head. Unable to hold on any longer, she ripped the hair from her braid and pulled at the strands.

She shrieked and fell over top of him. Every muscle tensed. Every bone ached, and her chest throbbed. She desperately wanted to wake from this nightmare. The anguish bore down upon her and compressed her lungs. She gasped. She clung to him, scratching the skin, wanting him to be here, with her.

"Please, God, bring him back." She grabbed his shoulders and shook. "Wake up, damn it. Wake up." She lay across him and buried her head into his neck, wheezing as bitter sobs burst from her lips.

"Nora? Nora, come now dear," Doctor Spencer pulled her from the bed.

"No." She wrestled with the doctor. She wouldn't leave Pa.

"He's gone."

She wrenched her arms from the doctor's hold and fell over top of her father. "He can't go. He can't. Pa, please, please." She clawed at the blood stained shirt, and wrapped her arms around his neck. "Wake up. You've got to wake up."

Strong arms guided her back from her father.

"I'm sorry, Nora."

She stared at her father, his chest still, his body covered in blood. Nora's knees buckled from the truth. Doctor Spencer caught her, and she wailed in his arms.

He helped her into the kitchen where Seth stood. The young boy had come back. He didn't say a word and she was glad. There was nothing to say. Someone had killed her father and now he was gone—gone from her forever.

She lifted a trembling hand to her eyes and wiped at the tears. She didn't care that they were covered in Pa's blood, or that her dress was ruined, stained beyond recognition. All she wanted was for someone to tell her this was a bad dream, for Pa to walk through the door alive and well. She sucked in a sob and bit the inside of her cheek.

The doctor came out of the bedroom and announced he'd prepared Pa for burial. Nora nodded, not knowing what to do next. She wanted to crawl into a dark hole and cry out all her sorrows. She wanted to scream at the top of her lungs and punch the wall. She wanted to die.

"Will you be okay, by yourself?" Doctor Spencer asked.

Dazed, she nodded. She wanted to be alone, and didn't hear the door close when they left. Pa's last words replayed in her mind, *I love you.* She'd never said it back. She never told him. She slid from the chair onto the floor, buried her head into Pal's fur.

"I'm sorry, Pa. I'm so sorry."

Otakatay heard the gunshot from the forest. It came from town. The wasichu didn't like to lose and he'd bet it was over a card game. There wasn't another shot fired and that told him it was intentional. The man didn't even know it was coming.

He slipped his knife into the leather casing tied around his shin. He had a job to do tonight. He sighed. The weight on his shoulders increased, and he was sure a mountain sat on top of them. He lifted his arms flexing the muscles. Tonight it would end. Tonight he'd have his last victim. The last throat he'd slice. The last scene he'd replay over and over. He touched the feather in his hair. *I do this for you.*

He tied Wakina's reins around a tree and walked toward town to find the cabin behind the blacksmiths. The piano from the saloon played a tinny, off key song that filled the otherwise silent street. He stayed in the shadows, watching as a few men left through the swinging doors and swayed down the street. There was no sign someone had been shot earlier. He shrugged. He didn't give a damn who had been killed or who had done it. All his senses focused on moving silently down the street to the cabin.

He eased up to the back window and peeked in. A man lay on the bed, and Otatakay immediately noticed the blood on the floor. This was the one who had been shot, the father. Was it a coincidence or pure fate that the father of the girl he was about to kill was dead? He examined the room. A brush and a few hair combs sat on the wooden dresser, and three dresses hung in the armoire.

With skilled movements he eased the window up, and silently climbed in. Light came from the other room, and he crept closer. He saw her sitting in a rocking chair in front of the fire. He stilled. It was her. It was the girl, Nora. A black dog lay at her feet, and he noticed the cuts and marks on his skin. The animal was injured and not a threat. He put him out of his mind.

He watched the girl. Blood smeared the front of her dress, and there was so much he wondered at first if she was injured. But after watching her, he realised that she was fine. Her pale skin was marked with red slashes of blood, and knotted black hair hung down her back. She rocked back and forth, and he saw the tears drip from her eyes onto her cheeks. Loud moans came from her lips as she brought her hands up to her face.

Why did it have to be her? He clenched his jaw. The lost look in her red-rimmed eyes told him she wasn't there at all. Killing her would be easy. She'd never see him coming. He pulled the knife from his back, gripping it within his hand.

Do it. Kill her. The heinous slayer inside of him screamed for retribution. He yelled, growled and whispered into the better part of his conscience. A veil of evil blanketed him and he was blind to what was right or wrong, the only thing he saw was death.

He shook his head, ignoring the executioner he'd become and focused on the girl. She was now on the floor, kneeling in front of the fire.

She hunched forward and he watched as her hands hovered above the fire. Her desolate sobs reached his ears, and a tiny part of him pitied her. Ina flashed across his mind, along with his promise, and he squeezed the knife. There was no time for pity, no time for caring. The assassin within him howled and he stepped toward her. The dog growled. He took another step when he saw her lean in toward the flames again.

What the hell was she doing? In two quiet steps he was behind her. The blade reflected the fire as he held it close. The dog growled again. She bent forward, and he knew she was going to burn them. He dropped his knife and sprung toward her. Grabbing her shoulders, he jerked her back as she placed her hands into the hot coals.

She screamed, and he didn't know if it was from the pain or the shock that he was there. He picked her up and set her in the rocker. He inhaled a couple times, before he took her hands and examined them. She'd burned them, not badly, but enough to need a salve to ease the pain and so infection didn't set in. He made the mistake of gazing into her eyes. Sorrow filled their navy depths and for the first time in his life, he didn't know what to do.

A part of him wanted to help her, while the other wanted to leave and never return. He wavered on the edge of good and evil. He stood up to go, when she brought her hands up to her face and wept within them. The sound tugged at the boy inside of him, and he remembered holding his Ina when she died. He pulled the medicine pouch from around his neck and emptied some of the herbs into his palm. He spat into his hand and mixed the concoction with his finger until it was a green paste.

Otakatay took her hands gently in his, and with tender movements rubbed the medicine into the burns. She sniffed, and he glanced at her. Eyes closed she winced, and he moved slower, barely touching the skin. Blisters formed, and he knew she was in pain.

"Please, please do not help me," she whispered, her voice hoarse.

He frowned and continued rubbing the herbs into her palms.

She tried to pull away, but he held her to him.

"Otakatay, please leave them. They are no good to me anymore." She glared at her hands. "They are worthless." She started to cry all over again.

He stopped and waited while her body trembled. She squeezed her hands together and yelled out from the pain, but didn't release them. A low moan came from her throat as she hung her head and sobbed.

He didn't know what to do, and he wasn't sticking around to find out what would happen next. He pulled the medicine pouch from around his neck and laid it on her lap.

"Mix small amounts with water or saliva, and rub it into your hands once a day." He didn't know if she heard him. He watched as she shook her head and muttered apologies to her father. The urge to hold her in his arms stole over him. He took a step back and ran his hand down the length of his face. He grabbed his knife, and looked at her one last time before he walked away.

Nora stood at the graveside while two men lowered her father into the ground. He'd been gone two days, but to her it felt more like an hour. The pain still raw, she brought the white handkerchief to her face and blotted her eyes. Jed purchased the wooden casket and she was grateful for the help. She couldn't afford it and without Pa's income, there would be no money now.

She scanned the faces gathered around, a handful of people had come to see Jack Rushton buried. Aside from Doctor Spencer and the sheriff, she didn't know any of them. They resembled gamblers, unwashed clothes hung from their skeletal frames. She figured they knew her father from the saloon. Her stomach spun. She thought he'd drink himself to death, but she'd been wrong.

She hung her head. He'd died from a wound she couldn't heal. A horrifying moment she wished over and over to have back. She'd have done things differently, given him whiskey so he couldn't fight her, or tried harder to save him. A tear slipped down her face. *I should've tried harder.*

The sheriff stood off to the side, still embarrassed he'd been drinking the night Pa was killed. He assured her that he was searching for the killer and wouldn't give up until justice was served. Nora wondered if the killer was among them now.

It could be any one of the people mulling about the open grave site. She took a second look at them. They fidgeted, stepped from one foot to the other and their bloodshot eyes focused on the ground. They were itching to drink. She doubted any of them could aim a gun, much less pull the trigger and kill someone. All they cared about was where they'd get the next drink.

She blew a shaky breath and clutched the handkerchief. Her hands still tender, she loosened her grip on the cloth. Two men shovelled dirt over the coffin. The *scrape, scrape* of the shovels and the silence after they dropped it down the hole, she'd never forget.

Oh, how she wanted to be told it was all a misunderstanding. None of it happened. Pa hadn't died and she wasn't alone. She thought of Otakatay. She didn't know why he'd come the night Pa died, but she was glad, his presence offered comfort.

Had he heard the shot? Did he see her trying to save him? He'd been there afterward. A steady hand to help her when she'd burned herself. She remembered very little of that night, but she'd never forget the concern in his eyes as he smoothed the salve over her throbbing hands.

The shovels pounded on the hill packing the dirt over where her father was buried. He was gone. Her chest tightened. A mound of soil and a small wooden cross were all that was left of Jack Rushton. She blinked back tears and blew a kiss toward the ground. *Goodbye, Pa. I love you.*

CHAPTER SEVENTEEN

It had been six days since Pa's death, and Nora still couldn't make it through a day without crying. Her evenings were plagued with nightmares that carried over into the morning and followed her throughout the day. She was helpless to the visions that swirled in her mind of her father lying dead before her.

She shivered. She was captured within herself, and each day that went by, the burden she carried weighed so heavy she was sure she'd crumble. The pressure pushed her lower and lower, until defeat and exhaustion had her screaming at the walls.

She placed some wood inside the stove and threw in a lit match. She slid the tea pot over the burner. The wood crackled and she inhaled the sweet aroma.

She brushed her hands along her dress and looked at the array of food on top of the counter. There was more in the icebox, a mourner's gift from the townspeople. She hadn't touched any of it and found herself giving it away instead. Seth chopped wood all morning for her, and to show her appreciation she gave him one of the half dozen pies she had. Jess had stopped by yesterday, and she'd insisted the woman take a chicken pot pie home for dinner. She gave her back the gun too, not wanting to be a part of the violence it held.

She stacked the unwashed cups and plates beside the metal bowl on the counter. She'd wash them later. She thought of Jess. The kind woman had begged her to come and live out on the ranch. She made a good argument, too. Nora shouldn't be living alone. They'd give each other company.

The idea was tempting, and she wanted to say yes, but regret over the past lingered within her soul and she declined. She liked the older woman, and didn't want to offend her, but she couldn't afford to be a burden to anyone ever again. She'd been the anchor Pa tugged behind him for years, keeping him from living a normal life. And she'd never forgive herself for it.

She held her hands out. The burns had healed, and she still had feeling in them thanks no doubt to Otakatay's medicine. *I will never use them again. I will live like a normal girl.* No one would ever know she possessed such power. She tucked her hands into her armpits.

There wasn't a cloud in the sky, and a part of her wanted to get out of the cabin. The thick, dense woods called to her. A walk through the forest might be what she needed. Staying cramped inside the house wasn't good. But as she glanced in the direction of the tall trees, she couldn't find the strength to leave. She wrapped her arms around her stomach and leaned against the wall. She missed her father so bad some days she thought she'd die from the pain.

She pulled back the curtain. Wagons rolled by, and people walked in and out of shops. Their lives hadn't been interrupted like hers. A little piece of her resented them for their smiles and carefree attitude. Would the aching inside her heart ever go away?

A tall, dark shadow crossed the street, and she recognized Otakatay immediately. He hadn't come back for his medicine pouch, and she was beginning to wonder if he ever would. She'd used all the herbs inside on her hands and wanted to replenish the leather sack, but didn't know the plant that had been inside.

He glanced in her direction, but she couldn't tell whether he saw her or not. Her heart skipped and she brushed the warm feeling aside. He'd threatened to kill her, scared the devil out of her and kissed her all in a matter of days. Who was he and why did he stir such odd feelings inside of her? She must be crazy to even think someone like him would have the slightest interest in someone like her. He was the opposite of everything she believed in. He killed people. She saved them. *Or at least I used to.*

She sighed and her breath fogged up the glass. She wiped it with her sleeve. Her left hand was marked with red slashes that were raised like a welt. A sick feeling settled low into her abdomen, and she inhaled through her nose to ease the queasiness. She should've saved pa.

He was right. She was cursed. The reason they had run from town to town. The reason her mother died. She'd been selfish and refused to listen. Remorse choked her, and she fought the scream welling up in her throat. She'd never forgive herself for Pa's death.

The tea kettle whistled, and as she poured herself a cup someone knocked on the door.

Joe stood on the porch, leaning into his crutches as sweat glistened from his forehead.

"Hello, Joe. Please, come in." She looked around him for June.

"Where's Miss June today?"

Joe shuffled into the cabin and sat down at the table. "She's busy, she's busy."

"Does she know you're here?"

He nodded and smiled.

"I can't believe you walked all the way over here on your own, Joe."

The poor boy was still trying to catch his breath, and her heart went out to him. How he must struggle. Everyday things she'd taken for granted didn't come easy for someone like him, and she felt horrible for the boy. She looked at his legs. *No, I will not even think of it.* She shoved the thought to the back of her mind.

"It was fun, fun." He tossed his head.

She smiled. "Would you like a cup of tea or some water?"

"I've never had tea, tea. Thank you, Nora."

He pulled a pack of cards from his front pocket and placed them on the table. Maybe a game was what she needed to take her mind off what she was going to do now. She took a dirty cup, dunked it in the cold water in the metal basin and dried it with a rag before she poured him a cup. She cradled the mug in her hand and sat down across from him. Joe's eyes watered and his lip trembled.

"Joe, are you okay?"

"I'm...I'm sorry about your Pa. I'm sorry about your Pa." He rocked back and forth.

Nora's vision blurred and she placed her hand over his. "Thank you, Joe."

He smiled, and it warmed her heart.

Curious, she asked, "Do you remember your mother?"

Joe didn't blink for a long while, and she grew nervous wondering if he was going into a fit.

He shook his head slowly.

"No. I don't remember her, I don't, I don't."

She could see the sadness reflected in his eyes. She had no intention of upsetting him. "I don't remember my mother either."

He squeezed her hand and blinked back tears. For all the things Joe lacked, the boy sure made up for them with compassion. He had a heart of gold, and she hoped Elwood would never steal that from him.

She grabbed the cards and shuffled them. "Let's play, shall we?"

Joe clapped his hands. "Yay, Yay!"

The sun was descending, casting gray shadows around them as she walked Joe back to the hotel. Pal trotted along beside them. The animal hadn't left her side since she'd healed him, and she was grateful. The long nights alone would be unbearable without him.

Joe gazed up at the sky, his blonde brows furrowed, and he moved his sticks faster.

"Joe, is something wrong?"

"It's getting dark, dark, dark." He tossed his head, and his eyelids fluttered.

She placed her hand on his shoulder. "We're almost to the hotel."

He didn't answer, and she moved her hand from his shoulder to his arm, offering support in case he fell. Joe's crutches made loud aggravated sounds as he ran them along the boardwalk. She scanned the street and noticed Fred Sutherland standing in the doorway of the mercantile.

"Good evening, Mr. Sutherland," she said as they passed.

"Good evening." He stepped in front of them. His brown eyes assessed her, and she stepped back. He was staring at her so intently she wondered if she had something on her face. She moved to go around him. He smiled, and pulled two candy sticks from his pocket.

"I know Joe has a sweet tooth, but I wasn't sure if you did."

Her hand shook as she grabbed the peppermint stick. "Thank you."

"Candy, candy." Joe almost jumped into Mr. Sutherlands arms.

The man laughed as he handed the candy over.

"Enjoy." The bell over the door jingled as he went inside.

The hair on Nora's neck prickled, and she pulled Joe along the boardwalk wanting to put some distance between them. Why she felt unsure around him all of a sudden, she didn't know. Goosebumps covered her arms and she pulled her sweater closed.

She glanced back. She could count on one hand the times she'd spoken to Mr. Sutherland. Maybe this was his usual demeanour. He'd been kind enough, and when she'd sold her mother's jewelry he was quite pleasant. She shrugged off the notion that the mercantile owner was anything but kind and continued walking.

Joe sucked on his candy with enthusiasm, and she smiled. The boy was a delight to be around, and she hadn't missed Pa as much while visiting with him today. She wondered why he was so afraid of the dark and decided to ask. "Joe, why don't you like the dark?"

He moved the stick to the other side of his mouth. "It's scary, scary."

"Yes, it can be."

"I go there when I'm bad, when I'm bad."

"When you're bad?"

He nodded.

She wanted to know what Elwood did to Joe when he was bad. Where did he take the boy that was dark and scary? She examined him with her eyes, searching for signs he'd been mistreated.

"Where do you go when you're bad?"

Joe pointed east to the mountain where the mine was. "There in the cave, cave."

"Elwood puts you in a cave?"

"Only when I'm bad, I'm bad."

He wouldn't. She stared up into the hills. He was a nasty man, but to harm a child, one with deficiencies like Joe, was heartless. She tried to process what Joe had told her. Had the doctor known? What about the townspeople, did they know? Were they all looking the other way while Elwood abused his own flesh and blood?

Nora's face heated as burning anger blazed through her. She wanted to confront the bastard. She wanted to stick up for Joe. Why hadn't she noticed before? Why hadn't she questioned Joe about Elwood? Guilt blanketed her, and she tried to push the feeling of suffocation away. *Poor Joe.*

She wanted to hug him, to tell him that not all people out there were as mean and vile as his own father. She thought of Pa, and her chest ached. He might've been a drunk, and he'd said unkind things, but he'd never struck her or left her behind.

She helped Joe to the back door of the hotel and was taken aback when he embraced her.

"Bye, Nora, Nora."

She hugged him back. If he could stand straight he'd be taller than her by at least a head. She blinked back the tear waiting to drip past her lashes.

"Goodbye, Joe. Please come by again."

He shook his head. "I go home tomorrow, tomorrow."

"Oh, I see. Well, next time you're in town, come and visit."

He nodded and went into the hotel.

She waited for the door to close behind him before she left. She followed the path behind the buildings back to the cabin, and was pulled into the shadows.

"Well hello, Nora."

Elwood's spicy cologne filled her nostrils, and she squirmed.

"Let me go." She tried to pull herself free of his grip.

He backed her into the side of the hotel and leaned in. The two men he'd had with him at the cabin stood blocking the entrance from the street. "Poor, Nora, you're all alone now, and need someone to take care of you." His fingers skimmed her cheek.

"Thank you for your concern, but I'll be fine." She tried to scoot around him, but he blocked her with his other arm.

"You'd have everything if you married me."

She searched the forest on her left and the street on her right for anyone she could call out to, but with Elwood's thugs blocking them from any prying eyes it was useless.

She tipped her chin and said hotly, "And why would I marry you?"

"Because bad things can happen to a woman living alone, I could protect you."

"I don't need protection."

"Don't you?" His finger skimmed her cheek.

"Please, let me go."

"I'm the wealthiest man within miles."

"What does money have to do with marriage?"

"Why everything, dear, and by marrying me you'll never be without it."

"If you think I'd marry you," She struggled to move away from him, "then you're dumber than I thought."

He laughed, a deep hollow sound, and she watched as his eyes hooded with desire. He brought her hands above her head and rammed his knee between her legs. She moved her head from side to side trying to get away from him. He gripped her chin in his hand and squeezed.

"You will have no choice," he sneered, nuzzling his lips into her neck.

She pressed into the wall behind her, the uneven wood pinched her back as she fought the urge to vomit all over him. The man repulsed her, and she rolled her hips trying to avoid his touch.

He caught her breast within his hand and squeezed.

She whimpered.

A low growl came from beside them.

"Savage, go on. Get outta here." He waved his hand behind him and continued to grind his groin up against her.

Nora pressed her nails into his hand trying to rip the flesh. She wiggled her head from his, avoiding his lips.

The dog barked and growled again, a low rumble that even had the hairs on her neck standing.

Elwood spun around. "What in hell?"

Pal was hunched low to the ground, his hind legs straight. Saliva dripped from his fangs as he showed his teeth.

"You son of a bitch." He kicked Pal catching him in the teeth.

The dog lunged for his foot, biting right through the boot. He shook his head, attacking the bastard's leg.

The two men ran toward them guns drawn.

"Don't shoot him. You may miss and hit me," Elwood screamed.

She eased away from him and faded into the shadows. Once she was a safe distance from them, she called Pal off.

"I'll kill that damn mutt yet, and then there will be no one to protect you." He wiped his mouth and spat. "I will marry you, Miss Rushton, if it's the last thing I do." He limped away smirking and his men helped him inside.

She wasn't waiting around for Elwood or his men to come back. She crumpled the hem of her skirt in her hand and ran all the way home, Pal beside her. She locked the door to the cabin and pressed her forehead against it. It wasn't until her heart resumed its normal rhythm that she knelt in front of her protector and hugged him.

CHAPTER EIGHTEEN

Otakatay packed up his bedroll and tied it to the saddle. He couldn't stay here any longer. He couldn't kill the girl. Unfamiliar emotions stirred inside him, and he didn't like it one bit. He was a killer, a breed. Not wanted anywhere but in hell.

He'd begun to care, to feel pity for Nora, and it pissed him off. He clenched his jaw. He didn't need some sniveling little girl getting inside of his head, making him feel things he had no right to feel. He had to get away and fast. He needed to find another victim, one whose face he hadn't seen.

He'd fought with himself for days about why he should kill her— why it was the right decision. She would be the last one. He'd have his money, have his freedom. He'd fulfill his promise. He flexed his hands.

He was going crazy. The killer in him shrieked of the good that would come from taking her life, he wanted her blood. Otakatay battled back and forth until all he saw when he closed his eyes was Nora's face. All he heard were her cries of agony, of hopelessness, and he understood. He remembered.

He pulled the blade from the deerskin case. It fit perfectly within his palm, and he stared hard at his reflection. The assassin he'd become cried out and he fought to control it. To calm the need for revenge—for the satisfaction of knowing she would be the last. *I've seen her face.* He'd heard her voice, kissed her lips. Sweat beaded on his forehead, and he tightened his grip.

He couldn't change the past, couldn't stop what he'd done, or what he'd become. He was Otakatay one who kills many, and he had. The last victims had been innocent—their only fault was a red mark upon their scalps. He killed for a purpose, and he'd paid the price. He'd never forget. Both the sleeping and waking nightmares would haunt the rest of his days.

Nora had the mark, the sign that could change his future forever. The answer to what he desired most. How could he walk away from everything he'd fought so hard for? The memories of the others plagued his mind, yet he'd had to do it to accomplish his goal.

He rocked back on his heels and threw the knife. The tree spat wood from the trunk as the blade struck it. Why couldn't he do it? Why couldn't he kill her? The act consumed him, kept him from sleep, from thinking of anything but her and the blue eyes set within a porcelain face. He made a promise, and this was all he needed to fulfill it. She'd be the last one.

"Shit."

There was no one to help him, to listen. There hadn't been since Ina died. He'd grown accustomed to living alone, to relying on no one. He closed his eyes. If he concentrated hard enough, he could see his mother's face. He could hear her, and on the days he felt most alone, he was sure he smelled her spicy, earthy scent.

He thought of his brother, Little Eagle and his heart ached. He hung his head and allowed the despair to fill him, drowning all thoughts of goodness from his mind. He wasn't good. Hell, he wasn't even close. Yet the one thing he strived for, the one purpose he had was what pushed him to do the things he'd done.

After seven years, he was so close to having enough money to fulfill his promise. Now, he was wrapped in a cloak that clouded his judgement and whispered words he did not want to hear. His mind was foggy, and the battle between the monster he'd become and the boy he once was raged inside of him.

He made a fist. He couldn't will them, or his mind to kill Nora. He yearned for a fight, for a way to get his emotions out, to calm the beast that screamed inside his head. He needed to smash something. He turned toward town. It'd be easy enough to find someone there to fight. The wasichu were always looking to put the lowlife breed in his place. He pulled the knife from the tree and placed it back inside the case. His body vibrating, he kicked leaves over top the ashes, when he heard someone approach.

"You haven't done your job," the wasichu said as he came through the trees. He stood face to face with Otakatay.

He growled, and did nothing to hide the angry expression on his face.

"The day is not over."

There was no need to tell the wasichu how he'd backed out the other night. How instead of killing her he'd helped her.

"You've had five days."

"It will get done."

"It damn well better. I've paid you half already, and I want her dead!"

The wasichu was no better than he was. In fact he was worse. He hid behind men like Otakatay to get the dirty work done, while sitting back and living as if he were the kindest of fellows. He was a deceiver, a manipulator, and Otakatay despised him.

The wasichu picked up a rock and tossed it in the air catching it in his palm. "If you do not kill her by tomorrow evening, I will find someone who will."

"Do you really believe she is a witch?"

He often wondered if any of the women held the magic the man spouted of, or if there was another reason, a personal reason for his wanting them killed. His people didn't believe in those types of things, and he found it hard to understand they even existed.

"Yes, of course I do. They're evil."

"Evil lurks on the earth in the killers I hunt, in rabid animals, and in men who pretend to be something they are not." He scowled at the wasichu, seeing right through him to the cold-hearted son of a bitch he was. "Evil is not in the face of a woman."

"What do you know? You're a bounty hunter. A damn breed." The man scrutinized him. "You haven't seen what they can do. I've been there. I've watched them kill by touching a person."

The urge to bust the wasichu's clean-shaven jaw vibrated over him. *In time, I will end his life.*

"It's in their hands. Their hands hold the power. They all have to die. They must," the wasichu went on half hysterical, and Otakatay watched as his eyes glazed and his face flushed crimson.

"Her father is dead."

"Yes, and soon she will be, too." He threw the rock onto the ground.

"Did you kill him?"

"Of course not," he scoffed. "Jack Rushton was at death's door anyway. If it wasn't a bullet that killed him, it would've been the alcohol."

Otakatay waited. He didn't care that the man was a drunk or that he'd been shot. All he wanted to know was if this wasichu had done it.

"You will do it. You will kill her."

He didn't know if it was the matter-of-fact way the man said the words, or because it was an order that caused him to bite down hard, and clench his fists. No one told him what to do. This was a job, nothing more. He chose to do it, and damn it, he'd choose when to end it.

"I want her scalp." He poked Otakatay's chest with his finger. "You will kill Nora Rushton, and you will do it by morning."

The fight he'd been looking for had presented itself. Otakatay smirked pulled back his arm and punched the man in the jaw. The wasichu stumbled backward, landing on his ass. A red welt brightened his chin and bled down the front of his shirt. He gaped up at Otakatay with dumb surprise.

"I work on my own terms." He glared. "Not yours." He grabbed the wasichu's throat and lifted him to his feet. "You touch me again white man, and you will die." He pressed his fingers into his neck.

The man nodded, his eyes bulging out of his head.

Otakatay released him with a shove.

The wasichu brushed the leaves and twigs from his pants. Fury and indignation shot from his eyes when he stared at Otakatay. He worked his hands at his sides, and Otakatay waited for him to charge. He wanted to smash the wasichu's face a few more times. He wanted to beat the life right out of the snake. But without saying another word, the white man pivoted on one heel and left.

Otakatay took a deep breath. The wasichu was the evil one, but he no longer held the money over his head. He'd find another way to get the remaining funds he needed. He'd stop by the sheriff's office and take a look at the wanted posters on the wall. It would be another month before his promise was fulfilled.

He rummaged through his saddle bags and pulled out the last of his pemmican. He bit into the dried meat and climbed onto Wakina. He thought of Nora. The wasichu would kill her.

He sat tall in the saddle, staring at the mountains ahead of him. He wouldn't allow the white man to take Nora's life. She was pure and innocent. A gem he'd not only had the pleasure to see but also to touch.

Thunder clapped in the sky, and he smelled rain. Dark clouds moved from the east toward town. This was going to be one hell of a storm. He took another bite of the meat and leaned forward to give Wakina the rest. They'd find shelter until dark, and then he'd warn the girl before he left town.

Nora placed a log on the fire and listened as the orange flames crackled, eating up the dry wood. The wind whistled through the cabin walls, and she sat back in the rocker while wrapping the quilt tighter around her legs. She hadn't been able to sleep in her room since Pa died, and tonight with the storm, she'd decided to sit by the fire with Pal.

A loud crack followed by an intimidating bang shook the cabin walls. Nora jumped. Pal whined beside her.

"It's okay. It's only rain," she said soothingly, unsure if it was for the dog's benefit or hers.

She glanced out the window and saw her reflection. It was darker than Pal's fur, and she couldn't help the slight shiver that shook her body. With her toes she pushed the chair back and forth, allowing the heat from the fire to warm her. Pa would've stayed in on a night like this and kept her company. Thunder clapped again, and Pal inched closer to her feet. She yawned and leaning her head back, she closed her eyes.

She needed to find a job. She had no money, and in time she'd have to restock the ice box. She'd stacked as much food as she could in there, but soon it would start to go bad and she'd have to throw it out. She'd find a job. She couldn't sit around here all day and do nothing. She couldn't stay in the cabin when all she thought of was Pa and how it was her fault he died.

She rocked the chair. Pal had nestled himself over her feet, keeping them warm, and she left them there not wanting to disturb him. She covered her mouth with her hand to stifle a yawn. The rain pelted the roof. The familiar and comforting *tap tap* lulled her to sleep.

Nora woke to Pal's growl. The room was black. She sat still. Someone was in the cabin. The hairs on her neck stood and her heart raced. The fire had burned down and the coals glowing orange offered little light in the room. She tucked her bottom lip between her teeth. Pal growled louder and the whites of his fangs glowed. She took a deep breath, held it and stood.

The blanket fell to her feet, and she turned around. A tall, wide shadow stood in front of her, and before she could scream the shadow lunged forward placing a hand over her mouth. She shrieked into the large palm cupped over her lips and went hysterical, thrashing her arms against a hard chest.

"It is me," a familiar voice whispered.

She inhaled through her nose as he pushed her closer to the fire so she could see his face. A loud sigh muffled against his hand when she recognized Otakatay standing before her. He stared into her eyes, waiting until she calmed down before he slowly removed his hand.

"You scared me half to death."

"There is no time. You must leave." He glanced around the cabin as if he were searching for something.

"Leave? But why?"

His eyes met hers, raw and obsessive.

Nora's stomach flipped. Terrified of what the feeling meant, she looked away.

"Someone is going to kill you."

Her head shot up. "What? Why would someone want to kill me?" *Did someone know? Had Jess or Joe told? It's what Pa feared all along.* She chewed her lip while trying to understand what he'd said.

"Because of something he thinks you have."

The room grew bright as lightning flashed outside followed by an ominous clap of thunder. The walls moved and she swayed to her right.

He caught her arm. She blinked up at him and tried to focus on his face.

"But I have nothing."

"You must go." He pulled her toward the door. "Now! You must go tonight."

Things were happening too fast. She needed to know why and how he knew someone wanted her dead. She tugged her arm free and planted her feet into the wooden floor.

"But where would I go?"

He paused. "Where is your family?"

"I have no one."

Lightning illuminated the room, and she saw the hint of sadness cross his face. She touched his cheek. His skin was soft except for the whiskers, and she skimmed her thumb over his lips.

She couldn't explain why she'd touched him so intimately, other than she was drawn to him. Touching him felt right. She wasn't afraid of him, and she knew he wasn't the vile beast he proclaimed to be.

He moved closer, his hard chest pressed against hers. He bent and his black hair tickled her cheek. She felt his breath upon her lips and closed her eyes. He released her and stepped back, his shoulders rigid.

"You must go."

She stood motionless and watched as sadness, anger and confusion crossed his handsome face.

"I have nowhere to go."

"Then I will take you." He gripped the door handle as lightning cast the room in yellow shades. "I will be back." He opened the door and took off into the storm.

She glanced down at Pal beside her. The wind howled outside, and the rain banged against the cabin walls. Two gunshots drown out the storm. Without thinking, she opened the door and ran out into the pouring rain. Pal darted past her and around the corner of the cabin. She followed him while the rain pelted her, soaking her dress. She stopped and the blood rushed from her head to her feet. *Oh no. Not him. Please not him.*

Pal sniffed Otakatay's body as it lay in the mud. He'd been shot. She ran over and without examining him, she reached underneath his arms and pulled him toward the cabin. He was heavy, and she didn't know if she'd be able to get him inside.

Rain ran down her face and dripped off of her nose. Her hair was drenched, and she couldn't see it was so dark. She pushed her bare feet into the mud and pulled Otakatay another foot closer to the door. Pal whined and stared off into the blackness behind the cabin.

She huffed and tugged on him once more, moving him another two feet. If it wasn't for the mud, she didn't think she'd be able to move him at all. The wet dirt offered a slick path so it was easier to pull him. Pal came around, bit into Otakatay's shirt, and helped Nora drag him into the house.

She lit the lamp and carried it to the door. Pal stood outside on the porch and when she called him inside he took off, disappearing into the darkness. She yelled after him, but he didn't return and she needed to help Otakatay.

She knelt beside him and ripped open his shirt. Nora gasped when she saw the scars embedded on his chest, stomach and arms. *What happened to him?* The bevelled lines marked his skin in a criss-cross fashion, and her heart broke for him and what he must've been through. Her hands heated and her fingers pulsed. She clenched them and held them at her sides. *No. I will not do it. I will help him without using my gift.*

She put a pot of water on the cook stove to heat and gently washed his muddy chest. One of the bullets had gone clean through his shoulder. The other was still lodged in the center of his chest. She searched the house for a bottle of whiskey. She knew Pa stashed one around here somewhere. She removed the blanket from the basket beside the sofa and found the half-filled bottle nestled inside.

She dipped a clean cloth into the whiskey and blotted at the wound on his shoulder. Blood trickled down his arm, and she knew it would need stitches. She'd tend to that later, for now she needed to get the bullet out of his chest.

She felt Otakatay for one of his knives and pulled the large blade from his leg. She dipped it into the liquid. The water boiled, and she removed the pot and placed it beside her on the floor. His chest rose and fell in uneven breaths. She could taste the fear on her tongue. *I will save you.*

Nora's hands throbbed with urgency. She opened and closed them a few times before she pressed the tip of the knife into the hole in his chest. She stopped to see if he could feel anything, but he laid still, an ashen color already beginning to settle over his skin.

She dug the knife deeper and moved it around, trying to locate the bullet. Blood poured from the wound. Nora's hands shook wildly, and she dropped the knife. She squeezed her eyes shut, willed her hands to stop—to let her be normal, to save him without the power.

A lone tear slid down her cheek and fell onto her hand. She gaped at him. The ripped flesh was swollen and bloody. She didn't have a choice. She couldn't save Pa, he wouldn't let her. Otakatay was unconscious, there would be no fighting.

She couldn't remove the bullet with the knife, she didn't know how. She needed to save him and soon. She couldn't watch another person die without trying to help them first.

She blocked all reason from her mind and placed her hands over the wound. Strong blistering pain slammed into her and almost knocked her backward. The wound was deep, and she needed to work fast. She pressed both hands, one on top of the other over the hole again.

The nauseous feeling filled her belly as a fire exploded in her chest. She wheezed as the force sucked the air from her lungs. A piercing spasm radiated up and down her arms, zigzagged across her breasts and into her back. She bent forward and tried to ease the burning in her muscles.

When she inhaled, her lungs pinched as painful tremors rippled through her body. The enormity of it was too much. She didn't know how long she could hold on. Mouth dry, she tried to focus on his face as the room spun around her.

She pushed up onto her knees and forced her body to press into his. The heat in her hands intensified as she healed the deadly wound. Everything around her grew fuzzy, and she swayed to one side. She grew weaker and struggled to keep her hands on his chest. Her stomach lurched, and she held on until she felt the skin close underneath her palms. She removed them just in time to crawl to the basket she'd found the whiskey in, and vomited until she had nothing left inside of her.

Sweat ran from her forehead, and she trembled from the damp sensation. Her stomach convulsed a few more times. She laid her head on the blanket. The rain hitting the cabin was the last thing she remembered before she passed out.

CHAPTER NINETEEN

Nora woke with a start. Her chest ached, and her arms were numb. She flexed her hands to get some of the feeling back. She remembered Otakatay and crawled toward him. The room was still covered in shadows, but she knew it wouldn't be long before the sun rose.

The wound on his chest was no longer visible, and she laid her palm to his forehead. He was warm. She removed the cloth from his shoulder and shivered. Red and swollen, the wound was infected. There was no way she'd be able to heal him after closing the chest wound a few hours before. Her hands ached, and her arms were useless. She was drained and would have to wait until her body had recuperated.

"Otakatay." She nudged him. "Otakatay, please I need you to wake up."

He opened his eyes.

"I need your help to get you to the bed."

He nodded, and by the glossy look in his eyes, she wasn't sure he knew where he was.

She placed her arm under his and helped him to his feet. Her muscles cried out in agony as she ushered him toward the bedroom. He lost consciousness just as she sat him on the straw filled mattress. She eased him onto his back and propped a pillow under his head. She went to work removing his muddy pants and boots. As she unbuttoned his denims, she realized he was naked underneath.

Oh, no. Her hands hovered above his groin. She shook her head and frowned. She didn't have time for this nonsense. She threw the blanket over his middle and pulled the pants off. She was being ridiculous. This was a life and death matter. But she couldn't bring herself to steal a peek at his private area. She straightened the quilt the best she could. She picked up his dirty clothes and boots before she left the room.

She threw the pot of bloody water out into the yard and bolted the door, sighing when the wooden latch slid into place. She hadn't forgotten why Otakatay had come. Nora shivered and peeked through the curtain. *But who?*

There was still some water left in the bucket on the counter, and she dumped it into the pot to heat. She searched the cupboards for the lye soap and wrapped it in the wash cloth. The floor was a mess, with mud and blood smeared into the wood. She stared at it for a moment, deciding to come back and clean it later.

Nora dunked the cloth into the hot water and lathered the soap. She ran the cloth along his hard body, trying not to gape at the defined muscles on his stomach and chest. Nora's fingers skimmed the slashes on his shoulders and arms. There were so many she wondered how he lived through them all. She took the whiskey bottle, squeezed her eyes shut and poured it over the shoulder wound.

Otakatay bolted upright, knocking her backward, and yelled out in Lakota.

"I'm so sorry, but I have to clean the wound." She pressed him back down onto the pillow.

Amid red cheeks and clammy skin, glassy eyes gazed back at her. She laid her hand on his arm. He was sweating.

"One more time," she whispered.

He nodded and lay back down. She watched as his jaw clenched, and he closed his eyes. She leaned in and quickly tipped the bottle sloshing brown liquid onto the hole to run down his arm and chest.

A guttural moan came from his closed mouth, and his whole body tensed.

She took the whiskey soaked cloth and dabbed at the wound.

A strong hand gripped her wrist. "Burn it. Heat the knife and close it."

Was he insane? She couldn't do that. "I will stitch it instead."

"Do as I say," he growled.

"It is infected."

He squeezed her wrist, and she thought he was going to get off the bed and cauterize the wound himself when he passed out instead.

She sighed, doused the cloth in whiskey and placed it on the back of his shoulder, where the bullet had exited. She needed to stitch the torn flesh before he woke and demanded she melt it together with the blade of his knife.

Waves of nausea rocked her stomach causing her face to lose all color.

He was still too warm. She finished cleaning the area, pulled out her needle and thread, and dipped both into the whiskey.

Black eyes glared at her, and she jumped.

"Why do you not listen? Burn the damn hole."

"I...I don't think I can."

"It will get the infection out."

She held up the needle and thread. "But I cleaned these so I can stitch you."

He shook his head.

She wanted to brush the black strands that clung to his cheeks and neck.

"Where is the knife?"

"Please, Otakatay. Please don't make me do this."

He watched her for a long while before he said, "I will show you. Get my knife."

With no other choice, she grabbed the large blade sitting on the bedside table and handed it to him. He struggled to sit up and winced when he moved his arm. With his good hand he gripped the knife.

"You must build a fire and heat the end until the blade glows red."

She swallowed and nodded.

"Then you will place it over the hole until the skin is closed."

Nora's cheeks flushed. *How am I going to do this?* She glanced at Otakatay. *What if I throw up all over him or worse yet, pass out?*

He handed her the knife.

She willed her legs to walk into the kitchen. It wasn't more than a few minutes before the flames had grown, pushing heat into the room. She placed the blade into the fire and watched as it turned a bright orange-red. She wrapped her hand in the apron she was wearing, so she didn't burn it and pulled the knife from the heat. She hurried back into the room where Otakatay lay and stood over him.

"Do it. Quickly, do it now." He closed his eyes and clenched his jaw.

She focused on the bright tip of the knife as she moved closer to the swollen flesh. *I can't do this.* She chewed on her lip, and her hand shook.

Otakatay opened his eyes, and before she could pull away he grabbed her hand and pressed it into the wound.

His face contorted, and he let out what sounded to her like a warrior's cry before he passed out.

The smell of burning flesh filled her nostrils, and her stomach reeled. She swallowed past the bile in her throat and pushed the knife into his shoulder. The skin around the blade bubbled, and she closed her eyes. She inhaled before removing the knife and opening her eyes. The skin was red and rigid over the hole. She took the whiskey-doused cloth and laid it against the closed wound. *I have to do this one more time. Oh, dear God.*

He watched helplessly as his brother Little Eagle struggled to carry a bucket of rocks down the narrow path to the opening of the tunnel. He was six, tiny for his age, and not strong enough for this kind of labor. Throughout the dark, wet mountain deep holes were used for discipline, and digging. Little Eagle was edging his way around one that had been blasted yesterday. It was a fresh hole, and it was deep.

He wanted to go to him, to help his brother. He struggled, trying to loosen the ropes tied around his feet and wrists. He was his protector, his shadow. He yanked on the rope again.

He stopped hammering and watched Little Eagle take careful steps around another hole.

A loud crack echoed throughout the cave, and he didn't have to turn to see what it was. The leather whip the guard held flew high in the air and snapped.

He flinched.

"Get back to work," the man yelled.

He couldn't take his eyes of off his brother until he'd passed the hole—until he was safe. The whip lashed out biting into his flesh. He dug his teeth into his bottom lip and refused to look away.

Little Eagle glanced up at him, and he watched in horror as his brother lost his balance. The heavy bucket pulled him toward the hole. In an instant he was gone.

"Noooo," He screamed, and grasped at the air around him. He tried to yank free from the rope that tied him to the others, but he didn't move.

Otakatay woke to Nora pressing a damp cloth to his forehead. The dream was so vivid, so real it was as if he were there in the mountain all over again and saw his brother fall.

"You had a bad dream," she said. "Are you okay?"

He didn't answer. He didn't know what to say. If only it was a dream and not true. If only he'd been there to help him—to save him. He closed his eyes. He was a failure. Sorrow filled him, flooding his senses, and he couldn't see past the shame he felt to look at Nora's face.

He took her hand from his forehead and moved it onto the bed.

No longer a boy, he was an assassin with a vengeance. He killed to keep a promise. It was what kept him sane all these years. He pushed rational thoughts from his mind and brought forth the animal he'd come to know. The beast, who craved blood, thirsted for money and valor. He snarled and growled plotting revenge on those who'd done him wrong.

He looked into Nora's blue eyes. She shouldn't be near him—in the same room as a killer who slaughtered so many.

"Otakatay, are you okay?"

Concern etched her pretty face, and he closed off any feelings he might have for her. He needed to go. He needed to leave here and kill the man who had shot him last night. *Two times. I was shot twice.* He inspected his bare chest.

The sun shone through the bedroom window, bright and welcoming. He didn't know if it was morning or afternoon. The single thought that plagued his mind was where the other bullet had entered. He was sure it had gone into his chest, but when he searched his chest all he saw were old scars.

"I was shot twice."

He watched as her eyes darted about the room. She was nervous. The warrior within him came alert, and he scrutinized her every move.

"I was shot two times. Where is the other wound?"

"I think you need to rest." She tried to stand, but he grabbed her wrist.

"Sit."

She slumped back down.

"Where was I shot besides my shoulder?"

"Umm. You were...uh...you were shot once."

He didn't believe her. He remembered a burning pain in his chest, the first place he'd been hit. The shoulder had been the second.

"No, I was shot here." He placed his palm over the center of his chest. The room dipped. He shook his head and focused on Nora.

Her face was white, and she chewed on her lip. She knew something, and he was about to get it out of her.

"Why is there no hole in my chest?"

He shook his head, battling the darkness that wanted to overcome him.

"You must be mistaken. You were shot once."

"You're one of them. You're the witkowin."

She was silent.

"I know I was shot here." He patted his chest. "Tell me what happened, now." His tone changed from calm to intense, a predator stalking his prey.

"You need to rest."

"You need to tell me what the hell is going on. Why is there no damn hole in my chest when I know I was shot there?"

The pain in his shoulder radiated down his arm causing his fingers to ache. He blinked trying to focus on her face, but his eyes wanted to close. He felt her hand on his forehead as her soothing voice faded into blackness.

CHAPTER TWENTY

Nora sat on the edge of the bed and watched as Otakatay's broad chest rose and fell in even cadence. He remembered the gunshot to his chest. *And I almost blurted out that I healed him.* She frowned. *Idiot.* Pa had drilled into her head to be careful, to keep the power her hands held to herself. The reason she'd been confined to four walls and a yard. And she didn't listen, yet again.

Otakatay had come to warn her last night. *Did he know who wanted to kill me?* She remembered the night Pa died. The sheriff still had no leads. What if the person who killed Pa wanted her dead also? Pa had no enemies, other than Elwood Calhoun, but almost everyone disliked the rich miner.

She crossed him off her list of potential murderers immediately and eyed Otakatay lying on the bed. Would he harm her if he knew? Could he have been the one who killed Pa? He had come to the cabin that night. *And thank goodness he did. I'd have burned my hands beyond repair.* He may be rough around the edges, but something told her he didn't kill Pa.

But one question remained. Did Otakatay know who did? She pressed her lips together. He was a bounty hunter after all, he hunted killers. She smoothed his thick black hair between her fingers. He knew who wanted her dead, so he had to know who killed Pa, and she was determined to find out who it was. She took the cloth from the basin, wrung it out and laid it gently on his forehead.

He desperately wanted her to see the horrible man he was, but when she observed him all she saw was sadness—broken and ragged. He held some sort of spell over her, and she wanted nothing more than to help him become whole again.

She sensed he battled with something evil, and she'd watched several times as he tried to harness whatever demon thrashed about inside of him. He bore marks upon his entire upper body, and pain melded with sorrow as she wondered how he ever survived such an ordeal.

Were those scars the reason he held such hatred for the white man? Had her people done this to him? With the tip of her finger, she traced a long scar from the rippled muscles on his stomach all the way up to his neck disappearing into the pillow he lay on.

She swallowed. Every muscle on his body was defined, and she stared in awe. She rubbed her legs together, as unfamiliar sensations pulsed in her most private place. She'd never seen anything like him. He was perfect. Her face heated as she covered him with a thin blanket. She needed some air.

She took his pants, shirt and boots into the kitchen. She needed wash water and the well was outside. *Someone wants you dead.* She peeked out the window and saw Jed working. She said a silent prayer, set her jaw and yanked the bucket from the counter.

She bolted outside. On her way to the well she picked up the other bucket to fill also. Jed waved to her. She smiled, and her lips quivered with uncertainty. She had to act normal. She couldn't go around acting leery of everyone. People would think she was crazy.

She set the buckets of water on the porch and scanned the yard, the street and the forest behind the cabin. There was no sign of Pal, and she worried he'd been hurt or worse yet, killed. She refrained from calling out his name and went inside instead. The wooden lock slid into place with a dull thud. She went to work washing Otakatay's clothes and scrubbing the floor. A knock on the door startled her. She peeked out the window and saw Seth standing there.

"Afternoon, Seth."

"Miss Nora."

The boy shifted from one foot to the other. "I found the bounty hunter's horse behind your cabin last night, and I took him to the Livery."

"Thank you."

"I know he's hurt. I heard the shots. But I won't tell anyone he's here."

She didn't know what to say. Seth had never spoken more than a sentence to her in the time she'd known him. She was a good judge of character, and Seth was genuine, he'd keep her secret.

She smiled. "I appreciate your help."

He nodded. "I'll feed and groom his horse until he's better." He tipped his hat and walked away.

He was a kind boy, and she was relieved to know he was there if she needed him.

Nora put another log onto the fire. The air still held a chill in the evenings, and she'd slipped into one of Pa's old sweaters to keep warm. Otakatay had slept the whole day, and the last time she checked on him he was still out. His skin was no longer warm, he'd been right to burn the wounds closed. Her stomach pitched remembering the sickening smell of burning flesh. She didn't want to do that ever again. Thank goodness he was on the mend and as she laid the thick quilt over top of him, she sighed.

The large pot of chicken soup simmered on the stove for hours, and she couldn't wait to taste it with the homemade bread Jess had left her. She pulled the kitchen curtain to the side and looked again for Pal, but there was still no sign of him.

Taking the ladle from the pot, she dumped a hearty portion into a bowl, and laid it outside on the porch. If Pal did come back during the night, he'd have something to eat. The gesture did little to ease the tension in her back. Where had he gone? She took one last look before closing the door for the night.

The cabin floor glistened, and no one would've guessed Otakatay had bled all over it last night. She crept into the bedroom and sat in the chair by the bed. She was exhausted and couldn't help yawning and stretching her tired muscles. Nora pulled the leather tie from her braid and placed it on the bedside table. She picked up her brush. The porcupine quills on the ivory handle massaged her scalp, and she closed her eyes.

"You're marked."

She jumped and fumbled to keep from dropping the brush, before placing it on her lap. Her eyes met his dark ones, and she smiled. "Oh, this?" She pulled back her hair to reveal the rose colored skin. "It's just a birth mark."

He frowned.

She almost went to him when he sat up and cringed from the pain. She couldn't help staring at his large muscles as they bunched and flexed before her. He reached for the glass of water beside the bed and took a sip.

"You bathed me?"

"Well, I...uh. Yes."

"Where are my clothes?"

He wasn't angry, and she realized it was the first time she'd seen a softer side to him.

"I washed them. They are hanging in the kitchen."

He nodded.

"I need to find Wakina."

"Oh, Seth came by earlier. Your horse is in the livery next door. You can go get him when you're well."

His dark eyes scanned the room, and she wondered how much he remembered of the last day and a half.

"I made soup. Are you hungry?"

"Yes."

She rushed into the kitchen and ladled a bowl for him, making sure to butter some bread, too.

"Here you go. Would you like me to feed you?"

"I'm not a damn cripple," he growled.

"I didn't mean—

"Are you not eating?" He positioned the bowl on his lap and dunked the bread into the soup.

"I didn't think—

He grunted.

She left and came back with her own bowl and bread. She shifted on the seat as he watched her sip from the spoon. His mouth twitched as he held the bowl to his lips and drank the soup.

"Do you frown often?" she asked, curious about the life he'd led before she'd met him.

He grunted again.

"Do you ever smile?"

"There is no reason to."

He put the empty bowl on the table beside the bed.

"Sure there is. Every time I hear a bird sing, I smile."

"That's because you are a little girl."

She straightened.

"I'll have you know I am nineteen years old. That hardly classifies me as a little girl."

He shrugged.

"How old are you?"

"Older than you, wicicala."

"What does that mean?"

"Young girl." He smirked.

She clamped her mouth shut. What was his problem? Why was he being so hard to get along with?

"That's your opinion."

He grunted again.

She put her bowl next to his, crossed her arms and glared at him.

"You are weak."

"I am many things, but I am not weak and I am not a *wicicaly* or whatever you call it."

"The truth lies within your eyes."

She bristled. "Pardon me, but who are you to judge?" She flung her arm at him. "You walk around like you're the damn reaper. Everyone who crosses your path is terrified of you." Her finger waggled in his face.

"And so I'm clear, I don't care what you think."

"Yes, you do."

She blinked back tears and glared at him. She'd saved his life, healed him with her own hands and this is how he repaid her? She shook her head.

"You know nothing about me."

"I know someone wants you dead."

She could feel the color drain from her face, and her head spun.

"How do you know this?" she whispered.

She was unsure if she wanted to know, but the question had been asked, and she waited for his answer.

"He hired me to do it," he answered bluntly, and his black eyes roamed her face.

"But why?" *Did he know?*

"You tell me."

Get a hold of yourself. He can't be trusted. "I don't know why."

Otakatay's black eyes traveled the length of her body, stopped at her face, and she was sure he could read her mind.

"I'd say you do."

"I don't know what you're talking about."

She stood and reached for the bowls. He grabbed her wrist.

She gasped.

"I'm not going to kill you, Nora."

She believed him. He didn't lie, he had no reason to. If he wanted to kill her, he'd have done it by now.

"Thank you."

He pulled her closer until his lips were an inch from her own. His eyes never left hers, as he brought their lips together in a passionate kiss. The bowls fell from her hands onto the floor. All that seemed to matter was him, and the way he made her feel.

His tongue slid along her bottom lip, and she opened her mouth. He deepened the kiss and her body buzzed with excitement. He released her wrist and combed his fingers through her hair. Cupping her head, he pressed her closer to him.

The kiss seemed to go on forever, and she ached for his touch. Her hands caressed his chest and the muscles tightened. He pushed her from him, panting, and frowned.

Nora's cheeks flushed. She straightened her skirt, picked up the broken bowls and, without saying a word left the room.

Otakatay shifted on the bed. He wanted her, and damn it he needed to get a hold of himself before he lost control. She was in danger, and he was the enemy. He cringed when he lifted his shoulder. He wasn't going to kill her—he couldn't, but it didn't mean he should go off and seduce her. Shit, he'd been too long without a woman.

The girl knew why she was hunted. He'd seen it in her eyes. She didn't trust him, and he didn't know why that bothered him. Hell, he was a reaper like she'd said. He had no feelings, there wasn't a kind bone left within his body. Except when he was with her, he struggled to remain the man he'd trained himself to be. He grasped at the horrible things he'd done, so he could justify keeping her at a distance.

He could hear her banging dishes around. She was kind, soft and sweet. Not something to be mixed with his hate hardened bitter self. He needed to leave, to get the hell away from her. He sat up, and a searing pain stabbed his shoulder. He cradled the limb in his good arm.

He'd come here to warn her, to take her with him somewhere safe. He couldn't leave. Not until he killed the bastard that shot him. Not until she was no longer in danger. Anger consumed him, and he ground his teeth. The wasichu shot him, he'd put money on it. He ran his hand through his long hair. Nora was a girl—a girl in danger. She'd die if he didn't help her.

Shit. He owed her nothing. Yet, he couldn't walk away without knowing she was safe. He didn't like her. He simply wanted her body and nothing else. Satisfied that he held no feelings other than wanting to bed the black-haired beauty, he sat back against the pillow.

His shoulder hurt like hell, and he wished he still had his medicine bag. The Slippery Elm was good for burns and cuts. He'd given it to Nora the night she'd burned her hands, and he hadn't seen it since. He glanced out the window. He'd seen the plant in the forest and was regretting not taking some of the sticky bark. It took two days to dry and be ground into powder. Two days he didn't have.

He flexed his shoulder. The muscle was tight and sore. He removed the white bandage she had wrapped around it and examined the rippled and deformed flesh. His shoulder didn't stand out at all against the rest of his scars. The skin around the burn was red, but there was no infection, and he took the bandage, dunked it into the basin of water beside the bed and blotted the burn.

He held his arm up, grinding his teeth through the pain in his shoulder. Otakatay's forehead bubbled with sweat, and his stomach convulsed from the stress he put on the injured arm, but he continued to exercise the muscle. The eagle feather fell into his eyes. He thinned his lips. He hadn't forgotten his promise. It had taken him so long to get here. To realize that what he had was enough for now. He'd been driven by revenge and hatred. He should've completed the promise years before.

CHAPTER TWENTY-ONE

Elwood sat with his foot elevated on the mahogany desk. Ten stitches below the toes and five more on the bottom of his foot. The bruised foot still throbbed, and he'd been dulling the pain with whiskey since the previous night. The damn dog would pay, and he'd make sure it was painful.

He hoped to have Nora with him when he returned to the mine, but the little bitch wanted nothing to do with him. The fact that she was all alone with no one to protect her sweetened his plan to take her as his wife. But now he realized that she wasn't going to come willingly.

He swirled the alcohol in his glass, spilling some over the sides to run down his fingers. He was resigned to making her his wife the old-fashioned way. He smiled. Oh what fun that would be. Visions of her on his bed naked with terror filled eyes flooded his mind, and he grew hard thinking about it. Yes, he'd devise a plan. If he could get her here and ruin her reputation, everything would fall into place. Soon she'd be overflowing with his seed and so ashamed she'd be begging him to marry her.

"Boss, the boy is giving us trouble again." Red stood in the doorway his hair disheveled and a cut below his bottom lip.

He downed the rest of the whiskey and snatched the braided leather belt hanging on the hook by the door. The leather rope gave him the power he needed to run the mine and the filthy brats that worked for him.

The door to Joe's room stood ajar, and Elwood could hear Levi yelling at the boy.

"What in hell is going on?" He limped closer to them.

"I'm tryin' to get the boy tied to his post, and he ain't cooperatin'," Levi said, out of breath and harried.

Joe stood in the corner of the room. Tears ran from his eyes and into the dirt smeared on his cheeks. He pointed a colt .45 at Levi.

"Where in hell did he get a gun?" Elwood demanded.

"I was tryin' to get him tied up, and he pulled it from my belt," Levi whined.

Elwood scowled at Red unsure if he should hit him or the boy first. "Joe, you put that gun down now, you hear?"

He shook his blonde head. "No, Pa. No. No. No."

The boy would get it once he got the damn gun from him. "Please, Son, hand over the gun."

"I don't want to be tied up, tied up. I don't like it, like it." He cried. "I want June-bug, June-bug."

"June lives in town. Joe, remember the deal we have. No seeing her if you don't obey."

Joe shook his head again and waved the gun around the room. Everyone dived out of the way, and Elwood had to keep from lashing out at the kid as pain sliced through his foot. He needed to get the gun from the boy and quick. "Okay, Joe. I won't tie you up. I promise."

Joe stopped crying, and a big smile spread across his face.

The mind of a simple child perplexed him.

Joe laid the gun on the bed.

"You little bastard." Levi threw his hand back and slapped Joe across the face sending him into the wall. The sticks fell from his armpits as he slid to the floor, clutching his cheek and whimpering.

"Levi, Red, I want you to go into town and get the girl. Bring her here unharmed."

"Yes, boss," Levi said.

"On your way out, check on the others. Make sure everyone is doing what they're told. I'm in no mood for trouble."

Both men nodded and left.

Elwood closed the door and, with his other hand, released the rope with a loud snap. He smiled when Joe jumped. Careful of his injured foot, he walked toward him. The damn kid wouldn't cross him again, not after tonight.

He cracked the whip.

CHAPTER TWENTY-TWO

He laid the dead rabbit on the table outside their house. Little Eagle sat beside him, a thin blanket wrapped around his narrow shoulders. Their mother had been dead two weeks, and their father hadn't returned. Left to fend for themselves, he had vowed to take care of his brother. There had been nothing left to eat in the shack after a few days, so he loaded the shotgun, and together they hunted for meat.

As the days passed, he prayed that their father never came back. He hated him, and because he took Ina from them forever, he wanted to kill him. He'd watch over Little Eagle. They didn't need anyone but each other, and together they'd make it.

He skinned the rabbit as a shiny black wagon bounced along the rutted road leading to their home. His father sat with another white man, on the seat up front. Buck Morgan had no friends, his father was a weasel, and he knew something wasn't right.

He tucked the blade beneath his sleeve and stood. He reached for Little Eagle, and with one arm pulled him close. He watched through hate-filled eyes as their father staggered down from the wagon and walked crookedly toward them. The air carried his familiar scent of sweat, unwashed clothes and alcohol.

He stepped back, taking his brother with him, and peered around his father's ripped and stained shirt to see the other man as he came closer. He couldn't help but gawk, and he forgot all about his father, when he saw the man's fancy suit. He'd never seen anything like him, or his shiny black buggy.

"Ina, Ina," Little Eagle cried into the back of his shirt as he hid behind him.

He reached back and patted the top of his brother's head.

"Un ohiti ke," he whispered. "Be brave."

The white man walked toward them.

He squeezed the knife and cupped his arm around Little Eagle to protect him. No one would harm his brother. He glared up at the well-dressed man and hissed, baring his teeth.

"What is this? Is your son part animal?" the man asked.

"He thinks he's tough, but once you knock him around a bit, he's like the rest of 'em half breeds. A coward," his father said, laughing before he took another drink from his bottle.

"What about the little one? Can he do the same amount of work?"

"I won't even charge ya for him. You can have him for free."

He studied his father then the other man. What did the man want? He took a step backward, pushing his brother with him toward the door. They wouldn't take Little Eagle, he'd protect him with his life. The rich man motioned to two large men behind him.

"Slim, Bob."

Slim had light hair, and Bob stringy and on top of his head, none at all. He hadn't even seen them he'd been so distracted by the rich man and his father.

He took another step back. Little Eagle whimpered into his shirt, and he wished there was something he could do to ease his fear. Large hands shoved him out of the way and yanked Little Eagle up into the air. Ear-splitting screams burst from his mouth. He watched helpless as Slim smacked Little Eagle on the side of the head.

He shouted, using the war cry his mother taught him, and ran up onto the tree stump catapulting himself into the air toward the man that held his brother. He slid the knife from his sleeve and into his hand, driving it into Slim's back. He yanked the blade from the flesh and swiped it across Slim's forearm.

The man dropped Little Eagle, and he dove for his brother, he had to protect him. He was struck from behind. Dark spots danced in front of him as he fell to the ground with a thud. The back of his head throbbed, and his arms hung to the sides, no longer able to fight. Two large hands picked him up and threw him into the back of the pretty black wagon. Little Eagle snuggled close burying himself into his neck and cried for Ina as it drove away.

Nora woke to Otakatay mumbling in Lakota. There was little light in the room, and she figured it was past midnight. She lit the lamp and pulled her tired muscles from the sofa and into the bedroom. She could see that he wasn't awake and knew without coming closer he was having another dream. She watched his face contort and twist. His arms jerked, and she went to him afraid he'd hurt himself more if she didn't wake him.

She put the lamp on the table and shook him.

"Otakatay, please wake up."

He stilled beneath her hand.

"You're dreaming. Wake up."

He opened his eyes and closed them again. "Leave."

She sat down in the chair and picked up the yarn and needles from the basket.

"Are you deaf? Leave." His tone left no room for challenge.

"No."

"No?"

Without looking at him, she said, "Yes, no."

"I don't want you here. Go away."

"I'm staying. Now if you'd like to go back to sleep, feel free. Or you can continue to pout. I don't care which you choose."

He grunted, said a few words she didn't understand, and she was sure she didn't want to, as he kicked his feet out from the quilt.

Minutes passed before she glanced up at him. He scowled at her.

"Tell me where you're from."

"Hell."

"Oh, nonsense. Where are your father and mother?"

"Dead and," he paused, "dead."

She stopped knitting and put the needles on her lap. "I'm so sorry. I didn't mean to bring up horrible memories for you."

He grunted again. "Buck Morgan wasn't worth the shit in the outhouse."

She didn't know what to say. He practically spat the words from his mouth as if they were poison. "He must've been an awful person for you to say that."

"Awful is too kind a word."

What had his father done to cause such hard feelings to come from his own son?

"How did he die?"

"I killed him."

"Oh."

She was silent while she debated her next question. Curiosity and the profound feelings she had for him all but shoved the words from her mouth. "Why did you kill him?"

"He was a snake who thought of himself and not his wife or two sons."

"You have a brother?"

He closed his mouth and held it shut, thinning his full lips. She met his eyes, and saw such anguish, such despair. How could she have been so daft? It was obvious that something had happened to his brother as well. The sheer magnitude of what he felt was reflected on his face. Pain and torment twisted his features and almost sent her fleeing the room to sob in a corner.

"Otakatay, I'm so sorry." She placed her hand over his.

He focused on her face, and she smiled.

"I cannot change the past."

She nodded thinking of Pa and how she'd love nothing more than to go back, and have him here once more. Life was not so easy, loved ones died. She wove the needle around the yarn and through the hole. She had no idea what she was making, and in truth it didn't matter. The hobby gave her something to do while she sat with Otakatay.

"When did your mother pass?" she asked, hoping to ease some of his pain by allowing him to talk about it.

"I was eleven winters."

"Was she sick?"

"My father killed her."

Wide eyed and mouth open, the shock of what he'd said was too much. She cleared her throat. She wanted to hold him and cry for all the horrible things he'd seen, all the unthinkable things that had happened to him. She didn't know where he'd gotten those scars, but she'd guess it was from when he was young. She couldn't imagine anyone inflicting that amount of torment on him now and living afterward.

"Is this where you were born?"

She glanced up from her knitting, taken aback by his question. He'd never asked about her past, she didn't think he cared.

"No, we moved here last year." She smiled sadly. "I've lived in every town from here to Texas." She took his silence to mean that he wanted to know more, and she continued. "Pa was always moving. He never liked to be somewhere too long. We were like gypsies, travelling from one place to the next. It was wonderful. I have fond memories of it." She had to keep from making a face as she lied, but there was no way she could tell him the truth. She didn't trust him.

"A simple yes or no would've worked."

Well, that didn't last long. Did he have a kind bone in his body? "Sorry I took up your valuable time," she huffed, and went back to knitting. She jerked the needle from the yarn. "You'd think you had somewhere to go."

"I do."

She glanced at him. "And where is that?"

"I need to kill the man who shot me."

He spoke in such matter-of-fact tones that, if it weren't for the gravity of what he'd said, she'd have burst out laughing.

"I see."

"Good. Now get my clothes."

"You are not going anywhere until your shoulder is healed."

He raised a brow.

"What good are you with one arm?"

"Want me to show you?" His dark eyes wandered her body.

She didn't miss the heated look he gave her, and it didn't take long to figure out what he meant.

She cleared her throat, shifted on her seat and went back to her knitting.

He swung his legs over the end of the bed, and she couldn't help but peek through her lashes as the blanket slid down his broad chest to rest on his lap. He yawned and stood, allowing the blanket to fall to the floor.

She buried her head in her hands. "What are you doing?"

"Stretching."

"Please, cover yourself." She waved her arm while still hiding her face.

He chuckled but didn't pick up the blanket.

He laughed? She opened her fingers enough for one eye to peek through. *Yup, he's naked, and damn it he was laughing.*

"Tsk, tsk, Wicicala."

"I am not a little girl." She shot up off the chair—her knitting fell to the floor. "I'm a grown woman."

He stepped toward her, and his chest skimmed her breasts.

"Prove it."

Without thinking, she ran her hand through his hair and pulled him toward her. She smashed her lips onto his in a feverish kiss. *No turning back now.* She thrust her tongue into his mouth and pressed her breasts up against his muscled chest. A low moan came from his throat, and he wrapped his arm around her waist lifting her from the ground.

She couldn't contain herself and ran her finger nails down his chest. He straightened, and she sensed his embarrassment. Not willing to end their embrace, she nipped at his bottom lip and was surprised when her hips rubbed against his groin. What was he doing to her? *I turn into a harlot in his arms.* But she felt whole and safe there. He sank into her and slowly pulled his lips from hers.

Nora's heart beat as fast as a wild mustang galloping across the prairies, and her breaths came in short puffs. Her breasts pulsed, and she yearned for more of him. She placed her hands on his chest.

He removed them, bringing them to her sides.

"They don't bother me," she whispered.

He coughed.

"They bother me." He picked up the blanket, and wrapping it around his middle he left the room.

She knew he didn't want her to follow, so she sat down in the chair. *I kissed him.* She touched her lips, still wet from his. She cared for him. Her stomach flipped, and she peeked at the doorway.

He aroused sensations within her she'd never felt before, making her hungry for his touch. How did this happen? She barely knew him. But as she licked her lips, remembering their kiss, warmth spread over her to linger in her most private place.

Otakatay peered out the window. He couldn't see a damn thing it was so dark. He needed to get out of this cabin. Being near Nora was no good, and he needed to stay on the path he'd set out for himself. He pulled the blanket tight around his waist. The little twit had actually risen to his challenge. He'd been playing with her, trying to get her to ask him to leave, and instead she'd surprised him with a kiss. An unbelievable kiss, one he'd think of over and over again for the rest of his life. He didn't need these distractions, especially the one that had just happened.

He rubbed his chest. He was shot here he knew it. He remembered the piercing pain when the bullet struck him. But where had the wound gone? He knew she was keeping that bit of information from him, and he figured it was because she was scared. A part of him wanted to know, to demand the information from her, while the other was intent on leaving and killing the son of a bitch who shot him.

He needed to finish this. *Wahi—I am coming.* The time had come, to become the venomous bounty hunter once again. He'd stalk his prey and use his knife to end lives. He made a fist. His shoulder was still sore, but he had to go. He had to place some distance between himself and Nora.

Tomorrow he'd leave and make sure she was in no more danger from the wasichu. As hard as it was for him to admit it, he liked the girl. She annoyed the hell out of him, and she talked endlessly, but she was soft and kind. He owed it to her to make sure she was safe, and he'd enjoy killing the white eyes.

He raised his arm and ground his teeth together. He embraced the sting in his muscle while he rotated his shoulder. The flesh burned, but he needed to work the arm so he could depend on it when needed. A paralyzed limb was no good in battle, and he continued to push the muscles as he moved his shoulder.

He glanced down at his chest and the unharmed skin. Aside from his scars, there wasn't even a mark that indicated a bullet had gone through. *Am I going crazy? I was shot here. I know it.* There was no way it could've disappeared so quickly. And why was he in no pain? He inhaled. It was as though it had never happened.

Too much for him to comprehend, he pulled the blanket up and over his shoulders. The room was chilly, and he placed another log onto the glowing embers. Nora knew what had happened the night he was shot. She was withholding where the other bullet struck him, but why? Was she afraid he'd kill her if he knew? *I told her I wouldn't.* She didn't know who hired him to kill the women like her, the ones with the witch-like tendencies. He scoffed. He never believed they held the power the wasichu had spouted of. The large bounty the wasichu paid for each scalp was why he did the work. He closed his eyes, and he'd never forget it.

The need for revenge pushed him to end lives and in return take what was owed. He had to finish the jobs, all of them, because he needed the money. He had to keep his promise. As it was he'd waited too long, been gone too many years. The guilt pushed aside any other emotions and lay heavy inside his stomach. He was a monster, and he had to end what he'd started.

He longed for peace. For a night filled with nothing but sleep. To rid himself of the demons that clawed their way through his soul and lashed out at the beast he'd become. He wished for a day he could laugh without a stab of blame piercing his chest. A moment he could embrace all that he'd done and start fresh—a clean slate.

There were times he'd fallen to his knees, the memories too much, the blood too vivid, the silence too loud, and he'd apologized—begged for their forgiveness only to be shadowed by the killer he was. The hunter who needed no condolence but the sound of justice as it screamed in his ears.

He pressed his face into his hands and rubbed his tired eyes. *It is who I am, what I've become.* He planned and plotted, and now it was time to end it. Now it was time to kill.

CHAPTER TWENTY-THREE

Nora waited for the door to close before she rushed to the window and watched Otakatay walk across the lawn. He woke while the chickadees sang, and the orange rays of dawn filtered through the windows of the cabin. Without even tasting the breakfast she'd put out, he'd left to saddle Wakina and find the man who shot him. There was no mention of him returning, only that he'd let her know when it was safe for her to venture out.

She shivered. Who shot him and wanted her dead? And how did they know of the powers she had? She couldn't see Jess saying anything to anyone about the day she healed her, and Joe, well she had faith in his promise, too. *Then who was it?*

Mr. Sutherland's face came to mind and his peculiar behaviour the other night. Her brows knitted together. He was a bit strange, but she didn't know him well enough to point a finger at him as the one who wanted her dead. She'd been in his store a few times before selling her mother's jewelry. He was quiet, and she figured that was because Willimena took over most conversations with her loud voice and overbearing mannerisms. She shook her head. He didn't seem the type to hire a bounty on women with a birthmark and a gift.

She wished her mother was still alive. She needed to ask her how she lived with such a secret. How she was able to heal and not be concerned with what people thought. Nora had been judged her whole life, if not by the people she healed, then by her own father. Pa's fear grew into resentment and then shame, until he couldn't be in the same room as her.

He preached to her about the Salem Witch trials back in 1692. How hundreds of people were persecuted without just cause. Husbands watched their wives hang from the gallows or burn at the stake. Many of the accused died within the filthy prisons.

He told the stories to her over and over again, trying to strike fear into her. But with the passing of decades people forgot about the deaths, and their concern turned toward the Indians and the need to place them on reservations. There was hardly any talk now of those who were different—of witches, or magic. But Pa still pushed her to be quiet about her gift, to never use it.

She'd shoved his concern aside, thinking he was being over protective. She never thought someone would want her dead and go far enough to hire a bounty hunter like Otakatay to kill her. Most people were kind after they were healed, thankful even. Yes, there were some who chased her, and some who wanted her for their own use, but there were so few she never heeded Pa's warnings.

She sighed and rubbed her hands together. She watched Otakatay walk inside the livery, and the ache in her chest intensified when he disappeared from her view. She saved his life, helped him when no one else could, and he'd tossed her aside as if she were nothing.

Sure, he said thank you, but she wanted more. She wanted, *love?* She frowned. He was not the kind who cared for someone like her. She couldn't deny that she had feelings for him, but the depth of her emotions even she couldn't see. *I kissed him for goodness sakes.* But was it love, or curiosity? She didn't know. He was a puzzle to her, and she yearned to put him back together.

Maybe it was her healing instinct that pushed her to want to help him. She watched while he fought nightmares. She'd seen his eyes cloud with anger and bitterness. And she hadn't missed the softness escape in fleeting moments before it was quickly hidden, tucked down far inside of him.

The empty room echoed the loneliness she felt, and she wrapped her arms around her middle for comfort. She took one last look out the window before she sat down at the table to eat the fried ham and toast she'd made earlier.

Nora was scrubbing the last plate, when a knock at the door startled her. She froze. Her hands remained in the soapy dish water as she waited, unsure of what she should do. If Pal were here he'd let her know who was there. Even though she'd only had the dog for a few weeks, she missed his companionship. She thought of him often and wondered where he was, and if he was okay.

Another knock.

"C'mon girl, I ain't standin' out here all damn day," Jess hollered.

She laughed and rushed to open the door.

"Bout bloody time." A bright smile spread across her wrinkled face.

"Hello, Jess. It's nice to see you."

She almost hugged her she was so thankful it wasn't the faceless man there to kill her.

"What brings you to town today?" she asked, stepping aside to allow her in.

"It's the first day of summer. Town celebrates it every year." She took off her hat and held it at her side. "There's always a picnic with games and later on a dance. I thought you'd want to go."

"Oh, I don't think—" she stammered. *Otakatay said to stay in the house. Not to venture out.*

"You're comin'. You need to get out of this blasted cabin."

She hadn't left the cabin in a while, and a few hours outside wouldn't hurt. She glanced out the window. It was close to lunchtime so surely no one would kill her in front of the whole town in broad daylight. Her cheeks heated. *Don't do it. Stay inside.* She folded her hands together and squeezed. Jess would be with her, it wasn't like she was going out alone. She inhaled and plastered a smile on her face.

"Let me grab my shawl."

It was a short walk to the lawn between the church and the school house. Tables were set with roasted chicken, ham, salad, bread and an array of delicious desserts. Even though she'd eaten breakfast an hour ago, Nora's mouth watered from the smells wafting toward her.

The whole town had shown up, and she smiled while she watched a potato sack race between the adults and kids. To her left was a baseball game, and to her right, four gentlemen were gearing up to play horseshoes. She tipped her face to the warm sun. Today she'd relax and enjoy Jess's company.

They zigzagged in between the blankets spread on the lawn until they found an empty spot near the school. She plopped down and smiled at Jess. The tension in her neck eased, and she set all apprehensions aside so she could enjoy the day.

Otakatay watched the town from the top of the hill. He ran his hand along Wakina's soft mane, glad he was okay. The young boy Seth had found Wakina wandering behind Nora's cabin the night he was shot and brought him to the livery to stay safe and be fed. He was grateful for the boy's fast thinking and caring nature. If not for him, Wakina could've wandered off or been taken by some wasichu.

He focused on the festivities below and tightened his grip on the reins. The town was unaware that a killer lurked amongst them or, he smirked, that one was watching. Tonight he'd kill the white man. He'd make sure Nora was safe, and then he'd carry on with his promise.

He forced himself not to glance at Nora's cabin. It was a warm day, and he wiped the sweat off his forehead. He hoped the girl listened to him and stayed inside despite the fun being had outdoors. She was safe as long as she didn't open the door. He felt bad for leaving her alone, especially with the white man hunting her, but he had no choice if he wanted to keep her safe.

Nora was different. There was no doubt about that. She was pushy, nosey, and irritating as hell, but something about her pulled at him. The first time they met he'd been drawn to her. There was something unexplainable in the way she held herself, watched him and even spoke. She radiated happy feelings, and it took everything within him not to succumb to the bright smile and warm exterior. The two days he stayed with her almost killed him.

He'd held himself at a distance for fear of being sucked into her smile and gentle attitude. He was none of those things. He stared up into the mountains. *Soon, I will rectify the wrong done.* He'd wasted enough time planning his revenge. Precious days had gone by while he lay in bed with a wounded shoulder. He'd been injured before and never stayed in bed longer than a day. He'd lost valuable time—time needed to finish what he'd started.

After he killed the wasichu, he'd leave the girl and all the soft memories she struck within him, and never return. Soon her face would disappear from his mind, and she'd be nothing more than a mere whisper, barely heard inside his heart. He tapped his heels into Wakina's sides and made his way back to the forest to wait for nightfall.

Nora spun around the street in Mr. Thompson's arms while the band played a lively tune. At first she'd been unsure about dancing with her father's old boss. He was married. His wife's rounded belly was ready to burst any day, but Mrs. Thompson smiled approvingly.

She hadn't laughed this much since she was little and Pa used to tell her funny stories by the campfire. Her cheeks ached as Jed swung her around. She lost her footing, and he slowed their pace and waited for her to catch up. She giggled as they took one more turn around the makeshift dance floor before the song ended, and they were both breathless.

The sun was low in the sky, and men hurried to light the lamps before darkness fell. The line up of young suitors waiting to dance with her seemed to be longer than when she left to dance with Jed. She placed a hand to her chest. She didn't have the energy for another dance. Not one of the men in the line even resembled Otakatay, and she couldn't help the disappointment that settled in her throat.

"I need to rest. I will come back shortly," she said to the waiting men.

A large hand gripped her arm, and before she could turn around, the doctor swung her into a waltz.

"Good evening, Doctor."

She smiled up at him and saw the horrible expression upon his face.

His eyes narrowed to slits of green that cut into her, and she shivered. *What was going on?* He worked his jaw, as she was assaulted by the vigorous puffs blowing from his nose.

The sound of his breathing grew louder as his hold on her tightened. She stiffened in his embrace and tried to pull away, but he jerked her closer. He was surprisingly strong. She took a deep breath and tried not to concentrate on the hammering inside her chest. Something was wrong, terribly wrong. She tried again to pull from his grip, but she couldn't move.

"Doctor Spencer, please let me go."

He glared down at her.

She watched as his eyes glazed and he laughed. It was an unforgettable sound, clipped and giddy at the same time.

"I know what you are," he said, and she was sure he'd gone mad the way his eyes flashed with fury.

"I don't know what you're talking about."

She wiggled trying to pull herself from him. People danced around them, and she didn't know if she should scream or finish the dance.

"You're evil."

Before she could answer, he pulled her into the center of the floor and shouted. "Nora Rushton is a witch."

Nora's heart stopped right there. The music ceased, and in a matter of seconds all eyes were on her and the doctor. *Oh no. God help me.* She licked her lips and tried to swallow past the dryness in her throat. She searched the crowd for Jess and let out a breath when the old woman ambled forward.

"What in tarnation are you talkin' about, Doc? Nora's a nice girl," Jess said.

"This is not something you accuse a kind woman like Nora of," Jed said.

The doctor yanked on her braid pulling it free from the leather strings. She watched as the brown strip fell to the ground, silently mourning its loss. He pulled at her hair loosening the braid until her black tresses hung down over her shoulders and back. He jerked her close, pulled the hair above her left ear and revealed the birthmark.

"See this?" he asked the crowd. "This is the mark they all have. That's how you know they're one of them. It's the mark of the devil."

"What's this all about, Frank? Nora's never done anything to deserve such harsh accusations." Sheriff Reid stepped forward. "Lots of people have birthmarks."

The doctor's fingers dug into her arm, and she bit her lip to keep from crying out. Her lungs burned, and she tried to take a breath but couldn't. People swayed before her as she tried to scan the faces in front of her. The townspeople demanded he let her go, and she dropped her shoulders, releasing some of the tension. She took a step toward Jed and his wife, but was jerked back by the hair.

Jess pulled her Colt. "You let that girl go, Doc, or you'll be spittin' lead for a week."

"I know what she is. You should all fear her," he screamed.

Nora yelped from the snap of pain in her head as he pulled her hair again.

"What proof do you have to support these claims?" Jed asked.

When the sheriff took a step toward them, the doctor raised his gun and shot Jess. Nora's heart lodged in her throat, and her stomach dipped. In the distance she heard the women and children screaming, but all she cared about was getting to Jess, helping her.

Out of the corner of her eye she saw the sheriff dive for the doctor, and the moment his grip loosened on her arm she yanked it free. With one swift motion Nora dived for Jess, blood poured from her side. The *click* from other guns rang in her ears, but she didn't turn to see if someone was aiming at her. She needed to concentrate. She needed to save her friend's life. Without thinking of the consequences, she placed her hot hands over her friend's wound.

Nora's head spun as she clenched her muscles, feeling Jess's pain climb up her arms and slam into her side. She gasped while her ribs screamed in agony. Unable to stay upright, the pain too much, she hunched over and pressed her hands into the flesh. Nora's throat burned, and her vision blurred as she demanded the torn edges of skin close together.

She blinked. *Do not pass out.* Spasms shot across her chest and into her back, and she swayed to the side. Sharp talons ripped through her insides, stealing her breath and rocking her back onto her heels. She couldn't take the pain any longer and was about to remove her hands when she felt the wound close beneath them.

She fell to the side, laying on the dirt road and wheezed. Her hands shook restlessly, and she had no energy left to even lift them. Nora's stomach lurched. She turned her head and vomited until there was nothing left.

Every muscle in her body trembled, and her arms tingled, numb from the healing. A deafening silence surrounded her, and before she could remember where she was, before she could think of an explanation, rough hands jerked her to her feet.

"I told you. I told you all. She is a witch," Doctor Spencer shouted.

"He's telling the truth. We've seen it," a woman's voice called from somewhere in the crowd.

"She works for the devil," another shouted.

"I say we hang her. Tonight. Now," Doctor Spencer said.

Women screamed, children cried, men aimed their guns.

"Kill the witch," a woman in the crowd yelled.

The townspeople went hysterical and shouted for her life.

"She's all possessed, like," another yelled.

"Devil woman!" they chanted.

Nora's legs wobbled beneath her as each insult hit her like a bullet and punctured her tough exterior. She was so weak there was no way she could fight them all off. A tear slid down her cheek, and she had nothing left within her to even wipe it away. *Otakatay.* She didn't know why she silently called for him, but she closed her eyes and pictured his face. She sucked in gulps of air in an effort to calm herself and harness the fear as it ran rampant inside her. The doctor pulled her through the crowd as they spat and cussed at her.

"You damn fools she's not evil," Jess called from somewhere.

"Hang her, too. She's been touched by the girl," a man she'd never seen before yelled, and the crowd shouted as two men grabbed Jess and hauled her to a waiting tree with two ropes tossed over a high branch.

Pa had been right all along. He'd been right. It didn't matter that she saved Jess's life, she was different and they were afraid of her. There was no one to protect her, no one to come to her aid, and now Jess would pay the price for being her friend.

"Please," she begged, as they dragged her to the tree. "Please this is wrong. Take me. Do not hurt Jess." But her pleas fell on deaf ears as they screamed for them to be hung.

She dug her feet into the ground as they pulled her toward the waiting ropes. Crazed people, ones she'd spoken to this afternoon, pulled her hair and ripped her dress. She spotted Fred and Willimena Sutherland standing away from the crowd, fear etched on both their faces. They were afraid of her, and she felt sorry for them. A woman reached through the crowd and scratched her, cutting her cheek. She placed her forearm over her face to try and shield herself from the angry crowd.

Two horses waited under the hanging ropes, and before she was lifted onto one, someone tied her wrists behind her back. Colors blurred before her, and she prayed she'd pass out. She didn't want to be conscious when they slipped the noose around her neck. She didn't want to feel the rope tighten around her throat as the air was sucked out of her lungs forever.

A gunshot rang out, and she flinched. The sheriff rode up on a black horse, his hand held high as smoke billowed from the barrel of his gun.

"There will be no hanging." He waved the gun at the crowd and women shrieked, clutching their children close. "Let them go. We will do this the right way when the judge comes through next week."

"You saw what she is. She's dangerous. What if she casts a spell?

She could kill us all," the doctor shouted. "Your children, your wives, we're all in danger. She's capable of anything. Look at the power she holds. She's evil, and we invite that here if we don't hang her!"

The crowd fired up again, demanding Nora's life. She watched horrified as the sheriff put his gun down, defeat written all over his aged face. He looked into her eyes, and she read the apology within them. The two men holding Jess tossed her onto the horse beside Nora. She couldn't stop the tears as they fell from her eyes.

"You better hope I die, cause if I don't I'll be shovin' the barrel of my 22 up your ass, you rotten son of a bitch," Jess said to the man placing the noose around her neck.

"Let her go, she's done nothing wrong," Nora begged.

They ignored her, and the crowd chanted, "Kill the witch."

She turned to Jess, her face wet with tears. "I'm so sorry."

"Darlin', don't be sorry. I'll be seein' my Marcus soon."

"This is wrong. You're innocent," she sobbed.

"Hush now. You be strong. Don't let these bastards see your tears. Then they've won. Hold your chin up."

Nora took a deep breath and willed the tears to stop. She turned toward the crowd and glared.

"That's my girl." Jess looked down at the two men beside her. "You damn heathens can rot in hell." She glanced up at Nora. "I love ya, girly." She winked before the horse shot out from under her, and she dropped.

Nora screamed as she watched her friend wiggle on the rope. She sucked in a sob as the doctor placed the rope around her neck. She struggled, and he smacked her across the face. *Otakatay, Otakatay.* She chanted his name in her mind and closed her eyes.

"You all must die. Every last one of you. Like the bitch that killed my wife," the doctor sneered.

"I am not that woman. Please, can't you see? I cannot harm anyone. I can only help them. My hands only heal."

"She said the same thing, she begged for her child, for her daughter. I would've killed the damn kid too but the bitch hid her."

"Who are you talking about?"

"The woman who stole my life," he stared at her, and she didn't miss the hollow look, "She was supposed to stop the bleeding, she was supposed to save my son. Instead she killed them."

"What was her name? What was her name?" she screamed.

He didn't answer, only tightened the noose around her neck.

Nora struggled against the thick rope. "Please, please tell me what her name was."

"Hannah." He slapped the horse, and Nora fell.

CHAPTER TWENTY-FOUR

Otakatay didn't have much time. He'd been in town to kill the wasichu when he heard the riot and went to investigate. Thank goodness he did. The horse under Nora had fled, and his heart stopped when he saw her dangling from a noose.

He let out a shrill war cry, and Wakina galloped into the centre of the crowd. He aimed his shotgun at the rope and fired. Relieved when it split and Nora fell to the ground. He glanced at the other woman swinging from the tree, when he heard the gun cock behind him. Out of the corner of his eye, he saw a man raise his gun. Otakatay turned and threw his knife into the man's chest, knocking him backward.

He leaned to the right in his saddle, his hair almost touching the ground, as Wakina cantered through the crowd. People ran in every direction.

"The witch has brought evil upon us with this Savage! Run," screamed a woman to his left.

If they only knew how close to the truth she really was. He yanked his knife from the man's chest and threw it at another man intending to fire his gun at him. The knife pierced his neck before he fell to the ground.

Otakatay jumped from his horse and ran toward the doctor who had his hands around Nora's throat. He ripped him from her and punched him in the stomach. He grabbed the knife from his back and smiled at the surprise in the wasichu's eyes.

"Thought you killed me?"

The doctor went for his gun, and Otakatay sprang forward, knocking him over. They rolled on the ground as the wasichu's fists pummeled his face. Each blow fueled his rage.

He growled and drove his elbow into the doctor's throat, stealing his air as he kicked beneath him. He glanced at Nora. She wasn't moving. He needed to get to her. He glared down at the man beneath him.

"Tonight you die," he said and without a second thought, he sliced his throat.

Blood soaked the front of the doctor's clean white shirt as life faded from his eyes.

He stood leaving the evil man to his fate, and went to Nora.

The street was empty except for the Sheriff, and he ignored the lawman as he knelt beside her. He placed his head to her chest and blew a sigh of relief when he heard her heart. Dirt smeared into the blood on her cheeks, blending with scratches on her face and arms. She'd taken a beating. He'd watched from the trees while the people tried to inflict wounds on her pretty face. Anger filled him, and he clenched his jaw.

He peered up at the old woman swinging from the rope. He straddled Wakina and cut the rope, taking the weight of the woman in his arms. Nora saved her life only to have them hang her any way. He still couldn't understand what he'd seen. How she'd done it. He closed the woman's eyes and placed her gently on the ground.

The sheriff cleared his throat, and Otakatay faced him.

"I will take care of her," he said motioning to Jess's body.

The lawman should've stopped the hanging, but he'd not been strong enough to go against the frantic crowd. Otakatay had seen the defeat written all over his aged face. The sheriff had watched as they strung the women up and never did a damn thing. He failed as a lawman, and Otakatay had no respect for him.

He opened and closed his hands, squeezing them until they hurt. He wanted to lash out at the old man, inflict pain on him, pain like Nora had felt. But the guilt of what he allowed to happen today was worse than any flesh wound he'd receive. The sheriff would replay this night over and over in his head for the rest of his life.

Otakatay went to Nora. The skin on her neck was red and swollen where the rope had bit in. She'd need some salve to heal the burn marks. *She'd need more than that.* He grazed the side of her face with his finger. She didn't deserve to be treated like this. She was kind, soft and sweet. She was white, the same color as they were, and yet they turned on her as though she were a killer, a murderer, *a breed.*

He lifted her into his arms and faced the sheriff.

"Go," the man said with sadness in his eyes when he glanced at Nora. "Take her somewhere safe."

Otakatay nodded.

The sheriff held out his arms, and he was reluctant to hand her over. Not after the man did nothing to save her. The monster within Otakatay shadowed his face, casting any illusions aside that he was agreeable.

The sheriff took a step back.

He walked toward Wakina, who knelt so he could get on without putting Nora down. He didn't spare the sheriff another glance, just kicked his heels into the horse's side and sped off into the forest.

Otakatay travelled the better part of the night to the cave nestled in the side of the mountain. After he laid her on the ground and covered her with his blanket, he made a fire to keep them warm. She hadn't stirred since he rescued her, and he wondered if she was ever going to wake up. He placed his head on her chest. The beat was stronger than before, and he exhaled.

He doubted she'd be able to talk for a few days, because of the noose. He cringed. He knew what it felt like to have a rope around his neck—to be tied up as if you were a dog.

He poked the fire with a branch and watched as the orange flames licked the air. He was so close to finalizing his plan. To seeing retribution for the years of suffering he and the others had gone through.

Little Eagle.

He stroked the feather in his hair. He'd never forgive himself for what had happened. He was supposed to keep him safe. Despair crawled through his veins to circle his heart and squeeze. There was no way he could take it back. No way to save him from the fall. He hung his head.

He escaped when the others hadn't, and he'd promised to return, to come back and save them. He ran his hand down his face. But he'd been gone so long. Would they remember? Would they still hope he'd return? He didn't know, and with each passing day he grew more restless.

He needed land and the money to buy it. They'd have nowhere to go, and he wanted to bring them somewhere safe. After years of killing outlaws, he'd built up a substantial amount of cash, but it was nowhere near the amount he required for his plan to work. For a while he thought all hope was lost, until he came upon the white man searching for someone to kill the witkowan.

He gazed out into the darkness and sighed. Desperation pushed him to do the things he'd done. The nightmares reminded him of the vengeance he carried and gave him the will to go forward. There was no choice but to throw aside the person he once was. He chose another name, one that was fitting to the beast he'd become, and he embraced the evil that it brought.

He forced himself not to care, not to love, but instead only to hate and to kill. He looked at Nora. To kill ones like her. He couldn't take back what he'd done. He couldn't forgive himself for it either. The wrongs he'd committed, and the lives he'd left behind haunted him. Blame and remorse filled him, and he gnashed his teeth together. Misery pooled inside his lungs, drowning him, and he sucked in a painful breath.

Nora stirred.

He wondered if the power she held was real. *It had to be.* He watched the old woman rise after being shot. He tried to wrap his mind around how she'd done it. How she was able to close the wound as if it hadn't been there.

He glanced down at his chest. He'd known all along she'd saved his life, but didn't understand it. He still couldn't. How was it possible? A low whimper grabbed his attention, and he watched as she slowly sat up. She was in pain, and he poured water from his canteen into the metal cup. He placed the cup on a rock beside the fire to heat.

"What happened?" she asked her voice no more than a whisper. She brought her hand to her throat.

"Your voice will return. Try not to talk."

The water boiled, and he sprinkled some of the ground witch hazel into the cup. The bark was good for many ailments, including a sore, inflamed throat. He wrapped a red bandana around the cup and handed it to her.

"Drink this. It will help."

"Jess?"

He didn't answer her right away. The old woman didn't make it. He'd saved Nora instead.

"She is gone."

She nodded and bit her lip.

"Drink."

She took the cup, smelled the drink and made a face at the awful scent.

"It works." He pulled some pemmican from his sack.

She hesitated, but the pain must've been too much because she took a long drink, and her body trembled from the horrible taste.

"What happened?"

"Don't talk," he growled a scowl on his face.

"Please tell me."

He ignored her, hoping she'd stay silent.

"Otakatay—

He brought his finger to his lips. "Shush."

"How did you find me?"

He rolled his eyes. He should've known she'd not listen and be quiet. Hell, she never shut up.

He groaned. "I shot the rope."

"You were there?"

He nodded.

"You saw what happened?"

He nodded again. How was it that he could be quiet, but she couldn't?

"Did you see? Did you see everything?"

He knew what she was getting at, but if she wanted to talk and not listen to him, he'd bait her a bit.

"I did. You're a witch."

Nora's eyes grew wide, and he watched amused as her mouth worked but nothing came out.

Finally, she is quiet.

"I am not a witch."

Well, that didn't last long. "I'd say you are by what I saw."

"I am not," her voice cracked, and she looked away. "I cannot confide in you."

"I saved your life. I'd say you can."

She was silent for some time, and he knew by the way her brow furrowed she was contemplating what he'd said.

"You owe it to me to explain."

Blue eyes watched him from across the fire, and he was sure he'd never seen anything as beautiful. He sat up taller and ignored the hammering of his heart.

"I am a healer."

"What's the difference?"

"There is a huge difference." She tried to shout, but it came out raspy and broken. She took another sip from the cup and shuddered.

It was awful stuff, but it worked.

"I am not a witch. I cannot cast spells or hurt people. I only have the ability to heal them."

He narrowed his eyes.

"I speak the truth."

He believed her, but it still didn't make sense.

"How do you do it?"

"My hands hold the power."

"You can heal anything?"

"No. I cannot heal the mind."

He nodded.

"Only flesh wounds?"

"Yes, and ones you cannot see, the ones inside."

He'd seen it with his own eyes. Hell, it was done to him and he still couldn't figure it out.

"You healed me?"

"Yes," she said with a loud sigh.

"So I was shot in the chest?"

"You would've died."

"Why didn't you let me?"

"Because I..." she averted her eyes, "because I could help."

He thought she wanted to say something else but changed her mind at the last minute.

"Why didn't you save your father?"

Nora's face changed immediately. Remorse shadowed her eyes, and she blinked away the tears he'd seen there.

"He didn't want me to."

He wasn't expecting her to say that. He took a bite of the pemmican he'd been holding, not because he was hungry, but for something to do. The space between them seemed to close in, and he moved back.

"Why not?"

"Because of me, we had to move from town to town all the time." She hung her head, and he had to lean in to hear her next words.

"He resented me for it."

Otakatay understood resentment, he understood the anger that came along with it, but what he didn't get was how anyone could resent her. She wasn't evil or horrible. She didn't hurt people. She healed them. She may be annoying, couldn't follow instructions even when her life depended on it, and she never shut the hell up, but those weren't reasons to hate her.

As far as he could see, her father was an imbecile. Hate came from deep within and if not careful it could consume a person, make them do things they never thought possible. *I would know.*

"Your father was an ass."

She shook her head.

"No, he had his reasons, and I didn't make it easy on him. But..." She stopped.

He waited.

"But I wish he'd have let me save him. I miss him so much."

One tear slid down her cheek, and he wanted to wipe it away, but held himself still instead.

"Drink." He motioned to the cup and was thankful that she listened and took a sip.

Nora's body trembled. The drink Otakatay had given her was horrible, and with each sip she had to concentrate so she didn't throw up all over the place. Her throat hurt so bad she was sure she'd never talk the same again. Her tongue was swollen, and the scratches on her neck pulsed. A cool cloth would help, but there didn't seem to be any water in the cave other than what was in her cup. She grazed her fingers over the hot skin on her neck and was surprised when he handed her one of his shirts.

"Wrap this around your neck. It will help until I can find more witch hazel for your cuts."

"Is that what I am drinking?"

He nodded.

"It relieves the swelling."

She took the shirt from him and wound it around her neck. Visions of last night crammed her mind. The noose, the crowd, the people she'd seen and conversed with that day, clamouring for her death. They attacked her, pulled her hair and ripped her dress.

She shook her head. She'd always be different, and she'd have to hide because of it. She thought of her mother. The doctor had killed Hannah Rushton years ago. He'd stolen from Nora a mother's love and warm embrace. He took from her father the chance to say goodbye and gave him a life filled with loneliness.

Anger twisted around her spine, and she straightened. She wanted to see the doctor pay for all that he'd done. She wanted him to feel the same pain her mother did hanging from the rope. The fear and revulsion of those who once were your friends, but found out you were different and called for your life. She peeked at Otakatay across the fire.

"What happened to the doctor?"

He glanced up at her, and she didn't miss the indignation as it shot from his eyes. "I killed him."

Relief spread over her, and she lifted her lips. "Thank you."

He shrugged.

She sighed.

"Are you hungry?"

He shifted his weight from left to right.

She sensed he needed to leave, and so she nodded.

He grunted and pulled his knife from the leather holder on his shin.

"Stay," he said and before she could reply he was gone.

Nora sighed and placed the cup down beside her. She was not drinking anymore. Another sip and she'd be heaving in the bushes. She thought of Jess and the last time she'd seen her. She closed her eyes as images of her friend dangling from a rope filtered through her mind.

She couldn't hide from the guilt as it slammed into her, and she let the tears fall. Jess always made her smile, and she'd cherish the little time they had together. She wiped her cheeks. Jess would curse her out for carrying on so, for being weak. She could hear her now. "Damn, girl, quit your cry babying." Jess would sure give heaven a new meaning. Nora smiled.

"You are with your Marcus," she whispered. "But I will miss you."

She moved closer to the fire. Her dress wasn't good for anything but the rag pile now. Ripped and stained, she wished she could take it off and burn it. She studied the cave Otakatay had brought her to. She didn't know where she was. He'd saved her, and each time she thought of him her heart swelled with warmth.

She was resigned to the fact that she had feelings for him. There had been something there the first time she saw him in the forest, and he threatened to kill her. But the time she'd spent with him had opened up a wave of feelings she didn't think existed, or at least she'd never felt before.

Last night she wanted to see his face in the line of men waiting to dance with her. When the town attacked her, she'd called out for him. And when there was nothing left to do but accept her fate, she closed her eyes and pictured his face. *Is it love that I feel?* She had no clue. She'd never been in love before.

She was sure of one thing and that was Otakatay. He'd been there when she burned her hands, tenderly spreading salve on them. He rescued her, risked his life to save her own, and for that she was thankful. But what she felt for him was more than mere appreciation. He was a Bounty Hunter, and he'd killed innocent women, but she knew in her heart he was not that man.

She saw within his eyes a sorrow, a misery so bleak that it broke her heart. When he kissed her, the world seemed to stop and all she could think of was him. She yearned for his touch, his eyes upon her, his scarce smiles.

She stared out into the forest. Dawn was approaching and the sun shone through the trees, bright and warm. *I love him.* It came as no surprise now that she'd accepted it, yet she didn't know what to do with her feelings.

All she'd ever wanted was someone to share her love with— someone to rely on, and to build dreams with. She couldn't tell him how she felt for fear he'd cast her aside. Otakatay never showed her any emotion other than when they kissed, and she'd been too caught up in her own feelings to watch for his.

She rubbed the edges of the soft shirt wrapped around her neck. It was deerskin, and she wondered where he'd gotten it. She inhaled the scent of leather and smoke embedded into the fabric. *Otakatay.*

She closed her eyes.

"What are you doing?"

He startled her, and she jumped, almost burning herself on the fire.

Black eyes stared down at her. He held the shot gun in one hand, and a skinned rabbit in the other.

"You cleaned it already?"

He shrugged.

"I didn't think you'd want to watch."

How did he know? She loved animals and knew their purpose, but she couldn't watch one be slaughtered.

He tied the rabbit to a long stick, added two more logs onto the fire and sat down beside her.

She inched away from the animal and fidgeted with her dress.

"You feel sorry for the rabbit?" he asked, amused.

She nodded.

"We need to eat."

"I know that," she snapped, "but why couldn't we eat berries or that stuff you were chewing on earlier?"

He grunted.

"Pemmican takes a long time to make, and berries won't fill you."

"What's in the pemmican?"

"Boiled fat, dried strips of pounded meat and some berries."

She made a face. It didn't sound appealing.

He shook his head, reached into his sack, pulled out a piece and handed it to her.

She lifted it to her nose and inhaled. The meat smelled musty. She closed her eyes and took a bite. She tasted the fat right away, but the berries added a sweet flavor, and she took another bite. It was delicious.

"You made this?"

"No, I trade for it on the reservations."

"Oh, I see."

She chewed on the dried meat enjoying every piece.

"Otakatay, did you ever live on a reservation?"

He shook his head.

"How come?" She didn't agree with what the government had done. They'd forced all the natives onto reserved land. The way she saw it, they stole their way of life. The government took their pride and smashed it.

"I am half white. I choose where I want to live."

The pemmican no longer appealed to her, and she put it on her lap.

He grasped his knife, and she saw the scars on his forearm, the same ones that marked his back and chest.

"How did you get those?"

He froze, and she watched as his eyes flickered with anger. She was sure he was going to lash out at her. She braced herself for the fight.

"A coward gave them to me," he sneered. "He believes in nothing but torturing the weak to gain riches."

"How awful." Nora's chest ached, and she laid her hand over his.

He tensed, but didn't pull away.

It wasn't pity she felt for him, but a deep sadness for the suffering he'd gone through. She ran her hand along his arm, pushed the sleeve up and revealed two nasty tracks. Nora's hands heated. She refrained, he wouldn't want her to.

She didn't care that he was full of marks, or that he was an Indian. She loved him. Her finger traced a long scar. How could someone do this to another person? Her eyes watered. What reason could they possibly have? She leaned over and touched her lips to a scar.

"Otakatay."

His forearm tightened but he didn't pull away. She ran her lips over the beveled and deformed skin, tasting her own tears. She wanted to weep for the agony of what he must've felt. He placed his hand in her hair, brushing the locks with his fingers.

She sat up and gazed into his eyes, the dark depths softened, and he rubbed his thumb across her cheek, wiping away a tear. At that moment she knew the love she felt for him was real, and he pulled her to him. She couldn't stop the swell of emotions as they burst from her and lit up her soul.

A whisper of a breath sat between their lips as he lowered his mouth onto hers in a feathery kiss. Supple lips melded with hers, and all she could think about was him and this moment. The kiss stole her senses, her fears—her heart. He'd been there when no one else had. He'd saved her, protected her.

Otakatay.

The fire crackled, the rabbit forgotten. He leaned into her, until she lay on the ground, and he hovered over her. Not once pulling their lips away. He deepened the kiss, tasting her, and she hummed beneath him. Nora's breasts tingled, while the spot between her legs heated and pulsed. She wanted him.

He unwound the shirt from her neck, while his other hand still cradled her head. He trailed kisses down her chin and onto her neck, stopping at the swollen spots to lick them. She ran her hand through his hair and onto his back. The muscles bunched, and she pressed him to her.

She didn't want this moment to end. She wanted to stay in his arms forever. His hand cupped her breast, and she arched her back. He was so tender, so gentle. She hadn't seen this side of him, and she smiled, knowing it was there all along.

He undid the buttons on her dress and massaged her bare breast with his hand, pinching the nipple. Oh, she was going to come undone. She could feel the hardness of his groin press into her. She needed to touch him. Feel his flesh beneath her palms—against her breasts. She tugged at the front of his shirt and was relieved when the buttons flew off.

She kissed his cheek, his neck and her hands rubbed the muscles on his back. She could feel the scars, there were so many.

He pulled away and was on his feet before she knew what had happened.

"Otakatay?" She sat up, holding her dress closed.

"Damn it. What are you doing to me?" The dark look she'd seen so many times before filled his eyes and cut into her.

"I...I thought—

"You thought what?" He pulled the burned beyond eating rabbit from the fire and threw it aside. "I am no good for you."

"Yes, you are." She stood and went to him.

He shoved her aside.

"No. I'm not. I am a killer, damn it."

He stood on the other side of the fire. His chest rose and fell. Rejection punched her hard in the stomach, and she wrapped her arms around her torso.

"I know what you are, and you're not that person, Otakatay."

His face changed. She watched as he masked off the man she'd just kissed, and brought forth the animal she'd seen in him on their first encounter. She took a step back.

"You're afraid, and you should be. I am a monster. I've killed women like you."

"But...but I love you," she whispered.

He grunted.

Nora's bottom lip quivered. He didn't want her not even a little bit, and she couldn't control the pain as it leaked from her eyes.

"Tomorrow, I will take you somewhere safe."

She hung her head, unable to meet his glare.

He snatched up his shotgun and left.

CHAPTER TWENTY-FIVE

Elwood paced the length of his office. The damn bastards were causing more problems. He hung the leather coil back on the hook. Blood had turned the tightly braided rawhide red. Bits of flesh still hung from it, and he smiled. He'd had to set a few of them straight tonight, and he'd beaten one so badly he didn't think the filthy Navajo would make it through the night. He'd have to replace him and soon.

Over the last year they'd been dropping like flies, some by his hand or his men's, and some from sickness. He'd told Levi and Red to toss the bodies in a pit on the other side of the mountains leaving them for the bears and cats that roamed the hills. He couldn't be bothered with digging graves. Once they were dead they were of no use to him.

Last month one of the savages found a fresh vein of coal. It brought a welcome change from the half-empty carts he'd seen lately, and he wanted more of it. He enforced longer shifts and less sleep. Those brats didn't need to rest; they were young and should be able to work a whole damn day without tiring.

He'd had to set a few straight about the rules again tonight. The tall one decided to fight, and Elwood made an example of him. He demanded respect and fear from the lowlifes. He owned them and when they forgot that, he had a way of reminding them.

He opened the drawer and pulled out a bottle of whiskey. Not bothering with a glass, he took a long swig. The liquor scalded his throat and set fire to his stomach. He glanced out the window while taking another drink. Levi and Red hadn't come back from town with Nora, and he was growing impatient. He ran his finger nails along the top of his desk, making a scratch-like sound. He wanted Nora. He'd wanted her for a long time, and he was getting damn tired of waiting for the little imp to change her mind.

He was a handsome man and could have any woman he wanted. But he wanted Nora, and damn it, he'd get her one way or the other. He'd given her flowers and jewelry. He'd asked her to dinner, but her father had said no, and dumped the gifts in the garbage. He even got rid of Jack Rushton, and she still wanted nothing to do with him.

He clenched his fist and groaned. The killing was supposed to fix everything. Nora's father was a drunk. He thought that with Jack out of the way, Nora would succumb to his charms. But she'd still denied his requests. Now there was no one left to protect her, and he'd have his way with her. She'd be his wife, the perfect trophy to perch on his arm. And when he tired of her, he'd cast her to the hills, too.

A loud knock on the door echoed throughout the room.

"Come in," he called.

Levi and Red sauntered in, their hair a mess and their clothes soiled. Both needed a bath and shave, but he had other things on his mind and didn't give a damn if they wanted to look like hell.

"Where's the girl?" he asked peering around them.

"Well, we went to town like you asked, and..." Levi glanced at Red.

"The townspeople were gonna hang her," Red finished.

"What? Why?"

"They were callin' her a witch. They hung that old Jess Chandler too," Levi said.

Jess's death was a welcome surprise. He'd battled the old crow for years to get her land, and now he'd have it.

"Where is Nora now? Did they kill her?"

He stood. He still had his stitches, but his foot didn't ail him as much as before, and he could walk without limping.

"Nah, but you ain't gonna like what we have to tell ya."

"Well, get on with it you fools."

"Some Indian rode in and saved her. Shot up the place too," Red said.

"Indian?" Elwood whispered. "Who?"

"He looked an awful lot like Hawk."

Elwood hadn't heard the name for almost ten years. The defiant half-breed had escaped killing his brother and two of his men. He hated that kid and wondered when he'd return. He knew the dirty Indian would want revenge for the beatings Elwood had given him and for what happened to his brother. How did Hawk know Nora? And how long had the renegade been in Willow Creek without Elwood or his men noticing?

Nora was his. He slammed his fist onto the desk.

"Find her. They can't be far."

CHAPTER TWENTY-SIX

Otakatay rummaged through his sack and pulled out the slippery elm. He'd found more after he left Nora's cabin two days ago. He'd take her to Denver when she woke. He figured that was the safest place for her to be. It was a city and no one would know her there. Denver was three days ride east, and he'd have to put his plans on hold. He couldn't be near her any longer.

He glanced at her, wrapped in his blanket fast asleep. Even now he was too close to her. He needed some distance from the desires she aroused within him. She'd become a distraction, one that he didn't need right now.

He shook his head. He'd been gone too long already, and he felt the weight of the time that had passed like a ton of rocks on top of his shoulders. He was so close even now, and yet Nora's safety stood in the way. He sighed. He'd have to wait another few days.

He yearned for the moment when he'd take his knife and put an end to the nightmares, when he could look at his reflection without cowering away in disgust. Was it even possible to know a night without reliving the past, a day where his soul could see beyond the evil desires within him? He didn't know, and he refused to allow himself a glimmer of hope.

He picked up the wooden bowl and grinder. With vehemence he ground the bark into a powder. His body buzzed for retaliation—for blood. *Soon I will have my revenge.* He dumped the powder into the leather sack and placed it on the ground.

Nora pushed herself up and rubbed the sleep from her eyes.

He concentrated on putting his things away and pulled the knife from the sheath on his back. Her beauty usually caught him off guard, but today he refused to look at her.

"Hello," she said.

He noticed her voice wasn't as bad as last night. He grunted.

She shifted and covered her legs with the long skirt. The rose-colored dress was torn. Dirt smeared the front. She had nothing else to wear. The fact that he cared about her dress, and he'd have to buy her a new one before they got to Denver, pissed him off. He was getting soft, and he couldn't have that. He flexed his arms. He was vengeance, fear, *a breed*, worth nothing more than flies on shit. And he'd do right to remember that.

She combed her fingers through her hair. The black strands hung to her waist in a blanket of long waves, and he was sure he'd never seen anything more mesmerizing.

She smiled, and he looked away. *What the hell am I doing?* He puffed out his chest. *I will not care for her. I will not.*

Light filled the cave, and she scanned the area. His bow and arrows, two shotguns and a knife were propped up against a wall.

"What's all that?" she asked.

"Weapons."

"I know that. Why do you have so many of them?"

"I am a bounty hunter. My job is to kill."

"Yes, so you've said." She scowled at him. "Can you shoot that?"

She pointed to the bow and arrows.

"Yes."

Why did she need to talk? He was trying to ignore her, and she wouldn't shut up. He glanced at the red bandana he'd used earlier to hold the hot cup and saw a second use for the cloth.

"Where did you learn?"

His Ina had taught him, but after years of being locked up and beaten, he'd had to retrain himself.

"I've always known."

She stared at him, and he recognized the pity in her eyes.

He sat up taller, and glanced at the bandana again. The idea had become very appealing. He worked his hands open and closed. His chest burned with anger. He didn't want her pity.

He didn't want anything from her. She thought she loved him. Hell, she was naive. He was not the type to love. He swept his hand through his hair. She had no idea who or what he was. He had no time for little girls with fantasies and professions of love. He wanted to spit, he was so disgusted. He took his knife and ran it across the whetstone.

"Are you angry with me?" She braided her hair.

He ignored her. Maybe if he didn't talk to her, she'd stop gazing at him with those innocent eyes of hers. Otherwise he'd be forced to use the bandana.

She finished her braid.

"Otakatay, have I done something to anger you? Please, I don't want what happened last night—

"Last night was a mistake."

She was quiet.

"You're a wicicala," he growled, "with little girl dreams."

Sparks flew from the blade while he sharpened it.

"I am not a little girl."

"So you've said. But when I look at you, that is all I see."

"Really?" She narrowed her eyes. "That's not what happened last night."

He grunted.

"You touched me with such gentleness. I know you're not the beast you proclaim to be."

He scowled, and his features faded revealing dark deadly corners.

"I've slashed the throats of women like you."

She went to stand, and he held up his hand to stop her.

"I know that, but I believe you had your reasons."

"I did it for money. I took their lives for paper!" He slipped his knife back inside the sheath on his back. "And I would've killed you, too."

"Why didn't you?" She threw his blanket from her and got to her feet. "Why, Otakatay, didn't you kill me?"

He spun from her. He knew why. He'd seen her face, gazed into her eyes. He didn't want to tell her. He called upon the revulsion, animosity and vile bitterness that lay dormant inside of him. He brought it forward and spun around. The knife he'd just put away, was cradled within his hand.

She stood still.

"Do not push me," he snarled.

"You're not going to kill me. You saved my life."

He ground his teeth together and clenched his jaw.

"You have feelings for me. Admit it." She tipped her chin and stood in front of him.

Before she could step back, he grabbed hold of her hair. He wrenched on it, placing the knife to her throat. "If there came a time when I allowed myself to care for someone, she would not be white," he said through clenched teeth.

He pushed her from him and picked up his rifle.

"Be ready to leave in an hour."

Nora watched him go. His cold words echoed in her mind and chilled her heart. A bottle of whiskey on an open wound would sting less. How could she think someone like him could care for someone like her, a little girl?

She winced. All he saw when he stared at her was a child. She was different. She was white and according to him no better than a snake.

With every insult he'd flung her way, a tear fell from her lashes. *Where will I go now?* He was taking her to the city, and she was reluctant to go. She wanted to stay with him but knew he'd take her willing or not.

She had no one now. Pa and Jess were gone, and she couldn't go back to Willow Creek. She'd have to start anew, and whether she liked it or not, that meant without Otakatay. She wiped her wet cheeks. *I have to stand on my two feet.* She swallowed back the sob and took a shaky breath. She'd get along fine. She had to. All she ever wanted was freedom, and after Otakatay dropped her in Denver, she'd have plenty.

The love she felt for him was real, and she'd draw on those emotions to get her through the next few months. A part of her wanted to make him see how much she cared, show him her love. *How do you show a blind man the sun?*

There was no other place she felt safe than in the circle of his arms. Even though the times he held her were brief, those were the times she'd felt passion and a sense of belonging. Until he was able to drive out the demons he battled, he'd never accept her or the love she was offering. *Oh, Otakatay why won't you let me love you?*

She picked up the blanket and peered out into the forest. She needed to get out of the cave, to go for a walk. She glanced down at her attire. A good washing may help the soiled dress, and she wanted to wipe the dirt from her cheeks and neck. She'd see if there was a stream nearby, a dip would do her some good.

Tall trees stood all around her, and she stopped to gaze at the beautiful landscape before her. She followed the path as it wound down the steep hill. Not familiar with the narrow trail, she wasn't prepared for the sharp turn and almost fell over the edge of the cliff. She placed a hand to her chest. *That was close.*

She reached the bottom and glanced up at the huge hill. Would she be able to find her way back? She paused when she heard the birds singing overhead. She smiled. She studied the path, copying it to her mind and headed in the direction the birds had flown.

It wasn't long before the forest opened into a peaceful meadow. Green and purple stalks of lilacs swayed in the light breeze and surrounded the lake. Nora plucked a flower and inhaled its sweet scent. She sat down by the water's edge and slipped off her boots. She lay back, resting her head on her arms and closed her eyes.

"Well, well, look who we found."

She hadn't been at the meadow more than ten minutes when she heard the slimy voice behind her, and sensed the danger it brought.

"I'd say the boss is gonna be pleased."

She picked up her boots and slowly stood. The hairs on her neck rose. She gulped. *Keep calm.* Nora spun around and collided with two men. She recognized them right away as the men who worked for Elwood.

"What is it you want?" she asked trying to keep her composure.

"We've found it," said Red.

Great. She scanned the meadow. There was nowhere to go. She smiled at them.

"Sorry, gentleman but I have to go." She tried to go around them.

"I don't think so," Levi said, and she dodged his large hands as he lunged for her.

The men stood on either side of her. *Could I make it to the cave?* She didn't think so. She gripped her boots tightly in her hands. There was no way she was going with them. She'd have to run. *It's now or never.* In one swift movement she swung her arms out clipping both men with her boots, and ran like hell.

The boots weighed her down, so she threw them to the side. She looked back and seeing them in hot pursuit, she picked up her pace. Nora's heart thudded in her throat as she burst from the meadow into the forest. The hard earth pierced her bare feet, but she didn't have time to stop. She could hear them behind her and they were getting closer. *Where was the path? Where was Otakatay?*

She jumped over a fallen log and kept going. Branches caught in her hair, pulling the strands from the braid, and she swatted at them. When she turned to see how far away they were, she tripped on a root and went tumbling head over feet. A jolt of pain burst from her ankle, and she cracked her head on something hard. She tried to get up, to grab onto something for support, but the trees would not stop spinning around her. Nora's middle pitched. She waved her arms hoping she'd connect with a branch, when someone yanked hard on her braid.

She screamed through clenched teeth.

"Got her," Red yelled.

Levi came through the trees. An eerie smile spread across his pockmarked face, and Nora shrank away from him. He pinched her cheeks together and squeezed until she felt teeth cut the inside of her mouth. He placed his wet lips onto hers.

She punched his wide chest and shook her head.

"Boss ain't gonna like that, Levi."

He pulled away, and Nora spat in his face.

"Do not touch me again," she hissed.

Red hugged her from behind, securing her arms.

"What the boss don't know won't hurt him. Besides, we had to chase her."

Levi wiped his face with his sleeve and puckered his lips for another kiss.

She waited until he was close enough then hauled off and kicked him in the groin.

"Son of a bitch," Levi screamed and fell to the ground.

She struggled to pull her arms from Red's grasp, but the brute held her to him. She was so busy trying to fight Red she didn't see Levi until she felt the burn when he slapped her across the face. Black dots danced in front of her. She opened her mouth to call for Otakatay, but was struck with another blow. The light faded to nothing.

Nora woke slung over the back of a horse, her wrists tied together. The uneven steps did nothing for her turning stomach, and she swallowed back the urge to puke. Her head hurt so bad she was sure someone had taken a log to it. She opened and closed her mouth feeling the puffy lip. She turned her head to see where they were heading and saw smoke billowing from a large hole in the mountain. She blinked and scanned the area. She was at the mine. Elwood's mine.

Damn it.

The mine was a fair size, and as they drew closer she was shocked at what she saw. For a wealthy man, Elwood did nothing to keep up the place. Dilapidated buildings littered the property along with broken rail carts and hundreds of rocks scattered all over.

She pushed herself up onto her elbows, ignoring the pain in her head and stared at four Indian boys. They stood on either side of two wagons sorting rocks from their buckets. Another boy carrying a bucket, walked out of a hole on the mountain. She watched, horrified, while he struggled to get it to the wagons.

There were no men here. An uneasy feeling crept over her, and she scanned the area again. All she saw working were boys, and all of them native. She looked up at the hill. Two man-sized holes were shored with wood to allow the boys to walk through, but it was the tiny tunnels inside the mountain that concerned her. She wondered how many boys were forced to go inside and crawl around the dark, dank caves.

She shuddered. *The poor darlings.*

She remembered what Joe had said. Elwood put him in a cave when he was bad. These were children. How could Elwood treat them like this?

A young boy, no more than seven, came running down the mountain. His clothes were ripped and soiled. He was screaming, and she saw the tears run down his hollow cheeks. She sucked in a breath as a man burst from a wooden structure a few feet from the small hole in the mountain and chased after him. It wasn't long before he had the boy by the neck and raised his hand to the child. Nora squeezed her eyes closed.

The others stopped their work, and Nora noticed their legs were tied together. These boys were slaves—prisoners. Elwood treated them like he did his dog. Thank goodness she'd healed Pal. She hoped he was still okay.

She squinted to get a better look at the boys. Slash marks covered the skin on their arms. Her eyes misted, and she pushed her head into the horse's side to stop the tears.

When she was pulled from the horse a piercing pain shot up her leg and throbbed in her ankle. She wobbled, and stood without putting any pressure on the sore limb. She steadied herself by reaching out to grab hold of the horse beside her. The sun shone bright, and she held her other hand up to block the powerful rays.

"Nora, darling," Elwood called as he walked down the verandah of a massive house.

So this is where all the money went. The house was built with logs and boasted large wood poles holding up a covered porch. Four long windows stared back at her from the front. The home was beautiful, but left an awful taste in her mouth when she considered how he treated the young boys. She peered around him for Joe. Where was he? She hadn't seen the boy at all and prayed he was all right.

"I'm glad to see you're unharmed after the horrible incident that happened in town." He kissed her cheek.

She yanked her face away.

"Why have you brought me here?"

"Why I want to marry you, of course."

"I've told you before. I will not marry you."

"Yes, but there is nowhere for you to go."

"I will be fine. Now please untie my hands."

She thrust her arms out in front of him.

"All in good time."

He smiled, and she wanted to slap him.

"I am not staying here and I will not marry you."

"There's no one else to protect you."

"Where is Joe?"

She heard Levi and Red snicker behind her, and her throat grew thick. *God, please let Joe be okay.*

"The boy is no concern of yours."

"What have you done with him?"

"Don't trouble yourself with thoughts of Joe."

"Where is he? I want to see him." Nora struggled against Levi's hold and yelled, "Joe, Joe."

Elwood backhanded her. "You will see Joe when I say so."

She tasted blood, but she wouldn't succumb to Elwood's demands. "You bastard. You abuse young boys to work at your mine."

He raised his hands and clapped three times.

"Well done. I knew you weren't as stupid as your drunken father."

She stiffened. Pa didn't deserve his insults. She lunged forward, but Levi had a hold of her arms and jerked her back.

"Why are you doing this? Those are children."

"Yes, yes they are, and they serve a purpose at my mine."

"What purpose is that?"

"Nora, you are so naive. Do you know how much money it would cost me to hire men? I'd have never gotten to be as wealthy as I am now if I'd had men working for me."

"You treat them like slaves. You're a snake." She tried to yank her wrists free, wanting to scratch his eyes out.

"Precisely, my dear, and I intend to keep doing so."

"You have no idea what you've done. Otakatay will come looking for me." She didn't think he would, he wanted to get rid of her, but she needed to scare Elwood.

"Is this the renegade who rescued you from hanging?"

"Yes, and he'll gut you like the pig you are for taking me, too." *He is probably well on his way and glad I am gone.*

Elwood's face changed from handsome to ugly and rigid. He stepped toward her, yanking her braid so her neck craned to the side. "This renegade, did he have you?"

She wanted nothing more than to be that close to Otakatay, but he'd pushed her aside. "Yes," she lied.

"You little bitch."

Elwood's eyes narrowed and his bottom lip curled. He raised his hand and slapped her across the face.

Tears filled her eyes and her cheek ached, but she refused to show any hint of defeat. *I will not cower.* Blood trickled down her chin, and she left it there meeting his crazed eyes instead.

"You gave yourself to a savage, a lowlife, but would not come to me?" he bellowed.

"I am not attracted to someone who beats children."

He brought his mouth down upon hers in a rough kiss.

She twisted away from him, but couldn't go far with Levi holding her.

"I'd never lay with you."

"Oh, Nora, you will. But first I must use you to lure in your dear Indian."

He took hold of her tied wrists and tugged her toward the center of the mine.

Fear slammed into her, knocking the air from her lungs. She hunched over, muscles cramped and her legs shook. Elwood had lost all sense, and he no longer resembled the well dressed man she knew. He gave her a chilling glare as his lips moved but nothing came out.

"He will come for me, and he will kill you," she lied again. "Otakatay will make you pay for what you've done."

"He will come, but he will die."

She dug her heels into the ground and almost came undone from the sharp stabs in her ankle and the bottoms of her feet. She knew without looking at them, they were cut and bleeding. Why did she take her boots off? She tried to jerk her wrists from him.

"He's a bounty hunter. There will be nowhere you can hide that he can't find you."

Elwood stopped and whirled toward her.

"Do you love him?"

She glared at him and remained silent.

"Do you love him?" he screamed, shaking her arms.

"Yes."

"And he loves you?"

Oh, she wished he did. She tipped her chin.

"Perfect."

He yanked on her wrists again and she hobbled, trying not to put weight on her injured ankle. They came to a thick pole anchored into the ground in the center of the mine. Blood smeared the wood, and long slash marks covered the entire surface.

He whipped the boys here.

Elwood untied her arms, wound them around the pole and tied them back together.

She looked up. The pole was so tall there was no way she'd be able to get loose. Defeat swelled in her stomach, and she tried to ease the heaviness with slow breaths.

"Now we wait for your beloved to come," Elwood whispered close in her ear. "You see, dear Nora, I know your Indian well, and I have a score to settle with him."

The scars on his back, the deformed skin on his arms and chest, oh dear God, he'd been here. Otakatay had been here.

"He doesn't love me. I lied. He will not come for me. He used me. He hates me." She spoke the truth, and the words hurt worse than any slap Elwood could give her.

"I think he will."

He motioned for Levi, and the man handed Elwood a blue strip of cloth. He jammed it into her mouth and tied it tight behind her head.

Nora screamed into the cloth.

"I can't have you giving my plan away. Levi, you watch her." He kissed her forehead before he left.

CHAPTER TWENTY-SEVEN

Otakatay stood in the meadow and stared down at Nora's boots. When he arrived back at the cave and discovered she was gone, he went searching for her. He traced her tracks to the clearing by the lake, when he saw four other footprints. Unease crept up his neck and squeezed as he assessed the rest of the area.

He didn't like the way the prints pushed into the ground. The front of the foot was deeper than the back, as if they anticipated she would run and they'd have to chase her. The size of both prints told him they belonged to men.

He studied the area some more and spotted the broken branches on the lilacs. He went to investigate and noticed more hanging twigs. She'd come through here. He followed her trail back into the forest, to an uprooted tree stump. Dirt was strewn around, and a petite hand print was embedded into the ground. *Nora.*

Four drops of blood lay next to it. She tried to fight them off, but she was no match for their size. She was in trouble, and he needed to find her. Wild rage trampled over him like a herd of mustangs.

The sun dipped behind a cloud and cast shadows from the trees onto the forest floor as he led Wakina up the hill. The trail they left wasn't hard to follow, and he got the impression they'd done it on purpose. He ground his teeth together. His fingers curled around the reins and squeezed. He'd enjoy killing the bastards.

As the trail veered north and climbed up the mountain, recognition flowed over him like lava. He touched the feather in his hair. *I promise.* He examined the familiar cliffs and hills. Dread, thick and moist, covered his skin. He'd been waiting for this day and braced himself for the battle to come.

He clicked his tongue, and Wakina continued to climb the trail.

He didn't know how Nora knew the mine owner, or if the bastard had seen them together and was acting on revenge, but he'd find a way to get her back, even if it meant trading his life for hers. His body hummed as he imagined the impact of what the night would hold.

Vengeance, untamed and barbaric raced through his veins. He yearned to release the rage, the hate. He was thirsty for tainted black blood, and only one person could quench that need. Elwood Calhoun, the rotten son of a bitch. He was next to the devil when it came to wickedness, and Otakatay was determined to send him straight to hell.

He mourned every day for those he'd left behind. They were boys—sold by their own for a petty bottle of whiskey, or a few coins. Shunned, the boys were tossed aside, never loved or cared for. Anger stirred in his stomach, and he bit back the curses he wanted to let fly.

Visions fogged his mind, and he tried to blink them away. But as he drew closer to the mine his senses tuned in, and he couldn't stop the images as they invaded his soul. His nostrils flared, and he smelled the rancid beef that had been slapped on the ground in front of him. The pain from not eating for days forced him to put the green meat into his mouth. His belly lurched. He heard the trickle of water running down the rocks, and the wretched moans of the others starving or being beaten. He wished he could go and help them.

He remembered the weight of their dead bodies as he carried the little ones, the weak ones and the ones his age to the edge of the cliff. He felt the tears fall from his eyes when he begged Elwood Calhoun to spare Little Eagle, to take him instead. His ears rang with the snap of the leather whip, the laughter that followed and the pain that was yet to come. He heard it all, felt it all, and his insides burned with anger—with retaliation.

Tonight he'd finish what he'd waited so long to accomplish. He'd kill Elwood Calhoun. He'd release the boys and bring them home. He ran his hand down Wakina's long mane. He'd save Nora. Chances were he wouldn't make it out alive, but he promised them, and damn it now was the time for him to own up to it.

Nora had been sitting on the ground for half the day, and she was sure her face was bright red from the hot sun beating down upon her. Sweat beaded in between her breasts, and the fly-away strands from her hair clung to her forehead and cheeks.

Her nose itched, and she tried to nestle her chin into her shoulder and relieve the irritating tickle, but all she did was cause a jolt of pain to shoot up her neck. The bandana in her mouth tasted of sweat and pig, and she'd tried several times to push it out with her tongue. The stench-filled cloth was loosening, but it was still too tight.

She glared at Levi. He tipped his chair back onto two legs, slumped against the rickety fence. He was snoring loud enough to wake the dead.

How he could stand this heat, she didn't know, but if she didn't get some water quick she was going to burst into flames.

She cleared her throat and was about to call out to him when another idea came to mind. She slid down onto her back and stretched, pulling at the rope around her wrists, she kicked the chair out from underneath him. The brute fell to the ground with a startled curse and rolled two times before he stopped.

She tried to hide her smile, but changed her mind and grinned at him through the bandanna. Even though it wasn't much, she tipped her chin and gave him a cool stare.

"You little wench," he spat. Dust flew from both his hands as he scrambled to his feet and charged straight at her.

She pulled herself back into a seated position as he pounced on top of her. Large hands wrapped around her throat, crushing her windpipe. She kicked her feet but wasn't strong enough to heave him off her. Black dots danced in front of her as she tried not to pass out. A gunshot split the hot afternoon air. The hands left her throat, and she sucked in fresh air.

"Levi, you touch her again and I'll put lead in your ass," Elwood said as he sauntered over.

The man glared at her, and she couldn't help but shiver. His empty, wooden eyes told her he wouldn't think twice about killing her. She gave him a nasty look, not willing to show defeat.

Elwood knelt beside her and removed the bandana. "Now, Nora, if you're a good girl, I will let you live after all of this."

"Go to hell," she hissed.

He laughed. "Ahh, you will be a fun one in bed." He traced his finger down her cheek. "And soon I will find out."

She jerked her face away and struggled against the pole, trying to loosen the ropes tied around her wrists. "I need some water."

Elwood motioned to Levi, and he dunked a tin cup into the bucket.

Nora's mouth watered.

Levi stood over her, filled his mouth with the water, smirked and spat it all over her.

She tucked her chin into her chest and prayed for the strength to go up against Elwood and his men.

"Thank you," she said curtly and turned toward Elwood. "You're wasting your time. Otakatay won't come. He doesn't care about me."

Elwood observed the hills and forest surrounding the mine. "He'll come, and I'll be waiting." He left her and headed toward the boys separating the rocks into carts.

She watched as he picked up a few, his face contorted with anger, spit flew from his mouth while he yelled at them to work faster. The boys never lifted their heads to make eye contact with him, and she noticed they flinched with each movement he made. She wished she could help them. Her hands heated, wanting to mend the open cuts she'd seen on their arms and legs. The warmth in her palms intensified, and she curled her fingers into a fist to stop the trembling.

Otakatay had lived here. He'd been Elwood's slave. It all made perfect sense now. She thought of Pal, how he was like a wild beast, attacking just for the taste of blood. Otakatay was no different. He killed for money, for a reason she didn't know, or was too oblivious to see.

There had to be an explanation. A fresh start maybe? She shook her head. That didn't seem to fit either. He could start over anytime, but he chose to hunt women like her. Doctor Spencer must've paid a handsome reward for the healers because it was the money that drove him to kill the women in the first place. If he killed for satisfaction, she'd be dead by now. But why did he need all that money? And why hadn't he come back to kill Elwood?

She surveyed the hills. There were five guards and Elwood. No one else was here. Otakatay could kill them all, and Elwood wouldn't know what hit him. So why hadn't he done it? Why was he hell-bent on travelling the continent searching for healers when the man who caused him such anguish was a few miles up the mountain from Willow Creek?

A loud slap permeated the air, and Nora snapped her head around to see where it had come from. A guard hovered above one of the boys at the rock station. The boy stooped over and clutched his cheek. She couldn't see his face for the long black hair hiding his features, so she twisted around to get a better look.

The boy glanced up, his hair falling to the side, and his eyes locked with hers. The truth unravelled like a ball of yarn. Chest tight, she bit her lower lip and held back the sob wanting to burst from her mouth. The money was for these boys—to help them.

Otakatay had tried to make her believe he was a monster, when all he ever wanted was to rescue these kids. She couldn't control the misery as it filled her eyes. How had she been so blind?

Hours had passed, and she was glad to see the sun settle in behind the mountains. Pain sliced through her shoulders, and she rotated them to ease the stiff joints. A flicker of color caught her eye, and she counted fifteen boys as they came out of the hole in the mountain.

Their ankles were chained together, and the clanking of metal links echoed toward her. Two men as dirty and unkempt as the boys walked alongside them. They were led to a building with missing planks and half a roof twenty yards from where she was tied. One by one the boys filed inside, while the men stood outside the doors.

As she scanned the surroundings for more children, she spotted another hole, no bigger than three feet high by two feet wide, in the side of the mountain. A portly guard sat outside of it. It wasn't long before more boys piled out of there, too. Some carried buckets, while the others carried a hammer and stake.

From what she could see, these boys were younger than the first ones, no older than six or seven. She inhaled, and her chest ached. Oh, dear God she wanted to help them. She jerked her arms, trying to get free. The rope bit into her flesh tearing the skin from her wrists.

The younger boys stared at her as they were ushered toward the same building as the others. Hope flashed in their eyes for a mere second before they realized she was tied up, a hostage like them. She couldn't bear to look into their eyes. No liveliness or youthful mischief swirled within the dark depths. All that stared back at her were empty, sad, desolate eyes of children forgotten. Boys that were tossed aside and not a second thought to anyone.

Her vision blurred, and she looked away, unable to see the torn and ratty clothes hanging from their bony, food deprived bodies. She couldn't gaze upon their broken and cut skin, the scars from so many beatings. And God help her, she couldn't see the despair clouding their eyes when they stared at her, knowing she couldn't do a damn thing to help them.

Hot rage bubbled and spit from her eyes as she glared at Elwood. Never in her nineteen years had she wanted to harm someone as much as she wanted to punish Elwood Calhoun for what he was doing to these boys.

She thought of Willow Creek. The townspeople assumed he was a rich miner with a simple son. They pitied him, gave him the best suite at the hotel, ordered in the finest whiskey while he was there. She was so disgusted she wanted to scream. They had no idea what he was doing up here on the mountain. How for years he'd tortured and beaten these young boys for his coal.

If she got out of here alive, she'd make sure those people knew what they'd harbored all these years. She'd make them feel the shame, helplessness and guilt she felt as this very moment.

There was a commotion by the door to the bunkhouse. She watched horrified as a little boy, no more than six came loose from his chains and ran toward her. She struggled with the rope around her wrists, wanting to reach out to him.

Tears soaked his dirty cheeks, and he yelled something in another language. Skinny arms wrapped around her neck as he burrowed himself within the curve of her hip and chest. Loud sorrowful sobs shook his little body, and she wished she could hold him in her arms. Her tears fell onto his knotty, unwashed hair.

"Shush, baby, it's okay," she crooned, rocking him from side to side as best she could. Nora's chest ached, and she didn't think she'd ever breathe the same again. The agonizing cries from the youngster tore at her soul, and she vowed to help him and the others. She'd find a way to rescue them.

The stocky guard yanked the boy from her chest and smiled down at her showing four rotten teeth. A high pitched scream came from the youngster as his arms and feet kicked the air.

"Leave him be," she yelled.

The man ignored her, walked past Elwood and threw the boy inside the building. He shut the door behind him.

"You bastard." She squirmed against the pole. "How can you do this to these children, they're innocent."

"I own them. Bought them fair and square," Elwood said nonchalantly.

"They're babies, missing their mothers."

He spun sadistic flat eyes toward her. "Some of their mothers sold them. So before you go and get all high and mighty, you may remember that I am doing these brats a favor. Half of them would be dead by now if it wasn't for me."

"But why them, they're so tiny and—

"Exactly! I can blast smaller holes, and these heathens can crawl in them. Less dynamite means more money."

"Yes, but men are a lot stronger than children."

He shrugged. "Maybe, but I'd have to pay them."

"So all of this is for the money. You're killing children for money?"

"They are Indians, and not worth shit. I'd save an outlaw before I'd help one of these lowlifes."

"Why do you hate them? What have they done to you?"

"They're thieves," he yelled. "Heartless killers who say they live off the land and then rape and murder our people." His arms flung out, and he glowered at the shack. "When I was twelve, those bastards slaughtered every man and woman on the wagon train we were on. They took my sister, and if we hadn't run, my brother and I would've died also."

Nora stared into eyes that bore hate of the vilest kind.

"Those dirty skinned Injuns," he pointed at the shack, "will pay for that day."

Elwood was a man who begrudged a whole race because of something a few had done.

"They are only boys. They have done nothing to you."

"Those boys will grow to be men, and kill our people. I plan to rid the territory of the red man, one filthy brat at a time."

Nora thought back to the boys she saw earlier. None of them looked older than fourteen. "What do you do when they get older?"

"Why kill them, of course."

"You're insane," she screamed, "I cannot wait for the day when you pay for all you've done."

He eyed her for a long while before he burst out laughing.

"My men are well trained. No one will touch me, not even your dirty Indian."

"I wouldn't be so sure. Otakatay is a killer, a hunter and he will show you no mercy."

"He won't make it past the shack." Elwood pointed to the building the boys were in.

Nora peered around him, and her breath caught in her throat when she saw three guards laying dynamite around the structure.

"You're going to kill those boys?"

"If your savage tries to release them, I will light the fuse."

"They are just children. Please, you can't do that. Please."

He shrugged. "I will find more on the reservations to replace them."

"I'll do whatever you want." She was on her knees. "I'll marry you, lay with you. Please, please take me instead."

"Now you beg for me to have you." Fire shot from his eyes. "You'd do it all to save them?"

"Anything. I will do anything. Please, don't hurt those boys."

"You're pathetic." He slapped her hard across the face. "Your skin is white. Yet you talk as if those brats are yours." He bent down until his face was almost touching hers and pinched her cheeks together. "I will have you no matter what. And then I will kill you too."

She didn't know what else to say. She yanked her face from his grip and wrestled with the ropes around her wrists. She needed to get free to save them, to save Otakatay.

Elwood pulled the bandana back over her mouth. He kissed her on the forehead and laughed all the way to the house.

She screamed through the cloth lodged between her teeth and kicked her legs out. How was she going to warn Otakatay? How was she going to rescue the boys? She lay limp against the pole, helpless. Bile crawled up her throat, and she swallowed past the angst—the utter disappointment of not being able to do something. She stared through tear-filled eyes at the shack.

God help us all.

CHAPTER TWENTY EIGHT

Otakatay stood among the corpses and skeletons. He'd gone to the open gravesite to pay his respects to those who hadn't survived long enough to see him return. He'd stood on the cliff high above the bodies, but needing to be closer, he climbed down the mountain.

There he saw Yellow Knee. He was a fresh body among the dead, and Otakatay ignored the sob lingering in his throat. The boy had been eight when he'd escaped and promised to return. Now, he'd never know freedom. He'd never breathe fresh air that wasn't tainted with rotten meat, vile bodies, and coal. He'd never taste the glory of independence. Otakatay had been too late for the young man. He'd failed him.

The pressure of what he'd done sank onto his shoulders, and he fell to his knees. The bow tied to his back cut into his skin, and he left it there. He hung his head. Remorse stirred in his gut, raw and spoiled. Guilt pressed into his back, curving it, as he moaned from deep within his soul.

Anguish clouded his vision, and he couldn't contain the sob as it burst from his clenched teeth. Tears overflowed onto his cheeks and chin. He placed his hand on Yellow Knee's cold one.

"I am sorry." He looked at the bones of the dead around him, "I am so very sorry."

He sat with Yellow Knee for the better part of an hour, before he carried the boy into the forest. There, he found a clearing, and laid him down on the ground. He pulled a bow from his pack and rested it gently on Yellow Knee's chest, he was a warrior. He couldn't let the mountain cat or any other animal feast on the child's body, so he gathered rocks to place around and over the boy.

"Wakan Tanan kici un—May the Great Spirit bless you." He placed the last rock over him and left.

Otakatay waited until it was dark and decided to come into the mine from the north side, where the graves had been. If Elwood and his men were watching for him, this would be the last place they'd guess he'd come from. He edged along the mountain until he could make out the house and other buildings below.

Three fires burned around the mine, lighting the area. He scanned the ground for any sign of Nora and stopped when he saw something move. He spotted the rose- colored dress immediately. She was tied to the whipping pole in the middle of the yard.

Rage rippled through him, and he flexed his hands. Had Elwood whipped her? He squinted to get a better look, but she was too far away. The miner would know great pain if he so much as touched one hair on her head. She hadn't moved. Her hands were tied to the pole, and her body slumped to the side. Time was running out.

He scrutinized the rest of the mine. He counted four men, two on either side of the shack, one by Nora, and one twenty feet below him. Quietly, he aimed his arrow at the man closest to him. He pulled the string back, paused, held his breath, and let go. He listened as the arrow whistled through the trees and struck its mark.

He jumped over a fallen log and took off down the hill toward the man. The arrow protruded from the man's back, and he was on the ground moaning in pain. Otakatay pulled his knife and placed it between his teeth. He rolled the guard over, and drove the blade into his heart.

One

He wiped the blood onto his denims and inched closer to the other buildings. He moved with ease, blending into his surroundings. He crouched within the bushes beside the shack, cupped his hand and hooted. The guard looked up into the trees. With great skill, he came from behind slit the man's throat and carried him into the forest. He left him there for the bears and the crows.

Two

The hinges on the wooden door creaked as he opened it. He stepped inside and tripped on something. He leaned over to get a closer look.

"Son of a bitch."

Elwood had laid dynamite around the building. He was going to kill the boys. He needed to get them out of here and fast. There was enough dynamite to kill them all and bring the building down on top of them. He turned toward the sleeping boys. He curled his lip. The mine owner would die tonight.

He stepped over the dynamite and waited until his eyes adjusted to the dark room. The stench invaded his senses, and he pushed all thoughts of the past from his mind. He needed to help the boys before all hell broke loose.

I promised.

Bodies were strewn all over the dirt floor fast asleep. Many were missing and had died since he'd been here. Shame settled in his gut. He searched the sleeping faces for any familiar ones and recognized a few. The rest had been too young when he'd escaped.

He knelt and woke an older boy. The smell from his unwashed body made Otakatay's eyes water.

The child opened his eyes and sat up.

"Do you speak English?" Otakatay whispered.

He nodded.

"Do you remember me?"

The boy's brown eyes narrowed, and he tilted his head to the side. "Cetan?"

Otakatay smiled. "Yes, it is me, Cetan."

The boy leapt into his arms.

He didn't care if the boy smelled. He wrapped his arms around him and squeezed. He'd take him and the others home. "What is your name?"

"Shinte Galeska—Spotted Tail."

"I need your help. You have to wake the others while I take care of the guard out front."

The boy nodded and scrambled to do as he was told.

Otakatay crept toward the door. The guard was directly on the other side. He paused, determining the best way to overtake him, when one of the boys began to cry. The door swung open, and he stepped back into the shadows.

The guard charged forward, whip in hand.

Otakatay lunged from the wall, knocking the man to the ground. He hadn't noticed how solid the guard was until his large chunky fists pummeled Otakatay's face. He could feel blood drip from a cut above his left eye. The blade of the knife poked into his leg, and he struggled to get it. The guard was a head taller than him and fifty pounds heavier.

He looked back at the boys and took a hard punch to the chin that snapped his neck back. He whirled around to face his attacker. Another blow to the jaw crushed his teeth together and sent painful vibrations up the side of his face. They wrestled with each other on the ground, and Otakatay was on the bottom. He glanced at the boys again. They were standing against the wall, watching the fight. Some were crying.

I promised.

Otakatay growled. He spat the blood from his mouth and heaved the giant off of his body. With panther-like skills he jumped on top of him, pulled his arm back and drove his elbow into the guard's nose, breaking it. Blood sprayed everywhere, and he hammered his fists into the man's face until he no longer fought back. The guard was out cold, or dead, and he didn't give a damn which it was. He huffed, as his chest rose and fell in uneven cadence. He wiped the blood from his mouth, and gathered the boys so he could usher them into the forest.

Halfway across the shack, a flicker of light eliminated the room. Fear knocked the air from his lungs. The guard had pulled himself to the open door, struck a match and was lighting the dynamite.

"Run! Run!"

Nora sat up. She could've sworn she heard Otakatay. A loud boom echoed throughout the mine as the darkness lit up with orange and red. Hot air blew across her face as the building the boys were in exploded.

"What the hell?" Levi said from behind her.

Oh, no. Not the children. She thrashed against the ropes as a black cloud rose into the sky. Every muscle in her tired body screamed in pain. The shack had been blown to bits. Charred wood and ashes floated in the black sky. She tried to hold on and fight back the tears, but the shock of it all was too much, and she sobbed into the bandana lodged in her mouth.

"What the bloody hell happened?" Elwood shouted, as he ran toward them, Red in tow.

"Not sure. It just exploded."

Nora laid her head on a rock as harsh sobs shook her body. She tried to suck in a breath that wasn't paired with an excruciating pain in her chest, but it was no use. Her shoulders ached, and her hands went numb. Nothing mattered anymore. Otakatay and the boys had died.

"They must've seen the Indian. Why else would they blow the building?" Levi said.

Elwood marched toward the burning wreckage. He picked up a piece of wood, and hollered out in pain. It was hot, and he dropped it, dancing around holding his hand.

He deserved more than a burned hand. He deserved to die. She glared at him.

The debris from the shack had fallen in large chunks where the building once was. There was no way anyone could sift through the mess until everything cooled off.

Levi fell to the ground beside her, an arrow wedged in his chest.

Elwood fired his gun into the forest around them. He ran toward them. "Where did it come from?"

"I don't know. It's that savage. He isn't dead. He's here." With one arm, he dragged himself to the fence and slumped against the pole. Blood flowed from the wound on his chest.

Elwood broke the arrow off and tossed the stick aside. He handed Levi a gun. "Shoot at anything that moves."

Levi nodded as sweat formed on his forehead, and he turned a pasty shade of gray.

Another arrow whizzed by, hitting Red in the throat.

She wasn't sure if he died right then or from the next arrow that struck him directly in the heart. She scrambled to the side, but she wasn't fast enough and his bloody body landed on her legs, pinning her to the ground.

"We're going to die," Levi whined. He waved the gun out in front of him and shot into the trees.

"No, we're not." Elwood pushed Red off of her legs and untied the rope that held her to the whipping pole. He tied her wrists in front of her and hauled Nora to her feet.

Nora's arms and legs were weak, and she stumbled as she tried to stand.

"Stand up, damn it." He lugged her up.

The bandana, moist from her tears and saliva, had stretched. She pushed it out of her mouth with her tongue. "Let go of me you rotten bastard."

She jerked her arms back, trying to loosen his grip.

He cuffed her with the butt end of his gun.

Pain vibrated up her cheek bone, buckling her knees and sent vomit up the back of her throat. She swallowed so she didn't throw up. He wrenched on her hair, and she stood.

Otakatay.

"If your lover shoots another damn arrow, I will kill you."

"Go to hell." She spat in his face.

He growled and punched her hard in the jaw.

Nora fell to the ground, the dirt floor swayed beneath her, and her vision blurred.

Elwood pulled her up again. He clamped his right arm around her waist and held her arms pinned to her sides.

"Hawk," he shouted into the forest. "Hawk, you low-life half-breed. Show yourself. Come down and face me."

Elwood was hysterical. He muttered to himself words she couldn't understand, and his left eye twitched while his head ticked to the side.

"Get your gun ready," he said to Levi.

The man bobbed his head up and down, while he aimed the short barrel at the trees in the distance.

Hours passed, and Otakatay still hadn't come through the forest. The first rays of light began to crest over the mountain as dawn approached. Elwood sat in a chair with Nora on the ground in front of him. She glanced at Levi. He hadn't moved in over an hour, and she wondered if he'd passed out or died.

Where was Otakatay? Had he left her here to fend for herself? Had he freed the children before the shack exploded and forgotten all about her? She didn't think he'd do such a thing, but the throbbing in her jaw and cheek had her second guessing him. She was exhausted, her muscles sore and tender. Every time she moved pain sliced across her arms and legs.

Over the last few hours she'd listened to Elwood mumble and convulse behind her. He'd gone crazy. He'd shoot at anything that moved and had reloaded his .42 several times since sitting in the chair.

The trees rustled in the distance, and she narrowed her eyes to get a better look. Elwood heard it too and fired at the bushes.

"You are wasting valuable bullets."

Nora spun to see Otakatay standing ten feet from her, his shot gun aimed at them. A purple bruise covered his right cheek, and a nasty cut over his left eye was caked with dry blood.

He was here all along.

Elwood stood and hauled her with him. He pointed his gun at Otakatay, and then changed his mind holding the barrel to Nora's temple instead.

"Levi, Levi," he yelled.

"Your friend is dead," Otakatay said.

Nora sensed the danger, as it oozed from his body, and she shivered. He resembled the killer she'd seen in the woods weeks before. The hunter and Elwood was his prey.

"If you shoot, I pull the trigger and kill the bitch."

"She is not mine. I don't give a damn what you do with her."

His words stung worse than any cut she'd ever received. Unable to look at him, she averted her eyes to the ground.

"Yes, she is. You rescued her from hanging. She said you've had her," Elwood sneered.

Otakatay laughed. "Those are fantasies of a little girl." His black eyes scrutinized her attire. "I would never sleep with a white woman."

"You're a liar. You've always been a liar," Elwood screamed. The sound reminded her of a cat in heat.

Otakatay cocked his shot gun and the click seemed loud enough to wake the dead. "Where is he?"

"I should've killed you back then," Elwood tightened his grip on her.

"Where is he?"

"He is dead."

Regret flickered across his black eyes, and he blinked.

Elwood fired his gun, and Otakatay dropped to the ground.

"No," she screamed, yanking herself from Elwood's hold. She ran to Otakatay and fell onto her knees beside him. Blood soaked his shirt above his forearm. He'd been shot in the lower shoulder. *Thank God.* Her hands heated and shook.

Elwood stood over them, his gun aimed at Otakatay.

"You will have to shoot me first," she said and sprawled across his chest.

Otakatay ignored the pain in his arm. He bit back the smile lingering at the corners of his mouth after Nora lay on top of him. She was quite the fighter, and he was proud of her. As he waited for the guard to die and dawn to approach, he'd watched her.

Elwood had hit her several times, and her pretty face showed the signs of his fists. She didn't cower from him, instead lifted her pert chin and challenged him, making the mine owner go even more insane.

He sensed Elwood standing over him now, about a foot from his legs. Nora was still stretched out on top of him.

"You stupid bitch." Elwood grabbed her hair, pulling so hard that she screamed out.

Otakatay flexed his muscles.

Elwood stood with his arm around her throat and aimed the gun at him.

Quick as a bolt of lightning, he kicked his leg out and tripped Elwood, sending both him and Nora to the ground as a shot went off.

He was on his feet, knife in hand, when he saw blood ooze from Nora's leg. Within minutes the front of her dress was soaked, and her bruised face lost all color. He let out a violent howl, and lunged at Elwood knocking him backward.

"I will enjoy this," he said between clenched teeth, and he pressed the blade into Elwood's throat.

A bone-chilling growl came from nearby. Otakatay twisted and was face to face with a black wolf.

"Attack, Savage. Attack," Elwood shouted, squirming beneath Otakatay.

The dog bared his fangs and growled as saliva dripped from his mouth. Black eyes narrowed in on Elwood, and he snarled, licking his teeth. The black hair on his back stood straight up, and he pawed at the ground.

Otakatay slid carefully off of Elwood, sensing the dog wanted nothing to do with him.

He went to Nora. She was passed out from the loss of blood. He ripped the bottom of her dress and tied it around her thigh to stop the bleeding. He pressed his head to her chest and was glad to hear the strong beats.

He smoothed the dark strands of hair away from her face and kissed her forehead. She'd fought for him. She was willing to give her life for him. He observed her tied wrists, the skin red and swollen, her bruised cheeks and pink lips. She never cared that he was a half-breed, that he'd killed women like her, or that he'd said hurtful things to her. She still cast her body over his injured one, willing to take a bullet for him.

He'd been wrong all along. She was his match. She was his woman, and he loved her. He lifted her into his arms, bit back a curse from the stinging in his arm and carried her toward the house.

The sharp growl from the wolf as he bit into flesh and Elwood's loud screams faded into nothing, and Otakatay never turned around.

He kicked open the door and walked through the well-furnished home into the kitchen. He laid Nora on top of an oiled wooden table. A bucket of water sat on the counter. He dunked the cloth in and squeezed out any excess moisture. He pulled her skirt up and cleaned the wound. The bleeding had stopped, so he left her side to build a fire in the hearth.

When the flames had grown hot enough, he heated the knife until the tip was bright orange. He bit down hard and dug the blade into the wounded flesh, searching for the slug. He blew out a relieved sigh when, less than a minute later, he pulled the lead ball from her leg.

She stirred, and he needed to get moving before she woke. He heated the blade again and without hesitation, he pushed it onto the hole, burning it closed.

Nora tossed her head from side to side and cried out while reaching for her leg. He didn't know what to say to ease the pain as she whimpered beside him, so he pulled her close and held her instead.

He brought his forehead to Nora's and whispered, "Techihila mitawin." He gazed into her sea-blue eyes and knew his heart would never beat the same again. "I love you, my woman," he repeated in English.

She gazed up at him, and her eyes watered.

"Nora, Nora," Joe called from behind them.

Otakatay helped her sit up.

"Joe, thank God you're okay," she said.

Otakatay released her and pivoted toward Joe. *It can't be.*

The boy had been beaten, his white shirt was ripped and blood stained. A frayed rope bound his wrists. He leaned into one stick, and Otakatay's chest ached when he stared at Joe's deformed legs. *Elwood said he was dead.* His stomach lurched, and his throat worked as he tried to swallow. Tears filled his eyes, and he held out his hand.

Joe took a step and recognition danced within his own eyes. "Cetan? Hawk, Hawk?"

He'd waited years to hear those words, and before he could catch himself, before he could reign in his emotions, a loud sob burst from his lips. In two strides he reached Joe and hugged him tight.

"How I've missed you."

"Hawk, Hawk. You came back," Joe cried.

"I will never leave you again. I promise."

Nora cleared her throat, confusion written all over her beautiful bruised face, and he went to her.

"I'd like you to meet my brother, Little Eagle."

She smiled as tears shone in her eyes.

He stared at her. Nora amazed him. She was in pain, and yet she was smiling. He left her to search the kitchen for clean bandages and found some strips of cloth in one of the drawers. He pulled the leather pouch from his pocket and rubbed the slippery elm onto the burn before wrapping it tight.

Nora flinched, but did not cry out. The love he felt for her brought more tears to his eyes.

Joe stood beside him, as Otakatay lifted Nora from the table, cradling her in his arms. Together they walked out of the house and watched as the boys ran from the forest shouting, "Hawk, Hawk."

Nora pulled his chin toward her. "I love you."

He smiled and touched his lips to hers.

EPILOGUE

One year later

Nora stood on the porch and peered out at the land surrounding her home. It had taken them six months to get things in order on the ranch. The addition to the house was complete. The day Hawk rescued the boys, her life changed forever.

She smiled.

Sheriff Reid, Fred Sutherland and a few others from Willow Creek had shown up at the mine that awful day. They'd seen the smoke from the explosion and wanted to make sure everything was all right. The men were ashamed and mortified at what Elwood had done. They promised Hawk, Nora and the boys a place within Willow Creek. Most of the townspeople were welcoming, with apologies and tearful hugs when they saw the boys.

Sheriff Reid handed Nora the deed to Jess's ranch. Happy to have somewhere to go and pleased to be continuing Jess and Marcus's dream, Nora took the deed and wrote Hawk's name alongside hers. They owned it together. With the reward money Hawk had acquired they purchased more livestock and built onto the home for the boys.

"Our little one is hungry," Hawk said from behind her.

She faced him and smiled.

He held their daughter, Morning Star, bundled in the crook of his arm. At two months old, she was all her father. Black hair and tanned skin, but she did have Nora's blue eyes, and behind her left ear, folded in the crease, she too was branded.

She was beautiful, and some days Nora sat staring at her for hours.

"You cannot feed her?" she teased, as she ran her fingers along the top of the baby's head.

He smiled, and she knew she'd never tire of seeing his face light up with joy.

"No, I cannot." He kissed the top of Morning Stars head and placed her into Nora's arms. "I don't remember, Wife, if I've told you yet today how much I love you?" he whispered into her ear.

Nora smiled. "Yes, my husband, you have, twice this morning. But I cannot remember if you've shown me."

His black eyes twinkled, and he kissed her neck, allowing her a taste of what was to come. "I will make sure to show you tonight."

She shivered in anticipation of their love making.

He laughed and wrapped his arms around her. "Wastelakapi—Beloved."

She tipped her head and kissed his chin. She knew the name he called her, and each time he said it she melted.

Since moving to the ranch, her husband had changed. No longer angry and bitter, he now had a different purpose—raising the boys and being a husband and father. His happiness overflowed onto her, and together they built a home filled with love and laughter.

"Hawk, Hawk. Come quick," Little Eagle called from the field.

He chuckled. "I must go and see what my brother wants."

"We'll sit and watch from here," she said.

He looked down at her, the passion and love vivid in the dark depths. He kissed her slowly, lingering a moment, before he ran down the steps toward his brother.

Nora's heart swelled while she watched her husband place his arm around Little Eagle and talk with him. He never tired of him, or his questions. Otakatay had found peace with his brother. She watched as Raven and White Bear sauntered over, and Hawk messed their hair affectionately. He'd taken the boys from the mine and given them a home.

Once a week, she taught them lessons from the school books she'd acquired by mail. She enjoyed the time she spent with them. Over the months Nora grew so close to each boy that they called her Mother. She loved each one as if he were her own.

Hawk was intent on showing them the Lakota way, but encouraged the white man's as well. He wanted them to be fluent in both worlds. He trained them to work with the horses. He showed them how to brand cattle and till the land surrounding their home. He taught them to take pride in what they had.

He worked long hours tending the livestock and the fields with the boys, and she missed him during the day. She counted the hours to when the house was quiet and everyone was asleep. In the privacy of their room, he'd take her in his arms and between tender kisses, he'd whisper in Lakota how much he loved her.

"Nora, Nora, Nora," Little Eagle shouted.

Pride filled her as she watched her brother-in-law run across the field without his sticks, his knees no longer deformed. She'd healed his legs a month after they'd come to the ranch.

"What is it, Little Eagle?"

It had taken her awhile to get used to his new name, but now she only saw him as such.

"A butterfly, a butterfly." He ran up the steps and stopped in front of her and Morning Star. Loud breaths came from his smiling lips as he opened his hand to reveal a squished orange and black butterfly.

"Oh, honey, I think the butterfly is dead."

His eyes watered, and his bottom lip trembled.

"It's okay, there are plenty more," she said and pointed to a yellow one flying around the oak tree in the yard. "Why don't you see if you can't find me another one?"

"Okay, okay." He dropped the butterfly onto the porch and took off into the field.

Nora picked up the pretty insect and sat back down in the rocking chair. She nestled Morning Star close and placed the butterfly on top of the blanket.

A dimpled hand reached out and touched the black-tipped wings.

The wings fluttered, and Nora smiled as the butterfly flew away.

~ * ~

If you enjoyed this book, please consider writing a short review and posting it on Amazon, Goodreads and/or Barnes and Noble. Reviews are very helpful to other readers and are greatly appreciated by authors, especially me. When you post a review, drop me an email and let me know and I may feature part of it on my blog/site. Thank you. ~ Kat

katflannery@shaw.ca

~ * ~

Watch for BLOOD CURSE, book 2 in the Branded Trilogy, coming in Fall 2014.

Dear Reader,

This story is very dear to me because of the emotions both main characters go through. Otakatay has been cast aside from his own people. He's grown up a slave where he fed his hate for white people and those around him. He trusted no one and relied on no one. There was never anyone there to give him guidance or to show him kindness.

Nora leads a very similar life in regards to her emotions. All she wants is the love of her father, who resents her for the gift she was born with. But Otakatay and Nora both took different paths in how they dealt with these situations. She has not allowed her father to alter her way of thinking. She doesn't care what color you are, if you're rich or poor. Everyone is equal to her, everyone deserves a chance. But she is still judged. She is still an outcast, who has experienced hatred at its worst.

When I see the way our world is, full of hate and anger, I cringe. I watch people, myself included judge others by the way they look, or how they behave. The old adage "Walk a mile in someone else's shoes" fill my head and bring me back to reality that I am no better than the next person.

It was love that healed Otakatay and saved Nora, and it is with love and empathy that we can look at those around us who are different and hold out our hand.

I hope you enjoyed LAKOTA HONOR.

Love

Kat

About the Author

Kat Flannery has loved writing ever since she was a girl. She is often seen jotting her ideas down in a little black book. When not writing, or researching, Kat enjoys snuggling on her couch with a hot chocolate and a great book.

Her first novel, CHASING CLOVERS became an Amazon's bestseller in Historical and Western romance. This is Kat's second book, and she is currently hard at work on the third.

When not focusing on her creative passions, Kat is busy with her three boys and doting husband

www.katscratch.blogspot.com

IMAJIN BOOKS

Quality fiction beyond your wildest dreams

For your next eBook or paperback purchase, please visit:

www.imajinbooks.com

www.twitter.com/imajinbooks

www.facebook.com/imajinbooks

CPSIA information can be obtained at www.ICGtesting.com
Printed in the USA
LVOW04s1930101014

408245LV00009B/205/P